STUDY GUIDE

to accompany

ECONOMICS

DAVID N. HYMAN

Prepared by

DONALD P. MAXWELL
Central State University

1989

IRWIN

Homewood, IL 60430
Boston, MA 02116

Articles on pages 51, 69, 97, 126, 226, 240, 282, 294, 309,
324, 359, 373, 386, 428, 459, 513, 528, 568, 581, and 591
are reprinted by permission of the Wall Street Journal
© Dow Jones & Company, Inc., 1985, 1988.

Contents

TO THE STUDENT

This <u>Study Guide</u> to accompany Hyman, <u>Economics</u> is designed as a set of interactive modules covering the key concepts developed in the textbook chapters and appendices. These modules will help you understand and apply the concepts you need to know. The <u>Study Guide</u> is based on my experiences teaching university economics for over a decade.

Each chapter of the <u>Study Guide</u> begins with **Chapter Challenges**, which give you the important learning objectives of the corresponding textbook chapter. This is followed by **In Brief: Chapter Summary**, which asks you to complete the summary, and in doing so review key concepts. The **Vocabulary Review** that follows is a fill-in exercise that will reinforce your understanding of the key terms in David Hyman's <u>Economics</u> glossary. Next comes a set of problems and exercises, **Skills Review**, selected to reinforce the main learning objectives of the chapter. These questions are presented in the same order as the concepts appear in the textbook. Each block of questions in the Skills Review section is subtitled according to the learning concept to which it applies, so that you can concentrate on areas that require extra study. These problems and exercises involve graphing, filling in tables, completing sentences, matching, listing, and discussion. For most chapters, advanced questions are included. These offer additional challenges and the opportunity to apply more advanced analysis, such as algebraic analysis, to certain problems.

After the Skills Review, a minitest of 15 to 20 multiple choice questions, like those you will encounter on exams, is included in the **Self-Test for Mastery**. These questions will give you feedback to determine how well you have mastered the important concepts of the chapter. The self-test is followed by 3 to 5 discussion questions that ask you to apply the concepts of the chapter to issues and problems. Following this **Discussion** section, 20 chapters of the <u>Study Guide</u> include a **Pop Quiz**. This exercise asks you to read a recent <u>Wall Street Journal</u> news article and answer one or two discussion questions. At the end of each chapter or appendix is an answer key. **Chapter Answers** include answers to all sections of the Study Guide, including discussion questions, so that you can check your progress.

In using this <u>Study Guide</u>, I suggest you first read the textbook chapter, paying particular attention to the introductory statement of learning objectives for the chapter and the concept checks that appear throughout the chapter. Next, complete the fill-in summary section of the <u>Study Guide</u>. Go back to the textbook and read and study the section for any parts of the summary that you answered incorrectly. Answer the vocabulary exercise next, after you review the glossary terms in the margins of the text chapter.

The problems and exercises in the Skills Review correspond closely to the examples used by David Hyman in the textbook. Try to answer the questions in the Skills Review and go back to the text for additional study if you have difficulty understanding how to answer a question. You can use the answer key for help, but you will get the most benefit by first studying the text and then working the problems in the <u>Study Guide</u>, rather than by going directly to the answer key.

After completing the Skills Review, take the self-test of multiple choice questions and compare your answers to those in the answer key to see where you need to spend additional study time. Review the concepts in the text and <u>Study Guide</u> that you have not yet mastered. Now try to answer the discussion questions from the Discussion and Pop Quiz sections. Read the answers to the discussion questions in the answer section. If there are discussion questions that you do not understand, go back to the corresponding sections of the text and <u>Study Guide</u> for additional study.

ACKNOWLEDGMENTS

I would like to thank the editors and staff at Times Mirror/Mosby and Irwin for suggesting this project and providing advice and support throughout the preparation of the manuscript. In particular, I would like to thank Jean Babrick, Developmental editor for Supplements, and Denise Clinton, Sponsoring Editor, for their encouragement and assistance. I would like to thank David Hyman for making this possible. I also want to thank the copy editors, Elisabeth Heitzeberg and Sandy Gilfillan for their work on the manuscript. Finally, thanks to Kathy Lumpkin, Production Editor, and her staff for bringing the Study Guide to you.

The Study Guide was reviewed by an expert in the design of of educational supplements and by several experienced university economics instructors for general content, appropriateness, and accuracy. Special thanks go to the technical reviewers of the manuscript, Kathy Gillespie of St. Louis University and Ben Childers of the University of Missouri, Columbia. Additional and very sincere thanks go to **Irwin Feller**, Penn State University, **James Kahn**, State University of New York, Binghamton, **William Witter**, University of North Texas, and **Richard Spivack** of Bryant College for reviewing the entire manuscript and providing valuable feedback and suggestions.

Don Maxwell
Central State University

1

Economics: What It's All About

CHAPTER CHALLENGES

After studying your text, attending class, and completing this chapter, you should be able to:

1. Describe the mechanism of the economy and the discipline of economics.
2. Understand the concepts of scarcity and opportunity costs.
3. Discuss major branches of economic inquiry: microeconomics, macroeconomics, positive analysis, and normative analysis.

IN BRIEF: CHAPTER SUMMARY

Fill in the blanks to summarize chapter content.

Economics is a study concerned with the use society makes of its (1)_____ (scarce, abundant) resources in attempting to satisfy the (2)_____ (normal, unlimited) desires of its members. The economy represents the mechanism or structure that organizes scarce resources for the purpose of producing the goods and services desired by society. (3)_____ (Inflation, Scarcity) is the fundamental problem facing all economies. It is also the reason decisions or choices involve (4)_____ (opportunity costs, production costs).

The real cost or opportunity cost of any choice is the value of the sacrifice required in making that decision. That sacrifice represents the foregone opportunity to pursue the (5)_____ (next best, any) decision. A fundamental problem confronting an economy is how to best meet the desires of individuals in a world of scarcity. Economies do this by addressing several basic questions: (a) What will be produced? (b) How will goods and services be produced? (c) To whom will goods and services be distributed? An economy's answers to the first two questions reveal the (6)_____ (fairness, efficiency) with which resources are used to satisfy the desires of society. The third question requires that society make value judgments regarding the distribution of income.

The two major branches of economic analysis are macroeconomics and microeconomics. (7)_____ (Macroeconomics, Microeconomics) is concerned with the economic behavior of individual decision-making units in the economy. (8)_____ (Macroeconomics, Microeconomics) is concerned with the effects of the aggregate economic behavior of all individuals, firms, and institutions. Inflation and unemployment are two topics that are studied in (9)_____ (macroeconomics, microeconomics), whereas the determination of prices and an analysis of markets are subjects dealt with in (10)_____ (macroeconomics, microeconomics).

Positive economic analysis seeks to determine (11)_____ ("what ought to be", "what is"). (12)_____ (Positive, Normative) economic analysis emphasizes the "should" or "ought to" approach. Positive analysis tries to uncover cause-and-effect relationships that are subject to empirical observation and verification. In contrast, normative analysis depends upon the analyst's (13)_____ (value judgment, mathematical skills). Disagreements arise among practitioners in any discipline. With positive analysis, it is possible to resolve disagreements empirically. With normative analysis, disagreements stem from different value systems and must be resolved in ways other than looking at the "facts."

VOCABULARY REVIEW

Write the key term from the list below next to its definition.

Key Terms

Economy   Macroeconomics
Economics   Unemployment rate
Scarcity   Inflation
Opportunity cost   Positive analysis
Microeconomics   Normative analysis

Definitions

1. _____: the cost of choosing to use resources for one purpose measured by the sacrifice of the next best alternative for using those resources.

2. _____: economic analysis concerned with the individual choices made by participants in the economy--also called <u>price theory</u>.

3. _____: the rate of upward movement in the price level for an aggregate of goods and services.

4. _____: seeks to forecast the impact of changes in economic policies or conditions on observable items, such as production, sales, prices, and personal incomes, and then tries to determine who gains and who loses as a result of the changes.

5. _____: the mechanism through which the use of labor, land, structures, vehicles, equipment, and natural resources is organized to satisfy the desires of those who live in a society.

6. _____: the imbalance between the desires of society and the means with which those desires are satisfied.

7. _____: evaluates the desirability of alternative outcomes according to underlying value judgments about what is good or bad.

8. _____: a study of society's use of scarce resources in the satisfaction of the unlimited desires of its members.

9. _____: economic analysis that considers the overall

performance of the economy with respect to total national production, consumption, average prices, and employment levels.

10. _____: measures the ratio of the number of people classified as unemployed to the total labor force.

SKILLS REVIEW

Concept: Describe the mechanism of the economy

1. List the three basic questions that all economies must answer:

    a. _____
    b. _____
    c. _____

Concept: Opportunity cost

2. Identify the likely opportunity costs associated with the following decisions.

    Hint: Think in terms of what would likely be sacrificed in pursuing a decision. In other words, what would have been the next best use of your time, money, or resources?

    a. You decide to attend a university full time.
    b. Your decision to purchase a new home results in a larger portion of your income committed to mortgage payments.
    c. You are having such a good time in the Caribbean, that you decide to extend your vacation by taking an additional week of vacation at no pay.
    d. As a manager, you decide to commit some of the corporation's resources to a plant expansion project.

3. Advanced Problem. Suppose that you are a farmer capable of producing corn or soybeans. Over the years you have maintained records regarding your total production of both crops. Assume that you have made full and efficient use of your resources throughout this period. Furthermore, assume that the only reason corn relative to soy production has changed is because of your desire to grow the combination of crops that produce the highest net farm income. Referring to your production data below, determine the opportunity cost of producing an additional bushel of soybeans. If the current price of a bushel of corn is $7, what is the dollar value of that opportunity cost?

Production Data
(000s of bushels)

	Soy	Corn
1981	100	20
1982	50	40
1983	25	50
1984	0	60
1985	75	30
1986	150	0
1987	125	10

a. Opportunity cost measured in bushels of corn: _____ bushels

b. Opportunity cost measured in dollars: $ _____

Concept: **Positive and normative analysis**

4. In the blanks provided, indicate whether the following statements involve positive (P) or normative (N) analysis:

   a. ____ Fred ought to get his act together.
   b. ____ My professor arrives for class late every morning.
   c. ____ The drought in the Midwest is increasing corn prices.
   d. ____ Government is too obtrusive and therefore its power should be reduced.
   e. ____ Lower state income tax rates are always preferable to higher rates.
   f. ____ Poverty is a serious problem in the United States.

5. Monitor your own statements as you interact with friends, family members, or fellow students and try to determine if your statements are based upon fact or observation or value judgments. For one day, carry a sheet of paper divided into two columns--label one column "fact" and the other "value judgment." Record your interactions with others and think about whether positive or normative statements are being made.

SELF-TEST FOR MASTERY

Select the best answer.

1. Which of the following best describes the study of economics?

   a. A study concerned with how to make money
   b. A fuzzy combination of Wall Street and insurance
   c. A study of how society uses its goods and services in determining the proper distribution of income
   d. A study of how society uses its scarce economic resources in satisfying the unlimited desires of society

2. The mechanism through which resources are organized in order to satisfy the desires of society is known as:

   a. A corporation.
   b. Government.
   c. An economy.
   d. A factory.

3. Scarcity means that:

   a. Resources are in finite supply.
   b. Poverty takes its toll on those with limited means.
   c. Choices are unnecessary.
   d. An imbalance exists between desires and the means by which those desires are satisfied.

4. The real cost of a choice or decision is its opportunity cost. Which of the following best defines opportunity cost?

   a. The actual dollar outlay required to produce a good or service
   b. The value of the forgone next best alternative
   c. The value to the resources required to implement the decision

d. The value of the loss that occurs when a speculative investment does not meet profit expectations

5. If a state government had a limited amount of tax and other revenue but decided to substantially increase the amount of appropriations to public education, appropriations to other functions such as corrections, health, and welfare would diminish. What concept is represented by this statement?

a. Opportunity costs
b. Normative analysis
c. Efficiency
d. None of the above

6. Microeconomics is a branch of economics that:

a. Studies the impact of inflation on the unemployment rate.
b. Studies the behavior of individual decision-making units in the economy.
c. Studies the effects and consequences of the aggregate behavior of all decision-making units.
d. Is only concerned with the determination of income.

7. Macroeconomics is a branch of economics that:

a. Studies the effects and consequences of the aggregate behavior of all decision-making units in the economy.
b. Is only concerned with the determination of individual market prices.
c. Studies the behavior of individual decision-making units in the economy.
d. Studies neither inflation nor unemployment.

8. Topics such as business cycles, unemployment, and inflation are studied in _____, whereas the determination of prices and the study of individual markets are studied in _____.

a. Positive analysis/normative analysis
b. Normative analysis/positive analysis
c. Microeconomics/macroeconomics
d. Macroeconomics/microeconomics

9. The rate of unemployment is defined as:

a. The number of job seekers.
b. The number of individuals who have been laid off or are unemployed but seeking work.
c. The number of job seekers as a percentage of total employment.
d. The number of individuals who have been laid off or are unemployed but seeking work expressed as a percentage of the labor force.

10. With respect to inflation, which of the following is true?

a. A one-time price increase of bananas constitutes inflation.
b. Inflation represents a widespread and continuing increase in prices.
c. Inflation represents the main or fundamental problem faced by all economies.
d. Inflation is studied in microeconomics.

11. Which of the following involves value judgments?

a. Normative analysis
b. Positive analysis

    c.   The search for a superconducting material operable at room temperature

    d.   The decision to install lifeline (discount) electric utility rates for the elderly

    e.   A and d

12.   _____ makes "ought to" or "should" statements, whereas _____ makes statements based upon observable events and therefore can be subjected to empirical verification.

    a. Positive analysis/normative analysis
    b. Normative analysis/positive analysis
    c. Macroeconomics/microeconomics
    d. Microeconomics/macroeconomics

THINK IT THROUGH

1.   Define economics, including its branches, microeconomics and macroeconomics. What are some topics typically addressed by each of these branches?

2.   Explain why scarcity and opportunity costs are related. Give an example from your personal or business experiences of the opportunity cost of a decision.

3.   As you will discover later in the text, under certain assumptions it can be shown theoretically that a perfectly competitive economy will produce a distribution of income where labor receives an income based upon its productive contribution to the enterprise. This is consistent with the protestant ethic which states that hard work and reward should go hand in hand. This statement involves both positive and normative analysis. Discuss.

CHAPTER ANSWERS

In Brief: Chapter Summary

1. Scarce   2. Unlimited   3. Scarcity   4. Opportunity cost   5. Next best
6. Efficiency   7. Microeconomics   8. Macroeconomics   9. Macroeconomics   10. Microeconomics   11. "What is"   12. Normative   13. Value judgments

Vocabulary Review

1. Opportunity costs 2. Microeconomics   3. Inflation   4. Positive analysis
5. Economy 6. Scarcity   7. Normative analysis 8. Economics 9. Macroeconomics   10. Unemployment rate

Skills Review

1.   a.   What will be produced?
    b.   How will goods and services be produced?
    c.   To whom will goods and services be distributed?

2.   a.   If you attend a university full time, there are a number of potential sacrifices all of which have value. The most obvious sacrifice is the potential income you could have earned had you been employed full

time. You may have less time to spend with your family and friends, as well as less leisure time. Direct outlays on tuition, room, and board could have been invested or saved.

b. As recently as the early 1970s it was not uncommon for homeowners to allocate only 15% of their incomes to mortgage payments. Today it is more common for families to spend as much as 25% to 35% of their incomes for housing. If you commit a much larger share of your income to housing, given scarcity (or a limited income), you must cut your spending elsewhere. The reduction in the value of goods and services consumed as a result of purchasing a more expensive home represents the opportunity cost of your decision.

c. If you choose to take a week of vacation without pay, you obviously sacrifice the income you would have earned otherwise. That extra week, as a result, is much more costly to you than the previous week of vacation.

d. If corporate funds are to be used for a specific project, they cannot be used for alternative investment projects. Depending on the needs of the firm, the funds could be invested in financial assets generating an interest income. The funds could be used for other investment projects yielding income. Businesses interested in achieving the highest level of profit will usually allocate funds to the projects yielding the highest return because to do otherwise would mean that the firm would be sacrificing opportunities to earn profit.

3. a. Two fifths of a bushel of corn. Historical production data reveal that for every 10,000-bushel increase in corn production, there is a 25,000-bushel decrease in soy output. Because the farmer is fully using his or her resources and employing these resources efficiently, the only way soy production can be increased is by withdrawing resources from corn production and employing those resources in soy production. Consequently, for every bushel increase in corn production, there is a 2.5-bushel decrease in soy production. In other words, for every additional bushel of soy produced, corn production must be reduced by two fifths of a bushel.

b. Two fifths of a bushel times $7 per bushel = $2.80. The opportunity cost of producing a bushel of soy measured in dollars represents the dollar value of that sacrificed output of corn.

4. a. N   b. P   c. P   d. N   e. N   f. N

Self-Test for Mastery

1. d   2. c   3. d   4. b   5. a   6. b   7. a   8. d   9. d   10. b   11. e
12. b

Think it Through

1. Economics is a study of how society uses its scarce resources to satisfy the unlimited wants of its members. Macroeconomics is a study of the effects of the aggregate economic behavior of all decision-making units in the economy, whereas microeconomics is concerned with an analysis of the decision making of individual firms, households, or other decision-making units. Business cycles, inflation, and unemployment are topics covered in macroeconomics. Microeconomics, also known as price theory, analyzes among other things individual markets and the determination of prices.

2.   If there were no scarcity, the opportunity costs of decisions requiring the use of resources would be zero. There would be such a thing as a "free lunch." If resources were available everywhere and in unlimited supply, the farmer in the above example could at any time produce more soy or corn without having to sacrifice the output of the other.

3.   The first statement regarding a competitive economy's ability to reward labor on the basis of labor's productive contribution is deduced from economic theory, which itself is a collection of postulates based upon empirically verifiable observations. In this sense, this statement involves positive analysis. The second statement declares that this method of income distribution is "good." But this is based upon a value system consistent with the protestant ethic, which is only one of many possible value systems. It is therefore a normative statement.

8

Basic Tools for Analyzing Economic Relationships

IN BRIEF: APPENDIX SUMMARY

Fill in the blanks to summarize appendix content.

Describing data graphically requires a number of considerations. Does the variable take on positive values only or does it also take on negative values? What is the unit of measurement? For what purpose are the data to be plotted? If you want to present a cause-and-effect relationship between two variables, a plot of the variables on a (1)_____ (set of axes, bar graph) would be appropriate. If you are interested in the cause-and-effect relationship of a third variable, a (2)_____ (bar graph, set of axes) cannot be used. If you are only interested in presenting the fluctuation in a variable over time, a plot on a set of axes is usually all that is required, although a bar graph can be employed.

Because most economic variables take on positive values, a set of axes having an origin in the extreme (3)_____ (northeast, southwest) corner is required. As you read vertically upward or horizontally rightward from the origin, units of measurement become increasingly positive. Each axis is defined in terms of a unit of measurement. Units of measurement can be discrete or continuous. A (4)_____ (discrete, continuous) variable is expressed in units that are indivisible. A (5)_____ (discrete, continuous) variable is divisible into fractions of a whole.

A plot of a specific set of values or (6)_____ (coordinates, intersections) of two variables on a set of axes produces a curve when the points are connected by a line. The curve can reveal important information regarding the association among the two variables plotted. If the variable on the vertical axis increases when the variable plotted on the horizontal axis increases, there is a (7)_____ (positive, negative) relationship between the two variables. If the variable on the vertical axis decreases when the variable plotted on the horizontal axis increases, the relationship is a (8)_____ (positive, negative) one. If there is no change in the variable plotted on the vertical axis when the variable on the horizontal axis changes, there is no relationship between the variables.

The (9)_____ (intersection, slope) of a curve describes the rate of change in the variable on the vertical axis given a change in the variable on the horizontal axis. A curve describing a positive relationship between variables has a (10)_____ (positive, negative) slope. A curve describing a negative relationship has a (11)_____ (positive, negative) slope, and a curve indicating no relationship between the two variables has a slope of zero. On a bowl-shaped or inverted bowl-shaped curve, a slope of zero represents the point at which the curve (or the value of the variable plotted on the vertical axis) reaches a maximum or minimum value. Two curves that just touch each other but do not intersect have (12)_____ (unequal, equal) slopes at that point of tangency. If two curves (13)_____ (intersect, are tangent), the two slopes at that point can both be positive or negative or one can be positive and the other negative, but they cannot be equal to each other as is the case with (14)_____ (an intersection, a tangency).

VOCABULARY REVIEW

Write the key term from the list below next to its definition.

Key Terms

Origin	Coordinate
Curve	Positive relationship
Slope	Negative relationship
Bar graph	Discrete variable
Intersection	Continuous variable
Tangency	Time series data

Definitions

1. _____: Measures the rate at which the variable on the vertical axis rises or falls as the variable on the horizontal axis increases.

2. _____: Data that show fluctuations in a variable over time.

3. _____: The point on a set of axes at which both variables, $\underline{X}$ and $\underline{Y}$, take on a value of zero.

4. _____: A graph that shows that value of $\underline{Y}$ as the height of a bar for each corresponding value of $\underline{X}$.

5. _____: The point at which two curves cross on a set of axes.

6. _____: Variable $\underline{Y}$ increases whenever variable $\underline{X}$ decreases and vice versa.

7. _____: Variable $\underline{Y}$ increases whenever variable $\underline{X}$ increases and vice versa.

8. _____: A variable that can realistically and meaningfully take on minute fractions of a variable.

9. _____: A point at which two curves just touch but do not intersect.

10. _____: A pair of numbers that corresponds to a pair of values for variables $\underline{X}$ and $\underline{Y}$ when plotted on a set of axes.

11. _____: A variable that cannot vary by fractions of units.

12. _____: A straight or curved line drawn to connect points plotted on a set of axes.

SKILLS REVIEW

1. a. Using the production data from question 3 in the Skills Review section in Chapter 1, construct the following bar charts:

	Soybeans (000s of bushels)	Production Data Corn (000s of bushels)
1981	100	20
1982	50	40
1983	25	50
1984	0	60
1985	75	30
1986	150	0
1987	125	10

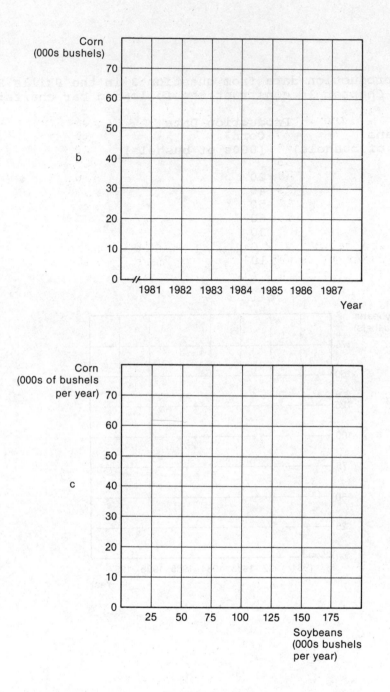

b.   Which of the above bar charts depict time series data and which
     depict a functional relationship representing the concept of
     opportunity costs?

          1.   Figure A _____
          2.   Figure B _____
          3.   Figure C _____

2. The following data represent quantities of tennis rackets demanded by consumers and supplied by producers at various prices:

Tennis Rackets
(000s per month)

Price per Racket	Quantity Demanded	Quantity Supplied
$10	75	15
20	65	20
30	55	25
40	45	30
50	35	35
60	25	40
70	15	45

a. In the figure below, plot a curve showing the relationship between price and quantity demanded by consumers. The relationship is a _____ relationship and has a _____ slope.

Price per racket

Quantity of rackets demanded (000s per month)

b. In the figure below, plot a curve showing the relationship between price and quantity supplied by producers. The relationship is a _____ relationship and has a _____ slope.

Price per racket

Quantity of rackets supplied (000s per month)

c. In the figure below, plot both curves from parts a and b above. The coordinate at which the two curves cross is called a/an _____. At what price and quantity supplied and demanded do the two curves cross? Price_____, quantity demanded_____, quantity supplied_____.

Price per racket

Quantity of rackets supplied and demanded (000s per month)

3. Suppose that you are a manager for a producer of business forms and you have noticed that over time your sales of business forms appear to increase as the rate of growth in the nation's output or GNP increases. That observed relationship is depicted in the table below:

	Rate of Growth in GNP (%)	Sales of Business Forms
Year 1	3.0	15,000
2	3.5	17,000
3	2.0	11,000
4	5.5	25,000
5	6.0	27,000

a. In the figure below, plot a time series curve describing the behavior of the rate of growth in GNP.

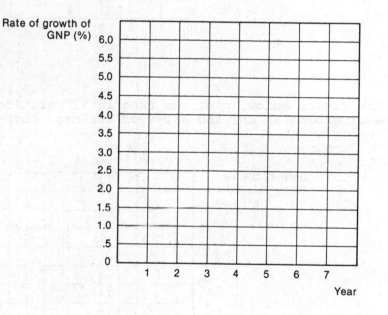

b.   In the figure below, plot a time series curve describing the behavior
of business forms sales.

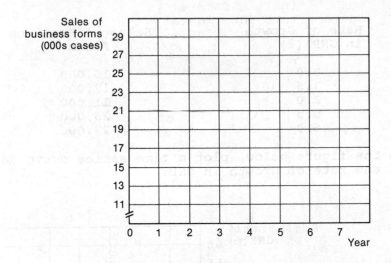

c.   In the figure below, plot the functional relationship between the
rate of growth in GNP and sales of business forms.

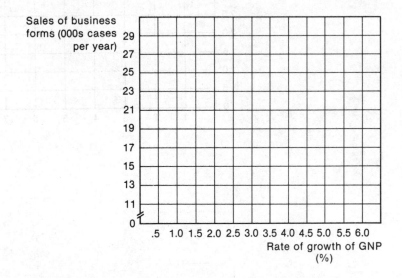

d.   <u>Advanced Question.</u> If the rate of growth in GNP is expected to be
4.5% in year 6, what would you predict to happen to business form
sales?

4.   a.   For the figures below, indicate whether a tangency exists or an
intersection occurs at:

        Point A in left figure: _____
        Point B in right figure: _____

16

b. For the figures below, indicate whether the curves at the point of tangency or intersection have a positive or negative slope.

    Curve 1 in left figure: _____
    Curve 2 in left figure: _____
    Curve 1 in right figure: _____
    Curve 2 in right figure: _____

5. Referring to the figures below, indicate whether the slope at the designated points are positive, negative, or zero.

1. _____
2. _____
3. _____
4. _____
5. _____
6. _____
7. _____
8. _____
9. _____

6. __Advanced Problem__. Suppose two variables are related to each other by the following equation:

$$Y = a + bX, \quad \text{where } a = 10 \text{ and } b = 1/2$$

a. Complete the table. (Use the Y1 column for the case where a = 10.)

X	Y1	Y2
100		
200		
300		
400		
500		
600		
700		
800		

b. Plot the relationship between X and Y1 in the figure below.
    (1) The slope = _____.
    (2) The intercept (value of Y1 at X = 0) = _____.

c. Assume that the constant term a in the above equation increases from
    10 to 60. Complete column Y2 above and plot the new relationship in
    the figure in part b. The curve has shifted _____. The
    slope = _____ and the intercept = _____.

SELF-TEST FOR MASTERY

Select the best answer.

1. Which of the following does not indicate a functional relationship between
    variables X and Y?

    a. As X increases, Y increases
    b. As X decreases, Y increases
    c. As X increases, Y remains unchanged
    d. As X decreases, Y decreases

2. When a value for X is paired with a value for Y on a set of axes, this
    combination of values is known as:

    a. A tangency.
    b. An intersection.
    c. A coordinate.
    d. The origin, if at least one value is zero.

3. A curve represents a set of coordinates that are connected by a line.
    Which of the following statements is true?

    a. A curve by definition cannot be a straight line.
    b. A curve must have either a positive or negative slope.
    c. A line of zero slope is not a function and therefore is not a curve.

d. A curve may be a straight or a curved line. If it is a curved line, it is possible to have a positive, negative, or zero slope at different points on that curve.

4. If Y increases as X is increased, there is a _____ relationship between X and Y. If Y decreases as X is increased, the functional relationship is said to be a _____ one.

   a. Adverse, positive
   b. Negative, positive
   c. Obtuse, negative
   d. Positive, negative

5. A function exhibiting a positive relationship between X and Y has a _____ slope and a curve that is _____.

   a. Positive, upsloping
   b. Negative, downsloping
   c. Positive, downsloping
   d. Negative, upsloping

6. A function exhibiting a negative relationship between X and Y has a _____ slope and a curve which is _____.

   a. Positive, upsloping
   b. Negative, downsloping
   c. Positive, downsloping
   d. Negative, upsloping

7. Which of the following defines the origin?

   a. The origin is the beginning of a set of time series data.
   b. The origin is the coordinate on a set of axes where the value of variables X and Y are both zero.
   c. The origin is the coordinate on a set of axes where the values of variables X and Y represent the initial values of the data plotted.
   d. The origin is that point on the northeast corner of a set of positive axes.

8. The slope can be defined as the:

   a. Change in Y/change in X.
   b. Rate of change in Y over time.
   c. Rate of change in X over time.
   d. None of the above.

9. A _____ variable is indivisible into fractions of a unit, whereas a _____ variable is divisible into fractions of a whole.

   a. Continuous, discrete
   b. Discrete, continuous
   c. Positive, negative
   d. Time series, constant

10. Which of the following variables have discrete units of measurement?

    a. Automobiles
    b. Gasoline
    c. Coffee beans
    d. The nation's money supply

11. Of the following variables, which one is a continuous variable?

    a. Computer
    b. House
    c. Basketball
    d. Natural gas

12. When two curves just touch each other, they have _____ slopes.

    a. Equal
    b. Unequal
    c. Positive and negative
    d. Only zero

13. The point at which two curves just touch each other is called:

    a. A tangency.
    b. The origin.
    c. A data point.
    d. An intersection.

14. The point at which two curve cross is called:

    a. A tangency.
    b. The origin.
    c. A data point.
    d. An intersection.

15. The values of X and Y at an intersection:

    a. Will be the same on both curves.
    b. Will be the same on both curves for the X variable only.
    c. Will not be the same on both curves.
    d. Depend upon the placement of the origin.

THINK IT THROUGH

1. Referring to the data below, plot the price and quantity demanded data on the axes below. On the same set of axes, plot the price and quantity supplied data and interpret the meaning of the intersection. Suppose a third variable changes, such as the introduction of VCRs, and as a result the quantity of movie tickets demanded at each price level declines by 20,000 tickets per week. What happens to the curve representing the demand data? What happens to the intersection?

Price per Ticket	Quantity Demanded	Quantity Supplied
	(000s per week)	
$2	80	20
3	70	30
4	60	40
5	50	50
6	40	60
7	30	70

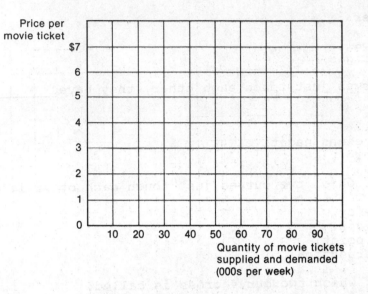

Price per movie ticket

Quantity of movie tickets supplied and demanded (000s per week)

2.   The following data represent the relationship between interest rates and building permits issued for new residential construction in a local housing market. Plot the relationship on the axes below and determine if a positive or negative relationship exits. Because of a regional recession, assume that local incomes decline and outmigration of people reduce the demand for new housing and thus reduce building permits issued by 100 permits per month at each mortgage rate. Plot the new relationship on the same set of axes and compare the position and slope of the new curve to the one that you previously plotted.

Mortgage Rate %	Permits Issued (000s per month)
8.5	1050
9.0	1000
9.5	950
10.0	900
10.5	850
11.0	800
11.5	750

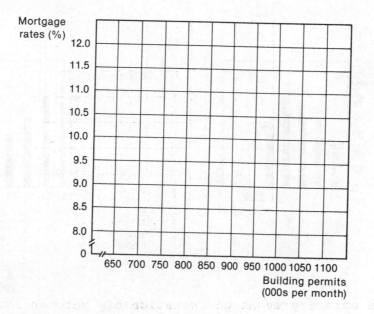

ANSWERS TO CHAPTER APPENDIX

In Brief: Appendix Summary

1. A set of axes or a bar graph 2. Bar graph 3. Southwest 4. Discrete 5. Continuous 6. Coordinates 7. Positive 8. Negative 9. Slope 10. Positive 11. Negative 12. Equal 13. Intersect 14. Tangency

Vocabulary Review

1. Slope 2. Time series data 3. Origin 4. Bar graph 5. Intersection 6. Negative relationship 7. Positive relationship 8. Continuous variable 9. Tangency 10. Coordinate 11. Discrete variable 12. Curve

Skills Review

1.   a.

b. (1) Time series
   (2) Time series
   (3) Functional relationship

2. a. Price per racket

Negative, negative

b. Price per racket

Positive, positive

c. Price per racket

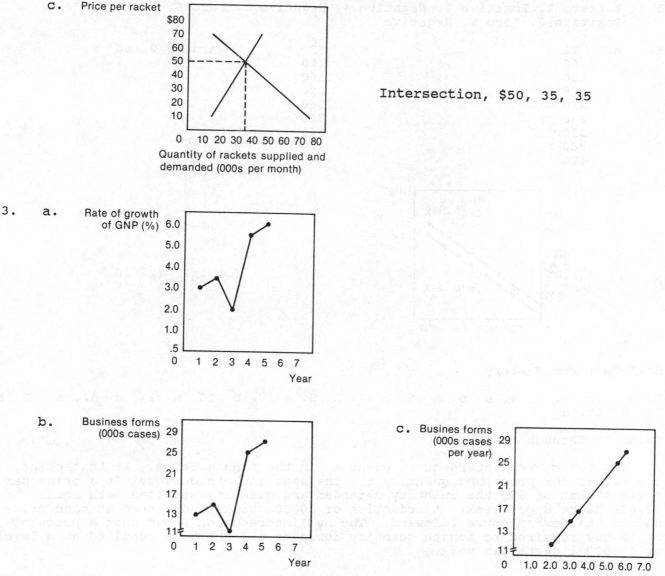

Quantity of rackets supplied and demanded (000s per month)

Intersection, $50, 35, 35

3. a. Rate of growth of GNP (%)

Year

b. Business forms (000s cases)

Year

c. Busines forms (000s cases per year)

Rate of growth of GNP (%)

d. From the functional relationship in part c above, it can be seen that a positive relationship exists between the rate of growth in GNP and sales of business forms. The slope of the curve is the change in business form sales for each percentage change in the rate of growth of GNP. Business form sales increase by 4,000 cases for each 1% increase in the GNP growth rate. If you expect that the growth rate of GNP will be 4.5% in year 6, then sales of business forms can be predicted to fall from 27,000 to 21,000 cases.

4. a. Tangency, intersection
   b. Negative, negative, positive, positive

5.   1. Zero 2. Positive 3. Negative 4. Negative 5. Zero 6. Positive 7. Positive 8. Zero 9. Negative

6.   a.   Y1   c.   Y2   Upward, 1/2. 60
            60   110
           110   160
           160   210
           210   260
           260   310
           310   360
           360   410
           410   460

b. Y_1, Y_2

(1) 1/2   (2) 10

Self-Test for Mastery

1. c 2. c 3. d 4. a 5. a 6. b 7. b 8. a 9. b 10. a 11. d 12. a 13. a 14. d 15. a

Think It Through

1.   The two curves intersect at point A in the figure below. At that point, the values for price and quantity are the same on both curves. At a price per movie ticket of $5, the quantity demanded and quantity supplied both equal 50,000 tickets per week. A reduction of 20,000 tickets demanded at each price shifts the demand curve leftward. The new intersection shows that a price of $4 is now required to equate quantity demanded and quantity supplied at a level of 40,000 tickets per week.

26

2. The relationship between mortgage rates and new building permits issued is a negative one. If building permits issued decline at each mortgage rate by 100 permits per month, the new curve lies to the left of the old curve but has the same slope.

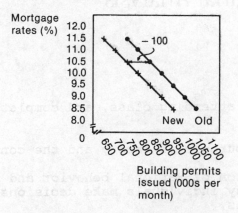

27

2

The Economic Way of Reasoning: Models and Marginal Analysis

CHAPTER CHALLENGES

After studying your text, attending class, and completing this chapter, you should be able to:

1. Understand the purpose of theory and the concept of an economic model and its uses.
2. Develop the notion of rational behavior and a general method of analyzing the way individuals make decisions, which is called marginal analysis.

IN BRIEF: CHAPTER SUMMARY

Fill in the blanks to summarize chapter content.

Economic analysis helps us understand the world around us. It helps us understand the functioning of the various sectors in the economy and the choices made by individual decision-making units. (1)_____ (Assumptions, Economic theories) simplify reality so that the underlying cause-and-effect relationships among variables can be understood. (2)_____ (Economic variables, Data) are quantities or dollar amounts that have more than one value. Theories are necessary in order to better understand the complexities of reality.

(3)_____(A bar graph, An economic model) is a simplified way of expressing a theory. It can be expressed verbally, graphically, in tables, or mathematically. Assumptions underlie a theory because theories are (4)_____(depictions of, abstractions from) reality, and it is necessary to establish the environment and motivation of people for which the theory holds. Economic models can be used to develop hypotheses. (5)_____ (An assumption, A hypothesis) is a statement of relationship between two variables that can be tested by empirical verification. Deductive reasoning is used when taking a general body of knowledge or theory and using implications of the theory to construct hypotheses. Hypotheses that have been subjected to repeated empirical verification and have withstood the test of time become (6)_____ (hypotheses, economic principles or laws). A good model is one that can generate accurate predictions. But even a model that does not predict perfectly can still be useful in helping us understand the causal relationships among variables and the consequence of the assumptions underlying the model. The causal relationships that we want to understand are difficult to isolate unless we make the assumption of (7)_____(_ceteris paribus_, the invisible hand). Otherwise, we cannot be sure that we have identified the exact relationship between the two variables of interest.

Economic analysis makes the assumption of rationality. Rationality means that most people behave as if they are comparing the additional gains or benefits from a choice or decision to the sacrifices or opportunity costs associated with that decision. The opportunity cost of a decision is known as its marginal (8)_____(benefit, cost). If the marginal benefits of a decision exceed the marginal costs, the individual's net gain or benefit (9)_____(increases, decreases). If the marginal cost of a decision exceeds the marginal benefits, the decision would not be undertaken because the individual would experience a net (10)_____(loss, gain). If a choice or decision is pursued to the point where marginal benefits and marginal costs are equal, the individual achieves the (11)_____(maximum, minimum) net gain.

VOCABULARY REVIEW

Write the key term from the list below next to its definition.

Key Terms

Marginal analysis	Ceteris paribus
Theory	Behavioral assumptions
Variable	Rational behavior
Economic model	Marginal benefit
Hypothesis	Marginal cost

Definitions

1. _____: a quantity or dollar amount that can have more than one value.

2. _____: "other things being equal"--used to acknowledge that other influences aside from the one whose effect is being analyzed must be controlled for in testing a hypothesis.

3. _____: establishes the motivation of persons for the purpose of understanding cause-and-effect relationships among economic variables.

4. _____: a decision-making technique involving a systematic comparison of benefits and costs of actions.

5. _____: the additional benefit obtained when one extra unit of an item is obtained.

6. _____: the sacrifice made to obtain an additional unit of an item.

7. _____: an abstraction or simplification of actual relationships; establishes cause-and-effect relationships.

8. _____: statement of a relationship between two or more variables.

9. _____: seeking to gain by choosing to undertake actions for which the extra benefit exceeds the associated extra cost.

10. _____: a simplified way of expressing economic behavior or how some sector of the economy functions.

SKILLS REVIEW

Concept: Economic models and uses

1. Develop a hypothesis regarding the level of family spending on goods and services and the level of family income. Describe that hypothesized relationship by setting up two columns of data reflecting the variables in your hypothesis. Is the hypothesized relationship a positive or negative relationship? Suppose that you gathered actual data on your variables and for some families your hypothesized relationship did not hold. Of what use is the ceteris paribus assumption in trying to isolate the relationship between family spending and income?

Family Spending on Goods and Services ($)	Family Income ($)

2. Suppose that you want to investigate the relationship between prices of restaurant meals and the quantity of meals demanded by local area households. Economic theory implies that there is a negative relationship between price and quantity demanded but that income, tastes, preferences, and other variables also influence quantity demanded. Clearly state your hypothesis and its underlying assumptions.

Concept: Marginal analysis

3. During the presidential campaign, Republican George Bush recommended that his party's platform include a proposal for child care payments of up to $1,000 to low-income working families and a tax credit for other families with children under age 4 in which at least one parent works. Assume that you are a single parent with young children. Using marginal analysis, assess the impact of such a program on your decision to work or to work additional hours.

4. Assume that the price you are willing to pay for an additional unit of a good measures the marginal benefit received. How could you measure the marginal cost of the decision to consume that extra unit?

5. A rational decision maker comparing the extra gains and losses of a decision will _____ net gains if the decision or choice is pursued to the point where _____ equals _____. Explain the logic of this statement.

6. Advanced Question. You are an administrator of the Environmental Protection Agency concerned with allocating cleanup funds from the agency's Superfund for the removal of toxic wastes. The following data represent the marginal benefits and costs associated with removing units of pollution from a polluted river. Your task is to decide if there is a net gain to society from cleaning the river and what level of pollution reduction would maximize that net gain.

Units of Pollution Reduction	Marginal Benefits (millions of dollars)	Marginal Costs (millions of dollars)
0	$ 0	$ 0
1	10	2
2	8	4
3	6	6
4	4	8
5	2	10

a.   Is there a net gain to society from cleaning the river? Discuss.

b.   Nets gains are maximized at a level of pollution reduction of
       _____, where marginal benefits and marginal costs are _____.

SELF-TEST FOR MASTERY

1.   The decision-making technique involving a systematic comparison of the
      benefits and costs of actions is known as:

      a.   Deductive reasoning.
      b.   Total gains analysis.
      c.   Marginal analysis.
      d.   _Ceteris paribus._

2.   A/An _____ is a simplification of reality seeking to uncover the
      underlying cause-and-effect relationships among economic _____.

      a.   Assumptions/variables
      b.   Economic theory/assumptions
      c.   Hypothesis/theories
      d.   Economic theory/variables

3.   Which of the following is true regarding economic variables?

      a.   Economic variables have more than one value.
      b.   Economic variables are quantities or dollar amounts.
      c.   Economic variables are necessary to economic theories and models.
      d.   All of the above.

4.   A/An _____ is a simplified way of expressing an economic theory.

      a.   Economic model
      b.   Assumption
      c.   Abstraction
      d.   Economic principle

5.   Which of the following assumptions is necessary in order to isolate the
      relationship between two variables?

      a.   "All things allowed to vary"
      b.   "All things held constant"
      c.   "_Ceteris paribus_"
      d.   B and c

6.   If gasoline prices rise, the quantity of gasoline demanded will fall.
      This statement is a/an:

      a.   Assumption.
      b.   Theory.
      c.   Abstraction.
      d.   Hypothesis.

7.   Economic hypotheses that have been subjected to repeated empirical
      investigation over time and have not been rejected, become:

      a.   Economic policy
      b.   Assumptions

31

c. Economic principles or laws
d. None of the above

8. If household purchases of automobiles are determined by both the level of household income and the interest rate and you want to isolate the relationship between interest rates and auto sales, you must assume:

   a. That the interest rate remains unchanged.
   b. That auto sales remain unchanged.
   c. That household income remains unchanged.
   d. None of the above because you would want to know both the effect of interest rates and income on auto sales.

9. Which of the following best defines rational behavior?

   a. Seeking to gain by choosing to undertake actions for which the marginal benefits exceed the associated marginal costs
   b. A comparison of the total gains and losses from a decision
   c. Decisions that avoid habit or impulse purchases
   d. Improving net gain by pursuing decisions in which the marginal costs of a decision exceed the marginal benefits

10. _____ can be defined as the extra benefit received from undertaking some action.

    a. Total benefit
    b. Total gain
    c. Marginal benefit
    d. Total net gain

11. _____ can be defined as the extra cost associated with some action.

    a. Total cost
    b. Marginal cost
    c. Total loss
    d. Total net loss

12. The total net gain from a decision or action reaches a _____ when a decision or action is pursued to the point where _____ equals _____.

    a. Maximum, total cost, total benefit
    b. Minimum, marginal benefit, marginal cost
    c. Minimum, total benefit, marginal benefit
    d. Maximum, marginal benefit, marginal cost

13. The sacrifice made to obtain an additional unit of an item is known as:

    a. Opportunity cost.
    b. The maximum tradeoff.
    c. Marginal cost.
    d. A and c.
    e. B and c.

THINK IT THROUGH

1. Define the concepts of economic theory and economic models. Discuss the importance of assumptions underlying models and theories.

2. Pollution is harmful to society, and the reduction of pollution levels increase society's total benefits. But if a 50% reduction in the pollution level resulted in an equality between the marginal benefits and marginal costs associated with pollution reduction, society would be better off if pollution were not eliminated completely. Reconcile the two statements.

3. A rational person would never engage in habit or impulse buying. Discuss.

4. A hypothesis requires the use of the <u>ceteris paribus</u> assumption. Why? Give an example.

5. A theory must depict reality. Do you agree? Explain.

CHAPTER ANSWERS

In Brief: Chapter Summary

1. Economic theories 2. Economic variables 3. Economic model 4. Abstractions from 5. Hypothesis 6. Economic principles or laws 7. <u>Ceteris paribus</u> 8. cost 9. Increase 10. Loss 11. Maximum

Vocabulary Review

1. Variable 2. <u>Ceteris paribus</u> 3. Behavioral assumptions 4. Marginal analysis 5. Marginal benefit 6. Marginal cost 7. Theory 8. Hypothesis 9. Rational behavior 10. Economic model

Skills Review

1. <u>Hypothesis</u>: Other things held constant, family spending on goods and services is expected to be positively related to family income.

   If upon gathering data on family spending and income it is found that the relationship between spending and income is not positive, that does not mean that your hypothesis is invalid. To determine the validity of your hypothesis, you must isolate the relationship you are interested in from all other variables that might influence family spending. If you do not, you cannot be sure that an increase in family spending is the result of increases in income or some third variable.

2. <u>Hypothesis</u>: Other things being the same, the price of restaurant meals and the quantity of restaurant meals demanded are expected to be inversely (negatively) related.

   The <u>ceteris paribus</u> assumption is necessary to control for other factors that influence quantity demanded, such as income and tastes and preferences. For instance, prices could be falling but incomes could fall as well. A family might dine out less often even at lower prices if their income has fallen.

3. As a working parent and particularly a single working parent, one of the major costs associated with work is child care. If you worked full time

at the minimum wage of $3.35 per hour and paid $450 per month for child care for two children, you would have $86 dollars left over to support you and your family. There is little incentive to work full time for a month just to bring home $86. But suppose that as a result of new legislation, $100 of that monthly child care bill is paid for by the government. You are now left with $186 per month. This amount, although insufficient to meet the minimum needs of a family of three, is nevertheless still very important. If you were deterred from working before the new law, publicly subsidized child care payments increase the net gain to you from work and might induce you to seek employment. If you are already working, these payments might induce you to work additional hours because now the net gains from work are higher.

The marginal benefits from working an additional hour include among other things the value of goods and services that can be purchased with the income earned from that hour of work. The marginal cost of work involves the sacrifices incurred in order to work. These sacrifices include the loss of leisure time, the loss of time spent with family and friends, and the resources spent on such things as child care and transportation that could have otherwise been spent on goods and services.

Child care subsidies can be viewed as reducing the marginal cost of an hour of work or as increasing the marginal benefits realized from work. A reduction in day care costs increases the amount of the hourly wage available for non-day care expenditures. In this sense, the marginal benefit of an hour of work increases. Regardless of how the problem is viewed, total net gains from work increase. This will likely increase employment among single parents.

4. The marginal cost of a decision to consume a unit of a good is the sacrificed next-preferred goods that could have been consumed. The dollar value of this forgone consumption is a measure of marginal cost.

5. Maximize, marginal costs, marginal benefits

    If marginal benefits exceed marginal costs from some action, a person can add more to his or her total benefits than total costs by undertaking the action. In other words, net benefit or gain increases. As long as marginal benefits exceed marginal costs, total net gains can be increased by pursuing an activity. When an activity has been pursued to the point where marginal benefits and costs are equal, no further increases to net benefits can be realized because the addition to total benefits would just be offset by the addition to total costs of the action.

6. a. Yes, because marginal benefits from pollution reduction up to a point exceed the sacrifice incurred in reducing pollution.

    b. 3, equal at $6 million. At this point, society's total benefits and costs equal $24 million and $12 million, respectively. Society's net gain is therefore $12 million. No other level of pollution reduction will result in as large of a net gain.

Self-Test for Mastery

1. c 2. d 3. d 4. a 5. d 6. d 7. c 8. c 9. a 10. c 11. b 12. d 13. d

Think it Through

1. Economic theory is a simplification of reality seeking to establish and explain important cause-and-effect relationships in the economy. An economic

model is a simplified way of expressing a theory. A model can be presented verbally, in tables, in graphs, or mathematically. Assumptions are necessary for both theories and models because they outline the environment or motivation of people for which the theory and model hold.

2. If pollution reduction were undertaken to the point where marginal benefit and marginal cost were equal and that happened to be at a 50% level of pollution reduction, then no further net gains to society could be realized by additional reductions in pollution. In fact, if additional pollution reduction beyond the 50% level resulted in marginal costs exceeding marginal benefits, society would experience a net loss and be worse off than when there was more pollution.

3. In fact it might be quite rational for a person to engage in habit or impulse buying if that person experiences psychic loss, dissatisfaction, or stress associated with certain actions or choices. A person may buy the first used car he or she sees but may be doing so in part because of a distaste for bargaining and haggling. A person may shop only locally because of an aversion to driving in traffic.

4. A hypothesis is a statement of relationship between two economic variables. To be certain that you have isolated the cause-and-effect relationship between the two variables, it is necessary to hold the effect of other influencing variables constant.   Otherwise, you cannot be sure that the relationship you have hypothesized is valid or instead results from some third variable that you have not considered.

5. A good theory yields accurate predictions, but even a theory that predicts inaccurately is of value in establishing cause-and-effect relationships and determining the significance of assumptions.

3
Production Possibilities and Opportunity Cost

CHAPTER CHALLENGES

After studying your text, attending class, and completing this chapter, you should be able to:

1. Show how limited available technology and scarce resources imply limited production possibilities over a period.
2. Demonstrate that the use of productive capacity to make more of any one good or service available involves sacrificing the opportunity to make more of other items available.
3. Discuss the basic determinants of a nation's production possibilities and how these can expand over time.
4. Understand the concept of productive efficiency and discuss its significance.
5. Demonstrate that when you use income over a period to buy more of one item, you sacrifice the opportunity to buy more of some other item over the period.

IN BRIEF: CHAPTER SUMMARY

Fill in the blanks to summarize chapter content.

(1)_____(Economy, Production) is the process of using economic resources or inputs in order to produce output. Economic resources consist of labor, (2)_____(capital, money), natural resources, and entrepreneurship. The quantity and productivity of economic resources and the extent and efficiency with which they are employed determine the output potential of a nation during a given period of time. Constraints in the availability or use of resources represent the (3)_____ (opportunity costs, scarcity) confronting nations. (4)_____ (Technology, A larger labor force) allows us to delay the sacrifices implied by scarce resources by increasing the productivity of resources. Improvements in resource productivity mean that a nation can produce more output with a given endowment of resources.

A (5)_____(marginal benefit, production possibilities) curve is a convenient tool for showing the implications of scarce resources. Assuming (a) a given quantity and productivity of resources, as well as a given state of the art with respect to technology and (b) full and efficient employment of resources, it can be shown that a nation can produce more of one class of goods only by (6)_____(sacrificing, increasing) the production of other goods. That sacrifice is a nation's (7)_____ (dollar outlay, opportunity cost) of producing more of a given good. As a nation produces more of a good, the opportunity cost (8)_____(rises, falls) because resources that are increasingly (9)_____(less, more) productive must be transferred from the production of other goods. This implies that a given increase in the production of one good will require ever (10)_____(smaller, larger) reductions in output of other goods. The law of increasing costs exists because resources (11)_____(are, are not) equally adaptable to all employments.

A point on the production possibilities curve represents a combination of the two classes of goods in question where output is at a maximum. A point inside the curve implies either (12)_____(unemployed, fully employed) resources or (13)_____(efficiently, inefficiently) employed resources. A point outside the curve represents a combination of goods that is (14)_____(attainable, unattainable) in the short run. But with an increase over time in the quantity and productivity of resources, together with improvements in technology, a point outside the curve is attainable in the long run.

Maximum production is attainable in the short run when resources are employed fully and efficiently. Productive efficiency means that a nation (15)_____(can, cannot) reallocate resources among the production of goods and services and achieve a gain in the output of one good only by causing a reduction in the output of another. Specialization and the division of labor are critical for the attainment of maximum productive efficiency.

The process of economic growth can be shown as (16)_____(inward, outward) shifts over time in the production possibilities curve. A nation can generally produce more of all goods over time as long as it experiences resource growth and an improvement in the quality of resources and technology. A nation's growth is influenced by its willingness to forgo some (17)_____(future, current) production of consumable output so that resources can be used for the production of (18)_____(consumable outputs, capital). Production of capital today increases the production possibilities in the future not only by increasing the quantity of capital but also by increasing the productivity of other resources.

The problem of scarcity confronting nations also confronts the individual. An individual has a limited amount of income per time period with which to consume and save. Given the prices of goods and services, that limited income can purchase, at a maximum, those combinations of goods and services which require the full expenditure of income. A curve representing these various combinations of goods and services is known as a (19)_____(budget line, production possibilities curve). An increase in income over time allows the individual to consume more of all goods. This is shown by an (20)_____ (inward, outward) shift of the budget line. Holding income constant but allowing prices to fall likewise (21)_____(increases, decreases) the quantities that can be purchased. This too shifts the budget line (22)_____(inward, outward). Rising prices or inflation will shift the budget line (23)_____ (inward, outward) if income remains constant. Finally, given a limited income and constant prices, the only way an individual can consume more of one good is by reducing consumption of other goods. The opportunity cost of consuming more of one good is the (24)_____(increase, reduction) in consumption of quantities of other goods.

37

VOCABULARY REVIEW

Write the key term from the list below next to its definition.

Key Terms

Economic resources   Production possibilities curve
Labor   Law of increasing costs
Capital   Productive efficiency
Natural resources   Division of labor
Entrepreneurship   Economic growth
Technology   Budget line

Definitions

1. _____: the inputs used in the process of production.

2. _____: the specialization of workers in particular tasks that are part of a larger undertaking to accomplish a given objective.

3. _____: shows an individual's opportunities to purchase two goods if he or she spends an entire month's income on these two goods at their current prices.

4. _____: the equipment, tools, structures, machinery, vehicles, materials, and skills created to help produce goods and services.

5. _____: shows the maximum possible output of one good that can be produced with available resources given the output of the alternative good over a period.

6. _____: the talent to develop products and processes and to organize production of goods and services.

7. _____: the expansion in production possibilities that results from increased availability and increased productivity of economic resources.

8. _____: the knowledge of how to produce goods and services.

9. _____: the physical and mental efforts of human beings in the production of goods and services.

10. _____: attained when the maximum possible output of any one good is produced given the output of the other goods. At this point it is not possible to reallocate economic resources to increase the output of any single good or service without decreasing the output of some other good or service.

11. _____: acreage and the physical terrain to locate structures, ports, and other facilities; also, natural resources that are used in crude form in production.

12. _____: the opportunity costs of extra production of any one good in an economy will increase as more and more specialized resources best suited for the production of other goods are reallocated away from their best use.

SKILLS REVIEW

Concept: **Scarce resources and limited production possibilities**

1. List four economic resources:

   a. _____
   b. _____
   c. _____
   d. _____

2. Which of the following uses of resources will likely increase labor productivity? (+, Increase; 0, No change.)

   a. _____ Expenditures on capital
   b. _____ Expenditures on more fashionable clothes
   c. _____ Expenditures on health care
   d. _____ Expenditures on education and training
   e. _____ Expenditures on military goods

Concept: **Production possibilities and opportunity cost**

3. The data in the table below represent the production possibilities for a nation producing two classes of goods.

Production Possibilities	Consumer Goods	Capital Goods
	(millions of units)	
A	0	90
B	20	80
C	40	65
D	60	47
E	80	26
F	100	0

   a. On the axes below, plot a production possibilities curve from the data in the table above.

b.   What is the meaning of a point <u>on</u> the production possibilities curve?
c.   What is the opportunity cost associated with an increase in the
     production of consumer goods by 20 million units?
             (1) From point B to C? _____ units of capital
             (2) From point C to D? _____ units of capital
             (3) From point D to E? _____ units of capital
             (4) From point E to F? _____ units of capital
d.   Do opportunity costs rise or fall as additional units of consumer
     goods are produced? Explain.

4.   Referring to the figure below:

     a.   Interpret the meaning of point A.
     b.   Interpret the meaning of point B.

Concept: Determinants of a nation's production possibilities

5.   Indicate whether the following events would cause the production
     possibilities curve to shift outward (O) or would leave it unchanged (U):

     a.   _____ Increased production of houses at full employment
     b.   _____ Increases in the quantity of resources
     c.   _____ Improvements in the quality and productivity of economic
                  resources
     d.   _____ A reduction in prices
     e.   _____ Increases in income
     f.   _____ Improvements in technology

6. a. On the axes below, draw a production possibilities curve for a nation. Now assume that economic growth is taking place. Draw a new production possibilities curve on the same axes reflecting this growth.

b. On the axes below, draw a production possibilities curve for a nation. Assume as above that the nation is experiencing growth, but also assume that the economy is investing more heavily in capital and technology than the economy shown above in part a. Draw a new production possibilities curve reflecting this.

7. a. If a nation used resources for capital or technological improvements for a specific industry, such as the aircraft industry, what are the implications regarding future levels of production not only in the aircraft industry but for other industries as well?

    b. Show the shift in a nation's production possibilities curve that results from the use of resources discussed above.

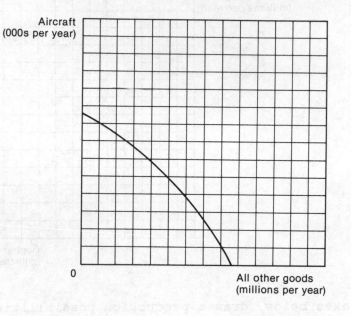

Aircraft
(000s per year)

0

All other goods
(millions per year)

Concept: Limited income and opportunity cost

8. Suppose that as a university student you receive $50 per month from your parents to be used as spending money. You spend all of your money each month on beer or compact discs (CDs). Assume that the price per six-pack of beer is $2.50 and the price of a CD is $10.

    a. Determine six combinations of beer and CDs that cost a total of $50. List the combinations in the table below.

Combination	Beer (six packs)	CDs (units)
A	_____	_____
B	_____	_____
C	_____	_____
D	_____	_____
E	_____	_____

    b. Plot these combinations below. The curve that you have plotted is called a _____.

Beer (six-packs per month): 50, 45, 40, 35, 30, 25, 20, 15, 10, 5, 0

CD's (units per month): 1 2 3 4 5 6 7 8 9 10 11 12

c. On the figure in part b, show what would happen to the curve if:
    (1) your parents began to send $100 per month
    (2) your total funds are still $50, but the price of beer increases to $5 and the price of CDs decreases to $5.

9. Advanced Question

    a. Derive the equation for the budget line in Question 8, part b.
    b. In question 8, part c1 alters the equation for the budget line in what way? Part c2 alters the equation in what way?

SELF-TEST FOR MASTERY

Select the best answer.

1. Which of the following can be defined as the process of using economic resources to produce outputs?

    a. Economics
    b. Production
    c. Economy
    d. Technology

2. Economic resources consist of:

    a. Money, credit, and capital
    b. Labor, capital, and money
    c. Labor, capital, natural resources, and money
    d. Labor, capital, natural resources, and entrepreneurship

3. Which of the following best defines capital?

    a. Money
    b. Plant and tools

    c.   Investment funds available for speculative financial outlays
    d.   Goods or skills that are produced in order to produce goods and
          services

4.   Scarcity exists in the short run because:

    a.   At a given point in time technological growth increases at a constant
          rate.
    b.   At a given point in time the quantity and quality of resources and
          the state of technology are fixed.
    c.   Resources are usually employed inefficiently.
    d.   The world's resources are in finite supply.

5.   A nation must sacrifice the output of some goods in order to produce other
    goods during a given period of time if:

    a.   There is less than full employment of resources.
    b.   Resources are inefficiently employed.
    c.   There is both full and efficient use of economic resources.
    d.   A nation relies on capital goods production.

6.   If a nation is currently operating at a point on its production
    possibilities curve, in order to increase production of one good, the
    production of other goods must be:

    a.   Held constant.
    b.   Increased.
    c.   Decreased.
    d.   None of the above.

7.   If a nation is currently operating at a point inside its production
    possibilities curve, it:

    a.   Has full employment.
    b.   Has unemployed and/or inefficiently employed resources.
    c.   Is operating at full potential.
    d.   Must reduce the output of one good in order to produce more of
          another good.

8.   The law of increasing costs states that:

    a.   Opportunity costs rise as more of a good is produced.
    b.   Opportunity costs fall as more of a good is produced.
    c.   Rising resource prices are inevitable because of scarcity.
    d.   Economic growth is always associated with inflation.

9.   The law of increasing costs is the result of the fact that:

    a.   Resources can be easily adapted to the production of any good.
    b.   Scarcity reduces supply and increases costs.
    c.   Resources are not equally adaptable to all employments.
    d.   People reach a point of satiation at which they no longer purchase
          goods.

10.   Economic growth is the process whereby the production possibilities curve
    shifts:

    a.   Inward
    b.   Outward
    c.   Either inward or outward
    d.   Outward, then inward

11. Points outside of the production possibilities curve are _____ in the _____.

   a. Attainable/short run
   b. Unattainable/short run
   c. Attainable/long run
   d. Unattainable/long run
   e. B and c

12. Production efficiency is achieved:

   a. If resources are reallocated among the production of goods and services and the output of one good can be increased without decreasing the output of other goods.
   b. If there is no waste in the production process.
   c. If resources are reallocated among the production of goods and services and the output of one good can be increased only by reducing the output of other goods.
   d. At a point within the production possibilities curve.

13. If nation A commits a larger share of its resources to capital and technological improvements than nation B, then over time _____ will realize _____ outward shifts in its production possibilities curve.

   a. Nation B/larger
   b. Nation A/smaller
   c. Nations A and B/the same
   d. Nation B/smaller

14. An individual's ability to consume goods and services depends upon:

   a. Income only.
   b. The rate of inflation.
   c. The individual's income and the prices of the goods and services consumed.
   d. Tastes.

15. A/An _____ is a curve indicating an individual's ability to consume various combinations of two goods or services over a period of time.

   a. Production possibilities curve
   b. Income curve
   c. Price line
   d. Budget line

16. The budget line shifts _____ when there is a/an _____ in income.

   a. Inward/increase
   b. Outward/decrease
   c. Inward/decrease
   d. Outward/decrease or increase

17. An individual's ability to increase the consumption of goods and services is _____ when the price of one or both goods _____.

   a. Increased/decrease
   b. Decreased/decrease
   c. Increased/increase
   d. Unchanged/increase unless income decreases

18. The sacrifice or opportunity cost associated with an individual's consumption of an additional good :

   a. Is the reduction in other goods consumed when the individual does not spend all of his or her income.
   b. Is the increase in other goods consumed when unused income is spent.
   c. Is the reduction in other goods consumed when an individual has no additional income.
   d. None of the above

THINK IT THROUGH

1. Explain why a nation's endowment of economic resources necessitates choices between current and future uses of resources.

2. Explain under what conditions a nation incurs an opportunity cost as it produces more of a good. How does the law of increasing cost fit into your discussion?

3. How do technology and capital expenditures improve the quality or productivity of "other" economic resources?

4. Assume that the United States contributes disproportionately more resources to the defense of Western Europe than do the other NATO allies, and as a consequence these other countries can invest a larger share of their resources in capital and other goods and services. Use production possibility curves to show both the short- and long-run consequences regarding the economies of the United States and Western Europe.

POP QUIZ   Read the news brief at the end of this chapter and answer the questions below.

1. Explain the nature of the short-run opportunity cost associated with the housing boom of the 1970s.

2. What are some of the long-run consequences of the housing boom? In other words, short-run choices affect long-run choices. Explain.

CHAPTER ANSWERS

In Brief: Chapter Summary

1. Production 2. Capital 3. Scarcity 4. Technology 5. Production possibilities curve 6. Sacrificing 7. Opportunity cost 8. Rises 9. Less 10. Larger 11. Are not 12. Unemployed 13. Inefficiently 14. Unattainable 15. Can 16. Outward 17. Current 18. Capital 19. Budget line 20. Outward 21. Increases 22. Outward 23. Inward 24. Reduction

Vocabulary Review

1. Economic resources 2. Division of labor 3. Budget line 4. Capital 5. Production possibilities curve 6. Entrepreneurship 7. Economic growth 8.

Technology 9. Labor 10. Productive efficiency 11. Natural resources 12. Law of increasing costs

Skills Review

1. a. Labor b. Capital c. Natural resources d. Entrepreneurship

2. a. + b. 0 c. + d. + e. 0

3. a.

    b. A point on the production possibilities curve represents a maximum level of production over a period of time for consumer and capital goods. At this level of production, resources are fully and efficiently employed.
    c. (1) 15   (2) 18   (3) 21   (4) 26
    d. Rise. Opportunity costs rise because in order to produce more and more consumer goods, increasing quantities of resources have to be reallocated from the capital goods industry to the consumer goods industry, and these resources are increasingly less adaptable to consumer goods production.

4. a. A point inside the curve represents a level of production involving unemployed resources or inefficient production or both.
    b. A point outside the curve is unattainable in the short run because of resource constraints. In the long run, however, it is possible to reach point B if the productivity and quantity of resources increase.

5. a. U b. O c. O d. U e. U f. O

6. a.

47

b.

All other goods
(millions per year)

New

Old

0   Capital goods
(millions per year)

7. a. Even if capital or technological improvements were made only in the
        aircraft industry, the levels of production in other industries would
        likely increase. The capacity to produce in the aircraft industry
        has increased, which means that more aircraft <u>can</u> be produced than
        before. Since capital increases the productivity of other resources,
        more aircraft could be produced with the same quantity of resources
        previously employed in the aircraft industry, or the same number of
        aircraft could be produced as before but now with fewer resources.
        These resources, therefore, could be used elsewhere in producing other
        goods and services.

    b.

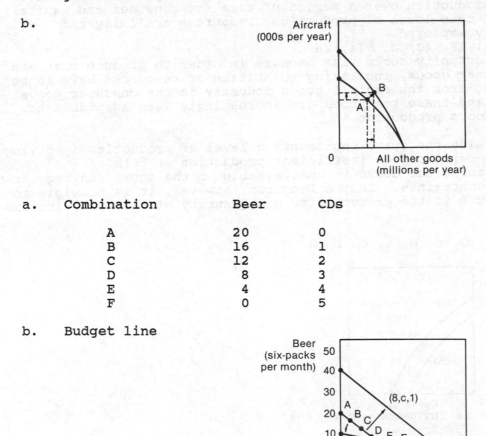

Aircraft
(000s per year)

B

A

0   All other goods
(millions per year)

8. a.

Combination	Beer	CDs
A	20	0
B	16	1
C	12	2
D	8	3
E	4	4
F	0	5

    b. Budget line

Beer
(six-packs
per month)

50
40
30
20
10

(8,c,1)

A
B
C
D E F

(8,c,2)

0   2   4   6   8   10

CD's
(units per
month)

    c. (1) (on figure above)
        (2) (on figure above)

9.   a.   Assume that the student's income (I) is spent in its entirety on beer
         (B) and compact discs (CDs). Furthermore, assume the price of beer
         (PB) and the price of a CD (PCD) are $2.50 and $10, respectively.

              I = (PB)(B) + (PCD)(CD)

         Solve the above equation for (B).

              B = I/PB - (PCD/PB)(CD)

         Notice that the vertical intercept of the budget line is the level of
         income divided by the price of beer. Also notice that the slope of
         the budget line is negative and equals the ratio of prices of the two
         goods.

     b.   (1) An increase in income will increase the intercept term or
              constant term in the above equation. The budget line will shift
              upward.
         (2) A decrease in the price of CDs and an increase in the price of
              beer will make the slope less negative and will decrease the
              intercept term. The budget line becomes flatter, with the
              vertical intercept decreasing.

Self-Test for Mastery

1. b 2. d 3. d 4. b 5. c 6. c 7. b 8. a 9. c 10. b 11. e 12. c 13.
d 14. c 15. d 16. c 17. a 18. c

Think it Through

1.   A nation's endowment of resources, whether plentiful or limited, is a
constraint to future growth. With full and efficient use of resources, a
nation can produce only so much over a given period of time. Using resources
today for capital means giving up the consumption of other goods today. But
capital increases the future capacity to produce and also increases the
productivity of economic resources. Because of this, a nation that forgoes
consumption today and invests in capital will be able to consume more tomorrow.

2.   A nation incurs a sacrifice or opportunity cost associated with the use of
resources when (a) there is full employment of resources and (b) efficient
production of output. If this were not the case, a nation could produce more
of one good without necessarily reducing the consumption of other goods by
either employing its resources more fully or by more efficiently producing its
output.
     At full employment and efficient production, a nation incurs rising
opportunity costs if it produces more and more of a given good because of the
law of increasing costs. Because resources are not completely adaptable to all
uses, they must be withdrawn in increasing amounts from other industries in
order to produce given quantities of the good.

3.   Both capital and technology increase the productivity of the production
process. More output can be produced with the same amount of resources. A
farmer with a tractor is far more productive than one with a digging stick.
This is the story of American agriculture. The enormous productivity increases
in the U.S. farm sector have been made possible by the mechanization of
agriculture.

4.   The United States not only sacrifices output of consumer goods and services in the short run but also sacrifices a higher rate of future economic growth and living standards.

Military goods (millions per year)

United States

A (Present)

(Future)

0   Capital and other goods (millions per year)

Western Europe, in contrast, is able to consume both more capital and other goods in the short run and because of greater capital investments will realize a faster rate of GNP growth in the future.

Military goods (millions per year)

Western Europe

(Future)

A (Present)

0   Capital and other goods (millions per year)

Pop Quiz

1.   The housing market boomed in the 1970s because of distortions caused by high marginal tax rates and inflation. It was not uncommon for a homeowner in the 1970s to face a negative real rate of mortgage interest. Even though family size and real median family income were falling and energy costs were rising significantly, these distortions were significant enough relative to these demographic and economic factors to result in not only a large increase in the quantity of housing, but also an increase in the average size per home. A sizable portion of the nation's savings went into housing rather than into business capital investment. Inflation had the effect of reducing the private after-tax return on business investment. In the short run, the additional housing was acquired at the expense of less business investment.

2.   The short-run choice of more housing and less business investment implies long-run consequences. A nation that underinvests in productive capital will experience a slower rate of economic growth and lower living standards in the future. Edwin Mills estimated the socially-optimal combination of investment funds and concluded that the housing stock is 25% too large and other forms of capital stock need to be increased by 12%. If the economy operated with the socially-optimal composition of investment, Mills estimates that GNP would be $3.606 trillion in 1983 rather than $3.278 trillion--a difference of $4,410 per family. Thus, long-run living standards were sacrificed for short-run consumption of additional housing.

More Costly Housing No Cause for Alarm

By DWIGHT R. LEE

Home ownership is the American dream, and a vibrant housing industry is associated with a healthy economy. Yet concern has been expressed recently that this dream is increasingly out of reach for many young Americans. A study cited in Housing Affairs Letter in March finds the homeownership rate among households in the 25-29 age bracket fell 17% between 1980 and 1987, and "finds [the] less affluent paying an increasing percentage of income for a dwindling supply of affordable housing." Yesterday, Michael Dukakis, campaigning at a housing redevelopment project in Cincinnati, spoke of "the problem of home ownership for young families."

But is less affordable housing a problem that warrants concern? Before concluding that it is, consider that homeownership was more affordable in the 1970s for reasons that were harmful to the economy then and for which we are still paying a price today. There are reasons for applauding the fact that homeownership has become a more costly dream and that the housing industry is not as robust as it was in the '70s.

Record in Housing Starts

The 1970s saw both a record number of housing starts and a steady increase in the size of houses. This occurred despite the fact that after-tax real income actually declined for the family of median income during the '70s and average family size was decreasing.

On the basis of sound economic decision-making, fewer new houses would have been constructed and those that were constructed would have been smaller. But economic circumstances in the 1970s were not conducive to sound decision-making. The housing boom can be explained by two factors that spelled gloom for the overall performance of the economy: high marginal tax rates and inflation.

Both distort economic decisions and by doing so make the economy less productive. High marginal tax rates reduce the private cost of consumption while at the same time reducing the private return on productive activities. Inflation, in addition to creating noise in the crucial allocative signals of changing relative prices, discourages commitments to long-term investments by increasing the uncertainty in future price levels. During the '70s, while reducing overall economic performance, high marginal tax rates in combination with inflation gave an artificial boost to the housing industry.

Consider being faced with a 40% marginal income-tax rate (common in the '70s), an inflation rate of 10% (exceeded at times during that decade), and a new mortgage. The interest rate on the mortgage will be about 14% (a 4% real rate plus 10% to account for inflation), and the after-tax interest rate will be 60% of that, or 8.4%. But since inflation is decreasing the value of money by 10% a year, the real after-tax interest rate is not 8.4%, but negative 1.6%. This negative interest rate serves as a tremendous subsidy to the purchase of a new house. And it is a subsidy that increases with both the inflation rate and the marginal tax rate.

During the '70s, this subsidy not only increased artificially the number of houses demanded, it also had a perverse effect on the size of houses. By any realistic standard, the size of newly constructed houses should have decreased. The average family size declined from 3.24 people in 1970 to 2.76 in 1980. The cost of home heating and cooling skyrocketed with the price of energy. And median family income, after adjusting for inflation and taxes, was $436 less in 1980 than in 1970. Nonetheless, during the 1970s the size of the average new house increased to 1,760 square feet from 1,510 square feet. Rather than expanding the nation's productive capital, Americans were putting their savings into larger houses for smaller families to be heated and cooled by increasingly costly energy.

These 1970 distortions in the housing industry are of more than just historical interest. The 1970s may be history, but we are still paying dearly for the distortions just described.

The housing industry attracts a significant percentage of the nation's saving in direct competition with other capital goods such as new plants and equipment. And while inflation and high marginal tax rates were increasing the private after-tax return on housing investment in the 1970s, they were decreasing the private after-tax return on business capital investment.

Since business capital is carried on the books at its historical cost, depreciation expense always understates the real replacement cost of capital during inflation, and therefore taxable profits are overstated. Also, the capital gains tax is assessed against increases in the nominal value of capital stock, which is always greater than increases in the real value during inflation. Again, taxable profits are overstated and investment in business capital is discouraged. So the success of the housing industry in the 1970s came at the expense of the type of investment that would have increased the productivity of the economy and meant higher incomes in the 1980s.

In a study published earlier this year, economist Edwin S. Mills estimated that if investment funds had been allocated between housing and other forms of capital investment in the proportion that maximized their combined social return, then the housing stock would have been approximately 25% smaller, and other forms of capital stock about 12% larger, than was the case in 1983. Mr. Mills also estimated that had we benefited from such an investment mix, gross national product would have been $3.606 trillion in 1983 (in 1983 dollars) instead of the $3.278 trillion actually achieved. This is a difference of about $4,410 for each family in the U.S.

It should be pointed out that Mr. Mills's study considers the effect of the distortion in investment not only over the 1970s, but also over several previous decades. But because of the high inflation rates and high marginal tax rates during the 1970s, a significant proportion of the distortion—and its adverse consequences for our current GNP—occurred in the 1970s.

Fortunately for the future productivity of the economy and for our incomes, the inflation rate was down to a little less than 5% in 1987 and marginal tax rates have been reduced significantly by the 1986 tax reform. A bias in favor of housing still exists because mortgage-interest payments remain fully deductible against taxable income. But this bias is now far less than it was in the 1970s.

Misplaced Concern

While good for the economy, lower inflation and reduced marginal tax rates have indeed increased the private cost of homeownership. This higher cost affects all home buyers, but since marginal tax rates declined more at higher income levels than at lower income levels, the increased cost is greater for higher-income families. According to a study published earlier this year by economist Theodore Crone, tax reform (assuming a 5% inflation rate and a 10.4% mortgage-interest rate) has increased the first-year cost of homeownership by 6.9% for a family with a $20,000 annual income and by 23.1% for a family with a $40,000 annual income.

It is more difficult for all young families to purchase their first home now than it was in the '70s. And when they are able to buy a home, it is more likely to be a smaller home than their counterparts were buying a decade ago. Considered in isolation this may appear to be cause for concern. But such concern is seen to be misplaced when the changes in economy that explain the higher cost of homeownership are considered. Indeed, young families are better off today than they were 10 years ago for the same reason it is more costly for them to buy that first home.

Mr. Lee is Ramsey professor of economics at the University of Georgia and a visiting professor at the Center for the Study of American Business at Washington University in St. Louis.

4

Market Transactions: Basic Supply and Demand Analysis

CHAPTER CHALLENGES

After studying your text, attending class, and completing this chapter, you should be able to:

1. Discuss the purposes and functions of markets.
2. Explain how a demand curve illustrates the law of demand and distinguish between a change in demand and a change in quantity demanded.
3. Show how a supply curve illustrates the law of supply and distinguish between a change in supply and a change in quantity supplied.
4. Describe the conditions required for market equilibrium and locate the equilibrium point on a supply and demand diagram.
5. Explain the consequences of shortages and surpluses in markets and how prices adjust in a free and unregulated competitive market to eliminate shortages or surpluses.
6. Show how changes in supply and demand affect market equilibrium.

IN BRIEF: CHAPTER SUMMARY

Fill in the blanks to summarize chapter content.

Understanding the concept of a market and the role it plays in the allocation of resources and the distribution of output is critical to an understanding of how economies function. (1)_____ (Markets, Trade publications) communicate information to buyers and sellers alike. The forces of supply and demand, which are basic to every market, interact to produce a (2)_____ (market quantity, market price) that acts as a vehicle for communicating the wants of buyers to sellers. (3)_____(Cost-benefit analysis, Supply and demand analysis) is a method of isolating the forces of supply and demand so that the factors determining market prices can be understood. This allows us to better understand the communication and rationing functions of the price system.

Demand constitutes amounts of goods and services that buyers are willing and able to buy at a given price during a given period. A (4)_____(demand schedule, demand curve) is a table of data showing the relationship between the prices of a good and the associated quantities demanded, holding all other influencing factors unchanged. A (5)_____(demand curve, demand schedule) is a plot of the price-quantity demanded coordinates. The demand schedule and its demand curve show that price and quantity demanded are negatively related. This relationship is known as the law of (6)_____(increasing returns, demand). When there is a change in price, quantity demanded changes. This is called a (7)_____(change in demand, change in quantity demanded). A change in demand determinants other than the price of the good will shift the demand curve. A shift in the demand curve means that, at a given price, quantity demanded will either increase or decrease. This is called a (8)_____(change in demand, change in quantity demanded). Changes in

52

demand are caused by changes in (a) income, (b) wealth, (c) the prices of related goods, (d) price expectations, (e) tastes, and (f) the number of buyers in the market.

Supply represents the quantities that sellers are willing and able to produce and make available to the market at a given price during a given period. A (9)_____(supply schedule, supply curve) is a table of data showing the relationship between the prices of a good and the associated quantities supplied by sellers, all other influences on supply remaining the same. A (10)_____(supply curve, supply schedule) is a plot of the price-quantity supplied coordinates. The relationship between price and quantity supplied is a positive one and is called the law of (11)_____ (monetary incentives, supply). A (12)_____(change in quantity supplied, change in supply) is caused by a price change. This is shown by a movement along a given supply curve. A (13)_____(change in quantity supplied, change in supply) is the result of influences other than price, such as (a) the price of inputs, (b) prices of other goods, (c) technology, (d) price expectations, and (e) the number of sellers in a market. These nonprice influences shift the supply curve.

The forces of supply and demand interact to produce a market (14)_____ (outcome, equilibrium), or state of balance, where the quantities demanded by buyers are just equal to the quantities supplied by sellers. In a state of equilibrium, buyers and sellers have no incentive to alter levels of consumption or production. It is the market (15)_____(price, quantity) that equates the quantities supplied and demanded.

A price above a market equilibrium price results in a (16)_____(shortage, surplus) because the quantity supplied at this price exceeds the quantity demanded. A price below the equilibrium price causes a (17)_____(shortage, surplus) because the quantity demanded exceeds the quantity supplied. In a competitive market, a seller tries to get rid of surpluses by (18)_____(increasing inventories, cutting prices). Falling prices will reduce surpluses. When the price falls enough to equal the market equilibrium price, the (19)_____ (shortage, surplus) is eliminated completely.

Shortages require some form of rationing. Sellers ration the limited supply of goods among competing buyers by (20)_____(increasing, decreasing) prices. But price increases reduce the quantities demanded and increase the quantities supplied, which in turn reduce the shortage. Shortages are completely eliminated when the price has risen (21)_____(above, equal to) the market equilibrium price. Market prices remain unchanged in a competitive market unless the underlying forces of supply or demand change. A change in demand, a change in supply, or a change in both supply and demand (22)_____ (can, cannot) alter the market equilibrium price and quantity.

VOCABULARY REVIEW

Write the key term from the list below next to its definition.

Key Terms

Market
Change in quantity
  demanded
Supply and demand
  analysis

Market equilibrium
Quantity supplied
Demand
Supply
Law of supply

Quantity demanded
Demand schedule
Law of demand
Complements
Demand curve
Surplus
Change in relative
  price
Change in demand

Supply schedule
Supply curve
Change in quantity
  supplied
Substitutes
Change in supply
Shortage
Equilibrium

Definitions

1. _____: an increase or decrease in the price of a good relative to an average of the prices of all goods.

2. _____: a graph that shows how quantity demanded varies with the price of a good.

3. _____: a table that shows how the quantity supplied of a good is related to the price.

4. _____: the quantity of a good sellers are willing and able to make available in the market over a given period at a certain price, other things being equal.

5. _____: a relationship between the price of an item and the quantity supplied by sellers.

6. _____: other things being equal, the higher the price of a good, the greater the quantity of that good sellers are willing and able to make available over a given period.

7. _____: an arrangement through which buyers and sellers meet or communicate for the purpose of trading goods or services.

8. _____: explains how prices are established in markets through competition among many buyers and sellers, and how those prices affect the quantities traded.

9. _____: attained when the price of a good adjusts so that the quantity buyers are willing and able to buy at that price is just equal to the quantity sellers are willing and able to supply.

10. _____: exists if the quantity demanded exceeds the quantity supplied of a good over a period of time.

11. _____: prevails when economic forces balance so that economic variables neither increase nor decrease.

12. _____: exists if the quantity supplied exceeds the quantity demanded of a good over a period of time.

13. _____: a change in the relationship between the price of a good and the quantity supplied in response to a supply determinant other than the price of the good.

14. _____: a change in the amount of a good buyers are willing and able to buy in response to a change in the price of the good.

15. _____: a change in the relationship between the price of a good and the quantity demanded caused by a change in a demand determinant other than the price of the good.

16. _____: goods whose use together enhances the satisfaction a consumer obtains from each.

17. _____: goods that serve a purpose similar to that of a given good.

18. _____: a graph that shows how the quantity supplied varies with the price of a good.

19. _____: other things being equal, the lower the price of a good, the greater the quantity of that good buyers are willing and able to purchase over a given period.

20. _____: a change in the amount of a good sellers are willing to sell in response to a change in the price of the good.

21. _____: a relationship between the price of an item and the quantity demanded.

22. _____: a table that shows how the quantity demanded of a good would vary with price, given all other demand determinants.

23. _____: the amount of an item the buyers are willing and able to purchase over a period at a certain price, given all other influences on their decision to buy.

SKILLS REVIEW

Concept: Demand, law of demand, changes in demand and quantity demanded

1. The following is a demand schedule for corn:

Price per Bushel	Quantity Demanded (000s bushels per week)	
	(a)	(b)
$4.00	850	
3.75	900	
3.50	950	
3.25	1,000	
3.00	1,050	
2.75	1,100	
2.50	1,150	

a. Plot the demand curve on the diagram below.

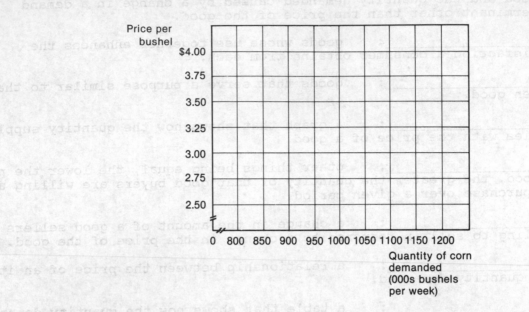

Price per bushel

$4.00
3.75
3.50
3.25
3.00
2.75
2.50

0 800 850 900 950 1000 1050 1100 1150 1200

Quantity of corn demanded (000s bushels per week)

b. What kind of relationship exists between the price per bushel of corn and the quantity of corn demanded?
c. Assume that the prices of other vegetables are falling relative to the price of corn. Will this cause the demand curve to shift? Why?
d. Assume that the quantity of corn demanded decreases by 50,000 bushels at every price level. Show the impact of this by completing column b above.
e. Show the impact from part d on the demand curve that you plotted in part a.

2. List six nonprice determinants of demand:

a. _____
b. _____
c. _____
d. _____
e. _____
f. _____

3. Indicate for each of the following if a demand curve for automobiles will shift to the right (R), left (L), or remain unchanged (U):

a. _____ Auto prices fall
b. _____ Price of gasoline triples
c. _____ Incomes decrease
d. _____ Stock market gains increase wealth
e. _____ Public transit fares fall to zero
f. _____ Auto price increase expected

Concept: Supply, law of supply, changes in supply and quantity supplied

4.   The following is a supply schedule for corn:

Price per Bushel	Quantity Supplied (000s of bushels per week)	
	(a)	(b)
$4.00	1600	_____
3.75	1400	_____
3.50	1200	_____
3.25	1000	_____
3.00	800	_____
2.75	600	_____
2.50	400	_____

   a.   Plot the supply curve on the diagram below.

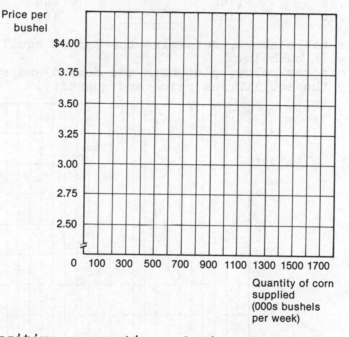

Price per bushel

$4.00

3.75

3.50

3.25

3.00

2.75

2.50

0 100 300 500 700 900 1100 1300 1500 1700

Quantity of corn
supplied
(000s bushels
per week)

   b.   Is there a positive or negative relationship between the price of
        corn and the quantity of corn supplied? Explain.
   c.   Suppose a serious drought reduces corn output at each price by
        100,000 bushels. Show the impact in column b above by completing the
        table.
   d.   Plot the new supply curve from column b on the diagram from part a.

5.   List five nonprice determinants of supply:

   a.   _____
   b.   _____
   c.   _____
   d.   _____
   e.   _____

6.   Which of the following will cause the supply curve for hamburgers to shift
     to the right (R), left (L), or remain unchanged (U)?

   a.   _____ Increase in the price of hamburger meat
   b.   _____ Increase in the price of hamburgers

57

c. _____ Increase in the price of chicken nuggets
d. _____ Introduction of new cost-saving technology
in the hamburger industry

Concept: **Market equilibrium price and quantity; shortages and surpluses**

7. The table below contains the price, quantity supplied, and quantity demanded data from column a of questions 1 and 4.

Price per Bushel	Quantity Demanded		Quantity Supplied	
	(000s of bushels per year)			
	(a)	(b)	(c)	(d)
$4.00	850	_____	1600	_____
3.75	900	_____	1400	_____
3.50	950	_____	1200	_____
3.25	1000	_____	1000	_____
3.00	1050	_____	800	_____
2.75	1100	_____	600	_____
2.50	1150	_____	400	_____

a. From the table above, determine the market equilibrium price and quantity in bushels.
b. On the diagram below, plot both the demand and supply curves. Identify the equilibrium price and quantity.

Price per bushel

$4.00
3.75
3.50
3.25
3.00
2.75
2.50
0

200 400 600 800 1000 1200 1400 1600 1800 2000 2200

Quantity of corn demanded and supplied
(000s of bushels per week)

c. At a price of $3.75, a _____ exists in the amount of
_____ because quantity demanded is _____ than quantity supplied.
d. At a price of $2.75, a _____ exists in the amount of
_____ because quantity demanded is _____ than quantity supplied.
e. What is meant by the statement that competitive markets are self-equilibrating?

Concept: **Changes in supply and demand and market equilibrium**

8.   Referring to the supply and demand schedules in question 7 above:

   a.   Suppose that an increase in income causes the demand for corn to increase by 250,000 bushels at each price. Show the change in question 7, column b. Plot the new demand curve on the diagram in question 7.
   b.   The market equilibrium price has _____ from $_____ to $_____. Market equilibrium output has _____ from _____ bushels to _____ bushels.
   c.   Suppose that because of excellent weather, corn production increases at every price by 500,000 bushels. Show the change by completing column d from question 7. Plot the new supply curve on the diagram in question 7.
   d.   Comparing the original equilibrium--demand curve a and supply curve c--to the new equilibrium with supply curve d, market equilibrium price has _____ from $_____ to $_____. Market quantity has _____ from _____ bushels to _____ bushels.
   e.   Comparing the original equilibrium--demand curve a and supply curve c--to a new equilibrium with demand curve b and supply curve d, market equilibrium price has _____ from $_____ to $_____ and market quantity has _____ from _____ to _____ bushels.

9.   Indicate below if the market price and quantity of concert tickets increases (+), decreases (-), or is indeterminate (0):

		Price	Quantity
a.	Stock market losses reduce wealth	_____	_____
b.	Income increases	_____	_____
c.	Season ticket prices are expected to rise	_____	_____
d.	Musicians union wins large pay increase	_____	_____
e.	Price of movie tickets falls	_____	_____
f.	Population migrating to an area increases	_____	_____

10.   <u>Advanced Question.</u> Let the following equations represent demand and supply curves for some good:

   Demand curve: $Qd = a - bP$
   Supply curve: $Qs = c + dP$

        where   a, b, c, and d are positive constants
                     Qd = quantity demanded
                     Qs = quantity supplied
                     P = price

   a.   Solve the above equations for the market equilibrium price.
   b.   Solve for the equilibrium quantity.
   c.   Interpret the equations for price and quantity. What causes price or quantity to rise or fall?

SELF-TEST FOR MASTERY

Select the best answer.

1. In a free and unregulated competitive economy:

   a. Wants are communicated to producers by the purchase orders of wholesalers.
   b. Wants of buyers are communicated to sellers through the determination of prices in markets.
   c. Sellers use market survey instruments to determine what and how much to produce.
   d. Markets play an insignificant role.

2. The quantities of goods that buyers are willing and able to purchase at a specific price over a period of time, other influences held unchanged, is a definition for:

   a. Quantity demanded.
   b. Supply.
   c. Total sales.
   d. Demand.

3. The demand _____ is a table of price and quantity demanded data in which the ceteris paribus assumption is employed. The _____ is a plot of that data.

   a. Table/scatter diagram
   b. Schedule/marginal cost curve
   c. Curve/schedule
   d. Schedule/demand curve

4. The law of demand states that, other things being the same:

   a. Price and income are positively related.
   b. Income and sales are positively related.
   c. Price and quantity demanded are positively related.
   d. Price and quantity demanded are inversely related.

5. Which of the following will not cause a change in demand?

   a. Change in income
   b. Change in the price of the good in question
   c. Change in the prices of related goods, such as complements or substitutes
   d. Expectation of higher prices

6. If two goods are substitutes and the price of one good increases, the demand for the other good will:

   a. Not change.
   b. Increase.
   c. Not be related.
   d. Decrease.

7. If two goods are complementary goods and the price of one good increases, the demand for the other will:

   a. Not change.
   b. Increase.

c.   Not be related.
d.   Decrease.

8.   If a good is a normal good, an increase in income will:

a.   Increase supply.
b.   Decrease demand.
c.   Increase demand.
d.   Decrease supply.

9.   The quantities of a good that sellers are willing and able to produce and make available to the market at a specific price over a given period, other things being constant, is a definition of:

a.   Demand.
b.   Equilibrium.
c.   Demand curve.
d.   Supply.

10. The law of supply states that, other influences being unchanged:

a.   Price and quantity demanded are inversely related.
b.   Price and quantity supplied are inversely related.
c.   Income and quantity supplied are unrelated.
d.   Price and quantity supplied are positively related.

11. A change in quantity supplied can be caused by a change in

a.   Price.
b.   Income.
c.   Technology.
d.   Price of inputs.

12. A shift in a supply curve is known as a:

a.   Supply shift.
b.   Change in quantity supplied.
c.   Rotation.
d.   Change in supply.

13. Which of the following will not cause a leftward shift in the supply curve?

a.   Decrease in input prices
b.   Increase in the prices of other goods that could be produced with the same resources and technology
c.   Expectation of lower product prices
d.   Decrease in the number of sellers

14. Market equilibrium occurs when:

a.   The forces of supply and demand oppose each other.
b.   The forces of price and quantity oppose each other.
c.   A market price just equates quantity demanded and quantity supplied.
d.   A market quantity just equates quantity supplied and quantity demanded.

15. A price above the market equilibrium price results in:

a.   A shortage.
b.   Inflation.

     c.   Excess demand.
     d.   A surplus.

16.   A price below the market equilibrium price results in:

     a.   A shortage.
     b.   Inflation.
     c.   Insufficient demand.
     d.   A surplus.

17.   An increase in the demand for a good will _____ price and _____ quantity.

     a.   Decrease/decrease
     b.   Increase/decrease
     c.   Increase/increase
     d.   Decrease/increase

18.   A decrease in supply of a good will _____ price and _____ quantity.

     a.   Decrease/decrease
     b.   Increase/decrease
     c.   Increase/increase
     d.   Decrease/increase

19.   An increase in both demand and supply will _____ price and _____ quantity.

     a.   Decrease/ decrease
     b.   Have an indeterminate effect on/increase
     c.   Increase/increase
     d.   Increase/have an indeterminate effect on

20.   If the price of movie tickets increases significantly, then the price of VCRs will probably _____ and the market quantity of VCRs will _____ .

     a.   Increase/decrease
     b.   Increase/increase
     c.   Decrease/decrease
     d.   Decrease/increase

THINK IT THROUGH

1.   A market economy is a type of economy that relies on the market to .... (Complete the statement as thoroughly as you can.)

2.   Use supply and demand analysis to assess the impact of the drought that occurred in the farm belt in the Spring and Summer of 1988.
     a.   Discuss the impact of the drought on the market for corn.
     b.   Discuss the probable impact on feedlots that use corn as feed.

3.   If a market is currently in equilibrium and an increase in demand occurs, what happens to the market price? Explain.

4.   If the price of golf course greens fees increases nationally, using supply and demand analysis, discuss the impact on the market for golf balls.

5.   Suppose that you operate a dry cleaning firm in a small city and you and the other dry cleaners are earning handsome profits. Because of the profit potential, a national dry cleaning firm enters the area and opens several new dry cleaners. Assess the impact on the market for dry cleaning in this city.

POP QUIZ   Read the news brief at the end of this chapter and answer the question below.

Identify the forces affecting the supply and demand for gasoline and explain the probable impact on market price and quantity.

CHAPTER ANSWERS

In Brief: Chapter Summary

1. Markets   2. Market price   3. Supply and demand analysis   4. Demand schedule   5. Demand curve   6. Demand   7. Change in quantity demanded   8. Change in demand   9. Supply schedule   10. Supply curve   11. Supply   12. Change in quantity supplied   13. Change in supply   14. Equilibrium   15. Price   16. Surplus   17. Shortage   18. Cutting prices   19. Surplus   20. Increasing   21. Equal to   22. Can

Vocabulary Review

1. Change in relative price   2. Demand curve   3. Supply schedule   4. Supply   5. Quantity supplied   6. Demand schedule   7. Market   8. Supply and demand analysis   9. Market equilibrium   10. Shortage   11. Equilibrium   12. Surplus   13. Change in supply   14. Change in quantity demanded   15. Change in demand   16. Complements   17. Substitutes   18. Supply curve   19. Law of demand   20. Change in quantity supplied   21. Quantity demanded   22. Demand schedule   23. Demand

Skills Review

1.   a.

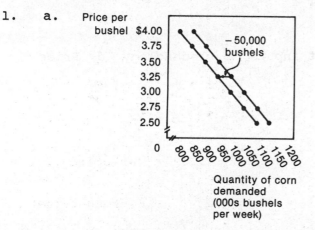

   b.   Negative or inverse
   c.   If other vegetables are considered substitutes for corn, the demand for corn falls and the demand curve shifts leftward as the prices of other vegetables are falling.

d.
    (b)
    800
    850
    900
    950
  1000
  1050
  1100

e. The demand curve shifts leftward as shown in the diagram above in part a.

2. a. Income b. Wealth c. Prices of substitutes and complements d. Price expectations e. Tastes f. Number of buyers

3. a. U b. L c. L d. R e. L f. R

4. a.

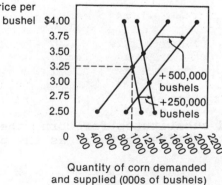

Price per bushel
$4.00
3.75
3.50
3.25
3.00
2.75
2.50

− 100,000 bushels

Quantity of corn supplied
(000s bushels per week)

b. Positive, higher prices increase the willingness and ability of suppliers to increase production.

c.
    (b)
  1500
  1300
  1100
   900
   700
   500
   300

d. The supply curve shifts leftward as shown in the diagram above in part a.

5. a. Prices of other goods b. Prices of inputs c. Technology d. Price expectations e. Number of sellers

6. a. L b. U c. L d. R

7. a. $3.25, 1,000,000

b. Price per bushel
$4.00
3.75
3.50
3.25
3.00
2.75
2.50

+ 500,000 bushels
+ 250,000 bushels

Quantity of corn demanded and supplied (000s of bushels)

64

    c.   Surplus, 500,000 bushels, less
    d.   Shortage, 500,000 bushels, greater
    e.   Competitive markets are self-equilibrating because market forces will eliminate shortages and surpluses. Shortages are eliminated as market prices rise and surpluses are eliminated as suppliers lower prices to sell excess inventory.

8.   a.   (b)   b.   Increased, $3.25, $3.50, increased,
             1100   1,000,000, 1,200,000
             1150
             1200
             1250
             1300
             1350
             1400

  c.   (d)   d.   Decreased, $3.25, $2.75, increased,
             2100   1,000,000, 1,100,000
             1900
             1700   e.   Decreased, $3.25, $3, increased,
             1500   1,000,000, 1,300,000
             1300
             1100
              900

9.

	Price	Quantity
a.	−	−
b.	+	+
c.	+	+
d.	+	−
e.	−	−
f.	+	+

10. Market equilibrium requires that Qd = Qs. Setting the supply and demand curves equal to each other:

$$a - bP = c + dP$$

and solving for P, the market equilibrium price, gives:

a. $P = (a - c)/(d + b)$

Substituting this expression for P into either the demand or supply equation and solving for Q, the market equilibrium quantity, yields:

b. $Q = (ad + bc)/(d + b)$

c.   Q is positive and P must be positive. P is positive if the intercept of the demand curve a exceeds the intercept of the supply curve c. This always is expected to be the case. Changes in the nonprice determinants of supply and demand influence the supply and demand equations by changing the value of the intercept terms, a or c. For instance, an increase in income would increase a assuming the good is a normal good. If it is an inferior good, the increase in income will reduce a. As can be seen from the equations above, an increase in a will increase P and Q. A decrease in a will decrease P and Q. An increase in c caused by a nonprice determinant of supply causes P to decrease and Q to increase.

1. b 2. d 3. d 4. d 5. b 6. b 7. d 8. c 9. d 10. d 11. a 12. d 13. a 14. c 15. d 16. a 17. c 18. b 19. b 20. b

Think it Through

1.   A market economy is a type of economy that relies on the market to allocate resources and distribute output. The impersonal interaction of the forces of supply and demand communicate the wishes of consumers to sellers via the market price. Changes in demand alter the price, and it is the change in price that causes a supplier to respond by altering production. As producers alter levels of production, they alter their levels of employment of resources. Thus markets determine what is to be produced and in what quantities. Resources flow to markets experiencing increases in quantity and away from markets experiencing decreases in production. Output is distributed based upon a buyer's ability to pay. Other things being constant, rising market prices reduce the ability to pay, whereas decreases in market prices increase the ability to pay.

2.   a. As is shown in the diagram below, the drought reduces the supply of corn increasing the price per bushel of corn and reducing the market quantity of corn.

Price per bushel

Quantity of corn supplied and demanded (000s bushels per week)

    b.   If corn is an input to feedlot operations and the price of corn is increasing, the supply of feedlot services will decrease, causing the price of those services to increase and the quantity of feedlot services to fall.

Price per day

Quantity of feedlot days supplies and demanded

3.   If demand increases, then at the current market price there is a shortage because quantity demanded exceeds quantity supplied. In order to ration the limited number of goods or services among many buyers, the price of the good or service is increased. Increases in price reduce quantity demanded but increase quantity supplied. This in turn reduces the shortage. As long as a shortage exists, the rationing function of prices implies that prices will continue to rise. Prices will no longer increase when the shortage is eliminated. The shortage no longer exists at the new market equilibrium.

4.   Greens fees and golf balls are complementary goods. If the price of greens fees increases, the demand for golf balls will decrease. As can be seen in the figure below, a decrease in the demand for golf balls reduces the market price and quantity.

Price per package

Quantity of golf balls supplied and demanded (millions of packages)

5.   If several new dry cleaners open for business, the local market supply of dry cleaning services will increase. This causes a decrease in the price of dry cleaning services, but an increase in total market quantity.

Price per garment cleaning

Quantity of garment cleaning services demanded and supplied (000s garments per week)

Pop Quiz

Gasoline prices have remained "firm" in spite of a $4 decline in the price of crude oil. In the long run, the price of crude oil is an important determinant of gasoline prices, but in the short run other forces affecting the supply of and demand for gasoline may be changing and thus offsetting the effect of lower crude prices on gasoline prices. On the demand side of the gasoline market, demand is expected to increase 2% in 1988 in part because many states raised speed limits, resulting in increased fuel consumption. Further, a decline in the international value of the dollar made foreign vacations more expensive relative to domestic vacations. The American Automobile Association projected that 10 million more automobile vacations would be taken in 1988 than in 1987.

On the supply side of the gasoline market, the summer drought reduced shipments of gasoline on the Mississippi River by 50,000 barrels per day. Gasoline barges required several more days between river terminals than normal. Coastal refineries had to purchase and bring in fresh water because river levels were not high enough to prevent the intrusion of salt water. Several refineries experienced breakdowns. Refineries were able to produce only 294 million gallons daily at capacity and quantity demanded was 319 million gallons per day. The number of refineries has fallen by about one-third from 213 in the early 1980s. Finally, the yield of gasoline per barrel of crude has fallen because of the government's ban on the use of lead additives.

In short, demand is strong and expected to grow, but supply is constrained--there are bottlenecks in delivery and refineries are operating at capacity. These forces would normally result in an increase in market price and in time market quantity, but the decline in crude prices and the 11% increase in the stocks of crude oil have been an offsetting factor. Also, the industry is

becoming less competitive; 80% of all gasoline used in the U.S. is produced by just 15 refineries. Major oil companies have been eliminating the independent retail segment of the market and have increasingly marketed and sold at retail the gasoline output of their refineries.

Array of Forces Bolstering The Pump Price of Gasoline

By Allanna Sullivan

Staff Reporter of The Wall Street Journal

For years, the cost of a road trip to, say, Yellowstone National Park has been largely determined by the councils of OPEC. But not this summer.

Long-term changes in the gasoline business—as well as some special, short-term factors—have drastically altered the dynamics of pricing in the more than $150 billion-a-year gasoline market. "Things aren't crystal clear anymore," says Thomas Burns, manager of economics at Chevron Corp. "The underlying reasons for price moves are more obscure."

The effect, however, is clear enough: Retail gasoline prices have remained firm, despite depressed prices for crude oil. In the long run, of course, the price of crude will continue to control whether gasoline prices rise or fall. But this summer, at least, "the gasoline market is marching to its own drummer," says Trilby Lundberg, whose Lundberg Letter tracks retail gasoline prices across the country.

Gasoline prices currently average around $1 a gallon nationwide, up about one cent from a year ago, even though the spot-market price of crude has dropped more than $4 a barrel in the same period, to $15.45 as of Friday. What's more, U.S. gasoline inventories have fallen sharply in recent weeks, to almost 10% below last year's levels, while stocks of crude oil are nearly 11% higher than they were a year ago. (Last week's explosion of a huge North Sea oil platform could help to shrink those inventories somewhat by eliminating for a time 300,000 barrels a day of production from the glutted crude market.)

The Role of Big Oil

One reason for the resilience of gasoline prices, some independent marketers say, is that the major oil companies' grip on the market is growing tighter in many areas. The majors can exclude costly middlemen by refining and selling their own products, in addition to producing the crude from which they're made. With their lower costs and deeper pockets, the major companies have been gobbling up larger chunks of regional markets at a time when independent station owners and marketers are abandoning their businesses because of slim profit margins.

Steven Riggins, whose family runs 16 gas stations in New Jersey, says half of the independent gasoline wholesalers in his market have dropped out in just the past year. As a result, he notes, he's stuck with buying more often from major companies, and pricing is less competitive. "There's definitely not the pick anymore," he says.

Demand, which averaged 7.2 million barrels a day in 1987 and is expected to jump a hefty 2% this year, is also bolstering gasoline prices. Even as the price creeps up, gasoline remains a bargain in the minds of most U.S. motorists. Only five years ago, regular unleaded in such areas as New York City cost $1.24 a gallon, compared with a top price there of $1.07 a gallon today. And with many states abolishing the 55-mile-an-hour speed limit, autos are soaking up more fuel.

Moreover, the declining value of the U.S. dollar is promoting more domestic vacations while attracting tourists from overseas. The American Automobile Association expects Americans to take 10 million more driving vacations this year than the 243 million taken last year. Through May, the Automobile Club of New York had fielded nearly 120 million requests for highway-travel information, up 7% from a year ago. "Our branches have never been so crowded," says a club spokesman.

The supply side, too, is keeping gasoline prices strong. On a regional basis, a number of special factors are tipping the balance against the consumer. For one thing, the delivery each day of at least 50,000 barrels of gasoline along the Mississippi River has been slowed because of drought conditions in that area. The tugboat Amoco Missouri River, for instance, is spending 15 days rather than the usual five to push its gasoline barges between two terminals.

Another drought-related problem: Low river levels are permitting saltwater to reach farther north in Louisiana. This has forced some coastal refineries to use barges, at great expense, to bring in the fresh water needed for their operations.

Meanwhile, a spate of breakdowns and maintenance stoppages has caused at least five major refineries to cut back on gasoline production in recent weeks. The explosion in May of Shell Oil Co.'s huge Norco, La., refinery alone took 130,000 barrels of gasoline a day off the market. "The Shell explosion sure hasn't helped," says Ted Eck, chief economist for Amoco Corp.

Indeed, even while operating nearly flat out last month, U.S. refineries were able to supply only about 294 million gallons of gasoline daily—against demand of 319 million gallons a day. The shortfall was filled from inventories and through imports from Venezuela, Brazil and Canada.

Fewer Refineries

A broader factor in the production squeeze is that the number of refineries in the U.S. has dwindled by almost a third, to 213, since the abolition earlier this decade of oil price controls, which virtually assured refiners of a profit. Of the survivors, no more than 15 provide 80% of the gasoline used by U.S. motorists, says Vic Rasheed, executive director of Service Station Dealers of America, a Washington-based trade group.

As refining capacity has shrunk, so, too, has the yield of gasoline from a barrel of crude, thanks to a government ban on using lead additives to boost octane. This problem is likely to become only more acute as motorists clamor for greater quantities of high-octane premium gasoline to fuel increasingly popular high-performance automobiles.

"The industry is producing (gasoline) at close to sustainable capacity already," says Rodger W. Murtaugh, vice president of operations, planning and transportation for Amoco. He calls current gasoline supplies "tight but manageable."

Mr. Burns, the Chevron economist, says similarly that, after years of glut, gasoline supplies are in "fairly good balance." But this, he adds, means "any accumulation of small things can tip that balance."

5

Using Supply and Demand Analysis

CHAPTER CHALLENGES

After studying your text, attending class, and completing this chapter, you should be able to:

1. Demonstrate how market equilibrium prices deal with the problem of scarcity by rationing goods and services and explain why prices would be zero for nonscarce goods.
2. Explain how supply and demand conditions affect the price and sales potential for new products.
3. Show how wages and interest are determined in competitive markets.
4. Use supply and demand analysis to show how government control of prices in competitive markets can result in shortages or surpluses.
5. Discuss nonprice rationing systems and show how these alternatives work when the rationing function of prices in markets is impaired.

IN BRIEF: CHAPTER SUMMARY

Fill in the blanks to summarize chapter content.

Supply and demand analysis is a useful tool for analyzing personal, business, and social problems and issues. It shows the importance of prices in the allocation of resources. Prices help us deal with the problem of scarcity in both the allocation of resources and the distribution of output. Do prices have a role when scarcity does not exist? Goods in abundant supply such as air are called (1)_____ (essential commodities, nonscarce goods) because there is no positive price for which quantity demanded exceeds quantity supplied. If a positive price is not possible, markets do not develop. Markets develop only when positive prices are possible.

But even at positive prices, a market may not develop if the minimum price required by sellers exceeds the maximum price that buyers are willing and able to pay for the first unit of output. A market for new products can only develop when demand and supply have reached a point where the (2)_____(maximum, minimum) price buyers are willing and able to pay for the first unit of output exceeds the (3)_____(maximum, minimum) price sellers are willing to take for that unit.

In addition to the markets for goods and services, supply and demand analysis can be used to assess changes in competitive labor and credit markets. The price per unit of labor is called the (4)_____(labor cost, wage). When the supply of labor equals the demand, there is a market wage and quantity of labor employed. Everyone who wants to work at that wage is employed. If the demand for the product produced by that labor increases, the demand for labor by employers will likewise increase. This causes the wage to (5)_____(rise, fall) and the quantity of labor employed to (6)_____(decrease, increase). In a recession, as the demand for goods and services falls, the demand for labor declines, causing both wages and employment to also (7)_____(rise, fall).

Changes in the demand and supply of loanable funds determine interest rate movements. In an economic expansion, individuals, businesses, and government as a group borrow more. Interest rates (8)_____(rise, fall) as the demand for loanable funds increases. If the supply of loanable funds increases, say as a result of an increase in savings by both businesses and individuals, interest rates will (9)_____(rise, fall) and (10)_____(more, less) credit will be extended by lenders.

Prices are not always allowed to perform the rationing function. Society will often sanction government price controls as an attempt to aid certain interest groups, such as farmers, unskilled workers, and low-income renters and borrowers. (11)_____ (Price ceilings, Price floors) are government-mandated prices that are set below market equilibrium prices. A price below the market price causes (12)_____(surpluses, shortages). Rent controls, while helping those fortunate enough to pay controlled rents, cause (13)_____(surpluses, shortages) of low-income housing and reduce the incentive of landlords to maintain properties. Usury laws that prevent interest rates from rising to their market levels, while benefiting those people able to obtain the regulated credit, will cause a (14)_____ (surplus, shortage) of loanable funds. The least credit worthy (and also the lowest income) members of society will have difficulty finding credit. Price ceilings will cause (15)_____ (surpluses, shortages) only when the regulated price is (16)_____(below, above) the market price. If market interest rates were to fall, for example, below the usury ceiling, there would be no (17)_____(shortage, surplus) of loanable funds.

When shortages develop there must be a way to allocate the limited goods and services among the buyers. A market system relies on prices to do this. But with price ceilings, prices are not allowed to perform that function. Waiting in line, eligibility criteria, and ration stamps are three methods of nonprice rationing. All three are less efficient than prices in responding to shortages. There will still be those people willing and able to pay prices above the controlled price. In response to this potential market, illegal or (18)_____ (new markets, black markets) develop.

(19)_____(Price ceilings, Price floors) are controlled prices that are set above the market price. Prices above market equilibrium prices cause (20)_____(surpluses, shortages). Whereas prices fall to eliminate the surplus, other means have to be used to deal with surpluses, such as with agricultural price-support programs. Farmers either have to be rewarded to reduce plantings or the surpluses have to be purchased, stored, and distributed by government. Resources that could have been used elsewhere in the economy are being used to eliminate or deal with surpluses that would have been efficiently eliminated by a functioning price system. Although farmers as a special interest group benefit, consumers lose in that they pay (21)_____(lower, higher) prices, and the allocation of resources in the economy is (22)_____(less, more) efficient.

Minimum wage laws set minimum wages at a level above the market wage in most labor markets. The intent of such legislation is to increase the income of the poorest members of society, those individuals who also happen to have the lowest skill levels. But as was the case with agricultural price supports, (23)_____(surpluses, shortages) develop. The unemployment rate among the unskilled is (24)_____(lower, higher). The minimum wage benefits those lucky enough to find employment at that wage, but causes (25)_____(more, less) unemployment in that segment of society that can least afford to be unemployed.

Price controls distort the economy. They benefit some at the expense of others and prohibit a competitive economy from efficiently rationing resources. If the motives underlying price controls are socially desirable, society would gain if methods other than price controls could be employed to make certain interest groups better off without impairing the functioning of a competitive economy.

VOCABULARY REVIEW

Write the key term from the list below next to its definition.

Key Terms

Nonscarce good	Price ceiling
Wages	Nonprice rationing
Credit	Black market
Interest	Price floor

Definitions

1. _____: a good for which the quantity demanded does not exceed the quantity supplied at a zero price.

2. _____: establishes a maximum price that can legally be charged for a good or service.

3. _____: the price paid for labor services.

4. _____: the price for the use of funds, expressed as a percentage per dollar of funds borrowed.

5. _____: a minimum price established by law.

6. _____: a market in which sellers sell goods to buyers for more than the legal prices.

7. _____: the use of loanable funds supplied by lenders to borrowers, who agree to pay back the funds borrowed, according to an agreed-upon schedule.

8. _____: a device that distributes available goods and services on a basis other than willingness to pay.

SKILLS REVIEW

Concept: The determination of wages and interest rates in competitive markets

1. You are a manager of a business and you are trying to decide if you should borrow funds for plant expansion today at the current interest rate of 12%. The morning newspaper reports that the Federal Reserve System has announced that within the next month it will begin to expand the funds that banks have on hand to extend credit.

a.   Show the impact on the supply of loanable funds curve in the diagram below.

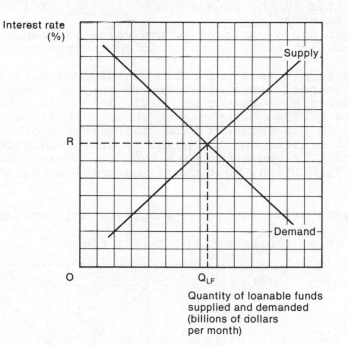

Interest rate
(%)

R

O   Q$_{LF}$

Quantity of loanable funds
supplied and demanded
(billions of dollars
per month)

b.   How will your analysis of future interest rates influence your decision to borrow today?

2.   You are a college sophomore trying to decide if you should major in mechanical engineering. Employability and income prospects are important considerations in your choice. As shown in the diagram below, the market for engineers is currently producing high entry market wages.

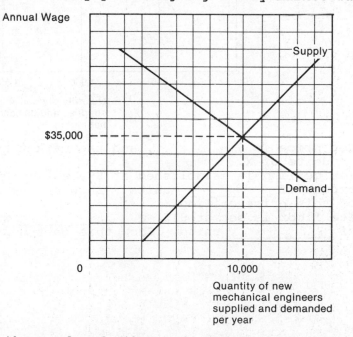

Annual Wage

$35,000

0   10,000

Quantity of new
mechanical engineers
supplied and demanded
per year

a.   If you and thousands of other college students are induced by the high entry wages to become majors in engineering, in time the supply

73

of engineers will _____. Show the future supply curve on the diagram above.

b. Entry wages in the future would _____, and the total employment of engineers would _____.

c. How might these expected future wages and employment levels influence your decision today to major in engineering?

3. <u>Advanced Question</u>. As a portfolio manager you must react to anticipated changes in interest rates with respect to your company's holding of financial assets such as stocks, cash, and bonds. Based on the current interest rate of 10%, our research shows that for each one percentage point change in the interest rate, the quantity of loanable funds supplied changes by $2 billion and the quantity of loanable funds demanded changes by $3 billion. If you anticipate that the demand for loanable funds will increase by $5 billion, what would you predict regarding the future rate of interest?

Concept: Government price controls--shortages and surpluses

4. The diagram below represents the market for good X.

Price per units

Quantity of good X supplied and demanded per month

a. The market price is $_____, and the market quantity equals _____ units of X.

b. If a price ceiling is established at $5, a _____ would exist in the amount of _____ units. Show on the diagram above the impact of this price ceiling.

c. If a price floor is set at $15, a _____ would exist in the amount of _____ units. Show this on the graph above.

5.   Given the market for unskilled labor in the diagram below:

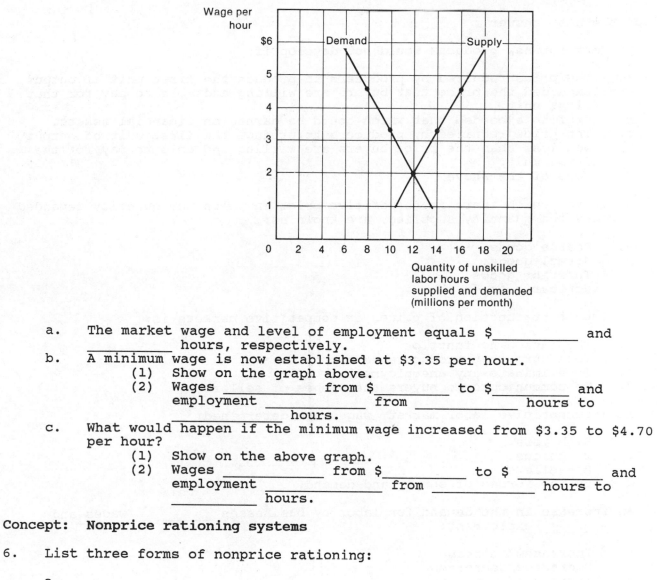

Wage per
hour

Quantity of unskilled
labor hours
supplied and demanded
(millions per month)

a.   The market wage and level of employment equals $_____ and
        _____ hours, respectively.
b.   A minimum wage is now established at $3.35 per hour.
      (1)   Show on the graph above.
      (2)   Wages _____ from $_____ to $_____ and
            employment _____ from _____ hours to
            _____ hours.
c.   What would happen if the minimum wage increased from $3.35 to $4.70
      per hour?
      (1)   Show on the above graph.
      (2)   Wages _____ from $_____ to $_____ and
            employment _____ from _____ hours to
            _____ hours.

Concept: **Nonprice rationing systems**

6.   List three forms of nonprice rationing:

      a.   _____
      b.   _____
      c.   _____

SELF-TEST FOR MASTERY

Select the best answer.

1. Markets for new products would not develop if:

    a. The price required by producers to produce the first unit of output exceeded the price that buyers are willing and able to pay for that first unit.
    b. Profits exceeded that which could be earned on financial assets.
    c. The price required by producers to produce the first unit of output was less than the price buyers are willing and able to pay for the first unit.
    d. None of the above

2. Goods for which there is no positive price in which the quantity demanded exceeds the quantity supplied, are known as:

    a. Scarce goods.
    b. Normal goods.
    c. Inferior goods.
    d. Nonscarce goods.

3. An important function of prices in competitive markets is:

    a. The rationing function.
    b. To ensure that producers make profits.
    c. To eliminate any unemployment.
    d. To communicate to buyers the wishes of sellers.

4. In a competitive labor market, wages are determined:

    a. By buyers.
    b. By unions.
    c. By sellers.
    d. By the forces of supply and demand.

5. An increase in the demand for labor by businesses _____ wages and _____ employment.

    a. Increases/decreases
    b. Decreases/decreases
    c. Increases/increases
    d. Decreases/increases

6. If because of a recession the demand for loanable funds decreases, what would happen to market interest rates and the quantity of credit extended?

    a. Interest rates would increase and the quantity of credit would decrease.
    b. Interest rates would decrease and the quantity of credit would not change.
    c. Interest rates would not change but the quantity of credit would fall.
    d. Both interest rates and the quantity of credit would decline.

7. Usury laws that prevent interest rates from rising to market levels are called:

    a. Monetary regulations.

b.   Price ceilings.
c.   Price floors.
d.   Rationing methods.

8.   Rents controls:

a.   Are price ceilings.
b.   Cause shortages of low-income housing.
c.   Result in the deterioration of low-income housing through the lack of maintenance.
d.   All of the above.

9.   The minimum wage law is an example of:

a.   An employment enhancement strategy.
b.   A price ceiling.
c.   A price floor.
d.   A well-designed policy intended to reduce teenage unemployment.

10. Price ceilings cause:

a.   No change in market quantities.
b.   Shortages.
c.   Quantity supplied to increase.
d.   Surpluses.

11. Price floors cause:

a.   No change in market quantities.
b.   Shortages.
c.   Quantity demanded to increase.
d.   Surpluses.

12. Agricultural price supports:

a.   Benefit farmers.
b.   Harm consumers.
c.   Require the use of scarce resources to deal with surpluses.
d.   All of the above

13. If in some labor markets the market wage for unskilled labor exceeds the minimum wage:

a.   Unemployment would result.
b.   Wages would rise.
c.   The minimum wage law would not have an adverse impact on unemployment.
d.   Wages would fall.

14. Which of the following cannot be considered true regarding price controls?

a.   Some people within special interest groups gain.
b.   Some people within the targeted special interest groups may actually lose.
c.   Resources are more efficiently used in the economy.
d.   Resources are less efficiently used in the economy.

15. Which of the following is not a nonprice form of rationing?

a.   Grouped staging
b.   Waiting in line

c. Ration stamps
d. Eligibility criteria

16. Price ceilings create an environment conducive to the development of:

a. New products.
b. Black markets.
c. Higher employment.
d. A saving ethic.

THINK IT THROUGH

1. Discuss the importance of the price system in a market-based economy.

2. Discuss how interest rates are determined in a competitive market for loanable funds. Identify the gainers and losers from usury laws. Under what conditions would the usury laws be ineffective? If it is socially desirable to make credit available at below-market interest rates, what are other ways to benefit the targeted interest group without resulting in as much economic inefficiency as usury laws.

3. In 1988 Democrats in Congress began a push to increase the minimum wage from its present level of $3.35 per hour to around $5 per hour. Identify the likely gainers and losers. If it is socially desirable to increase the incomes of the unskilled beyond the levels that would prevail in a competitive labor market, what are other ways of doing this so that unskilled workers can be better off without causing as much inefficiency as would be the case with price controls?

4. In the early 1970s, President Nixon installed a series of wage and price controls. Prices were temporarily frozen on all goods and services. The supply of and demand for gasoline put upward pressure on gasoline prices, but these prices were temporarily controlled. In effect, the price freeze acted as a price ceiling. What do you think occurred in the gasoline market? Explain.

CHAPTER ANSWERS

In Brief: Chapter Summary

1. Nonscarce goods 2. Maximum 3. Minimum 4. Wage 5. Rise 6. Increase 7. Fall 8. Rise 9. Fall 10. More 11. Price ceilings 12. Shortages 13. Shortages 14. Shortage 15. Shortages 16. Below 17. Shortage 18. Black markets 19. Price floors 20. Surpluses 21. Higher 22. Less 23. Surpluses 24. Higher 25. More

Vocabulary Review

1. Nonscarce good 2. Price ceiling 3. Wages 4. Interest 5. Price floor 6. Black market 7. Credit 8. Nonprice rationing

Skills Review

1. a.

Interest rate (%)

Old supply   New supply

R
R₁

Demand

O Q_{LF} Q_{LF}^1

Quantity of loanable funds
supplied and demanded
(billions of dollars
per year)

   b.   If you expect interest rates to fall, then other things being equal,
        you could lower borrowing costs by delaying borrowing until interest
        rates have fallen.

2. a.   Increase

Annual wage

Old supply   New supply

$35,000

Demand

0   10,000

Quantity of mechanical engineers
supplied and demanded
per year

   b.   Decease, increase
   c.   You might be deterred from becoming an engineering major in
        anticipation of lower market wages that might prevail at the time you
        graduate and enter the labor force. This, of course, assumes that
        nothing else is expected to influence wages in the future and that
        you are placing a very high priority on entry level wages relative to
        other benefits received from an occupation or course of study.

3.   This question can be solved graphically or algebraically with just the
     information given. Assume that the demand and supply curves for loanable
     funds are linear. This means that the slopes of both curves are constant.
     Assume also that no other influences are shifting the supply or demand
     curves other than the increase in demand of $5 billion. We are told that
     the current interest rate is 10%. This is the rate at which the supply
     and demand curves intersect. Increasing or decreasing the interest rate
     by one percentage point increases or decreases the quantity of loanable
     funds supplied by $2 billion and decreases or increases the quantity of
     loanable funds demanded by $3 billion. As can be seen in the figure
     below, this produces supply and demand curves that intersect at a market
     interest rate of 10%. Shifting the demand curve rightward by $5 billion
     increases the market interest rate to 11%.

Interest rate (%)

Quantity of loanable funds
supplied and demanded
(billions of dollars
per month)

Another way to solve the problem would be to use the equilibrium price equation derived in question 10 from Chapter 5. Except in this case let's call the price the interest rate.

Let R = (a - c)/(d + b), where R = the interest rate

A change in R = 1/(d + b) x the change in (a - c)

Recall that we are assuming constant slopes. Therefore d and b remain unchanged. The a term is the constant term that reflects noninterest rate influences on the demand for loanable funds--that shifts the demand curve. Since we are making the _ceteris paribus_ assumption, the c term is held constant.

A change in R = 1/(2 + 3) x $5 billion
= 1%

Interest rates are expected to rise from 10% to 11%

4. a. $10, 1000
    b. Shortage, 1000

Price per unit

Quantity of good X
supplied and demanded
per month

    c. Surplus, 1000

5.   a. $2, 12 million
     b. (1)

Wage per hour

Quantity of
unskilled labor hours
supplied and demanded
(millions per month)

       (2) Increase, $2, $3.35, decreases, 12 million, 10 million
    c. (1) Answer on the above diagram
       (2) Increase, $3.35, $4.70, decreases, 10 million, 8 million

6.   a. Waiting in line
     b. Ration stamps
     c. Eligibility criteria

Self-Test for Mastery

1. a   2. d   3. a   4. d   5. c   6. d   7. b   8. d   9. c   10. b   11. d   12. d   13. c   14. c   15. a   16. b

Think it Through

1.   Your answer needs to emphasize the rationing function of prices. Price changes will in time eliminate shortages or surpluses. The price system allocates resources efficiently. Prices represent the vehicle by which the wishes of buyers are communicated to sellers. In short, prices coordinate the purchase plans of buyers with the production plans of sellers.

2.   In a competitive market for loanable funds, the forces of supply and demand determine the market rate of interest and the market quantity of credit. Usury laws benefit those lucky enough to obtain loans at the controlled rate (those people with higher incomes and credit ratings), but impose costs on those who must go without credit (those people with lower incomes and poorer credit ratings). One alternative to regulated interest rates might be subsidies to low-income borrowers or those with poor credit ratings to be used to defer the cost of borrowing at the market rate of interest. Lenders could be encouraged to make loans to these people if lenders were protected from loan defaults by some form of government guarantee. This alternative would still require the use of scarce resources that would not have been required in a market involving no intervention. But at least the price system can perform its rationing function.

3.   An increase in the minimum wage will increase the incomes of those able to find employment at that wage. But the level of unemployment will increase among those least able to afford the loss of a job--the poor and unskilled. Incomes and employability can be increased a number of ways without having to resort to price controls. Job training programs that increase the productivity of the unskilled will increase their prospects for employment and better wages. Income transfers (such as Aid to Families with Dependent Children) can be used to supplement the incomes of the poor and unskilled. Again, these alternatives require the use of scarce resources but at least do not prevent the price system from functioning.

4.   Severe gasoline shortages developed at the frozen price. Because prices
could not perform their rationing function, people waited endlessly in line at
service stations all across the nation. The problem continued to be serious
until the price controls were removed.

6

The Price System: How It Functions and When It Fails

CHAPTER CHALLENGES

After studying your text, attending class, and completing this chapter, you should be able to:

1. Examine the framework of a pure market economy and show how the circular flow of income and expenditure in a capitalistic economy keeps it functioning.
2. Provide an overview of the price system as a mechanism for coordinating decisions and allocating resources to influence what is to be produced, how it is produced, and how output is distributed.
3. Point out the defects of a pure market system by showing how the price system doesn't attain all possible gains from resource use and how it sometimes results in low living standards for large numbers of people.
4. Briefly outline the functioning of the modern mixed economy.

IN BRIEF: CHAPTER SUMMARY

Fill in the blanks to summarize chapter content.

(1)_____ (Capitalism, Socialism) is an economic system characterized by private ownership, freedom of choice and enterprise, and a limited economic role for government. A capitalistic economy relies on the (2)_____ (benevolence of sellers, price system) to answer the "what, how, and to whom" questions basic to all economies. (3)_____ (Profit, Money) is the guiding force in capitalistic systems. It is what induces sellers to acquire resources to produce goods that are profitable to produce and to withdraw resources from other uses that are less profitable or involve no profit. (4)_____ (Economic chivalry, Economic rivalry) is also an essential characteristic in which there are large numbers of both buyers and sellers in markets and in which economic power is dispersed among many sellers and buyers such that no one seller or buyer dominates market outcomes.

For a market system to operate efficiently, it must not only produce output efficiently, but buyers and sellers must also be allowed to engage in mutually gainful trades or transactions. An economy attains the state of (5)_____ (allocative efficiency, production efficiency) when it is producing the maximum output for a given quantity of resources and buyers and sellers have engaged in mutually beneficial trades to the point where no further mutual gains can be achieved.

Transactions in a (6)_____(money, barter) economy do not involve the exchange of money for goods, but the exchange of goods for goods. It is an inefficient form of exchange because of the high transaction costs involved in finding "producers-consumers" with which to trade. Barter requires a (7)_____ (single coincidence of wants, double coincidence of wants). Money greatly facilitates the exchange process because it allows individuals to specialize in the production of a single good, to convert any surplus into money by selling it in the market, and to spend the money on goods and services produced by other sellers. With money, a double coincidence of wants (8)_____(is, is not) required.

A (9)_____(supply and demand diagram, circular flow diagram) is a useful way of identifying the major sectors in a pure market economy and the relationships among those sectors. Businesses purchase resources from households in order to produce the output of goods and services consumed by households. Households derive their income from the sale of resources to the business sector. It is in this market for resources that supply and demand conditions determine the market prices that businesses must pay for resources and therefore the market wages, rents, and interest plus profits received by households. A household's income is the result of the quantities of resources sold in the resource market and the market prices at which those resources sell.

Households use their income, in part, to purchase the output of business. Household expenditures become the firm's sale revenue. The revenue from sales is used by businesses to purchase the resources necessary to produce output. In the markets for goods and services, supply and demand determine prices, which in turn influence the quantities of goods and services demanded and supplied.

In a pure market economy, the price system answers the three basic questions: What is produced? How are goods produced? To whom are goods distributed? Goods are produced if they are profitable to produce. Resources are used first to produce the most (10)_____(profitable, desirable) goods and services. Profitability depends, in part, upon the prices prevailing in both product and resource markets. Because of economic rivalry, successful producers are those that are able to earn enough income over time to continue in business. Sellers who introduce new technology can realize lower costs and, as a result, higher profits. But increased production resulting from higher profits increases market supply and reduces prices. This requires other sellers to adopt the new technology just to maintain profits. The (11)_____(newest, least costly) methods of production are adopted and quickly disseminated among other sellers. The market distributes goods based upon a buyer's willingness and ability to pay. Ability to pay is determined by household income and the prices of goods and services purchased.

Markets often fail to achieve allocative efficiency. Private firms will not produce some goods that benefit society because prices cannot be used to exclude those unwilling to pay. These goods are known as (12)_____(private goods, public goods). Markets may overproduce or underproduce if market prices do not reflect all benefits and costs associated with the production or consumption of output. (13)_____(Negative, Positive) externalities occur when costs accrue to parties other than sellers and buyers. Sellers in this case make decisions based upon marginal costs that do not reflect these external or "third-party" costs. Their costs are lower than if all costs were considered and that induces them to produce (14)_____(less, more) than they would otherwise. In contrast, the production or consumption of goods may confer benefits on third parties, implying that market demand curves do not reflect all benefits associated with goods, but just those benefits received by the buyer of the good. (15)_____(Negative, Positive) externalities result in too (16)_____(much, little) output in that persons other than direct consumers benefit from the good. Sellers respond only to the effective demands registered by buyers, not third parties.

Externalities occur because property rights do not exist or because the property rights are not enforced. Property rights are not enforced when the

84

transaction costs involved in enforcing these rights are very
(17)_____(high, low). Some of the environment, such as air and navigable
waterways, involve common ownership and are often polluted because no one
individual has a property right or the capacity to enforce the right.

Other problems of a market system involve the absence of competition in markets
and the ability of sellers to control market outcomes to the disbenefit of
society. A market system can produce a skewed distribution of income in which
a small percentage of families receive a much larger percentage of income and
own an even larger percentage of the nation's wealth. A market system does not
guarantee the absence of unemployment or poverty. Because of market
shortcomings, modern economies rely on (18)_____(significant, limited)
government intervention in the economy to improve upon the allocation of
resources or to correct other market problems. These modern market economies
are known as (19)_____(mixed economies, pure market economies) because
decisions regarding resource use are made by both the private and public
sectors of the economy.

VOCABULARY REVIEW

Write the key term from the list below next to its definition.

Key Terms

Capitalism	Market failure
Mixed economy	Public goods
Price system	Externalities
Allocative efficiency	Property rights
Barter	Transaction costs
Money	

Definitions

1. _____: costs incurred in enforcing property rights to
traded goods, locating trading partners, and actually carrying out the
transaction.

2. _____: goods consumed equally by everyone whether they
pay or not.

3. _____: what sellers usually accept as payment for goods
and services.

4. _____: attained when all possible mutual gains from
exchange can be enjoyed.

5. _____: a mechanism by which resource use in an economy
is guided by prices.

6. _____: privileges to use or own goods, services, and
economic resources.

7. _____: characterized by private ownership of economic
resources and freedom of enterprise in which owners of factories and other
capital hire workers to produce goods and services.

8. _____: the process of exchanging goods and services.

9. _____ :   occurs when the price system fails to allocate resources so as to achieve allocative efficiency.

10. _____ :   costs or benefits of market transactions that are not reflected in the prices buyers and sellers use to make their decisions.

11. _____ :   an economy in which governments as well as business firms provide goods and services.

SKILLS REVIEW

Concept: **Framework of a pure market economy; circular flow of income and expenditure**

1. List six characteristics of a pure market economy:

   a. _____
   b. _____
   c. _____
   d. _____
   e. _____
   f. _____

2. In the diagram below, match the flow or box with one of the following:

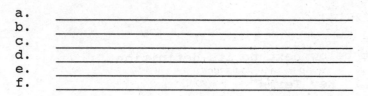

   a. _____   1. Market for goods and services
   b. _____   2. Resource market
   c. _____   3. Rents, interest, wages, and profits
   d. _____   4. Economic resources
   e. _____   5. Goods and services
   f. _____   6. Expenditures on goods and services

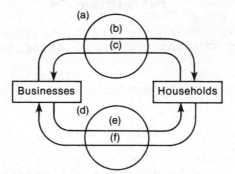

Concept: **Defects of a pure market economy**

3. List four failings of a market economy:

   a. _____
   b. _____
   c. _____
   d. _____

4. The diagram below represents the market for electricity. Electric power
    companies are burning bituminous coal and emitting sulfur into the
    atmosphere, creating acid rain that destroys forests and kills lakes.

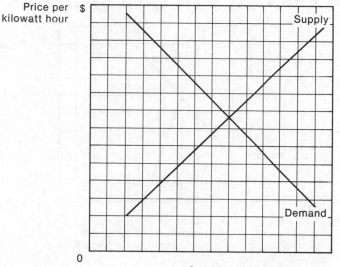

Price per $
kilowatt hour

Supply

Demand

0

Quantity of kilowatt hours
supplied and demanded
(millions of hours per month)

a. This is an example of a good involving _____ externalities.
b. On the diagram, show what would happen if these electric power
    companies were required to install scrubbers to remove sulfur from
    their emissions?
c. Market price of electricity _____ and market quantity
    _____.
d. Why is government required to correct the market failure?

5. Suppose the following diagram represents the market for AIDS therapy.
    Private pharmaceutical companies and health suppliers are in a race to
    discover and market a successful treatment. The demand for AIDS therapy
    reflects only the private demand of those infected with the virus and
    willing and able to pay for the treatment. Society as a whole, however,
    benefits from successful AIDS therapy because individuals who would have
    otherwise been infected are not infected because of the treatment that
    persons with AIDS are receiving.

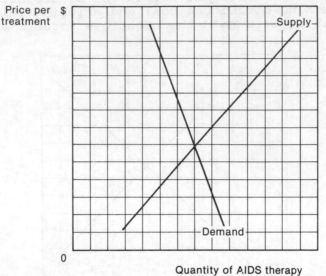

Price per $
treatment

Supply

Demand

0

Quantity of AIDS therapy
supplied and demanded
(000s treatments per month)

a. This is an example of a good involving _____ externalities.
b. Presently, there are too _____ resources allocated to AIDS therapy.
c. If government subsidizes AIDS research and the development of successful treatments, show on the diagram the likely impact on the market for AIDS therapy.
d. Market price of AIDS treatment _____ and market quantity _____.
e. Why must government be involved?

6. Advanced Question. The Sleaze E Chemical Company is presently dumping untreated effluent into a river. Downstream residents and other users of the river suffer from pollution. You are a policy maker in charge of determining the socially desirable level of pollution for the river and the appropriate effluent tax or charge per gallon of untreated effluent to impose on Sleaze E. You want to impose a tax high enough to induce Sleaze E to treat its discharge up to the point at which the proper level of pollution is reached.

Sleaze E Treated Discharge (000s gallons)	Units of Pollution Reduction	Marginal Benefits	Marginal Costs
0	0	$0	$0
10	1	10	2
20	2	8	4
30	3	6	6
40	4	4	8
50	5	2	10

a. Using the marginal benefits and marginal costs columns, determine the units of pollution reduction that maximize the net gain to society. Assume that the marginal benefit and cost data include external costs and benefits. How many gallons of discharge will Sleaze E have to treat in order to reach that level of pollution reduction?

b. The diagram below represents the relationship between Sleaze E's marginal cost of treating discharge and the quantity of discharge treated. What tax per unit of untreated effluent would be sufficient to induce Sleaze E to treat its effluent up to the level desired by society?

Marginal cost of treatment

Marginal cost of cleaning effluent

Treated discharge (000s gallons)

SELF-TEST FOR MASTERY

Select the best answer.

1. Which of the following is not true of a pure market system?

    a. Private ownership
    b. Freedom of enterprise and choice
    c. Significant economic role of government
    d. Presence of economic rivalry

2. A pure market economy relies on which of the following to answer the three basic questions: (1) What is produced? (2) How are goods produced? (3) To whom are goods distributed?

    a. Barter
    b. Money
    c. Property rights
    d. Price system

3. The catalyst or driving force in a market system that induces sellers to acquire resources to produce products is:

    a. Money.
    b. Profit.
    c. Price.
    d. Benevolence.

4. Economic rivalry means:

    a. That there are large numbers of consumers, but not sellers in markets.
    b. That the survival of the fittest criterion of business behavior is operative in the economy.
    c. There are large numbers of buyers and sellers in markets such that no one buyer or seller dominates market outcomes.
    d. That competitive firms produce profitable goods.

5. When an economy is operating at a point on its production possibilities curve and buyers and sellers have engaged in trade to the point where no further mutual gains from trade are possible:

    a. Production efficiency is said to exist.
    b. All firms are earning excess profits.
    c. Allocative efficiency is said to exist.
    d. Distributive efficiency is said to exist.

6. The advantage of a money economy as compared to a barter economy is :

    a. The avoidance of a double coincidence of wants.
    b. That money allows economic specialization and the division of labor.
    c. That money greatly facilitates the process of exchange.
    d. All of the above

7. In a circular flow diagram of the economy, households represent the _____ side of the resource market, whereas business represents the _____ of the market for goods and services.

    a. Demand/demand
    b. Supply/supply
    c. Demand/supply
    d. Supply/demand

8. In a circular flow diagram of the economy, households provide _____ and receive _____, which when _____ become the _____ of businesses.

    a. Goods/money/saved/capital
    b. Money/bonds/employed/capital
    c. Economic resources/money income/expended/sales revenue
    d. Money income/employment/used/property

9. Economic rivalry in a pure market economy ensures that:

    a. Only the healthiest firms use the most advanced technology.
    b. New cost-saving technology is rapidly disseminated among sellers in the economy.
    c. Firms will adopt the least-cost combination of resources.
    d. B and c
    e. A and c

10. Goods are distributed in a pure market economy:

    a. By government.
    b. By both the private and public sectors.
    c. On the basis of the buyer's willingness and ability to pay for goods and services.
    d. To those with the highest wages.

11. Private businesses will not allocate resources to the production of goods when prices cannot be used to exclude those unwilling to pay. These goods are known as:

    a. Inferior goods.
    b. Public goods.
    c. Loss goods.
    d. External goods.

12. Goods that when consumed or produced impose costs on third parties involve:

    a. Public external effects.
    b. Positive externalities.
    c. Marginal costs.
    d. Negative externalities.

13. Goods that when consumed or produced confer benefits on third parties involve:

    a. Public external effects.
    b. Positive externalities.
    c. Marginal benefits.
    d. Negative externalities.

14. Goods involving positive externalities result in :

    a. An efficient allocation of resources.
    b. Productive efficiency, but not allocative efficiency.
    c. An overallocation of resources to the production of the good.
    d. An underallocation of resources to the production of the good.

15. Externalities exist because:

    a. Businesses are often operated by uncaring individuals.
    b. Businesses do not investigate production problems as thoroughly as they should.
    c. Property rights are completely assigned and enforced.
    d. Property rights either do not exist, are not enforced, or are too costly to enforce.

16. High transaction costs associated with the assignment and enforcement of property rights increase the likelihood that:

    a. Externalities will not exist.
    b. Government will not intervene in the economy.
    c. Externalities will exist.
    d. Allocative efficiency will be achieved.

17. Actual market economies give rise to all but one of the following:

    a. A skewed distribution of income
    b. Poverty among plenty
    c. Full employment
    d. Less than competitive markets

18. In a market economy subject to market failures, society's well-being can be improved:

    a. By no government intervention.
    b. By government intervention that corrects resource misallocation and modifies other market outcomes consistent with the desires of society.
    c. By the price system.
    d. If decisions regarding public goods production are left to the private sector.

19. Modern market economies that rely on both the private and public sectors of the economy to answer the three basic questions are known as:

    a. Modern market economies.
    b. Pure market systems.
    c. Pure capitalistic economies.
    d. Mixed economies.

THINK IT THROUGH

1. Distinguish between concepts of productive efficiency and allocative efficiency.

2. During inflationary periods of the 1970s, a number of barter services were established as a means of eliminating inflation. These barter arrangements made use of computers to register the goods and services that the users were willing to supply and the goods that would be acceptable in exchange. Would such a barter system be as efficient as one with money? Explain.

3. A basic function of government in a pure market economy is to facilitate the functioning of the economy, but not to modify market outcomes. Discuss.

4. For a pure market economy, explain why producers employ the least costly techniques of production. If the price of labor rises relative to the price of capital and other inputs, how would this affect a competitive seller's combination of resources employed in production?

5. Education in the United States is provided by both the private and public sectors. Why?

POP QUIZ   Read the news brief at the end of this chapter and answer the question below.

In addition to the sources of market failure discussed in the text, markets may also fail to allocate resources efficiently if they do not operate competitively. Briefly describe the credit-card industry and indicate how resource allocation might be affected.

CHAPTER ANSWERS

In Brief: Chapter Summary

1. Capitalism 2. Price system 3. Profit 4. Economic rivalry 5. Allocative efficiency 6. Barter 7. Double coincidence of wants 8. Is not 9. Circular flow diagram 10. Profitable 11. Least costly 12. Public goods 13. Negative 14. More 15. Positive 16. Little 17. High 18. Significant 19. Mixed economies

Vocabulary Review

1. Transaction costs 2. Public goods 3. Money 4. Allocative efficiency 5. Price system 6. Property rights 7. Capitalism 8. Barter 9. Market failure 10. Externalities 11. Mixed economy

Skills Review

1. a. Private ownership
    b. Freedom of choice and enterprise
    c. Limited economic role for government
    d. Reliance on the price system to allocate resources
    e. Profit motive
    f. Economic rivalry

2. a. 2 b. 3 c. 4 d. 1 e. 5 f. 6

3. a. Externalities
    b. Lack of competition in markets
    c. Skewed distribution of income
    d. Doesn't eliminate poverty or unemployment

4. a. Negative
    b. If power companies are required to bear the cost of cleaning their emissions, the market supply curve would shift leftward.

Price per kilowatt hour

New supply Old supply

P_2
P_1

Demand

0   Q_2 Q_1

Quantity of kilowatt hours supplied and demanded (millions of hours per month)

    c. Increases, decreases
    d. Individual property rights do not exist to the atmosphere and to most lakes and a good portion of timber lands. Where property rights do exist in the ownership of forests and lakes, it is far too costly for any one property owner to identify the source of pollution and to seek remedy in court. Therefore government must intervene and enforce the collective property rights of society to commonly owned resources. Government can also reduce the transaction costs of enforcing property rights for individual property owners. In both cases, government improves resource allocation.

5. a. Positive
    b. Few
    c. Government subsidies increase the net gain to those conducting AIDS research and developing therapies. In time there will be a rightward shift in the supply curve.

93

Price per treatment

Quantity of AIDS therapy supplied and demanded (000s treatments per month)

d. Decreases, increases

e. A market system relies on pricing to allocate resources. Market prices do not reflect the external benefits accruing to third parties. Markets will underproduce goods involving positive externalities. Governments can produce net gains for society by engaging in activities that reallocate more resources to the production of goods with positive externalities.

6. a. Marginal benefits and costs become equal at three units of pollution reduction. This is the level of pollution that maximizes society's net gain. Sleaze E will have to treat 30,000 gallons of discharge for this level of pollution reduction to be realized.

b. $10. A tax of $10 per unit of untreated discharge will result in a net gain to Sleaze E for each unit of treated discharge up to 30,000 gallons. This is because the marginal cost of treating a gallon of effluent is less than the additional benefit associated with not having to pay the pollution tax on that gallon. This holds true up to the level of 30,000 gallons at which the marginal cost of treatment is $10. Treatment beyond this level would not take place because Sleaze E would be better off by paying the tax than treating the discharge.

Self-Test for Mastery

1. c 2. d 3. b 4. c 5. c 6. d 7. b 8. c 9. d 10. c 11. b 12. d 13. b 14. d 15. d 16. c 17. c 18. b 19. d

Think It Through

1. Production efficiency occurs when an economy is operating on its production possibilities curve. Here, resources are efficiently and fully employed. But allocative efficiency is not achieved if any trades can occur between buyers and sellers such that some people can be made better off without making anyone worse off. Allocative efficiency is reached only when trades and exchanges have taken place to the point at which the gains to some parties can only come at the expense of others.

2. Barter systems, whether or not they are operated by computers, must develop "prices" or exchange ratios for the goods involved. This requires scarce resources. A double coincidence of wants is required, which reduces the efficiency of exchange. A middleman must be paid to provide a service that is naturally provided as part of the functioning of a market economy using money.

3. In a pure market system, there are no failures. There are no externalities, markets provide employment for everyone willing and able to work at prevailing wages, all markets involve economic rivalry, and incomes are based strictly on the resources that households supply to the market and the prices at which they sell. In short, it is assumed that allocative efficiency

is achieved by the market without government interference. Government, nevertheless, performs a vital economic role by assigning property rights and enforcing those rights via a system of laws, courts, and police protection. Government also provides money and the basic infrastructure of roads, water supply, sewerage, etc., necessary for the efficient functioning of a market system.

4.   Economic rivalry implies that sellers must operate at least cost. If they did not, in time they would incur insufficient profits to remain in business. Firms that stay in business in a pure market system are those that are able to use the least costly combination of inputs and technology in order to at least generate a minimally sufficient level of profit. If the price of labor rises relative to the cost of other inputs, a least cost producer will substitute the relatively less costly resources for labor. By making capital more productive relative to labor, technology reduces the cost of capital relative to labor in the production of output. This is what happened in American agriculture. Technology made farm labor more expensive relative to capital, inducing farmers to mechanize.

5.   Education is a good involving positive externalities. A market system produces too little education from society's point of view. Government can increase the net gain to society by providing more education than that provided by a market system alone. But this does not necessarily mean the we have to have the current public-private system in order to achieve this outcome. Education could be entirely publicly provided or it could be provided entirely by a private sector encouraged to produce more with subsidies. Alternatively, students could be given education vouchers that supplement their own funds for education. These funds could be spent entirely in the private sector or even in the current public-private system.

Pop Quiz

Jeff Bailey poses an important question regarding the social consequences of the current structure of the credit-card industry: "A plastic OPEC?" Although 3000 financial institutions are issuing Visa and MasterCard, the ten largest credit-card issuers now have a 50% share of the market, up from about one-third in 1980. While other rates of interest have fallen markedly in the 1980s, credit-card rates have remained in the 17.5% to 20% range. These dominant credit-card issuers are oligopolists and have avoided a rate war by refusing to lower rates. Instead, they compete by spending huge sums in advertising on television and through direct mailings, whereas most of the other more price competitive issuers have inadequate resources to compete through advertising. Critics argue that there is not "prominent disclosure" of interest rates and fees and that issuers should be required to prominently display this information. Other critics contend that if the industry does not engage in price competition, rate caps should be employed, limiting the interest income earned by the large issuers.

Dominant credit-card companies are able to prevent interest rates from reflecting changes in the supply of and demand for consumer credit. If rates do not change to equate supply and demand, then there is a misallocation of resources in that there is either a shortage or surplus of consumer credit. If rates are prevented from falling given a decline in demand, less credit is demanded than would be the case if interest rates fell to restore equilibrium in the market. If consumers are being persuaded through mailings or other advertising to make choices with incomplete or misleading information, then consumer choices will result in a combination of goods and services consumed that is inferior to the combination chosen when consumers have access to full and complete information. Also, Jeff Bailey notes that for the dominant card issuers, the credit-card business is "hugely" profitable--three times as profitable as banking in general in terms of pretax profits as a percent of outstanding loans. These excess profits are received at the expense of possibly ill-informed consumers. This constitutes a redistribution of income from credit-card holders to issuers.

Major Credit-Card Issuers Tighten Grip On Market Despite High Interest Charges

YOUR

MONEY

MATTERS

By Jeff Bailey

Staff Reporter of The Wall Street Journal

A plastic OPEC?

Some banking industry critics contend that something close to that is emerging in the credit-card business. They are worried that a small number of card issuers are increasingly dominating the business and keeping card interest rates high.

"The business is really an oligopoly," says Rep. Charles E. Schumer, a New York Democrat who backs legislation that would force bank-card issuers to disclose their interest rates and fees rates more prominently. "There isn't true (price) competition," he says.

What bothers Mr. Schumer and other critics is that, since 1980, the 10 largest Visa and MasterCard issuers have expanded their combined share of the hugely profitable business to about half of the market from one third. And despite all the talk about credit-card wars, they have managed to do so without a rate battle.

Indeed, instead of falling sharply along with other interest rates, as many people expected, credit-card rates have edged down only slightly during the 1980s. A look at the top 10 card issuers shows current rates bunched in a range of 17.5% to 20%.

Rates Set Independently

The two bank card associations, Visa International and MasterCard International, along with the banks, see nothing wrong with that. They say interest rates are set independently and certainly aren't ever discussed among issuers. "We would never talk to anybody about pricing," says Ira Rimmerman, who heads Citicorp's card business.

That apparently includes consumers, too. Most promotions aimed at getting consumers to take new cards are distinguished by features other than the basic price of using the card, such as the size of the credit limit, the color of the card, free travel insurance and extra frequent flier miles. The issuers who do promote their cards based on a low interest rate repre-

sent only a tiny segment of the market.

With a lack of competition on pricing, the dominant issuers have little incentive to lower their rates. In fact, "the industry's resolve to *not* lower rates has stiffened," says a banker who runs one of the 10 biggest card operations.

That resolve was in question a year and a half ago when American Express Co. introduced its Optima bank card at 13.5%. Rate wars were predicted. But Optima has since won little of the market and earlier this month raised its rate to 14.25%.

In the meantime, borrowing by plastic is actually getting more expensive because

> **ISSUERS** that do promote their credit cards based on a low interest rate represent only a tiny segment of the market.

provisions of the 1986 tax law are rapidly phasing out deductions for credit-card interest payments. They'll be gone completely by 1991. Borrowing nevertheless has continued to grow.

Consumers are at least partly to blame for the fact that out of some 3,000 financial institutions issuing Visa and MasterCards, a handful dominate the business. For one thing, few people shop for cards. Instead, they are more likely to respond to direct-mail solicitations, the vast majority of which come from the major credit-card companies.

Generally, as few as 1% of consumers respond to a mailing. But some big issuers are able to back up mailings with heavy advertising and thus increase response rates. Citicorp, which aims to add three million new accounts this year, says its television advertising campaign—"Not just MasterCard. Citibank MasterCard"—has helped response rates to its mailings, though it won't say by how much.

Those consumers who seek out banks that charge lower rates find that they often require a better credit history and won't offer the big credit limits that larger issuers will. Despite its 10.92% rate and a periodic listing in this newspaper and other

publications, Arkansas Federal Savings in Little Rock has attracted less than $3 million in credit-card loans. But Arkansas Federal is among those with more stringent credit requirements and lower credit limits.

Card issuers have found, too, that many consumers disregard interest rates because they never intend to borrow money by plastic, but then do. "Most people believe they will pay the balance every month," says Philip J. Purcell, who oversees Sears, Roebuck & Co.'s Discover bank-card business. Only about half do, according to Visa.

Pretax Profits

It's clear why the large credit-card issuers want to increase their share of the business. Combined Visa and MasterCard loans total nearly $100 billion. And the profits on that business are huge. Citicorp's pretax profit on its $16 billion in credit-card loans appears to run at about $800 million a year, a figure that Citicorp's Mr. Rimmerman doesn't dispute. BankAmerica Corp., with about $6 billion in loans, makes more than $300 million before taxes. And First Chicago Corp., with about $4.5 billion in loans, makes more than $200 million before taxes.

For the larger issuers, the credit-card business brings in revenue generally totaling 21% of their loans outstanding. This includes interest payments and annual fees from cardholders and merchants. After subtracting the cost of funds, loan losses and operating costs—including processing, labor and marketing—the pretax profit is roughly 5% of the loans outstanding. That figure is roughly three times the level of a healthy bank's overall profit margin.

But some public officials would like to see the government trim card issuers' earnings. Rep. Schumer says that if the prominent disclosure of interest rates and fees on credit cards doesn't lead to more price competition, he would favor a national cap on credit-card rates.

Jerry Cosentino, Illinois state treasurer, isn't waiting. He wants a rate cap now and last year pulled state funds out of First Chicago to protest its 19.8% rate on credit cards. "They're gouging the consumer every day. There is so much greed in those top 10 issuers," he says. "It's like a conspiracy."

7

Elasticity of Supply and Demand

CHAPTER CHALLENGES

After studying your text, attending class, completing this chapter, you should be able to:

1. Explain the purpose and concept of price elasticity of demand.
2. Show how price elasticity of demand can be calculated for points on a given demand curve and discuss some uses of elasticity.
3. Explain how to use other elasticity measures, including the income elasticity of demand, the cross-elasticity of demand, and the price elasticity of supply.
4. Show how the price elasticities of demand and supply are relevant for explaining the impact of taxes on market prices of goods and services.

IN BRIEF: CHAPTER SUMMARY

Fill in the blanks to summarize chapter content.

The laws of supply and demand indicate the direction in which quantity supplied or demanded changes in response to a price change but they do not reveal the sensitivity of sellers or buyers to given price changes. The concept of elasticity is employed to gauge the sensitivity of buyers and sellers to price changes. Specifically, the (1)_____(income, price) elasticity of demand is a number measuring the sensitivity of buyers to a 1% change in price. If the percentage change in quantity demanded is (2)_____(greater, smaller) than the percentage change in price, demand is said to be elastic, and the price elasticity of demand coefficient is (3)_____(greater, smaller) than 1 (ignoring the minus sign). If the percentage change in quantity demanded is (4)_____(greater, smaller) than the percentage change in price, demand is said to be inelastic, and the price elasticity of demand coefficient is (5)_____ (more, less) than 1 (ignoring the minus sign)but greater than 0. A coefficient equal to (6)_____(1, 0) means that demand is unit elastic. Unit elasticity means that a given percentage change in price will result in (7)_____(a greater, the same) percentage change in quantity demanded.

The price elasticity of demand is determined by taking the percentage change in (8)_____(price, quantity demanded) divided by the percentage change in (9)_____ (price, quantity demanded). The elasticity coefficient or number is influenced by (a) the availability of substitutes, (b) time, and (c) the percentage of income spent on a good. Demand becomes (10)_____(more, less) elastic with increases in the availability of substitute goods, time, and increases in the proportion of income spent on the good. Decreases in the availability of substitutes, time, or the percentage of income expended on a good cause demand to become (11)_____(more, less) elastic.

The price elasticity of demand is not the slope of the demand curve. For a linear demand curve with a constant slope, the price elasticity of demand changes from being (12)_____ (inelastic, elastic) in the upper portion of the demand curve to being (13)_____(inelastic, elastic) in the lower segment of the curve. Exceptions to this would be the cases of perfectly elastic and perfectly inelastic demand curves. A vertical demand curve is perfectly inelastic and has a price elasticity coefficient of (14)_____(1, 0). A horizontal demand curve is perfectly elastic and has a price elasticity coefficient of (15)_____(0, infinity).

A useful application of the price elasticity of demand is an analysis of the behavior of total revenue or expenditures given percentage price changes. If demand is elastic over the range of a price decrease, total revenues and expenditures will (16)_____(fall, rise). This is because the increase in quantity demanded more than offsets the decline in price. If demand is inelastic over the range of a price increase, total revenue and expenditures also (17)_____(fall, rise). In this case, the price increase more than dominates the decline in quantity demanded. Therefore price and total revenue or expenditures are positively related when demand is inelastic and are negatively related when demand is elastic. When the price elasticity of demand is unit elastic, a change in price (18)_____(increases, has no impact on) revenue or expenditures.

Other elasticity concepts include the income elasticity of demand, the cross-elasticity of demand, and the price elasticity of supply. The income elasticity of demand measures the sensitivity of consumer purchases to changes in income. If the income elasticity coefficient is (19)_____ (greater, smaller) than 0, the good in question is a normal good. If the coefficient is (20)_____(greater, smaller) than 0, the good is an inferior good. The cross-elasticity of demand is a way to identify goods as being substitutes, complements, or unrelated. If the cross-elasticity is (21)_____ (negative, positive), the two goods in question are substitutes. The percentage quantity demanded of one good increases when the price of the other good increases by a given percentage. Two goods are complements when the cross-elasticity coefficient is (22)_____(negative, positive). In this case, the percentage quantity demanded of one good decreases when the price of the other good increases by a given percentage. Two goods are unrelated when the cross-elasticity is (23)_____(1, 0).

The price elasticity of supply measures the sensitivity of sellers to percentage price changes. If the percentage change in quantity supplied is greater than the percentage change in price, supply is (24)_____ (elastic, inelastic), with an elasticity coefficient greater than 1. If the percentage change in quantity supplied is less than the percentage change in price, supply is (25)_____(elastic, inelastic), with an elasticity coefficient greater than 0 but less than 1. A coefficient of 0 represents unit supply elasticity, where quantity supplied does not change given a change in price. Supply is (26)_____(more, less) elastic when (a) the additional costs of producing a unit of output rise slowly with increases in output and (b) sufficient time is allowed for the firm or industry to respond to price changes. As with demand, supply can also be perfectly inelastic or perfectly elastic. A vertical supply curve, one that is perfectly (27)_____ (elastic, inelastic), has a supply elasticity coefficient of 0. A horizontal supply curve is perfectly (28)_____(elastic, inelastic) with a coefficient of infinity.

Price elasticities of supply and demand can be used in determining the portion of a tax levied on producers that is shifted to buyers. A tax per unit of output levied on sellers will shift the supply curve (29)_____ (downward, upward) by the amount of that tax per unit. Prices rise, but if they rise less than the tax, some of the tax is borne by sellers and the remainder is borne by consumers. A firm would be successful in passing or shifting all of the tax to consumers when the demand curve is perfectly (30)_____ (inelastic,

elastic) or when the supply curve is perfectly (31)_____(inelastic, elastic). In the opposite case, where the demand curve is (32)_____(horizontal, vertical) and the supply curve is (33)_____(horizontal, vertical), the entire tax would be borne by sellers. With conventionally sloped demand and supply curves, both sellers and buyers bear a portion of the tax.

VOCABULARY REVIEW

Write the key term from the list below next to its definition.

Key Terms

Price elasticity of
  demand
Elastic demand
Inelastic demand
Total revenue
Unit elastic demand
Total expenditure
Income elasticity of
  demand

Normal goods
Inelastic supply
Inferior goods
Price elasticity of
  supply
Elastic supply
Unit elastic supply
Tax shifting
Cross-elasticity of
  supply

Definitions

1. _____: goods that have positive income elasticity of demand.

2. _____: prevails if the price elasticity of demand for a good is a number that exceeds 1, ignoring the minus sign.

3. _____: occurs when a tax levied on sellers of a good causes the market price of the good to increase.

4. _____: a number representing the percentage change in quantity demanded of a good resulting from each 1% change in the price of a good.

5. _____: a number used to measure the sensitivity of consumer purchases of one good to each 1% change in the prices of related goods.

6. _____: prevails when the price elasticity of supply is equal to or greater than 0 but less than 1.

7. _____: the dollars sellers of a product take in; the amount sold over a period multiplied by the price (PQ).

8. _____: prevails if the price elasticity of demand for a good exactly equals 1 when the minus sign is ignored.

9. _____: goods that have negative income elasticity of demand.

10. _____: a number used to measure the sensitivity of

changes in quantity supplied to each 1% change in the price of a good, other things being equal.

11. _____: prevails if the price elasticity of demand for a good is equal to or greater than 0, but less then 1, ignoring the minus sign.

12. _____: prevails when the price elasticity of supply is greater than 1.

13. _____: over any given period, the number of units of a product purchased multiplied by the price of the product (PQ); equals the total revenue of sellers.

14. _____: a number that measures the sensitivity of consumer purchases to each 1% change in income.

15. _____: prevails when elasticity of supply just equals 1.

SKILLS REVIEW

Concept: Price elasticity of demand; measurement, uses, determinants

1. Referring to the diagram below:

   a. Calculate the price elasticity of demand over the demand curve segment a-b. _____ Demand is _____.
   b. Calculate the price elasticity of demand over segment e-f. _____ Demand is _____.
   c. Calculate the price elasticity of demand over segment c-d. _____ Demand is _____.
   d. Total revenue (P X Q) at point
      a = _____
      b = _____
      c = _____
      d = _____
      e = _____
      f = _____
   e. A decline in price from $6 to $5 _____ total revenue by $_____.
   f. A decline in price from $2 to $1 _____ total revenue by $_____.
   g. A decline in price from $4 to $3 _____ total revenue by $_____.

101

2. Will the following make the elasticity of demand more elastic or less elastic?

    a. _____ Decrease in the percentage of income spent on a good
    b. _____ Import tariffs reduce the availability of substitute goods
    c. _____ More time to respond to price changes
    d. _____ Increase in the availability of substitutes

3. Given your knowledge of the determinants of the price elasticity of demand, which of the following goods are likely to have elastic demands and which are likely to be inelastic?

    a. _____ Diamonds
    b. _____ Hamburgers
    c. _____ Toothpaste
    d. _____ Automobiles
    e. _____ Gasoline
    f. _____ Cigarettes
    g. _____ Movies

Concept: Other concepts of elasticity; measurement, uses, determinants

4. Suppose you observe that as incomes increase by 10%, the quantity of some good purchased:

    a. Increases by 20%. Determine the income elasticity of demand. The good in question is a/an_____ good.
    b. Decreases by 5%. Determine the income elasticity of demand. The good is a _____ good.

5. Determine the cross-elasticity of demand if a 5% decrease in the price of good X:

    a. Increases the quantity of good Y purchased by 15% ____. Good Y is a _____ to good X.
    b. Decreases the quantity of good Y purchased by 5% ____. Good Y is _____ to good X.
    c. Does not change the quantity of good Y purchased ____. Good Y is _____ to good X.

6. Referring to the diagram below:

    a. Calculate the elasticity of supply over the supply curve segment a-b. ____ Supply is _____.
    b. Calculate the elasticity of supply over segment e-f. ____ Supply is _____.
    c. List two determinants of the elasticity of supply:
        (1)_____
        (2)_____

Price per unit

Quantity supplied per unit of time

Concept: Price elasticity of demand and supply; impact of taxes on prices

7. Referring to the diagram below:

a. Show the impact on the supply curve for cigarettes of a tax of $1 per pack.
b. Market price _____ from $_____ to $_____.
c. Consumers pay _____ cents of the tax and sellers pay the other _____ cents.
d. Assume that cigarette smoking is such an addiction that the demand for cigarettes is perfectly inelastic.
    (1) Show a perfectly inelastic demand curve on the diagram.
    (2) How much of the tax is paid by consumers? _____ cents By sellers? _____ cents

8. For which of the following diagrams is a per unit tax completely borne by:
    a.   Consumers?_____
    b.   Sellers?_____

9. <u>Advanced Question</u>. The market demand and supply equations from Chapter 4, question 10, are as follows:

    Qd = a - bP
    Qs = c + dP

    where a, b, c, and d are positive constants
    Qd = quantity demanded
    Qs = quantity supplied
    P = price

    Suppose that in the absence of per unit taxes on output, Qs is a positive function of P. If a tax, T, is levied on sellers, Qs becomes a function of the after-tax price rather than the before-tax price, P.

    a.   Modify the supply equation to incorporate a per unit tax, T.
    b.   Derive an expression for the market equilibrium price.
    c.   How can that expression be used to determine the portion of a tax, T, that is shifted to buyers?

SELF-TEST FOR MASTERY

Select the best answer.

1. The price elasticity of demand is measured by:

    a.   Dividing the percentage change in quantity demanded into the percentage change in income.
    b.   Dividing the percentage change in quantity demanded into the percentage change in supply.

c. Dividing the percentage change in price into the percentage change in quantity demanded.

d. Dividing price into quantity demanded.

2. If the price elasticity of demand is greater than 1, it is said to be:

a. Unit elastic.
b. Elastic.
c. Inelastic.
d. A normal good.

3. If the price elasticity of demand is greater than 0, but less than 1, it is said to be:

a. Unit elastic.
b. Elastic.
c. Inelastic.
d. A normal good.

4. A _____ elastic demand curve is one where the price elasticity coefficient is infinity.

a. Unit
b. Less
c. Completely
d. Perfectly

5. A demand curve for insulin is likely to be:

a. Perfectly inelastic.
b. Perfectly elastic.
c. Somewhat elastic.
d. Moderately inelastic.

6. Moving from the upper range of a linear demand curve southeast to the lower portions is associated with a price elasticity of demand that becomes increasingly:

a. Elastic.
b. Inelastic.
c. Large.
d. Difficult to estimate.

7. Which of the following is a determinant of the price elasticity of demand?

a. Time
b. The percentage of income spent on the good
c. The availability of substitutes
d. All of the above

8. Other things being equal, an increase in the availability of substitutes:

a. Has no impact on the price elasticity of demand.
b. Decreases the price elasticity of demand.
c. Increases the price elasticity of demand.
d. None of the above

9. If demand is elastic and the price falls, total revenue will:

a. Not change.
b. Increase.

c. Decrease.
d. Increase if the supply elasticity is not 0.

10. If demand is inelastic and the price falls, total revenue will:

    a. Not change.
    b. Increase.
    c. Decrease.
    d. Increase if the supply elasticity is not 0.

11. A good having a positive income elasticity of demand is called a:

    a. Positive good.
    b. Public good.
    c. Inferior good.
    d. Normal good.

12. A good having a negative income elasticity of demand is called a:

    a. Positive good.
    b. Public good.
    c. Inferior good.
    d. Normal good.

13. Two goods that are substitutes in consumption have a _____ cross-elasticity of demand.

    a. Positive
    b. Elastic
    c. Inelastic
    d. Negative

14. Two goods that are complements in consumption have a _____ cross-elasticity of demand.

    a. Positive
    b. Elastic
    c. Inelastic
    d. Negative

15. Which of the following is not a determinant of the price elasticity of supply?

    a. Availability of substitutes
    b. Time
    c. The marginal cost associated with producing additional units of output
    d. Percentage of income spent on a good
    e. A and d

16. A perfectly elastic supply curve is:

    a. Positively sloped.
    b. Vertical.
    c. Negatively sloped.
    d. Horizontal.

17. If the supply of some good is unit elastic and the price of the good increases by 10%:

    a. Quantity supplied increases by more than 10%.

b. Quantity demanded decreases by at least 10%.
c. Quantity supplied increases by 10%.
d. Quantity supplied does not change.

18. If a per unit tax is levied on sellers and the demand for the good is perfectly elastic, sellers:

a. Will pass all of the tax to consumers in the form of higher prices.
b. Will not be able to shift the tax.
c. Will share the burden of the tax equally with buyers.
d. None of the above

19. If a per unit tax is levied on sellers and the demand for the good is perfectly inelastic, sellers:

a. Will pass all of the tax to consumers in the form of higher prices.
b. Will not be able to shift the tax.
c. Will share the burden of the tax equally with buyers.
d. Will pay most of the tax.

20. If a per unit tax is levied on sellers and the supply and demand curves are conventionally sloped, sellers:

a. Will pass all of the tax to consumers in the form of higher prices.
b. Will not be able to shift the tax.
c. Will share the burden of the tax equally with buyers.
d. Will share the burden of the tax with buyers.

THINK IT THROUGH

1. You have been asked by a physician to determine if his fees should be increased. He wants to generate additional revenues. Based upon what you know about the determinants of the price elasticity of demand, determine first if the demand for physicians services is elastic or inelastic and then determine what fee change will increase the physician's revenues.

2. The demand for unskilled labor is generally regarded as elastic. Why? An increase in the minimum wage will increase wages for those employed, but will reduce the total wages paid to unskilled labor as a whole. Why?

3. How could knowledge of the price, cross-price, and income elasticities of demand for various goods be useful in helping a discount store manager predict the probable consequences of price changes?

4. Sumptuary taxes are taxes intended to discourage the consumption of goods considered harmful to individuals. A tax per quart of whiskey is such a tax. Based upon what you know about determinants of the price elasticity of demand, is a per unit tax on whiskey likely to curb consumption?

CHAPTER ANSWERS

In Brief: Chapter Summary

1. Price 2. Greater 3. Greater 4. Smaller 5. Less 6. 1 7. The same 8. Quantity demanded 9. Price 10. More 11. Less 12. Elastic 13. Inelastic

14. 0 15. Infinity 16. Rise 17. Rise 18. Has no impact on 19. Greater 20. Smaller 21. Positive 22. Negative 23. 0 24. Elastic 25. Inelastic 26. More 27. Inelastic 28. Elastic 29. Upward 30. Inelastic 31. Elastic 32. Horizontal 33. Vertical

Vocabulary Review

1. Normal goods 2. Elastic demand 3. Tax shifting 4. Price elasticity of demand 5. Cross-elasticity of demand 6. Inelastic supply 7. Total revenue 8. Unit elastic demand 9. Inferior goods 10. Price elasticity of supply 11. Inelastic demand 12. Elastic supply 13. Total expenditure 14. Income elasticity of demand 15. Unit elastic supply

Skills Review

1. a. 3.67, elastic
   b. 0.27, inelastic
   c. 1, unit elastic
   d. (a) $60, (b) $100, (c) $120, (d) $120, (e) $100, (f) $60
   e. Increase, $40
   f. Decrease, $40
   g. Changes, $0

2. a. More
   b. Less
   c. More
   d. More

3. a. Elastic
   b. Elastic
   c. Inelastic
   d. Inelastic
   e. Inelastic
   f. Inelastic
   g. Elastic

4. a. +2, normal
   b. -1/2, inferior

5. a. -3, complement
   b. +1, substitute
   c. 0, unrelated

6. a. 1, unit elastic
   b. 1, unit elastic
   c. (1) Additional cost of producing a unit of output as more output is produced
      (2) Time

7. a.

Price per pack

New demand New supply

Tax = $1

Old supply

Old demand

Quantity of cigarette packs supplied and demanded (millions of packs per year)

   b. Increase, $1, $1.75
   c. 75, 25
   d. (1) Shown on diagram above
      (2) 100, 0

108

8.   a.   Figures (1) and (2)
     b.   Figures (3) and (4)

9.   a.   Let Qs = c + d (P - T)
     b.   Equilibrium requires setting Qd = Qs.   Therefore:

$$a - bP = a + d (P - T)$$

          Solving for P gives:

$$P = (a - c + dT)/(b + d)$$

     c.   Let the change in P = [d/(b + d)] x change in T

          If d/(b + d) is greater than 0 but less than 1, both sellers and
          buyers share the tax burden. If d/(b + d) equals 0, the tax is borne
          by sellers. If d/(b + d) equals 1, the tax is borne by buyers. When
          d/(b + d) is 0, d = 0 or b equals infinity. d = 0 when supply is
          perfectly inelastic. b = infinity when demand is perfectly elastic.
          d/(b + d) is 1 when b = 0 or when d = infinity. b = 0 when demand is
          perfectly inelastic and d = infinity when supply is perfectly
          elastic.   Conventionally sloped supply and demand curves yield a
          value for d/(b + d) greater than 0 but less than 1.

Self-Test for Mastery

1. c 2. b 3. c 4. d 5. a 6. b 7. d 8. c 9. b 10. c 11. d 12. c 13.
a 14. d 15. e 16. d 17. c 18. b 19. a 20. d

Think it Through

1.   People perceive physician services as having no close substitutes.
Because care usually cannot be delayed, the demand for physician services is
regarded as inelastic. If the physician wants to increase revenues from his
practice, he should increase his fees.

2.   Unskilled labor is considered to have an elastic demand, in part because
many types of labor can be substituted for unskilled labor, but unskilled
workers are not substitutes for those requiring special skills, education, or
training. Also, there is typically a ready pool of unskilled labor that can be
employed with minimal training cost to the firm.

     If the demand for unskilled labor is elastic and the minimum wage
increases, total wages (minimum wage x quantity of labor hours employed) paid
to unskilled labor as a group will decrease, even though those employed at the
minimum wage are better off. This occurs because the unemployment caused by
the minimum wage more than offsets the impact of the higher wage on the total
wages paid to labor.

3.   Knowledge of price elasticities of demand for various goods would allow
the manager to predict percentage changes in quantities demanded for given
percentage price changes. Cross-price elasticities would allow predictions
regarding the quantities demanded of complementary and substitute goods.
Income elasticities of demand would allow predictions for those goods that are
normal or inferior. This would be useful, for instance, in areas experiencing
a significant influx of higher income households. All of this assumes that the
national or regional data used to estimate these coefficients are applicable to
a local economy. In other words, the relationships that hold for the economy
as a whole are assumed to pertain to the local economy as well.

4. For whiskey consumers, there are probably few close substitutes for whiskey. The demand for whiskey is probably inelastic. A sumptuary tax would primarily increase the price of whiskey, having only a modest negative impact on the quantity of whiskey demanded.

8

Consumer Choice and the Theory of Demand

CHAPTER CHALLENGES

After studying your text, attending class, and completing this chapter, you should be able to:

1. Explain the difference between total and marginal utility and show how the way marginal utility varies with purchases can reflect a person's preferences.
2. Describe the conditions for consumer equilibrium as expressed by the equimarginal principle for purchases.
3. Show how total and marginal benefits relate to total and marginal utility.
4. Demonstrate that buying any particular good up to the point at which its marginal benefit equals its price maximizes the total net benefit of giving up money to purchase the good.
5. Analyze the impact of changes in prices and incomes on consumer choices.
6. Derive a demand curve for a good for an individual consumer from data on marginal benefit and show how marginal benefit, and therefore demand, shifts when income changes.
7. Derive a market demand curve from the demand curves of individual buyers.

IN BRIEF: CHAPTER SUMMARY

Fill in the blanks to summarize chapter content.

An understanding of the demand side of the market requires an understanding of consumer choice. Marginal analysis is used to explain the choices made by consumers. Consumers seek to maximize their net gain from consumption. The consumption of goods increases a consumer's total satisfaction or (1)_____ (marginal, total) utility. But the additional satisfaction realized from the consumption of each additional unit of a good decreases. The law of diminishing (2)_____ (returns, marginal utility) states that marginal utility falls as more of a good is consumed over a period. Consumers will try to allocate their income such that they consume goods up to the point where the marginal utility per dollar expended on a good (3)_____(equals, is greater than) the marginal utility per dollar spent on each and every other good. This is known as the equimarginal principle. Consuming according to the equimarginal principle will maximize a consumer's utility.

To a consumer, total and marginal utility is valued by the (4)_____ (minimum, maximum) sum of money that the consumer is willing and able to give up to have the total quantity or additional unit, respectively. Because of (5)_____ (declining, increasing) marginal utility, the maximum sum that consumers are willing and able to give up to obtain an additional unit of a good (6)_____ (increases, declines) as more of the good is consumed. This is known as the law of declining marginal benefit. As long as buyers consume goods for which marginal benefits (7)_____(are less than, exceed) the price of the good, their net benefits increase. Net benefit is maximized

when consumption is carried to the point where marginal benefit (8)_____
(is still greater than, equals) the price. On units of goods consumed up to
the point where marginal benefits equal price, the consumer realizes a surplus.
Consumer surplus is the total benefit received in excess of the
(9)_____(dollar expenditure, marginal benefit) necessary to obtain the
goods.

Consumers will not necessarily prefer to purchase an additional unit of a good
having a high marginal benefit over one yielding less additional satisfaction
if the price of the former good is high. Nor will a consumer purchase any
units of a good when the price (10)_____(exceeds, is greater than) the
marginal benefit received. This is because the value of the goods and services
that the consumer will have to give up are worth more than the marginal
benefits received from consuming the good. Consumers will prefer those goods
for which marginal benefits exceed the price by the greatest margin.

Income affects a consumer's ability to pay. Total and marginal benefits are
the maximum sum of dollars that buyers are willing and able to give up to
obtain some total or additional quantity of a good. An increase in income
therefore increases the consumer's ability to give up dollars for benefits.
For (11)_____(inferior goods, normal goods), an increase in income causes
the marginal benefit curve to shift upward. At any quantity, the maximum
additional dollars that a buyer is willing and able to give up for an
additional unit of output increases. For (12)_____(inferior goods,
normal goods), an increase in income shifts the marginal benefit curve
downward. The maximum additional dollars that a buyer is willing and able to
give up for an additional unit of output decreases.

(13)_____(Market, Individual) demand curves can be derived from the
individual's marginal benefit curve. A price-quantity demanded coordinate on a
demand curve represents a point of consumption at which a utility-maximizing
consumer has equated price and marginal benefit. If the price falls, the
buyer's marginal benefit temporarily exceeds price. The consumer can increase
net benefits by increasing consumption to the point where price and marginal
benefit are once again equal. Thus lower prices are associated with higher
quantities demanded. This assumes that income, tastes, and other influences
are held unchanged.

Price changes have two effects: the income effect and the substitution effect.
A decrease in price, for instance, increases the purchasing power of a given
income and increases the consumer's ability to consume more of all normal
goods, including the one for which prices have decreased. This is known as the
(14)_____(substitution, income) effect. A decrease in price relative
to the prices of other goods will induce the buyer to substitute the relatively
less costly good for more expensive goods. With the income effect neutralized,
the (15)_____(substitution, income) effect means that price and quantity
demanded are always inversely related. For normal goods, the income effect
(16)_____(complements, offsets to some extent) the substitution effect
in that both effects work to increase quantities consumed as the price
decreases. For inferior goods, the income effect (17)_____
(complements, to some extent offsets) the substitution effect of a price
change. For a special variety of goods called Giffen goods, the income effect
(18)_____(more than offsets, does not offset) the substitution effect,
causing prices to be positively related to quantity demanded!

The market demand curve is a horizontal summation or aggregation of the demand
curves of individual buyers in the market. The market demand is downsloping
and shifts when individual demand curves shift.

112

VOCABULARY REVIEW

Write the key term from the list below next to its definition.

Key Terms

Preferences   Net benefit
Utility   Marginal benefit
Total utility   Paradox of value
Marginal utility   Income effect
Law of diminishing   Substitution effect
  marginal utility   Total benefit
Consumer equilibrium Market demand curve
Equimarginal principle Consumer surplus

Definitions

1. _____: the change in consumption of a good only as a result of the variation in the purchasing power of money income caused by a price change.

2. _____: the change in consumption of a good only as a result of a change in its price relative to the prices of other goods.

3. _____: shows the relationship between the price of a product and the total quantity demanded by all consumers willing and able to purchase the product at each price, other things being equal.

4. _____: states that the marginal utility of any item tends to decline as more is consumed over any given period.

5. _____: the maximum sum of money a consumer is willing and able to give up to obtain another unit of a good.

6. _____: the difference between the total benefit of a given quantity purchased by a consumer and the expenditure necessary to purchase that quantity.

7. _____: people are willing to give up zero or very small amounts of money to obtain certain items that provide them great total benefit.

8. _____: total satisfaction enjoyed from consuming any given quantity of a good.

9. _____: the maximum sum of money a consumer would give up to obtain a certain quantity of a good.

10. _____: the total benefit of the quantity of a good purchased less the dollar sacrifice necessary to purchase that quantity.

11. _____: the extra satisfaction received over a given period by consuming one extra unit of a good.

12. _____: the satisfaction consumers receive from items they acquire, activities they engage in, or services they use.

13. _____: states that to maximize utility, a consumer must equalize the marginal utility per dollar spent on each good.

14. _____ : individual likes and dislikes.

15. _____ : attained when a consumer purchases goods over a
period until the marginal utility per dollar is the same for all goods
consumed.

SKILLS REVIEW

Concept: Total and marginal utility

1. The table below contains quantity and total utility data for consumption
of good X.

Units of Good X	Total Utility	Marginal Utility
1	50	_____
2	90	_____
3	120	_____
4	140	_____
5	150	_____
6	150	_____
7	140	_____

a. Complete the marginal utility column above.
b. Plot the total and marginal utility data on the diagrams below.

Marginal untility
(units)

Quantity of good X
consumer per time period

c. Marginal utility is the _____ of the total utility curve. When total utility reaches a maximum, marginal utility equals _____.

Concept: Equimarginal principle

2. Assume that an individual has an income of $150 per week to be spent on either ballpark tickets or sweaters. The price of each ballpark admission is $5 and the price of a sweater is $25. The individual is assumed to spend all income each week. Given the total utility data below:

a. Complete the marginal utility (MU) columns.
b. Complete the marginal utility per dollar (MU/P) columns.
c. Determine the individual's utility-maximizing combination of ballpark tickets and sweaters. _____ tickets and _____ sweaters
d. Determine the total utility (TU) associated with the combination of goods consumed from part c. _____ units of utility

	Ballpark Tickets				Sweaters		
Units	TU	MU	MU/P	Units	TU	MU	MU/P
1	60	___	___	1	400	___	___
2	115	___	___	2	750	___	___
3	165	___	___	3	1050	___	___
4	210	___	___	4	1300	___	___
5	250	___	___	5	1500	___	___
6	285	___	___	6	1650	___	___
7	315	___	___				

Concept: Total and marginal benefits; the impact of price and income

3. The following represent total and marginal benefit data for a consumer:

Units of Good X	Total Benefits ($)	Marginal Benefits ($)
1	$250	
2	380	___

115

3	490	_____
4	580	_____
5	650	_____
6	700	_____
7	730	_____

a. Complete the marginal benefits column.
b. Plot the marginal benefits curve below.

c. If price equals $90 per unit, how many units of good X would be consumed?_____units. At this level of consumption, total benefits equal $_____, consumer surplus equals $_____.
d. If price equals $50 per unit, how many units of good X would be consumed?_____units. At this level of consumption, total benefits equal $_____, consumer surplus equals $_____.
e. If price equals $200, how many units of the good would be consumed?_____ units Why?

116

f. Plot the price-quantity demanded coordinates from parts c and d above in the diagram below. This curve is called a/an _____.

Price per unit

Quantity of good X demanded per time period

4. The following diagram represents the price and marginal benefits curve associated with a consumer's purchases of a good.

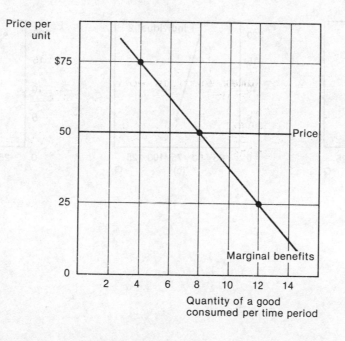

Price per unit

Quantity of a good consumed per time period

a. In the diagram, show the impact of an increase in income if the good is a normal good. Quantity consumed _____.

b. In the diagram, show the impact of an increase in income if the good is an inferior good. Quantity consumed _____.

5. a. For normal goods:
        (1) A decrease in price, via the income effect, will _____ quantity demanded.
        (2) A decrease in price, via the substitution effect, will _____ quantity demanded.
        (3) The net effect of a price decrease is an _____ in quantity demanded.

    b. For inferior goods:
        (1) A decrease in price, via the income effect, will _____ quantity demanded.
        (2) A decrease in price, via the substitution effect, will _____ quantity demanded.
        (3) The net effect of a price decrease is an _____ in quantity demanded.

    c. For Giffen goods,
        (1) A decrease in price, via the income effect, will _____ quantity demanded.
        (2) A decrease in price, via the substitution effect, will _____ quantity demanded.
        (3) The net effect of a price decrease is an _____ in quantity demanded.

Concept: Market demand curve

6. Derive the market demand curve in diagram d below from the individual demand curves shown in figures a, b, and c.

P
$20
15
10
5
0   25 50 75 100 125 150 175 200 225 250 275   Q
(d)
Market

P = Price per unit
Q = Quantity demanded per time period

SELF-TEST FOR MASTERY

Select the best answer.

1. The total satisfaction received by a consumer from a given quantity of consumption per time period is known as:

    a. Marginal utility.
    b. Marginal benefit.
    c. Total benefit.
    d. Total utility.

2. The additional satisfaction received by a consumer from the consumption of an additional unit of a good is known as:

    a. Marginal utility.
    b. Marginal benefit.
    c. Total benefit.
    d. Total utility.

3. Which of the following defines the law of diminishing marginal utility?

    a. Total utility rises at an increasing rate as additional units of a good are consumed
    b. Marginal utility rises at an increasing rate as additional units of a good are consumed.
    c. Marginal utility falls as more of a good is consumed over a period.
    d. Total utility falls as more of a good is consumed over a period.

4. If the marginal utility per dollar (MU/P) of good A exceeded the MU/P of good B, a consumer could increase utility by:

    a. Not altering the combination of goods A and B consumed.
    b. Consuming more of good B and less of good A.

119

c.   Consuming less of both goods A and B.
d.   Consuming more of good A and less of good B.

5.   Utility is maximized in the consumption of goods when:

a.   The marginal utility per dollar is the same for each good.
b.   Goods are consumed to the point of satiation.
c.   The marginal utility of each good is the same.
d.   The satisfaction from each good is equal.

6.   The maximum sum of money that consumers are willing and able to pay for the additional satisfaction associated with the consumption of an extra unit of output is called:

a.   Income.
b.   Total benefit.
c.   Marginal benefit.
d.   Marginal utility.

7.   The marginal benefit curve is downsloping because:

a.   Of the law of diminishing returns.
b.   It is the slope of the total utility curve.
c.   Most goods are normal goods.
d.   Of the law of diminishing marginal utility.

8.   A consumer can maximize net benefits by consuming a good to the point where marginal benefit:

a.   Equals the price.
b.   Equals marginal utility.
c.   Equals total benefit.
d.   Is equal for all goods.

9.   If goods A and B are associated with marginal benefits of $5 and $10, respectively, for the first unit consumed, a consumer would _____ if the price of good A equaled $6 and the price of good B equaled $12.50.

a.   Purchase both goods A and B
b.   Not purchase either good
c.   Prefer A to B
d.   Prefer B to A

10. Which of the following terms represents total benefits received in excess of the dollar expenditure necessary to obtain goods?

a.   Consumer excess
b.   Net gain
c.   Consumer surplus
d.   B or c

11. If the excess of marginal benefits over the product price for good A exceeds that of good B, a consumer:

a.   Is indifferent regarding the purchase of goods A and B.
b.   Would prefer A to B.
c.   Would not prefer either good.
d.   Would prefer B to A.

12. An increase in income shifts the marginal benefit curve _____, resulting in an increase in consumption if the good in question is a _____ good.

    a. Upward, inferior
    b. Downward, normal
    c. Upward, normal
    d. Upward, Giffen

13. The income effect reinforces the substitution effect for:

    a. Normal goods.
    b. Inferior goods.
    c. Giffen goods.
    d. Public goods.

14. The income effect to some extent offsets the substitution effect for:

    a. Normal goods.
    b. Inferior goods.
    c. Public goods.
    d. All goods and services.

15. The income effect more than offsets the substitution effect for:

    a. Normal goods.
    b. Inferior goods.
    c. Public goods.
    d. Giffen goods.

16. A market demand curve:

    a. Is a horizontal summation of individual demand curves.
    b. Is downsloping.
    c. Is the culmination of utility-maximizing choices by consumers.
    d. All of the above.

THINK IT THROUGH

1. You go to a restaurant, look at the menu, and find that the price of a cheese omelette is $3.50 and the price of a short stack of pancakes is $2. Your marginal benefits associated with the next order of an omelette or pancakes are $5 and $2.75, respectively. Which do you prefer? Why?

2. Explain the logic underlying the equimarginal principle.

3. You complain because your spouse always purchases the more expensive good when confronted with a choice. Assume that price and product quality are not always positively related. Is your spouse a utility maximizer? Discuss.

4. Why are people often willing and able to spend large sums on goods with limited usefulness like gold money clips when these same people are willing to spend little if any money for essential goods like air or water?

Read the news brief at the end of this chapter and answer the question below.

Explain, using supply and demand analysis, why condominium prices are rising everywhere but the Midwest.

CHAPTER ANSWERS

In Brief: Chapter Summary

1. Total 2. Marginal utility 3. Equals 4. Maximum 5. Declining 6. Declines 7. Exceed 8. Equals 9. Dollar expenditure 10. Exceeds 11. Normal goods 12. Inferior good 13. Individual 14. Income 15. Substitution 16. Complements 17. To some extent offsets 18. More than offsets

Vocabulary Review

1. Income effect 2. Substitution effect 3. Market demand curve 4. Law of diminishing marginal utility 5. Marginal benefit 6. Consumer surplus 7. Paradox of value 8. Total utility 9. Total benefit 10. Net benefit 11. Marginal utility 12. Utility 13. Equimarginal principle 14. Preference 15. Consumer equilibrium

Skills Review

1. a. | Units | MU |
|---|---|
| 1 | 50 |
| 2 | 40 |
| 3 | 30 |
| 4 | 20 |
| 5 | 10 |
| 6 | 0 |
| 7 | -10 |

b.

c. Slope, zero

2. a. and b.

Tickets			Sweaters		
Units	MU	MU/P	Units	MU	MU/P
1	60	12	1	400	16
2	55	11	2	350	14
3	50	10	3	300	12

4	45	9	4	250	10
5	40	8	5	200	8
6	35	7	6	150	6
7	30	6			

c. 5, 5
d. 1750

3. a.

Units	MB ($)
1	
2	130
3	110
4	90
5	70
6	50
7	30

b.

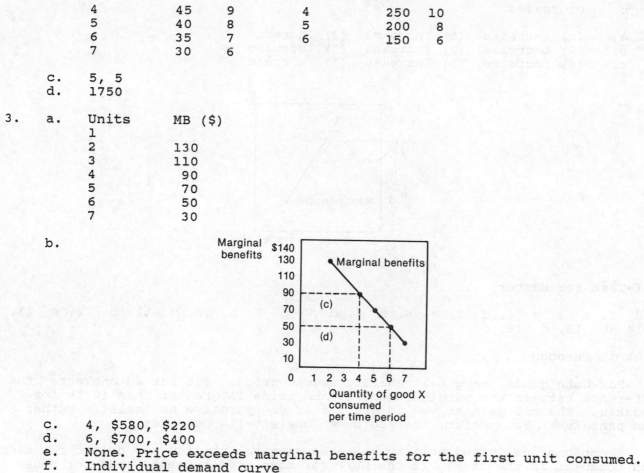

c. 4, $580, $220
d. 6, $700, $400
e. None. Price exceeds marginal benefits for the first unit consumed.
f. Individual demand curve

4. a. Increases

123

b. Decreases

5. a. (1) Increase (2) Increase (3) Increase
    b. (1) Decrease (2) Increase (3) Increase
    c. (1) Decrease (2) Increase (3) Decrease

6.

Self-Test for Mastery

1. d 2. a 3. c 4. d 5. a 6. d 7. d 8. a 9. b 10. d 11. b 12. c 13. a 14. b 15. d 16. d

Think it Through

1. For both goods, marginal benefits exceed price. But for an omelette, the difference between the marginal benefit and price is greater than it is for pancakes. The net gain to you is greater if you purchase an omelette rather than pancakes. You prefer, therefore, an omelette to pancakes.

2. A consumer maximizes utility when the marginal utility per dollar for each good consumed is the same. If the MU/P for some good exceeded that for other goods, dollars could be reallocated away from other goods and spent on the good with the higher MU/P. A consumer could increase utility by reallocating a given income. The reverse holds true for goods having a smaller MU/P.

3. Your spouse probably gets satisfaction from purchasing more expensive goods. It might be the perception of higher quality or an attempt to keep up with the Joneses or the need to not feel "cheap" that gives your spouse "tastes" for higher priced goods. Remember that a consumer's preferences depend on both prices and marginal benefits associated with goods. For higher priced goods, your spouse is simply expressing a willingness and ability to pay a higher maximum sum--a higher marginal benefit curve. But for the higher priced good to be chosen, the excess of marginal benefits over the price must be larger than for lower priced goods, or it would be irrational to purchase the more expensive good.

4. Plentiful goods such as air or water command either no market price or a very minimal price. The additional benefit of a gallon of water is very small. The price you are willing to pay is likewise very small even though the total benefit associated with water consumption is quite large. Because of their scarcity, the additional benefit of a gold clip is high. Some people are willing to pay high prices for gold money clips even though the total benefits received from the clips are very small relative to the consumption of water.

Pop Quiz

Single-family homes and condominiums are substitutes in consumption. If two goods are substitutes, an increase in the price of one good causes the demand

124

for the other good to increase. In all regions of the country except the Midwest, the median prices of single-family homes have been increasing. Prices have increased 10.5% in the South, 5.8% in the West, and 2% in the Northeast. As the price of single-family homes increases, the demand for condominiums increases. As the demand for condominiums rises relative to the supply of condominiums, condominium prices rise and market quantity increases.

Prices for Condominiums
Are on the Rebound

CONDOMINIUM prices declined in the early 1980s because of overbuilding: too many condos, not enough buyers. Now the glut is drying up—and prices are on the rise.

In the Northeast, South and West, prices for condos have increased on average about 18% over the five quarters through March 31, according to the National Association of Realtors.

The reason for the reversal: In many markets, the rising costs of single-family homes have sent buyers searching for less expensive alternatives, and condos have been the answer. As a result, their prices have jumped.

During the first quarter of 1988, this was especially true in the South, where median prices soared 10.5%, to $65,300 from $59,-100. In the West, prices rose 5.8%, to $105,100 from $99,300. And in the Northeast, where more than half of all condos are now sold, prices rose 2%, to $111,100 from $108,900.

The only region where prices are continuing to decline is the Midwest, where they dipped to $57,600 from $58,700. That's because the region still has a healthy supply of affordable single-family homes.

Indifference Curve Analysis

IN BRIEF: APPENDIX SUMMARY

Fill in the blanks to summarize appendix content.

(1)_____(Marginal, Indifference curve analysis) is a technique for analyzing the choices that consumers make between alternatives. The indifference curve and budget constraint are the essential elements of the analysis. Applied to goods, an indifference curve shows the various combinations of two goods that can be consumed while maintaining (2)_____(the same level, different levels) of utility. The curve is negatively sloped because in order to keep utility unchanged, the consumer must give up some consumption of a good in order to increase the consumption of another good. The slope of the indifference curve becomes less negative as more of the good on the horizontal axis is consumed. The slope is called the (3)_____(marginal utility, marginal rate of substitution). It indicates the quantity of one good that a consumer is willing to give up to have a unit of another good, while maintaining the level of utility. The marginal rate of substitution of x for y (MRSxy) (4)_____ (decreases, increases) as more of good X is consumed. This is known as the diminishing marginal rate of substitution. The consumer is willing to give up large quantities of Y in order to have the first few units of good X. As more and more units of X are consumed, the consumer is willing to sacrifice smaller and smaller quantities of good Y. Marginal utility and marginal benefits fall as additional units of X are consumed. But reducing the consumption of Y increases the marginal utility and benefit of Y. At the margin, units of X become increasingly less valuable in terms of the sacrifice of good Y. Indifference curves (5)_____(closer to, further from) the origin are associated with higher levels of utility.

(6)_____(The budget constraint, Income) determines the consumer's ability to maximize satisfaction from the consumption of goods X and Y. The budget constraint is determined by the income per period available to the consumer and the relative prices of the two goods consumed. The slope of the budget line is negative and is the ratio of the price of good X to the price of good Y. Changes in (7)_____(income, prices) shift the budget line, whereas changes in (8)_____(income, prices) alter the slope.

Consumer equilibrium occurs when the market value of good Y that you are willing to give up just equals what the market requires you to pay for a unit of good X. This occurs where the budget line (9)_____ (intersects, is just tangent to) the highest indifference curve. Here the marginal rate of substitution equals the ratio of the price of good X to the price of good Y. The consumer spends all income and allocates it in a way that maximizes utility. It can be shown that the MRSxy also equals the ratio of the marginal utility of good X to the marginal utility of good Y. MUx/MUy also equals the price ratio. The point of tangency between the indifference curve and budget constraint is equivalent to the equimarginal principle when the slope of the indifference curve is interpreted as the ratio of these marginal utilities.

An increase in income shifts the budget constraint curve (10)_____ (outward, inward) parallel to the old budget line such that a new point of tangency is reached on a higher indifference curve. For instance, if goods are normal, an income increase will cause the consumption of both goods to (11)_____(fall, rise). A decrease in the price of X will cause the budget line to become less steep. The consumption of X increases, and the consumer attains a higher level of utility. A demand curve for good X can be derived by changing the price of good X, all other things being equal, and determining the consumer's utility-maximizing quantity demanded. Plotting these price-quantity demanded coordinates yields the consumer's individual demand curve.

VOCABULARY REVIEW

Write the key term from the list below next to its definition.

Key Terms

Indifference curve analysis   Consumer equilibrium
Market basket   Budget constraint
Indifference curve   Indifference map
Marginal rate of   Diminishing marginal
   substitution   rate of substitution

Definitions

1. _____: the marginal rate of substitution of good X for Y will tend to decline as more X is substituted for Y along any consumer's indifference curve.

2. _____: represents the combination of goods purchased that maximizes utility subject to the budget constraint.

3. _____: a technique for explaining how choices between two alternatives are made.

4. _____: as defined by a consumer's income and its purchasing power; indicates that income must equal expenditure.

5. _____: a graph of various market baskets that provide a consumer with equal utility.

6. _____: the quantity of one good a consumer would give up to obtain one more unit of another good while being made neither better off nor worse off by the trade.

7. _____: a combination of goods and services.

8. _____: a way of describing consumer preferences.

SKILLS REVIEW

1. In the diagram below, draw a budget constraint where the consumer has income of $100 per week and the prices of goods X and Y are both $5.

a. The consumer's utility-maximizing combination of goods X and Y are _____ units of good X and _____ units of good Y.

b. Show on the diagram above the effect of an increase in income to $150 per week. The consumption of good X _____ to _____ units and the consumption of good Y _____ to _____ units. The goods must be _____ goods.

c. Holding income at $150 per week, show the impact of a price reduction of good X to $2.50. The consumption of good X _____ to _____ units; the consumption of good Y _____ to _____ units.

2. Referring to the diagram below, let income equal $120 and assume that the prices of X and Y equal $10.

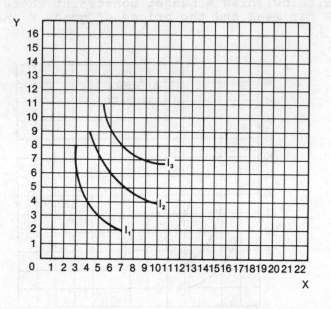

a. Determine the utility-maximizing combination of goods X and Y.
   _____ units of X, _____ units of Y

b. Let the price of X fall to $6. The utility-maximizing quantity of X consumed is _____ units. Of Y consumed the utility-maximizing quantity is _____ units.

c. Let the price of X rise from $10 to $20. The utility-maximizing combination of X and Y is _____ units of X and _____ units of Y.

d. Construct this consumer's individual demand curve in the diagram below for good X from the information in parts b and c above.

130

SELF-TEST FOR MASTERY

Select the best answer.

1. Which of the following are true regarding an indifference curve?

   a. The slope is negative.
   b. The MRSxy increases as more of good X is consumed.
   c. The MRSxy decreases as more of good X is consumed.
   d. Indifference curves farther from the origin imply a higher level of utility.
   e. A, c, and d.

2. The budget constraint:

   a. Has a positive slope.
   b. Must be curvilinear if the prices of the two goods are held unchanged.
   c. Has a slope equal to $-(Px/Py)$.
   d. None of the above.

3. Increases in income shift the budget constraint:

   a. Inward.
   b. Outward.
   c. To a different slope.
   d. Such that it no longer limits consumer purchases.

4. A change in price of either good X or Y will:

   a. Shift the indifference curve.
   b. Shift the budget constraint.
   c. Rotate the indifference curve.
   d. Rotate the budget constraint about one of its two intercepts.

5. Consumer equilibrium occurs when:

   a. The budget constraint and the indifference curve intersect.
   b. Two indifference curves intersect.
   c. The highest indifference curve on the indifference curve map is attained.
   d. The budget constraint is just tangent to the highest indifference curve.

6. In an indifference curve system, an increase in the price of good X will _____ the budget constraint toward the origin and _____ the quantity of good X consumed.

   a. Rotate, decrease
   b. Rotate, increase
   c. Shift, decrease
   d. Shift, increase

7. In an indifference curve system, an increase in income will _____
    the budget constraint away from the origin, and the quantity of good X
    consumed will _____ if good X is a normal good.

    a. Rotate, decrease
    b. Rotate, increase
    c. Shift, decrease
    d. Shift, increase

8. Which one of the following is true regarding consumer equilibrium?

    a. MRSxy = MUx = MUy
    b. MRSxy = (MUx/MUy) = (Px/Py)
    c. (Px/Py) + MRSxy = (MUx/MUy)
    d. None of the above

THINK IT THROUGH

1. Every point on a consumer's individual demand curve represents a utility-
maximizing decision. Discuss.

2. Explain how market demand curves can be derived from individual demand
curves.

APPENDIX ANSWERS

In Brief: Appendix Summary

1. Indifference curve analysis 2. The same level 3. Marginal rate of
substitution 4. Decreases 5. Further from 6. Budget constraint 7. Income
8. Prices 9. Is just tangent to 10. Outward   11. Rise

Vocabulary Review

1. Diminishing marginal rate of substitution 2. Consumer equilibrium 3.
Indifference curve analysis 4. Budget constraint 5. Indifference curve 6.
Marginal rate of substitution 7. Market basket 8. Indifference map

Skills Review

1.

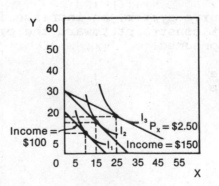

    a. 10, 10
    b. Increases, 15, increases, 15, normal
    c. Increases, 25, increases, 17 1/2

2.

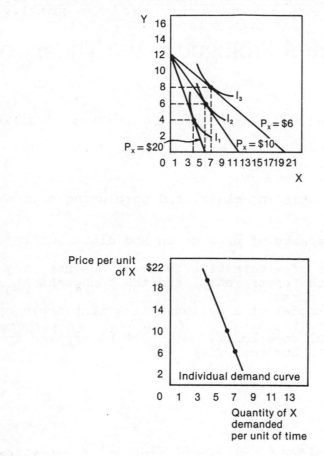

a. 6, 6
b. 7, 8
c. 4, 4

d.

Self-Test for Mastery

1. c   2. c   3. b   4. d   5. d   6. b   7. d   8. b

Think it Through

1.   A coordinate on the consumer's individual demand curve represents a utility-maximizing response to a given price of the good relative to other product prices, other things being equal. This is true of other coordinates on the demand curve. Each point on the demand curve represents a state of consumer equilibrium.

2.   Market demand curves represent the utility-maximizing responses of all consumers to relative prices. It can be derived by horizontally summing the individual demand curves of all consumers in the market.

9

The Business Firm: A Prologue to the Theory of Market Supply

CHAPTER CHALLENGES

After studying your text, attending class, and completing this chapter, you should be able to:

1. Explain how various aspects of production and distribution are integrated within a single firm.
2. Outline the advantages of alternative forms of business organization (the sole proprietorship, the partnership, and the corporation) and discuss the functions of business firms.
3. Describe a simplified model of a business firm that explains market supply.
4. Show how the concept of opportunity cost must be applied to accurately measure the profit of a business firm.

IN BRIEF: CHAPTER SUMMARY

Fill in the blanks to summarize chapter content.

Business firms, each of which is under one management, are engaged in earning profits for the owners by producing items for sale in markets. They operate one or more plants producing one or more products and in some cases are vertically integrated. Vertical integration means that all stages of operation, including the acquisition of raw materials, the processing of resources to produce output, and the distribution and marketing of goods are handled by (1)_____ (several firms, a single firm). A (2)_____ (conglomerate, corporation) is a firm that produces many kinds of goods and services. Firms selling (3)_____(different, similar) products are in the same industry.

A firm can be structured as a sole proprietorship, a partnership, or a corporation. A (4)_____(partnership, corporation) is a legal person. It has some distinct advantages over other business enterprises. Corporations can issue both stocks and bonds and the owners of the corporation (the stockholders) have (5)_____(limited, unlimited) liability. Both of these characteristics greatly (6)_____ (reduce, increase) the amount of funds that can be attracted for expansion and growth. Stockholders can easily sell their rights in the firm. Individuals can reduce the risk associated with owning firms by diversifying their holdings. This increases the total amount of funds available for stock ownership. Another factor that induces individuals to provide more funds to the corporation is (7)_____(limited, unlimited) liability. This too reduces the risk of ownership in that a stockholder's liability relates to the amount of stock held. Other business enterprises are at (8)_____ (an advantage, a disadvantage) compared to corporations in that they have unlimited liability and cannot issue stocks and bonds.

In corporations, ownership and management (9)_____(are, are not) separated. If management pursues goals that are inconsistent with the owners' goals, profits decrease because managers use corporate resources to attain managerial goals that would have otherwise been used to further the goals of the owners. Also, owners must use resources to monitor management to ensure that the owners' goals are met. Another disadvantage of corporations is that they are not only subject to a corporate income tax, but the (10)_____(retained earnings, dividends) paid to stockholders are subject to individual income taxes as well. Thus the income of the corporation is taxed twice. This (11)_____(is, is not) the case for other business enterprises.

The functions of business firms include the production of goods and services, the assignment of tasks to either employees or to outside firms for various stages of production, and a determination of the appropriate division of labor within the firm. Managers assist in these functions by helping to decide what and how much to produce and whether certain operations should be handled internally or contracted out. Operations are likely to be (12)_____ (contracted out, kept within the firm) if a reliable flow of materials and services is considered important and there is a possibility that outside suppliers might prove unreliable. A firm might want to control a strategic input and thus put other firms in the industry at a disadvantage. Or a firm might put a premium on internal communication or the ability to easily adapt to new technology. All of these things would probably induce a firm to vertically integrate--to handle all production stages within the firm. Managers also have to assign labor-specific tasks or responsibilities so that the firm can operate at least cost. Managers reward efficient employees with a compensation system designed to maintain and enhance labor productivity.

In studying the behavior of firms, it is necessary to abstract from the complexities of the modern economy and make some assumptions regarding the structure or goals of firms so that the basic features of firm behavior can be understood. It is assumed that there (13)____(is, is no) separation between ownership and management. Firms are assumed to be (14)_____ (multiproduct, single product), having owner-operators who make decisions regarding resource use and production that maximize (15)_____(revenues, profits).

Profit is defined as total revenue less total costs in which total costs include (16)_____(in addition to, only) the accounting costs, (17)_____(but not the, the) cost of owner-supplied resources. (18)_____ (Total, Accounting) costs are the explicit outlays by the firm for resources bought in resource markets. Owner-supplied inputs are not purchased by the firm but entail opportunity costs. These (19)_____ (explicit, implicit) costs must be imputed or estimated. They are estimated by determining the opportunity cost of the owner-supplied inputs. Revenues in excess of accounting and implicit costs are called (20)_____(economic, normal) profit. (21)_____(Economic, Normal) profit is treated as a cost (the implicit costs associated with owner-supplied resources). It is a return to the owner-operator just equal to the opportunity cost of self-owned resources.

VOCABULARY REVIEW

Write the key term from the list below next to its definition.

Key Terms

Business firm
Plant
Vertical integration
Conglomerate
Industry
Sole proprietorship
Partnership
Corporation
Dividend
Retained earnings
Limited liability

Manager
Personnel management
Multiproduct firm
Single-product firm
Profit
Economic cost
Implicit cost
Accounting cost
Normal profit
Economic profit

Definitions

1. _____: that portion of a firm's costs that is not included in accounting costs. A measure of the implicit cost of owner-supplied resources in a firm over a given period.

2. _____: profit in excess of the normal profit; the difference between total revenue and the opportunity cost of all inputs used by a firm over a given period.

3. _____: the portion of a corporation's profit paid to its stockholders.

4. _____: the portion of corporate profits not paid out as dividends.

5. _____: the monetary value of all inputs used in a particular activity or enterprise over a given period.

6. _____: the cost of nonpurchased inputs to which a cash value must be imputed because the inputs are not purchased in a market transaction.

7. _____: a group of firms selling a similar product in a market.

8. _____: a business that is legally established under state laws that grant it an identity separate from its owners.

9. _____: an organization under one management set up for the purpose of earning profits for its owners by making one or more items available for sale in markets.

10. _____: a business owned by one person.

11. _____: a physical structure in which a firm's owners or employees conduct business.

12. _____: a business owned by two or more persons, each of whom receives a portion of any profits.

136

13. _____: a firm that owns plants used in various stages of its production.

14. _____: measures the explicit costs of operating a business, those which result from purchases of input services.

15. _____: a firm's operating plants that produce many different kinds of goods and services.

16. _____: a person who coordinates decisions within the firm.

17. _____: a firm that produces only one type of item for sale.

18. _____: a firm that produces several different items for sale.

19. _____: a legal provision that protects the owners of a corporation (its stockholders) by putting a ceiling equal to the purchase price of their stock on their liability for debts of the corporation.

20. _____: the difference between the revenues a firm takes in over any given period and the costs incurred in operating the firm over the same period.

21. _____: the process by which managers monitor worker performance and provide rewards for workers who perform efficiently.

SKILLS REVIEW

Concept: Alternative forms of business organization

1. Which of the following characteristics are associated with corporations (C), sole proprietorships (PR), and/or partnerships (PT)?

   a. _____ Limited liability
   b. _____ Unlimited liability
   c. _____ Separation of ownership and management
   d. _____ Presence of owner-operators
   e. _____ Ability to issue stock and bonds
   f. _____ Can pay dividends
   g. _____ Income is subject to personal income
              taxes only
   h. _____ Income is subject to taxation twice
   i. _____ Is a legal person

Concept: Functions of business

2. List three functions of business firms:

   a. _____
   b. _____
   c. _____

3. List three ways in which managers assist business firms in the fulfillment of their functions:

    a. _____
    b. _____
    c. _____

4. You manage a U.S.-based corporation, the XYZ Aluminum Company, and you are trying to decide whether to mine your own raw input, bauxite, internally or to purchase it from outside firms. Assume that bauxite is found only in Africa and must be processed into aluminum ingots before shipment to fabrication plants in the United States. For each of the scenarios below, are you _more_ or _less_ inclined to contract out? Explain.

    a. _____ War develops, closing sea lanes.
    b. _____ Civil wars are no longer occurring in African nations, raising the possibility of long-term peace and political stability.
    c. _____ There are no substitutes for bauxite in the production of aluminum.
    d. _____ XYZ is battling with four other companies for a larger share of the aluminum market.
    e. _____ XYZ finds that closer managerial communication among the various stages of production enhances the firm's efficiency.
    f. _____ XYZ patents a process that reduces the cost of mining bauxite.
    g. _____ Because the world supply of bauxite and aluminum ingots is produced by firms specializing in the production of these inputs, they produce a large volume, realizing efficiencies associated with large-scale production and specialization.

Concept: Cost and profit measures

5. Given the data in the table below for Fred's Bar and Grill, determine Fred's:

    a. Accounting cost _____
    b. Explicit cost _____
    c. Implicit cost _____
    d. Normal profit _____
    e. Total cost _____
    f. Economic profit _____

Fred's Bar and Grill
(annual data)

Wages	$25,000
Depreciation	15,000
Interest paid	7,000
Other expenditures for inputs	17,000
Imputed cost of owner-supplied labor	20,000
Imputed cost of owner-supplied plant	6,000
Imputed interest associated with owner-supplied resources	2,000
Total revenue	108,000

6. Discuss the implications if Fred's Bar and Grill earned $85,000 of revenue instead of $108,000.

SELF-TEST FOR MASTERY

Select the best answer.

1. A business firm that engages in several stages of production from the acquisition of resources to the distribution of output is known as a:

    a. Conglomerate.
    b. Single-product firm.
    c. Multiproduct firm.
    d. Vertically integrated firm.

2. A business firm that sells output in many different industries is known as a:

    a. Conglomerate.
    b. Single-product firm.
    c. Multiproduct firm.
    d. Vertically integrated firm.
    e. A and c.

3. Which of the following best describes an industry?

    a. A collection of markets
    b. A group of firms
    c. A group of firms selling similar products
    d. A collection of markets for unrelated goods

4. Unlimited liability is a characteristic of:

    a. Corporations.
    b. Sole proprietorships.
    c. Partnerships.
    d. B and c.

5.   The ability to issue stock and bonds is a characteristic of:

     a.   Corporations.
     b.   Sole proprietorships.
     c.   Partnerships.
     d.   B and c.

6.   The separation of ownership and management is a characteristic of:

     a.   Corporations.
     b.   Sole proprietorships.
     c.   Partnerships.
     d.   B and c.

7.   Which of the following is a legal person?

     a.   Corporation
     b.   Sole proprietorship
     c.   Partnership
     d.   None of the above

8.   The main advantage of a corporation over other forms of business enterprise is that:

     a.   Other forms of business enterprise have their incomes taxed twice.
     b.   Other forms of business enterprise have limited liability.
     c.   Corporations have unlimited liability.
     d.   Corporations can raise larger sums of money for expansion and growth.

9.   That portion of corporate income which is not paid as dividends or used to meet the corporation's tax liability is called:

     a.   Depreciation.
     b.   Retained earnings.
     c.   Normal profit.
     d.   Implicit cost.

10. A business firm is less likely to contract out for production or services if:

     a.   Communication within the firm between various production stages is relatively unimportant.
     b.   Controlling a strategic input is unimportant to the firm.
     c.   Adapting to changing technology is considered unimportant.
     d.   There is a possibility that outside suppliers might prove unreliable.

11. A business firm is more likely to contract out when:

     a.   Communication within the firm between various stages of production is important.
     b.   Controlling a strategic input is considered important.
     c.   Adapting to changing technology is important.
     d.   Outside suppliers are reliable.
     e.   All of the above

12. Abstracting from the complexities of the modern economy to better understand the essential features of business firm behavior, several simplifying assumptions are made. Which of the following is not one of these?

   a. Ownership and management are not separated.
   b. The firm is a single-product firm.
   c. The goal of the firm is to maximize profits.
   d. The firm is vertically integrated.

13. The total actual payments made by a firm to acquire inputs are known as:

   a. Accounting costs.
   b. Normal profit.
   c. Implicit costs.
   d. Marginal costs.

14. Accounting costs are also called:

   a. Explicit costs.
   b. Total costs.
   c. Total normal costs.
   d. Imputed costs.

15. The cost of nonpurchased owner-supplied resources is known as:

   a. Implicit costs.
   b. Explicit costs.
   c. Accounting costs.
   d. Total costs.

16. Implicit costs are measured by the:

   a. Accounting costs less the imputed costs.
   b. Imputed costs plus the explicit costs.
   c. Total revenues less total costs.
   d. Opportunity cost of owner-supplied resources.

17. Total costs are the sum of:

   a. Accounting costs and explicit costs.
   b. Accounting costs and the opportunity costs of owner-supplied resources.
   c. Imputed costs and the opportunity costs of owner-supplied resources.
   d. Accounting costs and implicit costs.
   e. B and d.

18. A return to the owner just equal to the opportunity costs of the owner's self-owned resources provided to the firm is called:

   a. Total revenue.
   b. Imputed revenue.
   c. Normal profit.
   d. Economic profit.

19.   Economic profit is defined as:

   a.   A return to the owner just equal to the opportunity costs of the owner's self-owned resources provided to the firm.
   b.   Total revenue less accounting costs.
   c.   Total revenue less the sum of accounting costs and implicit costs.
   d.   Normal profit plus imputed revenues.

THINK IT THROUGH

1.   Of the three forms of business enterprise, why are sole proprietorships and partnerships so numerous and corporations so large?

2.   The microcomputer industry is populated by many more firms operating at a single stage of production than by vertically integrated firms.   Explain why.

3.   Why is it necessary to consider implicit costs in decisions?

4.   You are considering owning and operating a day care center.   You determine that the annual cost to hire labor is $35,000.   You plan to use one of your rental houses for the location of the center.   You estimate that $25,000 of capital equipment is required.   Because you have only $5,000 in cash, you expect to borrow $20,000.   The interest cost on the loan would be $2,000 per year.   Other miscellaneous inputs are expected to cost $15,000 annually.   You would consider it a success if you just break even the first year--if your revenues just cover your costs.   You estimate that you can do this if revenues for the first year are $52,000.   Discuss.

CHAPTER ANSWERS

In Brief: Chapter Summary

1. Single firm 2. Conglomerate 3. Similar 4. Corporation 5. Limited 6. Increases 7. Limited 8. Disadvantage 9. Are 10. Dividends 11. Is not 12. Kept within the firm 13. Is 14. Single product 15. Profits 16. In addition to 17. The 18. Accounting 19. Implicit 20. Economic 21. Normal

Vocabulary Review

1. Normal profit 2. Economic profit 3. Dividend 4. Retained earnings 5. Economic cost 6. Implicit cost 7. Industry 8. Corporation 9. Business firm 10. Sole proprietorship 11. Plant 12. Partnership 13. Vertical integration 14. Accounting cost 15. Conglomerate 16. Manager 17. Single-product firm 18. Multiproduct firm 19. Limited liability 20. Profit 21. Personnel management

Skills Review

1.   a. C b. PR, PT c. C d. PR, PT e. C f. C g. PR, PT h. C   i. C

2.   a.   Production of goods and services
     b.   Assignment of tasks to employees of the firm or to outside firms
     c.   Determination of the appropriate division of labor and specialization of resources

3.   a.   Helps decide what and how much to produce
     b.   Helps decide whether or not to contract out for production or
          services
     c.   Assigns labor-specialized tasks, monitors their efforts, and rewards
          them accordingly

4.   a.   Less. If you rely on African suppliers to ship ingots to the United
          States, there is likely to be an interruption in supply. Whereas if
          you develop the resource yourself, you might be able to stockpile
          ingots or build fabrication plants in Africa in anticipation of
          impending events.

     b.   More. The likelihood of interruptions in the availability of ingots
          is lessened.
     c.   Less. If you must have ingots to produce aluminum and if survival is
          considered important, it might be wise to develop the capability to
          mine and process bauxite.
     d.   Less. One way to lessen competition is to gain control over an input
          strategic to all competitors.
     e.   Less. If least-cost production is important and it is found that for
          XYZ internal communication is critical to achieving that goal, it
          might make sense to vertically integrate.
     f.   Less. If XYZ can mine and process bauxite at less cost than outside
          suppliers because of this new technology, it can reduce costs by
          vertically integrating. It could even compete as a seller in the
          bauxite market.
     g.   More. Outside suppliers specializing in the production of aluminum
          ingots can deliver the ingots to you less expensively and more
          reliably than if you were vertically integrated.

5.   a. $64,000
     b. $64.000
     c. $28,000
     d. $28,000
     e. $92,000
     f. $16,000

6.   Fred would incur an economic loss of $7,000. Total revenues are less than
     total costs by $7,000. The opportunity cost of Fred's self-owned
     resources used in the firm are $28,000, but only $21,000 of this is earned
     in the current employment of these resources. Fred would in time probably
     consider employing his self-owned resources elsewhere.

Self-Test for Mastery

1. d 2. e 3. c 4. d 5. a 6. a 7. a 8. d 9. b 10. d 11. d 12. d 13.
a 14. a 15. a 16. d 17. e 18. c 19. c

Think it Through

1.   Sole proprietorships and partnerships involve limited resources and
maximum freedom and are easy to establish. There are simply many more firms
that have modest resource requirements than there are firms that require very
large sums of money. The largest firms are corporations because of their
ability to attract funds for expansion and growth.

2.   The microcomputer industry has chip makers, producers of microprocessors,
assemblers of cards or boards, component manufacturers such as producers of
disk drives and modems, final assemblers, sales distributors, etc. In this
case, technology is changing very fast and involves many small upstart
companies. Because of the number of firms, the supply of inputs is reliable

and available at competitive market prices. To stay abreast of the technology
and to purchase inputs at minimum prices, many companies rely on a large
network of outside suppliers.

3.   It is necessary to consider implicit costs in a decision because if you
did not, you would not be considering the total costs of some action or
alternative. You would likely make a decision that would not result in the
best use of your resources. You would be sacrificing more productive uses of
your resources.

4.   In this case, you are not considering total costs , but rather accounting
costs. If you indeed realize revenues of $52,000, you are covering accounting
costs but not providing any revenues toward your implicit costs of owner-
supplied resources. You have sacrificed the opportunity to have used your own
resources in their next-best employment. To break even, your revenues must be
high enough to cover both accounting and implicit costs.

10
Production and Cost

CHAPTER CHALLENGES

After studying your text, attending class, and completing this chapter, you should be able to:

1. Analyze productive relationships and show how the law of diminishing marginal returns implies a certain pattern of variation in output in the short run when the use of some inputs cannot be varied.
2. Explain the distinction between variable cost and fixed cost and describe the pattern of variation in total cost and other cost concepts as a single-product firm varies production.
3. Explain the relationship between cost and productivity of inputs.
4. Explain how long-run cost curves can be derived
5. Show how marginal cost is affected by changes in input prices.

IN BRIEF: CHAPTER SUMMARY

Fill in the blanks to summarize chapter content.

To understand the supply side of product markets, it is necessary to first examine productivity and costs associated with producing output. Inputs are used in the production process to produce output. Some inputs are in fixed quantities over a period, whereas other inputs can be varied. (1)_____ (Fixed, Variable) inputs can be varied over the short run. Some resources are fixed in the short run. These resources are known as (2)_____ (fixed, variable) inputs. In the (3)_____(long run, short run), all inputs are variable.

In the short run, if a variable input such as labor is increased to produce output, while other resources such as plant and equipment are held constant, then in time the extra output resulting from each additional unit of the variable input will decline. This is known as the law of diminishing marginal (4)_____(utility, returns). The total product curve will in time increase at a (5)_____(decreasing, increasing) rate as additional units of the variable input are employed. The slope of the total product curve (change in total output/change in a unit of variable input) is known as the (6)_____ (total, marginal) product of a variable input. Marginal product begins to (7)_____(decline, increase) at the point at which diminishing marginal returns set in. Average product, or output per unit of the variable input, (8)_____(falls, rises) as long as marginal product is greater than average product and (9)_____(declines, increases) when marginal product is less than average product. Diminishing marginal returns occur when a variable input is continually added to a fixed quantity of other inputs. This is because continued employment of the variable input will eventually strain and surpass a plant's capacity to productively utilize the variable input.

Short-run costs can be derived from the short-run productivity relationships. (10)_____(Fixed, Variable) costs are the costs of the variable inputs. These costs (11)_____ (do not vary, vary) with the level of output. They are determined by the quantity of variable inputs, valued at their market prices, required to produce output. (12)_____(Fixed, Variable) costs are the costs associated with fixed inputs. They (13)_____(do, do not) vary with levels of output. Total costs are the sum of variable costs and fixed costs. Other short-run cost concepts include (14)_____(average total, total) cost, which is the sum of average fixed cost and average variable cost. (15)_____(Total, Average) fixed cost is total fixed costs divided by total output. (16)_____(Marginal, Average variable) cost is total variable costs divided by total output. Finally, (17)_____(marginal, average variable) cost is the cost associated with production of one additional unit of output.

The behavior of short-run costs and the shape of the short-run cost curves are related to the behavior of the short-run productivity relationships. Although total product initially increases at an increasing rate, total variable costs and total costs increase at a/an (18)_____(decreasing, increasing) rate. But when diminishing marginal returns set in, total product increases at a/an (19)_____(decreasing, increasing) rate and both the total and variable cost curves increase at a/an (20)_____(decreasing, increasing) rate. When the average productivity of the variable input is increasing, a unit of output can be produced with increasingly smaller quantities of the variable input. The average variable cost and average total cost therefore (21)_____ (decrease, increase). When average product declines, the average variable and average total cost (22)_____(decrease, increase). When the marginal product of a variable input is rising, an additional unit of output can be produced with smaller quantities of the variable input. The marginal cost of producing that additional unit of output (23)_____ (decreases, increases). When marginal product declines, marginal cost (24)_____(decreases, increases). Thus short-run costs depend upon the quantity and productivity of the resources employed and the market prices at which they sell.

In the long run, (25)_____(only variable inputs, all inputs) are variable. Costs are not only influenced by the rate at which plants are utilized, but also by the size and number of plants operated. If the manager's objective is to find the combination of inputs that minimizes costs, the (26)_____ (largest, least cost) plant size must be utilized and it must be operated at minimum average cost. Long-run minimum average costs are attained at the minimum point on the average cost curve of the most efficient size plant. Declining long-run average costs are known as (27)_____ (diseconomies, economies) of scale, whereas increasing long-run average costs are called (28)_____(diseconomies, economies) of scale. Constant returns to scale mean that a number of plant sizes have the same minimum average total cost.

VOCABULARY REVIEW

Write the key term from the list below next to its definition.

Key Terms

Production	Fixed costs
Inputs	Variable costs
Production function	Total cost
Short run	Average cost
Variable input	Average variable cost

Fixed input
Law of diminishing
marginal returns
Total product curve
Point of diminishing
returns
Total product of a
variable input
Long run
Marginal product
Marginal cost

Average fixed cost
Long-run cost
Average product
Economies of scale
(increasing returns to
scale)
Diseconomies of scale
(decreasing returns to
scale)
Constant returns to
scale

Definitions

1. _____: costs that do not vary as a firm varies its output; also called overhead costs.

2. _____: costs that change with output; the costs of variable inputs.

3. _____: the total output produced over a given period divided by the number of units of that input used.

4. _____: corresponds to the level of usage of the variable input at which its marginal product begins to decline.

5. _____: the sum of the value of all inputs used to produce goods over any given period; the sum of fixed costs and variable costs.

6. _____: the process of using the services of labor and capital together with other inputs, such as land, materials, and fuels, to make goods and services available.

7. _____: states that the extra production obtained from increases in a variable input will eventually decline as more of the variable input is used with the fixed inputs.

8. _____: the increase in output from one more unit of an input when the quantity of all the inputs is unchanged.

9. _____: a period of production long enough that producers have adequate time to vary all the inputs used to produce a good.

10. _____: fixed costs divided by the number of units of output produced over a given period.

11. _____: the extra cost of producing one more unit of output.

12. _____: the labor, capital, land, natural resources, and entrepreneurship that are combined to produce products and services.

13. _____: total cost divided by the number of units of output produced over a given period; also called unit cost.

14. _____: describes how output varies in the short run as more of any one input is used with fixed amounts of other inputs under current technology.

15. _____ : variable cost divided by the number of units of output produced over a given period.

16. _____ : describes the relationship between any combination of input services and the maximum attainable output from that combination.

17. _____ : the amount of output produced over any given period when that input is used along with other fixed inputs.

18. _____ : a period of production during which some inputs cannot be varied.

19. _____ : an input whose quantity can be changed.

20. _____ : an input whose quantity cannot be changed.

21. _____ : the minimum cost of producing any given output when all inputs are variable.

22. _____ : reductions in unit costs resulting from increased size of operations; also called economies of mass production.

23. _____ : increases in average costs of operation resulting from problems in managing large-scale enterprises.

24. _____ : prevail when economies of scale no longer exist and when average costs do not increase as a result of diseconomies of scale in the long run.

SKILLS REVIEW

Concept: Productive relationships in the short run

1. The following represents daily production data for a small manufacturer of cup holders.

Units of Labor	Total Product	Marginal Product	Average Product
		(number of cup holders)	
0	0		
1	50		
2	130	___	___
3	230	___	___
4	320	___	___
5	400	___	___
6	465	___	___
7	525	___	___
8	575	___	___

a. Complete the marginal and average product columns in the table above.

b. Plot the total product (TP), marginal product (MP), and average product (AP) curves in the diagram below.

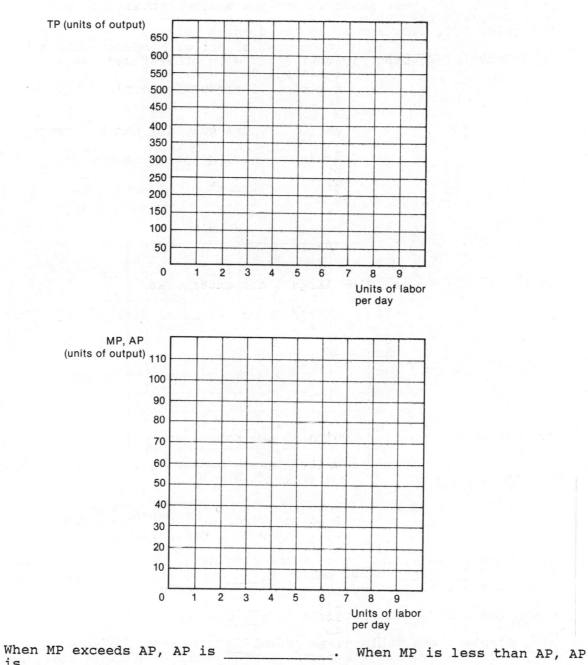

c. When MP exceeds AP, AP is _____. When MP is less than AP, AP is _____.

d. When TP is rising at an increasing rate, MP is _____. When TP is rising at a decreasing rate, MP is _____.

Concept: Costs in the short run

2. Using the production data above and assuming that total fixed costs (TFC) equal $50 and the price per unit of labor is $20:

    a.   Complete the table below.
    b.   Plot TFC, TVC, and TC in the diagram below.

Units of Output	Labor (units)	TFC $	TVC $	TC $
0	0			
50	1	___	___	___
130	2	___	___	___
230	3	___	___	___
320	4	___	___	___
400	5	___	___	___
465	6	___	___	___
525	7	___	___	___
575	8	___	___	___

Output
(units per day)

    c.   When TP is rising at an increasing rate, TVC and TC are rising at a _____ rate. When TP is rising at a decreasing rate, TVC and TC are rising at an _____ rate.

3. Given the cost and output data in question 2,

    a.   Complete the table below (round to two decimal places).
    b.   Plot the average fixed cost (AFC), average variable cost (AVC), average total cost (ATC), and marginal cost (MC) in the diagram below.

Units of Output	AFC $	AVC $	ATC $	MC $
0				
50				
130	___	___	___	___
230	___	___	___	___

320	___	___ ___	___
400	___	___ ___	___
465	___	___ ___	___
525	___	___ ___	___
575	___	___ ___	___

AFC, AVC, ATC, MC

Output
(units per day)

c. When MP is rising, MC is _____ and both TVC and TC are rising at a/an _____ rate. When MP is falling, MC is _____ and both TVC and TC are rising at a/an _____ rate.

d. When AP is rising, AVC is _____. When AP is falling, AVC is _____.

e. When MC is below AVC, AVC is _____. When MC is above AVC, AVC is _____. When MC is below ATC, ATC is _____. When MC is above ATC, ATC is _____.

4. If total fixed costs are $80 and marginal costs are given below:

a. Complete the table below (round to two decimal places).
b. Plot TFC, TVC, TC, AVC, ATC, and MC on the diagrams below.

Units of Output	MC $	TVC $	TFC $	TC $	AFC $	AVC $	ATC $
0		___	___	___			
1	75	___	___	___	___	___	___
2	65	___	___	___	___	___	___
3	55	___	___	___	___	___	___
4	65	___	___	___	___	___	___
5	75	___	___	___	___	___	___
6	85	___	___	___	___	___	___
7	95	___	___	___	___	___	___

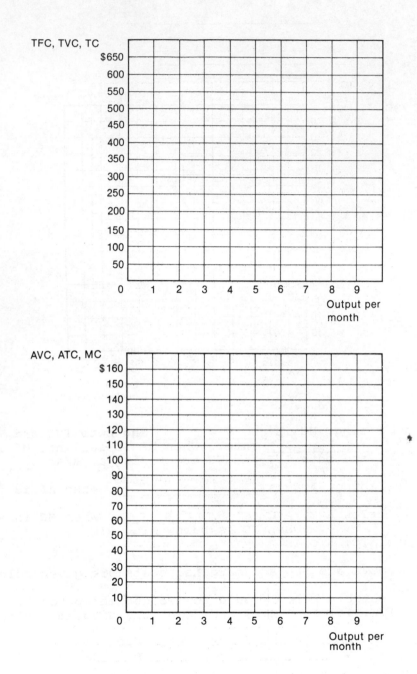

TFC, TVC, TC

$650
600
550
500
450
400
350
300
250
200
150
100
50

0   1   2   3   4   5   6   7   8   9

Output per month

AVC, ATC, MC

$160
150
140
130
120
110
100
90
80
70
60
50
40
30
20
10

0   1   2   3   4   5   6   7   8   9

Output per month

5.   Advanced Question. If TFC equals $100 and TVC increases by $30 for every one unit increase in output:

a.   Find equations for TFC, TVC, TC, AFC, AVC, ATC, and MC.
b.   Plot TFC, TVC, TC, AVC, ATC, and MC on the diagrams below for levels of output from one to five units.
c.   Does the MC curve ever intersect the ATC curve?

c. The figure below represents a set of short-run average total cost for various plant sizes. Determine the long-run ATC curve by drawing over those segments of short-run ATC's that are part of the LRAC.

4. Determine for each of the following whether it exhibits long-run increasing, constant, or decreasing returns to scale (or economies of scale, or constant returns to scale).

5. For the three cost curves shown in the diagram above, which firm is likely to be... whether they are likely to be...

Concept: **Costs in the long run**

6.   a.   The figure below represents a set of short-run ATC curves for various
           plant sizes.   Determine the long-run ATC curve by tracing over those
           segments of the short-run ATCs that make up the long-run ATC.

     b.   Determine for the levels of output designated on the long-run ATC
          below whether there are economies of scale, diseconomies of scale, or
          constant returns to scale.
                    (1) _____
                    (2) _____
                    (3) _____

     c.   For the three long-run ATC curves below, determine whether there are
          likely to be few or many producers or both and whether they are
          likely to be large or small or both.
                    (1) _____
                    (2) _____
                    (3) _____

ATC $
(3)

Long-run ATC

0   Output

7. a. Economies of scale exist because:
        1. _____
        2. _____
        3. _____
        4. _____

    b. Diseconomies of scale exist because:
        1. _____
        2. _____

SELF-TEST FOR MASTERY

Select the best answer.

1. A period of time during which some inputs are variable and some are fixed
    is known as the:

    a. Market period.
    b. Short run.
    c. Interim period.
    d. Long run.

2. A period of time during which all inputs can be varied is known as the:

    a. Market period.
    b. Short run.
    c. Interim period.
    d. Long run.

3. A _____ input is one that varies with output in the short run.

    a. Marginal
    b. Economic
    c. Fixed
    d. Variable

4. A _____ input is one that does not vary with output in the short
    run.

    a. Marginal
    b. Economic
    c. Fixed
    d. Variable

5. The law of diminishing marginal returns states that:

a. Total product begins to fall as a result of continued employment of a variable input.
b. Marginal product increases when the employment of variable inputs increases and falls when the employment of variable inputs falls.
c. The extra production obtained from increases in a variable input will eventually decline as more of the variable input is used with the fixed inputs.
d.. The total production obtained from increases in a variable input will eventually decline as more of the variable input is used with the fixed inputs.

6. Marginal product is defined:

a. As total product divided by total output.
b. As total product divided by the change in total output.
c. As the change in total product divided by total product.
d. As the change in total product divided by the change in variable input.

7. Average product

a. Increases when marginal product is greater than average product.
b. Is defined as total product divided by the quantity of variable input employed.
c. Reaches a peak when marginal product and average product are equal.
d. All of the above.

8. _____ costs do not vary with the level of output.

a. Accounting
b. Explicit
c. Variable
d. Fixed

9. Total costs equal the sum of:

a. Variable costs and fixed costs.
b. Marginal costs and imputed costs.
c. Average variable costs and marginal costs.
d. Economic costs less implicit costs.

10. Average variable costs can best be defined as:

a. Total variable costs times the average level of production.
b. Total product divided by total variable costs.
c. Average total costs less average fixed costs.
d. None of the above.

11. Marginal cost is the:

a. Change in production costs divided by output.
b. Change in total variable cost divided by a change in total product.
c. Change in total cost divided by a change in total product.
d. B and c.

12. The marginal cost curve:

    a. Intersects the total variable cost and total cost curves from below at their minimum points.
    b. Falls when the point of diminishing marginal returns is reached.
    c. First rises and then declines.
    d. Increases when the average total cost curve lies above the average variable cost curve.

13. When the marginal product is rising, _____ is _____.

    a. Average total cost, rising
    b. Average variable cost, rising
    c. Marginal cost, rising
    d. Marginal cost, falling

14. When marginal product is falling, marginal costs are _____ and both the total cost and total variable cost curves are _____ at a/an _____ rate.

    a. Falling, falling, decreasing
    b. Falling, rising, increasing
    c. Rising, falling, decreasing
    d. Rising, rising, decreasing

15. The point of diminishing returns occurs when:

    a. The average product curve has reached a peak.
    b. The marginal cost curve has reached a trough.
    c. The total product curve has reached a peak.
    d. The marginal product curve has reached a trough.

16. Economies of scale mean that:

    a. Short-run average total cost decreases.
    b. Long-run average total cost decreases.
    c. Long-run total costs decrease.
    d. Long-run marginal costs exceed long-run average total costs.

17. The rising portion of the long-run average total cost curve is called:

    a. Diseconomies of scale.
    b. Economies of scale.
    c. Mass production economies.
    d. Constant returns to scale.

18. An industry with firms having long-run average total cost curves that initially decline sharply, flatten out over a range of output, and then begin to increase suggest that the industry is probably composed of firms:

    a. That are both large and small, producing at the minimum long-run average cost.
    b. That are large and few in number.
    c. That are numerous and very small.
    d. That must be large to realize economies of scale.

19. Which of the following is not considered a cause of economies of scale?

    a. Specialization and division of labor
    b. Inability to shift to new production methods as the firm becomes larger

c. Ability to purchase inputs in large quantity at quantity discounts
d. As output is increased, a proportionate increase in inputs is not required.

20. Which of the following has been suggested as a cause of diseconomies of scale?

a. Inability to purchase inputs at a discount
b. Ability to shift to new production methods as the firm becomes bigger
c. Impaired managerial communication
d. Government regulation

THINK IT THROUGH

1. A producer never produces at a level of output where marginal product is negative. Why?

2. Explain how changes in wages influence the average variable cost and marginal cost associated with the use of labor in producing output.

3. Why are fixed costs irrelevant to decisions in the short run involving marginal costs?

4. In many American industries a handful of very large capital-intensive firms dominate sales. Why?

5. Clearly explain why total variable costs rise at an increasing rate when the point of diminishing returns is reached.

CHAPTER ANSWERS

In Brief: Chapter Summary

1. Variable 2. Fixed 3. Long run 4. Returns 5. Decreasing 6. Marginal 7. Decline 8. Rises 9. Declines 10. Variable 11. Vary 12. Fixed 13. Do not 14. Average total 15. Average 16. Average variable 17. Marginal 18. Decreasing 19. Decreasing 20. Increasing 21. Decrease 22. Increase 23. Decrease 24. Increases 25. All inputs 26. Least cost 27. Economies 28. Diseconomies

Vocabulary Review

1. Fixed cost 2. Variable cost 3. Average product 4. Point of diminishing returns 5. Total cost 6. Production 7. Law of diminishing marginal returns 8. Marginal product 9. Long run 10. Average fixed cost 11. Marginal cost 12. Imports 13. Average cost 14. Production function 15. Average variable cost 16. Total product curve 17. Total product of a variable input 18. Short run 19. Variable input 20. Fixed input 21. Long run cost 22. Economies of scale 23. Diseconomies of scale 24. Constant returns to scale

Skills Review

1. a.

MP	AP
50	50
80	65
100	76.67
90	80
80	80
65	77.50
60	75
50	71.88

b.

c. Rising, falling
d. Increasing, falling

2. a.

TFC	TVC	TC
50	0	50
50	20	70
50	40	90
50	60	110
50	80	130
50	100	150
50	120	170
50	140	190
50	160	210

b.

c. Decreasing, increasing

3. a.

AFC	AVC	ATC	MC
1.00	.40	1.40	.40
.38	.31	.69	.25
.22	.26	.48	.20
.16	.25	.41	.22
.13	.25	.38	.25
.11	.26	.37	.31
.10	.27	.36	.33
.09	.28	.37	.40

b.

c.   Falling, decreasing, rising, increasing
d.   Falling, rising
e.   Falling, rising, falling, rising

4. a.

TVC	TFC	TC	AFC	AVC	ATC
0	80	80			
75	80	155	80	75	155
140	80	220	40	70	110
195	80	275	26.67	65	91.67
260	80	340	20	65	85
335	80	415	16	67	83
420	80	500	13.33	70	83.33
515	80	595	11.43	73.57	85

b.

5. a.   TFC = $100
TVC = $30 TP
TC = $100 + $30 TP
AFC = $100/TP
AVC = $30
ATC = $100/TP + $30
MC = $30

b.

TP	TFC	TVC	TC	ATC	AFC	AVC	MC
0	100	0	100				
1	100	30	130	130	100	30	30
2	100	60	160	80	50	30	30
3	100	90	190	63.33	33.33	30	30
4	100	120	220	55	25	30	30
5	100	150	250	50	20	30	30

c.   For MC and ATC to intersect, MC = ATC. Let:

$$MC = \$30 = \$100/TP + \$30 = ATC$$

As TP approaches infinity, $100/TP approaches zero. ATC approaches MC as TP approaches infinity, but never touches it.

6.   a.

b.   (1) Economies of scale
     (2) Constant returns to scale
     (3) Diseconomies of scale
c.   (1) Many small firms
     (2) Both large and small firms
     (3) A few large firms

7.   a.   (1) Can increase output without proportionately increasing inputs
     (2) Quantity discounts
     (3) Specialization and division of labor
     (4) Ability of use new methods of production
b.   (1) Strained managerial communication
     (2) Shirking of labor and difficulty of monitoring performance

Self-Test for Mastery

1. b 2. d 3. d 4. c 5. c 6. d 7. d 8. d 9. a 10. d 11. d 12. a 13. d 14. d 15. b 16. b 17. a 18. a 19. b 20. c

Think it Through

1.   A negative marginal product means that using more variable inputs reduces output! No manager would increase total costs in order to reduce output.

2.   Average variable costs equal total variable costs divided by output. Total variable costs equal the quantity of variable inputs purchased times the respective input prices per unit. With regard to labor:

$$AVC = (\text{Units of Labor} \times \text{wage})/TP$$

or

$$AVC = \text{Wage}/(TP/\text{units of labor}) = \text{Wage}/AP$$

An increase in wages increases AVC and a decrease in wages decreases AVC. Notice that an increase in wages will not increase AVC if average labor productivity increases more than wages.

Similarly, marginal cost can be expressed as:

$$MC = (\text{Change in the units of labor} \times \text{wage})/\text{change in TP}$$

or

$$MC = \text{Wage}/(\text{change in TP}/\text{change in the units of labor})$$

$$= \text{Wage}/MP$$

MC rises when wages increase and falls when wages decrease unless the marginal product of labor changes sufficiently to offset the impact of wages.

3.   If a decision involves whether or not to increase output by a unit, fixed costs are unimportant in that they are "sunk" costs. If a goal of the firm is to maximize profits in the short run, the relevant comparison is between the marginal costs of producing that unit and the revenues received from the sale of that unit. Fixed costs influence average total costs but not marginal costs.

4.   These industries comprise a few very large firms that have long-run average total cost curves that decline over a very large range of output. They must be large in order to realize economies of scale. This is because the least-cost combination of inputs requires a capital-intensive operation with large fixed costs in plant and equipment. It takes a large level of production to spread the overhead costs. Large-scale production runs take advantage of cost-saving technology. Purchasing inputs in mass quantity allows the firm to realize quantity discounts. And the larger the firm, the greater the extent to which the division of labor and the specialization of resources can be achieved.

5.   When the point of diminishing returns is reached, production requires increasing quantities of a variable input in order to produce a given quantity of output. Therefore, the cost of the variable input must rise at an increasing rate for given increases in output.

Isoquant Analysis: Choosing the Method of Production

IN BRIEF: APPENDIX SUMMARY

Fill in the blanks to summarize appendix content.

Indifference curve analysis can be used to analyze the choice of production methods. The analysis assumes that firms have a goal to minimize the costs of producing a given output.

An (1)_____(isoquant, isocost line) represents various combinations of two inputs that can be used to produce a given level of output. It is (2)_____ (positively, negatively) sloped because the use of additional labor requires a/an (3)_____(reduction, increase) of capital in order to keep output unchanged. The slope is called the marginal rate of technical substitution (MRTS) of labor for capital. Because of the law of diminishing marginal (4)_____(returns, utility), the slope of the isoquant becomes (5)_____(less, more) negative as more labor is employed. This is because the MRTS of labor for capital equals the ratio of minus the change in capital to the change in labor. This ratio in turn equals the ratio of the marginal product of labor to the marginal product of capital. Therefore as more labor is used and less capital is employed along an isoquant, the marginal product of labor (6)_____ (decreases, increases), and the marginal product of capital (7)_____(decreases, increases), causing the isoquant slope to become (8)_____(less, more) steep. An isoquant map shows isoquants at various distances from the origin. Isoquants lying farther from the origin represent (9)_____(higher, lower) levels of output.

Total costs can be thought of as the quantity of inputs employed in producing a given output multiplied by their respective market resource prices. An (10)_____(isoquant, isocost line) can be derived by solving the total cost equation for capital in terms of labor. The slope of the isocost line is (11)_____ (positive, negative) and equals the ratio of the price of labor to the price of capital. Changes in the price of capital and the price of labor will (12)_____ (shift, alter the slope of) the isocost line. Changes in total cost (13)_____ (shift, alter the slope of) the isocost line--higher costs shift the line outward from the origin and vice versa.

Costs are minimized when an isoquant for a given level of output is just tangent to the isocost line (14)_____ (farthest, closest) to the origin. This occurs where the MRTS of labor for capital equals the ratio of the price of labor to the price of capital. The cost-minimizing combination of capital and labor used in producing a given output is influenced by the prices of labor and capital and technology that influences marginal products and the MRTS.

Write the key term from the list below next to its definition.

Key Terms

Isoquant   Marginal rate of technical
Isocost line   substitution (MRTS) of labor for
Isoquant map   capital

Definitions

1. _____: a measure of the amount of capital each unit of labor can replace without increasing or decreasing production.

2. _____: gives all combinations of labor and capital that are of equal total cost.

3. _____: a curve showing all combinations of variable inputs that can be used to produce a given quantity of output.

4. _____: shows the combinations of labor and capital that can be used to produce several possible output levels.

SKILLS REVIEW

1. Given the isoquant map in the diagram below:

a. Derive the isocost line, assuming that the price per unit to labor is $10, the price per unit of capital is $20, and total cost equals $300. Plot the line on the diagram.

b.   Find the cost-minimizing combination of labor and capital:
     (1) _____ units of labor
     (2) _____ units of capital
     (3) _____ level of output at this combination of inputs
c.   Show the effect on the diagram of an increase in the price of labor
     to $15. The cost-minimizing combination of labor and capital changes
     to _____ units of labor and _____ units of capital.
d.   Show the effect on the diagram of an increase in the price of capital
     to $30, assuming the price of labor is $10. The cost-minimizing
     combination of inputs changes to _____ units of labor and
     _____ units of capital.

SELF-TEST FOR MASTERY

Select the best answer.

1.   An isoquant is :

     a.   The level of production possible from a given stock of resources.
     b.   A curve giving various combinations of two inputs that are equal in
          total cost.
     c.   A curve showing all combinations of variable inputs that can be used
          to produce a given quantity of output.
     d.   The producer's demand curve for labor and capital.

2.   A _____ gives all combinations of labor and capital that can be used
     to produce several possible output levels.

     a.   Isoquant
     b.   Isocost
     c.   Isoquant map
     d.   Isocost map

3.   The slope of an isoquant is negative and equal to:

     a.   The ratio of the change in capital to the change in labor.
     b.   The ratio of the marginal product of labor to the marginal product of
          capital.
     c.   The marginal rate of technical substitution of labor for capital.
     d.   B and c.
     e.   All of the above.

4.   Which of the following concepts best explains the curvature of an
     isoquant?

     a.   Equimarginal principle
     b.   Law of decreasing costs
     c.   Law of diminishing marginal returns
     d.   Law of diminishing marginal utility

5.   The slope of an isocost line is:

     a.   The ratio of the marginal products of labor and capital.
     b.   The product price divided by the price of labor and capital.
     c.   The change in capital divided by the change in labor.
     d.   Negative and equal to the price per unit of labor divided by the
          price per unit of capital.

6. A/An _____ in the price of labor makes the isocost line _____ steep.

   a. Increase, more
   b. Decrease, more
   c. Increase, less
   d. Change, increasingly

7. A/An _____ in the price of capital makes the isocost line _____ steep.

   a. Increase, more
   b. Decrease, more
   c. Decrease, less
   d. Change, neither more nor less

8. The cost-minimizing combination of labor and capital can be found where

   a. The MRTS of labor for capital = the change in capital/change in labor.
   b. The MRTS of labor for capital = the ratio of input marginal products.
   c. The MRTS of labor for capital = the ratio of the price of capital to the price of labor.
   d. The MRTS of labor for capital = the ratio of the price of labor to the price of capital.

THINK IT THROUGH

1. Explain why the slope of the isoquant becomes increasingly less steep as more labor is used relative to capital.

2. What condition must be satisfied in order to find the cost-minimizing combination of labor and capital? Explain.

APPENDIX ANSWERS

In Brief: Appendix Summary

1. Isoquant 2. Negatively 3. Reduction 4. Returns 5. Less 6. Decreases 7. Increases 8. Less 9. Higher 10. Isocost line 11. Negative 12. Alter the slope of 13. Shift 14. Closest

Vocabulary Review

1. Marginal rate of technical substitution of labor for capital 2. Isocost line 3. Isoquant 4. Isoquant map

Skills Review

a.

Units of capital

```
21
19   (a) P_L = $10, P_K = $20
17   (c) P_L = $15, P_K = $20
15   (d) P_L = $10, P_K = $30
13   (a)
11  (c)
 9
 7  (d)
 5                    120
 3                   110
 1                      100
 0  2  6 10 14 18 22 26 30 34 38
```

Units
of labor

b.   (1) 18   (2) 6   (3) 120
c.   12, 6
d.   18, 4

Self-Test for Mastery

1. c   2. c   3. e   4. c   5. d   6. a   7. b   8. d

Think it Through

1.   Output is constant along a given isoquant. An increase in labor times the marginal product of labor must equal the decrease in capital times the marginal product of capital in order to keep the production level unchanged. But as more labor is added and capital is reduced, the marginal product of labor decreases and the marginal product of capital increases. This is due to the law of diminishing marginal returns. Since the slope of the isoquant is the ratio of the marginal product of labor to the marginal product of capital, the slope becomes less negative as more labor is used.

2.   To find the least-cost combination of labor and capital, the MRTS of labor for capital must equal the ratio of the price of labor to the price of capital. The rate at which it is technically feasible to substitute labor for capital is just equal to the rate at which labor can be exchanged for capital as determined by market prices and the total cost of production. The cost-minimizing condition can be alternatively expressed as follows:

(MP of labor/price of labor) = (MP of capital/price of capital)

Costs are minimized in producing a given output when the last dollar's worth of labor and capital yields the same marginal product.

11

The Profit-Maximizing Competitive Firm and Market Supply

CHAPTER CHALLENGES

After studying your text, attending class, and completing this chapter, you should be able to:

1. Explain the concept of perfect competition in markets.
2. Explain why the demand curve for a competitive firm is perfectly elastic at the market equilibrium price.
3. Explain how the total profit a competitive firm can earn over a given period varies with the output actually sold given the market price of the product.
4. Use marginal analysis to explain how the firm chooses its output so as to maximize profits.
5. Use graphs to show the actual profits a firm earns and to show how the market price of the product affects the profitability of the firm.
6. Explain under what conditions the firm will cease operations in the short run.
7. Show how a supply curve can be derived for a competitive firm that maximizes profit from selling a single product and how the market supply curve can be derived from the supply curves of individual firms in an industry.
8. Demonstrate how changes in input prices affect the supply curve in the short run.

IN BRIEF: CHAPTER SUMMARY

Fill in the blanks to summarize chapter content.

In order to construct a theory of supply, it is necessary to make simplifying assumptions. The goal of the firm is (1)_____ (profit maximization, market share). The firm produces a single product and operates in a perfectly competitive market. The assumptions underlying perfect competition are: (a) (2)_____(few, many) sellers, (b) (3)_____ (homogeneous, heterogeneous) goods, (c) (4)_____ (large, very small) market shares, (d) firms are (5)_____ (unconcerned, concerned) about the decisions of competing firms, (e) information is (6)_____(costly, freely available), and there is (f) freedom of (7)_____(entry and exit, enterprise). The firm is a price taker, producing the quantity of output that maximizes profit or minimizes losses in the short run.

The market demand curve for an industry is downward sloping, but the demand curve faced by a competitive firm is horizontal or perfectly (8)_____ (inelastic, elastic). The firm can sell any quantity it desires at the market price without influencing market supply and hence the equilibrium price. A firm maximizes profit in the short run by producing at that level of production where total revenue exceeds total cost by the (9)_____ (greatest, smallest) amount. At zero output, total costs (10)_____ (exceed, are

less than) total revenues because of fixed costs and zero sales revenue. At
high levels of output, total costs (11)_____ (are also less than,
will also exceed) total revenue because of the law of diminishing marginal
returns. In between are levels of production where total revenues exceed total
costs, but there is only one level of output where economic profit is at a
maximum. If market prices are low enough, there may be no levels of output
where total revenues exceed total costs.

Marginal analysis can also be used to determine the profit-maximizing level of
production in the short run. A producer will increase or decrease output if
there is a net gain from doing so. If the additional benefits from altering
production (12)_____(exceed, equal) the additional costs, then it would
be rational to change the level of output to the point where the net gain from
doing so is at a maximum. If the marginal revenue associated with the sale of
an additional unit of output (13)_____(exceeds, is less than) the
marginal cost of producing that unit, more is added to revenue than to costs
and profit must (14)_____(decrease, increase)--marginal profit is positive.
If marginal cost (15)_____(is less than, exceeds) marginal revenue,
profit can be increased by reducing output. Cutting output by one unit reduces
total costs more than total revenues and as a result (16)_____ (decreases,
increases) profit. Where marginal revenue and marginal cost are equal,
marginal profit is (17)_____ (zero, negative), meaning that a one-unit
increase or decrease in output will have no effect on profit. At this level of
output, either profits are maximized or losses are minimized. For a perfectly
competitive firm, price and marginal revenue are equal because the slope of the
total revenue curve, marginal revenue, is constant and equal to the market
price. Therefore the rule for maximizing profit in the short run for a
competitive firm is either (18)_____ (MR = MC or P = MC,MR = AC or P =
MR).

A competitive firm will operate in the short run and produce output as long as
the market price exceeds the minimum average (19)_____(variable, total)
cost. If price exceeds average variable cost, a portion of the firm's
(20)_____ (marginal, fixed) costs will be covered by revenue. Even
though the firm is not earning sufficient normal profits to retain the services
of the entrepreneur for very long, it can minimize losses by producing at a
positive level of output and deferring some of the firm's overhead or fixed
costs. If the market price is (21)_____(above, below) average variable
cost, the loss-minimizing strategy would be to shut down in the short run and
not produce any output. This is because the firm's loss would be limited to
the payment of fixed costs. If the firm produced output, its losses would
(22)_____ (exceed, be less than) its fixed costs.

At prices above the minimum average variable cost, the firm is induced to
produce output. As prices rise it is profitable to increase production. For
the firm, the supply curve is that segment of the firm's (23)_____
(average variable, marginal) cost curve that lies above the (24)_____
(average variable, marginal) cost curve. The market supply curve is an
aggregation or summation of the supply curves of all the individual firms in
that industry.

Factors that influence and shift the market supply curve are: (a) the number of
firms, (b) the average productive capacity of firms, (c) the prices of
(25)_____(fixed, variable) inputs, and (d) technology. An increase or
decrease in the number of firms will shift the market supply curve to the right
or left, respectively. A change in productive capacity will shift the marginal
cost curve to either the right or the left. A decrease in variable input
prices or an improvement in technology will shift the marginal cost curve
(26)_____ (downward, upward) and vice versa. Because the market
supply curve is an aggregation of individual firms' supply curves, shifts in
their marginal cost curves shift the market supply curve and affect market

equilibrium prices. While a change in the price of a variable input affects marginal cost and the market supply curve, a change in the price of a fixed input has no effect on marginal costs, market supply, or price, but does influence the producer's (27)_____(market share, profits).

VOCABULARY REVIEW

Write the key term from the list below next to its definition.

Key Terms

Perfectly competitive market   Marginal profit
Competitive firm   Shutdown point
Average revenue   Short-run supply curve
Marginal revenue   Market supply curve

Definitions

1. _____: one that sells its product in a perfectly competitive market in which it is a price taker.

2. _____: total revenue per unit of a good sold.

3. _____: the change in profit from selling an additional unit of a good, representing the difference between the marginal revenue from that unit and its marginal cost.

4. _____: the portion of a firm's marginal cost curve above the minimum point of its average variable cost curve.

5. _____: gives the sum of the quantities supplied by all firms producing a product at each possible price over a given period.

6. _____: exists when (1) there are many sellers in the market; (2) the products sold in the market are homogeneous; (3) each firm has a very small market share of total sales; (4) no seller regards competing firms as a threat to its market share; (5) information is freely available on prices; (6) there is freedom of entry and exit by sellers.

7. _____: the extra revenue obtained from selling an additional unit of a good.

8. _____: the point a firm reaches when price has fallen to a level below that which just allows the firm to cover its minimum possible average variable cost.

SKILLS REVIEW

Concept: Perfectly competitive market

1. List six conditions necessary for the existence of a perfectly competitive market.

    a. _____
    b. _____
    c. _____
    d. _____
    e. _____
    f. _____

Concept: Perfectly elastic demand curve; economic profit and output

2. If you operate a business in a perfectly competitive market and the current market equilibrium price is $12 per unit:

    a. Show on the diagram below the demand curve you face.

    b. On the diagram above, show the effect of an increase in price from $12 to $15.
    c. On the diagram above, show the effect of a decrease in price from $12 to $10.

3. a. Find total revenue from the quantity and P1 columns in the table below and enter the results in the TR1 column. Plot the total revenue curve, TR1, in the diagram below the table.

Quantity	P1	P2	P3	TR1	TR2	TR3
0	$12	$___	$___	$_____	$_____	$_____
10	12					
20	12					
30	12					
40	12					
50	12					
60	12					

Total revenue $1000 950 900 850 800 750 700 650 600 550 500 450 400 350 300 250 200 150 100 50 0

10 20 30 40 50 60 70 80 90

Quantity sold
(units per time period)

b. Assume price increases from $12 to $15. Enter the price in column P2 in the table above and find TR2. Plot the new total revenue curve, TR2, on the figure above.

c. Assume price decreases from $12 to $10. Enter the price in column P3 in the table above and find TR3. Plot TR3 on the diagram above.

4. Consider the following quantity and total cost data:

Quantity	Total Cost
0	$ 50
10	120
20	220
30	330
40	450
50	600
60	780

a. Plot the total cost curve, TC, on the figure above in question 3.

b. Referring to TC and TR1, at zero output, economic profit (or loss) equals $_____.

172

c.   As output increases, what happens to profit (or loss)?

Quantity   Profit (Loss)

10        $_____
20   _____
30   _____
40   _____
50   _____
60   _____

d.   At what level of output are profits at a maximum? _____ units
e.   Referring to TC and TR3, what relationship exists between output and profit or loss? The profit-maximizing or loss-minimizing level of output is _____ units.

Concept: Marginal analysis and profit maximization

5.   a.   Complete the table.

Q	P1	TR1	MR1	P2	TR2	MR2	P3	TR3	MR3
0	$12	$___	$___	$15	$___	$___	$10	$___	$___
10	12	___	___	15	___	___	10	___	___
20	12	___	___	15	___	___	10	___	___
30	12	___	___	15	___	___	10	___	___
40	12	___	___	15	___	___	10	___	___
50	12	___	___	15	___	___	10	___	___
60	12	___	___	15	___	___	10	___	___

b.   In the diagram below, plot the MR curves: MR1, MR2, and MR3.

6. a. Complete the table.

Q	TC	TVC	MC	AVC	ATC
0	$ 50	$_____			
10	120	_____	$_____	$_____	$_____
20	220	_____	_____	_____	_____
30	330	_____	_____	_____	_____
40	450	_____	_____	_____	_____
50	600	_____	_____	_____	_____
60	780	_____	_____	_____	_____

b. Plot the MC, AVC, and ATC curves in the diagram below.

c. On the figure above, show the MR1 curve from question 5 (b) (P1 = MR1 = $12). Profit is maximized where _____ equals _____ at _____ units of output.

7. <u>Advanced Question</u> A perfectly competitive firm's MR and MC curves can be expressed as follows:

MR = P   where P and Q are price and quantity,
MC = a + bQ   a is a constant term reflecting the
                forces that influence marginal cost
                other than quantity, and b is the slope
                of the MC curve reflecting the extent to
                which diminishing marginal returns are
                encountered.

a. Find an expression for the profit-maximizing quantity.
b. If price increases, the profit-maximizing quantity _____ and vice versa.
c. If marginal costs increase due to influences other than quantity--if a increases--the profit-maximizing output _____ and vice versa.
d. If new technology reduces the effect of diminishing returns such that the slope, b, of the MC curve decreases, the profit-maximizing output _____.

174

Concept: **Shutdown point; a competitive firm's short-run supply curve**

8. a. On the figure above, show the marginal revenue curve, MR2, from question 5 (P2 = MR2 = $15). The profit-maximizing output is _____ units, and profit equals $_____ .

    b. On the figure above, show the marginal revenue curve, MR3, from question 5 (P3 = MR3 = $10). The profit-maximizing (or loss-minimizing) output is _____ units, and profit (or loss) equals $_____ . Will the firm shut down at this price? Why or why not?

    c. If the market price falls to $7, will the firm shut down? Why or why not?

9. a. Complete the profit-maximizing quantity column in the table below using the results derived in questions 6 and 7.

Price	Profit-Maximizing or Loss-Minimizing Quantity (units)
$15	_____
12	_____
10	_____
7	_____

    b. In the figure below, plot the price and quantity supplied data from the completed table above.

    c. The curve that you have plotted above is called the firm's _____ and is that segment of the _____ curve lying above the _____ curve.

Concept: Market supply; determinants of market supply

10. Assume there are 100 firms comprising an industry with cost curves identical to that plotted in question 6.

a. Complete the table below.

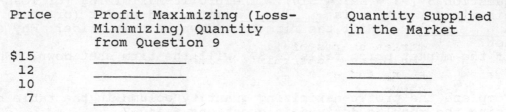

Price	Profit Maximizing (Loss-Minimizing) Quantity from Question 9	Quantity Supplied in the Market
$15	_____	_____
12	_____	_____
10	_____	_____
7	_____	_____

b. Plot the market supply curve from the data above.

11. List four factors that shift the market supply curve and indicate for each one, whether the effect of an increase or improvement in the factor shifts the supply curve up or down or right or left, whichever is appropriate.

a. _____
b. _____
c. _____
d. _____

176

SELF-TEST FOR MASTERY

Select the best answer.

1. Which of the following is a characteristic of perfectly competitive markets?

    a. Many sellers
    b. Very small market shares of firms
    c. Information on prices is freely available
    d. Freedom of entry and exit
    e. All of the above

2. The demand curve faced by a perfectly competitive firm:

    a. Is perfectly inelastic.
    b. Is horizontal.
    c. Is downward sloping.
    d. Is perfectly elastic.
    e. B and d

3. An increase in market price shifts the firm's demand curve _____ and rotates its total revenue curve _____.

    a. Downward, counterclockwise
    b. Upward, clockwise
    c. Upward, counterclockwise
    d. Downward, upward parallel to the old total revenue curve

4. At a zero level of output, the loss incurred is equal to

    a. Variable costs.
    b. Fixed costs.
    c. Marginal costs.
    d. Price.

5. If market price is high enough, profits increase as output increases up to a maximum level of profits and then begins to decline as output continues to increase. Which of the following concepts accounts for this relationship?

    a. The law of supply
    b. The law of marginal profit
    c. The law of diminishing marginal returns
    d. Marginal analysis
    e. None of the above

6. For the case of perfect competition, which of the following is true?

    a. Price always equals average revenue.
    b. Profit maximization occurs at the level of output where MR = MC.
    c. Profit maximization occurs at the level of output where P = MC.
    d. A and c.
    e. All of the above.

7. When price exceeds marginal cost, a profit-maximizing producer will:

    a. Increase production.
    b. Decrease production.
    c. Lower price and increase production.
    d. Leave the level of output unchanged.

8. When price is less than marginal cost, a profit-maximizing producer will:

    a. Increase production.
    b. Decrease production.
    c. Raise the price and decrease output.
    d. Leave the level of output unchanged.

9. If at the level of output where MR = MC the market price is less than a competitive firm's ATC but is greater than its AVC:

    a. The firm would continue to operate indefinitely.
    b. The firm would shut down.
    c. The firm would continue to operate in the short run.
    d. The firm would increase output to increase sales and profit.

10. If at the level of output where MR = MC the market price is less than the competitive firm's AVC:

    a. The total fixed-cost loss exceeds the operating loss and the firm will shut down.
    b. The variable-cost loss is less than the fixed-cost loss and the firm will continue to operate in the short run.
    c. The firm can minimize losses by producing where MR = MC.
    d. The firm can minimize losses by raising prices.
    e. The firm will raise prices and increase production.

11. A firm's short-run supply curve is:

    a. The segment of the variable cost curve below the total cost curve.
    b. The marginal cost curve.
    c. The market supply curve.
    d. The section of the marginal cost curve below the average total cost curve.
    e. The segment of the marginal cost curve above the minimum point of the average variable cost curve.

12. Which of the following does not influence the firm's short-run supply curve?

    a. The number of firms
    b. The productivity of the firm
    c. The prices of variable inputs
    d. Improvements in technology

13. The market supply curve is a horizontal summation of:

    a. Industry output.
    b. The marginal cost curves of all the firms selling in the market.
    c. The total cost curves of all the firms selling in the market.
    d. Prices times quantity demanded for all the firms selling in the market.
    e. The short-run supply curves of all the firms selling in the market.

14. An increase in the number of firms in an industry:

   a. Shifts the market supply curve upward at each level of output.
   b. Shifts the market supply curve downward at each level of output.
   c. Shifts the marginal cost curve upward.
   d. Shifts the market supply curve rightward at each price.
   e. Shifts the market supply curve leftward at each price.

15. An increase in wages will:

   a. Shift the market supply curve upward at each price.
   b. Shift marginal cost curves downward at each level of output and shift the market supply curve leftward.
   c. Shift the total cost curve upward, shifting the market supply curve to the right.
   d. Shift marginal cost curves upward at each level of output and shift the market supply curve leftward.

16. A decrease in the price of a variable input will shift the market supply curve _____ and cause the equilibrium price to _____.

   a. Rightward, fall
   b. Leftward, fall
   c. Rightward, rise
   d. Leftward, rise
   e. The supply curve will not shift, and the market price will not change.

17. An increase in insurance premiums (a fixed input) will shift the market supply curve _____ and cause the equilibrium price to _____.

   a. Rightward, fall
   b. Leftward, fall
   c. Rightward, rise
   d. Leftward, rise
   e. The supply curve will not shift, and the market price will not change.

THINK IT THROUGH

1. Why is the market for wheat considered to be a competitive market?

2. This is a free country. You can raise or lower the price of a good or service if you wish. Why then do we say that the competitive firm is a price "taker" rather than a price "maker"?

3. Discuss the rationale underlying the MR = MC rule for profit maximization. If it is a rule for the maximization of profits, then how can it also be a rule for the minimization of losses?

4. You are a manager in a firm within a competitive industry that is heavily reliant upon electricity as a source of power to propel the assembly line. An embargo of oil from the Middle East causes increases in the price of oil and its substitutes such as natural gas and coal. Coal-fired electric power plants will experience an upward shift in their marginal cost curves, resulting in an increase in the price of electricity. What are the implications for your industry and your firm?

CHAPTER ANSWERS

In Brief: Chapter Summary

1. Profit maximization 2. Many 3. Homogeneous 4. Very small 5. Unconcerned 6. Freely available 7. Entry and exit 8. Elastic 9. Greatest 10. Exceed 11. Are also less than 12. Exceed 13. Exceeds 14. Increase 15. Exceeds 16. Increases 17. Zero 18. MR = MC or P = MC 19. Variable 20. Fixed 21. Below 22. Exceed 23. Marginal 24. Average variable 25. Variable 26. Downward 27. Profits

Vocabulary Review

1. Competitive firm 2. Average revenue 3. Marginal profit 4. Short-run supply curve 5. Market supply curve 6. Perfectly competitive market 7. Marginal revenue 8. Shutdown point

Skills Review

1. a. Many sellers b. Homogeneous goods c. Firms with very small market share d. Firms unconcerned about rivals e. Information on prices is freely available f. Freedom of entry and exit

2.

3.

P2	P3	TR1	TR2	TR3
$15	$10	$ 0	$ 0	$ 0
15	10	120	150	100
15	10	240	300	200
15	10	360	450	300
15	10	480	600	400
15	10	600	750	500
15	10	720	900	600

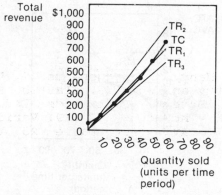

Total revenue

Quantity sold (units per time period)

4. a. TC plotted on figure above.
    b. -$50
    c. Profit (Loss)   d. 40
          $ 0   e. There is a loss at every
            20   output, but the loss is
            30   minimized at an output of
            30   20 units.
             0
           (60)

5. a.

TR1	MR1	TR2	MR2	TR3	MR3
$ 0	$12	$ 0	$15	$ 0	$10
120	12	150	15	100	10
240	12	300	15	200	10
360	12	450	15	300	10
480	12	600	15	400	10
600	12	750	15	500	10
720	12	900	15	600	10

    b.

Price per unit

Quantity (units per time period)

6. a.

TVC	MC	AVC	ATC
$ 0	$	$	$
70	7	7	12
170	10	8.50	11
280	11	9.33	11
400	12	10	11.25
550	15	11	12
730	18	12.10	13

b.

MC, ATC, AVC $20
18 MC
16 MR₂
14 ATC
MR₁ 12 AVC
10 MR₃
8
6
4
2
0

10   30   50   70   90

Quantity
(units per time
period)

c.   MR, MC, 40

7.   a.   Set marginal revenue equal to marginal cost and solve for the profit-maximizing quantity.

$$MR = MC$$
$$P = a + bQ$$

$$Q = (P - a)/b$$

b.   Increases   c. Falls   d. Increases

8.   a.   50, 150
     b.   20, -20 ; No, because the operating loss is less than the fixed-cost loss.
     c.   At $7, the firm is indifferent because the operating loss is equal to the fixed-cost loss. Any price below this, however, will force the firm to shut down because the operating loss will exceed the fixed-cost loss.

9.   a.   Profit-Maximizing (Loss-Minimizing)
          Quantity (units)

                 50
                 40
                 20
                 10

b.

Price per unit $16
14
12
10
8
6
4
2
0

Firm's supply curve

10   30   50   70   90

Quantity supplied
(units per time
period)

c.   Short-run supply curve, MC, minimum point of the average variable cost curve

182

10. a.
Quantity Supplied (Firm)	Quantity Supplied (Market)
50	5,000
40	4,000
20	2,000
10	1,000

b.

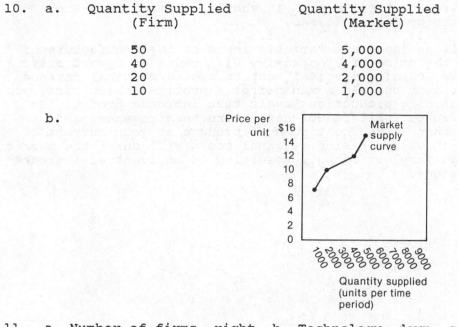

11. a. Number of firms, right b. Technology, down c. Prices of variable inputs, up d. Average productive capacity, right

Self-Test for Mastery

1. e 2. e 3. c 4. b 5. c 6. e 7. a 8. b 9. c 10. a 11. e 12. a 13. e 14. d 15. d 16. a 17. e

Think it Through

1.   There are a number of characteristics similar to those required for perfectly competitive markets. There are many producers, so no one farmer can change production enough to affect market prices. Wheat farmers are price takers and have very small market shares. Wheat is not strictly homogeneous in terms of quality, but the wheat produced by one farmer is a very close substitute if not a perfect substitute for the wheat produced by other farmers. Wheat farmers can sell all they produce at the market price and are therefore unconcerned with decisions of rival farmers. Information regarding wheat prices is freely available in that prices are published daily in most newspapers and announced on many television stations. There are certainly freedom of entry and exit, but the financial investment required to enter the wheat-farming industry as a competitive producer would probably be sizable and thus to some extent would impede entry.

2.   Because there are many firms with very small market shares producing goods that are perfect substitutes for each other, any one firm choosing to raise price above the market price would experience a loss of most if not all sales. Consumers would simply go elsewhere and buy the identical product at the lower market price.

3.   If marginal revenue exceeds marginal cost, an increase in output by a unit will increase revenues more than costs and will either increase profits or reduce losses, depending on whether or not the market price exceeds average total cost. If marginal revenue is less than marginal cost, a one-unit decrease in output will increase profits or reduce losses. If marginal revenue equals marginal cost, a one-unit change in output will change revenues and costs by the same amount, leaving the profit or loss unchanged. At this point profits are at a maximum or losses are at a minimum again, depending on whether

or not the price exceeds average total cost. It should be noted that the losses being referred to are operating losses.

4.   Because electricity is an important variable input to the manufacture of your good, an increase in the price of electricity will cause an upward shift in your marginal cost curve, causing marginal cost to exceed marginal revenue at your current rate of production. As a manager of a profit-seeking firm, you have to make decisions regarding production levels that increase profit. In this case, a reduction in output will reduce costs more than revenues and result in a higher profit than if you continued to produce at your current level of output. For the industry, rising marginal costs will shift the market supply curve upward at each level of output, resulting in an eventual increase in the market price of the good.

12

Long-Run Supply in Competitive Markets

CHAPTER CHALLENGES

After studying your text, attending class, and completing this chapter, you should be able to:

1. Explain the concept of long-run competitive equilibrium in a market and analyze the characteristics of the equilibrium for product prices.
2. Show how profits and losses act a signals that cause shifts in market supply in the long run.
3. Derive long-run supply curves for products sold in perfectly competitive markets and show how long-run supply differs from short-run supply.
4. Analyze the long-run impact of taxes and subsidies on prices and quantities traded in perfectly competitive markets.
5. Evaluate outcomes in markets in the long run using normative criteria.

IN BRIEF: CHAPTER SUMMARY

Fill in the blanks to summarize chapter content.

Firms in a competitive industry are in long-run equilibrium when there is neither entry to nor exit from the industry and when firms within the industry are neither expanding nor contracting. In long-run competitive equilibrium, economic profits are (1)_____(zero, positive), but the opportunity costs of the owner's self-owned resources (2)_____(are not, are) being covered. The existence of short-run economic profits in a competitive industry induces firms to (3)_____(enter, exit) the industry. Entry of new firms (4)_____ (decreases, increases) market supply and (5)_____ (increases, reduces) market prices and economic profits in the long run. Prices (6)_____(fall, rise) until entry stops. This occurs at a market price equal to minimum (7)_____(average variable, average total) cost in the long run. Here economic profits equal zero although normal profits are being earned. Consumers are paying a price equal to the minimum possible average cost of production.

Assuming competitive long-run equilibrium initially, the impact of an increase in market demand for a good (8)_____ (decreases, increases) the market price, causing existing firms to experience economic (9)_____ (profits, losses) and the incentive to (10)_____(decrease, increase) production. Firms (11)_____(decrease, increase) output because marginal revenue has risen relative to marginal cost. But short-run profits induce firms to (12)_____ (exit, enter) the market, causing the market supply curve to shift (13)_____ (leftward, rightward). As market supply (14)_____ (rises, falls) relative to market demand, the equilibrium price (15)_____(rises, falls) until the economic profits are eliminated-- where price equals both short- and long-run marginal cost and minimum average cost. If the expansion of the industry does not affect input prices, the price will return to its former level. The long-run market supply curve is

(16)_____ (horizontal, upward sloping) for the above case of constant costs. If industry expansion is significant enough to cause the market prices of inputs to rise, the marginal and average cost curves will shift upward. Thus prices will not have to fall as much in the long run to restore market equilibrium. For the case of increasing costs, the long-run market supply curve is (17)_____(horizontal, upward sloping).

An improvement in technology increases the productivity of inputs and reduces both marginal and average costs. As average costs (18)_____(fall, rise) relative to the market price, firms realize economic (19)_____(losses, profits). Also, as marginal costs fall relative to marginal revenue, firms have an incentive to (20)_____(contract, expand) production. The economic profits result in new firms entering the industry and cause an increase in market supply. As supply rises relative to demand, prices fall, but in this case prices will fall (21)_____(below, to) their initial level because the long-run minimum average cost has (22)_____(declined, increased) due to the technological improvement and prices must equal this minimum to establish the new equilibrium.

For the case of constant costs, an increase in a tax per unit of output will shift the long-run average cost curve upward by the amount of the tax. If firms were in long-run equilibrium prior to the tax, the tax would impose losses on the firms, causing some of them to (23)_____(enter, exit) the industry. Market supply would (24)_____(rise, fall) and price would (25)_____(rise, fall) eventually to equal the higher average costs. Prices would therefore increase by the upward shift in the average cost curve or by the increase in the tax since average costs and taxes increase by the same amount. For the case of increasing costs, market prices would increase by (26)_____ (less, greater) than the tax per unit because the industry decline would reduce input prices and keep average costs from increasing as much as in the constant-costs case.

A competitive market in long-run equilibrium achieves allocative efficiency when the marginal benefit associated with the use of resources (27)_____(equals, is greater than) the marginal cost of those resources. The value consumers place on an additional unit of a good consumed is just equal to the producer's opportunity cost of the resources employed to produce that unit. Net gains to both consumers and producers are maximized. A point on the market demand curve represents marginal benefit--the (28)_____ (minimum, maximum) price that the consumer is willing and able to pay for an additional unit of a good rather than go without. The market supply curve, being a summation of individual firm marginal cost curves, represents the marginal cost of producing an additional unit of output. Market equilibrium occurs where the demand and supply curves intersect or, in terms of benefits and costs, where the marginal benefit and marginal cost curves intersect. A perfectly competitive market results in a level of output where marginal benefit and marginal cost are (29)_____(unequal, equal) and net gains to producers and consumers are at a maximum. Consumers are maximizing utility and producers are maximizing profit, although in the long run only normal profits are earned and consumers pay a price equal to the lowest possible average cost of production.

VOCABULARY REVIEW

Write the key term from the list below next to its definition.

Key Terms

Long-run competitive equilibrium
Constant-costs industry
Long-run industry supply curve
Increasing-costs industry

Definitions

1. _____: one for which the prices of at least some of the inputs used increase as a direct result of the expansion of the industry.

2. _____: a relationship between price and quantity supplied for points where the industry is in long-run equilibrium.

3. _____: exists in an industry when there is no tendency for firms to enter or leave the industry or to expand or contract the scale of their operations.

4. _____: one for which input prices are unaffected by the quantity produced or the number of firms in the industry.

SKILLS REVIEW

Concept: **Long-run equilibrium for a firm and market; role of profits and losses**

1. a. On the diagram below, draw the competitive firm's demand curve and label the curve dl.

b. Given the figure above, determine whether the firm is realizing economic profits or losses.
(1) The firm's short-run economic profits (losses) = $_____
(2) The firm's level of output = _____ units
(3) Market price = $_____
(4) Market quantity = _____ units

c. (1) In time, _____ (entry, exit) will occur because of the presence of economic _____ (profits, losses).
(2) Show graphically in the figure above the long-run adjustment of both the market and the firm assuming the firm operates in a constant-costs industry.
(3) As a result of _____ (entry, exit), economic _____ (profits, losses) will _____ (rise, fall). (Entry, Exiting) will continue until market price _____ (rises, falls) sufficiently to eliminate economic _____ (profits, losses).

d. In the long run, price equals both short- and long-run _____ and _____. Consumers pay a price equal to the minimum _____. Producers earn _____ economic profits but continue to earn _____ profits. Referring to the figure above, in long-run equilibrium the firm's economic profit (or loss) equals $_____ and its level of production is _____ units. Market price and quantity are $_____ and _____ units, respectively.

2. a. On the diagram below, draw the firm's demand curve and label it d2.

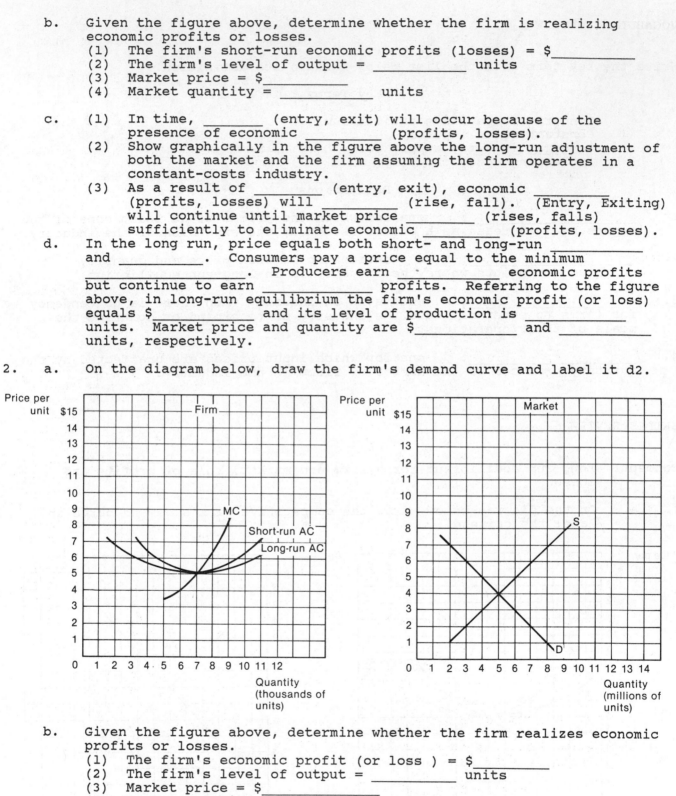

Price per unit $15 — Firm
MC
Short-run AC
Long-run AC
Quantity (thousands of units)

Price per unit $15 — Market
S
D
Quantity (millions of units)

b. Given the figure above, determine whether the firm realizes economic profits or losses.
(1) The firm's economic profit (or loss) = $_____
(2) The firm's level of output = _____ units
(3) Market price = $_____
(4) Market quantity = _____ units

c. (1) In time, _____ (entry, exiting) will occur because of the presence of economic _____ (profits, losses).

(2) Show graphically in the figure above the long-run adjustment of both the market and the firm assuming the firm operates in a constant-costs industry.

(3) As a result of _____ (entry, exiting), economic _____ (profits, losses) will _____ (rise, fall). _____ (Entry, Exiting) will continue until market price _____ (rises, falls) sufficiently to eliminate economic _____ (profits, losses).

d. In long-run equilibrium, price equals both short-and long-run _____ and _____. Consumers pay a price equal to the minimum _____. Producers earn _____ economic profits but continue to earn _____ profits. Referring to the figure above, in long-run equilibrium the firm realizes economic _____ (profits, losses) of $_____ and produces _____ units of output. Market price and quantity equal $_____ and _____ units, respectively.

Concept: Long-run market supply curves

3. a. Given the figure below representing a competitive firm and market in long-run equilibrium, show the short-run impact of an increase in market demand of 20 million units at every price.

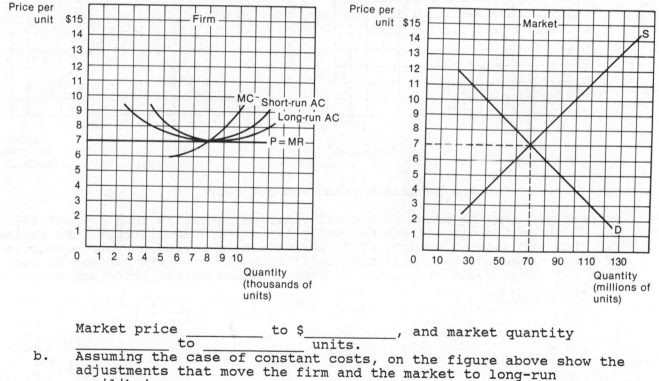

Market price _____ to $_____, and market quantity _____ to _____ units.

b. Assuming the case of constant costs, on the figure above show the adjustments that move the firm and the market to long-run equilibrium.

c. Show the long-run supply curve in the figure above. The long-run supply curve has a _____ slope.

4. For the case of an increasing-costs industry, show graphically on the
    figure below:

    a. The short-run effect of an increase in market demand of 40 million
        units at every price.
    b. The impact of industry expansion on the firm's costs (assume that the
        marginal and average cost curves shift upward by $1 at each level of
        output).
    c. The adjustment of the firm and market to long-run equilibrium.
    d. The long-run market supply curve. The long-run market supply curve
        has a _____ slope.

Concept: **Impact of taxes on market price and quantity**

5. Suppose you are the owner of a small vineyard operating in a competitive
    market in California and are currently in long-run equilibrium. An excise
    tax (tax per unit of output) of $1 per bottle is levied on your production
    of wine. Assuming that all other California wineries are subject to the
    same tax, what would you expect to happen to the market price and quantity
    of wine?

a. Using the figure below, show the short-run impact of the tax.

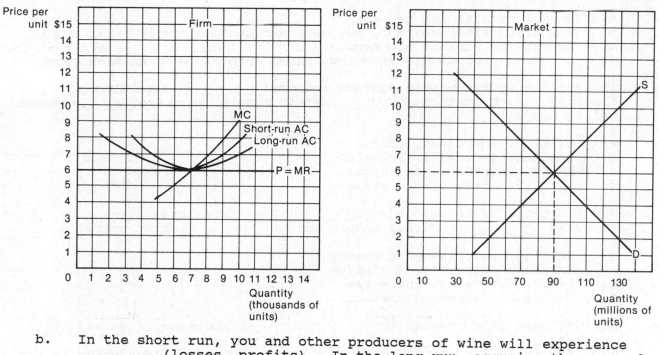

b. In the short run, you and other producers of wine will experience _____ (losses, profits). In the long run, assuming the case of a constant-costs industry, firms _____ (enter, exit), causing market price to _____ by $_____ to $_____ and market quantity to _____ to _____ units. Prices _____ (rise, fall) by what percentage of the $1 excise tax? _____%

SELF-TEST FOR MASTERY

Select the best answer.

1. Long-run competitive equilibrium occurs when:

   a. Firms are neither entering nor exiting the industry.
   b. Firms within the industry are neither expanding nor contracting.
   c. Economic profits are zero.
   d. The opportunity costs of the owner's self-owned resources are just being covered.
   e. All of the above.

2. In long-run competitive equilibrium, price equals not only _____, but also _____.

   a. Average variable costs, marginal cost
   b. Marginal cost, minimum possible average cost
   c. Marginal cost, total benefit
   d. The lowest price available to the consumer, total revenues to the firm.

3. Which of the following is correct regarding profits in long-run competitive equilibrium?

   a. Normal profits are zero.
   b. Normal profits are zero, but economic profits are being covered.
   c. Accounting profits are zero.
   d. Economic profits are zero, but normal profits are being covered.

4. The existence of economic profits induces _____ from/into an industry, which in turn _____ market supply and _____ market price.

   a. Exiting, increases, increases
   b. Exiting, decreases, increases
   c. Entry, increases, increases
   d. Entry, increases, decreases

5. The existence of losses induces _____ from/into an industry, which in turn _____ market supply and _____ market price.

   a. Exiting, increases, increases
   b. Exiting, decreases, increases
   c. Entry, increases, increases
   d. Entry, increases, decreases

6. For the case of a constant-costs industry, an increase in demand will:

   a. Result in a higher price in the short run and a lower price in the long run as compared to the current market price.
   b. Increase the firm's profits in the long run.
   c. Result in a higher price in the short run and the same price in the long run as compared to the current market price.
   d. Cause short-run profits but long-run losses.
   e. C and d.

7. The long-run market supply curve for a constant-costs industry is:

   a. Vertical.
   b. Upward sloping.
   c. Downward sloping.
   d. Horizontal.

8. For the case of an increasing-costs industry, an increase in demand will:

   a. Result in a higher price in the short run, but in the long run price will fall to a level above the original market price.
   b. Result in short-run profits but long-run losses.
   c. Increase profits in the long run.
   d. Cause an expansion of the industry that will increase input prices and shift the firm's average cost curve downward.

9. The long-run market supply curve for an increasing-costs industry is:

   a. Vertical.
   b. Upward sloping.
   c. Downward sloping.
   d. Horizontal.

10. An improvement in technology in an industry:

    a. Shifts the marginal cost curve upward and causes production and
        profit to rise.
    b. Shifts the average cost curve upward due to increased labor
        productivity.
    c. Results in short-run economic profits and a decline in price below
        the initial market price in the long run.
    d. Produces an upward sloping market supply curve.

11. For the case of a constant-costs industry, a per-unit tax levied on a
    good:

    a. Shifts the competitive firm's average cost curve down by less than
        the amount of the tax and increases the market price.
    b. Increases supply and causes the price to fall.
    c. Shifts the competitive firm's average and marginal cost curves upward
        by the amount of the tax per unit and in the long run results in an
        increase in the market price that is equal to the unit tax.
    d. None of the above.

12. For the case of an increasing-costs industry, a per-unit tax:

    a. Results in an increase in the long-run market price equal to the tax
        per unit.
    b. Results in an increase in the short-run market price equal to the tax
        per unit.
    c. Results in an increase in the long-run market price less than the tax
        per unit.
    d. Results in an increase in the long-run market price greater than the
        tax per unit.

13. Net gain is maximized where:

    a. Price equals marginal revenue.
    b. Marginal cost equals marginal benefit.
    c. The average variable cost is low.
    d. Economic profits are high.

14. A market demand curve can be thought of as a marginal benefit curve
    because:

    a. The price reflects the opportunity costs of scarce resources.
    b. Quantities consumed yield benefits.
    c. The price represents a measure of the additional benefit received
        from consuming one unit of a good--the price on a demand curve
        represents the maximum price that the consumer is willing and able to
        pay rather than go without.
    d. Price times marginal benefit equals total net gain.

15. Allocative efficiency occurs where:

    a. Marginal benefits equal marginal costs.
    b. Net benefits are maximized from the allocation of resources.
    c. The maximum price that consumers are willing and able to pay for an
        additional unit of a good just equals the price required by firms to
        produce that unit.
    d. All of the above.

16. Competitive markets can maximize the net gain to both buyers and producers because:

    a. Marginal benefits exceed the supply of the good.
    b. The market demand curve reflects marginal benefits and the market supply curve reflects marginal costs, and in equilibrium, supply equals demand; hence marginal benefits equal marginal costs.
    c. They are efficient and do not waste resources.
    d. Optimal exchange takes place to the point where total benefits equal total costs.

THINK IT THROUGH

1. Oil prices are determined by the world supply of and demand for oil. In the early 1970s, the member nations of OPEC reduced production of the world's available supply of oil. Although the oil industry is not perfectly competitive, the forces of supply and demand determine prices. Using your knowledge of the short- and long-run adjustments in markets, what would you predict to happen to oil prices in the short run and the long run as a result of OPEC's restriction of output?

2. Discuss the impact of technological improvement on the competitive firm, the competitive market, and the long-run market supply curve.

3. How do perfectly competitive markets maximize the net gains to producers and consumers?

CHAPTER ANSWERS

In Brief: Chapter Summary

1. Zero 2. Are 3. Enter 4. Increases 5. Reduces 6. Fall 7. Average total
8. Increases 9. Profits 10. Increase 11. Increase 12. Enter 13. Rightward
14. Rises 15. Falls 16. Horizontal 17. Upward sloping 18. Fall 19. Profits
20. Expand 21. Below 22. Declined 23. Exit 24. Fall 25. Rises 26. Less
27. Equals 28. Maximum 29. Equal

Vocabulary Review

1. Increasing-costs industry 2. Long-run market supply curve 3. Long-run competitive equilibrium 4. Constant-costs industry

1. a.

b. (1) Profits, $9,000 (2) 9,000 units (3) $7 (4) 6 million
c. (1) Entry, profit
    (2) On figure above
    (3) Entry, profits, fall; Entry, falls, profit
d. Marginal cost, minimum possible average cost; possible average cost
    of production; zero, normal; $0, 7,000 units; $5, 8 million

2. a.

b. (1) Loss, $9,000 (2) 6,000 units (3) $4 (4) 5 million
c. (1) Exiting, losses
    (2) On figure above
    (3) Exiting, losses, fall; Exiting, rises, losses
d. Marginal cost, minimum possible average cost; possible average cost
    of production; zero, normal; $0, 7,000 units; $5, 4 million

3. a.

195

Increases, $8, increases, 80 million
b.   On figure above
c.   On figure above, zero or horizontal

4.   a.

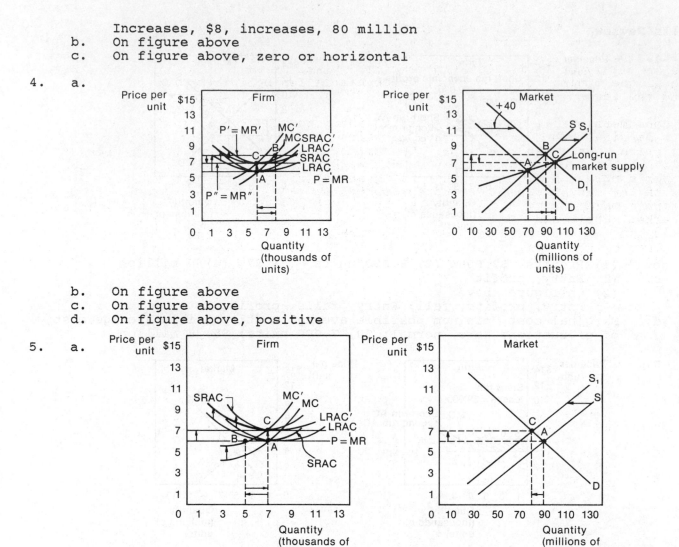

b.   On figure above
c.   On figure above
d.   On figure above, positive

5.   a.

b.   Losses; exit, increase, $1, $7, decrease, 80 million; rise, 100%

Self-Test for Mastery

1. e 2. b 3. d 4. d 5. b 6. c 7. d 8. a 9. b 10. c 11. c 12. c 13. b 14. c 15. d 16. b

Think it Through

1.   In the short run, the restriction of oil production reduces market supply relative to market demand and increases the price per barrel of oil. This results in greater short-run profits associated with the production of oil and in the long run results in firms entering the industry such as wildcats and other independent oil producers. It will also cause existing oil producers other than the members of OPEC to expand exploration and production efforts. The latter represents a movement up the supply curve in response to higher prices, and the former represents a rightward shift in the supply curve. As the supply curve shifts rightward, the market price in the long run will fall.

2.   Technological improvement increases the productivity of variable inputs, causing the marginal and average cost curves to shift downward. The minimum possible average cost of production likewise falls. As marginal costs fall relative to marginal revenue, the firm has an incentive to increase production

in order to maximize short-run profits. But short-run profits induce entry into the industry, shifting the market supply curve rightward and reducing the market price. In the long run, (assuming a constant-costs industry) the market price is likely to fall below the original market price because price will fall to equal the minimum average cost, which has fallen below its original level due to the technological improvement.

3.   Consumers maximize utility by consuming goods to the point where price equals marginal benefit. Producers maximize profits by producing to the point where price equals marginal cost. The market equilibrium occurs where demand equals supply. But since a point on the market demand curve represents the consumer's marginal benefit of consuming an additional unit of a good and a point on the market supply curve represents the price necessary to just cover the firm's marginal cost, marginal benefits and marginal costs are equal where the market supply and demand curves intersect. When the market is in equilibrium, net gains to consumers and producers are maximized from the allocation of resources.

13
Monopoly

CHAPTER CHALLENGES

After studying your text, attending class, and completing this chapter, you should be able to:

1. Explain the concept of pure monopoly and how it can be maintained in a market.
2. Show how the demand curve for a product sold by a monopoly firm implies that the firm can control the market price.
3. Show how the marginal revenue from a monopolist's output is less than the price the monopolist charges for its product, and how the marginal revenue is related to the price elasticity of demand for the monopolist's product.
4. Show how a profit-maximizing monopoly seller chooses how much of its product to make available to buyers in markets, and demonstrate how the decision of how much to sell is inseparable from that of how much to charge.
5. Compare market outcomes under pure monopoly with those that would prevail under perfect competition.
6. Discuss the social cost and possible social benefit of monopoly.

IN BRIEF: CHAPTER SUMMARY

Fill in the blanks to summarize chapter content.

A pure monopoly exists when there is a single seller of a product or service for which there are (1)_____ (close, no close) substitutes. The monopolist controls the market price by restricting output and preventing entry into the industry. Barriers to entry include government franchises and licenses, patents and copyrights, (2)_____ (control of an important resource, government influence), and economies of scale made possible by large size. Some monopolies that exist because of economies of scale are regulated by government so that the economies associated with large-scale production can be passed on to consumers in the form of lower prices than would be possible if the industry were made up of many small firms operating inefficiently small plants. These monopolies are called (3)_____ (natural, pure) monopolies.

The monopolist faces (4)_____ (a horizontal, the market) demand curve because it is the only seller in the market. Because the market demand curve is downward sloping, prices must be lowered in order to increase sales. Therefore marginal revenue (5)_____ (increases, falls) as output sold increases and is also (6)_____ (less, greater) than the product price. A monopoly firm will maximize profits by finding the level of output where marginal revenue (7)_____ (is greater than, equals) marginal cost. Once the profit-maximizing level of output is found, the monopolist will set a price on the market demand curve at a level that will ensure that quantity of output will be sold. Because price (8)_____ (equals, exceeds) marginal revenue and because at the profit-maximizing output marginal revenue equals marginal cost, price must also (9)_____ (equal, exceed) marginal cost. The monopolist will never operate where marginal revenue is negative. This means that the monopoly seller will operate on the (10)_____(inelastic, elastic) portion of the market demand curve where marginal revenue is positive and increases in output resulting from decreases in price will increase total revenue. No unique monopoly supply curve can be found because it is possible to have more than one price associated with the same level of monopoly output.

As compared to perfect competition, the monopolist charges a (11)_____ (higher, lower) price by (12)_____ (expanding output above, restricting output below) the level that would prevail in a competitive market. The monopolist's price (13)_____(equals, exceeds) marginal cost, whereas the competitive market results in a price (14)_____(equal to, greater than) marginal cost. Because of the presence of barriers to entry, the monopolist (15)_____(cannot, can) earn economic profits in the long run. With perfect competition, economic profits are competed away in the long run due to entry into the competitive industry. Further, the monopolist's price (16)_____ (equals, exceeds) the minimum possible average cost of production. Consumers pay more for the good than they would have to pay in a competitive market. Monopolization of markets in effect redistributes income from consumers to the owners of monopoly firms. Since price exceeds marginal cost, the marginal benefit to a consumer from the consumption of an additional unit of the monopolist's good will (17)_____ (be less than, exceed) the opportunity costs of the resources used to produce that good. Society's net gain (18)_____ (is, is not) maximized. That loss of potential net benefit is the (19)_____ (external, social) cost of monopoly and is measured by the triangular area between the demand and marginal cost curves from the monopolist's level of output to the level of output that would prevail in a perfectly competitive market.

Other comparisons between monopoly and perfect competition include analyses of the impact of taxes and price ceilings on a monopolist vs. a competitive firm and the effect of a price-discriminating monopolist on market quantity and price. An increase in a tax per unit of output increases the market price by an amount (20)_____(greater than, equal to) the increase in the tax for the case of perfect competition, but will result in an increase in price by (21)_____(less, greater) than the increase in the tax for a monopolist. A price ceiling (22)_____(increases, reduces) output in a perfectly competitive market, but (23)_____(increases, reduces) it in a monopoly. Price discrimination by a monopolist can result in a level of output (24)_____(greater than, equal to) that produced by a competitive market, but price will equal marginal cost (25)_____ (for all units, only for the last unit) of output sold. All other buyers have to pay a price in excess of marginal cost. Price discrimination is feasible if the firm can control the price, the good produced (26)_____(is, is not) resalable, and customers can be differentiated according to their willingness and ability to pay.

VOCABULARY REVIEW

Write the key term from the list below next to its definition.

Key Terms

Pure monopoly   Natural monopoly
Monopoly power   Social cost of monopoly
Barrier to entry   Price discrimination

Definitions

1. _____: the ability of a firm to influence the price of
its product by making more or less of it available to buyers.

2. _____: a constraint that prevents additional sellers
from entering a monopoly firm's market.

3. _____: a measure of the loss in potential net benefits
from the reduced availability of a good stemming from monopoly control of
price and supply.

4. _____: a firm that emerges as a single seller in the
market because of cost or technological advantages contributing to lower
average costs of production.

5. _____: occurs when there is a single seller of a product
that has no close substitutes.

6. _____: the practice of selling a certain product of
given quality and cost per unit at different prices to different buyers.

SKILLS REVIEW

Concept: Pure monopoly

1. List four characteristics of a pure monopoly.
   a. _____
   b. _____
   c. _____
   d. _____

Concept: A monopoly firm's demand, marginal revenue and total revenue

2. The following price and quantity demanded data are for a monopolistic
market.

Price per Unit	Quantity Demanded (000s units)	Total Revenue	Marginal Revenue
$10	1	$ _____	
9	2	_____	$ _____
8	3	_____	_____
7	4	_____	_____
6	5	_____	_____
5	6	_____	_____
4	7	_____	_____

   a. Complete the marginal revenue and total revenue columns in the above
   table.

b. Plot the firm's total revenue curve in a in the figure below, and
    plot the demand and marginal revenue curves in b.

a. Total revenue
    (000s) $30
               28
               26
               24
               22
               20
               18
               16
               14
               12
               10
                8
                6
                4
                2
                0
                    1   2   3   4   5   6   7   8
                                        Quantity
                                        (000s units)

b.
           $10
             9
             8
             7
             6
             5
             4
             3
             2
             1
             0
                 1   2   3   4   5   6   7   8
            −1
            −2
                                        Quantity
                                        (000s units)

c. Total revenue _____ when marginal revenue is positive and
    _____ when marginal revenue is negative. The elastic
    segment of the demand curve is that section over the range of output
    where marginal revenue is _____ and total revenue is
    _____.

201

Concept: Profit maximization of a monopolist

3.   Consider the monopoly seller's cost and demand data in the table below.

Quantity Supplied (000s)	TC (000s)	AC	MC	Quantity Demanded (000s)	Price	TR (000s)	MR	Profit (Loss) (000s)
1	$12	$12.00		1	$10	$_____		$____
2	14	7.00	$2	2	9	_____	$____	____
3	17	5.67	3	3	8	_____	____	____
4	21	5.25	4	4	7	_____	____	____
5	26	5.20	5	5	6	_____	____	____
6	32	5.33	6	6	5	_____	____	____
7	39	5.57	7	7	4	_____	____	____

a.   Complete the table.
b.   Determine the monopolist's profit-maximizing price and quantity.
      Price = $_____, quantity = _____ units, and total profit
      = $_____ .
c.   Plot the total revenue and total cost curves in a in the figure below
      and identify the profit-maximizing level of output and the level of
      profits. Plot the marginal cost, average cost, demand, and marginal
      revenue curves in b and identify the level of profits and the profit-
      maximizing level of output and price.

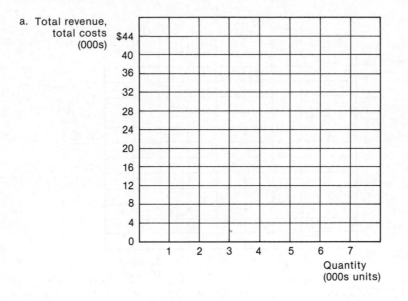

a. Total revenue, total costs (000s)

202

b.

Quantity
(000s units)

d. A monopolist maximizes profits by producing at a level of output where _____ equals _____ .

e. The monopolist shown in b in the figure above is operating on the _____ segment of the market demand curve.

4. <u>Advanced Question</u> Below are expressions for a monopolist's demand, marginal revenue, and marginal cost curves.

    Demand   P = a - bQ
    Marginal revenue   MR = a - 2bQ
    Marginal cost   MC = c + dQ

a. Find and interpret an equation for the profit-maximizing level of output.

b. Find and interpret an equation for the monopolist's price.

c. If a = \$20, b = .1, c = \$5 and d = .25, find the profit-maximizing price and quantity.

Concept: **Comparison of monopoly and perfect competition**

5. Referring to b in the figure above:

a. Price _____ (exceeds, equals, is less than) marginal cost and is _____ than would be the case for perfect competition. For perfect competition, price _____ marginal cost.

b. Price _____ (exceeds, equals, is less than) marginal revenue, whereas with perfect competition, price _____ marginal revenue.

c. Price _____ (exceeds, equals, is less than) average cost, whereas with perfect competition, price _____ the minimum average cost of production.

d. Output for a monopolist occurs where _____ equals _____ . A monopoly firm produces _____ output than a perfectly competitive industry.

e. In the long run, monopolists may earn _____ profits, but a perfectly competitive firm earns only _____ profits.

6.   Suppose a tax of $1 per unit of output is levied on the monopolist shown
     in the figure below.

Quantity
(000s units)

a.   Show the effect of a $1 per unit tax on the marginal and average cost
     curves above.
b.   The profit-maximizing price _____ and the level of output
     _____. Price _____ (increases,decreases) _____
     than the $1 tax. With perfect competition in long-run equilibrium,
     the price _____ (increases, decreases) by an amount _____
     the $1 tax.

SELF-TEST FOR MASTERY

Select the best answer.

1.   Which of the following is not a characteristic of a pure monopoly?

     a.   Single seller
     b.   No close substitutes
     c.   Barriers to entry
     c.   Control over price
     d.   Operates on the inelastic portion of the demand curve

2.   Which of the following are not barriers to entry?

     a.   Government franchises and licenses
     b.   Copyrights and patents
     c.   Control of an important resource
     d.   Advantages of government lobbying efforts
     e.   Economies of scale

3. Monopolies that are allowed to exist because of scale economy advantages but are regulated by the government are called:

    a. Normal monopolies.
    b. Natural monopolies.
    c. Pure monopolies.
    d. Regulated monopolies.
    e. None of the above.

4. A monopolist's marginal revenue is:

    a. Equal to the product price.
    b. Greater than the market price.
    c. Less than the price on the market demand curve.
    d. Measured by the change in output divided by the change in total revenue.
    e. C and d.

5. Marginal revenue is more steeply sloped than the demand curve because:

    a. Price must be lowered in order to increase sales and the lower price pertains not just to the additional units sold but to the monopolist's total output.
    b. The monopolist restricts output.
    c. The monopolist raises price and reduces marginal revenue.
    d. The monopolist restricts output and to do that it must raise price, which applies to all units sold.

6. The monopolist maximizes profit when:

    a. Marginal revenue equals average cost.
    b. Price equals marginal revenue.
    c. Marginal revenue equals marginal cost.
    d. Price equals marginal cost.
    e. Total revenue equals total cost.

7. At the monopoly seller's profit-maximizing output:

    a. Price exceeds marginal revenue.
    b. Price exceeds marginal cost.
    c. Price exceeds average cost.
    d. Economic profits are being earned.
    e. All of the above.

8. A monopolist operates on the _____ portion of the market demand curve because that is where marginal revenue is _____ and total revenue is _____.

    a. Elastic, positive, increasing
    b. Elastic, negative, increasing
    c. Inelastic, negative, decreasing
    d. Inelastic, positive, decreasing

9. A monopolist's supply curve:

    a. Is the segment of its marginal cost curve above its average variable cost curve.
    b. Is the market supply curve because the monopolist is the sole producer of output in the industry.
    c. Is represented by the price - marginal revenue coordinates from a zero level of output to the level where price equals marginal cost.

d.   None of the above.

10.   Compared to the case of perfect competition, a monopolist that does not experience significant economies of scale:

a.   Charges a higher price.
b.   Produces a lower level of output.
c.   Earns long-run economic profits.
d.   Operates at a level of output where average cost is not minimized.
e.   All of the above.

11.   The social cost of monopoly is the:

a.   Sacrificed net benefit to society that results from the monopolist restricting output below the competitive output.
b.   Cost incurred by the Justice Department to control monopoly behavior.
c.   Income that consumers lose as a result of paying higher monopoly prices.
d.   Explicit outlays by the monopolist to acquire scarce resources.

12.   The social cost of monopoly is measured by:

a.   The accounting costs of the monopolist's production.
b.   The area underlying the marginal revenue curve.
c.   The triangular area between the demand and marginal cost curves from the monopolist's level of output to the level of output that would prevail in a perfectly competitive market.
d.   The area above the average cost curve and below the demand curve.

13.   A per-unit tax on output _____ the monopolist's price by _____ the tax.

a.   Decreases, an amount equal to
b.   Increases, an amount less than
c.   Increases, an amount greater than
d.   Increases, an amount equal to

14.   A price ceiling _____ output in a competitive market but _____ it for a monopoly.

a.   Decreases, increases
b.   Decreases, decreases
c.   Increases, decreases
d.   Increases, increases

15.   Price discrimination by a monopolist can result in a level of output _____ that produced by a competitive market, but price will equal marginal cost _____.

a.   Greater than, only occasionally
b.   Equal to, for all levels of output
c.   Less than, for all levels of output
d.   Equal to, only for the last unit of output sold

16.   Which of the following best defines price discrimination?

a.   Charging different prices on the basis of race
b.   Charging different prices for goods with different costs of production
c.   Selling a certain product of given quality and cost per unit at different prices to different buyers

d.   Charging different prices based upon cost-of-service differentials

17.   Which of the following is not a condition necessary to enable a monopolist to engage in price discrimination?

a.   Must operate on the inelastic portion of the demand curve
b.   Must be able to set the price of the product
c.   The product must not be resalable
d.   Must be able to differentiate customers according to willingness and ability to pay

THINK IT THROUGH

1.   A monopolist produces a good for which no close substitutes exist. The monopolist therefore faces an inelastic demand. True or false? Explain.

2.   Discuss the social cost of monopoly. How does society benefit from efforts by government to reduce, eliminate, or regulate monopolies?

3.   Compare a perfectly competitive industry with one in which a monopolist is engaged in price discrimination.

4.   Society is generally better off with perfect competition than with pure monopoly. But why does government promote regulated monopolies or natural monopolies in some industries rather than insist upon perfect competition?

CHAPTER ANSWERS

In Brief: Chapter Summary

1. No close 2. Control of an important resource 3. Natural 4. The market 5. Falls 6. Less 7. Equals 8. Exceeds 9. Exceed 10. Elastic 11. Higher 12. Restricting output below 13. Exceeds 14. Equal to 15. Can 16. Exceeds 17. Exceed 18. Is not 19. Social 20. Equal to 21. Less 22. Reduces 23. Increases 24. Equal to 25. Only for the last unit 26. Is not

Vocabulary Review

1. Monopoly power 2. Barrier to entry 3. Social cost of monopoly 4. Natural monopoly 5. Pure monopoly 6. Price discrimination

Skills Review

1.   a. Single seller b. No close substitutes c. Can control price d. Barriers to entry

2.   a.   Total Revenue   Marginal Revenue
            $10,000
            18,000 $8
            24,000   6
            28,000   4
            30,000   2
            30,000   0
            28,000   -2

b.

c. **Increases, decreases; positive, rising**

3. a.

TR	MR	Profit (loss)
$10,000		($2,000)
18,000	$8	4,000
24,000	6	7,000
28,000	4	7,000
30,000	2	4,000
30,000	0	(2,000)
28,000	-2	(11,000)

a. **$7, 4,000 units, $7,000**

c.

208

Quantity
(000s units)

d. Marginal revenue, marginal cost
e. Elastic

4. a. The profit-maximizing output equation can be found by first setting marginal revenue equal to marginal cost and then solving for output.

MR = MC
a - 2bQ = c + dQ

Q = (a - c)/(d + 2b)

An increase in a--an upward shift in the demand and marginal revenue curves--will increase the profit-maximizing output. An increase in c--an upshift in the marginal cost curve--will decrease the profit-maximizing quantity. As can be seen in the denominator of the quantity equation, changes in the slopes of the demand, marginal revenue, and marginal cost curves will also influence the profit-maximizing output.

   b. Substituting the profit-maximizing quantity equation, Q, for Q in the demand curve yields the price required to maximize profit.

P = a - bQ
P = a - bQm   where Qm=(a - c)/(d + 2b)
P = [bc + a(b + d)]/(d + 2b)

An increase in c or a will result in the monopolist raising price. Changes in the slopes of the curves will also likely affect the monopolist's price.

   c. Qm = 33.33 units; Pm = $16.67

5. a. Exceeds, greater; equals b. Exceeds, equals c. Exceeds, equals d. Marginal revenue, marginal cost; less e. Economic, normal

6. a.

Quantity
(000s units)

b.   Increases, decreases; less; increases, equal to

Self-Test for Mastery

1. d 2. d 3. b 4. c 5. a 6. c 7. e 8. a 9. d 10. e 11. a 12. c 13. b 14. a 15. d 16. c 17. a

Think it Through

1.   False. The monopolist will never operate on the inelastic portion of the market demand curve because marginal revenue is negative and increases in production reduce total revenues while costs continue to increase.

2.   The social cost of monopoly is the sacrificed net benefit that could have been realized if the market operated at the higher competitive level of output where price equals marginal cost. Social policies designed to replace monopoly with competition or to regulate monopolies such that output is not restricted and price equals marginal cost will allow society to realize the maximum net benefits from the allocation of resources. This assumes that the monopolies in question exist for reasons other than significant scale economies.

3.   A price-discriminating monopolist produces at the same level of output as does a perfectly competitive industry--where price equals marginal cost, or in other words, where the market demand curve intersects the marginal cost curve. The monopolist, however, is able to redistribute the net gains to society of this level of output away from consumers to the monopolist's owners. Price equals marginal cost as it does for perfect competition, but only for the last unit of output sold.

4.   Some monopolies exist largely because of scale economies. They must be large in order to realize an efficient use of plant and an efficient scale of operation. Even though economic profits are earned, a monopolist with significant scale economies might produce more output at a lower price than would be the case if the industry were made up of many small, inefficiently sized firms. States allow utilities such as electric power companies to exist as regional monopolies, but the states regulate prices so that the benefits of large-scale production can be passed on to consumers.

14

Monopolistic Competition and Oligopoly

CHAPTER CHALLENGES

After studying your text, attending class, and completing this chapter, you should be able to:

1. Explain the concept of monopolistic competition in markets and show how outcomes in such markets differ from those expected under perfect competition and pure monopoly.
2. Explain the concept of oligopoly and analyze market outcomes under oligopoly.
3. Explain the concept of a cartel and show how it differs from a pure monopoly.
4. Understand the impact of competition through advertising and improvements in product quality in imperfectly competitive markets, and explain how imperfectly competitive firms decide to price their products.

IN BRIEF: CHAPTER SUMMARY

Fill in the blanks to summarize chapter content.

Perfect competition and pure monopoly represent extreme market structures. Virtually all markets fall somewhere in between. Monopolistic competition and oligopoly are two such imperfectly competitive markets. Monopolistic competition is characterized by (a) (1)_____ (few firms, a large number of firms) with small market shares, (b) the production of goods that (2)_____ (are not, are) perfect substitutes, (c) (3)_____ (concern, lack of concern) regarding rivals' reactions to price and production policy, (d) relative freedom of entry and exit, and (e) (4)_____ (no, significant) opportunity or incentive to collude to limit competition.

In the short run, the monopolistic competitor finds the profit-maximizing price and quantity by producing at a level of output where (5)_____(marginal revenue, price) equals marginal cost. The firm must set a price to achieve sales at this level of output because it faces a (6)_____ (market, downward-sloping) demand curve. The demand and marginal revenue curves are flatter or (7)_____(less, more) elastic than in the case of monopoly because the goods in question, while not perfect substitutes, are nevertheless substitutes in consumption. In contrast, the monopolist produces a good for which there are no close substitutes. A perfectly competitive firm faces a horizontal demand curve because the goods produced in the market by various firms are perfect substitutes.

Short-run profits or losses will have the same effect on the monopolistic competitor as they do on the perfect competitor. Economic profits result in (8)_____(exiting from, entry into) the industry, whereas losses result in (9)_____ (exiting from, entry into) the industry. (10)_____(Profits, Losses) that cause firms to enter an industry will shift an existing firm's demand and marginal revenue curves leftward until they are just tangent to the firm's (11)_____(marginal, average) cost curve. (12)_____ (Profits, Losses) cause exiting of firms in the long run and cause a rightward shift in a firm's demand and marginal revenue curves until they are again just tangent to the (13)_____(marginal, average) cost curve. In the long run, the monopolistically competitive firm will earn (14)_____ (zero economic, zero normal) profits and will charge a price (15)_____(greater than, equal to) average cost, but the price charged will (16)_____ (equal, exceed) both marginal cost and the minimum average cost of production. The industry operates in long-run equilibrium with too (17)_____(many, few) firms, each having (18)_____(insufficient, excess) capacity.

Whereas neither the perfectly competitive firm nor the monopolist has an incentive to advertise, the monopolistic competitor often uses substantial resources to advertise, establish brand names, and develop and improve products. In the short run, such efforts can shift the demand and marginal revenue curves (19)_____(rightward, leftward) and may even make them steeper or (20)_____(more, less) elastic. But the selling costs associated with product promotion and advertising increase average costs as well. In the long run, however, entry or exiting ensure that such efforts (21)_____ (produce, have no lasting effect on) economic profits. The consumer benefits from the information content in advertisements and the variety of products that are produced as firms try to differentiate their products. But prices (22)_____(may be higher, are always lower) as a result of the product promotion and differentiation.

(23)_____(Monopolistic competition, Oligopoly) is a market structure with (24)_____(a few, many) dominant firms having large market shares and producing either standardized or differentiated goods. Other characteristics include the necessity of considering rivals' reactions and the presence of barriers to entry. There is no single behavioral model of oligopoly. The oligopolistic market results in different outcomes depending upon how rivals react to a given oligopolist's decision to change price or promotion policy and other decisions. If each oligopolist assumes that rival oligopolists will not react to a price cut, then each firm believes it can increase market share by reducing price. This results in (25)_____ (price leadership, a price war), causing the price to fall to the (26)_____(average, marginal) cost of production. A (27)_____(cartel, contestable) market is one in which oligopolists reduce price to average cost in order to eliminate the incentive for new firms to enter the market.

Price warring and contestable markets benefit consumers through lower prices, but deplete economic profits. Since oligopolists have large market shares and are few in number, there is an incentive to collude to restrict industry output and increase market price and profit. In effect, there is an incentive to coordinate their activities such that they can jointly produce an outcome identical to that of (28)_____(monopoly, monopolistic competition). A (29)_____(cartel, contestable market) is created by an agreement among oligopolists to restrict market output and share in the sales and profits resulting from the higher market price. There is an incentive to form cartels if barriers to entry (30)_____(exist, do not exist), market and firm production targets can be agreed upon, and the agreement can be enforced. But once a cartel is formed, members have an incentive to cheat and to produce beyond their quota in order to increase profits. Cheating will work for a firm only if the change in market supply resulting from its increase in production (31)_____ (influences, does not influence) the market price and if it can be carried out undetected.

Two other models of oligopoly are the price leadership and price rigidity models. In a (32)_____ (price leadership, cartel) oligopoly, the dominant oligopolist takes the lead and establishes the market price and the less dominant firms follow shortly with similar prices. This behavior avoids price warring and brings some stability to the industry. Even though the dominant firm's price may not maximize the profits of the other oligopolists, the fear of predatory pricing by the dominant firm may be great enough to keep the other firms in a price follower pattern.

If oligopolists react to a price cut by reducing prices but do not match price increases, a kink in the demand curve results where there is a noticeable change in the elasticity of demand. Demand is more elastic above the kink and less elastic or even inelastic below the kink. A change in price above or below the kink will likely reduce total revenues. Therefore the price tends to (33)_____(be flexible, remain rigid) at the kink. Changes in costs that shift the marginal cost curve over a given range (34)_____(may not have any, always have an) impact on the profit-maximizing level of output and price and are another reason why the price is rigid.

VOCABULARY REVIEW

Write the key term from the list below next to its definition.

Key Terms

Imperfect competition	Oligopoly
Monopolistic competition	Price war
Product group	Contestable market
Excess capacity	Cartel
Selling costs	Price leader

Definitions

1. _____: exists when more than one seller competes for sales with other sellers of competitive products, each of whom has some control over price.

2. _____: represents several closely related, but not identical, items that serve the same general purpose for consumers.

3. _____: all costs incurred by a firm to influence the sales of its product.

4. _____: a market structure in which a few sellers dominate the sales of the product and where entry of new sellers is difficult or impossible.

5. _____: a market in which entry of sellers is easy and exit is not very costly.

6. _____: a group of firms acting together to coordinate and control price as if they were a single monopoly.

7. _____: exists when many sellers compete to sell a differentiated product in a market in which entry of new sellers is possible.

8. _____: the difference between the output corresponding to minimum possible average cost and that produced by the monopolistically competitive firm in the long run.

9. _____: a bout of continual price cutting by rival firms in a market; one of many possible consequences of oligopolistic rivalry

10. _____: one dominant firm in an industry that sets its price to maximize its own profits, after which other firms follow its lead by setting exactly the same price

SKILLS REVIEW

Concept: **Monopolistic competition; comparison to perfect competition and pure monopoly**

1. List five characteristics of a monopolistically competitive market.

   a. _____
   b. _____
   c. _____
   d. _____
   e. _____

2. The diagram below represents a monopolistically competitive firm in short-run equilibrium.

a. Short-run profits are maximized where _____ equals _____. The profit-maximizing price = $_____, and quantity = _____ units.

b. This firm has short-run economic _____ (profits, losses) equal to area _____ in the figure above.

c. In the long run, _____ causes the firm's demand and marginal revenue curves to shift _____ until the demand curve is just tangent to the _____ curve.

d. Show the long-run equilibrium on the figure above.

214

e.   In long-run equilibrium:
          (1)   Price _____ marginal cost
          (2)   Price _____ average cost
          (3)   Price _____ minimum average cost
          (4)   Economic profits = $_____

3.   The figure below represents a monopolistically competitive firm in short-
      run equilibrium.

a.   The profit-maximizing or loss-minimizing level of output and price
      are _____ units and $_____, respectively.
b.   The firm has short-run economic _____ (profits, losses) equal to
      area _____ in the figure above.
c.   In the long run, _____ causes the firm's demand and marginal
      revenue curves to shift _____ until the demand curve is just
      tangent to the _____ curve.
d.   Show the long-run equilibrium on the figure above.
e.   In long-run equilibrium:
          (1)   Price _____ marginal cost
          (2)   Price _____ average cost
          (3)   Price _____ minimum average cost
          (4)   Economic profit = $_____

4.   As compared to perfect competition, monopolistic competition results in:

a.   (Same, higher, lower) price.
b.   (Same, higher, lower) output.
c.   (Same, higher, lower) average cost.
d.   (Same, more efficient, less efficient) capacity utilization.
e.   (Same, more, less) economic profit.
f.   (Same, more, less) net benefits to society.
g.   (Same, more, less) product promotion and development.

5. List four similarities and four dissimilarities between monopolistic
    competition in long-run equilibrium and pure monopoly.

    a. Similarities
        (1) _____
        (2) _____
        (3) _____
        (4) _____
    b. Dissimilarities
        (1) _____
        (2) _____
        (3) _____
        (4) _____

Concept: Oligopoly; oligopoly behavior and market outcomes

6. List three characteristics of oligopoly.

    a. _____
    b. _____
    c. _____

7. The figure below represents an oligopolist in short-run equilibrium in an
    industry in which each oligopolist believes that a price decrease will <u>not</u>
    be matched by rival oligopolists.

    a. The oligopolist maximizes profit by equating _____ and
        _____. Economic profits equal area _____, price
        = $_____, and quantity = _____ units.

216

b.   Suppose this oligopolist cuts price in order to increase market
share. Show the effect graphically in the figure below.

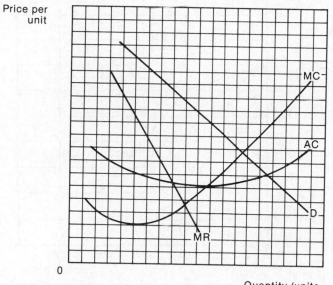

c.   If other oligopolists react by also cutting prices, the oligopolist
that initiated the price reduction must _____ (match, not match)
the price decrease in order to maintain market share. If a price war
develops, price could potentially fall to a level equal to
_____. Show the effect of price warring in the figure above.
What happens to economic profit?
d.   Price wars create an incentive for rival oligopolists to
_____. A formal agreement of output restriction and market
sharing is known as a _____. The intent of such a
restriction and market sharing is to approximate the market outcome
of a _____.

8. Consider the following figure of an oligopolist.

a. Explain the behavioral reactions of rival oligopolists that produce the "kink" in the demand curve.

b. Profits are maximized at a level of output where _____ equals _____. Price = $_____ and quantity = _____ units.

c. Show on the figure above the effect of an increase in marginal cost of $5 at each level of output and a decrease of $5. An increase in marginal cost of $5 at each level of output causes the profit-maximizing price and quantity to _____. A decrease in marginal cost of $5 at each level of output causes the profit-maximizing price and quantity to _____.

d. Prices are _____ (rigid, flexible) given certain shifts in the marginal cost curve in the discontinuous section of the marginal revenue curve.

SELF-TEST FOR MASTERY

Select the best answer.

1. Which of the following is not a characteristic associated with monopolistic competition?

   a. There is a large number of firms with small market shares.
   b. Goods produced by firms within the industry are not perfect substitutes.
   c. Firms are unconcerned with the reaction of rival firms.
   d. There are barriers to entry.
   e. There is no opportunity or incentive to collude to limit competition.

2. The demand and marginal revenue curves faced by a monopolistic competitor are flatter or more elastic than the demand and marginal revenue curves faced by a monopolist because:

    a. The demand for the good is very responsive to changes in income.
    b. The goods produced in the industry, while not perfect substitutes, are nevertheless close substitutes.
    c. The goods in the industry are unique and are not substitutes.
    d. Entry and exiting by firms makes consumers more responsive to price changes.

3. A monopolistically competitive firm maximizes profit at the level of output where:

    a. Price equals marginal revenue.
    b. Price equals marginal cost.
    c. Marginal cost equals average revenue.
    d. Marginal revenue equals marginal cost.

4. In the short run, economic profits cause _____ the monopolistically competitive industry and a _____ shift in the demand and marginal revenue curves.

    a. Entry into, leftward
    b. Entry into, rightward
    c. Exiting from, leftward
    d. Exiting from, rightward

5. In the short run, losses cause _____ the monopolistically competitive industry and a _____ shift in the demand and marginal revenue curves.

    a. Entry into, leftward
    b. Entry into, rightward
    c. Exiting from, leftward
    d. Exiting from, rightward

6. In a monopolistically competitive industry, short-run losses or economic profits will cause the demand curve to shift to the point where in long-run equilibrium, it:

    a. Intersects the supply curve.
    b. Intersects the average variable cost curve.
    c. Is just tangent to the average cost curve.
    d. Is just tangent to the marginal cost curve.

7. Monopolistic competition and perfect competition are similar in which of the following ways?

    a. In long-run equilibrium, economic profits are zero.
    b. Price exceeds marginal cost.
    c. Price equals minimum average cost.
    d. There is relative freedom of entry and exit.
    e. A and d.

8. Which of the following market structures is associated with significant advertising and product development?

    a. Perfect competition
    b. Pure monopoly
    c. Monopolistic competition

d. Oligopoly
e. C and d

9. Because the monopolistic competitor charges a price _____ marginal cost, net benefits to society _____.

   a. Equal to, are maximized
   b. Less than, are maximized
   c. Equal to, are not maximized
   d. Greater than, are not maximized

10. Which of the following is not a characteristic associated with oligopoly?

    a. Few firms
    b. Standardized or differentiated goods
    c. Lack of concern regarding a rival's behavior
    d. Large market shares
    e. Barriers to entry

11. If each oligopolist in a given industry believes that its rivals will not match price cuts:

    a. Price wars can develop resulting in economic profits for all but the smallest oligopolists.
    b. There is no incentive to reduce prices and risk a price war.
    c. A price war can develop, resulting in prices falling to a level equal to average cost.
    d. A kink appears in the oligopolist's demand and marginal revenue curves.

12. If each oligopolist in a given industry matches price cuts but does not match price increases:

    a. Price wars develop, resulting in zero economic profits.
    b. Prices become rigid at the intersection of the marginal revenue and average cost curves.
    c. Prices become flexible due to the price-cutting behavior.
    d. Prices become rigid at the kink in the demand curve.

13. Prices are rigid at the kink of an oligopolist's demand curve because:

    a. Of the distinct change in the elasticity of demand at the kink.
    b. Changes in fixed costs have no impact on the profit-maximizing price.
    c. Changes in marginal cost in the discontinuous section of the marginal revenue curve do not alter the profit-maximizing price and output.
    d. A and c.
    e. All of the above.

14. A contestable market is one in which

    a. There are significant transaction costs associated with exiting an industry.
    b. Entry is difficult, but exiting is costless.
    c. Entry is easy and exiting is not very costly.
    d. Rival oligopolists engage in predatory pricing.

15. In order to prevent entry into a contestable market, oligopolists:

    a. Set prices very high to earn monopoly profits.
    b. Set prices equal to marginal costs to maximize profits.
    c. Set prices to reduce normal profits to zero.

d.   Set prices at a level equal to average cost.

16.   Price warring creates an incentive by oligopolists to collude. A formal agreement to restrict output and share markets is called a:

a.   Pure monopoly.
b.   Restrictive oligopoly.
c.   Cartel.
d.   Quota.

17.   Which of the following conditions are necessary for a cartel to exist?

a.   Barriers to entry
b.   Agreement on total market production levels
c.   Agreement on individual firms' share of total output
d.   Ability to police and enforce the agreement
e.   All of the above

18.   An oligopolistic market in which the dominant oligopolist establishes the industry price, which subsequently is matched by the other oligopolists, is characterized by:

a.   Illegal collusion.
b.   Price leadership.
c.   Predatory pricing.
d.   Price discrimination.

THINK IT THROUGH

1.   Discuss the advantages and disadvantages of monopolistic competition relative to perfect competition.

2.   Which market structure best fits the video rental business in your community? Explain. What are your expectations for that industry as it attains long-run equilibrium?

3.   Discuss the natural forces that tend to make cartels unworkable over the long run.

4.   Why is it difficult to compare the market outcomes of oligopoly to those of other market structures?

POP QUIZ   Read the news brief at the of this chapter and answer the
                  questions below.

1.   Using the information in the article, explain why OPEC is having difficulty maintaining the price of oil.

2.   According to the text, why are these difficulties expected?

CHAPTER ANSWERS

In Brief: Chapter Summary

1. A large number of firms 2. Are not 3. Lack of concern 4. No 5. Marginal revenue 6. Downward-sloping 7. More 8. Entry into 9. Exiting from 10. Profits 11. Average 12. Losses 13. Average 14. Zero economic 15. Equal to 16. Exceed 17. Many 18. Excess 19. Rightward 20. Less 21. Have no lasting effect on 22. May be higher 23. Oligopoly 24. A few 25. A price war 26. Average 27. Contestable 28. Monopoly 29. Cartel 30. Exist 31. Does not influence 32. Price leadership 33. Remain rigid 34. May not have any

Vocabulary Review

1. Imperfect competition 2. Product group 3. Selling costs 4. Oligopoly 5. Contestable market 6. Cartel 7. Monopolistic competition 8. Excess capacity 9. Price war 10. Price leader

Skills Review

1. a. There is a large number of firms with small market shares.
    b. Goods are close but not perfect substitutes.
    c. There is lack of concern regarding the reaction of rivals.
    d. There is freedom of entry and exit.
    e. There is no opportunity or incentive to collude to limit competition.

2. a. Marginal revenue, marginal cost; $ad, ah units
    b. Profits, cdef
    c. Entry, leftward, average cost

    d.

    e. (1) Exceeds (2) Equals (3) Exceeds (4) $0

3. a. ai units, $ad
    b. Losses, defg
    c. Exiting, rightward, average cost

d.

Price per unit

Units of output per time period

e.   (1) Exceeds (2) Equals (3) Exceeds (4) $0

4.   a.   Higher b. Lower c. Higher d. Less efficient e. Same f. Less g. More

5.   a.   (1) Price exceeds minimum average cost.
         (2) Price exceeds marginal cost.
         (3) Price exceeds the competitive price.
         (4) Output is less than the competitive output.

     b.   (1) Price equals average cost for monopolistic competition, but exceeds average cost for a monopolist.
         (2) Economic profit is zero for the monopolistic competitor but positive for the monopolist.
         (3) Monopolistic competition is associated with ease of entry, whereas monopoly has barriers to entry.
         (4) Monopolistic competitors have incentives to advertise and engage in product development, whereas monopolists have little if any incentive to promote or improve their product.

6.   a.   Few firms with large market shares
     b.   Standardized or differentiated goods
     c.   Barriers to entry

7.   a.   Marginal revenue, marginal cost; cfgh, $af, aj units

     b.

Price per unit

Units of output per time period

     c.   Match, average cost; economic profits fall to zero
     d.   Collude; cartel; monopolist

8.   a.   The kink in the demand curve results from rival oligopolists matching
          price cuts but not matching price increases. The logic is that the
          firm must match price cuts or lose market share. With price
          increases, a firm could increase market share by not matching the
          price increase and capturing a portion of the market share previously
          held by the oligopolist that raised its price. As a result, below
          the kink demand is much less elastic or inelastic because a price
          reduction does not increase sales very much since other oligopolists
          are also reducing prices. In contrast, an increase in price results
          in large sales losses because other firms have maintained their
          prices at the lower level. Here demand is much more elastic.
     b.   Marginal revenue, marginal cost, $30, 200 units

     c.

          Not change, not change
     d.   Rigid

Self-Test for Mastery

1. d 2. b 3. d 4. a 5. d 6. c 7. e 8. e 9. d 10. c 11. c 12. d 13.
d 14. c 15. d 16. c 17. e 18. b

Think it Through

1.   Monopolistic competition results in product differentiation. Perfect
competition is associated with a homogeneous good. Consumers benefit by having
a greater variety of goods. Consumers, however, pay a higher price for less
efficiently produced goods. Allocative efficiency is not achieved because the
price charged by the monopolistic competitor exceeds marginal cost. While
product advertising may increase the information available to consumers,
resulting in more efficient choices, the selling costs represent resources that
would otherwise be available for the production of goods in a perfectly
competitive economy.

2.   In a local market, the video rental industry is a monopolistically
competitive market. The are numerous firms each with a small market share.
Short-run economic profits attract new entrants to the industry. The product
is differentiated by advertising, the length of the rental period, store hours,
method of payment, and convenience in pickup and return. Even price
discrimination is practiced in that popular new releases have a less elastic
demand than older releases and often carry a higher rental fee. Because of the
number of firms and the certainty of entry in response to economic profits, it
would be very difficult to collude to limit competition. In the long run, the
video rental business will have too many firms, each with excess capacity and
earning only normal profits.

224

3. The monopoly price resulting from a cartel's restriction of output will likely not be the price that maximizes profit for the individual cartel members. Each firm will probably have somewhat different average and marginal costs of production. Beyond the firm's share of cartel profits resulting from the sale of a specified level of output at the cartel price, the firm could increase profits even more by reducing prices to other buyers. This will work only if the increase in production does not affect market price and the cartel either does not detect the clandestine price cutting or cannot enforce the cartel agreement. If several of the members are doing this, market price will fall and the cartel will effectively be broken.

4. The market outcomes of oligopoly depend, among other considerations, upon the reactions of rival oligopolists, the scope of the market--local, regional, national, or international--and the ease of entry and exit. An oligopolist may operate where price equals average cost or, because of scale economies, may even charge a price less than that of a perfectly competitive firm. On the other hand, an oligopolist may charge a price in excess of marginal and average cost and earn economic profits in the long run. There is no given model of oligopolistic behavior that fits all oligopolistic industries. Differences in firm behavior produce differences in outcomes. In order to assess oligopoly relative to other market structures, each oligopolistic market must be considered unique and studied individually.

Pop Quiz

1. World oil prices have declined by as much as $4 per barrel since 1986. This is attributed to the world oil "glut" caused in part by increased production by certain members of OPEC. The United Arab Emirates have openly stated that they intend not adhere to their production quota. Instead, they intend to produce almost 50% more oil per day than their current quota of 948,000 barrels per day. Kuwait's output is up considerably as is the Saudi's production. It is estimated that total OPEC oil output is 20 million barrels per day, which is about 2 million barrels per day greater than required from the OPEC countries. Current OPEC members are scrambling for larger markets by increasing production and discounting prices. The OPEC cartel is having trouble maintaining the price of oil because it is having difficulty controlling the production of its own members.

2. This behavior is not unexpected. If a cartel has no effective means of policing its members or erecting barriers to entry, the cartel will eventually break down as members disregard cartel agreements and pursue their own independent price-production strategy. If an individual OPEC country discounted oil prices on secret sales in excess of the quota and the increased production did not affect world oil prices, this country would likely be able to earn greater profits than under the OPEC agreement. If several countries are trying to do this, their combined production will likely decrease world oil prices, resulting in an effective breakdown of the cartel.

OPEC Output Jumps to Levels Of a Year Ago

Despite Glut, Price Decline, Daily Production Hits About 19 Million Barrels

---

By JAMES TANNER

Staff Reporter of THE WALL STREET JOURNAL

The Organization of Petroleum Exporting Countries suddenly is swelling the world oil glut by pumping out crude at the highest level in a year.

Trackers of the cartel's output say it now is up to 19 million barrels a day, despite the talk in OPEC about efforts to curb production excesses to stabilize deteriorating petroleum prices. Some authoritative estimates place output as high as 20 million barrels.

That is about 1.5 million barrels a day above OPEC's June level, and as much as two million barrels a day above the generally estimated need for OPEC oil for the third quarter.

Reasons for the spurting output—paced by OPEC's Middle East members, including Saudi Arabia—are not entirely clear. But, with petroleum storage tanks brimming world-wide, the production surge "helps explain the weakness in the oil market," a senior OPEC official conceded yesterday.

"We are not yet in a free-fall in prices, but we are seeing a free-for-all on OPEC production," added Lawrence Goldstein, the executive vice president of Petroleum Industry Research Foundation.

Few oil economists expect to see a repeat of the oil-price crash of early 1986. Nevertheless, petroleum markets remain stubbornly soft despite recurring signals of a possible turnaround, including major gains in petroleum demand and supply interruptions, such as last week's explosion that destroyed the Piper Alpha platform in the North Sea.

Prices Decline Again

On average, world oil prices are down more than $3 a barrel since Jan. 1 to the lowest level since 1986. They fell again yesterday, some by as much as $1 a barrel. In volatile trading on European spot markets, prices of North Sea Brent crude dropped below $14 a barrel, down between 40 cents and 45 cents from day-earlier levels. On the U.S. futures market, West Texas Intermediate bounced off a 21-month low during the day to close at $14.72 a barrel, down only six cents.

However, major U.S. petroleum refiners—including **Phillips Petroleum** Co., **Sun** Co., **USX** Corp.'s Marathon Petroleum unit and **Coastal** Corp.—reduced their field postings for West Texas Intermediate crude by $1, to $14.25 a barrel. At such a posting, this U.S. benchmark crude is down nearly $6 a barrel from last year's peak price.

Significantly, OPEC crudes generally have dropped below $13 a barrel, which had been believed to be the "trigger" point at which Middle East producers would agree to some action to curb production. Dubai, an important United Arab Emirates crude, currently is being traded at $12.20 to $12.45 a barrel, depending on the delivery date.

Focus on Emirates

The Emirates are, in fact, a target of some OPEC efforts to restore production discipline. In recent weeks, the Emirates had proclaimed the country would ignore its OPEC quota of 948,000 barrels a day and would produce 1.5 million barrels a day.

As a result, Subroto, OPEC's new secretary-general and the former oil minister of Indonesia, plans to visit there to meet with the Emirates' president to discuss oil-market conditions. Yesterday, OPEC sources said Mr. Subroto won't arrive in the Emirates until after going to Saudi Arabia next week for the Hajj, the Moslem pilgrimage to Mecca.

Another effort that may be pursued by OPEC, as previously reported, would be a possible meeting of the price-monitoring committee. This group of five leading oil ministers is charged with monitoring world oil prices and can recommend a course of action including an emergency conference of OPEC. But yesterday, chances of a meeting of the price committee appeared to be fading.

"I don't think the meeting will take place," a senior OPEC official said. But he said several oil ministers will be in Saudi Arabia for the Hajj. "Maybe they will talk about oil," he said.

Saudi Arabia is one of the puzzles in the current outpouring of oil. Previously, the kingdom stuck to its OPEC quota of 4.3 million barrels a day, while urging others to adhere also to their production allotments. Now, there is some question as to whether the Saudis have become frustrated at the lack of restraint and whether the country, like the others, now sees the OPEC quotas as a floor for production, rather than a ceiling on output.

"The Saudis are aggressively discounting" prices, said Bryan Jacoboski, senior oil analyst at PaineWebber Inc.

Estimate Above Quota

It isn't unusual for Saudi production to be up in the first week of a month because of normal commercial commitments and then adjusted later. In the first week of July, however, Saudi Arabia exceeded its production quota by nearly one million barrels a day, according to Petro-Logistics of Geneva, Switzerland, which estimates total OPEC output at 20 million barrels a day.

"But it may be too early to draw the conclusion that Saudi policy is to produce more than quota on a regular basis," reports Petro-Logistics, which also puts Kuwait's output up sharply.

There are still differences between the current scramble for market share by OPEC's members and that which led to the 1986 price collapse. But one thing worrying oil economists this time is that Saudi Arabia, Kuwait and the Emirates seem to be going their separate ways. "The Persian Gulf players aren't coming together with a cohesive point of view," said Mr. Goldstein of Petroleum Industry Research Foundation.

Oligopoly Strategies and the Theory of Games

IN BRIEF: APPENDIX SUMMARY

Fill in the blanks to summarize appendix content.

Oligopolists (1)_____(are, are not) mutually interdependent. Strategies of one oligopolist (2)_____ (do not influence, influence) the strategies of other oligopolists. The theory of games analyzes the impact of decisions assuming various reactions on the part of rivals. The payoff matrix shows the expected gains or losses from each possible strategy (3)_____ (assuming firms are unconcerned with the reactions of rivals, given the reactions of rivals). Among many possible strategies, one possibility is to choose the strategy that (4)_____(minimizes, maximizes) the worst possible outcome of all possible strategies. This is known as the maximin strategy. If the decisions involve whether to cut price or leave it unchanged, and if each oligopolist hopes that a price cut will not induce rivals to also cut prices, a maximin strategy on the part of each firm that causes rivals to cut prices will result in a price war. Each firm (5)_____ (increases, loses) profit. This creates an obvious incentive to reduce the uncertainty by (6)_____ (colluding and agreeing to maintain, increasing) price.

VOCABULARY REVIEW

Write the key term from the list below next to its definition.

Key Terms

Theory of games
Payoff matrix
Maximin strategy

Definitions

1. _____: the strategy that maximizes the minimum (or worst) outcomes of all possible strategies.

2. _____: shows the gain or loss from each possible strategy for each possible reaction by the rival player of the game.

3. _____: analyzes the behavior of individuals or organizations with conflicting interests.

SKILLS REVIEW

Suppose there are two newspapers in a community-<u>The Times</u> and <u>The Daily</u>. <u>The Times</u> is trying to decide whether it should cut price. It expects to increase profits by 10% if <u>The Daily</u> does not react by cutting prices. If <u>The Daily</u> does match the price cut, it expects profits to fall by 4%. If <u>The Times</u> maintains price and <u>The Daily</u> cuts price, profits are expected to fall by 8%.

    a.   Set up the payoff matrix.
    b.   Assuming each firm employs the maximin strategy, what will <u>The Times</u>
         do? How will <u>The Daily</u> react? What are the long-run consequences
         for the local newspaper market?

SELF-TEST FOR MASTERY

Select the best answer.

1.   The theory of games is useful:

    a.   In understanding the operations of a monopolist.
    b.   When the decisions of one firm are unrelated to the decisions of
         other firms.
    c.   In understanding the behavior of monopolistic competitors.
    d.   In understanding the behavior of oligopolists when their decisions
         are mutually interdependent.

2.   The payoff matrix:

    a.   Shows the potential profits or losses associated with a given price.
    b.   Shows the gains or losses associated with various strategies given
         various reactions by rival firms.
    c.   Ranks profitable strategies in descending order.
    d.   Shows the relationship between oligopolistic profits and product
         price.

3.   When each rival employs the maximin strategy to protect the level of
     profits:

    a.   Monopolistic profits arise.
    b.   Price wars develop, resulting in a decrease in profits and an
         incentive to collude.
    c.   One oligopolist succeeds at the expense of the others and becomes the
         industry leader.
    d.   Profits are maximized only when average-cost pricing accompanies the
         strategy.

APPENDIX ANSWERS

In Brief: Appendix Summary

1. Are 2. Influence 3. Given the reaction of rivals 4. Maximizes 5. Loses
6. Colluding and agreeing to maintain

Vocabulary Review

1. Maximim strategy 2. Payoff matrix 3. Theory of games

Skills Review

a.

		Times	
		Reduce price	No change
Daily	Reduce price	-4%	-8%
	No change	+10%	------

b. If both firms pursue the maximin strategy, they will cut prices, thus reducing profits and likely starting a price war. In the long run, the firms might decide that collusion is necessary to reduce the uncertainty and to protect profits.

Self-Test for Mastery

1. a 2. b 3. b

15
Antitrust Policy and Regulation of Markets

CHAPTER CHALLENGES

After studying your text, attending class, and completing this chapter, you should be able to:

1. Describe how governments use the law and the courts to prevent establishment of monopoly positions through unfair business practices. Also, discuss antitrust laws and how they affect business behavior and mergers.
2. Explain the characteristics of natural monopoly firms and discuss alternative policies of government control over the prices such firms are permitted to charge for their products. Also, demonstrate understanding of the concept of "fair-rate-of-return" pricing.
3. Describe the impact of government policies that limit the freedom of sellers to choose their own prices and to enter markets. Also, discuss the impact of eliminating government controls on prices and competition in markets.

IN BRIEF: CHAPTER SUMMARY

Fill in the blanks to summarize chapter content.

The goal of antitrust policy is to prevent abuses of market power in less competitive markets and to prevent the monopolization of markets that are presently competitive. The first antitrust law was the (1)_____ (Clayton, Sherman) Act of 1890. The intent of the law was to prohibit activities that restrain trade. The (2)_____ (Clayton, Sherman) Act of 1914 identified specific business practices that restrict competition, such as price discrimination, tying contracts, interlocking directorates, and anticompetitive mergers via the acquisition of corporate (3)_____ (assets, stock). The Federal Trade Commission, established in 1914, regulates methods of competition and today it (4)_____ (targets deceptive and false advertising, is mainly interested in violations of U.S. pricing statutes). The Robinson-Patman Act of 1936 was intended to protect small retailers from unfair competition from chain and discount stores. The Celler-Kefauver Act of 1950 closed a major loophole in the Clayton Act by making illegal the acquisition of (5)_____(stock, assets) that lessens competition.

The antitrust laws have been interpreted in different ways by the courts over the years. In 1911, (6)_____(U.S. Steel, Standard Oil) was broken up because it engaged in practices considered to constitute an intent to monopolize. In 1920, (7)_____ (U.S. Steel, Standard Oil) had a high market share but was not dissolved because it was found that it did not use its size to limit competition. In effect, the (8)_____ ("rule of reason," relevant market rule) was established in which it had to be shown that the monopolist or firm with a very large market share was a "bad" monopolist--

engaging in anticompetitive activities. This interpretation held until the Alcoa case of (9)_____ (1926, 1945). Alcoa had a 90% share of its market. It was found to have not engaged in anticompetitive activities, but it was found guilty of monopolization and broken up because its expansion of capacity was viewed as an attempt to monopolize the market. This essentially reversed the rule of reason--market share alone was enough to be convicted of monopolization. Another major interpretation relating to market share had to do with the concept of the "relevant" market. Although du Pont had a monopoly in the production of cellophane, if the definition of the relevant market was broadened to include all flexible wrappings, it had a much smaller market share. Du Pont was found (10)_____(guilty, innocent) of monopolization. Similar considerations were relevant when the Justice Department dropped its antitrust case against IBM in 1982.

Are high market concentration and profits evidence of monopoly power? In many cases the answer is yes, but not always. For instance, a firm may have a large market share because economies of scale require a large production run. The large firm may be large because it offers a superior product. High accounting profits do not necessarily mean high economic profits because implicit costs are not considered in accounting profit. If firms face competition from abroad, even firms with large domestic market shares must contend with numerous foreign firms. This tends to (11)_____ (lessen, increase) market power and the potential for market abuses. Concentration ratios can be misleading in that a firm with a small national concentration ratio may have a high ratio in some local or regional markets, allowing it to exercise market power.

An important portion of the market share concentration in business today is the result of mergers. Mergers can be horizontal, vertical, or conglomerate. (12)_____ (Horizontal, Vertical, Conglomerate) mergers occur between firms that operate at a given stage of production, such as refining in the oil industry, whereas (13)_____ (horizontal, vertical, conglomerate) mergers are between firms that operate at different stages of production, such as oil exploration and refining. (14)_____ (Horizontal, Vertical, Conglomerate) mergers are between firms in dissimilar industries.

Where economies of scale dictate the existence of a single producer and where the good or service is considered vital, the government allows the existence of the single firm, but regulates its profit and hence the rates or prices that it charges. These firms are called (15)_____ (oligopolies, natural monopolies). Marginal-cost pricing for such a firm is (16)_____ (unworkable, desirable) because a firm experiencing economies of scale has marginal costs that are below average costs. A price set below average cost would not allow the firm to realize enough normal profit to attract sufficient funds for expansion and modernization. Federal and state regulatory commissions today require utilities to employ (17)_____ (marginal-, average-) cost pricing to ensure that a "fair" rate of return is earned. The intent of this regulation is to ensure enough normal profits to allow the continuation of a vital service, but to not allow the utility to earn economic profits at the consumer's expense.

Regulation by federal and state governments in some industries such as airlines, railroads, and trucking, has actually prevented entry of potential new firms and prohibited price competition. The commissions set up to regulate these industries had the intent to ensure the continuation of a vital service at stable prices and to prevent monopolization. But in controlling service routes, rate structures, etc., they (18)_____ (promoted, in effect prevented potential) competition. Several of these industries have been deregulated, resulting in generally lower prices to the public, but in the airline industry there is concern regarding the quality of service and the threat of oligopolization as the market stabilizes.

VOCABULARY REVIEW

Write the key term from the list below next to its definition.

Key Terms

Antitrust statutes	Rule of reason
Horizontal merger	Vertical merger
Conglomerate merger	

Definitions

1. _____: holds that acts beyond normal business practice that unduly restrain competition for the purpose of excluding rivals can be used to infer intent to monopolize an industry.

2. _____: seeks to prevent "unfair" business practices that give rise to monopoly power.

3. _____: a merger of a firm with its suppliers.

4. _____: occurs when competing sellers in the same market merge into a single firm.

5. _____: a merger of firms selling goods in unrelated markets.

SKILLS REVIEW

Concept: Antitrust laws

1. Identify the antitrust legislation designed to prevent each of the following activities.

   Law/Date
   a. _____ anticompetitive price discrimination
   b. _____ anticompetitive mergers resulting from the acquisition of corporate assets
   c. _____ anticompetitive mergers resulting from the acquisition of corporate stock
   d. _____ monopolization that results in a restraint of trade
   e. _____ false and deceptive advertising
   f. _____ chain stores taking over markets from independent retailers
   g. _____ tying contracts
   h. _____ interlocking directorates

2. Which antitrust cases are associated with the following?

   Case/Date
   a. _____ establishment of the rule of reason
   b. _____ market share itself or how it is acquired, whether or not the firm engages in anticompetitive activities, is evidence of intent to monopolize

232

c. _____ the "relevant" market must be identified in order to use market share as evidence of monopolization

d. _____ mere size itself is not an offense

3. List five reasons why the presence of high market share and profits may not be evidence of monopoly power.

a. _____

b. _____

c. _____

d. _____

e. _____

Concept: Regulation of natural monopolies

4. The figure below represents an electric power company located in a region in which it is the sole supplier of electricity.

a. Identify the unregulated monopoly price, output, and economic profits/losses. Price = $_____, output = _____ units, profit/loss = $_____

b. Suppose you have just been elected to be a state regulatory commissioner. Because you are aware that the net benefits to society are maximized where price equals marginal cost, you decide to impose marginal-cost pricing on the electric power company. Identify the new price, quantity, and profit/loss. Price = $_____, output = _____ units, profit/loss = $_____

c. An average-cost ("fair" rate-of-return) pricing scheme results in price equal to $_____, quantity equal to _____ units, and $_____ profit/loss.

d. Identify and discuss the problems associated with average-cost pricing.

Concept: Deregulation of regulated industries

5. List four effects of the Airline Deregulation Act of 1978.

a. _____

b. _____

c. _____

d. _____

SELF-TEST FOR MASTERY

Select the best answer.

1. Which of the following acts made it illegal to "restrain trade"?

    a. Sherman Act of 1890
    b. Clayton Act of 1914
    c. Federal Trade Act of 1914
    d. Robinson-Patman Act of 1936
    e. Celler-Kefauver Act of 1950

2. Which of the following acts prohibited specific anticompetitive business practices such as price discrimination?

    a. Sherman Act of 1890
    b. Clayton Act of 1914
    c. Federal Trade Act of 1914
    d. Robinson-Patman Act of 1936
    e. Celler-Kefauver Act of 1950

3. Under which act is false and deceptive advertising prohibited?

    a. Sherman Act of 1890
    b. Clayton Act of 1914
    c. Federal Trade Act of 1914
    d. Robinson-Patman Act of 1936
    e. Celler-Kefauver Act of 1950

4. Which of the following acts is designed to protect small independent retailers from large chain store operations?

    a. Sherman Act of 1890
    b. Clayton Act of 1914
    c. Federal Trade Commission Act of 1914
    d. Robinson-Patman Act of 1936
    e. Celler-Kefauver Act of 1950

5. Which act prohibits anticompetitive mergers resulting from the acquisition of a firm's assets?

    a. Sherman Act of 1890
    b. Clayton Act of 1914
    c. Federal Trade Commission Act of 1914
    d. Robinson-Patman Act of 1936
    e. Celler-Kefauver Act of 1950

6. The "rule of reason":

    a. Holds that monopolists must be reasonably competitive when dealing with smaller rivals.
    b. Was established in the Alcoa case of 1920.
    c. Holds that acts beyond normal business practice that unduly restrain competition for the purpose of excluding rivals can be used to infer intent to monopolize an industry.
    d. Holds that the entire market must be considered rather than just the relevant market.

7. The "rule of reason" was established in which of the following cases?

    a. Standard Oil case of 1911
    b. U.S. Steel case of 1920
    c. Alcoa case of 1945
    d. Du Pont case of 1956

8. The concept that mere size was not an offense was established in the:

    a. Standard Oil case of 1911.
    b. U.S. Steel case of 1920.
    c. Alcoa case of 1945.
    d. Du Pont case of 1956.

9. The concept of the "relevant" market was important in which of the following cases?

    a. Standard Oil case of 1911
    b. Du Pont case of 1956
    c. IBM case, which was terminated in 1982
    d. U.S. Steel case of 1920
    e. B and c

10. High market concentration and profit are not necessarily evidence of monopoly power because:

    a. Of the presence of economies of scale.
    b. The firm may simply produce superior products.
    c. A firm with a high domestic concentration ratio might nevertheless face significant competition from imports.
    d. High accounting profits do not necessarily mean high economic profits.
    e. All of the above.

11. A merger of two firms operating in different markets producing dissimilar goods is called a:

    a. Horizontal merger.
    b. Vertical merger.
    c. Multinational merger.
    d. Conglomerate merger.

12. A merger of two firms operating in the same market is known as a:

    a. Horizontal merger.
    b. Vertical merger.
    c. Multinational merger.
    d. Conglomerate merger.

13. If marginal-cost pricing is imposed on a natural monopolist, one that experiences declining average costs of production:

    a. The firm will earn only normal profits.
    b. The firm is induced to produce the level of output that maximizes society's net benefits.
    c. Losses are imposed on the firm.
    d. The firm will have trouble attracting equity funds.
    e. C and d.

14. Average-cost (or "fair" rate-of-return) pricing

    a. Allows the firm to realize normal profits but no economic profits.
    b. Results in losses that have to be made up with tax revenue.
    c. Results in the maximum net gain to society.
    d. Creates an incentive for the firm to minimize average costs.

15. Which of the following is incorrect with respect to average cost pricing?

    a. Average-cost pricing creates an incentive to be efficient and minimize average costs.
    b. Average-cost pricing results in prices greater than marginal cost, meaning that society would experience a net gain if more of the good could be produced at a lower price.
    c. Average-cost pricing results in the use of excess capital as a way of increasing the rate base in order to get higher rates or prices.
    d. None of the above.

16. Some transportation industries, such as airlines, railroads, and trucking, were regulated:

    a. Because violent unions required the government to intervene in order to establish stability.
    b. To ensure or guarantee service and to prevent the monopolization of the industry.
    c. Because such industries are considered natural monopolies.
    d. To avoid the destructive effects of price wars.

17. Regulation in the transportation industries resulted in:

    a. Price competition and freedom of entry and exit.
    b. Lower prices.
    c. The absence of both price competition and the freedom of entry and exit.
    d. The establishment of the FTC as the major oversight body in charge of reviewing rate structures.
    e. B and d.

18. The Airline Deregulation Act of 1978 has resulted in all but one of the following.

    a. A reduction in fares
    b. A more complex price structure
    c. An increase in the quality of service
    d. Increased entry to and exit from the industry

THINK IT THROUGH

1. Discuss the how the interpretation of the antitrust laws has changed over time and identify the important court cases associated with the changes.

2. Large market share and high profits are evidence of the exercise of monopoly power. True or false? Explain.

3. If perfectly competitive markets result in allocative efficiency, then why does the government grant exclusive operating rights to utilities? The government is in effect sponsoring a monopoly.

4.   Interstate trucking was deregulated in the 1970s, but many states continue to regulate intrastate trucking. Discuss the intent or objectives of regulatory commissions. Can you think of any reasons why some of the strongest objections to the deregulation of intrastate trucking often come from trucking firms with dominant market shares rather than small firms?

POP QUIZ   Read the news brief at the end of this chapter and answer the questions below.

Certain industries are exempt from antitrust legislation. The insurance industry was exempted in 1944 by the McCarran-Ferguson Act. Critics of the insurance industry argue that the exemption should be removed. Why? How might society benefit?

CHAPTER ANSWERS

In Brief: Chapter Summary

1. Sherman 2. Clayton 3. Stock 4. Targets deceptive and false advertising
5. Assets 6. Standard Oil 7. U.S. Steel 8. "Rule of reason" 9. 1945 10. Innocent 11. Lessen 12. Horizontal 13. Vertical 14. Conglomerate 15. Natural monopolies 16. Unworkable 17. Average 18. In effect prevented potential

Vocabulary Review

1. Rule of reason 2. Antitrust statutes 3. Vertical merger 4. Horizontal merger 5. Conglomerate merger

Skills Review

1.   a.   Clayton Act of 1914 b. Celler-Kefauver Act of 1950
     c. Clayton Act of 1914 d. Sherman Act of 1890 e. Federal Trade Commission Act of 1914 f. Robinson-Patman Act of 1936 g. Clayton Act of 1914 h. Clayton Act of 1914

2.   a.   Standard Oil (1911) b. Alcoa (1945) c. Alcoa (1945), du Pont (1956), IBM (suit terminated in 1982) d. U.S. Steel (1920)

3.   a.   Economies of scale require a large production run and may result in a lower price than if the industry was made up of several inefficiently sized firms.
     b.   The firm might produce a superior product.
     c.   Accounting profit is likely to be larger than economic profit.
     d.   The presence of foreign competition will likely result in more competition among firms having high domestic concentration ratios than among firms having lower ratios but no foreign competition.
     e.   A firm may have a low national concentration ratio but have a regional monopoly.

4.   a.   ag, ak, profit (fghi)
     b.   ac, ap, loss (cdno)
     c.   ae, am, 0
     d.   Average-cost pricing does not create an incentive for a firm to minimize average costs, but rather creates an incentive to

overcapitalize--to build an inefficiently sized plant to pad the rate base in order to win higher rates from the regulatory commission.

5.   a. Lower fares b. More complex fares c. Increased entry and exit d. Reduced quality of service

Self-Test for Mastery

1. a 2. b 3. c 4. d 5. e 6. c 7. a 8. b 9. e 10. e 11. d 12. a 13. e 14. a 15. a 16. b 17. c 18. c

Think it Through

1.   Standard Oil was found guilty in 1911 of monopolization and broken up. It engaged in business practices, in excess of those considered normal, that resulted in a restraint of trade. The "rule of reason" was established in which a firm could be found guilty of monopolization if it engaged in activities beyond normal business practices where the effect was to lessen competition. Although U.S. Steel was a firm with a large share of the market, in 1920 it was found innocent of monopolization because it did not engage in anticompetitive business practices. From 1920 until the Alcoa case of 1945, the interpretation of the antitrust laws was that size is itself not an offense, but anticompetitive business practices together with size were sufficient to show the intent to exercise market power. In 1945, this interpretation changed in the Alcoa case in that Alcoa was not found to have engaged in anticompetitive business practices, but was convicted of monopolization because of Alcoa's large market share and the way in which Alcoa's production capacity was acquired. The concept of the relevant market became important in the Alcoa case of 1945, the du Pont case of 1956, and the IBM case terminated in 1982. To be convicted of monopolization, the firm has to have a very high share in the relevant product market, not just a large market share in general.

2.   False. A large market share and high profits may many times indicate the exercise of monopoly power, but there are a number of reasons other than the exercise of market power why a firm could have a large market share and high profits. For instance, accounting costs do not include implicit costs and therefore accounting profits will likely always be higher than economic profits. A firm may have a low national market share but be a monopolist in regional or local markets. A firm with economies of scale may have a large market share in order to operate at an efficient level of production. Because of the scale economies, the firm may even charge a price lower than that charged by many small but inefficiently sized firms. A firm might have a large market share because of its reputation for quality and service.

3.   Utilities are natural monopolies--they realize significant economies of scale and require a high rate of production and hence a large market share in order to produce at low average cost. But they are still monopolies and will charge prices to maximize profits if unregulated. Their service or good is usually considered vital to the community. Regulatory commissions want to promote the continuation and stability of the utility's service or good, but they also want the cost advantages of a monopoly utility passed on to customers in the form of lower prices. Utilities must be allowed to earn at least a normal profit ("fair" rate of return) in order to attract equity funds for modernization and expansion. Therefore regulators choose a second-best option by imposing on utilities average-cost pricing rather than the socially preferable marginal-cost pricing.

4.   Objectives of regulation regarding the trucking industry include (a) ensuring the continuation of a vital service, and (b) avoiding price warring or monopolization that might threaten the availability of the regulated good or

service. Trucking regulation has been in the form of strict control over rates and service routes, thus prohibiting price competition and entry of new firms. Established firms, often having large market shares of the intrastate trucking business, are sheltered and protected by the very commissioners who are ostensibly acting in the public interest to promote lower rates and reliable and universal service. Thus the sheltered firm may have much to lose if the market is opened up to competitive pricing and entry.

Pop Quiz

The 1944 act exempting the insurance industry from antitrust prosecution and the 1980 prohibition against FTC investigation of the industry has given insurers license to operate together to jointly determine coverage and rates. Critics contend that the industry is a collusive oligopoly that in the mid-1980s dramatically cut liability coverage and raised rates. It is argued that the insurers were raising rates not because of mounting liability insurance losses, but because they were trying to increase profits. Although there are 1400 member insurers of the industry's trade association, only 8 to 12 of the 1400 effectively guide the "standards" established by the association. It is argued that these few insurers put undue pressure on the trade association to write into the standards certain restrictions such as pollution exclusions. It is also suspected that the insurers conspired to limit liability coverage and raise rates to induce state legislators to pass laws establishing maximum liability awards.

These critics further argue that the removal of the antitrust exemption would result in "...greater prudence at the companies and, ultimately, steadier competition in a broader array of products and price ranges." If, indeed, insurance companies are conspiring in the manner described in the article, subjecting them to antitrust prosecution would be desirable. Greater competition would likely result in greater product differentiation and product availability and would likely result in lower premiums or premiums that at least reflect past claims records.

Unaccustomed Risk

Insurers, Long Free Of Antitrust Curbs, Face Rising Challenges

Congress May Cut Immunity, And 19 States Are Suing; The Spark: Soaring Rates

Giant Firms' Dominant Role

By PETER WALDMAN
Staff Reporter of THE WALL STREET JOURNAL.

The insurance industry has long held a cozy place in the heart of Congress.

In 1944, lawmakers exempted insurers from federal antitrust laws, allowing the state-regulated companies to share data and jointly fix premiums and policy provisions. In 1980, Congress broadened that immunity by prohibiting the Federal Trade Commission from investigating even non-antitrust aspects of the industry, squelching what had been a useful source of consumer information.

In return, the giant companies have long contributed generously to congressional campaigns.

Now, however, Congress is making the industry squirm. Faced with mounting evidence that some insurers have used their antitrust immunity to raise prices and limit coverage, the judiciary committees of both houses are considering bills to curtail that exemption. The bills still face several hurdles, but they could be signaling a shift in the regulatory winds.

'Committed' Congressman

"I've never seen [Rep. Peter] Rodino as committed to an antitrust issue as this," says one longtime congressional aide describing the attitude of the New Jersey Democrat who heads the House Judiciary Committee.

Documents obtained by The Wall Street Journal corroborate how the industry has worked in concert—perfectly legally—to fix prices, set restrictive policy terms and even influence legislation by reducing the availability of insurance. Congress granted the industry special immunity in the McCarran-Ferguson Act of 1944, which exempts the "business of insurance" from antitrust prosecution, provided the states regulate it. The immunity, however, specifically excludes acts of "boycott, coercion or intimidation."

Specifically, the suits charge that Insurance Services Offices Inc., a trade group based in New York, succumbed to pressure from a small group of member companies in 1984 and rewrote industrywide policy standards to exclude coverage for pollution damages and for "retroactive" losses—losses occurring before the starting date of a policy. These exclusions amounted to an illegal industry boycott, the suits charge.

The ISO says it began revising general-liability policy terms as early as 1977. Through the late 1970s and early 1980s, however, high interest rates were spurring a price-cutting frenzy among insurers striving to sell more policies and thereby raise capital for investment. Under those circumstances, proposals to adopt coverage restrictions that might have driven down premium income didn't get far.

"We have serious doubts about the fundamental soundness of an approach which is likely to create market problems," Lyman Baldwin Jr., a senior vice-president of the Hartford Fire Insurance unit of ITT Corp., wrote in a 1979 letter to ISO President Daniel McNamara.

But by 1983, interest rates had dropped, and many insurers were reeling from the price war. That year, the industry's profits on general-liability insurance plunged to just $118 million from $847 million in 1979, according to the federal General Accounting Office. Efforts to revise policies and raise rates began in earnest.

The seemingly small changes in coverage for pollution and retroactive losses severely hurt some municipalities, small businesses and nonprofit organizations, which suddenly were paying much higher premiums for less coverage.

Milford, Mass., for example, had to pay $125,000 for liability insurance in 1987, four times more than in 1984. Yet, under its new policy, Milford had no coverage for pollution-related accidents, such as gas or sewage leaks, nor for any claims reported after the policy expired, even if the damages occurred while it was in force.

Likewise, the Texas Easter Seal Society, which has never been sued for any reason, watched its liability premiums soar nearly tenfold in the past three years, to $117,000, for reduced coverage. That additional money spent on insurance could provide therapy services for 100 disabled people, says Lila Coughran, the chapter's executive director.

Many federal and state regulators have testified against that exemption before Congress. "It is not cynical to suspect that at least some insurers have taken advantage of McCarran-Ferguson immunity to harm consumers," Daniel Oliver, the FTC chairman, told the Senate Judiciary Committee last year.

The Insurance Crisis

Though critics have charged for years

that the industry's exemption allows a small cartel of dominant companies to manipulate the market, their cries for reform went largely unheeded until the insurance crisis of the mid-1980s. Then, seemingly overnight, insurers slashed coverage, jacked up premiums on many types of policies—and sparked heated debate.

Insurers, backed by the Reagan administration, blamed the crisis on a rash of unexpected court decisions that greatly expanded their liability for certain claims. In particular, some judges in the late 1970s reversed prior industry and judicial interpretations and decided that damages from gradual, long-term pollution leaks were covered under standard liability policies. Courts also stunned insurers by upholding their liability for unpredictable, so-called cumulative injuries such as asbestosis.

Traumatized by these and other decisions, the industry said it needed to move fast to rewrite policies and raise rates. If the public didn't like that, the companies reasoned, it could press for changes in state tort laws.

Critics' View

But consumer groups, trial lawyers and some politicians—with their own axes to grind—or pockets to fill—blame the crisis not on the courts but on collusion. Insurers, these critics contend, were merely exploiting their antitrust exemption to increase profits after years of reckless price-cutting. In 1986, when, for want of liability insurance, cities were curtailing services, directors were quitting corporate boards and charities were folding, the attorneys general of California, Texas and some other states launched a joint investigation of a possible conspiracy.

Their findings, lodged in antitrust suits filed last spring by 19 states against 32 insurer defendants, focus on the industry's cooperative practices expressly forbidden for most industries. Even the defendants' version of the facts of the case depicts a small old-boy network of giant-company executives who, by cajoling and sometimes bullying the industry's main trade group, jointly limited the liability insurance available in the U.S.

Seeking Common Goals

In addition to the state suits, other cases show how insurers use the antitrust exemption to fight for common goals. In one instance, several insurers, including the Aetna Casualty & Surety unit of Aetna Life & Casualty Co. and Fireman's Fund Insurance Co., agreed to interpret Pennsylvania's no-fault auto-insurance law in a way that barred work-loss benefits for survivors of auto-accident victims. The state's supreme court ruled against that interpretation in 1980, but not before the insurers had saved millions of dollars in payouts.

Subsequently, in 1981, the husband of an

Unaccustomed Risk: Insurers Face
Possible Loss of Antitrust Shield

auto-accident victim filed an antitrust suit against the Pennsylvania insurers, but a federal district judge dismissed it. The judge ruled that the "wholly intra-industry agreement" was akin to rate-making and therefore exempt from the antitrust laws under the McCarran-Ferguson Act.

In another case, five medical-malpractice insurers, including St. Paul Fire & Marine Insurance Co. and Continental Casualty Co., simultaneously sent policy-cancellation letters to about 6,500 doctors, dentists, hospitals and clinics in West Virginia, after the state legislature passed a law they didn't like. Although that law, which was due to take effect in June 1986, limited awards in malpractice judgments, it also required insurers to base rates on policyholders' past claims records.

While both the law and the cancellations were pending, the state legislature, in a special session, repealed the rate-setting provision. West Virginia's attorney general filed an antitrust suit against the insurers and won a state-court order enjoining them from canceling policyholders en masse. The suit is still in litigation.

Multistate Suits

In the multistate suits, the states contend that four big U.S. insurers, along with several U.S. and British reinsurers, coerced the ISO into adopting the retroactivity and pollution exclusions in late 1984. Earlier that year, the ISO had issued standard forms without such restrictions.

Legal memorandums prepared for the ISO by its own attorneys indicate that some defendants used threats and other tactics to pressure the trade group into adopting the additional exclusions. Thomas Greene, a U.S. reinsurance broker who, the suits allege, was "enlisted" to pressure the ISO by defendants General Reinsurance Corp. and Hartford Fire Insurance, told the group's directors in June 1984 that without the added exclusions, the new policies "just [wouldn't] fly in the reinsurance market," according to an ISO memo. The broker added that there was "no chance" the reinsurers would "break ranks and give you what you want."

Reinsurers, many of whom are associated with Lloyd's of London, cover a portion of the risk underwritten by insurance companies and share in the premium. At the height of the alleged conspiracy, ISO documents show that senior ISO staff members traveled to London to confer with reinsurers about the new policy forms. At a dinner given by some British companies at London's posh Garrick Club, the ISO officials found their hosts "almost militant" in support of coverage restrictions in the new forms, the state complaints say.

ISO legal memorandums also show that in mid-1984, a senior ISO staffer tried to get Hartford Fire, a staunch proponent of added, industrywide restrictions, to compromise on less stringent provisions. But Hartford "refused to budge," according to the memorandums.

Coercion Denied

Hartford Fire and other defendants deny jointly coercing the ISO to adopt the narrower coverage. "We were proceeding to achieve Hartford's objectives for The Hartford"—to get a policy "tool we could use in a very difficult marketplace," says Stephen Martin, Hartford's vice president for government relations.

The defendants also argue that because any threats by reinsurers to boycott the U.S. market would have affected only other insurance companies, the state plaintiffs lack standing to sue. They add that the final policy revisions were scrutinized by state regulators, a few of whom rejected the new forms. Essentially, the defendants contend, the ISO did merely what state regulators expressly license it to do: It melded its members' needs and opinions into policy standards for the market.

"In any meeting where people have different views, it's only natural that people of similar views are going to line up and present their views together," says Robert Pike, the general counsel of defendant Allstate Insurance Co., a unit of Sears, Roebuck & Co.

But the very fact that such collusive actions may have been legal is exactly what makes the states' allegations so damning, industry critics say. Of the ISO's 1,400 member companies, the same eight to 12 insurers controlled its executive committee throughout the four years during which it rewrote the new liability forms, according to a complaint filed by Texas. Moreover, five of those same companies—Hartford, Aetna Life & Casualty, Liberty Mutual Insurance Co., Travelers Insurance Co. of Travelers Corp. and USF&G Corp.—served on all the major committees responsible for drafting the new policies, according to the complaint.

"Many companies don't have the re-sources to devote to the ISO function," Hartford's Mr. Martin explains.

ISO Staff's Influence Weak

Theoretically, the ISO's own independent staff is supposed to bridle committee members' self-interest. But ISO documents show how weak its influence really is. In the summer of 1984, for example, ISO President McNamara wrote a "staff recommendation" advising the trade group's leadership to postpone adoption of the coverage restrictions, pending further study. This suggestion was promptly rejected by the chairman of the ISO's Commercial Lines Committee, who feared more study would cause "unacceptable delay," according to ISO legal memorandums.

Critics of the McCarran-Ferguson immunity say the state suits, and other evidence of concerted action, show how the law has fostered a herdlike mentality in the insurance industry. Although few argue that its repeal will solve the underlying economic forces driving the industry's vicious market cycles, many critics contend that antitrust restrictions would spur greater prudence at the companies and, ultimately, steadier competition in a broader array of products and price ranges.

"Absent the implicit assumption that collective wisdom is favored over independent analysis, we would see less lock-step conformity," says John Van de Kamp, California's attorney general.

The congressional bills wouldn't wipe out the McCarran-Ferguson Act. Instead, they would repeal the industry's immunity for price-fixing and other "monopolistic" practices while safeguarding state regulation and certain "pro-competitive" joint activities such as collection of actuarial data. Overall, though, insurers would be held to a much tighter standard in matters of collusion.

That might not be so bad, some insurance executives say. Right or wrong, McCarran-Ferguson has become such an embarrassment that the exemption may well have outlived its usefulness, they concede. "We may have come to the time where the misconceptions that stem from the McCarran-Ferguson Act are more than the industry can tolerate," says the general counsel of one defendant in the state suits.

16

Market Failure and the Role of Government in Allocating Resources

CHAPTER CHALLENGES

After studying your text, attending class, and completing this chapter, you should be able to:

1. Explain the concept of an externality and show how externalities prevent free and competitive markets from allocating resources efficiently.
2. Describe the causes of externalities and show how government can help achieve efficiency by intervening in markets when externalities exist.
3. Explain the concept of a public good and show how provision of public goods by government can result in net gains to consumers.
4. Describe and evaluate social regulation by government to correct for market failure.

IN BRIEF: CHAPTER SUMMARY

Fill in the blanks to summarize chapter content.

Markets often fail to allocate resources efficiently. Governments may be able to correct the misallocation, thus enhancing society's well-being. Externalities are a common cause of market failure. (1)_____ (Positive, Negative) externalities are costs associated with the use of resources that are not reflected in price and are imposed on third parties--those other than the buyers or sellers of the good. Marginal social costs (2)_____ (are less than, exceed) the producer's marginal cost by the marginal external cost. Because profit-maximizing producers equate marginal cost and marginal revenue rather than the (3)_____ (higher, lower) marginal social cost and marginal revenue, too (4)_____ (much, little) is produced and market price (or marginal benefit) is (5)_____ (above, below) the marginal social cost. Thus society would benefit if (6)_____ (more, less) of the good were produced.

(7)_____ (Positive, Negative) externalities are benefits associated with the use of resources that are not reflected in price and accrue to third parties. Marginal social benefits (8)_____ (are less than, exceed) marginal benefits by the marginal external benefit. Since the market equates marginal benefit and marginal cost rather than the (9)_____ (lower, higher) marginal social benefit and marginal cost, the market (10)_____ (underproduces, overproduces) output, which results in a price that is too (11)_____ (high, low). It allocates too (12)_____ (many, few) resources to the production of the good. Society would gain if (13)_____ (more, less) of the good were produced.

Both negative and positive externalities result because (14)_____ (prices, property rights) either do not exist, are poorly defined, or are not enforced. Common property resources such as navigable rivers are often polluted in the absence of government regulation because no one individual has a property right to the river and therefore cannot prevent others from imposing

242

external costs such as pollution on users of the river. The producer of a positive externality does not have a property right to the (15)_____ (benefits conferred, costs imposed) on others. There is no way to be compensated for these external benefits by the market.

Government can potentially correct an externality by internalizing the externality--forcing the external costs of negative externalities on those that generate them and requiring those that benefit from positive externalities to compensate the producer of the benefits. A (16)_____ (corrective subsidy, corrective tax) can be used to internalize a negative externality. A tax equal to the marginal (17)_____ (social, external) cost of some action will cause the firm's marginal cost to equal the marginal social cost. A profit-maximizing firm will be induced to (18)_____ (cut, increase) output and (19)_____ (lower, raise) price. The adjusted market price now equals the marginal social cost, and the level of output is the level that maximizes the net gain to society from the use of resources. The tax revenue can be used to compensate those that have suffered as a result of the negative externality.

A corrective (20)_____ (subsidy, tax) can be used to internalize a positive externality. A (21)_____ (subsidy, tax) to consumers equal to the marginal external benefit would cause the marginal benefit or demand curve to shift to the higher marginal social benefit curve. Consumers would be induced to purchase (22)_____ (less, more) of the subsidized good, ultimately causing market price and quantity to (23)_____ (decrease, increase). Price would (24)_____ (rise, fall) to equal marginal social benefit, which would also equal marginal cost. Again society's net benefit is maximized. Alternatively, a subsidy could be given to the producer, causing the producer to (25)_____ (increase, decrease) output, but price would (26)_____(rise, fall) and be less than the marginal social benefit. Subsidies can be financed via specific taxes levied on the beneficiaries of the positive externality. If the beneficiaries cannot be easily identified or the extent of the benefit cannot be precisely measured, then general tax revenues can be used.

Public goods are (27)_____ (rival, not rival) in consumption, are (28)_____ (subject, not subject) to the exclusion principle, and are associated with (29)_____ (zero, positive) marginal costs of production. If the public good is provided to one, it is provided to all and at zero marginal cost. A profit-maximizing firm equating price and marginal cost would not produce a good at zero price. Even if a positive price could be charged, there is no way to exclude nonpayers from enjoying the benefits of the good. The market will therefore (30)_____ (produce, not produce) public goods. Yet these goods bestow benefits on society.

Government can reallocate resources from private goods production to public goods production by taxing the private sector and using the tax revenues to purchase or produce public goods. In order to maximize net benefits from the use of resources, government should produce public goods up to the point at which marginal (31)_____ (social, external) benefits (the sum of individual marginal benefits) equal the marginal social cost of providing the public good. Beneficiaries can be forced to share the cost of the public good through taxation. Taxation is necessary because of the (32)_____ (democratic process, free-rider problem). If some people pay for the public good and it is provided, it is provided to all whether they pay or not. Since people can receive the benefits without having to contribute, many people have to be coerced to pay, and this is done via a mandatory tax.

Markets also fail in other areas, such as providing the socially desirable levels of product safety, occupational safety, and racial integration. Often these failures stem from lack of information or faulty information used by consumers and producers in making decisions. (33)_____ (Antitrust legislation, Social regulation) is the use of government power to intervene in markets to achieve social goals such as product and occupational safety, the absence of discrimination, and an equitable distribution of income.

VOCABULARY REVIEW

Write the key term from the list below next to its definition.

Key Terms

Negative externality   Corrective tax
Marginal external cost   Corrective subsidy
Positive externality   Private goods
Marginal external benefit   Pure public good
Internalization of an   Free rider
    externality   Social regulation

Definitions

1. _____: the extra benefit that accrues to third parties when a positive externality is present.

2. _____: a tax levied on polluters to simulate a charge equal to the marginal external cost of their actions.

3. _____: an amount paid to consumers or producers of a good equal to the marginal external benefit of the good.

4. _____: a good that provides benefits to all members of a community as soon as it is made available to any one person.

5. _____: the extra cost imposed on third parties when a negative externality is present.

6. _____: a benefit associated with the use of resources that is not reflected in prices. Also called external benefit.

7. _____: a person who seeks to enjoy the benefits of a public good without contributing to its costs.

8. _____: a cost associated with the use of resources that is not reflected in prices. Also called external cost.

9. _____: the use of government power to intervene in markets so as to reduce the risk of accidents and disease and to achieve other social goals such as equality of opportunity for all persons.

10. _____: goods whose benefits are rival in consumption and for which exclusion of those who refuse to pay is relatively easy.

11. _____: occurs when the marginal cost or marginal benefit of a good has been adjusted so that market sale of the item results in the efficient output.

SKILLS REVIEW

Concept: Externalities and government intervention in markets

1. The diagram below represents the market for the propellant used in aerosol sprays. Aerosol use has been responsible for the release of fluorocarbons into the atmosphere, causing a depletion of the earth's protective ozone layer. It is speculated that this will increase the incidence of cancer.

Price per case

Quantity (millions of cases per year)

a. On the figure above, find the market price and quantity. Price = $_____, quantity = _____ cases
b. The production and use of aerosol propellants with fluorocarbons result in _____ externalities.
c. Assume that the marginal external cost is $10. Show the marginal social cost curve in the figure above. The efficient levels of output and price that maximize society's net benefits are _____ cases and $_____, respectively. The market _____ (overproduces, underproduces) the propellant and charges a price that is too _____ (low, high).
d. Society would be better off with an/a _____ in output and an/a _____ in price. Government could intervene to achieve this outcome by using a corrective _____ (tax, subsidy) equal to the marginal _____ (social, external) benefit of $_____. Show this graphically on the figure above.

2. An urban highway is built in a metropolitan area through a portion of the city previously having poor access to the central business district. The direct beneficiaries are the users of the highway, who include the residents in the proximity of the highway. But the presence of the highway results in the development of commerce and industry near its major intersections, which benefits the local residents whether or not they use the highway. Assuming that highways are produced by the private sector, the metropolitan market for highways is shown in the figure below.

Toll or price per lane mile

Quantity (lane miles per year)

a. On the figure above, find the market toll and quantity of lane miles.
    Price or toll = $_____, quantity = _____ lane miles
b. The production and consumption of highways result in a
    _____ externality.
c. Assume that the marginal external benefit of the highway per resident
    is $20. Also assume that there are 1000 residents. Show the
    marginal social benefit curve on the figure above. The efficient
    levels of output and price is _____ lane miles and
    $_____, respectively. The market _____
    (overproduces, underproduces) highways and charges a price that is
    too _____ (low, high).
d. The community would be better off with an/a _____ in lane
    miles and an/a _____ in tolls. Government could intervene in
    the market and use a corrective _____ (tax, subsidy) equal to the
    marginal _____ (social, external) benefit of $_____.
    Show this graphically on the figure above.
e. The _____ (tax could be levied on, subsidy could be
    given to) consumers equal to their individual marginal _____
    (social, external) benefit of $_____.

3. Advanced Question   The following equations are for a market in which a
    negative externality results from the production of the good.

        MB = a - bQ   (market demand)
        MC = c + dQ   (market supply)
        MEC = e   (marginal external cost)

        where   e is a positive constant
                        Q = output
                        P = price per unit
                        MC = marginal cost (private)
                        MB = marginal benefit = marginal social
                                              benefit

a. Find the market equilibrium price and quantity equations.
b. Find the equations for the socially efficient price and quantity.

246

c. Market price is too _____, and market quantity is too _____.
d. A tax per unit of the good equal to _____ will correct the misallocation of resources.

Concept: Public goods and government provision

4. A community's siren system for early warning of tornadoes is made available by the public sector rather than by the private sector.

    a.   Characteristics of   Characteristics of
         a Private Good   the Siren System

         (1) _____   (1) _____
         (2) _____   (2) _____
                                      (3) _____

    b.   Why is the early warning system provided by the government?
    c.   The efficient level or optimal provision of early warning sirens is at that level where _____ equals _____.

5. The following data represent the community's total social benefits (TSB) and total social costs (TSC) associated with an early warning system.

Sirens per Square Mile	TSC ($ thousands)	MSC	TSB ($ thousands)	MSB	Net Benefit ($ thousands)
0	0		0		
1	3		30		____
2	9	____	54	____	____
3	18	____	72	____	____
4	30	____	84	____	____
5	45	____	90	____	____
6	63	____	90	____	____

    a.   Complete the table and plot the marginal social cost and marginal social benefit curves on the figure below.

247

b.   The efficient provision of early warning capability is _____ sirens. MSC = $_____ , MSB = $_____. Show this graphically in the figure above.

c.   If there are 500 residents in the community and all benefit from the warning system, a voluntary contribution of $_____ per person could be used to finance the system.

d.   A voluntary contribution scheme will likely _____ (succeed, fail) because of the _____ problem. If a voluntary system will not work, how can the system be financed?

SELF-TEST FOR MASTERY

Select the best answer.

1.   A cost associated with the use of resources that is not reflected in price is known as a/an:

   a.   Positive externality.
   b.   External benefit.
   c.   Negative externality.
   d.   External cost.
   e.   C and d.

2.   A benefit associated with the use of resources that is not reflected in price is known as a/an:

   a.   Positive externality.
   b.   Public good.
   c.   External cost.
   d.   Negative externality.

3.   Which of the following must be added to marginal benefit in order to get marginal social benefit?

   a.   Marginal cost
   b.   Price
   c.   Marginal social cost
   d.   Marginal external benefit

4.   The sum of the firm's marginal cost and the marginal external cost is called:

   a.   Total cost.
   b.   Total marginal cost.
   c.   Marginal social benefit.
   d.   Marginal social cost.
   e.   Opportunity cost.

5.   The presence of negative externalities results in _____ output and a _____ price than is desirable for society.

   a.   More, higher
   b.   Less, lower
   c.   More, lower
   d.   Less, higher

6. The presence of positive externalities results in _____ output and a _____ price than is desirable for society.

   a. More, higher
   b. Less, lower
   c. More, lower
   d. Less, higher

7. Government can correct a negative externality by using _____, which result in a _____ market output and a _____ market price.

   a. Subsidies to consumers, larger, lower
   b. Corrective taxes, smaller, lower
   c. Corrective subsidies to suppliers, larger, higher
   d. Corrective taxes, smaller, higher

8. Government can correct a positive externality by using _____, which result in a _____ market output and a _____ market price.

   a. Corrective subsidies to consumers, larger, lower
   b. Corrective taxes, smaller, lower
   c. Corrective subsidies to suppliers, larger, lower
   d. Corrective subsidies to suppliers, larger, higher
   e. Corrective taxes, smaller, higher

9. Externalities are caused by:

   a. The absence of property rights.
   b. Poorly defined property rights, resulting in disputes.
   c. The lack of enforcement of existing property rights.
   d. All of the above.

10. A good whose benefits are rival in consumption and for which exclusion of those who refuse to pay is relatively easy is called a:

    a. Normal good.
    b. Rival good.
    c. Public good.
    d. Private good.

11. A good that provides benefits to all members of a community as soon as it is made available to any one member is called a:

    a. Pure public good.
    b. Rival good.
    c. Normal good.
    d. Private good.

12. Which of the following is not true of public goods?

    a. Public goods are not rival in consumption.
    b. Consumers cannot easily be excluded from the benefits of the good.
    c. Once the good is provided to one member of a community, it can be provided to each additional member at zero marginal cost.
    d. A system of voluntary financing of the public good can easily be established by those that benefit from the good.

13. The marginal social benefit of a public good:

a. Is the difference between the marginal benefit and marginal cost.
b. Is the sum of the individual marginal benefits enjoyed by all consumers.
c. Is the marginal social benefit less the marginal social cost of a private good.
d. Is the market demand curve for the public good.

14. Voluntary cost sharing by the beneficiaries of a public good will not work because:

a. Income is insufficient to justify the good.
b. Of the constant price problem.
c. Of the free-rider problem.
d. Of rising opportunity costs.
e. None of the above.

15. The market system produces _____ pure public goods.

a. Just the correct quantity of
b. Excess quantities of
c. Insufficient quantities of
d. No

16. Market failure results from all but one of the following,:

a. The absence of property rights
b. The lack of information
c. Inaccurate information
d. Profits that are too low

17. Social regulation refers to:

a. Specific antitrust statutes.
b. Corrective taxes and subsidies.
c. Government intervention in markets to achieve certain social goals, such as product and occupational safety.
d. Government's "big brother" attempt to interfere with the efficient functioning of the free enterprise system.

THINK IT THROUGH

1. Explain the following statement. "The socially optimal or efficient level of pollution is not at a zero level."

2. Explain why the market will likely underallocate resources to the prevention of contagious diseases.

3. If a negative externality results from the lack of property rights or the lack of enforcement of those rights, what role can government play in reducing or eliminating externalities?

4. Explain how government can improve the efficiency of the economy's use of resources by providing information that either is not provided by the market or is provided in insufficient quantities or is misleading.

CHAPTER ANSWERS

In Brief: Chapter Summary

1. Negative 2. Exceed 3. Higher 4. Much 5. Below 6. Less 7. Positive 8.
Exceeds 9. Higher 10. Underproduces 11. Low 12. Few 13. More 14. Property
rights 15. Benefits conferred 16. Corrective tax 17. External 18. Cut 19.
Raise 20. Subsidy 21. Subsidy 22. More 23. Increase 24. Rise 25. Increase
26. Fall 27. Not rival 28. Not subject 29. Zero 30. Not produce 31. Social
32. Free-rider problem 33. Social legislation

Vocabulary Review

1. Marginal external benefit 2. Corrective tax 3. Corrective subsidy 4. Pure
public good 5. Marginal external cost 6. Positive externality 7. Free rider
8. Negative externality 9. Social regulation 10. Private good 11.
Internalization of an externality

Skills Review

1.

a. $40, 6 million b. Negative c. 5.5 million, $45, overproduces, low
d. Decrease, increase, corrective tax, marginal external cost, $10

2.

a. $100,000; 45 b. Positive c. 50, $110,000; underproduces, low d.
Increase, increase, corrective subsidy, marginal external benefit, $20,000
e. Subsidy could be given to, marginal external benefit, $20

3.   a.   Setting the marginal benefit and marginal cost equations equal to
          each other and solving for quantity yields

              Q = (a - c)/(d + b)

251

Substituting the equilibrium quantity equation in place of Q in the marginal benefit equation gives the market price

$$P = (ad + bc)/(d + b)$$

b. Adding the MEC to the marginal cost equation gives

$$MC = (c + e) + dQ$$

Setting this equation equal to the marginal benefit equation and solving for P and Q as above results in

$$Q = (a - c - e)/(d + b)$$
$$P = (ad + bc + be)/(d + b)$$

Since e is a positive constant, the presence of negative externalities decreases the socially optimal quantity and increases the socially optimal price.

c. Low, high

d. Marginal external cost or e

4. a.

Characteristics of a Private Good	Characteristics of the Siren System
(1) Rival in consumption	(1) Nonrival in consumption
(2) Can exclude nonpayers	(2) Cannot exclude nonpayers
	(3) Zero marginal cost after provision to first individual

b. The siren system is provided by the public sector because a market cannot develop for a good that cannot be withheld from those that do not pay. Individuals have no incentive to purchase the good for a positive price because if it is purchased by one person, it is consumed by all others whether they pay or not.

c. Marginal social benefit, marginal social cost

5. a.

Sirens per Square Mile	MSC	MSB	Net Benefits
		($ thousands)	
0			0
1	3	30	27
2	6	24	43
3	9	18	54
4	12	12	54
5	15	6	45
6	18	0	27

        b.   4, $12,000, $12,000
        c. $24
        d.   Fail, free rider. A mandatory tax can be used to force the free
              riders to share the marginal social cost of the warning system.

Self-Test for Mastery

1. e 2. a 3. d 4. d 5. c 6. b 7. d 8. c 9. d 10. d 11. a 12. d 13.
b 14. c 15. d 16. d 17. c

Think it Through

1.   A good entailing a negative externality (pollution) is overproduced by the
market. A corrective tax equal to the marginal external cost will cause a
reduction in the market quantity of the good to the socially desired level but
will not necessarily result in zero pollution unless the tax provides
sufficient revenues for the cleanup of the pollution that continues to take
place as a result of the production of the good at the socially desirable
level. A producer in the long run might find that it is less costly to install
pollution abatement facilities than it is to pay the tax. But this involves a
comparison of the marginal benefits to the firm of pollution abatement with the
marginal costs of cleaning up the pollution. There is no reason to believe
that the firm's profit-maximizing level of pollution abatement will result in
zero pollution.

2.   The prevention of contagious diseases benefits the potential victims of
the disease in that they continue to be healthy and productive citizens.
Prevention also benefits society at large in that the economy and its
institutions function more fully and efficiently with healthy and productive
members of society than with individuals some of whom are out of the labor
force or are disabled or less productive because of diseases. Individuals in
the economy benefit from the economic activity and growth allowed in part by
the prevention of diseases even if those individuals would have never
contracted the disease. A market responds primarily to those who presently
have the disease and require treatment, not to potential victims and other
indirect beneficiaries. The marginal social benefits of disease prevention
exceed the marginal benefits reflected in the market. The market will
underproduce disease prevention.

3.   Government could reduce the incidence of externalities by clearly defining
and enforcing property rights where they exist and creating property rights
where they do not exist. The commonly owned environment--the atmosphere,
bodies of water, etc--is often polluted because no one individual has the right
to prevent some other individual from polluting it. Class action suits by
individuals without private property rights can enforce the collective property
rights of society. Also, government can sell property rights to the highest
bidder or allot them on the basis of many allocation schemes. Government can
exercise the collective property right in the commonly owned property by
passing legislation to impose costs on those that pollute. Government provides
a system of courts to resolve property right disputes and enforce property
rights.

4.   The positions of both the marginal social benefit and marginal social cost
curves depend in part on the accuracy and availability of information
regarding, among other things, the quality, reliability, and safety of the
good. The efficiency of consumer choice depends upon the availability of
complete and accurate product information. Producers likewise require data for
decisions but will produce only that information from which they can benefit.
The market will not provide the necessary information to assess the extent of
external costs or external benefits. By providing accurate, timely, and
comprehensive information in excess of that provided by the market, government

can improve the choices made by consumers, the decisions made by business, and the resource reallocation decisions of the government. Individual users of the government information benefit, but society as a whole benefits because of the more efficient use of scarce resources. Governments provide information on the climate, product safety, the purity and safety of drugs and food, contagious diseases, demographics, and the economy.

17

Externalities and the Environment: Policy Analysis

CHAPTER CHALLENGES

After studying your text, attending class, and completing this chapter, you should be able to:

1. Explain the costs and benefits of pollution control and the tradeoffs involved in government policies designed to protect the environment.
2. Discuss some of the problems involved in estimating the costs and benefits of pollution control and in choosing policies that result in the efficient level of environmental protection.
3. Describe actual and proposed policies designed to control pollution, and evaluate their impact on the environment and resource allocation.
4. Describe economic incentives to use natural resources and discuss policies that prevent overuse or depletion of these resources.

IN BRIEF: CHAPTER SUMMARY

Fill in the blanks to summarize chapter content.

Pollution is an economic problem. It results in benefits to the polluter in the form of lower costs of production but imposes external costs on third parties. Pollution control creates benefits by reducing or eliminating the damage to resources that otherwise would occur. But scarce resources are required to clean up the pollution. Society's net benefit from environmental protection is maximized if pollution control is produced up to the level where the marginal social cost of controlling pollution (1)_____(is less than, just equals) the marginal social benefit to society. This would be the "efficient" level of pollution control. There is no reason to believe that this level of control (2)_____ (would not, would) eliminate pollution completely. In other words, an (3)_____ (efficient, inefficient) level of pollution is associated with an efficient level of pollution control.

Estimating the marginal benefits and costs of pollution control is (4)_____ (an, not an) easy task. Estimates of the marginal benefits must include the value of the benefits associated with the reduction in the incidence of pollution damage to people, material inputs, natural resources, and agricultural resources. If pollution causes death, a value must be placed on the reduction in death due to pollution control. If pollution affects the productivity or useability of resources, a value must be placed on the reduction in the incidence resource damage. In short, estimates of marginal benefits (5)_____(may not be, are) reliable, and it is likely that the public sector will choose a level of pollution control that is (6)_____(efficient, inefficient). The market will underproduce pollution control (or overproduce pollution), and government can improve upon the market's allocation of resources even if government is unable to precisely "maximize" net benefits.

Emission control policies include emission charges, regulation, and the use of property rights. An/A (7)_____ (emission charge, property right) is a charge per unit of pollution. The fee or charge can be set at a level where a profit-maximizing firm will be induced to clean up its emissions to some socially-desirable level. If a charge is high enough, it will be less costly to treat the emissions than to pollute and pay the charge. An effect of the emission charge is that it (8)_____ (allows, does not allow) firms flexibility in the methods used to clean up their discharge. A firm (9)_____ (does not have, has) an incentive to clean up pollution in the most efficient manner.

(10)_____ (Emission charges, Regulation) have/has been the dominant form of pollution control in the United States. The Environmental Protection Agency places limits on the amount of a pollutant that can be emitted. For instance, drinking water has a prescribed set of maximum chemical contaminant levels. If the emission limits are exceeded, a firm faces fines. The disadvantages of regulation are that there are no incentives to employ the most efficient pollution abatement techniques. The regulations also are often (11)_____ (flexible, inflexible) because they (12)_____ (allow several methods, prescribe a particular method) of compliance. In addition, firms have an incentive to just meet the allowed contaminant levels (13)_____ (but not, and often) to reduce emissions beyond that level. Therefore, if the marginal social benefits of pollution control vary regionally, inflexible national pollution standards are (14)_____ (inefficient, efficient).

Another way to control pollution would be for government to assign, lease, or sell pollution rights. The right to pollute could be limited to achieve the socially-preferred level of pollution. If pollution rights are sold, the level of demand for those rights determines their price. Some firms would pay the price necessary to pollute, whereas others would find it less costly to clean up their emissions. (15)_____ (Disadvantages, Advantages) of pollution rights include the ability of government to strictly control the level of pollution through the issuance of pollution rights. In addition, firms would have the flexibility to purchase the right to pollute or to seek the most cost efficient method of pollution abatement.

The EPA has recently instituted new programs in an effort to make their regulations less rigid. In many regions of the country, emissions offsets are employed. A new firm entering a region has to pay other firms already established in the region to reduce their emissions. In this way, the increase in pollution caused by the new firm is "offset" by a decrease in the emissions of existing firms. This is equivalent to (16)_____ (emission charges, the sale of existing property rights). The EPA also allows firms to exceed some contaminant levels if they emit other contaminants in amounts less than the maximum allowable limits. In fact, a firm can earn credits for emitting less than the allowable limits. These credits can be used later if the firm wants to exceed the limits or can be sold.

In the short run, the amount of proven reserves of depletable resources depend upon (17)_____ (the profitability of extracting them and making them available to the market; the finite stock of resources). An increase in its price will bring forth a greater quantity of the resource, and in the long run will result in additional exploration and search for new deposits of the resource, resulting in increased (18)_____(supply, demand). In addition, price increases give users of the resource an incentive to substitute less expensive resources and to develop technologies not requiring as much of the resource or allowing the use of other resources. Demand for a resource may actually fall in the long run, as was the case with oil.

Resources may be overexploited in the short run, imposing external costs on society.   These external costs stem from a reduction in the future use of the resource. Common property resources are overused because (19)_____(regulations, property rights) have not been established for the use of the resource.

VOCABULARY REVIEW

Write the key term from the list below next to its definition.

Key Terms

Pollution   Depletable resource
Emission charges   Renewable resource
Emission standards   Common property resource
Pollution right

Definitions

1. _____: prices established for the right to emit each unit of a pollutant.

2. _____: a government-issued certificate allowing a firm to emit a specified quantity of polluting waste.

3. _____: a resource (such as the ocean) whose use is not priced because property rights for payment of services have not been established.

4. _____: a natural resource that can be restocked over time, such as fish, timber, and wildlife.

5. _____: a resource for which there is a given amount of known reserves available at any point in time.

6. _____: limits established by government on the annual amounts and kinds of pollutants that can be emitted into the air or water by producers or users of certain products.

7. _____: waste that has been disposed of in the air, in water, or on land that reduces the value of those resources in alternative uses.

SKILLS REVIEW

Concept: Efficient level of environmental protection

1. You are an administrator with the EPA and are responsible for determining the efficient level of pollution control (sulphur removal) from smokestack emissions of coal-fired electric power plants. These emissions result in acid rain and the deterioration of forests and lakes.

    a. What are some of the benefits associated with controlling smokestack emissions?

b. The costs of controlling the emissions is the _____ cost of the resources used for pollution control in their next-best use. Explain.

c. Below are total social benefits and costs associated with reducing sulphur emissions.

Percent Reduction Sulphur Emissions	Total Social Benefits ($millions)	MSB	Total Social Costs ($millions)	MSC	Net Benefit
0%	0		0		____
10	180	____	60	____	____
20	350	____	140	____	____
30	510	____	240	____	____
40	660	____	360	____	____
50	800	____	500	____	____
60	930	____	660	____	____
70	1,050	____	840	____	____
80	1,160	____	1,040	____	____
90	1,260	____	1,260	____	____
100	1,350	____	1,500	____	____

(1) Complete the table.
(2) Plot the marginal social benefit and marginal social cost curves on the graph below.

Dollars per percent change (milions of dollars)

Reduction in sulphur emissions (%)

(3) The efficient level of pollution control is a _____ % reduction where _____ equals _____ and _____ are maximized. MSB = $_____, MSC = $_____, Net Benefits = $_____.

(4) Identify the efficient level of pollution control on the graph above.

258

Concept: Pollution policies

2. Assume that for the example above each firm faces identical costs
    associated with removing a given percentage of sulphur from smokestack
    emissions. Below are pollution control data for a representative electric
    power company.

Sulphur Reduction Percent	Units	Total Cost ($thousands)	MC per Unit Removed
0%	0	0	
10	50	25	_____
20	100	60	_____
30	150	105	_____
40	200	160	_____
50	250	225	_____
60	300	300	_____
70	350	385	_____
80	400	480	_____
90	450	585	_____
100	500	700	_____

a. Complete the table.
b. Plot the firm's marginal cost of pollution removal on the following
    graph.

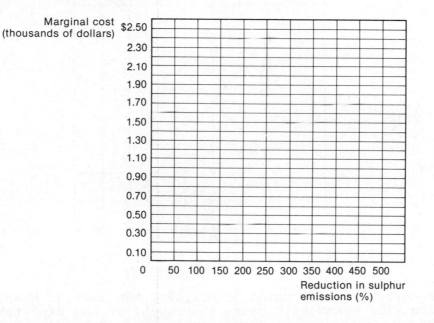

c. From question 1, it was found that the socially-desirable level of
    sulphur reduction was _____ %. For the power company above, this
    means reducing sulphur emissions by _____ units. An emission
    charge of $_____ would induce the power company to reduce
    emissions to the efficient level. Explain.
d. Show the emissions charge on the figure above and identify the
    efficient level of pollution (emission of sulphur).
e. If, because of new and more accurate estimates of the marginal social
    benefits of emission control, the EPA decided to reduce emissions
    further, it could _____ the emission charge.

3. List three advantages of using emissions charges as a means of controlling pollution.

    a. _____

    b. _____

    c. _____

4. List three disadvantages associated with regulation as a means of controlling pollution.

    a. _____

    b. _____

    c. _____

5. List two advantages associated with the assignment or sale of property rights as a means of controlling pollution.

    a. _____

    b. _____

Concept: Depletable and renewable resources

6. The market for oil, a depletable resource, is shown in the figure below.

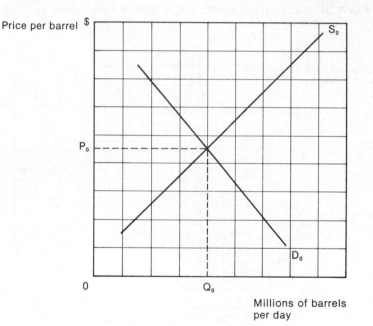

    a. At the current market price of oil, P_0, the current quantity of oil demanded will eventually cause the supply of the depletable resource, oil, to _____. Show graphically. This causes the price of oil to _____.

    b. The _____ in the price of oil will, in the long run, likely result in an/a _____ in supply, thus causing the market price to _____. Explain.

    c. How will consumers of oil react in the long run to the increase in the price of oil today, and what are the implications for the market price and quantity?

7.   The marginal benefits associated with catching fish from a common-property lake (one in which property rights do not exist) is shown below.

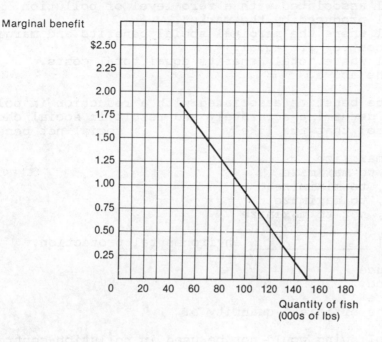

Marginal benefit

Quantity of fish
(000s of lbs)

a.   What quantity of fish will fishermen remove from the lake? _____ lbs.   Why?
b.   In order to maintain a given quantity of fish for future fishermen, a maximum catch of 80,000 lbs would leave a reproduction stock of fish just large enough to achieve future desired levels of fish production.   The current catch of _____ lbs represents an _____ (overuse, underuse) of the renewable resource.   Explain how property rights could be used to correct the problem.
c.   Show on the graph above the effect of using property rights to correct the inefficient use of the lake.

SELF-TEST FOR MASTERY

Select the best answer.

1.   Pollution is an/a:

   a.   Public good.
   b.   Negative externality.
   c.   Positive externality.
   d.   Opportunity cost.

2.   An emission creates pollution :

   a.   All of the time.
   b.   When the efficient level of pollution is reached.
   c.   When the emission causes damage to resources.
   d.   If it is emitted into the atmosphere.

3. The efficient level of pollution control is :

    a. That level associated with a zero level of pollution.
    b. That level produced by the market.
    c. That level where the marginal social benefits and marginal social costs of control are equal.
    d. At a level where total benefits equal total costs.
    e. None of the above.

4. Estimates of the benefits associated with a reduction in pollution are _____ to determine accurately and result in social choices regarding pollution control that are likely _____ social net benefits.

    a. Easy, to maximize
    b. Easy, not to maximize
    c. Difficult, to minimize
    d. Difficult, to maximize
    e. Difficult, not to maximize

5. The market will _____ environmental protection.

    a. Underproduce
    b. Not produce
    c. Overproduce
    d. Produce the efficient quantity of

6. Which of the following would not be used in pollution control?

    a. Corrective subsidies
    b. Regulation
    c. Emission charges
    d. Property rights

7. Which of the following is considered an advantage of emission charges?

    a. The charge can be set at a level to induce a profit-maximizing firm to either clean up or restrict pollution to the desired level.
    b. The firm has an incentive to employ the most efficient technique of pollution cleanup.
    c. Charges allow flexibility by firms in various regions to deal with the pollution problem in the most appropriate way.
    d. All of the above.

8. The predominant method of pollution control in the United States:

    a. Is regulation.
    b. Is emission charges.
    c. Is property rights sales.
    d. Is corrective taxes.

9. Regulation as a means of eliminating or reducing pollution:

    a. Is efficient because it results in the maximum net benefits to society.
    b. Is inefficient because it is often inflexible, requiring a single method of compliance rather than allowing the firm to seek the cost efficient method of pollution abatement.
    c. Is effective because it creates incentives by firms to reduce pollution by more than the allowable limits.
    d. Is the only practical method of pollution control when the point

source of pollution can be identified and the emission can be easily measured.

10. Common property resources are often polluted:

    a. Because emission charges are set too low.
    b. Because regulation needs to be extended to include more than privately owned property.
    c. Because of the absence of property rights.
    d. Because of industrialization.

11. The efficient level of pollution control can be achieved by imposing an/a_____ on the polluter _____ the polluter's marginal cost of pollution cleanup at the socially-desired level of pollution reduction.

    a. Regulation, increasing
    b. Regulation, decreasing
    c. Corrective subsidy, greater than
    d. Emission charge, greater than
    e. emission charge, equal to

12. The EPA's emission offset is equivalent

    a. to an emission charge.
    b. to a subsidy.
    c. to a tax.
    d. In effect to a sale of property rights.

13. Under which EPA program can a firm earn credits for emitting less than the allowable limits of pollution? The credits can be used by the firm to exceed the limits in the future or can be sold to other firms.

    a. Emission charge
    b. Emission offset
    c. The "bubble"
    d. Leasing of property rights

14. The supply of proven reserves of a depletable resource depends

    a. Upon the profitability of extracting the resource and making it available to the market.
    b. Exclusively upon the technological ability to extract the resource.
    c. Only on the finite supply of the resource.
    d. On the reserves presently being mined and the yet undiscovered reserves.

15. Other things constant, the supply of a depletable resource will in time _____, causing the price of the resource to _____, which in turn causes new exploration and the use of new extraction techniques and in the long run causes the supply of the resource to_____.

    a. Increase, rise, increase
    b. Increase, fall, decrease
    c. Decrease, rise, decrease
    d. Decrease, rise, increase
    e. Increase, fall, increase

16. Which of the following property resources are likely to be overused?

    a. A private lake
    b. Your backyard

        c.   A rancher's stock pond
        d.   Ocean fisheries

17. Common property resources are overexploited because:

        a.   Of the absence of regulation.
        b.   Of the absence of corrective subsidies.
        c.   Of the absence of property rights.
        d.   Of competing regional interests.
        e.   None of the above.

THINK IT THROUGH

1.   An environmentalist might argue that any emissions beyond that which can
be safely absorbed by the natural environment reduces society's well-being. Do
you agree? Explain.

2.   Discuss the dominant approach to pollution control in the United States.
What alternative approaches could be used? What are the advantages of these
other methods of pollution control?

3.   Can you think of any reason why it is necessary for federal and state
governments to "manage" wildlife populations? Explain. What alternatives
could be employed other than game limits?

CHAPTER ANSWERS

In Brief: Chapter Summary

1. Just equals 2. Would 3. Efficient 4. Not an 5. May not be 6.
Inefficient 7. Emission charge 8. Allows 9. Has 10. Regulation 11.
Inflexible 12. Prescribe a particular method 13. But not 14. Inefficient
15. Advantages 16. The sale of existing property rights 17. The profitability
of extracting them and making them available to the market 18. Supply 19.
Property rights

Vocabulary Review

1. Emission charges 2. Pollution right 3. Common property resource 4.
Renewable resource 5. Depletable resource 6. Emission standards 7. Pollution

Skills Review

1.   a.   A reduction in sulphur emissions will reduce the incidence of acid
           rain, which will reduce the deterioration of lakes and forests. The
           benefits of controlling sulphur emissions are the commercial and
           recreational values of lakes and forests, which would have otherwise
           diminished as a result of pollution.
      b.   Opportunity. Controlling pollution involves the use of scarce
           resources that have value in alternative uses.

c. (1)

Sulphur Reduction	MSB	MSC ($ millions)	Net Benefits
0%			$ 0
10	18	6	120
20	17	8	210
30	16	10	270
40	15	12	300
50	14	14	300
60	13	16	270
70	12	18	210
80	11	20	120
90	10	22	0
100	9	24	-150

(2)

(3) 50, MSB, MSC, Net Benefits; $14 million, $14 million; $300 million

(4) See figure above.

2. a.

Units	MC ($ thousands)
0	
50	0.5
100	0.7
150	0.9
200	1.1
250	1.3
300	1.5
350	1.7
400	1.9
450	2.1
500	2.3

b.

c. 50, 250; $1,300. As long as the charge exceeds the marginal cost of cleanup, a profit-maximizing firm will treat the effluent rather than pollute and pay the charge. If marginal cost exceeds the emission charge, the least-cost strategy would be to pollute and pay the charge. Therefore, a firm has an incentive to treat its discharge up to the point at which the emission charge equals the marginal cost of pollution treatment.

    d.   See figure above.

    e.   Increase

3.   a.   Emission charges can be set a level to achieve the desired level of pollution reduction.

    b.   Firms have the flexibility to employ techniques of pollution treatment that best fit their unique situation.

    c.   Firms have an incentive to minimize costs of cleanup that improve the economy's resource allocation.

4.   a.   Regulations are often inflexible requiring a single method of compliance rather than allowing the firm to seek the most cost-efficient solution.

    b.   Firms have no incentive to reduce pollution below the emission standards set by the EPA.

    c.   Regulations that are uniform nationally do not allow for regional variations in the marginal social benefits of pollution control.

5.   a.   Issuance of property rights or government certificates granting the right to pollute can be sold or issued in an amount that will limit pollution to the socially-desired level.

    b.   A market for these limited rights will develop in which some firms will find it more profitable to treat their effluent before discharge than to pay the market price for the right to pollute. Thus firms have an incentive to minimize costs associated with reducing emissions.

6.   a.   Decrease; increase

    b.   Increase, increase, fall. In the long run, there will be more exploration as a result of the higher prices, and new extraction technologies will likely be employed both of which increase the supply of oil. Other things being constant, this will reduce the price of oil.

    c.   Users of resources respond to rising prices by substituting relatively less costly resources and developing production techniques or products allowing the use of more plentiful and less costly resources. As in the case of oil, the higher short-run price of oil causes a movement up the demand curve in the short run, but it will also shift the demand curve leftward in the long run, causing long-run market price and quantity to fall.

7.   a.   150,000 lbs. With no cost or price associated with the use of the resource, fishermen will catch fish up to the point where their total

benefits are maximized, that is, where the marginal benefit curve intersects the quantity axis at a level of zero marginal benefits.

b. 150,000 lbs, overuse. Government certificates allowing the right to extract 80,000 lbs of fish annually could be sold. Assuming all benefits associated with fishing are private and there are no social goals involved other than preventing the overuse of the resource, the property rights scheme will result in the highest and best use of the resource (assuming competitive markets).

c.

Self-Test for Mastery

1. b 2. c 3. c 4. e 5. a 6. a 7. d 8. a 9. b 10. c 11. e 12. d 13. c 14. a 15. d 16. d 17. c

Think it Through

1. Emissions are a by-product of production. The production of goods benefits society. But if emissions result in pollution, there is an external cost that is not reflected in the firm's costs of production. The firm will allocate too many resources to the production of the good. It is "efficient" to require the firm to reduce pollution only up to the level that maximizes social net benefits. Requiring the firm to reduce pollution to zero will likely mean that the opportunity costs of the pollution control resources will exceed the benefits to society from the reduction in pollution.

2. Regulation is the dominant method of pollution control in the United States. Emissions standards are established for various pollutants, and fines are imposed if the standards are violated. The regulations tend to be inflexible and do not allow firms to respond in the most efficient manner to emission reduction. Emission charges could be used giving firms the incentive to seek the most cost efficient method of pollution reduction. They are flexible and can vary by firm and region. Property rights could be established and sold, giving those in the market for pollution rights the incentive to seek the least-cost solutions to pollution reduction. The quantity of those rights can be set to achieve the desired level of pollution.

3. It is necessary to regulate or manage wildlife populations because of the fear that breeding stocks would eventually be depleted, reducing the commercial and recreational values associated with hunting and fishing for future generations. Private landowners can prevent excessive hunting--they have a legal remedy. Public lands and lakes are common property resources for which no individuals own property rights. In the absence of government involvement, public lands would be overhunted and public lakes would be overfished as individuals hunt and fish to the point where their marginal benefits equal zero. This assumes that no price or any other cost is associated with the use of the resource.

The traditional approach to preventing overexploitation of wildlife populations is by regulation and establishing game limits. If the limits are exceeded, fines are imposed. Property rights are used to a limited extent. Certain hunting grounds may be opened only to a limited number of hunters. The rights to hunt are generally allocated on a lottery basis rather than sold in markets. User charges are used in the form of a license or stamp fee, but these are inflexible in the sense that they are not set to achieve specific game limits for each given species of game. If there are no social goals other than preventing the overexploitation of wildlife populations, a market for property rights or a hunting or fishing fee similar in concept to emission charges would achieve the desirable level of wildlife populations; furthermore, this would achieve it more efficiently than the current system of game limits and fines.

18

Subsidizing Agriculture and Industries: The Economics of Special-Interest Groups

CHAPTER CHALLENGES

After studying your text, attending class, and completing this chapter, you should be able to:

1. Discuss special interest groups, their goals, and the impact on prices and resource allocation of programs that benefit these interests.
2. Describe the process of rent seeking in which people compete for government subsidies and other programs that increase their incomes.
3. Evaluate the impact of agricultural policies that subsidize farmers in the United States.

IN BRIEF: CHAPTER SUMMARY

Fill in the blanks to summarize chapter content.

(1)_____ (Special interest groups, Lobbying associations), such as in agriculture, seek expenditures or special benefits from government that result in an increase in income. The costs of the benefits are dispersed over many millions of taxpayers and add little to a taxpayer's tax liability. Therefore, special interest legislation often encounters little resistance from the general public. Many individuals seek to use the power of government to increase their earnings above their opportunity costs. These people are (2)_____(income, rent) seekers. (3)_____(Wages, Rents) are receipts in excess of opportunity costs that can be created by government by limiting the right to perform a given activity. Agricultural allotments and exclusive franchises are created by government policy and have the effect of (4)-_____(decreasing farm incomes, creating rents).

Agriculture is a major special interest group in the United States. In 1933, the (5)_____(Agricultural Adjustment Act, Farm Price Support Act) was passed, controlling acreage in both production and prices. The primary goal of the Act was to prevent surpluses of agricultural commodities in order to keep prices and framers' incomes from falling. More specifically, the goal was to keep the purchasing power of the farmers' income from falling. This is accomplished if the price of agricultural products rise at a rate fast enough to compensate for the (6)_____(cost increases associated with producing the commodities; rise in the prices of the goods and services consumed by farmers). This is known as (7)_____(parity, a price support). As of the mid-1980s, the parity price ratio was at an all time (8)_____(low of under 60%, high of just over 90%).

Government price supports and acreage control programs are intended to increase farm incomes. Government agricultural price supports increase farm incomes but result in (9)_____ (shortages, surpluses) if the price supports exceed market prices. Prices are supported through the loan support program through which a farmer can borrow from the government at a specified price per bushel.

The agricultural commodity is used as collateral for the loan. The loan rate is generally set (10)_____(below, above) the market price per bushel. The farmer can choose to let the government keep the grain or repay the loan. The farmer will repay the loan only if the market price (11)_____(exceeds, is less than) the loan rate. Acreage control programs involve payments to farmers to (12)_____(expand, take land out of) production. The idea is to (13)_____(reduce, increase) supply and to keep market price, and hence farm incomes, at a higher level.

The government holds a large portion of the grain that it acquires off the market to prevent depressing prices and incomes. There are large storage costs and other costs associated with reducing these stocks of commodities. The (14)_____ (Target Price, Payment-in-Kind) program was an attempt to control farm production and to reduce government stocks of grain at the same time. Farmers that took acreage out of production were paid in kind with the government's stock of commodities.

Current methods of supporting farm incomes include (15)_____ (target prices, payment-in-kind) and direct subsidies. Target prices are government guaranteed prices. Farmers are generally required to restrict acreage in order to qualify for the Target Price program. If the guaranteed price exceeds the market price, farmers sell all of their output at the market price and the difference between the market and target price is made up by the government. Surpluses (16)_____ (develop, do not develop), but the acreage restrictions (17)_____ (do not necessarily, necessarily) limit or fix supply. The program, in effect, transfers income from taxpayers to farmers. Target prices result in (18)_____ (higher, lower) market prices than with traditional farm policies, but prices are not necessarily lower than would prevail in a competitive market.

Government policies can benefit special interest groups with direct subsidies and tax breaks. Subsidies increase the market price and quantity of the subsidized good if given to (19)_____ (consumers, producers), but they decrease market prices if given to (20)_____ (consumers, producers). The net price paid by consumers and received by producers is exactly the same, regardless if subsidies are given to producers or consumers. Both consumers and producers of the subsidized good benefit, as well as those that supply specialized inputs to the subsidized industry.

In addition to direct payments, subsidies can be in the form of (21)_____ (excise taxes, tax preferences). Certain activities, such as home ownership, are given preference in the tax code, which in effect "subsidizes" the activity through a lower tax liability. The losses in government tax revenues from the tax breaks are called (22)_____(tax expenditures, tax losses). Tax preferences benefit both buyers and sellers in the preferred markets, including the resource suppliers to those markets.

Some subsidies are "hidden" because they indirectly benefit certain groups. Examples of "hidden" subsidies include (23)_____ (agricultural loan supports, government loan guarantees) and government-provided insurance (flood insurance, for example). By transferring some of the risks associated with production in the private sector to the public sector, in effect the government is subsidizing business growth and development.

VOCABULARY REVIEW

Write the key term from the list below next to its definition.

Key Terms

Special interest group   Economic rents
Rent seeking   Parity
Parity price ratio   Target price
Acreage control program   Tax credit
Tax preference   Tax expenditure

Definitions

1. _____: an organization that seeks to increase government expenditures or induce government to take other actions that benefit particular people.

2. _____: the ratio of an average of the prices of goods sold by farmers to an average of the prices of goods on which farmers spend their incomes.

3. _____: an exemption, deduction, or exclusion from income or other taxable items in computing tax liability.

4. _____: the idea that the prices of agricultural commodities must rise as fast as the prices of goods and services on which farmers spend their incomes.

5. _____: a reduction in the tax liability for a person or corporation making certain purchases or engaging in certain activities.

6. _____: the process by which people compete to obtain government favors that increase the economic rents they can earn.

7. _____: guarantees sellers a minimum price per unit of output.

8. _____: earnings that exceed the opportunity cost of an activity.

9. _____: provide cash payments to farmers who agree to take some of their land out of production for certain crops.

10. _____: the losses in revenue to the federal government as a result of tax breaks granted to individuals and corporations.

SKILLS REVIEW

Concept: Special interest programs--Agriculture

1. The diagram below represents a market for an agricultural commodity in the absence of government intervention.

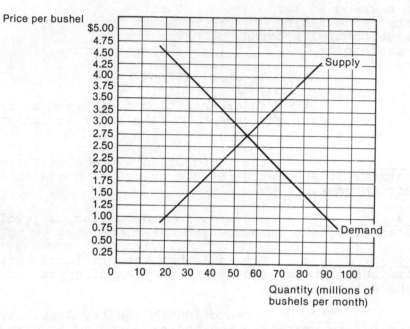

Price per bushel

Quantity (millions of bushels per month)

a. The current market price and quantity are $_____ and _____ bushels, respectively. Assume that the current market price results in a parity price ratio of 100%.

b. Because of improvements in production techniques, the supply of the commodity increases 10 million bushels at each price. Show this in the graph above and label the new supply curve, S1. After the change in supply, market price and quantity are $_____ and _____ bushels, respectively. Assuming all other prices are unchanged, the parity price ratio _____ (increases, decreases), which means that the farmers' purchasing power has _____ (increased, decreased).

c. Assume that farmers are able to win legislation ensuring a parity price ratio of 100%. This is accomplished through a commodity loan program that effectively establishes a price support. The supported price must equal $_____.   At the supported price, quantity demanded equals _____ bushels and quantity supplied equals _____ bushels resulting in a _____ (shortage, surplus) of _____ bushels. Show graphically in the figure above.

d. The cost to the taxpayer of the _____ (shortage, surplus) is $_____. Shade in the area representing that cost in the figure above.

e. The price support program results in _____ prices to consumers and _____ taxes incurred or_____ government services received by society.

f. An acreage restriction program could also be used to achieve a price sufficient to yield a parity price ratio of 100%. How much would supply have to be reduced at each price? _____ bushels. This program results in either _____ taxes or _____ government

272

services and _____ prices to consumers as well as _____ (shortages, surpluses).

2. The market below is for an agricultural commodity for which there is no government intervention.

Price per bushel

Quantity (millions of bushels per month)

a. The current market price and quantity are $_____ and _____ bushels, respectively.
b. Because the market price is considered by farmers to be too low, farm lobbies are able to win special interest legislation guaranteeing a price per bushel--a target price which is above the prevailing market equilibrium price. To qualify for the program, farmers must restrict acreage. Suppose the acreage restriction phase of the program reduces quantity supplied at each price by 25 million bushels. Show the new supply curve in the figure above and label it, S1. Market price _____ to $_____ and market quantity _____ to _____ bushels.
c. At a target price of $4 per bushel, farmers will produce and make available to the market _____ bushels and will receive a market price per bushel of $_____ and a subsidy per bushel of $_____. Show in the figure above. Consumers will pay a price of $_____, and taxpayers will pay a total subsidy of $_____. Quantity demanded will _____ quantity supplied.
d. As compared to price supports or acreage restriction programs, the Target Price program results in a _____ price to the consumer. As compared to a competitive market without government intervention, the Target Price program above results in _____ price to the consumer.
e. Target price programs, in effect, transfer income from _____ to _____.

273

Concept: Effects of subsidies, tax breaks

3.   The diagram below represents a competitive market for a good.

Price per unit

Quantity (thousands of
units per week)

a.   A subsidy of $1 per unit given to consumers results in a/an
      _____ in demand. Show in the diagram above.
b.   Market price _____ to $_____ and market quantity _____
      to _____ units. The net price (after deducting the subsidy) to
      the consumer at the new market quantity is $_____.
c.   Given the initial demand curve, D, show the effect graphically in the
      diagram if the $1 subsidy is given to producers instead of consumers.
d.   Market price _____ to $_____ and market quantity
      _____ to _____ units. The net price (after the subsidy
      is added) received by the producer is $_____.
e.   Subsidies to consumers, as compared to subsidies to producers, result
      in _____ market prices. The net price paid by consumers and
      the net price received by producers are _____ for
      subsidies to consumers or for subsidies to producers.

4.   List two indirect subsidies and give an example of each.

      a. _____
      b. _____

5.   Give two examples of hidden subsidies.

      a. _____
      b. _____

274

SELF-TEST FOR MASTERY

Select the best answer.

1. Special interest groups are composed of individuals that try to use the power of government to increase incomes above the opportunity cost of their activities. These individuals are:

   a. Acting in society's best interest.
   b. Called free riders.
   c. Rent seekers.
   d. Irrational.

2. An economic rent is a payment:

   a. In excess of the opportunity cost of an activity.
   b. Made to lease building space.
   c. Less than the cost of an activity.
   d. Equal to the opportunity cost of an activity.

3. Which of the following acts sought to maintain farm income by implementing price supports and acreage restrictions?

   a. Payment-in-Kind program of 1933
   b. Food Security Wheat Reserve Act of 1933
   c. Agricultural Adjustment Act of 1933
   d. Rent Seekers Act of 1933

4. Which of the following is not a goal of U.S. farm policy?

   a. Maintaining farming as a free and independent business
   b. Maintaining an adequate supply of food at reasonable prices
   c. Encouraging agricultural exports
   d. Reducing the size of family farms and increasing their numbers

5. The concept of parity:

   a. An equitable distribution of income among farmers.
   b. That farm commodity prices must keep in step with other prices in order to keep the farmers' purchasing power from falling.
   c. That a commodity price must be set above the market equilibrium price.
   d. None of the above.

6. As of the mid-1980s, the parity price ratio:

   a. Is at an all time low of 20%.
   b. Is at an all time high of 90%.
   c. Has risen above the 80% level.
   d. Is at an all time low of less than 60%.
   e. Has fallen to just below 80%.

7. Price supports result in _____ and _____ prices to consumers.

   a. Shortages, higher
   b. Shortages, lower
   c. Surpluses, higher
   d. Surpluses, lower

8. Acreage restriction programs are similar to price support programs in that prices to consumers are _____ than unregulated market prices, but they are different in that quantity supplied _____ quantity demanded.

    a. Lower, exceeds
    b. Higher, exceeds
    c. Lower, equals
    d. Higher, equals

9. Which of the following programs pays farmers with government stocks of commodities to restrict acreage?

    a. Target price program
    b. Price support program
    c. Government commodity program
    d. Payment-in-kind program
    e. Acreage allotment program

10. Which of the following programs guarantees farmers a price per bushel but allows market supply and demand to determine the market price?

    a. Target price program
    b. Price support program
    c. Government commodity program
    d. Payment-in-kind program
    e. Acreage allotment program

11. Which of the following programs effectively transfers income from taxpayers to farmers without necessarily resulting in commodity prices lower than would prevail in a competitive market?

    a. Target price program
    b. Price support program
    c. Government commodity program
    d. Payment-in-kind program
    e. Acreage allotment program

12. Subsidies given to consumers result in an/a _____ market price and an/a _____ in market quantity.

    a. Decrease, increase
    b. Increase, decrease
    c. Decrease, decrease
    d. Increase, increase

13. Subsidies given to producers result in an/a _____ in market price and an/a _____ in market quantity.

    a. Decrease, increase
    b. Increase, increase
    c. Decrease, decrease
    d. Increase, increase

14. The net price paid by a consumer under a consumer subsidy program is
_____ the net price paid by the consumer under a producer subsidy
program.

   a. Equal to
   b. Greater than
   c. Less than
   d. Equal to or less than
   e. Equal to or greater than

15. Which of the following is a deduction, exemption, or exclusion from income
in computing taxes?

   a. Tax credit
   b. Tax liability
   c. Tax preference
   d. Tax expenditure

16. Which of the following is a reduction in tax liability resulting from
engaging in some activity?

   a. Tax credit
   b. Tax liability
   c. Tax preference
   d. Tax expenditure

17. Which of the following is the loss in government tax revenue resulting
from a tax break?

   a. Tax credit
   b. Tax liability
   c. Tax preference
   d. Tax expenditure

18. Government loan guarantees are an example of a/an:

   a. Direct subsidy.
   b. Indirect subsidy.
   c. Lost subsidy.
   d. Hidden subsidy.

THINK IT THROUGH

1. Discuss the advantages of a target price program as compared to a price
support program.

2. You are on the staff of a U.S. congressman and have been asked to prepare
a statement regarding the gains and losses associated with a subsidy program.
Identify the typical benefits and costs as well as the gainers and losers.

3. Can you think of any reasons why a tax expenditure rather than a direct
subsidy would be employed to promote a given activity?

POP QUIZ   Read the news brief at the end of this chapter and answer the following questions.

1.   One of the goals of U.S. farm policy is to ensure adequate supplies of farm commodities at reasonable prices. According to the article, how has government contributed to the reduction in the soybean crop and the increase in soybean prices?

2.   Discuss how the special interest lobby, the American Soybean Association, contributed to the impending soybean shortages.

CHAPTER ANSWERS

In Brief: Chapter Summary

1. Special interest groups 2. Rent 3. Rents 4. Creating rents 5. Agricultural Adjustment Act 6. Rise in the prices of the goods and services consumed by farmers 7. Parity 8. Low of under 60% 9. Surpluses 10. Above 11. Exceeds 12. Take land out of 13. Reduce 14. Payment-in-Kind 15. Target prices 16. Do not develop 17. Do not necessarily 18. Lower 19. Consumers 20. Producers 21. Tax preference 22. Tax expenditures 23. Government loan guarantees

Vocabulary Review

1.   Special interest group 2. Parity price ratio 3. Tax preference 4. Parity 5. Tax credit 6. Rent seeking 7. Target price 8. Economic rents 9. Acreage control programs 10. Tax expenditure

Skills Review

1.   a. $2.75, 55 million

     b.

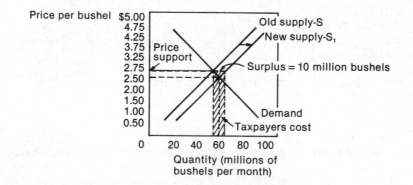

      $2.50, 60 million, decreases, decreased
     c. $2.75, 55 million, 65 million, surplus, 10 million
     d.   Surplus, $27.5 million
     e.   Higher, higher, fewer
     f.   10 million; higher, fewer, higher, an equality between quantity supplied and quantity demanded

278

2. a. $2.75, 55 million
    b.

        Increases, $3.38, decreases, 42.5 million
    c.   55 million, $2.75, $1.25; $2.75, $68.75 million; equal
    d.   Lower, the same
    e.   Taxpayers, farmers

3. a.   Increase

    b.   Increases, $6.50, increases, 11,000, $5.50
    c.   Shown in the graph above.
    d.   Decreases, $5.50, increases, 11,000, $6.50
    e.   Higher, the same

4. a.   Tax credits: investment tax credits, child care tax credits
    b.   Tax preferences: interest exemption on home mortgage interest

5. a.   Government loan guarantees
    b.   Government provided insurance, such as flood insurance

Self-Test for Mastery

1. c 2. a 3. c 4. d 5. b 6. d 7. c 8. d 9. d 10. a 11. a 12. d 13.
a 14. a 15. c 16. a 17. d 18. d

Think it Through

1.   A target price program does not result in surpluses, as is the case with
price supports. Government does not have any costs associated with purchasing,
storing, and disposing of surplus farm commodities. The commodity prices paid
by consumers are likely to be less with the target price program and may even
be as low as would prevail in an unregulated market. Nevertheless, with a
target price program, taxes must be used pay the farm subsidies. The program
redistributes income from taxpayers to farmers.

2.   The beneficiaries of a subsidy include the consumers of the good, the
producers of the good, and the resource suppliers to the subsidized industry.

If the subsidy is intended to correct a market misallocation of resources resulting from a positive externality, then society as a whole benefits as well. Because subsidy programs require tax funding, either taxpayers lose because of an increase in taxes or society loses through a reduction in government services. Income is effectively transferred from taxpayers to the beneficiaries of the subsidized good. If the beneficiaries of the subsidy have, on average, higher incomes than taxpayers, the distribution of income may become more unequal.

3. A direct subsidy is visible to voters, and beneficiaries usually can be readily identified. In contrast, an indirect subsidy is not as obvious to voters, and the benefits go to a general class of individuals or institutions engaging in certain activities. Furthermore, the tax expenditures resulting from these tax breaks are not appropriated on an annual basis, once enacted, there is no limit to the extent of the subsidy over time nor are there any criteria as to whether the tax expenditures have accomplished their goals. Also, tax expenditures do not show up in government budgets as expenditures-- they represent lost tax revenues that are not clearly visible to the general public. In short, it is politically easier and more expedient to encourage activities through the tax system than risk the annual public debates associated with annual program appropriations in Congress.

Pop Quiz

1. By the mid-1980s, U.S. farm policy was giving lavish subsidies in the form of price support loans and marketing loans to growers of certain crops in return for restricting acreage. These crops included corn, wheat, rice, and cotton. In contrast, soybean support prices were low, there were no marketing loans, and farmers were prohibited from growing soybeans on "set-asides" from other crop programs. It was simply more profitable to produce the crops with the more generous government subsidies than to produce soybeans. Soybean prices are strong and demand is growing, but shortages of soybeans are expected and the loss of foreign export markets anticipated. U.S. buyers of soybeans are making plans to import soy even though there is "idle" land from the set-asides that could be planted in soy. As recently as the 1970s, soybeans were America's major export crop. As of 1982, the United States was responsible for 86% of the world trade in soybeans. This share of the world market is expected to decline to 60% in 1989, in large part because of U.S. farm policy. As noted in the text, one of the goals of farm policy is to encourage exports.

2. The soybean lobby, the American Soybean Association, is not a powerful or cohesive lobby. There is regional factionalism regarding the proper policy. Southern farmers want marketing loans but no expansion of acreage. Midwestern farmers want to expand acreage without being penalized but oppose marketing loans. The soybean lobby previously supported limited acreage restrictions in hopes of reaping gains from rising market prices. The soybean lobby contributed to the shortages because it was not effective enough in maintaining the status of soybeans relative to other crops in terms of U.S. farm subsidies.

Coming a Cropper

Farm-Policy Fumbling On Soybeans Shrinks U.S. Share of Market

Despite the Demand, Farmers Idle Their Land and Grow Other Crops for Subsidies

Next: Chickens From Brazil?

By Scott Kilman
And Bruce Ingersoll
Staff Reporters of The Wall Street Journal

CAMERON, S.C.—On Cemetery Road, at the edge of this farming community of 536 people in Calhoun County, lies a pile of rubble—all that is left of a soybean processing plant that until last year had been the town's biggest employer. The cause of its demise: a 50% plunge in the size of the county's biggest cash crop, soybeans, over the past five years.

Here and elsewhere, in places from the Deep South to the Great Plains, the American soybean boom has gone bust.

Once the "miracle bean" stood as the brightest hope of American agriculture. Now U.S. output is falling for the third consecutive year; yesterday, the Agriculture Department forecast a 23% drop in the 1988 crop. This means that for the first time since American breeders redesigned the Manchurian native to thrive on these shores, America will have grown less than half the world's soybeans. With millions of fertile acres idle, the U.S. is close to running out of its second most valuable crop, after corn.

"We are just realizing that the U.S. isn't the only ball game in town," says John Hane, a Fort Motte, S.C., farmer. South American growers, he says, "are taking away our crop from us and making us look like asses."

Inflation and Shortages

Don't blame market prices or demand. On the contrary, prices for processed soybean products are strong and, partly because of the drought, headed higher; some farmers who use the beans for feed may lose money on their hogs and chickens. By the fall of 1989, there may be shortages of soybeans, used in cooking oils and other human food as well as in animal feed.

Despite all this, farmers seem reluctant to grow the crop without government assistance—help they frittered away in a splintered lobbying effort.

Foreign farmers are fast plowing new acreage for soybeans to meet demand around the world. American processors are laying plans to *import* soybeans that won't be grown on the U.S.'s idle acreage. At the Chicago Board of Trade, speculators swap rumors of bargeloads of South

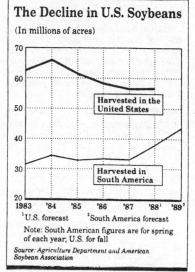

The Decline in U.S. Soybeans
(In millions of acres)

¹U.S. forecast   ²South America forecast

Note: South American figures are for spring of each year; U.S. for fall

Source: Agriculture Department and American Soybean Association

American soybean oil moving up the Mississippi River.

If all this seems weird, it is. The short, if cynical, explanation is that producers of corn, wheat, rice and cotton command powerful and cohesive lobbies. Soybean growers do not. But that is oversimple. The growers themselves, hoping to enjoy the best of both the subsidized and free-market worlds, pitched their own wrenches into the agricultural policy machinery and now suffer the consequences.

Trusting the Market

By 1984, policy makers were eager to refloat a floundering farm economy with lavish subsidies for corn, wheat, rice and cotton—which farmers call program crops. Income-support payments and price-support loans guaranteed growers of these crops profits in return for setting aside big chunks of their usual planting acreage. For rice and cotton growers came a bonus in the form of marketing loans, costly export subsidies that compensate farmers and exporters for selling U.S. commodities abroad at low prices.

Soybean growers lacked a consensus toward subsidies. For years, in fact, their strongest lobby had looked askance at subsidies, confident that market demand for the wondrous protein source would ensure higher profits. In the farm legislation that took effect in 1985, soybean support prices were low. No marketing loans were offered. Nor were farmers permitted to plant soybeans on land idled by corn, wheat and cotton "set-asides." Because government subsidies are based on an average of five consecutive harvests, planting soybeans for one season on program cropland would penalize a farmer for several years.

Since then, U.S. soybean acreage has shrunk by 15%. On world markets, American agriculture has been made to look much like General Motors in the 1970s, a lumbering giant slow to size up its competition. The vast, empty refining vats amid the rubble of Cameron's former Continental Grain Co. plant attest to the cost.

The plant sprang up in the 1960s, a few years before the buff-colored bean was engineered into a new source of protein for a hungry world. While U.S. farmers had planted a few soybeans in the past, processors lifted the crop from obscurity in the 1970s and made it America's biggest farm export. Its champions, ranging from farmers and processors to Agriculture Department officials, put technicians to work on recipes for tofu, meat lookalikes, gravies and bread—all made from soybeans.

"When you start thinking about future applications of soy protein, it can boggle the mind," gushed a promotional brochure by Archer Daniels Midland Co., the leading U.S. processor.

At the same time, costly overseas promotion made the soybean a staple of diets in Japan, Korea, West Germany and elsewhere. Prices in the 1970s doubled, showering farmers with cash they invested to double their production by 1979 to 2.26 billion bushels, the biggest crop ever. The American Soybean Association, a farmer lobby, chose to risk price swings in the market in order to avoid limiting production and exports.

Then came the farm crisis of the early 1980s and the 1985 farm act. By early 1988, the stage was set for a soybean shortage. In February, Rep. Jerry Huckaby, a Louisiana Democrat, tried to help soybean growers by introducing a bill to provide them with a marketing loan. Rep. Dan Glickman, a Kansas Democrat who chairs the House Agriculture subcommittee on wheat, soybeans and feed grains, held hearings on the soybean industry's dilemma, and he and others pressed ahead with legislation designed to increase soybean acreage.

Coming a Cropper: Farm-Policy Fumbling Shrinks U.S. Output and Growers' Share of Soybean Market

That began a political fiasco that killed the industry's chances for a 1988 recovery. In what a congressional aide called "the North-South war," the soybean association split along regional lines. Southern soybean farmers sought a marketing loan in hopes of lifting exports but wanted no expansion of soybean acreage, which might depress prices. At the same time, growers in the Midwest, where soybean yields are 50% higher, mostly wanted a chance to plant more beans without their subsidies being penalized. But they opposed a marketing loan for precisely the same reason the Southerners objected to increase acreage: It might depress prices.

"The politics of soybeans are very confused," says Illinois Rep. Edward Madigan, the ranking Republican on the House Agriculture Committee. Says soybean-association President James Lee Adams, of Camilla, Ga., "We were in a terrible quandary at the time."

After flip-flopping on the issue, the growers' group declared itself opposed to both a marketing loan *and* an acreage expansion in 1988. The waffling outraged legislators and doomed efforts to expand production. By then it was March, too late to change the farm program in time for 1988 plantings. "It would have just added to the confusion," Mr. Adams says.

Jumping Ship

Nevertheless, he concedes, "we haven't had our act together. . . . Making policy for the American Soybean Association is a lot like trying to load a wheelbarrow full of frogs. We get a few of us on board, and others start jumping ship."

With soybean stockpiles now expected to fall to a dangerously low three weeks' supply by next summer, the government has since sweetened the pot. Under the $3.9 billion drought-relief package enacted last month, farmers can without penalty shift at least 10% of their land from program crops into soybeans for one year, and perhaps as much as 25% at the Agriculture Secretary's discretion.

Changes in the farm program may be too little and too late. Some 14 million acres of U.S. soybeans have effectively shifted to South America. There, the plant-

ing season begins next month, and Argentina and Brazil are expected to increase their plantings by 20% and 15%.

In the U.S., corn subsidies are still so attractive that LeRoy, Minn., farmer Russell Roe plans to switch only 15% of his corn acreage to soybeans. U.S. soybean plantings are expected to rise by only two million to three million acres next spring, half the increase expected in competing South American nations.

Losing Market Share

Bit players such as Australia are weighing into soybeans, and nations unsuited to growing them are planting alternative crops. Heavily subsidized rapeseed production in Western Europe has risen 60% in the past four years, lessening the European Economic Community's dependence of U.S. soybean meal and strengthening it as a competitor in world vegetable oil.

The decline in America's share of the world soybean trade, totaling $10 billion a year now, will be tough to end. The U.S. share is expected to tumble to less than 60% in the coming year from 86% in 1982. The number of domestic processing plants—crushers and refiners—has fallen 28% in the past 10 years, to 88.

More are on the verge of closing. Decatur, Ill., a processing town deep in the Farm Belt, has conceded its title of "the soybean capital of the world." Ponta Grossa, Brazil, and Rosario, Argentina, are new contenders.

Here in Cameron and the rest of the Southeast, a major soybean-producing region, the cost of farm-policy machinations has run especially high. Mr. Hane, the Fort Motte farmer, planted only 250 acres in soybeans this spring, just one-third as much as six years ago. "When you plant soybeans, you are totally on your own," Mr. Hane says. "With the others, the government protects you from low prices."

Soybean seed sales skidded last spring in South Carolina, and dealers were forced to destroy tens of thousands of bags. Luther Wannamaker, president of his family's seed business, is glum about the prospects for soybeans. Farmers have planted pine trees on many former soybean fields under a government program that pays

them $45 an acre each year to idle land. Other acreage is in subsidized crops such as cotton. "Program crops are too attractive," Mr. Wannamaker says.

Only two of the five soybean processing plants within 100 miles of Calhoun County are still crushing soybeans. Lessened demand from the processors is further dulling the local price on beans, further dulling farmers' incentive to grow them here. Yet the drought, reduced competition and higher transportation costs have worked to increase the prices on soybean products. Livestock raisers are smarting from an 80% increase in the cost of soybean meal, a principal feed ingredient.

Steve Pittman, a Fort Motte, S.C. farmer, says rising feed costs will wipe out profit on his 450-hog operation this year. The plant closing is "a sad waste," he says. "We lost a golden opportunity."

Southeastern poultry producers fear withering soybean supplies will force up prices on other commodities. Joe Hatfield, president of Fieldale Farms Corp., a Baldwin, Ga., poultry grower, says the cost of feeding soybean meal to chickens could make them too expensive to export.

He also worries that Brazil might take advantage of its expanding soybean crop to develop its poultry industry—and exports. "We could be facing South American competition for chickens," he says.

At Sylvia's restaurant in downtown St. Matthews, the seat of Calhoun County, a knot of farmers mulls international trade issues over lunch. "We fought low prices. Then the weather," says Pallie Wiles, a soybean farmer in a John Deere cap. "Now it's the South Americans."

The closing of the Cameron plant dashed farmers' hopes of expanding markets for their promising new crop. With the plant vanished the jobs of 58 residents and the line of trucks that snaked into town during the annual harvest. Along Cemetery Road, "it's going to be right quiet this fall," says David Summers, president of the Golden Kernel Pecan Co., across the road from the plant site.

Says Mr. Wiles, "It's a tragedy, what's happening."

19

The Government Sector of the Economy: Expenditures, Revenues, and Public Choice

CHAPTER CHALLENGES

After studying your text, attending class, and completing this chapter, you should be able to:

1. Describe the economic functions of modern governments.
2. Explain how governments raise revenue and describe the major catagories of expenditure for the federal, state, and local governments in the United States.
3. Explain the principles used to evaluate taxes.
4. Explain the process of public choice under majority rule.

IN BRIEF: CHAPTER SUMMARY

Fill in the blanks to summarize chapter content.

The (1)_____(democratic, federal government) system consists of various levels of government, each with its own powers to provide services and to regulate the private sector. The basic functions of government include (a) the establishment of rights to use productive resources and the regulation of private actions, (b) provision of goods and services, (c) redistribution of income, and (d) (2)_____ (stabilization of the economy, provision of armed forces). Government-provided goods and services can be categorized in two basic ways. Some publicly provided goods are made available free of charge to all members of society, and the cost is financed with taxes or through borrowing. National defense, public health, and (3)_____(national parks, welfare benefits) are some examples of this type of good. Some tax-financed government goods and services are made available only to some individuals meeting certain eligibility criteria. Examples include education, Social Security pensions, and (4)_____(national parks, welfare benefits).

At the federal level of government, as of 1987, national defense spending was the (5)_____(largest, second largest) component of federal spending. Social Security benefits are also a major federal government outlay. State and local governments spend just over (6)_____ (two thirds, half) of the amount spent by the federal government. At the state and local levels of government, (7)_____(welfare, education) accounts for more than one third of all expenditures, followed by income support, social insurance, and welfare as the second major type of expenditure. Road maintenance and transportation is also an important function at the state and local levels of government.

In 1987, federal government tax revenues (8)_____ (exceeded, fell short of) expenditures by $152.6 billion. This is referred to as a budget deficit. Deficits have to be financed by borrowing. The U.S. Treasury does this by issuing U.S. government securities. Major federal taxes in order of importance include the personal income tax, (9)_____ (the payroll tax, sales taxes), corporate profits taxes and excise taxes. State and local governments incurred a budget (10)_____(deficit, surplus) of $45.5 billion in 1987. Major state and local sources of revenue by order of importance include (11)_____(income, sales) taxes, property taxes, federal grants, (12)_____(income, sales) taxes, fees and charges, and payroll taxes.

Taxes are evaluated on the basis of efficiency and equity. Taxes can be levied on the basis of the taxpayer's ability to pay or the benefits received from the government good or service. A person with a higher income may pay more taxes than an individual with a lower income, and yet the tax can still be a (13)_____ (progressive, regressive) tax in which individuals with higher incomes pay a smaller percentage of their incomes in taxes than lower-income persons. A (14)_____ (progressive, regressive) tax, such as the personal income tax, requires individuals with higher incomes to pay a larger percentage of their incomes in taxes. A flat-rate tax is an example of a (15)_____(regressive, proportional) tax in which persons with different incomes pay the same percentage of their income in taxes.

Economic decisions are based on (16)_____ (marginal, average) tax rates rather than (17)_____ (marginal, average) tax rates. Whether or not an individual engages in an activity or a change in some activity depends in part on the after-tax net gains. The decision to work an extra hour depends on the net take-home wage. What is important is not the worker's average tax per dollar earned, but the increase in tax associated with an additional hour of work. Taxes can result in efficiency losses from less employment, less productivity, and less saving and capital growth. This efficiency loss or (18)_____ (excess burden, tax loss) of a tax is the loss in net benefits from resource use caused by the distortion in choices resulting from taxation.

Public choices are made through voting. Under simple majority rule, as individuals pursue their most-preferred political outcome, a political equilibrium is reached at the median most-preferred outcome. This is known as the (19)_____ (plurality, median-voter) rule. A competitive market provision of goods allows consumers to purchase goods up to the point at which marginal benefits equal price. (20_____ (Consumers cannot, Each consumer can) maximize utility. But with politically supplied goods, only the median voter maximizes satisfaction. Some citizens will receive more of the public good than they desire and some less.

VOCABULARY REVIEW

Write the key term from the list below next to its definition.

Key Terms

Taxes	Marginal tax rate
Federal system	Excess burden
of government	Public choices
Government transfers	Simple majority rule
Budget deficit	Most-preferred political
Budget surplus	outcome
Regressive tax	Political equilibrium
Progressive tax	Median voter
Proportional tax	Median voter rule
Average tax rate	Government failure

Definitions

1. _____: payments that are financed by taxes and made directly to certain citizens or organizations for which no good or service is received in return at that time.

2. _____: that alternative for which the marginal benefit just equals the tax a voter would pay if he were able to purchase the good or service in a market at a price equal to his assigned tax per unit.

3. _____: a tax for which the percentage of income paid in taxes is the same no matter what the taxpayer's income.

4. _____: the loss in net benefits from resource use caused by the distortion in choices resulting from taxation.

5. _____: the extra tax paid on extra income or the extra dollar value of any other taxed item.

6. _____: the amount of taxes paid divided by the dollar value of the item taxed.

7. _____: choices made by voting.

8. _____: a tax for which the fraction of income used to pay it increases as income increases.

9. _____: a means for reaching public choices that enacts a proposal if it obtains affirmative votes from more than half the voters casting ballots in an election.

10. _____: a tax for which the fraction of income used to pay it decreases as income increases.

11. _____: an agreement on the quantity of a public good to supply through government, given the rule for making the public choice and given the taxes per unit of the public good for each voter.

12. _____: an excess of government revenues over government expenditures in a given year.

13. _____: given an odd number of voters, the voter whose most-preferred outcome is the median of all the most-preferred outcomes.

14. _____: the amount by which government expenditures exceed government revenues in a given year.

15. _____: states that when the marginal benefit of a pure public good declines for each voter as more of the good is made available, the political equilibrium under majority rule always corresponds to the median most-preferred outcome when there is an odd number of voters.

16. _____: numerous levels of government, each with its own powers, exist to provide services and regulate private affairs.

17. _____: exists when voters approve programs for which marginal costs exceed marginal benefits.

18. _____: compulsory payments associated with income, consumption, or holding of property that persons and corporations are required to make each year to governments.

SKILLS REVIEW

Concept: Economic functions of government

1.   List four functions of government and give an example of each.

     a. _____
     b. _____
     c. _____
     d. _____

2.   Government goods and services can be classified as (1) goods that are made
     available to all citizens free of charge and (2) goods and services that
     are available only to certain citizens based on specific eligibility
     criteria. For each of the goods or services below, indicate whether the
     good or service is of the first or second category. Use (1) for the first
     category and (2) for the second category.

     a. _____ National defense   b. _____ Medicaid
     c. _____ Roads   d. _____ Fire protection
     e. _____ Food stamps   f. _____ National parks
     g. _____ Police   h. _____ Social security
     i. _____ Education

Concept: Government revenues and expenditures

3.   List the federal government's tax revenues in order of importance.

     a. _____
     b. _____
     c. _____
     d. _____

4.   List the federal government's expenditures in order of importance.

     a. _____
     b. _____
     c. _____
     d. _____
     e. _____

5.   List state and local revenue sources in order of importance.

     a. _____
     b. _____
     c. _____
     d. _____
     e. _____
     f. _____

6.   List major categories of state and local expenditures in order of
     importance.

     a. _____
     b. _____
     c. _____

Concept: Principles used to evaluate taxation

7. Taxes are generally considered equitable if taxpayers pay taxes on the basis of their _____ or the _____ from the public good or service consumed.

8. Indicate for the taxes below whether they are progressive, regressive, or proportional taxes.

   a. _____ Federal personal income tax
   b. _____ Sales tax
   c. _____ Payroll tax (FICA)
   d. _____ Flat-rate tax
   e. _____ Cigarette excise tax

Concept: Public choice and voting

9. Below are the marginal benefits associated with various quantities of a public good for five voters. Assume that the public choice rule is the majority vote and the tax cost per voter per year is $100.

Marginal Benefits ($)

Units of the Public Good	A	B	C	D	E
0					
1	200	140	80	125	110
2	180	130	70	100	105
3	160	120	60	75	100
4	140	110	50	50	95
5	120	100	40	25	90
6	100	90	30	0	85
7	80	80	20	-25	80

   a. If each voter maximizes his net benefits, what is the most-preferred political outcome for each voter?

Voter	Units
A	_____
B	_____
C	_____
D	_____
E	_____

   b. At the following levels of public goods provision, indicate the vote for and against and whether the vote fails or passes.

Units	For	Against	Pass/Fail
0			
1	_____	_____	_____
2	_____	_____	_____
3	_____	_____	_____
4	_____	_____	_____
5	_____	_____	_____
6	_____	_____	_____
7	_____	_____	_____

c. Political equilibrium is achieved at what level of public goods provision? _____ units This quantity is the most-preferred political outcome of which voter?_____ This voter is called the _____ voter.

SELF-TEST FOR MASTERY

Select the best answer.

1. Welfare payments fall under which of the following government functions?

   a. Establishment of rights to use resources and the regulation of private actions
   b. Provision of goods and services
   c. Redistribution of income
   d. Stabilization of the economy

2. Education expenditures fall under which of the following government functions?

   a. Establishment of rights to use resources and the regulation of private actions
   b. Provision of goods and services
   c. Redistribution of income
   d. Stabilization of income

3. Payments made by government to certain persons or organizations for which no good or service is currently received in return are called:

   a. Government spending
   b. Welfare benefits
   c. Government off-budget expenditures
   d. Government transfer payments

4. Which of the following was the largest federal government expenditure in 1987?

   a. Income security
   b. Social Security
   c. National parks
   d. National defense
   e. Education

5. Which of the following was the largest source of tax revenue for the federal government in 1987?

   a. Excise tax
   b. Corporate profits tax
   c. Sales tax
   d. Payroll tax
   e. Income tax

6. Which of the following was the largest category of spending at the state and local levels of government in 1986?

   a. Highways
   b. Education
   c. Welfare

d. Police and fire protection
e. Hospitals

7. Which of the following was the largest source of state and local government revenue in 1987?

   a. Sales tax
   b. Income tax
   c. Gross production tax
   d. Excise tax
   f. Property tax

8. Two concepts of equity in taxation are the _____ and _____ concepts.

   a. Egalitarian, utopian
   b. Ability-to-pay, benefits received
   c. Democratic, Republican
   d. Progressive, regressive

9. A tax for which the fraction of income used to pay it decreases as income increases is called a:

   a. Progressive tax.
   b. Regressive tax.
   c. Proportional tax.
   d. Flat-rate tax.

10. A tax for which the fraction of income used to pay it increases as income increases is called a:

   a. Progressive tax.
   b. Regressive tax.
   c. Proportional tax.
   d. Value-added tax.

11. A flat-rate tax is an example of :

   a. A progressive tax.
   b. A regressive tax.
   c. A proportional tax.
   d. The U.S. income tax.

12. The appropriate tax concept to be used in marginal analysis is:

   a. The total tax liability from the full extent of an activity.
   b. The marginal tax rate.
   c. The average tax rate.
   d. The ability-to-pay concept.

13. A voter's most-preferred political outcome is:

   a. When taxes are shared equally by all voters.
   b. When total benefits equal the total cost of the public good.
   c. At the level of public goods provision where the voter's marginal benefit just equals his tax share per unit of the public good.
   d. Always satisfied more efficiently in the market.

14. If the public choice rule is the majority vote rule and voters know their respective tax shares and maximize net benefits, political equilibrium:

    a. Occurs at a level of provision where the median voter maximizes net benefits.
    b. Occurs at the same level of provision as would be the case for a competitive market equilibrium.
    c. Occurs at a level of provision where all voters maximize net benefits.
    d. None of the above.

15. An advantage of having nonpublic goods produced by the market rather than by government is that:

    a. Consumers can consume goods up to the point at which their net benefits are maximized.
    b. Taxes will be lower.
    c. Consumers can consume goods up to the point at which their marginal benefits equal the price of the good.
    d. A and c.
    e. None of the above.

16. _____ exists when voters approve programs for which marginal costs exceed marginal benefits.

    a. Anarchy
    b. Market failure
    c. The most-preferred political outcome
    d. Government failure

THINK IT THROUGH

1. Compare and contrast the expenditures and revenue sources of the federal government with those of the state and local levels of government.

2. Describe what is meant by efficiency and equity in taxation.

3. Explain why it is possible under a majority vote system for voters to pass legislation on single issues where voter contentment with legislative outcomes can range from a broad consensus to a great deal of dissatisfaction.

POP QUIZ   Read the news brief at the end of this chapter and answer the questions below.

1. What is the excess burden of a tax?
2. What is a major cost of compliance with the federal income tax? Do you think that the compliance cost of the federal income tax is a significant component of the excess burden associated with the tax? Explain.

CHAPTER ANSWERS

In Brief: Chapter Summary

1. Federal government 2. Stabilization of the economy 3. National parks 4. Welfare benefits 5. Largest 6. Half 7. Education 8. Fell short of 9. The payroll tax 10. Surplus 11. Sales 12. Income 13. Regressive 14. Progressive 15. Proportional 16. Marginal 17. Average 18. Excess burden 19. Median voter 20. Each consumer can

Vocabulary Review

1. Government transfers 2. Most-preferred political outcome 3. Proportional tax 4. Excess burden 5. Marginal tax rate 6. Average tax rate 7. Public choices 8. Progressive taxes 9. Simple majority rule 10. Regressive tax 11. Political equilibrium 12. Budget surplus 13. Median voter 14. Budget deficit 15. Median voter rule 16. Federal system of government 17. Government failure 18. Taxes

Skills Review

1. a.   The establishment of rights to use resources and the regulation of private actions
    b.   Provision of goods and services
    c.   Redistribution of income
    d.   Stabilization of the economy

2. a. 1 b. 2 c. 1 d. 1 e. 2 f. 1 g. 1 h. 2 i. 2

3. a.   Personal income tax b. Payroll taxes c. Corporate profits taxes d. Excise taxes

4. a.   National defense b. Social Security c. Interest payments d. Income security e. Medicare

5. a.   Sales taxes b. Property taxes c. Federal grants d. Income taxes e. Fees and charges f. Payroll taxes

6. a.   Education b. Income support, social insurance, and welfare c. Road maintenance and transportation

7. Ability-to-pay, benefits received

8. a.   Progressive b. Regressive c. Regressive d. Proportional e. Regressive

9. a. | Voter | Units |
        |-------|-------|
        | A | 6 |
        | B | 5 |
        | C | 0 |
        | D | 2 |
        | E | 3 |

    b. | For | Against | Pass/Fail |
        |-----|---------|-----------|
        | 1 | 4 | Fail |
        | 4 | 1 | Pass |
        | 4 | 1 | Pass |
        | 3 | 2 | Pass |
        | 2 | 3 | Fail |
        | 2 | 3 | Fail |

```
          1    4         Fail
          0    5         Fail

    c.   3 units, voter E, median
```

Self-Test for Mastery

1. c 2. b 3. d 4. d 5. e 6. b 7. a 8. b 9. b 10. a 11. c 12. b 13. c 14. a 15. d 16. d

Think it Through

1. The federal government provides national defense, Social Security, income security, interest payments on the public debt, and Medicare as well as other goods and services. These are financed with personal income taxes, payroll taxes, corporate profits taxes, and excise taxes. State and local governments provide education, income support, social insurance, welfare, road maintenance and transportation, police and fire protection, and other goods and services. State and local levels of government finance their activities with sales taxes, property taxes, federal grants, income taxes, fees and charges, and payroll taxes. The largest federal expenditure as a percentage of total spending is for national defense, whereas the largest state and local expenditure is for education. Sales taxes are the major revenue source at the state and local levels of government, but personal income taxes provide the most revenue to the federal government.

2. Taxes can create an excess burden when there are tax-caused changes in individual and business behavior resulting from changes in net wages, net interest rates, and other prices or incomes. Efficiency can be improved if the tax is used to correct a negative externality. An efficient tax is one that raises tax revenue without causing an excess burden. The two basic concepts of equity in taxation are the ability-to-pay and benefits received concepts. The benefits received principle cannot be used where the benefits cannot be closely correlated with an individual's activity. The ability-to-pay criterion states that a fair tax is one for which an individual's tax liability is correlated with his or her ability to pay. Thus, higher income persons should pay more in taxes than those with lower incomes. This criterion does not indicate whether proportional, progressive, or regressive taxes are preferable, because ability-to-pay can be measured in absolute dollars or as a percentage of income.

3. If the marginal benefits from a public good for most taxpayers are similar with little variability and the tax share per taxpayer is the same, the majority vote rule will result in a political equilibrium in which many or most voters have most-preferred political outcomes that are very close to the median voter outcome. Only the median voter achieves the most-preferred political outcome, but the extent of dissatisfaction with the vote is much less than if there is considerable dispersion of marginal benefits. If a larger percentage of voters have most-preferred political outcomes that depart widely from the median voter outcome, there will be far more dissatisfaction with the vote.

Pop Quiz

1. The excess burden of a tax is the loss in net benefits from resource use caused by the distortion in choices resulting from taxation.

2. According to Rose Gutfeld's article, a 3-year study funded by the IRS found that taxpayers used a total of 5.3 billion hours for filing federal income tax returns in 1986. This is unquestionably the major cost of compliance and is an important component of the excess burden associated with federal income taxes. The opportunity cost of compliance is the value of these billions of hours in their next-best alternative uses in either work or

leisure. The resources used for tax filing would have been used for other activities that increase total social benefits. The tax-compliance loss must be added to other distortions caused by the income tax in order to determine the extent of its excess burden. In fact, one of the objectives of the Tax Reform Act of 1986 was to simplify the tax-compliance process in order to reduce this aspect of the excess burden.

It Seems Like Days, but IRS Estimates Tax Filing Takes Only About Nine Hours

By Rose Gutfeld

Staff Reporter of The Wall Street Journal

WASHINGTON—Take heart, taxpayers. Filing a return may be unpleasant, but the Internal Revenue Service has found the task takes the average person a mere nine hours and five minutes.

Starting next year, estimates of the average time taxpayers spend on record keeping, learning about the tax law, preparing forms, copying them and sending them to the IRS will be printed on the instructions accompanying the returns and schedules. The nine-hour-plus estimate is for someone filing a 1040 without any schedules such as those for interest and dividend income.

Understated Burden

The agency has been required to come up with these so-called burden estimates for several years, but in the past it strenuously resisted efforts to have them listed on forms or instructions. Officials argued, among other things, that doing so would encourage tax protesters and others to stop working on their returns as soon as they had put in the stated time, whether they had completed the forms or not. Moreover, the estimates could be discouraging even to willing filers who found themselves spending more time than average.

At a news conference yesterday, though, Arthur Altman, chairman of the agency's forms coordinating committee, said previous reluctance reflected concerns that past agency estimates, which included only time needed for preparation, understated the burden on taxpayers. He said the agency doesn't think the new estimates will encourage protesters or be frustrating for slow filers.

The times released yesterday reflect the results of a three-year study conducted for the IRS by Arthur D. Little Inc. The study found that Americans, including individuals and businesses, spent a total of 5.3 billion hours on tax filings for 1986, with two-thirds of the burden falling on business taxpayers.

The study involved focus-group interviews, studies of taxpayer diaries and nationwide surveys of taxpayers. It found that for 1986 returns, taxpayers spent 1.5 billion hours on preparation alone, up from 796 million hours according to previous IRS estimates.

Tax Times

Estimated average times needed to complete and file the following tax forms

FORM	RECORD KEEPING	LEARNING ABOUT THE LAW OR THE FORM	PREPARING THE FORM	COPYING, ASSEMBLING AND SENDING THE FORM TO IRS
1040	3 hrs., 7 min.	2 hrs., 22 min.	3 hrs., 1 min.	35 min.
Sch. A (1040)	2 hrs., 47 min.	26 min.	1 hr., 1 min.	20 min.
Sch. B (1040)	33 min.	8 min.	16 min.	20 min.
Sch. C (1040)	7 hrs., 4 min.	1 hr., 11 min.	2 hrs., 9 min.	25 min.
Sch. D (1040)	1 hr., 2 min.	45 min.	54 min.	35 min.
Sch. E (1040)	3 hrs., 12 min.	1 hr., 2 min.	1 hr., 22 min.	35 min.
Sch. F (1040)	10 hrs., 53 min.	2 hrs., 2 min.	4 hrs., 10 min.	35 min.
Sch. R (1040)	20 min.	16 min.	22 min.	35 min.
Sch. SE (1040)				
Short	20 min.	11 min.	13 min.	14 min.
Long	26 min.	22 min.	37 min.	20 min.

Source: Internal Revenue Service

People with vivid memories of the 1988 filing season may be surprised to learn that, according to the IRS, they spent less time, on average, filling out tax forms this year, the first year of filing under the new law, than they did a year earlier. Among other reasons, under the new tax law, fewer people itemize their deductions, so more can use the simpler 1040A and 1040EZ forms. The time estimate for the 1040 form increased slightly under the new law.

Several professional tax preparers say they think the new time estimates generally are accurate, but they say a few are too low. "I wouldn't argue with many of those estimates," says David J. Silverman, a New York tax consultant. "But I would dispute the record keeping. Out of every 10 people who come into my office, seven have to go back and dig up additional stuff that's missing. That takes time."

A spokesman for H&R Block Inc. says people spend more than the estimated time on learning about the form. "You have to read a lot just to see if it applies to you," he says.

Of the main individual forms, the longest estimate applied to Schedule F, where farm income is listed. Record keeping alone for the form is put at 10 hours, 53 minutes, with the total time needed estimated at 17 hours, 40 minutes.

Schedule A, for itemized deductions, is supposed to take four hours and 34 minutes, while Schedule B, where interest and dividend income is listed, takes one hour, 17 minutes. The form for capital gains income or loss, Schedule D, should take three hours, 16 minutes.

Seeking Feedback

On next year's tax forms, the IRS also will solicit public comment on the time estimates and suggestions for simplifying the forms. Mr. Altman says the forms contain only subtle changes from this year's versions.

John D. Johnson, an assistant IRS commissioner, says the agency plans additional research into making tax forms as accessible as possible to taxpayers. The agency will attempt to measure filers' "tax literacy"—that is, how much of the tax forms they actually understand. Forms currently are aimed at people with a 10th-grade reading level. The agency also will consider the possibility of converting the tax forms to a more visual approach, through the use of flow charts or question-and-answer formats.

20

Input Markets and the Demand for Resources

CHAPTER CHALLENGES

After studying your text, attending class, and completing this chapter, you should be able to:

1. Explain the concept of a perfectly competitive input market.
2. Show how much of a particular input, like labor, a profit-maximizing firm chooses to buy over a certain period in a competitive market.
3. Show how a firm's demand for an input depends on the productivity of the input and on the price the firm receives from selling the product of the input.
4. Show how the market price of an input depends on its supply and demand.

IN BRIEF: CHAPTER SUMMARY

Fill in the blanks to summarize chapter content.

A competitive input market is one in which there is (1)_____ (lack of free, free) entry and exit of sellers of inputs, where the owners of resources (2)_____ (can, cannot) shift their resources to different locations in response to differences in input prices, and where buyers and sellers of resources (3)_____ (have, have no) control over resource prices. In competitive input markets, the forces of supply and demand determine market input prices and quantities employed.

The demand for an input is a derived demand--derived from the demand for the product produced by the input. The demand curve for an input is the (4)_____(marginal revenue product, marginal product) curve. Marginal revenue product is the input's marginal product times (5)_____ (average cost, marginal revenue). Marginal product is the extra production that results from the use of one additional unit of an input. For the case of a perfectly competitive product market, marginal revenue (6)_____ (is less than, equals) price. Therefore, for competitive input markets, marginal revenue product (7)_____ (is less than, equals) product price times the input's marginal product. Marginal revenue product is the contribution by an extra unit of an input to the firm's total revenue.

A profit-maximizing firm will employ an input up to the point at which the additional benefit from doing so (the marginal revenue product) (8)_____ (is greater than, equals) the additional costs (or marginal input costs). For the case of labor, a firm will employ labor up to the point at which the marginal revenue product of labor equals the wage, assuming a competitive input market. A firm's demand curve for labor is the marginal revenue product curve with the wage rate plotted on the vertical axis. Each point on the curve represents a profit-maximizing quantity of labor demanded at that wage rate.

An input demand curve will shift if the demand for the firm's output changes, if the prices of substitute or complementary inputs change, or if changes in technology affect the marginal product of the input. The demand for an input will increase (the demand curve will shift to the right) if the price of the product produced by the input (9)_____ (increases, decreases), if technological improvement (10)_____ (increases, decreases) the input's marginal product, if the price of a substitute input (11)_____ (increases, decreases), or if the price of a complementary input (12)_____ (increases, decreases). The opposite changes will cause the demand for an input to decrease and the input demand curve to shift to the left.

For the case of a monopoly product market, marginal revenue is (13)_____ (equal to, less than) price at each level of output, causing the monopolist's marginal revenue product curve for an input to lie (14)_____ (outside, inside) the market input demand for competitive firms. As a result, at a given wage the monopolist will maximize profit by hiring (15)_____ (more, fewer) units of the input than would be the case for competitive firms.

The market demand curve for an input is a summation of the individual firm-level demand curves for the input. It is downward sloping, as is the case for the firm's input demand curve. The supply curve for an input is upward sloping because higher input prices are necessary to cover (16)_____ (rising, falling) marginal costs associated with supplying the input. The market supply of and demand for an input determine the market price and quantity of the input. For example, if the demand for an input increases or supply decreases or some combination of the two, market input prices will (17)_____ (increase, decrease).

Economic rent exists when the market price of an input (18)_____ (equals, exceeds) the minimum price that sellers of the input will take. It represents a surplus over the opportunity costs associated with producing and providing an input and can be taxed away (19)_____ (reducing, without reducing) the quantity of inputs offered at the market price. Key facts regarding input markets include: (a) the prices of inputs are determined by the forces of supply and demand, (b) the price of an input equals its marginal revenue product for the case of competitive input markets, (c) the demand for an input is a derived demand, (d) productivity is a major determinant of input prices, and (e) for the case of competitive input markets, attempts by employers to pay less than the going market input price will fail.

VOCABULARY REVIEW

Write the key term from the list below next to its definition.

Key Terms

Input market   Marginal input cost
Competitive input market   Change in input demand
Derived demand   Market demand for an input
Marginal revenue product   Market supply of an input

Definitions

1. _____: a relationship between the price of an input and the quantity supplied for employment in all industries and other uses.

2. _____: the change in total revenue that results when one more unit of that input is hired.

3. _____: the sum of the quantities demanded by all industries and other employers using that input at any given price.

4. _____: the demand for an input that is derived from the demand for the product that the input is used to produce.

5. _____: a shift of an entire input demand curve caused by a change in one of the determinants of input demand other than price.

6. _____: a market in which neither individual buyers nor individual sellers can influence the prices of input services.

7. _____: the extra cost associated with hiring one more unit of an input.

8. _____: a market used to trade the services of productive resources for income payments.

SKILLS REVIEW

Concept: Perfectly competitive input markets

1. List the characteristics of a perfectly competitive input market.

   a. _____
   b. _____
   c. _____

Concept: Demand for an input by a profit-maximizing competitive firm

2. Company X is a profit-maximizing firm selling in a competitive product market and hiring in a competitive input market. Company X uses semi-skilled labor to produce dampers used in office building ventilation systems. Below are data regarding labor productivity for the firm. Assume that the current market price per damper is $500.

Workers	Total Product (dampers/week)	Marginal Product	Marginal Revenue Product
0	0		
10	15	_____	$_____
20	28	_____	_____
30	39	_____	_____
40	48	_____	_____
50	55	_____	_____
60	60	_____	_____

a. Complete the table and plot the marginal revenue product curve in the diagram below.

Marginal revenue product

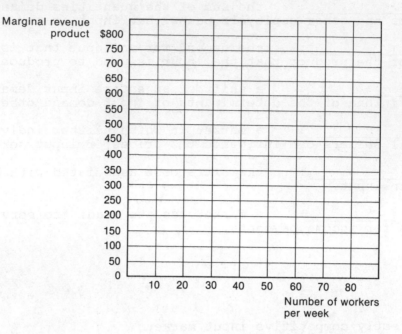

Number of workers per week

b. Assume that the prevailing weekly salary per semi-skilled worker is $550. Company X would employ _____ workers. The profit-maximizing level of employment occurs where _____ equals _____.

c. Suppose the market wage fell from $550 per week to $450 per week. Company X would employ _____ workers. If the market wage increased to $650, Company X would employ _____ workers.

d. Plot the quantities of labor demanded by Company X at the three wages considered in parts a and c in the figure below. For Company X, the input demand curve for semi-skilled labor is the _____ curve.

Wage per week

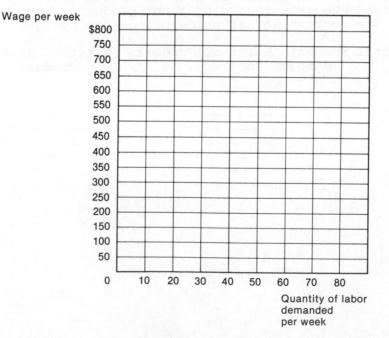

Quantity of labor demanded per week

298

Concept: Determinants of a competitive firm's input demand

3.   List three factors that will shift a firm's input demand curve.

a.   _____
b.   _____
c.   _____

4.   Given the data in question 2 above, show what happens to the firm's
marginal revenue product schedule and curve and its input demand curve for
labor if the price per damper falls to $400.

Workers	Marginal Revenue Product
0	
10	$_____
20	_____
30	_____
40	_____
50	_____
60	_____

a.   Complete the table.
b.   On the first figure shown, plot the marginal revenue product curve
associated with a price per damper of $400.
c.   On the second figure shown, plot the new demand for labor curve.
d.   The input demand curve shifts to the _____ (left,right).
e.   At a wage of $550 per week, would Company X continue to hire the same
number of workers given the reduction in the price of dampers?
Explain.
f.   The demand for an input is a _____ demand.

Concept: **The demand for an input by a profit-maximizing monopolist**

5.   The product and employment data below are for an entire market.

Q	Ql	Pc	Pm	MRm	MPL	MRPc	MRPm
0	0	$2	$2.00				
1	5	2	1.80	$____	____	$____	$____
2	11	2	1.60	____	____	____	____
3	18	2	1.40	____	____	____	____
4	26	2	1.20	____	____	____	____
5	35	2	1.00	____	____	____	____

Q = thousands of units of output per week
Ql = workers
Pc = competitive firm's product price
Pm = monopolist's product price
MRm = monopolist's marginal revenue
MPL = marginal product of labor
MRPc = competitive firm's marginal revenue product
MRPm = monopolist's marginal revenue product

a.   Complete the table.

b.   Plot the competitive market input demand curve on the figure below.

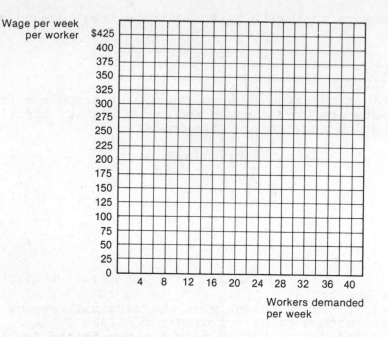

Wage per week per worker

Workers demanded per week

c.   Plot the monopolist's input demand curve on the above figure.
d.   At a wage of $250 per week, competitive firms will employ a total of
     _____ workers. At the same wage a monopolist will hire
     between _____ and _____ workers. Show this in the figure
     above. A monopolist hires _____ workers than a competitive
     firm.

Concept: Market input prices and quantities

6.   The competitive market for skilled workers is shown below. The companies
     hiring skilled labor are selling output in competitive markets.

Hourly Wage	Quantity of Labor Demanded	Quantity of Labor Supplied
	(millions of labor hours per day)	
$10.00	30	105
9.75	35	95
9.50	40	85
9.25	45	75
9.00	50	65
8.75	55	55
8.50	60	45
8.25	65	35
8.00	70	25

a.   In the diagram below, plot the demand and supply curves for labor and
     identify the market wage and level of employment. Wage =
     $_____, labor supplied _____ hours.

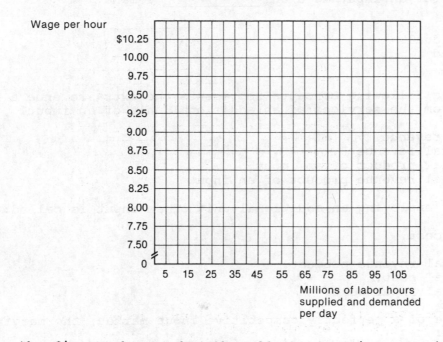

Wage per hour

Millions of labor hours
supplied and demanded
per day

b.   On the figure above, show the effect of an increase in the market
     demand for labor. Market wage rates _____ and employment
     _____.

c.   On the figure above, show the effect of an increase in the market
     supply of labor. Market wage rates _____ and employment
     _____.

d.   For those workers willing to work for a wage no less than $8.25 per
     hour but who receive the market wage of $_____, economic rent per
     labor hour equals $_____. A maximum tax per hour of
     $_____ could be levied on worker income without affecting the
     quantity of labor supplied.

e.   An increase in labor productivity will shift the _____ curve
     to the _____ (right, left) and will cause the market wage to
     _____ and market employment to _____.

f.   A decrease in the market prices of the goods produced by the
     employers of skilled labor will shift the _____ curve to the
     _____ (right, left) and will cause the market wage to _____
     and market employment to _____.

SELF-TEST FOR MASTERY

Select the best answer.

1.   Which of the following is not a characteristic of a competitive input
     market?

     a.   There is an absence of close substitute resources.
     b.   Both buyers and sellers of inputs are price takers.
     c.   There is freedom of entry into and exit from input markets.

301

d.   Resources are mobile in that they can be used in other employments and in other locations.

2.   The demand for an input is a/an _____ demand.

   a.   Normal
   b.   Individual
   c.   Derived
   d.   Market

3.   Which of the following concepts represents the extra revenue a firm receives from the services of an additional unit of an input?

   a.   Total revenue
   b.   Marginal revenue
   c.   Marginal product of an input
   d.   Marginal revenue product of an input

4.   The cost of employing an additional unit of an input is called:

   a.   Input cost.
   b.   Income.
   c.   Marginal revenue product.
   d.   Marginal cost.
   e.   Marginal input cost.

5.   For the case of a perfectly competitive input market, the marginal input cost equals:

   a.   The total cost of the input.
   b.   The price of the input.
   c.   The average cost of the input.
   d.   Marginal cost.

6.   For the case of a perfectly competitive product market, the marginal revenue product equals:

   a.   Revenue times marginal product.
   b.   Price times total product.
   c.   Marginal revenue times average product.
   d.   Price times marginal product.

7.   If at a firm's current level of employment the marginal revenue product of the last worker employed exceeds the marginal cost of labor, the firm should:

   a.   Decrease employment.
   b.   Maintain the existing level of employment.
   c.   Increase employment.
   d.   Produce less output and hire fewer workers.

8.   A profit-maximizing competitive firm will hire labor in a competitive labor market up to the point at which the _____ equals the _____.

   a.   Average revenue product, product price
   b.   Total product, wage
   c.   Marginal revenue product, wage
   d.   Marginal input cost, wage

302

9. A firm's demand curve for an input is its:

    a. Marginal cost curve.
    b. Market demand curve.
    c. Marginal product curve.
    d. Marginal revenue product curve.
    e. None of the above.

10. An increase in the demand for the product produced by an input:

    a. Will increase the supply of the input.
    b. Will decrease the supply of the input.
    c. Will increase the demand for the input.
    d. Will decrease the demand for the input.

11. If labor and capital are substitute resources in production, an increase
    in the price of capital will:

    a. Increase, the demand for labor.
    b. Increase, the supply of labor.
    c. Decrease, the demand for labor.
    d. Decrease, the supply of labor.

12. Technological innovation that increases the marginal product of labor
    will:

    a. Increase, the demand for labor.
    b. Increase, the supply of labor.
    c. Decrease, the demand for labor.
    d. Decrease, the supply of labor.

13. A monopolist's marginal revenue product curve :

    a. Is the monopolist's demand for an input.
    b. Equals marginal revenue times marginal product.
    c. Lies inside a competitive industry's demand curve for an input.
    d. Is equated to the marginal cost of labor in order to maximize profits
        from the employment of a variable input.
    e. All of the above.

14. The market supply of an input is upward sloping because:

    a. A supply curve must be upward sloping.
    b. Input suppliers face rising marginal costs as they make more of an
        input available to the market.
    c. Price and quantity supplied are inversely related.
    d. Price and quantity demanded are inversely related.

15. Economic rent is:

    a. A payment to landlords.
    b. The difference between what a resource supplier earns in the market
        and the minimum amount of income required by the resource supplier to
        maintain the same quantity of the input supplied.
    c. The maximum wage required by labor less the market wage.
    d. The minimum wage required by labor less the market wage.

16. What portion of an input supplier's income can be taxed away without affecting the quantity of inputs made available to the market?

    a. 0%
    b. 100%
    c. A portion equal to economic rent
    d. A portion equal to the input supplier's opportunity cost
    e. None of the above

17. An increase in the market demand for an input _____ market input price and _____ employment of the input.

    a. Increases, increases
    b. Decreases, decreases
    c. Increases, decreases
    d. Decreases, increases

18. An increase in the market supply of an input _____ market input price and _____ employment of an input.

    a. Increases, increases
    b. Decreases, decreases
    c. Increases, decreases
    d. Decreases, increases

19. If education increases the productivity of labor, the market _____ curve will shift _____ and cause the market wage to _____.

    a. Supply, leftward, increase
    b. Demand, leftward, increase
    c. Supply, rightward, decrease
    d. Demand, rightward, increase
    e. Demand, leftward, decrease

THINK IT THROUGH

1. Discuss intuitively how competitive input markets equalize wages of a given type of labor.

2. In the 1980s, the world price of oil fell dramatically. Discuss the likely impacts on input markets in the energy-producing regions of the United States.

3. Explain why movie or sports stars could have a much larger share of their income taxed than is currently the case without reducing the quantities of their services supplied.

4. Discuss the five key facts about input markets.

POP QUIZ   Read the news brief at the end of this chapter and answer the following questions.

1. According to the article, why are incomes of those with a bachelor's degree "exploding" in the 1980s?

2.   Using the analysis of this chapter, can you explain why college education results in higher income?

CHAPTER ANSWERS

In Brief: Chapter Summary

1. Free 2. Can 3. Have no 4. Marginal revenue product 5. Marginal revenue 6. Equals 7. Product price 8. Equals 9. Increases 10. Increases 11. Increases 12. Decreases 13. Less than 14. Inside 15. Fewer 16. Rising 17. Increase 18. Exceeds 19. Without reducing

Vocabulary Review

1. Market supply of an input 2. Marginal revenue product 3. Market demand for an input 4. Derived demand 5. Change in input demand 6. Competitive input market 7. Marginal input cost 8. Input market

Skills Review

1.   a.   Buyers and sellers of inputs are price takers
      b.   There is free entry into and exit of sellers from input markets.
      c.   Economic resources can be transferred to different
            employments and to different locations.

2.   a.   Marginal Product   Marginal Revenue Product
            1.5 $750
            1.3   650
            1.1   550
             .9   450
             .7   350
             .5   250

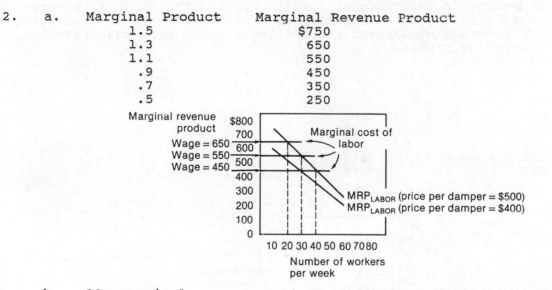

      b.   30; marginal revenue product of labor, wage per week per
            employee
      c.   40; 20
      d.   Marginal revenue product

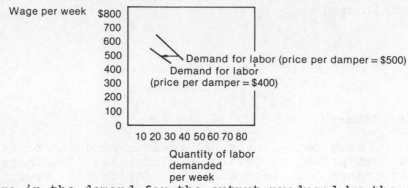

Wage per week

Quantity of labor demanded per week

3. a. A change in the demand for the output produced by the input
   b. Changes in the productivity of an input
   c. Technological changes affecting the marginal product of an input

4. a. Marginal Revenue Product
      $600
       520
       440
       360
       280
       200
   b. Answer on the first figure above.
   c. Answer on the second figure above.
   d. Left
   e. No. A decline in the price of dampers reduces the marginal revenue product relative to the marginal cost of labor. A profit-maximizing firm, by reducing employment, lowers labor costs more than revenues, thus increasing profit.
   f. Derived

5. a.

MRm	MPL	MRPc	MRPm
$1.80	200	$400	$360
1.40	167	334	234
1.00	143	286	143
.60	125	250	75
.20	111	222	22

   b.

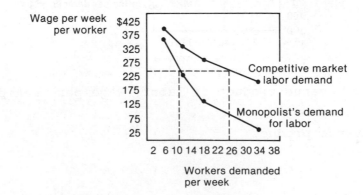

Wage per week per worker

Workers demanded per week

   c. Answer in figure above.
   d. 26; 5, 11; fewer

6. a. $8.75, 55 million

306

Wage per hour

$10.25
9.75
9.25
8.75
8.25
7.75

S_0
Supply of
S_1 labor

D_1
D_0
Demand for
Labor

5 20 35 50 65 80 95 110
   55   60

Millions of labor hours
supplied and demanded
per day

b. Rise, increases
c. Fall, increases
d. $8.75, $.50; $.50
e. Labor demand, right, rise, increase
f. Labor demand, left, fall, decrease

Self-Test for Mastery

1. a 2. c 3. d 4. e 5. b 6. d 7. c 8. c 9. d 10. c 11. a 12. a 13.
e 14. b 15. b 16. c 17. a 18. d 19. d

Think it Through

1.   Assuming free entry into and exit from a given labor market and the
mobility of labor, if wages in region A exceeded wages for identical labor in
region B, some workers would leave the low-wage region and move to the high-
wage region in pursuit of higher wages. This would cause a reduction in the
supply of labor in region B and an increase in the supply of labor in region A.
Assuming given labor demand curves for the two regions, market wages in region
A will fall while market wages in region B will rise. These changes will
continue until there are no further gains by labor from moving from one region
to the other. This occurs where the wage rates in the two regions for the
given type of labor are equalized.

2.   The large decline in oil prices reduced the marginal revenue products of
labor and other inputs used by the oil industry. As the marginal revenue
product of an input falls relative to the marginal cost of the input, profit-
maximizing firms reduce employment. The oil industry reduced employment and
cut production, causing regional recessions in those areas of the nation where
the oil industry represents a significant portion of the regional economy.

3.   Some top executives, sports and movie stars, and others receive such
enormous annual incomes that the payments they receive for their services far
exceed the minimum amount required by these individuals to make their services
available. It was recently reported that Michael Jackson earned $97 million
last year. Do you think that he would have withdrawn his services if he had
earned only $87 million? The difference between the incomes received and the
minimum incomes required by individuals to make their services available is
called economic rent. Economic rent can be taxed away in its entirety without
reducing the quantity of input services made available.

4.   Simple conclusions emerge regarding competitive input markets. The prices
of inputs used in production are determined by supply and demand. The price of
an input equals the input's marginal revenue product--an input is paid an
income equal to its contribution to the firm's revenues. The demand for an
input is derived from the demand for the output produced by the input.
Influences affecting product demand curves therefore influence input demand

curves. An input's productivity is an important determinant affecting input prices. In competitive input markets, firms are input price takers--attempts to pay an input price below the market price and marginal revenue product will fail.

Pop Quiz

1.   Income growth in the 1980s can in part be attributed to the increase in the number of men and women in the labor force having college degrees. The income gap between those having bachelor's degrees and those having just finished high school is widening in the 1980s. This gap is widening even faster among those with some years of job experience in addition to a college degree. Over the last 10 years, the work force has expanded faster than the number of new entrants with college degrees. Given the increasing emphasis on education in the high-tech workplace, bachelor's degrees are in strong demand. From the supply side of the labor market, the payback time from earning a degree is falling, thus increasing the perceived economic value of the degree to students. More people are responding to this incentive and the realization that education is increasingly necessary and are enrolling in universities.

2.   The price received by an input in a competitive labor market is equal to the input's marginal revenue product. Marginal revenue product equals the price of the output produced by the input times the input's marginal product. Anything that increases labor productivity will increase labor's marginal revenue product. If labor productivity increases, competitive firms hiring in competitive labor markets will increase employment. The market demand for labor rises, causing the market wage and level of employment to increase. It could be argued that a bachelor's degree (or rather the level of educational proficiency attained) increases labor productivity. With the widespread perception on the part of employers that bachelor's degrees are increasingly necessary and with more members of the labor force earning degrees, the demand for individuals with bachelor's degrees will increase, putting upward pressure on salaries.

Benefit of B.A. Is Greater Than Ever

Latest Data Show College Degree Greatly Increases Earnings Power

YOUR

MONEY

MATTERS

By GARY PUTKA

Staff Reporter of THE WALL STREET JOURNAL.

There may be something rising faster than the price of going to college, after all.

The price of not going.

In a ritual well known to strapped parents, the College Board recently released its annual survey showing tuitions rising faster than inflation. As is customary, the big admissions group gave no explanation for the 7% increase for 1988-89, the eighth year in a row that the rise in college tuition has outpaced inflation.

Pressed by Congress and others for the reasons, colleges have in the past blamed the need for more scholarships and higher faculty salaries. But a growing body of research suggests a more markets-like answer: College costs more because the product is worth more.

Measured in terms of income, returns on a bachelor's degree "have been exploding in the '80s," says Finis Welch, an economics professor at the University of California at Los Angeles who specializes in the labor market. Mr. Welch and other analysts, using census data, see a dramatic rise in the amount of income gained by going to college over a time period roughly coinciding with the big tuition increases.

Salary Gap

Male college graduates in the work force made 39.2% more than high school graduates in 1986, the latest year of Census Bureau reports, compared with 23.8% in 1979. For women, the difference rose to 40.5% from 27.9%.

More recent data, derived by University of Michigan economist Jonathan Bound from computer tapes of the Census Bureau's monthly surveys, indicate that the differences were more pronounced in 1987. Mr. Bound's figures show that the gap last year was 70% for women in their first 10 working years and 46% for males of that experience. Economists caution that when data for all workers is reported by the Census Bureau, the unusually large gap for women will probably shrink, though it still will be above the 1986 figure.

Moreover, Mr. Bound says the figures don't reflect another benefit of college, namely that the college educated are less likely to be unemployed than high school graduates. And Mr. Welch's research shows that the gap between more-seasoned workers is widening even faster, peaking at about 20 years' experience and remaining steady afterward.

No one is sure what's behind the growing income gap, but some economists point to a drop in high-paying factory jobs among high school graduates. Another reason may be the growing importance of high-tech employment demanding more education. Also, while the number of new college graduates has edged up only about 5% in the past 10 years to about 980,000 a year, the work force has expanded much faster. This has given a sheepskin a rarity value unimagined in the 1970s, when the well-educated flooded the labor market and the cabbie with a doctorate drove his way into national folklore.

"It's rather remarkable," says Richard Freeman, an economist whose 1976 book, "The Overeducated American," presented evidence on the decline of a diploma's value. Now director of labor studies at the National Bureau for Economic Research in Boston, Mr. Freeman says he had expected college's value to make a comeback, "but no one anticipated the magnitude" of the gains for college graduates.

Census data show that the median income of the college-educated man in 1986 was $34,391 versus $24,701 for those without college. That means that the college "payback time"—the number of years it takes a worker to recoup four years of tuition and lost earnings—has shrunk despite the soaring tuitions. Using tuition figures for public colleges, which educate about 77% of all students, the payback time is down to about 11 years, from about 17 in 1979, before the big tuition mark-ups.

Economists don't suggest that high school seniors are delving through census data and punching calculators before deciding whether or not to attend college. But they do say students and parents know what's going on around them—and act accordingly.

"People see some of the kind of job creation that's going on, and they realize without a college education they're up a tree," says Louis Morrell, treasurer of Radcliffe College, Cambridge, Mass. "People want it and they're willing to pay for it."

Relatively stable annual enrollment of about 12 million students in the 1980s wouldn't seem to support the idea of more clamoring for college. But enrollment has

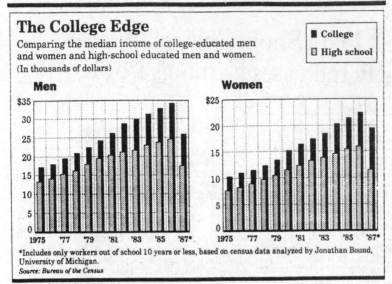

The College Edge

Comparing the median income of college-educated men and women and high-school educated men and women.
(In thousands of dollars)

Legend: ■ College ▨ High school

Men

Women

*Includes only workers out of school 10 years or less, based on census data analyzed by Jonathan Bound, University of Michigan.
Source: Bureau of the Census

held steady in the face of a 16% decline in the number of high school graduates since 1977. More college freshmen than ever say they're there to make more money, and according to the most recent Gallup survey on the subject, 64% of Americans rate a college education as "very important" in getting ahead, up from 36% in 1978.

"Costs have escalated at the very moment in history when more people believe that (college) is worth it," says Terry Hartle, education aide to Sen. Edward Kennedy of Massachusetts. "I don't think it's unrelated."

Market Forces

The figures tend to support the economic value of college. But they also suggest that prices in higher education are more subject to market forces than universities have generally acknowledged. Richard Rosser, president of the National Association of Independent Colleges and Universities, says many colleges struggle to hold the line on costs without sacrificing quality. And he adds that tuitions cover only a portion of total costs, with the balance coming from governments, private donations and investment earnings. "Colleges agonize over tuition decisions," he says. "What they're doing is simply covering the real cost of running our universities."

With soaring applications, officials of Ivy League and other top private colleges have long contended that they could raise tuitions by more than they have, and still retain enrollments. They say they have resisted doing so because of concern about the ability of some people to pay.

As for the future?

High Cost of College

Average annual price of four-year colleges

	TUITION AND FEES	
	PUBLIC	PRIVATE
1977-78	$ 621	$2,476
1978-79	651	2,647
1979-80	680	2,923
1980-81	706	3,279
1981-82	819	3,709
1982-83	979	4,021
1983-84	1,105	4,627
1984-85	1,126	5,016
1985-86	1,242	5,418
1986-87	1,337	5,793
1987-88*	1,359	7,110
1988-89*	1,566	7,693

NOTE: Figures are as reported in year of survey
*Weighted averages; all others unweighted
Source: College Board

Higher tuitions still, say the economists who study higher education, until quality, or at least the economic value of higher education, is perceived to decline. "Colleges will act like businessmen on a board," says Mr. Morrell of Radcliffe. "They price themselves according to what the value of the good is perceived to be, and they'll continue to do that until the market says it won't accept it."

21

Labor Markets, Labor Productivity, and Personnel Management

CHAPTER CHALLENGES

After studying your text, attending class, and completing this chapter, you should be able to:

1. Analyze the choice to work and show how a person's labor supply curve depends on his preferences and other influences, such as nonlabor sources of income.
2. Show how the market supply of labor services is influenced by population and other demographic variables.
3. Explain why different wages are paid for different jobs, occupations, or skills.
4. Show how labor productivity is a key determinant of the average level of wages in a nation.
5. Show how personnel management techniques can be used to motivate workers and increase the marginal revenue product of labor.

IN BRIEF: CHAPTER SUMMARY

Fill in the blanks to summarize chapter content.

An individual's decision to work an additional hour depends on the additional gains versus additional losses from doing so. The (1)_____(marginal benefits, marginal costs) of an additional hour of work include the extra monetary and nonmonetary satisfaction received. The additional cost of an hour of work is the (2)_____ (wage, value of a forgone hour of leisure). The opportunity cost of leisure time increases as the individual works more hours. As a result, higher wages or other nonmonetary benefits are (3)_____ (necessary, unnecessary) to compensate the worker for the rising opportunity cost of leisure time. The individual's labor supply curve is upward sloping if an increase in wages, or an increase in the marginal (4)_____ (benefits, costs) relative to the marginal cost of work, induces the individual to work additional hours.

There are both substitution and income effects associated with a change in the wage. An increase in the wage makes an hour of work more valuable in terms of the goods and services that can be purchased with the higher income earned. This causes the opportunity cost of an hour of leisure to increase. An individual will substitute an hour of work for an hour of leisure. The substitution effect results in (5)_____(less, more) hours worked as wages rise. The income effect has just the opposite impact on hours worked. An increase in wages means that the worker can consume the same quantities of goods and services with (6)_____ (fewer, more) hours worked. If the substitution effect outweighs the income effect, the supply curve of labor is (7)_____ (upward sloping, backward bending). If the income effect outweighs the substitution effect, the labor supply curve is (8)_____ (backward bending, upward sloping). If the income and substitution effects just offset each other, the labor supply curve is (9)_____ (positively sloped, vertical).

Market wages depend upon the supply of and demand for labor. The supply of labor is influenced by population and the rate of participation in the labor force. Birth and death rates, immigration, and emigration all influence the supply of labor. Labor productivity is a key determinant of the demand for labor. Increases in a nation's labor productivity (10)_____ (increase, decrease) labor incomes.

Differences in wages among workers and jobs can be explained by productivity or quality differences. Differences in quality are influenced by natural abilities or other characteristics of the individual and by the extent of training or education. Differences in wages can also be attributed to working conditions. Some jobs have negative (11)_____ (externalities, nonpecuniary wages) in that nonmonetary aspects of the job make it less desirable than another job paying exactly the same wage. In order to induce people to accept employment in less desirable occupations, a compensating wage differential must be paid to the worker to make the total compensation from the job (12)_____ (equal to, greater than) to other jobs paying a lower wage but having higher nonmonetary benefits. Some jobs have nonpecuniary benefits that are greater than those for other jobs. These jobs pay a lower wage in order to equalize the total compensation among jobs.

An objective of (13)_____ (production, personnel) management is to adjust the monetary and nonmonetary characteristics of a job in order to increase the marginal revenue product of labor. But first, personnel managers must hire and train workers. The signals from the job seeker's resume and interview offer an (14)_____ (efficient, low-cost; inefficient, high-cost) method of screening. Once hired, the worker has to be trained. This is often a costly process, and firms tend to give only firm-specific training. Where possible firms promote from within in order to avoid some of these training costs. A firm must monitor the actions of its workers to ensure that the owner's desires are met. Owners want to maximize profits, but when workers seek to maximize personal objectives that do not coincide with the owner's goal of profit maximization, workers shirk on the job. They engage in activities that increase their satisfaction (15)_____ (but that increase, and lower) production costs and (16)_____ (increase, lower) worker productivity. One way to reduce shirking is to design and implement compensation systems tying together the interests of workers, managers, and owners. Profit sharing and stock options are two examples.

VOCABULARY REVIEW

Write the key term from the list below next to its definition.

Key Terms

Nonwage money income	Nonpecuniary wages
Marginal cost of work	Compensating wage differential
Marginal benefit of work	Staffing
Labor supply curve	Signals
Substitution effect of a	Screening
wage change	Internal labor market
Income effect of a wage	Shirking
change	Backward-bending labor supply
Human capital	curve

312

Definitions

1. _____: represents the skills and qualifications of workers that stem from education and training.

2. _____: the nonmonetary aspects of a job that must be added to or subtracted from money wages to obtain total compensation per hour of work.

3. _____: implies that the substitution effect on a worker's labor services outweighs the income effect only at relatively low wages.

4. _____: a difference in money wages necessary to make total compensation for similar jobs equal when nonpecuniary wages are not equal to zero.

5. _____: the change in hours worked stemming from the change in income caused by the wage change.

6. _____: indicators displayed by job applicants and used by employers to predict the future satisfaction and productivity of a worker.

7. _____: the change in hours worked resulting only from a change in the opportunity cost of an hour of leisure.

8. _____: the process of recruiting and hiring workers to perform the various tasks required to produce goods and services.

9. _____: shows a relationship between a worker's hourly wages and labor hours supplied for work over a given period.

10. _____: a process in which an employer limits the number of applicants for a job to those it believes are the most likely to succeed in the company.

11. _____: the extra income received from extra work, including any nonmonetary satisfaction obtained from a job.

12. _____: behavior by workers that prevents a firm from achieving the maximum possible marginal product of labor over a given period.

13. _____: the value of extra leisure time given up to work.

14. _____: exists within a firm when it fills positions by hiring its own employees, rather than new employees, to fill all but the lowest-level positions.

15. _____: includes pensions, welfare payments and subsidies, interest, dividends, allowances, and any other type of income that is available independent of work.

SKILLS REVIEW

Concept: An individual's choice to work and labor supply curve

1. Fred's marginal benefits and marginal costs associated with additional
    hours of work are shown below. Assume Fred's marginal benefit from a hour
    of labor is the market wage and that after 8 hours of sleep, Fred has 16
    hours per day to allocate between work and leisure.

Hours per Day	Marginal Benefit	Marginal Cost
0		
1	$9	$1.50
2	9	3.00
3	9	4.50
4	9	6.00
5	9	7.50
6	9	9.00
7	9	10.50
8	9	12.00
9	9	13.50
10	9	15.00

a. Plot the marginal costs and marginal benefits on the figure below.

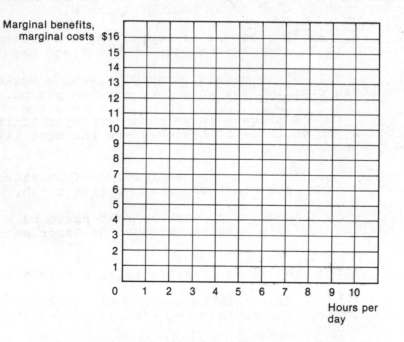

b. Fred maximizes net benefits from work by working _____ hours and
    consuming _____ hours of leisure. Show this in the figure
    above.
c. If the market wage increases to $12 per hour, Fred maximizes net
    benefits by working _____ hours and consuming _____
    hours of leisure. Show this in the figure above.
d. If the market wage falls to $6 per hour, Fred maximizes net benefits
    by working _____ hours and consuming _____ hours of leisure.
    Show this in the figure above.
e. Plot Fred's labor supply curve in the figure below using market
    wages of $6, $9, and $12.

314

Wage

$16
15
14
13
12
11
10
9
8
7
6
5
4
3
2
1
0

1 2 3 4 5 6 7 8 9 10

Hours per day

f. Fred's labor supply curve is his _____ curve.

2. <u>Advanced Question</u> Suppose Fred's marginal cost and marginal benefit can be expressed as follows:

$$MB = Wo$$
$$MC = a + bH$$ where Wo represents the given market wage and H is the number of hours worked

a. Derive an expression for the number of hours worked that maximizes net benefits.

b. What happens to the net benefit-maximizing level of hours worked given changes in a, b, and W? Interpret.

c. If a wage tax, t, is levied on the hourly wage, what happens to the benefit-maximizing level of hours worked? (Assume that t is greater than zero but less than 1.)

3. Answer the following questions on the basis of the figure below.

Wage per hour $

C

B

A

0   Quantity of
labor hours
supplied per month

a. At point A, there is _____ relationship between the hourly wage and the quantity of labor supplied. This is because the substitution effect _____ the income effect of a wage change.

b. At point B, there is _____ relationship between the hourly wage and the quantity of labor supplied. This is because the substitution effect _____ the income effect of a wage change.

c. At point C, there is _____ relationship between the hourly wage and the quantity of labor supplied. This is because the substitution effect _____ the income effect of a wage change.

Concept: Determinants of market wages

4. What factors influence the market supply of labor? Give an example of each.

a. _____

b. _____

5. Below is a market for sales clerks.

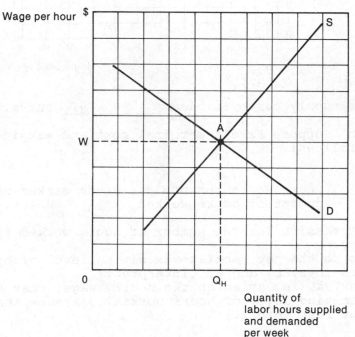

a. Assume that because of an increase in the birth rate some years ago, there is currently a large increase in the number of teenagers entering the labor force. The _____ curve for sales clerks shifts _____. Market wages _____, and employment _____. Show this graphically in the figure above.

b. Assume that because of new technology, the marginal products of sales clerks increase. The _____ curve for sales clerks shifts _____. Given the initial market equilibrium at point A, wages _____ and employment _____. Show this graphically in the figure above. Worker productivity and wage rates are _____ related.

SELF TEST FOR MASTERY

Select the best answer.

1. Which of the following is a definition for the marginal cost of work?

    a. The value of the time and toil involved in a job
    b. The wage
    c. The value of extra leisure time given up to work
    d. The additional production costs associated with the use of an additional unit of labor

2. The extra income received from extra work, including any nonmonetary satisfaction obtained from a job, is called:

    a. Total pecuniary benefits.
    b. The marginal benefit of work.
    c. External benefits.
    d. The wage rate.
    e. Nonpecuniary satisfaction.

3. In order to maximize the net benefits from work, an individual should work additional hours up to the point where:

    a. The total costs of labor equal the total benefits of labor.
    b. The wage equals marginal revenue.
    c. Marginal revenue is greater than marginal labor cost.
    d. The marginal cost of work equals the marginal benefit of work.

4. An individual's labor supply curve:

    a. Is upward sloping if the substitution effect outweighs the income effect of a wage change.
    b. Represents combinations of wage rates and quantities of labor hours supplied.
    c. Is an equilibrium relationship in that each coordinate point on the curve is a net benefit-maximizing quantity of hours supplied at that wage rate.
    d. May have sections that are upward sloping, downward sloping and even vertical.
    e. All of the above.

5. If the market wage rises such that an individual's wage exceeds the marginal cost of work and assuming that the substitution effect is dominant, the individual will maximize net benefits from work by:

    a. Working additional hours.
    b. Working fewer hours.
    c. Consuming more leisure.
    d. Consuming the same quantity of leisure.

6. The backward-bending portion of a labor supply curve occurs:

    a. When wages equal the firm's marginal product.
    b. Where the substitution effect outweighs the income effect.
    c. Only rarely and at low levels of income.
    d. Where the income effect outweighs the substitution effect.

7. Which of the following is a determinant of the market supply curve for labor?

    a. Population growth
    b. Rate of labor force participation
    c. Birth rate
    d. Extent of immigration
    e. All of the above

8. Investment in capital _____ labor productivity, resulting in a _____ shift in the market _____ curve for labor.

    a. Decreases, leftward, supply
    b. Decreases, rightward, demand
    c. Increases, rightward, demand
    d. Increases, leftward, demand

9. The "baby boom" caused the market _____ curve for labor to shift _____, resulting in a/an _____ in market wages, others things held constant.

    a. Supply, rightward, decrease
    b. Demand, leftward, increase
    c. Supply, leftward, increase
    d. Demand, rightward, decrease

10. Training and education:

    a. Are investments in human capital.
    b. Increase the productivity of labor.
    c. Increase a nation's living standards because of the increase in labor productivity.
    d. Are one explanation for wage differences between different jobs and workers.
    e. All of the above.

11. Which of the following is an example of nonpecuniary wages?

    a. Hourly wage rate
    b. Air-conditioned workplace
    c. Health and retirement benefits
    d. Stock options

12. Which of the following is an example of nonpecuniary job benefits?

    a. Flexible work hours
    b. Opportunities for advancement
    c. Nonhazardous job
    d. Pleasant job or local amenities
    e. All of the above

13. If two jobs, job A and job B, are identical with the exception that job B is associated with nonpecuniary job benefits, job A will pay _____ job B.

    a. A higher wage than
    b. A lower wage than
    c. The same wage as
    d. None of the above

14. Firms often have a preference for promoting existing employees to fill new or vacant positions. Which of the following terms represents this concept?

    a. Staffing
    b. Signals
    c. Screening
    d. Internal labor market

15. Shirking by management and labor results when:

    a. Lazy employees are hired.
    b. The interests of owners, management, and workers coincide.
    c. Goods and services are produced by government but never when private firms produce output.
    d. The interests of owners, management, and workers do not coincide.

16. Shirking on the job:

    a. Is a problem unless a compensation system is devised in which managers and workers are induced to pursue the owner's goals for the firm.
    b. Is an insignificant problem because monitoring eliminates it.
    c. Is most efficiently reduced with monitoring.
    d. Is most efficiently reduced by compensation systems such as stock options and profit sharing, particularly if monitoring is costly.
    e. A and d.

THINK IT THROUGH

1. Why does the opportunity cost of leisure rise as an individual works additional hours per day?

2. If two occupations located in the same city and requiring the same skills, education, and experience pay different wage rates, there must be discrimination. True or false? Explain.

3. If two individuals working in the same occupation receive different wage rates, there must be discrimination. True or false? Explain.

4. If workers and managers have goals other than the owner's goal of profit maximization, explain how shirking arises and its implications for the firm and for the economy's allocation of resources. How can owners deal with the shirking problem?

POP QUIZ   Read the news brief at the end of this chapter and answer the questions below.

1. According to the article, why has real hourly pay of blue-collar and clerical workers remained roughly constant over the last 15 years? (Indicate the influences affecting the demand for and supply of labor.)

2. Explain, in terms of supply of and demand for labor, why real wages are expected to rise in the future.

CHAPTER ANSWERS

In Brief: Chapter Summary

1. Marginal benefits 2. Value of a forgone hour of leisure 3. Necessary 4. Benefits 5. More 6. Less 7. Upward sloping 8. Backward bending 9. Vertical 10. Increase 11. Nonpecuniary wages 12. Equal to 13. Personnel 14. Efficient, low-cost 15. But that increases 16. Lower

Vocabulary Review

1. Human capital 2. Nonpecuniary wages 3. Backward-Bending labor supply curve 4. Compensating wage differential 5. Income effect of a wage change 6. Signals 7. Substitution effect of a wage change 8. Staffing 9. Labor supply curve 10. Screening 11. Marginal benefit of work 12. Shirking 13. Marginal cost of work 14. Internal labor market 15. Nonwage money income

Skills Review

1. a.

    b. 10, 6 c. 8, 8 d. 4, 12

    e.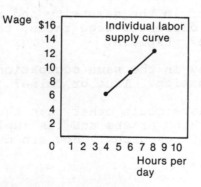

    f. Marginal cost of work

2. a. Net benefits from work are maximized where the marginal cost of work equals the marginal benefit of work. Setting MB equal to MC and solving for H yields the net benefit-maximizing level of hours worked.

    $$H = (W1 - a)/b$$

    b. A change in a shifts the marginal cost of work curve, whereas a change in b changes the slope of the curve. An increase in a or b decreases hours worked. Anything that causes Fred's marginal cost of work to increase relative to the prevailing wage will cause Fred to work less and vice versa. For instance, if Fred receives news that he has a terminal illness, the value of extra leisure time given up to work would increase. The marginal cost curve would shift upward, and Fred would work less. An increase in the market wage will increase Fred's hours worked and vice versa.

    c.   Fred's willingness to work an additional hour is based on the wage received and available for expenditure. Taxes reduce spendable wages. It is necessary to reduce the before-tax wage by the amount of the tax.

$$Wa = \text{After-tax wage} = (1 - t)W1$$

Inserting Wa in the expression above for the net benefit-maximizing hours worked gives

$$H = [(1 - t)W1 - a]/b$$

Since t is a positive fraction, Fred's hours worked after taxes are imposed are less than the hours worked before the imposition of a wage tax. The marginal benefits of work fall relative to the marginal cost of work, and Fred reduces hours worked.

3.   a.   Positive, outweighs b. No, just offsets the c. Inverse, is less than

4.   a.   Population. The "baby boom" affects the number of workers entering the labor force and results in a rightward shift in labor supply curves.

    b.   Rates of labor force participation. Even with a constant population, if more people are entering the labor force and seeking employment, labor supply curves will shift rightward.

5.   a.

      Market supply, rightward; decrease, increases

    b.   Market demand, rightward; increase, increases; positively

Self-Test for Mastery

1. c 2. b 3. d 4. e 5. a 6. d 7. e 8. c 9. a 10. e 11. b 12. e 13. a 14. d 15. d 16. e

Think it Through

1.   Assuming an individual sleeps 8 hours per day, there are 16 hours to be allocated between work and leisure. An additional hour worked means that an additional hour of leisure is sacrificed. Because of diminishing marginal utility (or benefits), the value of an hour of leisure rises as less leisure

time is available. Therefore the opportunity cost of an hour worked rises as more hours are worked and fewer hours are available for leisure.

2.   There may be discrimination, but the difference in wage could be due to compensating wage differentials paid to compensate the worker for undesirable aspects of the job or because of the presence of nonpecuniary job benefits that allow employers to pay a lower wage. In both cases, total compensation received by the worker is the same even though wages differ. The individual working in the job with nonpecuniary job benefits receives a portion of his total compensation from the pleasant or desirable nonmonetary benefits of the job.

3.   There may be discrimination, but a wage differential between two workers in the same occupation could also be due to differences in the productivity or quality of the two workers. It could also be due to regional differences in labor markets, including regional differences in product prices that may affect marginal revenue products. Regional amenities (weather, sports, fine arts, education, etc.) vary, thus affecting the nonpecuniary benefits associated with a given occupation located in different regions.

4.   Assume that individuals maximize utility whether they are owners, workers, or managers. Owners maximize utility in part by maximizing the return to their invested resources--by maximizing profits. Workers and managers maximize utility by engaging in activities that give satisfaction. This may include earning income, consuming goods and services, exercising power, achieving job security, achieving prestige, and so on. If a firm's compensation system is not designed to encourage both workers and managers to seek the owner's goal of profit maximization, workers and managers will shirk on the job. They will, within the constraints of the job, engage in activities that enhance their welfare but do not necessarily maximize the firm's profits. Managers may decorate their offices with expensive furniture and art and hire attractive but possibly inefficient secretaries. Workers will likely not maximize their effort per hour worked in earning a wage income and assuring themselves of job security and promotion opportunities. The marginal products of managers and workers alike will not be at their potential. The firm's costs of production will be higher, and owners will not receive maximum profit. The economy is less efficient in that resources are underemployed because maximum output is not being achieved from a given complement of resources. The economy is inside its production possibilities curve.

A firm can use stock options or an employment contract to encourage a manager to increase profits. If the manager's compensation is tied to the firm's profits, the manager will make more decisions consistent with the interests of the owner. Workers also can be motivated to seek the owner's profit goals with profit-sharing wage contracts.

Pop Quiz

1.   A number of factors have been responsible for the lack of growth in the real hourly wages of blue-collar and clerical workers over the last 15 years. On the supply side of the labor markets, the baby-boom generation increased the supply of labor and the labor force participation rate increased due to the entry of teenagers and women. Further, the decline in union power meant that unions were decreasingly able to manipulate the supply side of labor markets. On the demand side of the labor markets, the economy at times has been stagnant, resulting in a reduction in the demand for labor. Increased competition in international markets and deregulation held down prices and marginal revenue products. The rate of saving and investment in capital decreased, reducing the marginal products of labor. In short, the supply of labor was increasing faster than the demand for labor, keeping real hourly wages from rising.

2.   Real wages are expected to rise over the next few years because the labor force is expected to grow less rapidly due to a decline in population growth and immigration laws preventing the entry of illegal aliens. Another cause of the expected increase in real wages is an anticipated increase in saving and capital investment. The supply of labor is expected to fall relative to the demand for labor, causing wages to rise.

Wage Stagnation May Be Ending

By William A. Cox

The presumed American birthright of rising living standards has been on hold for 15 years. Average hourly pay of blue-collar and clerical workers is slightly lower in purchasing power now than it was in 1973 and has made no progress even in the prosperous mid-1980s. Counting managers, professionals, other self-employed people, and the rising share of employee compensation received as fringe benefits, real earnings per hour have increased only 0.7% a year from 1973 through 1987.

Income per capita has risen faster than income per hour because a larger share of the adult population is working more hours per capita. In other words, we are working harder for it, and this has its cost in leisure, child care, and home-cooked meals. Per-capita income also rose faster than hourly pay because of the faster rise in interest income and Social Security.

The reasons for stagnant real wages will be much debated in this election year. But this epoch may now be ending, regardless of who becomes the next president.

Erosion of Unions

The world's postwar economic boom foundered in the 1970s just when the U.S. labor force was growing at a pace unmatched since early in the century. Pay fell behind oil-fueled price rises partly because plentiful young workers were a drag on productivity. Young and other marginal workers, including swelling ranks of low-income single mothers, lost ground rapidly relative to others in the general retrenchment in the 1980s.

Intense foreign competition, due mainly to exchange-rate maladjustments, held down wages (as well as prices and profits) in the mid-1980s in all industries exposed to international competition. Some of the lag in average wages stemmed from erosion of union wage scales that were out of line with the rest of the economy. Union wages in manufacturing, construction and transportation have been undermined by spreading nonunion competition. Federal deregulation of the airline and trucking industries accelerated the breakdown of their sheltered wage and price structures by allowing new competition in markets that for decades had been protected.

An important fact explaining the stagnation of productivity and real wages is that bumper crops of new workers were not matched by faster additions to capital. Total hours worked in the private economy grew by only 0.5% a year from 1950 through 1968 but three times as fast from 1969 through 1986. But the wherewithal and motivation for business investment did not suddenly increase with swelling labor supplies. According to the Commerce Department, the net stock of fixed capital in private business expanded more slowly in the later period, as economic growth slowed and profitability declined. Since its peak postwar growth rates of the mid-1960s, net private capital has grown more slowly in each successive business upswing, including the present one. The amount of capital per hour worked has continued to grow, but only about half as fast as before 1968.

Given the drop in domestic saving and extremely high real interest rates since 1979, it is remarkable investment has not slowed by more. Private saving as a share of gross national product was sustained in the 1970s by rising corporate saving (undistributed profits), which offset the decline in personal saving. But corporate saving plunged during the 1980-82 recession and never recovered, while personal saving, after rising in 1978-81, resumed its fall.

The federal government, moreover, had deficits (dissaving) that averaged 0.1% of GNP from 1950 through 1969; during that period, deficits exceeded 1% of GNP only during five years of recession or war. But in 13 of the 19 years from 1970 to date, deficits have been at least 2% of GNP and usually much larger. Since 1980 they have averaged 4%.

As a result, net national saving—the sum of personal, corporate and government saving—which averaged 8% of GNP from 1950 to 1979, has fallen to 3.1% from 1980 through 1987. Partly for this reason, real interest rates (represented here by Treasury bill rates minus concurrent consumer inflation), which ranged between 1% and 2% traditionally and were negative during most of the 1970s, averaged 3.7% from 1979 through 1987.

Starting in 1979, the number of teenagers reaching working age began to fall. Labor-force growth plummeted from 2.9% annually in 1978 and 1979, peak years of the last business cycle, to 1.7% in 1985 through 1987. This scarcity of newly trained young workers will intensify until the mid-1990s, with little relief even then. The 1986 immigration law, moreover, limits labor-force growth further by curtailing illegal aliens' access to jobs.

The Labor Department recently forecast that labor-force growth will average only 1.2% annually from 1986 through 2000, assuming that the new law is partially effective in curtailing illegal workers. This means a return to labor-supply conditions of the 1950s, except that many more of the future new workers will be minority and female workers.

With labor scarcity wages will rise, especially for entry-level workers, regardless of minimum-wage legislation. Employers

> *Opportunities for inexperienced and poorly educated workers will be revolutionized. Conditions favor a reduction in the poverty rate among female-headed households.*

will have to take much more vigorous measures to recruit and train workers. Firms incurring those "start-up" costs will improve amenities to retain people. Opportunities for inexperienced and poorly educated workers will be revolutionized. This makes a shift from welfare to workfare very timely and suggests that improved child-care and work-sharing arrangements are the wave of the future. Conditions favor a reduction in the high rate of poverty among female-headed households.

Effects on wages of the deregulation moves of the late 1970s have nearly run their course. The exchange-rate maladjustment, which depressed U.S. industries, has now been corrected, and American producers are coming back strong. Thus wage catch-up is likely to replace wage givebacks as labor's agenda in the future.

The $64 billion question is whether supplies of home-grown saving available for investment will recover. The federal deficit has been reduced from 5.2% of GNP in 1983 to about 3.2% in 1988, although the improvement was more than offset by the remarkable drying up of private saving. The Gramm-Rudman-Hollings law requires the deficit to be eliminated, and steadily rising surpluses in the Social Security trust fund suggest that the overall budget may in fact be balanced sometime in the 1990s and could move into surplus for 20 years or so.

A big question mark hangs over the future of private savings, corporate as well as personal, both of which are at historic lows. But there may be hope. Corporate saving did not recover from its plunge of the early 1980s because of poor profits in industries facing international competition and woe in the financial sector. Profitability in manufacturing, insurance and commercial banking is now being restored. Even the personal saving rate could rise gradually as the baby-boomers finish acquiring initial stocks of automobiles, housing and equipment, and move into a stage of life characterized by greater saving.

A shift toward scarcer labor and more plentiful capital—the reverse of conditions that marked the past 15 years—would raise returns to labor relative to capital. Scarcity of labor is an imminent certainty. A rise in domestic saving, evolving over several years, could result in a long-term decline in real interest rates from today's inordinate levels. Rising wages and lower capital costs would strengthen incentives for labor-saving investment, boosting capital-labor ratios and productivity. Faster growing productivity is the missing link to convert faster rising wages into rising real living standards.

Foreign Debt

With today's global capital markets, however, an increase in American saving could flow into investments abroad if returns are higher there. The earnings would help to cover payments on the recent buildup of foreign-held assets in this country, but the productivity and wage gains would go to foreigners. The extent to which savings will flow abroad depends in part on the extent to which technology development creates attractive new investment opportunities in this country.

The bill to service the foreign-debt buildup of the 1980s is coming due. This will divert some future income gains abroad. How large this burden will become depends on two interrelated factors: How fast the U.S. saving rate rises and how fast the trade deficit declines. In any event, faster-growing productivity and real wages would make the burden easier to bear and leave more for renewed gains in American living standards.

Mr. Cox was deputy chief economist at the Commerce Department, 1978-81, and now specializes in economic policy at the Congressional Research Service.

22

Imperfectively Competitive Input Markets: Labor Unions, Monopsony, and Bilateral Monopoly

CHAPTER CHALLENGES

After studying your text, attending class, and completing this chapter, you should be able to:

1. Describe the goals and purposes of labor unions.
2. Show how labor union practices can influence wages and affect the productivity of workers.
3. Describe the hiring practices of a monopsony firm and show how such a firm sets input prices.
4. Show how conflicts in input markets arise when monopoly and monopsony are simultaneously present.

IN BRIEF: CHAPTER SUMMARY

Fill in the blanks to summarize chapter content.

Labor unions engage in collective bargaining to win higher wages and better working conditions and to achieve other goals. In (1)_____ (imperfectly competitive, competitive) product markets, labor unions can only succeed in getting higher wages if the entire industry is unionized. A union must erect barriers to entry to jobs for which it has been able to raise wages. It must also be able to prevent workers from making side agreements with employers.

The earliest unions in the United States were (2)_____ (craft, industrial) unions. The modern union movement began in 1886 with the (3)_____ (Congress of Industrial Organizations, CIO; American Federation of Labor, AFL), which included craft unions composed of skilled workers. In 1935, the (4)_____ (Congress of Industrial Organizations, CIO; American Federation of Labor, AFL) organized industrial unions. A/An (5)_____ (craft, industrial) union organizes all types of labor within an industry, regardless of skill level. In 1955, the AFL and CIO merged. Federal legislation prohibits closed shops and featherbedding, but allows states to pass right-to-work laws. The federal government can intervene and issue an injunction to delay a strike for a period of time. The labor movement has (6)_____ (declined since it peaked, expanded since it bottomed out) in the 1950s. As of 1984, only (7)_____ (35%, 16.1%) of U.S. workers belonged to unions.

Unions try to increase wages by (8)_____ (expanding, restricting) the supply of labor or imposing an above-market equilibrium wage through the collective bargaining process. Unions (9)_____ (can also; cannot, however,) raise wages by promoting demand for the products they produce. If collective bargaining ends in stalemate, arbitrators will be used to mediate the issues. Evidence indicates that the average wage differential between unionized and nonunionized industries is between (10)_____ (25% and 33%,

10% and 20%) with the differential being much larger for certain industries or occupations. Evidence also indicates that a unionized work force is (11)_____ (more, less) stable, reliable, and productive than a nonunionized work force.

A pure (12)_____ (monopoly, monopsony) exists when there is a single buyer of an input that has few if any alternative employment opportunities. A monopsonist can set wage rates and other input prices. Because the monopsonist is the sole employer of the market supply of an input, it must pay higher input prices to induce input suppliers to make additional inputs available. But the higher input prices have to be paid not only to the new employees but to all existing employees as well. The monopsonist's marginal input cost (13)_____ (equals, exceeds) the wage rate (or average input cost). A profit-maximizing monopsonist will hire inputs up to the point at which the (14)_____ (marginal cost of an input, wage) equals the input's marginal revenue product. A monopsonist pays a wage (15)_____ (equal to, below) the marginal input cost of labor and the worker's marginal revenue product. The (16)_____ (competitive labor market, monopsonist) hires fewer workers and pays a lower wage than employers in a (17)_____ (competitive, monopsonistic) labor market.

A (18)_____ (bilateral monopoly, pure monopsony) exists when the demand side of an input market is represented by a monopsonist and the supply side is represented by a monopoly seller. Through the collective bargaining process a monopoly seller of an input such as a labor union can win a wage above the wage desired by the monopsonist, resulting in (19)_____ (less, higher) employment and higher wages that are closer to or equal to the worker's marginal revenue product.

VOCABULARY REVIEW

Write the key term from the list below next to its definition.

Key Terms

Labor union	Pure monopsony
Monopsony	Monopsony power
Collective bargaining	Marginal input cost
Craft union	Average input cost
Industrial union	Bilateral monopoly
Closed shop	

Definitions

1. _____: exists when only one buyer and one seller trade input (or output) services in a market.

2. _____: a union that represents all workers in a particular industry, regardless of their craft or skill.

3. _____: a single firm that buys the entire market supply of an input that has few if any alternative employment opportunities.

4. _____: an organization of workers in a particular skilled job, such as plumbers, electricians, carpenters, or musicians.

5. _____: the ability of a single buyer to influence the prices of some of the input services it purchases.

327

6. _____: the process of negotiating for wages and
    improvements in working conditions between a labor union and employers.

7. _____: the change in total input cost associated with a
    change in input services hired.

8. _____: a single buyer with no rivals in an input market.

9. _____: the price of an input.

10. _____: an organization formed to represent the interests
    of workers in bargaining with employers for contracts concerning wages,
    fringe benefits, and working conditions.

11. _____: a union arrangement with an employer that permits
    hiring only of union members.

SKILLS REVIEW

Concept: Labor union practices

1. Match the union legislation listed below to the following descriptions.

    Norris-LaGuardia Act (1932)
    Wagner Act (1935)
    Fair Labor Standards Act (1938)
    Taft-Hartley Act (1947)

    a. _____ allowed states to establish right-to-work laws
    b. _____ outlawed featherbedding
    c. _____ outlawed child labor
    d. _____ limited the power of federal courts to intervene in
                       labor disputes
    e. _____ prohibited closed shops
    f. _____ was established to protect workers against unfair
                       labor practices
    g. _____ gave courts the right to issue injunctions to delay
                       strikes
    h. _____ guaranteed workers the right to form unions

2. The diagram below represents a competitive labor market with Wc and Lc representing the market wage rate and the level of employment, respectively.

Wage rate $

0   L$_c$

Quantity of labor
supplied and demanded
per week

a. Show on the figure above the effect of a union-imposed wage rate of Wu. Employment is _____ (higher, lower) than for the case of a competitive labor market.

b. Show on the figure above the effect of an union policy of limiting the quantity of labor supplied in order to increase wages to Wu. Employment is _____ (higher, lower) than for the case of a competitive labor market.

c. The union-desired wage of Wu could alternatively be achieved by promoting or advertising the product produced by the union's members. Show on the figure above the effect of this approach. Employment is _____ (higher, lower) than for the case of a competitive labor market.

Concept: **Hiring practices of a monopsonist**

3. A large textile firm has a plant located in a small rural town and is virtually the town's only employer. Residents of the town are too far away from other communities to commute to a job. Therefore they have no alternative employment opportunities. Below are data for the town's labor supply and the textile firm's marginal revenue product schedule.

Wages per Day	Labor Hours Supplied per Day	Total Cost of Labor	Marginal Input Cost of Labor	Marginal Revenue Product
$50	600	$_____		
55	700	_____	$_____	$175
60	800	_____	_____	155
65	900	_____	_____	135
70	1,000	_____	_____	115
75	1,100	_____	_____	95
80	1,200	_____	_____	75

329

a. Complete the table above and plot the marginal input cost of labor, labor supply, and marginal revenue product curves in the figure below.

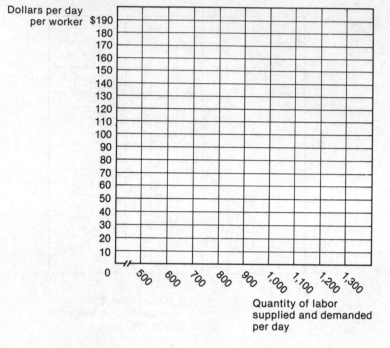

Dollars per day per worker $190 180 170 160 150 140 130 120 110 100 90 80 70 60 50 40 30 20 10 0

500 600 700 800 900 1,000 1,100 1,200 1,300

Quantity of labor supplied and demanded per day

b. A profit-maximizing monopsonist will equate _____ and _____ and hire _____ workers and pay a wage equal to $_____.

c. The monopsonist's wage _____ the worker's marginal revenue product.

d. Assume that the labor market above is a competitive labor market having the same demand for labor as the textile firm. As compared to a perfectly competitive labor market, a monopsonist pays a _____ wage and hires _____ workers. Show this in the figure above.

330

Concept: Simultaneous presence of monopoly and monopsony in input markets

4.   Assume that a monopsonist such as the one in the preceding problem is confronted by a union representing all workers in the town. The monopsony labor market is shown below.

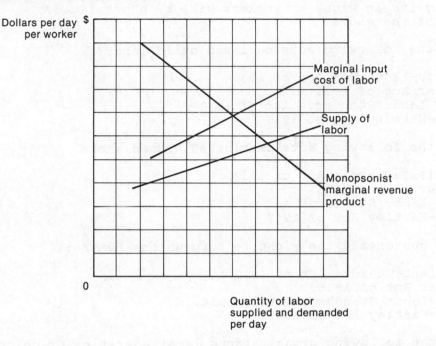

a.   Suppose now that a monopoly union is able to win a union-desired wage of Wu, which is above the wage preferred by the monopsonist, Wm. On the figure above identify the monopsony wage and employment and label them Wm and Lm, respectively. Show the effect on employment of a union wage, Wu, greater than Wm.

b.   For the case of bilateral monopoly, the wage will equal labor's marginal revenue product if the union wage is equal to or greater than the wage at which the _____ curve intersects the _____ curve.

SELF-TEST FOR MASTERY

Select the best answer.

1.   An organization formed to represent the interests of workers is called a/an:

   a.   Trade association.
   b.   Monopsony.
   c.   Labor union.
   d.   Industrial organization.

2.   A goal or objective of unions is to:

   a.   Improve job safety.
   b.   Increase wages.
   c.   Achieve job security.
   d.   All of the above.

3. If a union is successful in raising wages for some firms in a perfectly competitive industry:

   a. The firms will exit the industry in the long run.
   b. The firms will not be covering normal profits.
   c. The gains in wages by workers will be short lived.
   d. All of the above.

4. Which of the following acts outlawed child labor?

   a. Norris-LaGuardia Act of 1932
   b. Wagner Act of 1935
   c. Fair Labor Standards Act of 1938
   d. Taft-Hartley Act of 1947

5. Which of the following acts prohibited closed shops?

   a. Norris-LaGuardia Act of 1932
   b. Wagner Act of 1935
   c. Fair Labor Standards Act of 1938
   d. Taft-Hartley Act of 1947

6. Labor was guaranteed the right to form unions by the:

   a. Norris-LaGuardia Act of 1932.
   b. Wagner Act of 1935.
   c. Fair Labor Standards Act of 1938.
   d. Taft-Hartley Act of 1947.

7. Which of the following organizations is a federation of unions representing skilled labor as well as all types of labor in given industries?

   a. American Federation of Labor
   b. United Mine Workers
   c. United Rubber Workers
   d. Congress of Industrial Unions
   e. AFL-CIO

8. Union membership peaked in the _____, but was _____% of all workers in 1984.

   a. 1920s, 20%
   b. 1930s, 40%
   c. 1940s, 18.1%
   d. 1950s, 16.1%
   e. 1960s, 24.2%

9. Which of the following is not usually practiced by unions as a means to raise wages?

   a. Investing in capital to increase worker productivity
   b. Restricting the supply of labor
   c. Imposing a union wage through the collective bargaining process
   d. Advertising or promoting the product produced with union labor

10. If unions increase wages by restricting the supply of labor or by getting a higher wage through negotiation:

   a. Labor is unquestionably better off.
   b. Industry employment actually increases.

c. Industry employment decreases.
d. Total wages received by labor as a group must increase.

11. A union may support a restrictive tariff on the import of foreign products because:

   a. Domestic product prices are likely to increase.
   b. The marginal revenue product of labor in the protected industries will increase.
   c. Wages paid in the protected industries will rise.
   d. All of the above.

12. Empirical evidence indicates that unions have raised average wages in unionized as compared to nonunionized industries by:

   a. 5% to 50%.
   b. 10% to 20%.
   c. 25% to 33%.
   d. 16.1% to 24%.
   e. 13%.

13. Evidence indicates that union work forces are _____ reliable and stable than nonunionized work forces and collective bargaining may _____ labor productivity.

   a. Less, decrease
   b. More, decrease
   c. Less, increase
   d. More, increase

14. A single firm that buys the entire market supply of an input is called:

   a. A monopolist.
   b. An oligopoly.
   c. A multinational firm.
   d. A labor federation.
   e. A pure monopsonist.

15. A monopsonist pays a wage that is _____ than the marginal cost of labor and is _____ than the worker's marginal revenue product.

   a. Less, less
   b. Greater, less
   c. Greater, greater
   d. Less, greater

16. As compared to a competitive input market, a monopsonist pays a _____ wage and employs _____ workers.

   a. Lower, more
   b. Higher, fewer
   c. Lower, fewer
   d. Higher, more

17. A monopsonist employs an input up to the point at which the _____ equals the _____.

   a. Wage, supply curve
   b. Marginal cost, marginal product
   c. Wage, marginal cost
   d. Marginal input cost, marginal revenue product of the input

e.   None of the above

18.   The marginal input cost curve of a monopsonist:

   a.   Lies above the market input supply curve.
   b.   Is more steeply sloped than the market input supply curve.
   c.   Differs from the input supply curve because the monopsonist must not only pay higher input prices to attract additional inputs, but must also pay these higher prices to the suppliers of inputs currently employed.
   d.   Together with the marginal revenue product curve determines the profit-maximizing level of employment.
   e.   All of the above.

19.   Which of the following best defines a market in which only one buyer and one seller trade input services?

   a.   Monopoly
   b.   Monopsony
   c.   Bilateral monopsony
   d.   Bilateral monopoly

20.   With bilateral monopoly, if unions can _____ wages, employment will _____ and the wage will come closer to or even equal the worker's _____.

   a.   Increase, decrease, marginal input cost
   b.   Increase, increase, marginal product
   c.   Increase, increase, marginal revenue product
   d.   Increase, decrease, marginal revenue product

THINK IT THROUGH

1.   Explain why union attempts to raise wages in competitive firms will fail unless the entire competitive industry is unionized.

2.   Compare and contrast the case of a monopsonist selling in a competitive product market with the case of a monopsonist that is also a monopolist in its product market.

3.   Is it possible for the power of a monopoly union to just offset the power of a monopsonist such that wage and employment levels are the same as they would be in a competitive labor market? Explain.

4.   Discuss the social gains and losses associated with unionism.

CHAPTER ANSWERS

In Brief: Chapter Summary

1. Competitive 2. Craft 3. American Federation of Labor, AFL 4. Congress of Industrial Organizations, CIO 5. Industrial 6. Declined since it peaked 7. 16.1% 8. Restricting 9. Can also 10. 10% and 20% 11. More 12. Monopsony 13. Exceeds 14. Marginal cost of an input 15. Below 16. Monopsonist 17. Competitive 18. Bilateral monopoly 19. Higher

Vocabulary Review

1. Bilateral monopoly 2. Industrial union 3. Pure monopsony 4. Craft union
5. Monopsony power 6. Collective bargaining 7. Marginal input cost 8.
Monopsony 9. Average input cost 10. Labor union 11. Closed shop

Skills Review

1. a. Taft-Hartley Act b. Taft-Hartley Act c. Fair Labor Standards Act d.
    Norris-LaGuardia Act e. Taft-Hartley Act f. Wagner Act g. Taft-Hartley
    Act h. Wagner Act

2.

  a. lower b. lower c. higher

3. a.

Total Cost of Labor	Marginal Input Cost of Labor
$30,000	$
38,500	85
48,000	95
58,500	105
70,000	115
82,500	125
96,000	135

  b. Marginal input cost of labor, marginal revenue product of labor,
      1,000, $70
  c. Is less than
  d. Lower, fewer

4.   a.

Union negotiated wage

Dollars per day per worker

Marginal input cost of labor

W_u
W_m

Supply of labor

Monopsonist's marginal revenue product

0   L_m L_u

Quantity of labor supplied and demanded per day

   b.   Labor supply curve, marginal revenue product curve

Self-Test for Mastery

1. c 2. d 3. d 4. c 5. d 6. b 7. e 8. d 9. a 10. c 11. d 12. b 13. d 14. e 15. a 16. c 17. d 18. e 19. d 20. c

Think it Through

1.   In competitive long-run equilibrium, the firm is just earning normal profits and zero economic profits. If a union is successful in raising wages in a few of the industry's firms but not the entire industry, these firms will continue to sell at the prevailing market price but will have higher costs of production. The owners will not earn sufficient normal profits to keep them in the industry. In time, they will exit the industry and their employees will be unemployed or no longer working at the union wage. If all firms in the industry face a higher union wage, each firm's average cost and marginal cost curves rise. The minimum average cost of production is at a higher level, and in long-run equilibrium the product price will rise to equal the minimum average cost of production.

2.   A monopsonist selling in a competitive product market has a marginal revenue product curve for an input that is found by multiplying product price times the input's marginal product. A monopsonist that is also a monopolist in its product market derives its marginal revenue product curve by multiplying marginal revenue by marginal product. Since marginal revenue is less than product price at a given level of output, the monopoly monopsonist will have a marginal revenue product curve that lies inside the competitive monopsonist's marginal revenue product curve. A competitive monopsonist pays a lower wage and employs fewer workers than a competitive input market. But a monopoly monopsonist pays a lower wage and employs even fewer workers than a competitive monopsonist.

3.   Interestingly, it is possible to achieve the competitive market wage and level of employment in the case of a bilateral monopoly if the collective bargaining process results in a negotiated wage above the monopsonist wage such that the negotiated wage is at a level that equates the supply of and demand for labor (where the labor supply curve intersects the marginal revenue product curve). This assumes that competitive employers have the same aggregate marginal revenue product as the monopsonist. Wages and employment are at their competitive levels, and the wage equals the worker's marginal revenue product.

4.   Unions add to a firm's cost of production and reduce profits received by the owners of the firm. Consumers purchase the products produced by union

members at higher prices. But unions are responsible for increasing average
wages in unionized industries and for improving working conditions. Wages in
nonunionized industries are probably lower because unionization results in
fewer jobs. The unemployed seek employment opportunities in the nonunionized
labor markets, thus depressing market wages. Evidence indicates, however, that
union work forces are more reliable and stable and that collective bargaining
increases worker productivity.

23

Interest, Rents, and Profit

CHAPTER CHALLENGES

After studying your text, attending class, and completing this chapter, you should be able to:

1. Explain the concepts of capital and investment and show how the interest rate represents a crucial price influencing investment in new capital.
2. Analyze investment decisions and show how the interest rate affects those decisions.
3. Outline the influences on the supply of and demand for loanable funds that affect the equilibrium interest rate for various types of loans in a competitive market.
4. Explain how land rents are determined in competitive markets.
5. Understand how profit opportunities arise in an economy and how entrepreneurs seize those opportunities for personal gain.

IN BRIEF: CHAPTER SUMMARY

Fill in the blanks to summarize chapter content.

In addition to wages, other types of income include rents, interest, and profit. (1)_____ (Interest, Rent, Profit) is a payment for the use of borrowed funds. (2)_____ (Interest is, Rents are, Profits are) paid to acquire land. (3)_____ (Interest arises, Rents arise, Profits arise) from the production and sale of output and accrues to the owners of businesses.

Businesses invest in (4)_____ (stocks, physical capital) either to replace worn-out capital or to expand capacity. Individuals invest in (5)_____ (financial assets, human capital) to increase their productivity and value in the market place. (6)_____ (Saving, Borrowing) is the income not consumed during the year that is available for capital investment. Investment in capital will take place up to the point at which the marginal revenue product from additional capital is (7)_____ (greater than, just equal to) the marginal input cost of capital. Expressed in percentage terms, investment will take place up to the point at which the (8)_____ (marginal return on investment, marginal revenue product of an investment) is just equal to the market rate of interest.

The loanable funds market determines the market rate of interest which ,in turn, determines the profit-maximizing level of investment. A/An (9)_____ (decrease, increase) in the demand for loanable funds increases the market interest rate above the marginal return on investment and results in a/an (10)_____ (decrease, increase) in investment and vice versa. The expected marginal return on an investment is the present value of the stream of expected returns over the life of the investment project expressed as a percentage return. Future returns must be discounted to obtain their current or present value because dollars received in the future (11)_____ (are not worth as much as, are worth more than) the same amount of dollars received today. Dollars today could be invested at the prevailing market rate of interest, resulting in more future dollars. The (12)_____ (present value, cost) of an investment project is the sum of the discounted future returns over the life of the project. An increase in the interest rate (13)_____ (increases, reduces) the present value, whereas a decrease in the interest rate (14)_____ (increases, reduces) the present value. Firms will find it profitable to invest if the present value of an investment project (15)_____ (exceeds, is just equal to) its present cost. In perfectly competitive capital markets, the price of a capital asset is (16)_____ (less than, equal to) the present value of the asset.

The demand for and supply of loanable funds determine the market rate of interest and thus influence the present value of an investment project, affecting its profitability or desirability. The demand for loanable funds is (17)_____ (downward sloping, upward sloping) and can shift in response to changes in business expectations regarding future sales as well as improvements in technology that affect the marginal revenue product of new capital. Households and government likewise demand loanable funds, but for different reasons. The market supply of loanable funds is (18)_____ (downward sloping, upward sloping) because people require more than a dollar of future consumption for each dollar saved (or not consumed). The additional compensation is in the form of higher interest rates. Also higher interest rates increase the opportunity cost to firms of holding idle funds or using those funds internally. As businesses minimize their holdings of idle balances and internal funds in response to higher interest rates, more funds are made available to the loanable funds market.

While the general level of interest rates is determined by the supply of and demand for loanable funds, specific rates of interest are affected by such factors as the risk associated with an investment or a loan, the length of a loan or maturity of a bond, the amount of collateral pledged to a lender, and the tax treatment of the asset. Higher risk requires (19)_____ (lower, higher) interest rates to compensate risk-averse individuals; otherwise they will invest in less risky projects. A lender may charge a (20)_____ (lower, higher) interest rate on a personal loan that is not collateralized as compensation for a greater exposure to risk of default. A tax-exempt bond with a low interest rate can still compete with taxed financial assets having higher yields for a portion of the available pool of savings because the after-tax yields are the same for both assets.

Rents are determined by the supply of and demand for usable land. Demand for land is determined by the (21)_____ (marginal revenue product, marginal cost) of land. The supply of land, however, is fixed--the market supply curve is perfectly (22)_____ (elastic, inelastic). Market rents are determined entirely by the market demand for land. Anything that changes the price of a good produced with land or alters the marginal productivity of land, such as climate, location, and access to water, utilities, or highways, will affect the (23)_____ (marginal revenue product, marginal cost) of land and cause the market rent to change. In central cities, land is fixed in supply and the highest bidders for the central parcels will put the land to its highest-valued use--such as with high-rise office buildings. Land at the periphery of an urban area is too far from the central city to be used as office space. The bidders for outlying parcels will be farmers, ranchers, and residential developers. The land will be allocated to the highest bidder based on the use that has the (24)_____ (highest, lowest) marginal revenue product. Because rent is a payment in excess of that which is necessary to bring forth the current quantity of land supplied (the current quantity of land is fixed regardless of rent), landlords could be taxed the full amount of their rent received (25)_____ (reducing, without altering) the quantity of land made available.

Profit is the return or reward to the owner. (26)_____ (Economic, Normal) profit is a payment equal to the opportunity cost of the owner's self-owned resources. Normal profits are necessary in order to keep the owner from exiting the industry--from taking his self-owned resources elsewhere. Economic profit and losses allocate resources among industries as some industries expand and some decline. (27)_____ (Economic, Normal) profit results from innovations and anticipation of consumer demands, risk taking, and the exercise of monopoly power.

VOCABULARY REVIEW

Write the key term from the list below next to its definition.

Key Terms

Rent	Marginal return on investment
Capital	Discounted present value
Investment	Risk
Depreciation	Risk averse
Saving	

Definitions

1. _____: the amount of income not consumed in a given year.

2. _____: the percentage rate of return on investment of additional sums used to purchase more capital.

3. _____: the rate at which machines and structures wear out.

4. _____: the current value of funds to be received in future periods.

5. _____: the process of replenishing or adding to capital stock.

6. _____: measures the variation of actual outcomes from expected outcomes.

7. _____: an input created by people for the purpose of producing goods and services. It consists of tools, machinery, vehicles, structures, raw material, inventories, and human skills.

8. _____: describes an investor who, if given equal expected returns, would choose an investment with lower risk.

9. _____: the price that is paid for the use of land

SKILLS REVIEW

Concept: Investment decisions and the interest rate

1. The Awax Paint Company is considering whether or not to install a new metering device for 1 year. The cost of the system is $95,000. The expected return from the metering device at the end of the year is $15,000 plus a resale value of $90,000 for the used metering device.

    a. The marginal return to the investment is expected to be _____ %. If the market rate of interest is 8%, Awax _____ (will, will not) install the new metering system.
    b. If the market rate of interest rises to 13%, Awax _____ (will, will not) install the device.

2. If Awax's metering device had a useful life of 5 years and did not have any resale value at the end of this period, determine the present value of the measuring system from the data given below.

Expected Return		PV (10%)	PV (5%)
Year 1	$15,000	_____	_____
2	35,000	_____	_____
3	30,000	_____	_____
4	25,000	_____	_____
5	10,000	_____	_____

    Total PV (10%) = $_____   Total PV (5%) = $_____

    a. Complete the table.
    b. At a present cost of $95,000 and a market rate of interest of 10%, Awax _____ (will, will not) install the device because the present value of the system _____ the present cost.
    c. If the market rate of interest falls to 5%, Awax _____ (will, will not) install the device because the present value of the system _____ the present cost.
    d. The present value of a capital asset and the interest rate are _____ related.
    e. A decrease in the interest rate _____ the present value of proposed investment projects and results in a/an _____ in the volume of investment.

3. The diagram below represents the market for loanable funds and a given firm's marginal return on investment.

a. In part a of the diagram above, find the market rate of interest assuming the demand for loanable funds is given by Dlf-1. In part b of the diagram, find the firm's profit maximizing quantity of annual investment. Show this in the figure above. Interest rate = _____ %, annual investment = $_____

b. A firm will invest up to the point at which _____ equals _____.

c. Assume that the market demand for loanable funds increases to Dlf-2. Find the new interest rate and the firm's annual level of investment. Show on the above figure. Interest rate = _____ %, annual investment = $_____

d. An increase in the supply of loanable funds given the demand for loanable funds _____ the market rate of interest, causing a firm's current marginal return on investment to _____ the interest rate and resulting in a/an _____ in investment.

Concept: Rent determination in competitive markets

4. A large parcel of land exists at the periphery of an urban area, but is still used by farmers to grow crops. The data below represent the quantity of land supplied and demanded by farmers at this site.

Rent per Acre	Acres Supplied (per year)	Marginal Revenue Product (MRP)	Acres Employed
$100	1,000	$100	1,400
200	1,000	200	1,200
300	1,000	300	1,000
400	1,000	400	800
500	1,000	500	600
600	1,000	600	400
700	1,000	700	200

a. Plot the farmer's marginal revenue product schedule and supply curve on the figure below.

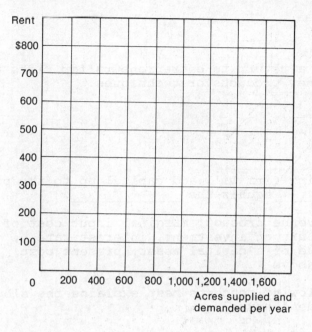

Rent

$800
700
600
500
400
300
200
100

0   200 400 600 800 1,000 1,200 1,400 1,600

Acres supplied and
demanded per year

b. The rent per acre at this site is $_____. Because the supply of land is perfectly _____, rent is determined entirely by _____. If there are no other bidders for the acreage, its highest-valued use is _____.

c. Suppose highways are extended to the site greatly improving access to the central city. Assume that at every acreage size employed a residential developer's marginal revenue product is double that of the farmer's marginal revenue product. Show the developer's marginal revenue product curve on the figure above. The market rent per acre _____ to $_____, and it highest-valued use changes from _____ to _____.

d. Rent is a payment _____ of the payment necessary to bring forth a resource. For the case above, the developer pays a total rent of $_____. What percentage of this amount could be taxed without affecting the quantity of land supplied or its highest-valued use? _____ %

SELF-TEST FOR MASTERY

Select the best answer.

1. A payment for the use of funds lent by one person for the use of others is called:

   a. Rent.
   b. Interest.
   c. Profit.
   d. Wage.

2.   A payment for the services of land is called:

      a.   Rent.
      b.   Interest.
      c.   Profit.
      d.   Wage.

3.   _____ is/are a return to entrepreneurs for risks associated with the introduction of new products or techniques.

      a.   Rents
      b.   Interest
      c.   Profits
      d.   Wages

4.   A profit-maximizing firm will add capital up to the point at which the _____ equals the _____.

      a.   Marginal revenue product, marginal input cost of capital
      b.   Marginal return on investment, interest rate
      c.   Present value of a capital asset, present cost
      d.   All of the above

5.   Which of the following concepts best explains the slope of the marginal return on investment curve?

      a.   Profit maximization
      b.   Law of diminishing marginal returns
      c.   Law of increasing returns
      d.   Equimarginal principle
      d.   Diminishing marginal revenue

6.   Present value can be defined as:

      a.   The total return associated with a project.
      b.   The end-of-the-period return discounted to its future value.
      c.   The sum of the discounted future returns associated with a capital asset.
      d.   The cost of the project.
      e.   The sum of the discounted future profits associated with a capital asset.

7.   The interest rate and the present value of a capital asset are:

      a.   Independent of each other.
      b.   Positively related.
      c.   Inversely related.
      d.   Unrelated.
      e.   Unimportant in investment decisions.

8.   An increase in the market demand for loanable funds _____ the market rate of interest causing the interest rate to _____ the current marginal return on investment and resulting in an/a _____ in investment.

      a.   Decreases, fall below, increase
      b.   Increases, equal, decrease
      c.   Decreases, fall below, decrease
      d.   Increases, rise above, decrease

9. An increase in the market supply of loanable funds _____ the market
    rate of interest, causing the interest rate to _____ the current
    marginal return on investment and resulting in an/a _____ in
    investment.

    a. Decreases, fall below, increase
    b. Increases, equal, decrease
    c. Decreases, fall below, decrease
    d. Increases, rise above, decrease

10. Of the following factors influencing interest rates, which one does not
    result in higher interest rates?

    a. Higher risk
    b. Less collateral pledged against a loan
    c. Longer-term loan or bond
    d. Tax-exempt status

11. The supply of land:

    a. Reflects the law of supply.
    b. Is perfectly elastic.
    c. Is upward sloping.
    d. Is perfectly inelastic.
    e. Is downward sloping.

12. A firm's demand for land:

    a. Is downward sloping.
    b. Is the firm's marginal revenue product curve for land.
    c. Shifts if the price of the product produced with the land changes.
    d. Determines the rent.
    e. All of the above.

13. Rent is determined:

    a. By the landlord.
    b. By shifts in supply of and demand for land.
    c. Entirely by the demand for land.
    d. Entirely by the supply of land.

14. The highest-valued use to which land is put is dependent upon:

    a. The marginal cost curves of the bidding firms.
    b. The marginal revenue curves of the bidding firms.
    c. The use desired by the supplier of land.
    d. The marginal revenue product curves of the bidding firms.

15. A tax on land rents:

    a. Will reduce the quantity of land supplied.
    b. Will result in an increase in rents.
    c. Will be passed forward to consumers.
    d. Will not affect the quantity of land supplied, nor will it increase
        rents.

16. Which of the following is defined as the opportunity cost of owner-
    supplied resources?

    a. Total cost
    b. Profit

c. Normal profit
d. Economic profit

17. The profit reported by business:

a. Is greater than economic profit.
b. Includes normal profit.
c. Accounts for some of the opportunity costs of owner-supplied resources.
d. All of the above.

18. Which of the following is not a source of economic profit?

a. Innovations and anticipation of consumer demands
b. Risk taking
c. Exercise of monopoly power
d. The owner's stock of self-owned resources

THINK IT THROUGH

1. Discuss intuitively how the principles of investment discussed in this chapter can be used in deciding whether or not to pursue a university degree.

2. Suppose that consumers are heavily indebted and have reached a point at which they must reduce their demand for loanable funds. Discuss the implications for the loanable funds market and for the level of business investment in physical capital.

3.   If the market supply of and demand for loanable funds determine the market rate of interest, then why are there many different rates of interest at any one time?

4.   Taxes levied on land are considered more efficient than taxes levied on improvements on the land (such as structures). Can you think of any reasons why?

CHAPTER ANSWERS

In Brief: Chapter Summary

1. Interest 2. Rents arise 3. Profits arise 4. physical capital 5. Human capital 6. Saving 7. Just equal to 8. Marginal return on investment 9. Increase 10. Decrease 11. Not worth as much 12. Present value 13. Reduces 14. Increases 15. Exceeds 16. Equal to 17. Downward sloping 18. Upward sloping 19. Higher 20. Higher 21. Marginal revenue product 22. Inelastic 23. Marginal revenue product 24. Highest 25. Without altering 27. Economic

Vocabulary Review

1. Saving 2. Marginal return on investment 3. Depreciation 4. Discounted present value 5. Investment 6. Risk 7. Capital 8. Risk averse 9. Rent

Skills Review

1. a. 10.53%, will b. Will not

2. a.
PV (10%)	PV (5%)
$13,636.36	$14,285.71
38,925.62	31,746.03
22,539.44	25,915.12
17,075.34	20,567.56
6,209.25	7,835.26
$88,386.01	$100,349.68

   b. Will not; is less than
   c. Will; is greater than
   d. Inversely e. Increases, increase

3. a.

    10%, $10 million
   b. Marginal return on investment, the market rate of interest
   c. 14%, $6 million
   d. Decrease, exceed, increase

4. a.

   b. $300; inelastic, the demand for land; in agricultural
      production
   c. Increases, $600, agriculture, residential development
   d. In excess of, $600,000; 100%

Self-Test for Mastery

1. b 2. a 3. c 4. d 5. b 6. c 7. c 8. d 9. a 10. d 11. d 12. e 13.
c 14. d 15. d 16. c 17. d 18. d

Think it Through

1.   An investment in a college degree generates a stream of benefits over time
and involves the explicit outlays of tuition, room, and board but also includes
as a cost the forgone income that could have been earned if the individual had
worked rather than attended college. Future benefits of a college degree
include both pecuniary and nonpecuniary benefits. A net benefit-maximizing
individual will compare the present value (or the sum of the discounted future
returns) resulting from a college degree to the present costs, which include
the forgone income mentioned above. If the present value of a degree is less
than the present cost, the individual will not invest in a degree. If the
present value is greater than the present cost, the individual will invest in a
degree. For instance, assuming only pecuniary benefits are considered, a very
highly paid executive will not likely take a 4-year leave of absence to earn a
degree. The present value of a bachelor's degree is not likely to outweigh the
current sacrifice of income.

2.   If consumers reduce their demand for loanable funds, market rates of
interest decrease. As interest rates decrease, firms find that projects that
were previously unprofitable at higher interest rates are now profitable
because interest rates have fallen below the marginal return on investment for
many projects. Alternatively, falling interest rates increase the present
value of an investment project relative to its present cost. Firms will
increase investment, and the aggregate level of investment in the economy may
rise or fall depending upon the relative sizes of the consumer and firm
effects.

3.   The average level of interest rates is determined by the demand for and
supply of loanable funds. Because different loans and financial assets have
different characteristics, they command different rates of interest at any
point in time. Interest rates are higher on financial assets that are riskier,
involve a longer term to maturity, are less collateralized, and do not receive
favorable tax treatment. Nevertheless, when the average rate of interest
changes, these specific rates of interest are likewise changing in the same
direction but with different lags and rates of change.

4.   Efficient taxes are able to raise tax revenues without distorting resource
allocation--without altering the allocation of resources that would prevail in
the absence of the tax. Because land is fixed in supply and the payment to
acquire land is economic rent, land could be taxed without altering the present
quantity of land supplied or the use to which it is put. Landlords cannot
escape the tax by taking their land elsewhere. Nor can the owner of the land
pass the tax to the renter in the form of higher rents. If this was tried, the
renter would find that the rent exceeded his marginal revenue product for the
land and would leave. But the land owner needs the land employed in its most
productive use in order to earn the highest rents to cover the tax.

Taxes on structures distort economic choices and resource allocation. Taxes on
improvements result in an allocation of resources that differs from what would
prevail in the market without taxes. Some improvements and structures are
mobile. A tax can be avoided by moving the improvements to an area with a
lower tax or no tax. In the long run, structures may be allowed to
deteriorate, thus reducing the productivity of the land upon which the
structure is located.

24

The Distribution of Income and the Economics of Poverty

CHAPTER CHALLENGES

After studying your text, attending class, and completing this chapter, you should be able to:

1. Discuss the facts about income distribution in the United States.
2. Document the extent of poverty in the United States.
3. Discuss government assistance programs to the poor and the impact of these programs on incentives and well-being of recipients.
4. Explain the causes of income inequality and evaluate the impact of policies designed to reduce poverty and alter income distribution.

IN BRIEF: CHAPTER SUMMARY

Fill in the blanks to summarize chapter content.

Income in the United States is not distributed equally. As a percentage of total money income, the lowest 20% of families in 1984 received (1)_____ (5%, 15%) of the nation's income, whereas the richest 20% of families received almost (2)_____ (43%, 33%) of total money income. The degree of inequality as reflected in the distribution of income has (3)_____ (decreased, remained relatively unchanged) from 1947 to 1984. The (4)_____ (welfare, Lorenz) curve is a useful tool for showing the degree of income inequality. The line of income equality results if a given percentage of families receive (5)_____ (that same, a greater) percentage of the nation's money income. For the United States the line is bowed outward, meaning that the distribution of income is skewed to the higher-income families. Policies designed to reduce the inequality will shift the Lorenz curve (6)_____ (away from, inward toward) the line of income equality.

As of 1985, about (7)_____ (6%, 14%) of the U.S. population were counted as poor--having incomes below the poverty income threshold. (8)_____ (The poverty threshold is, Welfare benefits are) determined by estimating the minimally acceptable food budget for a family of a certain size and multiplying by three. By this measure of poverty, the incidence of poverty fell dramatically from 1959 to the end of the 1970s (9)_____ (and continued to decline, but increased) in the early 1980s. Estimates of poverty do not take into account forms of government assistance other than cash assistance. If noncash government benefits were included, it is estimated that the poverty rate would fall to about (10)_____ (2%, 10%).

The incidence of poverty is (11)_____ (higher, lower) among blacks and Hispanics, female-headed households, and children than for the population as a whole. The (12)_____ (Hispanic minorities, elderly) have experienced the largest gains in reducing poverty, largely because of more generous private and public pensions (such as Social Security).

Programs designed to assist the poor are called welfare programs. Recipients must qualify for the programs based on a means test. Government assists the poor with cash and in-kind assistance. (13)_____ (Cash, In-kind) assistance programs include the AFDC and SSI programs. AFDC benefits vary widely by state and are at a level considerably below the poverty line. Examples of (14)_____ (cash, in-kind) assistance include Medicaid, food stamps, and housing assistance. In 1986, AFDC and SSI benefits equaled $20 billion and in-kind assistance totaled $55 billion.

A disadvantage of the assistance programs mentioned above is that there are considerable work disincentives. As the welfare recipient works and earns income, welfare benefits drop such that it is not uncommon for a welfare mother, for instance, to lose 80 cents in cash and in-kind benefits for every dollar earned. The losses in production from these disincentives are one form of inefficiency associated with assistance programs. Another form of inefficiency results from the (15)_____ (resource underemployment, distortion of choices) caused by in-kind transfers. If a poor family prefers less food than it could purchase with the food stamps, the stamps are less highly valued than an equivalent amount of cash. If the family received cash instead, it would purchase the desired amount of food and other goods and attain a higher level of utility. However, this apparently is not a big problem because food stamp benefits are low and most families would probably consume more food than allowed by their food stamps. Medicaid is offered to the poor at a zero price. This results in (16)_____ (overconsumption, underconsumption) of medical services, which probably raises the prices of health care services to all consumers.

There are equity-efficiency tradeoffs in the welfare system. Increasing welfare benefits require additional tax revenues. If tax rates are increased, incentives to work, save, and invest are reduced. Improving the equity of the distribution of income results in some efficiency (17)_____ (gains, losses). Apparently, the United States has chosen over the years to minimize the efficiency losses and has shifted the Lorenz curve inward toward greater income equality (18)_____ (by a considerable, by only a very modest) amount. The (19)_____ (antipoverty, negative) income tax proposal has been suggested as a way to reduce poverty without creating efficiency losses as large as is presently the case. Politically, it is not likely to be seriously considered because it involves transferring income to the nonpoor and would require high tax rates.

Because poverty results from the lack of marketable skills or the inability to work, government can do a number of things to increase worker productivity and opportunities to work. The government could provide educational opportunities or subsidies. Economic growth could be promoted as well as worker training. Where discrimination exists it can be reduced or eliminated. Evidence indicates that some of the wage or income differentials observed are probably the result of discrimination, (20)_____ (but a significant share, and only a very small percentage) of the differentials can be attributed to factors other than discrimination, such as education or work experience.

VOCABULARY REVIEW

Write the key term from the list below next to its definition.

Key Terms

Lorenz curve
Poverty income threshold
Welfare programs

Means test
Negative income tax
Discrimination in
    labor markets

Definitions

1. _____: occurs when minority-group workers with skills, experience, and training comparable to those of workers in other groups are paid lower wages and have less opportunity for employment and advancement.

2. _____: government programs to assist the poor in the United States who are unable to work.

3. _____: the income level below which a person or family is classified as being poor.

4. _____: provides for government payments to people whose income falls below certain levels.

5. _____: establishes the fact that people in the groups eligible for welfare payments have incomes below the amounts that are minimally acceptable.

6. _____: a plotting of data showing the percentage of income enjoyed by each percentage of households ranked according to their incomes.

SKILLS REVIEW

Concept: **Distribution of income, poverty and the poverty threshold income**

1. Given the data below on the distribution of family income, answers the questions below.

Percentage of Families	Percentage of Total Income
Highest 20%	43%
4th 20%	24%
3rd 20%	17%
2nd 20%	11%
Lowest 20%	5%

a.　On the figure below, plot the Lorenz curve for the data above.

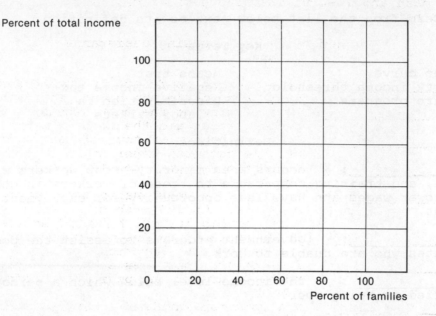

Percent of total income

Percent of families

b.　On the figure above, identify the line of income equality.

c.　On figure above, show the effect on the current distribution of family income of policies that reduce income inequality.

2.　Which groups of individuals in the United States in 1984 had the highest incidence of poverty?

Group	Percentage of the Group Classified as Poor
a. _____	_____ %
b. _____	_____
c. _____	_____
d. _____	_____

3.　If the federal government determines that the minimally acceptable food expenditure is \$3 per person per day, determine the poverty threshold income for a:

a.　Family of 2. \$_____

b.　Family of 3. \$_____

c.　Family of 4. \$_____

d.　Given the following distribution of four-person families, determine the poverty rate. (The poverty rate is the percentage of four-person families having incomes below the poverty-threshold income.)

Income	Families of Four
\$51,000 and above	2 million
Below \$51,000	27 million
Below \$27,640	19 million
Below \$13,140	3 million
Below \$ 6,280	1 million

Poverty rate = _____ %

Concept: **Programs to aid the poor**

4.   Match the cash and in-kind assistance programs listed below to the statements below.

   AFDC   Medicaid   Housing assistance
   SSI   Food stamps

   a.   _____   This program is federally funded and involves cash payments to the blind, aged, and disabled.
   b.   _____   This program is the most expensive of all federal programs that aid the poor.
   c.   _____   Only one person in four who are eligible for this program receives benefits.
   d.   _____   A program designed to aid families with dependent children.
   e.   _____   A program in which maximum benefits vary greatly by state. In 1987, these benefits were $144 per month in Mississippi but $833 in Alaska.
   f.   _____   This program provides the poor with stamps that can be redeemed for food.
   g.   _____   This program provides subsidized payments and rents to assist the poor in renting private housing.
   h.   _____   This program involves a service rendered for which the poor pay a zero price.

5.   In the long run, government must pursue certain fundamental policies if poverty is to be reduced or eliminated. What are they?

   a.   _____
   b.   _____
   c.   _____
   d.   _____

SELF-TEST FOR MASTERY

Select the best answer.

1.   What percentage of the U.S population was classified as poor in 1985?

   a.   5%
   b.   9%
   c.   14%
   d.   18%
   e.   22%

2.   In 1984, the highest 20% of the families in the income distribution received what percentage of total income?

   a.   20%
   b.   43%
   c.   67%
   d.   53%
   e.   38%

3.	In 1984, the lowest 20% of the families in the income distribution received what percentage of total income?

	a.	14%
	b.	21%
	c.	8%
	d.	5%
	e.	12%

4.	The distribution of income in the United States from 1947 to 1984:

	a.	Has become more unequal.
	b.	Has become significantly more equal.
	c.	Has been stable.
	d.	Has coincided with the line of income equality.

5.	Which of the following is a plotting of data showing the percentage of income enjoyed by each percentage of households ranked according to their incomes?

	a.	Income curve
	b.	Distribution curve
	c.	Phillips curve
	d.	Lorenz curve

6.	If a nation's Lorenz curve lies below the line of income equality:

	a.	Proportionately more of the nation's income is received by the highest 20% of families than the lowest 20%.
	b.	The income received by each 20% of families is 20% of the total income.
	c.	Proportionately more of the nation's income is received by the lowest 20% of families than the highest 20%.
	d.	Income is equally distributed.

7.	Poverty in the United States is defined as:

	a.	Unwholesome living conditions.
	b.	A level of income below the median income for all families.
	c.	A level of income below the minimally acceptable annual food budget of a family of a given size times three.
	d.	An income below 20% of the average family income.

8.	The percentage of the U.S. population living in households having incomes below the poverty threshold level has _____ from 1959 to 1984.

	a.	Decreased
	b.	Increased
	c.	Remained remarkably stable
	d.	Increased for 2 decades and fallen for 5 years

9.	Which of the following groups does not have a high incidence of poverty--a rate of poverty above the rate for the population as a whole?

	a.	The elderly
	b.	Female-headed households
	c.	Blacks
	d.	Hispanics
	e.	Children

10. Which of the following groups has experienced the largest drop since 1959 in the percentage of its members who are poor?

    a. The elderly
    b. Female-headed households
    c. Blacks
    d. Hispanics
    e. Children

11. Which of the following assistance programs to the poor is not an in-kind assistance program?

    a. Food stamps
    b. Medicaid
    c. Housing
    d. AFDC

12. The most costly program to aid the poor is:

    a. The food stamp program.
    b. Medicaid.
    c. Federal housing assistance.
    d. SSI.

13. A Census Bureau study found that if income was defined as including money income and in-kind transfers, the percentage of the population having incomes below the poverty threshold level would be about:

    a. 0%.
    b. 5%.
    c. 8%.
    d. 10%.
    e. 14%.

14. Which of the following best illustrates the work disincentives present in the current welfare system?

    a. The vicious circle of welfare teaches children to be lazy.
    b. For each additional dollar earned, a welfare recipient may lose as much as 80 cents in welfare assistance.
    c. Even though the poor are able-bodied, they choose to not work in order to rip off the welfare system.
    d. An average welfare recipient faces a tax rate of 15%.

15. Policies that increase welfare benefits and require tax rate increases to fund the expanded programs

    a. Increase both equity and efficiency.
    b. Decrease both equity and efficiency.
    c. Increase efficiency, but decrease equity.
    d. Increase equity, but decrease efficiency.

16. The negative income tax proposal:

    a. Provides for a minimum-guaranteed income.
    b. Involves high tax rates.
    c. Transfers income to higher-income families than currently receive benefits under existing welfare programs.
    d. Is very costly.
    e. All of the above.

17. Which of the following policies should be undertaken by government in order to reduce or eliminate poverty?

    a. Programs that support equality of opportunity
    b. Programs the promote economic growth
    c. Programs that encourage or provide education
    d. Programs that encourage or provide training
    e. All of the above

18. Which of the following acts outlawed discrimination on the basis of race, religion, sex, or national origin?

    a. The Anti-discrimination Statute of 1955
    b. The Equal Rights Amendment of 1982
    c. The Civil Liberties Union Act of 1978
    d. The Civil Rights Act of 1964

THINK IT THROUGH

1. Discuss how poverty is measured. Can you think of any limitations of the current method of defining poverty?

2. Discuss the nature of the efficiency-equity tradeoff associated with efforts to redistribute income.

3. Briefly discuss current programs to aid the poor and discuss the effectiveness of the programs in terms of the level of poverty and the distribution of income.

4. If poverty results from the lack of marketable skills, inability to work, or the lack of opportunity to work or attain skills, discuss the types of policies that government must pursue if it is to successfully reduce poverty.

POP QUIZ   Read the news brief at the end of this chapter and answer the following question.

Evidence indicates that some of the wage differential between males and females is likely the result of discrimination. Discrimination can be of the direct type where an employer exercises a sex bias in promotion, employment, and pay, or it can be a more subtle form of discrimination that still has the same consequences in terms of relative pay. According to the article, what is one source of this subtle discrimination, and how does it affect the pay of women?

CHAPTER ANSWERS

In Brief: Chapter Summary

1. 5% 2. 43% 3. Remained relatively unchanged 4. Lorenz 5. That same 6. Inward toward 7. 14% 8. Poverty threshold is 9. But increased 10. 10% 11. Higher 12. Elderly 13. Cash 14. In-kind 15. Distortion of choices 16. Overconsumption 17. Losses 18. Only by a very modest 19. Negative 20. But a significant share

Vocabulary Review

1. Discrimination in labor markets 2. Welfare programs 3. Poverty income threshold 4. Negative income tax 5. Means test 6. Lorenz curve

Skills Review

1.

2. a. Female-headed households with dependent children; 34%
    b. Blacks; 33.8%
    c. Hispanics; 28.4%
    d. Children; 20%

3. a. $6,570 b. $9,855 c. $13,140 d. 7.69%

4. a. SSI
    b. Medicaid
    c. Housing assistance
    d. AFDC
    e. AFDC
    f. Food stamps
    g. Housing assistance
    h. Medicaid

5. a. Promote equal opportunity
    b. Promote economic growth
    c. Provide or subsidize education
    d. Provide, encourage, or subsidize training

Self-Test for Mastery

1. c 2. b 3. d 4. c 5. d 6. a 7. c 8. a 9. a 10. a 11. d 12. b 13. d 14. b 15. d 16. e 17. e 18. d

Think it Through

1. The poverty rate of a given group or population in the United States is the percentage of the group or population having incomes below the poverty income threshold. The poverty income threshold is determined by estimating the minimally acceptable food expenditure per day per person and multiplying that amount by three. Therefore the poverty income threshold for a family depends on the size of the family. One limitation of this measure of poverty is that it does not include in-kind goods or services received by households. If these benefits were included, it is estimated that the poverty rate for the entire population would fall to 10%. Another limitation is that the measure is an absolute rather than a relative measure of poverty. Over time more families might have incomes above the poverty income threshold but still retain their

relative place in the distribution of income. In other words, they are likely to feel just as poor even though their absolute income level has risen.

2.   Programs designed to reduce poverty and redistribute income, if successful, will improve equity (assuming that society feels that some redistribution is socially desirable). However, programs require resources that must be withdrawn from the private sector of the economy. If tax rates are ultimately increased to fund these programs, economic efficiency is reduced. Since most taxes are not neutral in their impact, distortions will occur in decisions regarding work, saving, and investment. The economy is operating inside its production possibilities curve. But this is the tradeoff-- the opportunity cost of improving fairness in the economy is a lower level of production. The very fact that redistribution programs and tax laws have been in place for decades is evidence that society believes that some redistribution should take place.

3.   The current approach to aiding the poor is through cash and in-kind transfers. Cash assistance includes Aid to Families with Dependent Children (AFDC) and Supplemental Security Income (SSI). In-kind programs include Medicaid, which is the most expensive program for the poor, housing assistance, and food stamps. The nation's poverty rate fell in the 1960s and until the end of the 1970s. In the early 1980s, the poverty rate increased substantially and has fallen to the present but still remains above the all-time lows of the late 1970s. From the answer to question 1 above, note that improvements in absolute income levels do not guarantee that a family's relative position in the distribution of income will improve. In fact, the Lorenz curve has shifted inward only a slight amount since the advent of these poverty programs. In the 1980s, the distribution of income has likely become less rather than more equal.

4.   The government needs to treat the disease in addition to the symptoms. Poverty is the result of the lack of purchasing power. But the lack of purchasing power is related to the absence of marketable skills, the lack of opportunity to attain those skills or find employment, and both overt and subtle forms of discrimination. Evidence suggests that a considerable portion of the wage differentials among workers can be attributed to differences in skills, education, or experience. But there is an unexplained component of these differentials that may be due to discrimination. Government programs that assure equal opportunity, not only to education and training, but also to the workplace and that increase workers' marginal products, such as programs designed to encourage the consumption of additional training and education, will in the long run be more effective in combatting poverty than short-term cash or in-kind transfers.

Pop Quiz

There is evidence of subtle discrimination or bias while females are in school--from first grade through the university level. Females are given less attention than males, and are less likely to be praised by teachers. This impairs a female's self esteem and affects her expectations regarding her future. As a result, women are socially trained to be less assertive and more risk averse. They will not likely "...present themselves as effective managers." Boys receive more scolding in school than girls but this increases their aggressiveness and assertiveness. In college, females enroll in courses with large female enrollments to avoid being intimidated by male-dominated classes. Female-dominated courses often lead to some of the lower-paying occupations. In short, the socialization process "tracks" females into occupations that are crowded with women and consequently involve low pay.

Studies Link Subtle Sex Bias in Schools With Women's Behavior in the Workplace

By Sharon E. Epperson

Staff Reporter of The Wall Street Journal

What's holding women back as they climb the success ladder?

Classrooms may be partly to blame.

Overt discrimination it isn't, for schools are increasingly offering equal opportunities to girls and boys in both formal courses and extracurricular activities, including sports. But several studies suggest that, from first grade through college, female students are the victims of subtle biases. As a result, they are often given less nurturing attention than males.

Consider these findings from studies at schools in the U.S. and Britain. Compared with girls, boys are:

—Five times as likely to receive the most attention from teachers.

—Eight times as likely to call out in class, which helps to explain why they out-talk girls there by a ratio of 3 to 1. (When the teacher is female and the majority of the class is male, boys are 12 times as likely to speak up.)

—Twice as likely to demand help or attention from the teacher, to be seen as model students or to be called on or praised by teachers.

Researchers maintain that a chilly climate for women in the classroom undermines self-esteem and damages morale. They believe, too, that some of these patterns of student-teacher interaction may help set the stage for expectations and interactions later in the workplace.

Emotional Baggage

"Females aren't taught to be risk takers; they don't have the same autonomy as males," asserts Jane Ayer, associate dean of education and professor of counseling psychology at the University of Wisconsin, Madison. "And you take what you've learned about yourself in the classroom into the workplace."

In coed schools, researchers find that girls receive considerably less direct attention than boys. For instance, a study of teachers' interactions with pupils in more than a hundred fourth-, sixth- and eighth-grade math and language-arts classes found that boys receive significantly more praise, criticism and remedial help.

Reactions of both male and female teachers to their female students "aren't that great," says David Sadker, an American University professor of education who conducted the four-year study with his wife, Myra, also an education professor at American. Teachers often accept the girls' responses without offering constructive comment, Mr. Sadker explains.

"In the workplace," he argues, "women are less likely to present themselves as effective managers. A lot of it deals with passive roles" they assume at school.

In lower grades, other researchers have found, boys often also receive more attention through disciplinary action. These scoldings for disruptive activity can make boys "less sensitive to negative feedback from teachers" and may further their aggressive behavior, says Marlaine Lockheed, a senior research scientist for the World Bank who studied the matter while working for the Educational Testing Service in Princeton, N.J.

Yet another study, begun in 1981 by two researchers at the University of Illinois, has measured the self-confidence of 80 high-school valedictorians, salutatorians and honor students. The study found that, upon graduation, 23% of the men and 21% of the women believed they were "far above average" in intelligence. As college sophomores, only 4% of the women said they felt far above average, while 22% of the men rated themselves that way. By senior year in college, none of the women reported feeling far above average, compared with 25% of the men.

This apparent lack of self-esteem on the part of the women appears to be rooted in classroom interaction, says Bernice Sandler, executive director of the Association of American Colleges' project on the status and education of women. Researchers, she notes, have found that even in college classes "men receive more eye contact from their professors than women, are called on more often and receive informal coaching from their instructors."

Racial prejudice can make the situation even worse. "Minority women in higher education frequently face double discrimination—once for being female and once for being racially or ethnically different," noted a 1986 report by the college association's project on women. "For example, intellectual competence and leadership ability, along with other primary academic qualities, are associated not only with males but with white males."

A More Comfortable Setting

Researchers say sexual bias leads some women to opt for courses with a large female enrollment, where they will feel more comfortable voicing their opinions. Bertha French, a junior at the University of Virginia, Charlottesville, agrees. She notes that women usually dominate discussions in her mostly female French classes; the two or three male students don't speak up so much. "I think it's because it's not considered a masculine major," she says. In her male-dominated government classes, she adds, she and other female students sometimes feel intimidated.

At many schools, students, teachers and administrators often seem unaware of everyday inequities in the classroom. Faculty members may consider themselves too evenhanded to discriminate.

For example, the Sadkers' study included a math teacher who was active in the National Organization for Women. She told the Sadkers she probably wouldn't benefit from their training sessions on sexism in the classroom because she had been concerned about the issue for years. After viewing videotapes of her classroom interaction, however, she said she was "stunned" to find that she was talking to boys more than twice as much as to girls, and praising them four times as much.

Such disparities are the reason some educators stress the usefulness of single-sex schools, which are nonetheless on the decline. All-girl schools and women's colleges "create a more positive learning environment for females, who don't have to fear failing in front of males," maintains the University of Wisconsin's Ms. Ayer. She says she believes the schools help females to get away from traditional social conditioning and give them freedom "to show what they can do."

25

Gross National Product and the Performance of the National Economy

Studies and Subject See Chapter Summary
With Work Balance Problems and the Workplace

CHAPTER CHALLENGES

After studying this chapter, attending class, and completing this chapter, you should be able to:

1. Explain what GNP is and how it is measured and discuss the shortcomings of GNP as a measure of national well-being.
2. Understand the distinction between final products and intermediate products. Explain how gross national product can be measured as the sum of value added at each stage of production and how value added must equal the earnings accruing to owners of resources used in production.
3. Understand the distinction between nominal GNP and real GNP and explain how real GNP can be used to measure aggregate production over time.
4. Show how gross national product can be viewed as either a flow of expenditures or a flow of income.
5. Use a circular flow analysis to understand the interrelationships in the economy among households, business firms, financial transactions, governments, and international trade and explain how leakages and injections of spending affect the economy.
6. Understand how supply and demand analysis is used in macroeconomics and show how changes in aggregate demand or aggregate supply can cause real GNP and prices to change.

IN BRIEF: CHAPTER SUMMARY

Fill in the blanks to summarize chapter content.

The National Income and Product Accounts are designed to measure economic activity--flows of income and expenditures over a period of time. The broadest measure of economic activity is (1)_____(gross national product, aggregate output). GNP is the market value of an economy's (2)_____(total, final) goods and services produced over a period of 1 year. It is designed to measure economic activity that gives rise to income, output, and employment. Some transactions during the year do not affect production and employment and are thus excluded from GNP. These include changes in the value of existing assets, (3)_____ (nonfinancial, financial) transactions, sale of used goods, and most goods not sold in markets.

GNP can be thought of as the total value added in a nation over a given year. The market value of all products and services (4)_____(less, plus) the market value of all intermediate goods equals the value added in producing and making final goods and services available to the market. Value added (5)_____(is greater than, also equals) the payments to suppliers of labor, capital, and raw materials, including profit to entrepreneurs. Because GNP is defined in terms of its market value, inflation can cause the value of GNP to change. In order to remove this inflationary bias so as to uncover the movements in GNP that affect output and employment, it is necessary to deflate

GNP--to remove the effect of inflation. This is accomplished by dividing a general price index into (6)_____ (nominal, real) GNP. Doing so yields (7)_____ (real, nominal) GNP, a measure of the value of a nation's aggregate output of final products using market prices defined by the price index base year.

GNP should not be considered a perfect measure of a nation's well-being. It excludes nonmarket goods and services, such as the services of spouses in maintaining a home, that contribute to society's welfare. It also excludes the value of leisure, does not consider the impact of environmental damage caused by the production or consumption of output, (8)_____ (but does, and does not) reflect the market value of goods and services produced in the underground economy.

Gross national product can be measured by determining the total aggregate expenditures on final output during the year or by determining the income generated by the economy in producing that final output. GNP can be estimated by summing personal consumption expenditures of households, gross private domestic investment, government purchases of goods and services, and net (9)_____(exports, imports). Personal consumption expenditures are household expenditures on durable goods, nondurable goods, and services. Gross private domestic investment represents spending on producer durables, residential and nonresidential construction, and (10)_____ (the, changes in the) value of inventories. Government expenditures include the expenditures of all levels of government on goods and services (including labor services) less transfer payments. Net exports are total (11)_____ (exports, imports) less (12)_____(exports, imports).

Gross national product can also be determined by summing the incomes received by resource suppliers during the year. The five types of income are compensation of employees, proprietors' income, corporate profits, net interest, and rental income. Compensation of employees includes wages and salaries and employer-provided contributions to Social Security and pension plans. (13)_____(Enterprise income, Proprietors' income) is the income of unincorporated enterprises. Corporate profits are the incomes of corporations and equal the sum of dividends and retained earnings, and corporate profits taxes. Net interest includes the interest paid by business (14)_____ (and, but not) the interest paid by government. Rental income is received by those supplying land, mineral rights, and structures for the use of others. It (15)_____ (excludes, also includes) the imputed rent earned by homeowners. Adding these components of total income to indirect business taxes and depreciation gives GNP.

As can be shown in a circular flow diagram, total aggregate expenditures on final output generate the income necessary to sustain those expenditures. But if leakages from the circular flow exceed injections into the flow of spending, the level of economic activity will (16)_____(decline, increase). Leakages include net taxes, saving, and imports. These reduce the amount of funds available to purchase domestic output. Injections include gross private domestic investment, government spending on goods and services, and exports. These expenditures increase total spending on domestic output. If leakages are less than injections, economic activity will (17)_____(decline, increase). If leakages equal injections, the level of economic activity will just be maintained, neither increasing nor decreasing.

Gross national product and the level of prices can be modeled using an aggregate supply and demand model. The aggregate demand curve shows the relationship between the general price level and total expenditures on final output. The price level is (18)_____(positively, negatively) related to aggregate expenditures on final output. The aggregate supply curve shows a (19)_____(positive, negative) relationship between the price level and the total production of final output. Where the aggregate supply and demand curves intersect, the macroeconomy is in a state of balance or equilibrium. There is only one combination of GNP and the price level consistent with this state. A change in aggregate demand or a change in aggregate supply will alter the equilibrium level of GNP and prices.

VOCABULARY REVIEW

Write the key term from the list below next to its definition.

Key Terms

Gross national product
Net exports
National Income and
 Product Accounts
Aggregates
Net taxes
Intermediate products
Aggregate expenditure
Total value added in
 a nation
Nominal GNP
Real GNP
Aggregate real income
Personal consumption
 expenditures

Gross private domestic
 investment
Depreciation (capital
 consumption allowances)
Net private domestic
 investment
Government purchases of
 goods and services
Transfer payments
Leakages
Indirect business taxes
Corporate profits taxes
Disposable income
Injections

Definitions

1. _____: the market value of an economy's final goods and services produced over a period of 1 year.

2. _____: broad totals of economic variables such as production or unemployment.

3. _____: the market value of a nation's aggregate production of final output based on current prices for the goods and services produced during the year.

4. _____: the nominal (money) income of a nation, adjusted for inflation.

5. _____: investment purchases by business firms: expenditure on new machinery and equipment (producer durables), the value of new residential and nonresidential construction, and the change in business inventories during the year.

6. _____: expenditure on final products of business firms and all input costs, including labor costs, incurred by all levels of government in the United States.

7. _____: taxes levied on business firms that increase their costs and are therefore reflected in the market value of goods and services sold.

8. _____: the difference between taxes and transfer payments.

9. _____: a portion of income that is not used to purchase domestically produced goods during the year.

10. _____: the official system of accounting to measure the flows of income and expenditures in the United States.

11. _____: products produced by business firms for resale by other firms or for use as materials or services that will be included in the value of resold goods.

12. _____: a measure of the value of a nation's aggregate output of final products obtained by using market prices prevailing for products during a certain base or reference year.

13. _____: any excess of expenditure on exports over imports.

14. _____: an estimate of the value of capital goods that wear out or become obsolete over the year.

15. _____: payments for which no good or service is currently received in return and that therefore do not represent expenditures for the purchase of final products.

16. _____: those amounts corporations pay as taxes to governments out of their annual receipts from the sale of goods and services.

17. _____: the amount of income available for households to spend after receipt of government transfer payments and payment of taxes.

18. _____: a purchase made by business firms, governments, or foreign buyers that increases the flow of income in a nation.

19. _____: the difference between the market value of <u>all</u> products of business firms and the market value of all intermediate products.

20. _____: the sum of consumption, investment expenditures, government purchases, and net exports during the year.

21. _____: household and individual purchases of both durable and nondurable goods and services.

22. _____: gross private domestic investment less depreciation.

SKILLS REVIEW

Concept: GNP and its shortcomings

1. List four catagories of items excluded from GNP.

a. _____
b. _____
c. _____
d. _____

2. Indicate whether the following cause GNP to be understated or overstated as a measure of well-being.

    a. _____ GNP excludes most nonmarket goods.
    b. _____ GNP excludes the value of leisure.
    c. _____ The environmental damage that results from production is not accounted for in GNP.
    d. _____ GNP excludes the value of goods and services produced by the underground economy.

Concept: Nominal and real GNP

3. Consider the production and price data below for a nation producing only automobiles. (Assume that all automobiles are identical.)

Year	Price per Auto	Output (units)	Nominal GNP	Price Index	Real GNP
1	$10,000	1,000			
2	10,500	1,200	_____	_____	_____
3	11,000	1,400	_____	_____	_____
4	11,500	1,600	_____	_____	_____
5	12,000	1,800	_____	_____	_____

    a. Complete the nominal GNP column.
    b. Complete the price index column. Assume that year 3 is the base year. Price index = (current year price/base year price) x 100.
    c. Prices have increased _____ % from year 3 to year 5.
    d. Complete the real GNP column. (Hint: Divide the price index by 100 prior to dividing into nominal GNP.)

Concept: GNP and the flow of expenditures and income

4. The following are national income and product accounts for a nation for a given year.

National Income and Product Accounts

Government purchases of goods and services	$ 580
Indirect business taxes	230
Personal consumption expenditures	1,520
Depreciation	310
Proprietors' income	175
Employer contributions to public and private pension plans	325
Net interest	98
Gross private domestic investment	410
Rental income	45
Exports	460
Imports	260
Corporate profits	225
Wages and salaries	1,302

    a. Using the expenditure side of GNP, determine GNP. _____
    b. Using the income side of GNP, determine GNP. _____
    c. Net private domestic investment = _____
    d. Net national product = _____
    e. Net exports = _____
    f. Capital consumption allowances = _____

5. a. List the components of personal consumption expenditures.
        (1) _____
        (2) _____
        (3) _____
    b. List the components of gross private domestic investment.
        (1) _____
        (2) _____
        (3) _____
    c. List the components of corporate profits.
        (1) _____
        (2) _____
        (3) _____

Concept: Circular flow, leakages, and injections

6. Regarding a circular flow diagram:

    a. List the leakages from the flow of income.
        (1) _____
        (2) _____
        (3) _____
    b. List the injections to the flow of final expenditures on domestic output.
        (1) _____
        (2) _____
        (3) _____
    c. Economic activity _____ when leakages exceed injections.
        Economic activity _____ when leakages are less than injections.
        Economic activity _____ when leakages equal injections.
    d. Saving is composed of:
        (1) _____
        (2) _____
        (3) _____

Concept: Aggregate supply and demand

7. An aggregate demand-aggregate supply model for an economy is shown in the diagram below.

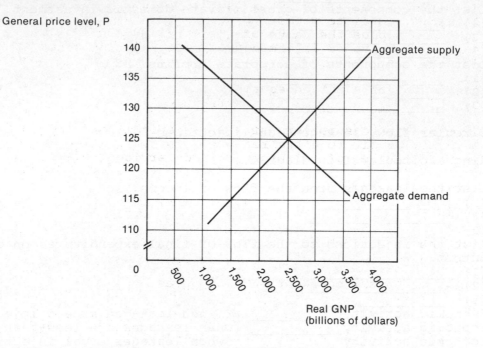

General price level, P

Real GNP
(billions of dollars)

a. Find the equilibrium level of real GNP and the price level. GNP = _____ , P = _____
b. If government reduces the level of government purchases, show the impact on the figure above. GNP _____ , and P _____
c. An increase in aggregate demand _____ GNP and _____ P.
d. An increase in aggregate supply _____ GNP and _____ P.
e. An increase in both aggregate demand and aggregate supply _____ GNP and _____ P.

SELF-TEST FOR MASTERY

Select the best answer.

1. Which of the following defines GNP?

   a. Total output produced by an economy
   b. Total final output produced by an economy
   c. The market value of the total final output produced by an economy during a given year
   d. The market value of the total output produced by an economy during a given year

2. Which of the following are excluded from GNP?

   a. Changes in the value of existing assets
   b. Financial transactions
   c. Sale of used goods
   d. All of the above

3. The value added for a nation equals:

   a. All goods and services less the intermediate goods used in
      production.
   b. The market value of all products and services less the market value
      of all intermediate goods.
   c. Input costs plus the value of intermediate goods.
   d. The market value of intermediate goods less the value of all goods
      and services.

4. The value added for a nation equals:

   a. GNP.
   b. The payments to suppliers of labor, capital, and raw materials,
      including profit to entrepreneurs.
   c. The market value of all products and services less the market value
      of all intermediate goods.
   d. All of the above.

5. Nominal GNP is:

   a. A preliminary estimate of GNP.
   b. GNP unadjusted for inflation.
   c. GNP adjusted for inflation.
   d. GNP less capital consumption allowances.

6. Real GNP is:

   a. The final estimate of GNP for a period.
   b. GNP unadjusted for inflation.
   c. GNP adjusted for inflation.
   d. Total income minus indirect business taxes.

7. GNP overstates economic well-being if:

   a. Nonmarket goods are included in GNP.
   b. Leisure time is not included in GNP.
   c. Production in the underground economy is included in GNP.
   d. The environmental damage caused by economic activity is not
      considered in GNP.

8. GNP can be estimated by summing :

   a. Personal consumption expenditures, net private domestic investment,
      and federal government spending.
   b. Personal consumption expenditures, gross private domestic investment,
      government spending on goods and services, and net exports.
   c. All services and goods purchased by households, businesses, and
      government.
   d. Household spending, investment, financial transactions, and
      government transfers.

9. What two items must be added to net interest, corporate profits,
   proprietor's income, rental income, and employee compensation in order to
   derive GNP?

   a. Depreciation and capital consumption allowances
   b. Capital consumption allowances and indirect business taxes
   c. Dividends and retained earnings
   d. Household consumption and business investment

10. Gross private domestic investment equals the sum of:

    a.   Changes in the value of inventories, new residential and nonresidential construction, and producer durables.
    b.   The value of inventories, residential construction, and machines.
    c.   Business structures and machines.
    d.   Plant and equipment.

11. Which of the following categories absorbs the largest percentage of household expenditures?

    a.   Nondurable goods
    b.   Services
    c.   Durable goods
    d.   Taxes

12. The most volatile components of GNP are:

    a.   Defense spending and net exports.
    b.   Personal consumption expenditures.
    c.   Services and government spending.
    d.   Investment and net exports.

13. Rental income is composed of:

    a.   Income from rental properties.
    b.   Lease payments and apartment rents.
    c.   Income received by suppliers of land, mineral rights and structures.
    d.   Imputed rent attributed to owner-occupied housing.
    e.   C and d.

14. Leakages from the flow of income include:

    a.   Saving.
    b.   Imports.
    c.   Taxes.
    d.   All of the above.

15. Which of the following is not an injection to the flow of spending?

    a.   Investment
    b.   Government spending
    c.   Imports
    d.   Exports

16. If leakages exceed injections, economic activity will:

    a.   Expand.
    b.   Remain unchanged.
    c.   Decline.
    d.   Experience a slight decline, then a robust expansion.

17. If injections exceed leakages, economic activity will:

    a.   Expand.
    b.   Remain unchanged.
    c.   Decline.
    d.   Expand, then decline upon reaching the point of diminishing returns.

18. If injections equal leakages, economic activity will:

    a. Expand.
    b. Remain unchanged.
    c. Decline.
    d. None of the above.

19. In an aggregate supply and demand model of the economy, an increase in aggregate demand will _____ GNP and _____ the price level.

    a. Decrease, decrease
    b. Increase, decrease
    c. Increase, increase
    d. Decrease, increase

20. In an aggregate supply and demand model of the economy, an increase in aggregate supply will _____ GNP and _____ the price level.

    a. Decrease, decrease
    b. Increase, decrease
    c. Increase, increase
    d. Decrease, increase

THINK IT THROUGH

1. Discuss two methods of estimating gross national product.

2. If capital consumption allowances exceed gross private domestic investment, what will happen to the nation's capital stock?

3. Discuss how the effect of inflation can be removed from GNP. Of what use is this?

4. Recently, the U.S. trade balance has improved. Exports are rising at a faster rate than imports. How is this likely to affect the U.S. economy?

5. Using the value added concept, explain why total expenditures on the nation's output of final goods and services are conceptually equal to the total income earned by suppliers of economic resources.

POP QUIZ   Read the news brief at the end of this chapter and answer the
                  following question.

Explain why measured real GNP might today overstate actual GNP. Should an increase in real GNP be interpreted as an improvement in quality of life?

CHAPTER ANSWERS

In Brief: Chapter Summary

1. Gross national product 2. Final 3. Financial 4. Less 5. Also equals 6. Nominal 7. Real 8. And does not 9. Exports 10. Changes in the 11. Exports 12. Imports 13. Proprietors' income 14. But not 15. Also includes 16. Decline 17. Increase 18. Negatively 19. Positive

Vocabulary Review

1. Gross national product 2. Aggregates 3. Nominal GNP 4. Aggregate real income 5. Gross private domestic investment 6. Government purchases of goods and services 7. Indirect business taxes 8. Net taxes 9. Leakages 10. National income and product accounts 11. Intermediate products 12. Real GNP 13. Net exports 14. Depreciation 15. Transfer payments 16. Corporate profits taxes 17. Disposable income 18. Injections 19. Total value added in a nation 20. Aggregate expenditure 21. Personal consumption expenditures 22. Net private domestic investment

Skills Review

1. a. Changes in the value of existing assets
    b. Sale of used goods
    c. Financial transactions
    d. Most goods not sold in markets

2. a. Understated
    b. Understated
    c. Overstated
    d. Understated

3.

Nominal GNP	Price Index	Real GNP
$10,000,000	90.9	$11,001,100
12,600,000	95.5	13,193,717
15,400,000	100.0	15,400,000
18,400,000	104.5	17,607,656
21,600,000	109.1	19,798,350

    c. 9.1%

4. a. $2,710
    b. $2,710
    c. $100
    d. $2,400
    e. $200
    f. $310

5. a. (1) Durable goods
        (2) Nondurable goods
        (3) Services
    b. (1) New residential and nonresidential construction
        (2) Producer durables
        (3) Changes in the value of inventories
    c. (1) Corporate profits taxes
        (2) Retained earnings
        (3) Dividends

6. a. (1) Saving
        (2) Net taxes
        (3) Imports
    b. (1) Gross private domestic investment
        (2) Government purchases of goods and services
        (3) Exports
    c. Declines, increases, remains unchanged
    d. (1) Personal saving
        (2) Business saving
        (3) Foreign saving

7. a. $2,500, 125
    b. Falls, falls

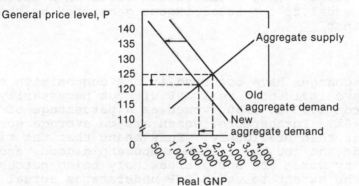

    c. Increases, increases
    d. Increases, decreases
    e. Increase, may either increase, decrease or leave unchanged

Self-Test for Mastery

1. c 2. d 3. b 4. d 5. b 6. c 7. d 8. b 9. b 10. a 11. b 12. d 13.
e 14. d 15. c 16. c 17. a 18. b 19. c 20. b

Think it Through

1. GNP can be estimated by summing the aggregate expenditures on the nation's
final output or by summing the income generated by the economy in producing
that output. The expenditure approach requires the summation of personal
consumption expenditures, government purchases of goods and services, gross
private domestic investment, and net exports. The income approach involves the
addition of the five types of income (proprietors' income, corporate profits,
compensation of employees, rental income, and net interest) to indirect
business taxes and capital consumption allowances.

2. Although gross private domestic investment is positive, net private
domestic investment is negative. Total investment is insufficient to replace
the capital that has worn out during the year's production of GNP. The total
capacity of the economy to produce output has declined. Future economic growth
will likely be impaired.

3. Real GNP can be derived by dividing a general price index into nominal
GNP. Changes in real GNP are the result of changes in output and not prices
because real GNP is valued at a given set of prices as determined by the base
year. Economists are interested in real GNP because changes in real GNP
reflect real changes in economic activity that produce output and employment
rather than the image of changes in economic activity caused merely by
inflation.

4.   If exports are rising faster than imports, net exports are rising. The
total level of aggregate expenditures on domestic output is therefore also
rising. In the context of the aggregate supply and demand model, aggregate
demand is rising, causing an increase in real GNP and the price level.

5.   Total expenditures on a nation's final output equal the market value of
the final output produced. But the market value of all final output less the
market value of all intermediate inputs must equal the value added at the last
stage of production. This value added is made possible by the combined
services of labor, raw materials, capital, and entrepreneurs. The value added
just equals the payments to suppliers of labor, capital, and raw materials,
including profits to owners. The sum of the value added at each stage of
production equals GNP, but it also equals the total aggregate income generated
in producing that value added. Thus total expenditures on a nation's final
output are conceptually equal to the total income generated by the economy in
producing that final output.

Pop Quiz

Since 1960, fundamental changes have occurred in the composition of the labor
force. These changes have influenced real GNP without necessarily improving
the quality of life. From 1960 to 1980, women as a percentage of the labor
force grew from 33% to 43%. Furthermore, women are on average working more
hours on the job per year than previously. This means that the time available
for non-paid work outside the job has fallen. Household goods and services
that were once produced by women are now increasingly being purchased in
markets. This reduces the extent to which GNP understates actual output,
because now a greater percentage of production involves market transactions
which are accounted for in measured real GNP. Laura Stern argues that the
household goods and services now purchased in markets are in many cases
inferior to home-produced items--child care, for instance. Measured Real GNP
rises as a result of this shift from nonmarket to market production, causing
real GNP to possibly overstate actual GNP. Quality of life does not
necessarily increase when measured real GNP increases.

I Work This Hard So I Can Eat Tuna Surprise?

By Laura Stern

Staring forlornly at the "meal" I've prepared for my family, at the end of a 10-hour day employed as an economist, I see convincing evidence here that the gap between measured gross national product and social welfare has widened radically. The omission of nonmarket activities (like a home-cooked meal) is a distortion of GNP that is readily admitted by economists, but the different composition of goods and services constituting GNP today has made the problem somewhat different. Although our rising real GNP (up 6.8% in 1984, less since) may give an impression of "material well-being," the taste of tuna and Tostitos that we chomp down for dinner tells the true story.

The advance of women into paid jobs is one of the fundamental changes of this generation. Women's share of the labor force grew to 43% from 33% between 1960 and 1980. Also, the average hours women work in a paid job have increased more than 50%, to 873 a year from 572, according to the Census Bureau. Since the number of hours in a day has remained remarkably stable at 24, it should come as no surprise that average nonmarket hours worked by women have declined to 1,497 in 1979 from 1,854 in 1959, according to a recent study by Victor Fuchs.

What kinds of nonmarket activities have been abandoned, hurriedly done or substituted for as a result of women exchanging non-paid for paid work? The list is long: housework, child care, chauffeuring of children to lessons or friends' houses, volunteerism, pickling and preserving, ironing, decorating, crafts, sports, sleeping, reading the paper, and so on.

Now, the astute reader will necessarily point out that many of the nonmarket activities previously performed by women have been replaced by market activities that will raise GNP and do represent an increase in the production of goods and services, or, as GNP represents, "a measure of national economic performance." Let's be serious—does a meal at Red Lobster truly compare with a meal of oysters Rockefeller served on rock salt, lovingly prepared at home, rock by rock? Is the perfunctory greeting from a housekeeper as a youngster bounds in the door from school nearly as meaningful as the harsh scream from Mom to "hang up your coat before you grab for the cookies"? Can the despair of finding out that you have no more clean underwear (albeit you own 13 luxurious pairs) ever be appropriately quantified?

What is being suggested is that with the changing composition of the labor force, and specifically the change in activities that women perform today, there are many missed activities that have made the nation worse off but have *not* lowered real GNP as it is currently measured. Our method of GNP accounting, then, rather than understating GNP as in the past, now probably overstates GNP due to the omission of activities not now being performed. Although poking holes in GNP accounting is nothing new, the changed role of women has radically affected the impact of this problem.

In Mr. Fuchs's study, entitled "His and Hers: Gender Differences in Work and Income, 1959-1979," he concludes that if you combine market and nonmarket hours, women worked more hours in 1979 than in 1959 and even more hours relative to men in 1979 than in 1959. Most distressingly, he found that the women-to-men ratio of total income rose very slightly or *not at all*, depending on the set of assumptions used. It was an immense relief to discover that my feeling this year of being "more tired and no richer" was not a figment of my imagination.

It is not being suggested for a minute that women abandon their roles in the labor force and defer career ambitions for the warmth of a baby bottom on a lap from 9 to 5. Rather, it is advisable to use caution in interpreting GNP statistics, and specifically to avoid automatically linking rises in GNP to improvements in quality of life. Future estimates of real GNP peg a trend growth of about 3% a year over the rest of the decade. This may be cause for celebration in some circles, but I'd settle for being able to stay conscious after 10 p.m. or having some time to make my infamous homemade graham cracker cake with mocha frosting. Mmm, remember that one?

Ms. Stern, a former university instructor, is a happy but tired public utility economist, wife and mother of three.

26

Business Cycles and Unemployment

CHAPTER CHALLENGES

After studying this chapter, attending class, and completing this chapter, you should be able to:

1. Discuss the phases of the business cycle and give examples of recent periods of recession and expansion of the U.S. economy.
2. Understand the concept of the unemployment rate and discuss different possible causes of fluctuations in the unemployment rate.
3. Define the concept of full employment and show how it is related to the natural rate of unemployment. Also, show how the actual unemployment rate is the sum of the natural unemployment rate and the cyclical unemployment rate.
4. Understand the concept of potential real GNP and the difficulties involved in estimating it.
5. Discuss the social costs of unemployment and programs designed to cushion those costs.

IN BRIEF: CHAPTER SUMMARY

Fill in the blanks to summarize chapter content.

The business cycle describes the ups and downs in real GNP over time. Although no two business cycles are identical, they all have four distinct phases: expansion, peak, contraction, and trough. An economy is in a recession or contraction when real GNP has declined for (1)_____(three, two) consecutive 3-month periods. Although real GNP fluctuates up and down, its long-run average annual growth trend is just over (2)_____(3%, 5%). When the economy is in a recession, such in the Great Depression of the 1930s or more recently the 1981-82 recession, unemployment (3)_____(rises, falls). As the economy expands out of a trough, the unemployment rate (4)_____(rises, falls).

The unemployment rate is the percentage of the labor force that is unemployed. The labor force includes all persons over the age of 16 with jobs and those actively seeking employment. A person is considered unemployed if the person is over age 16 and is available for work (5)_____(but not, and) actively seeking employment. The unemployment rate may understate or overstate the true extent of unemployment. The unemployment rate (6)_____ (does not, does) include discouraged workers. Also, part-time employment is considered as full-time employment, not as partial employment or unemployment. People may respond to unemployment surveys that they are looking for work when in fact their expectations of a job will likely not materialize because those expectations are unrealistic. The rate of unemployment is higher among (7)_____ (married, single) workers than among (8)_____ (married, single) workers. It is also higher among (9)_____(whites, blacks) than (10)_____(whites, blacks). Teenagers, particularly nonwhite teens, face some of the highest unemployment rates.

The three types of unemployment are frictional unemployment, structural unemployment, and cyclical unemployment. (11)_____ (Structural, Frictional) unemployment is due to the length of time it takes to find employment upon entering the labor force or between jobs. (12)_____ (Structural, Frictional) unemployment results from changes in the composition of output produced by the economy or by technological changes that cause some industries to expand and others to decline. Cyclical unemployment is unemployment caused by economic decline or recession. Most cyclical unemployment is the result of layoffs. Full employment is defined as a level of economic activity where the actual unemployment rate (13)_____ (is less than, equals) the sum of structural and frictional unemployment and exists even when the economy is operating at the peak of the business cycle--at a high rate of capacity utilization. When the sum of frictional and (14)_____ (structural, cyclical) unemployment is expressed as a percentage of the total labor force, the ratio is known as the natural rate of unemployment.

(15)_____(Actual, Potential) GNP is the level of output that results if the economy operates for an entire year at the natural rate of unemployment. The difference between potential and actual GNP is called the (16)_____(natural rate of unemployment, GNP gap). If actual GNP falls short of potential GNP, the sacrificed output constitutes a major cost of cyclical unemployment. For instance, for each 1% increase in the unemployment rate, real GNP falls by (17)_____(3.5%, 2.5%). This is known as Okun's Law. Using Okun's Law, the GNP gap for 1982 is estimated at approximately $300 billion. Other social costs of unemployment include the monetary and nonmonetary costs associated with suicide, crime, mental illness, physical illness, stress, and other problems attributed to unemployment.

Unemployment insurance was established in 1935 as part of the Social Security Act in order to soften the blow of unemployment. Generally, only those people who lose their jobs due to layoff, economic contraction, or (18)_____ (firings, plant closings) get unemployment benefits. Evidence shows that unemployment benefits, while softening the trauma of unemployment, (19)_____ (increase, decrease) frictional unemployment.

VOCABULARY REVIEW

Write the key term from the list below next to its definition.

Key Terms

Business cycle
Contraction
Recession
Layoff
Expansion
GNP gap
Recovery
Job separation
Labor force
Okun's Law
Unemployment rate
Unemployed person
Discouraged worker

Job search
Job finding
Frictional
   unemployment
Structural
   unemployment
Cyclical
   unemployment
Natural rate of
   unemployment
Full employment
Potential real GNP

Definitions

1. _____: the term used to describe the fluctuations in aggregate production as measured by the ups and downs of real GNP.

2. _____: an upturn of economic activity between a trough and a peak during which real GNP increases.

3. _____: the sum of the number of persons over age 16 with jobs and workers who are actively seeking a job but currently do not have one.

4. _____: the temporary suspension of employment without pay for a period of 7 consecutive days or more.

5. _____: occurs when a worker leaves a job for any reason: quitting, being fired, or being laid off.

6. _____: the amount of unemployment resulting from declines in real GNP during periods of contraction or recession or in any period when the economy fails to operate at its potential.

7. _____: the level that would prevail if the economy achieved the natural rate of unemployment over a period.

8. _____: the difference between potential and actual GNP.

9. _____: states that each 1% increase in the unemployment rate is associated with a 2.5% reduction in real GNP.

10. _____: a downturn from peak economic activity in the business cycle during which real GNP declines from its previous value.

11. _____: the term used to describe an expansion in economic activity after a trough if the expansion follows a period of contraction severe enough to be classified as a recession.

12. _____: measures the ratio of the number of people classified as unemployed to the total labor force.

13. _____: a worker who leaves the labor force (stops actively seeking work) after unsuccessfully searching for a job for a certain period.

14. _____: the process of looking for suitable work either by those just entering the labor force or by those having just experienced a job separation.

15. _____: the percentage of the labor force that can normally be expected to be unemployed for reasons other than cyclical fluctuations in real GNP.

16. _____: exists when the decline in real GNP measured at an annual rate occurs for two consecutive 3-month reporting periods.

17. _____: a person over age 16 who is available for work and has actively sought employment during the previous 4 weeks.

18. _____: occurs when an unemployed worker accepts an offer of a new job.

19. _____: occurs when the actual rate of unemployment is no more the natural rate of unemployment.

20. _____: represents the usual amount of unemployment resulting from people who have left jobs that did not work out and are searching for new employment, or people who are either entering or reentering the labor force to search for a job.

21. _____: unemployment resulting from shifts in the pattern of demand for goods and services or changes in technology in the economy that affect the profitability of hiring workers in specific industries.

SKILLS REVIEW

Concept: **Phases of the business cycle; record of recent fluctuations in the U.S. economy**

1.   Identify the phases of the business cycle in the diagram below.

a. _____
b. _____
c. _____
d. _____

2.   a.   During the 1930s, the unemployment rate _____ to _____ and real GNP _____ by _____ of its 1929 value.
     b.   As a result of World War II, the unemployment rate _____ and real GNP _____, but recessions did occur _____. The 1950s can be characterized as a period of _____, although _____ occurred in _____ and _____.
     c.   The 1960s was a period of economic expansion lasting from _____ to _____, which was due in part to _____.
     d.   The decade of the 1970s experienced periods of rising _____ and _____. The last half of the decade can be characterized as _____.
     e.   There have been _____ recessions in the 1980s, with the most severe recession since the Great Depression occurring from _____ to _____.

377

Concept: Unemployment rate

3. Find the size of the labor force, the number of unemployed persons, and the unemployment rate from the data below.

1.	Total population	200 million
2.	Persons over age 16 working	95
3.	Institutional population (prisons, hospitals, etc.)	12
4.	Discouraged workers	2
5.	Persons over age 16 actively seeking work and available for employment	5
6.	Part-time workers	1

   a. Total labor force = _____
   b. Unemployed persons = _____
   c. Unemployment rate = _____

4. List three reasons why the unemployment rate may not reflect the true extent of unemployment.

   a. _____
   b. _____
   c. _____

5. Identify each of the following as either frictional, structural, or cyclical unemployment.

   a. _____ You quit your job and spend time searching for new employment.
   b. _____ You are temporarily unemployed due to layoff.
   c. _____ Advances in office automation reduce the need for secretaries.
   d. _____ Movie theaters reduce employment because more people are watching home videos.
   e. _____ You graduate from high school and begin your search for a job.
   f. _____ A decline in demand for the nation's output causes both GNP and employment to decline.

Concept: Potential GNP, actual GNP, and GNP gap

6. Determine potential GNP and the GNP gap from the data below.

1.	Natural rate of unemployment	6%
2.	Actual rate of unemployment	5%
3.	Annual labor hours (4% unemployment)	200 billion
4.	Annual labor hours (5% unemployment)	250 billion
5.	Annual labor hours (6% unemployment)	300 billion
6.	Output per labor hour	$15
7.	Actual GNP	$ 4 trillion

   a. Potential GNP = _____
   b. GNP gap = _____
   c. If there are 100 million households, find the GNP gap per household.
      _____

d.   On the diagram below, shade in the area representing the GNP gap.

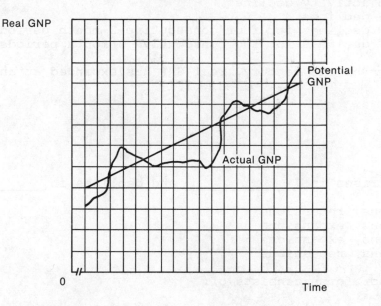

Real GNP

Potential GNP

Actual GNP

0

Time

Concept: Social costs of unemployment

7.   In addition to the GNP gap, other social costs of unemployment include the costs associated with:

a.   _____
b.   _____
c.   _____
d.   _____

SELF-TEST FOR MASTERY

Select the best answer.

1.   Which of the following best defines the business cycle?

a.   Recessions and expansions
b.   Ups and downs in business activity
c.   Ups and downs in real GNP
d.   None of the above

2.   The phase of a business cycle just following a trough is called a/an:

a.   Recession.
b.   Decline.
c.   Expansion.
d.   Peak.

3.   The economy is defined as being in a recession if:

     a.   Economic activity declines.
     b.   Real GNP declines.
     c.   Real GNP declines for four consecutive 3-month periods.
     d.   Real GNP declines for two consecutive 3-month periods.

4.   Since the turn of the century, real GNP has expanded at an average annual rate of:

     a.   2%.
     b.   3%.
     c.   4%.
     d.   5%.

5.   Unemployment rises in _____ and declines in _____.

     a.   Expansions, recessions
     b.   Recessions, expansions
     c.   Expansions, expansions
     d.   Recessions, recessions

6.   The total labor force consists of:

     a.   All persons working plus those not working.
     b.   All persons over age 16 working.
     c.   Discouraged workers, part-time and full-time workers, and the armed forces.
     d.   All persons over age 16 either working or actively seeking work and available for employment.

7.   The unemployment rate is defined as:

     a.   The percentage of the population that is unemployed.
     b.   The percentage of the labor force that is unemployed.
     c.   All unemployed workers, including discouraged workers, divided by the total labor force.
     d.   All unemployed workers, including discouraged workers, divided by the total population.

8.   Which of the following is not a reason why the unemployment rate may not reflect the true extent of unemployment?

     a.   Discouraged workers are excluded.
     b.   Part-time work is considered as full-time work.
     c.   People may respond to employment surveys that they are looking for work when in fact the likelihood of their finding employment that meets their expectations is remote.
     d.   None of the above.

9.   Which of the following groups experiences the highest unemployment rates?

     a.   Teenagers, whites, single persons
     b.   Middle-aged persons, blacks, single persons
     c.   Teenagers, blacks, married persons
     d.   Teenagers, blacks, single persons

10. Unemployment due to the length of time it takes to find employment upon entering the labor force or voluntarily between jobs is called:

    a.   Cyclical unemployment.
    b.   Frictional unemployment.
    c.   Structural unemployment.
    d.   Natural unemployment.

11. Unemployment that results from changes in the composition of output produced by the economy or from technological changes is called:

    a.   Cyclical unemployment.
    b.   Frictional unemployment.
    c.   Structural unemployment.
    d.   Natural unemployment.

12. Unemployment caused by economic decline or recession is called:

    a.   Cyclical unemployment.
    b.   Frictional unemployment.
    c.   Structural unemployment.
    d.   Natural unemployment.

13. Most cyclical unemployment is the result of:

    a.   Layoffs.
    b.   Voluntary job separations.
    c.   Job findings.
    d.   Firings.

14. The unemployment rate that exists even when the economy is at the peak of a business cycle is:

    a.   The sum of the frictional and structural unemployment rates.
    b.   The actual unemployment rate.
    c.   The cyclical unemployment rate.
    d.   The natural rate of unemployment.
    e.   A and d.

15. Today most economists consider the natural rate of unemployment to be:

    a.   4%.
    b.   8%.
    c.   6%.
    d.   2%.

16. _____ is the level of output that would result if the economy operated for an entire year at the natural rate of unemployment.

    a.   Real GNP
    b.   Natural rate of GNP
    c.   Capacity GNP
    d.   Potential GNP

17. The difference between potential GNP and actual GNP is the:

    a.   GNP gap.
    b.   Major economic cost of unemployment.
    c.   Forgone output resulting from the actual rate of unemployment exceeding the natural rate of unemployment.
    d.   All of the above.

18. Costs associated with unemployment include:

   a. The GNP gap.
   b. Costs associated with suicide and mental illness.
   c. Costs associated with stress, physical illness, and crime.
   d. All of the above.

19. Unemployment insurance:

   a. Covers all workers.
   b. Is federally administered.
   c. Primarily covers those workers who lose their jobs due to layoff, economic contraction, or plant closings.
   d. Was established in 1970.

20. Evidence shows that unemployment benefits:

   a. Decrease structural unemployment.
   b. Increase structural unemployment.
   c. Decrease frictional unemployment.
   d. Increase frictional unemployment.

THINK IT THROUGH

1. Define the unemployment rate and discuss why it may not accurately reflect the true extent of unemployment.

2. Discuss the factors that influence the unemployment rate.

3. Of what use is the concept of the natural rate of unemployment?

4. What are the social costs associated with unemployment?

5. Discuss one way in which society softens the blow of unemployment.

POP QUIZ   Read the news brief at the end of this chapter and answer the questions below.

1. According to the news brief, what is the natural rate of unemployment?

2. What forces have been responsible for the rise in the natural rate of unemployment in the 1960s and 1970s?

3. Are there any reasons to believe it is falling today?

CHAPTER ANSWERS

In Brief: Chapter Summary

1. Two 2. 3% 3. Rises 4. Falls 5. And 6. Does not 7. Single 8. Married
9. Blacks 10. Whites 11. Frictional 12. Structural 13. Equals 14.

Structural   15. Potential   16. GNP gap   17. 2.5%   18. Plant closings   19.
Increase

Vocabulary Review

1. Business cycle   2. Expansion   3. Labor force   4. Layoff   5. Job separation
6. Cyclical unemployment   7. Potential real GNP   8. GNP gap   9. Okun's law   10.
Contraction   11. Recovery   12. Unemployment rate   13. Discouraged worker   14.
Job search   15. Natural rate of unemployment   16.   Recession   17. Unemployed
person   18. Job finding   19. Full employment   20. Frictional unemployment   21.
Structural unemployment

Skills Review

1.   a. Peak   b. Recession   c. Trough   d. Expansion

2.   a.   Increased, 25%, fell, one third
     b.   Fell, increased, at the end of the war and in 1949; growth and
          stability, recessions, 1954, 1958
     c.   1961, 1970; military expansion and the Vietnam War
     d.   Inflation, unemployment; growth and rampant inflation
     e.   Two, 1981, 1982

3.   a.   100 million
     b.   5 million
     c.   5%

4.   a.   Discouraged workers are excluded.
     b.   Part-time work is counted as full-time work.
     c.   Survey responses may be misleading.

5.   a. Frictional   b. Cyclical   c. Structural   d. Structural   e. Frictional
     f. Cyclical

6.   a. $4.5 trillion   b. $.5 trillion   c. $5,000

     d.

7.   a.   Crime   b. Suicide   c. Mental illness   d. Physical illness

Self-Test for Mastery

1. c   2. c   3. d   4. b   5. a   6. d   7. b   8. d   9. d   10. b   11. c   12. a   13.
a   14. e   15. c   16. d   17. d   18. d   19. c   20. d

383

Think it Through

1.   The unemployment rate is the percentage of the total labor force that is unemployed. The labor force consists of all persons over age 16 either working or actively seeking employment but not currently employed. Unemployed persons are those individuals over age 16 available for work and actively searching for employment. The unemployment rate may not reflect the true extent of unemployment because discouraged workers are unemployed but not counted as part of the labor force. Also, part-time work is counted as full-time employment. Further, employment surveys include responses from individuals that may be misleading.

2.   The factors that influence the unemployment rate are the factors that influence frictional, structural, and cyclical unemployment. The rates of voluntary job separation and job finding affect frictional unemployment. The length of time that it takes to find a job varies with the business cycle. The decision to enter or reenter the labor force may also be associated with the level of economic prosperity. Technological progress often displaces certain workers who have skills specific to the obsolete technologies. Changes in society's preferences regarding the composition of GNP will cause some industries to expand and some to decline, even at a state of full employment in the economy as a whole. Broad forces causing economic contraction or expansion will decrease or increase the cyclical component of the unemployment rate.

3.   The natural rate of unemployment is a useful benchmark for determining the potential output of the economy. Policies that are intended to spur economic activity and reduce unemployment must have a benchmark indicating possible courses of action in the short run.

4.   The social costs of unemployment include the output that is forgone when an economy operates at a level of unemployment above the natural rate of unemployment. This is known as the GNP gap. Other social costs include the costs associated with crime, suicide, mental and physical illness, and stress.

5.   Unemployment insurance was established as part of the Social Security Act of 1935 in order to alleviate to some extent the problems associated with unemployment. Unemployment benefits replace some of the lost purchasing power resulting from unemployment, although there is not universal coverage of unemployed workers. Critics contend that the benefits are too high and available for too many weeks, thus reducing the urgency with which workers search for employment. Evidence seems to indicate that unemployment benefits increase frictional unemployment.

Pop Quiz

1.   According to the news item, the natural rate of unemployment is defined as the nonaccelerating-inflation unemployment rate. This rate of unemployment is assumed to be equally divided between frictional and structural unemployment. Most economists believe that this rate of unemployment is approximately 6%.

2.   The natural rate of unemployment rose from the 4 to 5% range because of the marked entry of women and baby boomers (teenagers) into the labor force in the 1960s and 1970s. In the 1970s, the labor force grew 24 million, double the increase in the 1960s and almost 3 and one-half times the increase in the 1950s. In 1978, 24.5% of the labor force was composed of 16- to 24-year-olds. These new entrants brought fewer skills and less experience to labor markets causing the rate of frictional unemployment to increase at given rates of inflation. As a result, the nonaccelerating-inflation rate of unemployment rose.

3.   Today, the natural rate of unemployment is likely falling and should continue to fall for a time. By 1990, it is expected that the natural rate of unemployment will again be down to the 4% range. Women have been integrated into the labor force and baby boomers are no longer teenagers, but in the most productive 25- to 44-year-old group. Labor force participants 16 to 24 years of age have become a smaller percentage of the labor force, falling to 19.2% last year. It is also suggested that the natural rate of unemployment is falling because firms, increasingly cost conscious, are unlikely to increase wages as rapidly as labor markets tighten, resulting in lower nonaccelerating-inflation rates of unemployment.

The Outlook

Has Unemployment Finally Hit Its Low?

NEW YORK

Has the U.S. unemployment rate, which hit a 14-year low of 5.3% in June, dropped about as far as it's going?

That it got that low surprises many economists. As long as 3½ years ago, with the economic expansion apparently aging and the jobless rate at 7.4% of the labor force, they suspected that unemployment had already hit bottom. And beginning in 1968, the lows in unemployment from one business cycle to the next had trended alarmingly higher, from 3.4% to 4.6% in 1973, to 5.6% in 1979, to 7.2% in 1981.

As the figures soared, the non-accelerating-inflation rate of unemployment—the rate that can't be reduced without speeding up inflation—was generally believed to have risen to about 6%. That 6% was evenly divided, most economists held, between frictional unemployment—workers voluntarily between jobs—and structural unemployment—workers with inadequate skills.

This concept of a natural rate of unemployment is admittedly vague; you can't pin it down with statistics. Audrey Freedman, a labor economist at the Conference Board, comments that it can't be known "until we get wage inflation due to tight labor-supply conditions"—a bit like saying you can't see that truck coming until it hits you.

But it's important. If unemployment has already fallen to its natural rate, it can't safely be reduced further. So, hunches about that natural rate strongly influence notions of appropriate fiscal and monetary policy.

Even though economists can't pinpoint the natural rate, most believe it rose in the 1970s and now has fallen.

"Before the baby-boomers and women entered the labor force in substantial numbers," says Roger H. Fulton, an economist at A. Gary Shilling & Co., "a general unemployment rate of 4%-5% was viewed as full employment. Because the two groups lacked experience and training, which limited the types of jobs they could handle, economists concluded that the economy could be faced with greater structural unemployment."

But today, Mr. Fulton notes, "women have become an integral part of the nation's work force and most baby-boomers have moved into the 25-44 year age group, generally considered to be the prime productivity age ranges. . . . And because of declining birth rates, teen-agers now comprise an abnormally small percentage of workers."

Edward Yardeni of Prudential-Bache Securities believes that these "demographic forces should push the unemployment rate down to 4% by 1990"—and perhaps sooner. He notes that during the 1970s, when "the baby-boomers overwhelmed the job market," the labor force grew 24 million, up from 12.3 million in the 1960s and only seven million in the 1950s. But last year, he says, 16-to-24-year-olds fell to 19.2% of the labor force from the 1978 peak of 24.5%.

"The 'birth dearth' which followed the baby boom is already helping push the unemployment rate back down toward levels not seen since the mid-1970s," he adds.

However, Mrs. Freedman contends that the non-inflationary rate of unemployment has dropped not because of demographic trends, which peaked in the mid-1970s, but because "employers' wage-setting practices have changed. They no longer engage in a great deal of wage imitation. Now, employers are not looking at each other but at their own companies' competitive situations and their own unit labor costs."

Still worried about foreign competition and still able to take advantage of labor unions' weakness, employers probably won't start bidding wars to get workers. "Corporate managers are unlikely to suddenly offer big wage hikes after they spent five years cutting costs," Mr. Yardeni says.

The point at which low unemployment becomes inflationary also is affected by what is driving it down. If it is low because of genuine prosperity, it isn't as inflationary as demand force-fed by government, whose borrowing tends to flood the economy with too much money.

Also important is how people react.

If consumers see inflation rising, they may step up their spending to try to beat price increases. The faster money is flowing through the economy, the more inflationary bang for a given rise in the number of bucks.

And if workers demand more pay, they also can boost inflation. So far, a Smith Barney research report sees "no clear proof that wage inflation is accelerating." Gregory Gieber, an economist at the securities firm, cites the year-to-year gains in a key private-sector employment-cost index. "After holding relatively flat around 3.2% from mid-1986 through the first quarter of 1988," he writes, "wage inflation jumped to 3.7% in the second quarter. . . . However, the rate is still low relative to the late 1970s-early 1980s and less than might be expected, based on historical relationships between economic or employment growth and wage rates."

The fact that New England's unemployment averaged only 3.4% last year may indicate that the jobless rate could fall considerably below 5% elsewhere, too.

But the closer to plant capacity the economy is operating, the faster low unemployment pushes up costs and prices. And operating rates are rising; in July, they reached 83.5%, the highest since March 1980. Meanwhile, productivity gains, which can offset rising costs, are lagging, held down by slow growth in the service sector. Productivity fell in the second period, and Merrill Lynch sees it up less than 1% in the second half.

The risk of inflation is clearly rising, and, once again, many analysts doubt unemployment can fall much further. Mr. Gieber calculates that unemployment, adjusted for the demographic changes, was 5.5% in July, matching its level in 1979, "when the economy appeared to be starting to overheat."

—HENRY F. MYERS

27

Inflation and Its Consequences

CHAPTER CHALLENGES

After studying your text, attending class, and completing this chapter, you should be able to:

1. Understand how price indexes are used to measure the price level.
2. Define the concepts of inflation and deflation and show how they are measured.
3. Distinguish nominal income from real income and nominal wages from real wages.
4. Explain the consequences of inflation for incomes and decisions.
5. Explain how inflation affects interest rates and explain the difference between real and nominal interest rates.

IN BRIEF: CHAPTER SUMMARY

Fill in the blanks to summarize chapter content.

A price index is used to measure the price level. The (1)_____ [producer price index, consumer price index (CPI)] is used to measure the impact of changes in prices on households. It is determined by dividing the (2)_____ (current, base-year) value of a market basket of products and services by the value of the same market basket in the (3)_____ (current, base) year. The quotient is then multiplied by 100. In the (4)_____ (current, base) year, the price index is always 100. The CPI is actually a weighted average of a number of component price indexes. The weights are determined from household expenditure surveys conducted every (5)_____ (year, 10 years). Other price indexes include the producer price index and the implicit GNP deflator. The (6)_____ (producer price index, implicit GNP deflator) measures the price level of producer goods such as materials, chemicals, intermediate products, and capital equipment. The (7)_____ (producer price index, implicit GNP deflator) is used in calculating real GNP.

Inflation is the percentage increase from period to period in a price index. If the price index is decreasing, the percentage change in the index is called (8)_____ (disinflation, deflation). From 1913 until 1950, the CPI exhibited periods of both inflation and deflation. (9)_____ (Deflation, Inflation) usually occurred immediately following wars and depressions. Since 1950, the CPI has shown a consistent (10)_____ (decrease, increase), although the rate of inflation has been variable. From 1960 to the 5-year period ending in 1980, the 5-year average rate of inflation increased from 1.3% to 8.9%. Between 1980 and 1985 inflation decreased to an average of 5.9%, and between 1985 and 1987 inflation decreased further to a 2-year average of (11)_____ (3.1%, 5.5%).

Price indexes can be used to remove the effect of inflation from nominal variables such as nominal income, nominal wages, and nominal GNP. Inflation

(12)_____ (increases, erodes) the purchasing power of a dollar. Since nominal variables are defined in terms of current dollars, changes in the purchasing power of nominal variables (13)_____ (are necessarily, are not necessarily) fully reflected by dollar changes in the variable. For instance, if a household's nominal income doubled over a 10-year period but the level of prices confronting the household also doubled, the household's purchasing power would (14)_____ (remain unchanged, double). Nominal values can be converted to real values by dividing the nominal variable by the relevant price index itself (15)_____ (multiplied, divided) by 100. By removing the effect of inflation, we can determine how much of an increase in a nominal variable is due to inflation and how much is due to real increases in purchasing power. During periods of rapid inflation, nominal wage inflation (16)_____ (lags behind, exceeds) price inflation, causing real wages to (17)_____ (rise, fall). In effect, income is redistributed from workers to employers. Over the long run, however, wage inflation has exceeded price inflation, resulting in an/a (18)_____ (increase, decrease) in real wages.

In addition to reducing purchasing power, inflation can redistribute income and wealth. Borrowers (19)_____ (lose, benefit) during a period of inflation because the future dollars that they pay in principal and interest are worth (20)_____ (more, less) in purchasing power than the dollars at the time they were borrowed. The government borrows vast sums of money to finance its annual budget deficit. During periods of inflation, the purchasing power of the federal debt actually decreases. Over time, inflation may transfer purchasing power (21)_____ (to, away from) government (or taxpayers that are not creditors of government) and (22)_____ (to, away from) those holding government debt. Because households headed by young individuals and those with middle incomes tend to have large debt as a percentage of income relative to other age and income groups, inflation benefits young and middle-income households relative to other households. In general, if inflation is unanticipated, debtors benefit at the expense of creditors.

(23)_____ (Anticipated, Unanticipated) inflation affects present choices. If expectations of inflation are in error, choices are likely to result in a (24)_____ (more, less) efficient allocation of the economy's resources. If anticipated inflation is greater than the nominal interest rate, the real rate of interest is negative. If anticipated inflation increases more than the nominal rate of interest, the real rate of interest (25)_____ (falls, rises). Planned investment spending depends in part on the real rate of interest. Changes in anticipated inflation that cause changes in real rates of interest will affect planned investment. If those expectations are in error, businesses will likely over- or underinvest.

Similarly, expected inflation might cause households to consume (26)_____ (later rather than now at current prices, now rather than wait for prices to rise). Given a level of income, an increase in consumption of goods and services means that saving will decline. If anticipated inflation reduces saving, economic growth is (27)_____ (promoted, impaired). Also during periods of anticipated inflation, individuals tend to purchase goods that rise in value as fast as or faster than the general price level. If funds are being used to purchase real estate, gold, art, and other similar goods, those funds are not available as saving for use by businesses for capital investment. Inflation also redistributes wealth to households having these inflation-hedging assets away from those having assets that do not inflate in value as rapidly.

VOCABULARY REVIEW

Write the key term from the list below next to its definition.

Key Terms

Price level — Purchasing power of a dollar
Price index — Nominal income
Inflation — Real income
Deflation — Nominal wages
Consumer price — Real wages
   index (CPI) — Nominal interest rate
Pure inflation — Real interest rate
Producer price — Implicit GNP deflator
   index

1. _____: an index number whose value varies with the ratio of nominal GNP to real GNP.

2. _____: measures movements in a broad aggregate of products purchased by producers rather than consumers.

3. _____: a measure of how much a dollar can buy.

4. _____: occurs when the prices of all goods rise by the same percentage over the year.

5. _____: the actual number of dollars received over a year.

6. _____: commonly used to measure the impact of changes in prices on households. The index is based on a standard market basket of goods and services purchased by a typical urban family.

7. _____: hourly payments to workers in current dollars.

8. _____: the rate of downward movement in the price level for an aggregate of goods and services.

9. _____: nominal wages deflated to adjust for changes in the purchasing power of the dollar since a certain base year.

10. _____: the rate of upward movement in the price level for an aggregate of goods and services.

11. _____: the annual percentage amount of money that is earned on a sum that is loaned or deposited in a bank.

12. _____: a number used to measure the price level. The value of the index is set at 100 in the base year.

13. _____: the actual annual percentage change in the purchasing power of interest income earned on a sum of money that is loaned out.

14. _____: an indicator of how high or low prices are in a given year compared to prices in a certain base year.

15. _____: the purchasing power of nominal income.

SKILLS REVIEW

Concept: Price indexes and inflation

1. a. Given the annual values of a given market basket of goods and
        services, compute the price index assuming the base year is year 3.

Year	Current Value of Market Basket	Price Index (base year = 3)
1	$18,000	_____
2	20,000	_____
3	24,000	_____
4	27,000	_____
5	29,500	_____
6	33,000	_____

    b. Determine the rate of inflation from the price index values above:

        (1) From year 3 to year 4 _____ %
        (2) From year 4 to year 5 _____ %
        (3) From year 5 to year 6 _____ %

2. If housing has a weight of 42.6% in the CPI and housing prices increase
    20% over the year, assuming all other prices rise at 5%, what is the rate
    of inflation for the year as measured by the rate of change in the
    CPI?_____ %

Concept: Nominal and real income

3. a. Suppose you cleaned your closet and found income tax records for
        several consecutive years. Assuming your nominal income was shown in
        the table below and given the consumer price index, determine your
        real income for each year in the table.

Year	Nominal Income	CPI (base year = year 1)	Real Income
1	$29,000	100	$_____
2	31,000	110	_____
3	34,100	125	_____
4	35,000	131	_____
5	37,200	144	_____
6	39,500	160	_____

    b. Are you better off in year 6 as compared to year 1?

4. The data below consist of a household's nominal hourly wage and the CPI
    for given consecutive years.

Year	Nominal Hourly Wage	CPI	Real Hourly Wage
1	$6.25	110	
2	7.50	115	_____
3	8.50	125	_____
4	10.00	133	_____
5	12.00	145	_____

    a. Complete the table.

b. Assume nominal wage growth is the result of two factors--inflation and increases in labor productivity. Determine what portion of the year-to-year change in the nominal hourly wage is due to inflation and what portion is due to increases in labor productivity.

Year 1 to 2: _____% due to inflation, _____% due to labor productivity.

Year 2 to 3: _____% due to inflation, _____% due to labor productivity.

Year 3 to 4: _____% due to inflation, _____% due to labor productivity.

Year 4 to 5: _____% due to inflation, _____% due to labor productivity.

Concept: Consequences of inflation

5. Identify how inflation affects purchasing power, the distribution of income and wealth, and economic choices.

a. Purchasing power:

b. Distribution of income and wealth:

c. Economic choices:

SELF-TEST FOR MASTERY

Select the best answer.

1. Which of the following is an indicator of how high or low prices are in a given year compared to prices in a certain base year?

a. Inflation
b. Deflation
c. Price level
d. Price index

2. Which of the following is defined as a rate of downward movement in the price level for an aggregate of goods and services?

a. Inflation
b. Deflation
c. Price level
d. Price index

3. Which of the following price indexes measures the impact of changes in prices on households?

    a. Inflation index
    b. CPI
    c. Producer price index
    d. Implicit GNP deflator
    e. Explicit GNP inflator

4. A price index has a value of _____ in the base year.

    a. 100
    b. 10
    c. 50
    d. 1000
    e. 0

5. A price index for a market basket of goods can be found by:

    a. Multiplying the value of the market basket by the rate of inflation.
    b. Dividing the value of the market basket by the rate of inflation.
    c. Dividing the current-year value of the market basket by the base-year value of the basket and multiplying the result by 100.
    d. Dividing the base-year cost of the basket by the current-year cost of the basket.

6. If the CPI in year 1 equals 100 and the CPI in year 2 equals 113, it can be concluded that:

    a. Year 2 is the base year.
    b. The rate of inflation from year 1 to year 2 is 113%.
    c. The rate of inflation from year 1 to year 2 is 13%.
    d. More information is needed to determine the rate of inflation.

7. Which of the following is not true regarding the consumer price index?

    a. The CPI is a weighted average.
    b. Most households actually experience rates of inflation somewhat different from that measured by percentage changes in the CPI.
    c. The CPI covers all goods consumed by households.
    d. Since 1950 the CPI has risen, although prior to that time there were times when consumer prices fell.

8. Beginning in 1960, the 5-year average rate of inflation in the United States:

    a. Has continually increased.
    b. Has continually decreased.
    c. Increased until 1975-1980 and then decreased to the present.
    d. Increased until 1980-1985 and then decreased to the present.

9. If the rate of inflation for a year is 10% but the rate of nominal income growth is 5%, real income:

    a. Will rise.
    b. Will fall.
    c. Will remain the same.
    d. Cannot be determined.

10. Over the long run _____ has exceeded _____, resulting in _____ real hourly wages in the United States.

    a. Inflation, the rate of wage growth, rising
    b. The rate of wage growth, inflation, falling
    c. The rate of wage growth, inflation, rising
    d. Inflation, the rate of wage growth, rising
    e. Income, wages, falling

11. During periods of rapid inflation, _____ lags _____, causing real wages to _____.

    a. Inflation, wage growth, rise
    b. Wage growth, inflation, rise
    c. Inflation, wage growth, fall
    d. Wage growth, inflation, fall

12. Debtors benefit during periods of unanticipated inflation because:

    a. The money they pay lenders is worth more than the money originally borrowed.
    b. Inflation outpaces wage growth.
    c. Interest rates fall.
    d. The purchasing power of the dollars borrowed is greater than the purchasing power of the dollars repaid to lenders.

13. Which of the following groups lose as a result of unexpected inflation?

    a. Lenders
    b. Savers
    c. Taxpayers holding government debt
    d. Retirees on fixed pensions
    e. All of the above

14. Which of the following defines the anticipated real rate of interest?

    a. The nominal interest rate less the expected rate of inflation
    b. Inflation less the nominal rate of interest
    c. The nominal rate of interest plus the ex post rate of interest
    d. The real rate of interest adjusted for inflation

15. Anticipated inflation:

    a. Affects the choices we make as individuals.
    b. Constitutes a perfect forecast of actual inflation.
    c. May result in too much saving.
    d. May cause errors in consumption, but planned investment levels will always be correct because profit-maximizing producers use marginal analysis.
    e. None of the above.

16. Anticipated inflation:

    a. Results in less funds available for productive investment.
    b. Causes individuals to buy inflation "hedges" such as real estate, art and gold.
    c. May cause individuals to consume now rather than wait until prices rise.
    d. If erratic causes problems for planning and designing long-term contracts.
    e. All of the above.

17. Extremely high inflation such as that experienced by Germany in 1922 is called:

   a. Deflation.
   b. Inflation.
   c. Stagflation.
   d. Disinflation.
   e. Hyperinflation.

THINK IT THROUGH

1.   It is likely that you experience a rate of inflation different from that derived from the rate of change in the consumer price index. Explain.

2.   Explain the difference between nominal and real GNP. Can you think of any reasons why it is necessary to distinguish between nominal and real GNP? Discuss.

3.   Explain what is meant by the following statement: " Inflation is a distorter of choices and a capricious redistributor of income."

CHAPTER ANSWERS

In Brief: Chapter Summary

1. Consumer price index (CPI) 2. Current 3. Base 4. Base 5. 10 years 6. Producer price index 7. Implicit GNP deflator 8. Deflation 9. Deflation 10. Increase 11. 3.1% 12. Erodes 13. Are not necessarily 14. Remain unchanged 15. Divided 16. Lags behind 17. Fall 18. Increase 19. Benefit 20. Less 21. To the 22. Away from 23. Anticipated 24. Less 25. Falls 26. Now rather than wait for prices to rise 27. Impaired

Vocabulary Review

1. Implicit GNP deflator 2. Producer price index 3. Purchasing power of the dollar 4. Pure inflation 5. Nominal income 6. Consumer price index (CPI) 7. Nominal wages 8. Deflation 9. Real wages 10. Inflation 11. Nominal interest rate 12. Price index 13. Real interest rate 14. Price level 15. Real income

Skills Review

1.   a.   Price Index (base year = year 3)
              75
              83.3
              100
              112.5
              122.9
              137.5

     b.   (1) 12.5%   (2) 9.2%   (3) 11.9%

2.   Compute a weighted-average inflation rate as follows:

              .426(20%) + .574(5%) = 11.39%

3. a.   Real Income

         $29,000.00
          28,181.82
          27,280.00
          26,717.56
          25,833.33
          24,687.50

    b.   You are worse off in year 6 as compared to year 1 because your real
         income has declined.

4. a.   Real Hourly Wage
              $5.68
               6.52
               6.80
               7.52
               8.28

    b.   In order to determine the year-to-year percentage change in nominal
         hourly wages due to increases in labor productivity, find the year-
         to-year change in real hourly wages and divide this by the year-to-
         year change in nominal hourly wages. Subtract the result from 1 to
         determine the year-to-year percentage change in nominal hourly wages
         due to inflation.

	Due to Inflation	Due to Increases in Productivity
Year 1 to 2	32.8%	67.2%
2 to 3	72.0	28.0
3 to 4	52.0	48.0
4 to 5	62.0	38.0

5. a.   Inflation reduces the purchasing power of a dollar and reduces the
         purchasing power of all nominal variables, such as nominal wages,
         nominal income, and nominal GNP.

    b.   Unexpected inflation harms creditors such as financial institutions,
         savers, and holders of government debt, but benefits borrowers,
         including the federal government. It also benefits those households
         with a high debt burden such as middle-income households and
         households headed by young individuals. Inflation redistributes
         wealth from households having assets that do not increase in value as
         rapidly as the price level to households having assets that rise in
         value at a rate faster than the general price level.

    c.   Anticipated inflation affects economic choices in the present.
         Expectations of inflation may cause an increase in consumption in an
         effort to beat the expected price increase. Or it may induce people
         to purchase inflation-hedging assets. Both forms of spending reduce
         current saving, impairing future economic growth. Errors are likely
         to be made in decision making because long-term plans and contracts
         will be based in part on an expected rate of inflation that may or
         may not materialize. Because of the uncertainty regarding future
         price levels, planned investment may be lower.

Self-Test for Mastery

1. c 2. b 3. b 4. a 5. c 6. c 7. c 8. c 9. b 10. c 11. d 12. d 13.
e 14. a 15. a 16. e 17. e

Think it Through

1.   The consumer price index is a weighted average of several price indexes
for certain classes of goods or services such as housing or food and beverages.
The weight for each class of goods represents the percentage of a typical urban
family's budget that is spent on that class of goods. For instance, the weight
for housing is .426, meaning that the typical urban family spends 42.6% of its
budget on housing. These weights are based upon a 1982 to 1984 survey. These
surveys are updated once a decade.

If you differ in any way in your spending as compared to the "typical" urban
family, you will face a different rate of inflation than that given by
percentage changes in the CPI. The further in time we are away from the date
of the survey, the less accurate are the weights. New products such as VCRs
and personal computers and the changing spending patterns in response to these
new goods would not be reflected in the weights of the CPI until the next
survey.

2.   Nominal GNP is the current-dollar value of GNP. Increases in prices or
output will cause GNP to rise. While economists and others are certainly
interested in inflation, it is of value to know how much real output the
economy produces from year to year. It is increases in real output not
inflation that ultimately result in increased employment and living standards.
To remove the effect of rising prices from nominal GNP in order to reveal the
changes in real output, nominal GNP can be divided by a price index (the
implicit GNP deflator) itself divided by 100. The result is real GNP, which is
a much better indicator of economic growth over time than is nominal GNP.

3.   See question 5 in the Skills Review section for the answer. Inflation is
"capricious" in its redistribution of income in that there are gainers and
losers and it is difficult to assess the net outcome. Further, these changes
in income distribution result not from deliberated public policy, but from
unanticipated changes in price levels.

28

The Forces of Aggregate Supply and Demand: Investigating the Causes of Cyclical Unemployment and Inflation

CHAPTER CHALLENGES

After studying your text, attending class, and completing this chapter, you should be able to:

1. Distinguish an aggregate demand curve from a market demand curve and explain why an aggregate demand curve is downward sloping.
2. Distinguish an aggregate supply curve from a market supply curve and explain the shape of an aggregate supply curve prevailing in the short run.
3. Use aggregate supply and demand analysis to show how we determine the equilibrium level of real GNP and the price level over a given year.
4. Use aggregate supply and demand analysis to show how changes in aggregate demand and aggregate supply affect the equilibrium levels of real GNP and the price level for a given year.
5. Use aggregate supply and demand analysis to explain the possible causes of recessions, excessive unemployment, and inflation.
6. Understand the classical model of macroeconomic equilibrium and explain why the self-correction mechanism implied by the model does not work quickly and reliably in modern economies to ensure full employment.

IN BRIEF: CHAPTER SUMMARY

Fill in the blanks to summarize chapter content.

Macroeconomics is concerned with explaining the forces affecting aggregate production and the general level of prices rather than with specific market quantities and prices. Aggregate supply and demand analysis is used to explain the factors that cause aggregate production and the price level to change. The aggregate demand curve shows the relationship between (1)_____ (the general price level, aggregate income) and the aggregate domestic production demanded. The aggregate quantity demanded is (2)_____ (positively, inversely) related to the general price level--the aggregate demand curve is (3)_____ (downward sloping, upward sloping). A change in the price level will change the aggregate quantity demanded, but influences other than the change in the price level that affect aggregate quantity demanded will (4)_____ (result in a movement along an aggregate demand curve, shift the aggregate demand curve).

The aggregate demand curve shows an inverse relationship between the price level and aggregate quantity demanded. As the price level rises, real wealth falls, causing saving to (5)_____ (increase, decrease) and consumption to (6)_____ (increase, decrease). Higher prices increase the demand for credit, thus increasing real interest rates which (7)_____ (increases, reduces) planned investment. Finally, a higher price level reduces exports and increases imports. Thus a higher price level (8)_____ (increases, reduces) aggregate purchases.

The aggregate supply curve shows an/a (9)_____(inverse, positive) relationship between aggregate output produced (real GNP) and the price level as potential real GNP is approached. As the price level rises, individual producers experience rising prices for the products that they produce. If input prices are not rising, opportunities for additional profits arise, causing some producers to increase production. Because producers confront (10)_____ (falling, rising) marginal costs with increases in output, they must have higher product prices to cover the (11)_____ (falling, rising) marginal and unit costs of production. At output levels associated with considerable cyclical unemployment, increases in production do not increase unit production costs. As potential real GNP is approached, unit production costs begin to (12)_____ (rise, fall). If output expands beyond potential real GNP, unit production costs rise even faster for given increases in output.

Macroeconomic equilibrium occurs when the quantity of real GNP demanded equals the quantity of real GNP supplied--where the aggregate demand and supply curves intersect.   In equilibrium, there are no tendencies for the price level or aggregate output level to change (13)_____(and there will be no, even though there may be) shortages or surpluses in individual product or resource markets. If aggregate demand rises relative to aggregate supply, unintended inventories fall, inducing firms to eventually (14)_____ (increase, decrease) production. If aggregate demand falls relative to aggregate supply, unintended inventories (15)_____ (rise, fall) causing firms to eventually (16)_____ (increase, cut) production and employment.

Factors that shift the aggregate demand curve include: (a) changes in investment demand by business, (b) changes in consumers' willingness to consume and save, (c) changes in exports sold or imports demanded, and (d) (17)_____ (changes in the price level, changes in government purchases of final products and input services). If changes in these factors reduce aggregate demand, the aggregate demand curve shifts to the left, causing real GNP to fall relative to potential real GNP. An/a (18)_____ (inflationary, recessionary) gap arises equal to the difference between the potential and actual levels of real GNP. If changes in these factors cause aggregate demand to increase and the aggregate demand curve to shift rightward, both real output and the price level will increase. Continual increases in aggregate demand cause (19)_____ (demand-pull, cost-push) inflation. The increase in the price level and the level of real GNP depend on the point on the aggregate supply curve at which the economy is operating. If actual real GNP exceeds potential real GNP, an/a (20)_____ (inflationary, recessionary) gap exists by the amount of the difference between the potential and actual levels of real GNP.

Changes in aggregate supply will alter the equilibrium level of real GNP and the price level. If aggregate supply decreases relative to aggregate demand, the price level will (21)_____ (fall, rise) while the level of employment and output will fall. If aggregate supply increases relative to aggregate demand, output (22)_____ (decreases, increases) and the price level falls. Rising input prices shift the aggregate supply curve (23)_____ (leftward, rightward), causing the price level to increase and employment and real GNP to (24)_____ (rise, fall). Continual decreases in aggregate supply cause (25)_____ (demand-pull, cost-push) inflation.

The (26)_____ (Keynesian, classical) model of macroeconomic equilibrium assumes that any departure of real GNP from its full-employment level will cause wages and prices to adjust in such a way as to quickly restore full employment. If the economy is initially at potential real GNP and aggregate demand increases, the price level will rise, inducing firms to increase production. But in time, input prices (27)_____ (fall, rise), shifting the

398

aggregate supply curve leftward, and real output falls back to its potential level. In the long run, real GNP is fixed at (28)_____ (an inflationary level, its potential level) regardless of the price level. The classical long-run aggregate supply curve is therefore (29)_____ (vertical, upward sloping) at the potential level of real GNP.

(30)_____ (Keynesian, Classical) macroeconomic analysis criticizes the (31)_____ (Keynesian, classical) model's assumption of flexible wages and prices. If wages and prices are rigid in the downward direction, a decline in aggregate demand will not result in sufficient wage and price level changes to restore full employment. As a result, Keynes argued that (32)_____ (government policies, the economy's self-adjustment mechanism) could be used to increase aggregate demand to move the economy toward its potential level of real GNP.

VOCABULARY REVIEW

Write the key term from the list below next to its definition.

Key Terms

Aggregate demand curve
Aggregate quantity demanded
Aggregate supply curve
Aggregate quantity supplied
Macroeconomic equilibrium
Recessionary GNP gap
Demand-pull inflation
Change in aggregate demand
Keynesian model of macro-
  economic equilibrium

Inflationary GNP gap
Change in aggregate
  supply
Cost-push inflation
Classical model of
  macroeconomic equi-
  librium
Long-run aggregate supply
  curve (LRAS)

Definitions

1. _____: inflation caused by increases in aggregate demand.

2. _____: a shift in the economy's aggregate demand curve, causing the economy to move to a new macroeconomic equilibrium.

3. _____: the difference between equilibrium real GNP and potential real GNP when the economy is overheated.

4. _____: the difference between the equilibrium level of real GNP and potential real GNP when the economy is operating at less than full employment.

5. _____: a shift in the economy's aggregate supply curve as the relationship is altered between the price level and real GNP supplied.

6. _____: occurs when the quantity of real GNP demanded equals the quantity of real GNP supplied.

7. _____: inflation caused by continual decreases in aggregate supply.

8. _____: the quantity of real GNP supplied by producers that is associated with a given price level.

9. _____: implied that excessive unemployment of workers and unused productive capacity would set up forces that would eventually result in increases in real GNP and eliminate the unemployment of workers.

10. _____: shows the aggregate output of final products, as measured by real GNP, that will be produced at each possible price over a given period.

11. _____: shows the relationship between the aggregate quantity supplied and the price level that would be observed if nominal wages and other money prices were flexible enough to allow the classical self-correction mechanism to work.

12. _____: the amount of real GNP that buyers are willing and able to purchase at each possible price level.

13. _____: assumes that because of rigid nominal wages the economy's self-correction mechanism cannot be expected to restore full employment when aggregate demand declines.

14. _____: shows how the amount of aggregate domestic production demanded, measured by real GNP, will vary with the price level.

SKILLS REVIEW

Concept: Slope of the aggregate demand curve; shifts in the aggregate demand curve

1. Assume that the economy is currently operating at a level of real GNP of $2200 billion with a price level equal to 120. Plot this coordinate on the figure below.

a. An increase in the price level to 180 will cause real wealth to
_____, causing saving to _____ and consumption to
_____ by $200 billion.

b. This price level increase will also cause real interest rates to
_____, resulting in a/an _____ in planned investment of
$100 billion.

c. The increase in the price level _____ imports by $80 billion and
_____ exports by $20 billion, causing net exports (exports minus
imports) to _____ by $100 billion.

d. The total change in aggregate quantity demanded due to the increase
in the price level to 180 is $_____. Plot this new price level-
aggregate quantity demanded coordinate on the figure above. The
aggregate demand curve has a/an _____ slope.

2. List four factors that shift the aggregate demand curve and indicate
whether an increase in the factor shifts the aggregate demand to the <u>right</u>
or <u>left</u>.

a. _____
b. _____
c. _____
d. _____

Concept: Aggregate supply

3. Match the statement with the proper segment of the aggregate supply curve
shown in the figure below.

a. _____ : Output can increase without much upward pressure on
unit costs of production.

b. _____ : Unit production costs rise very rapidly.

c. _____ : Higher prices are required by producers to cover the
rising unit costs of production as potential real GNP
is approached.

d. _____ : There is idle capacity and much cyclical unemployment.

e. _____ : The economy is overheated.

Concept: Changes in aggregate demand and macroeconomic equilibrium

4. a. Show on the figure below the effect of an increase in aggregate demand and label the new AD curve AD1. Identify on the figure the change in real GNP and the price level. Real GNP _____ potential real GNP, resulting in a/an _____ gap.

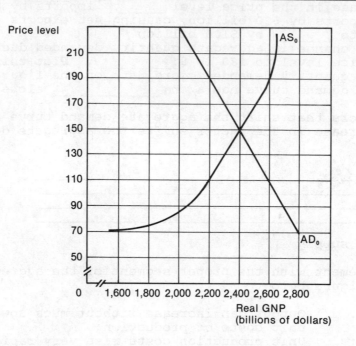

b. Given ADo as the initial aggregate demand curve, show on the figure above the effect of a decrease in aggregate demand and label the new AD curve AD2. Identify the changes in real GNP and the price level. Real GNP _____ potential GNP, resulting in a/an _____ gap.

Concept: Changes in aggregate supply and macroeconomic equilibrium

5. The economy shown in the figure below is currently operating at its potential level of real GNP.

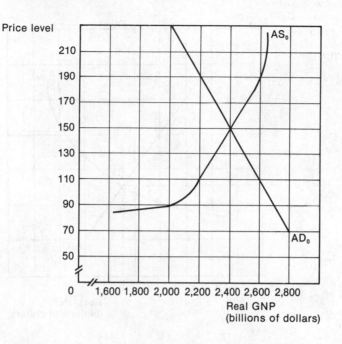

a. If the nation experiences a significant increase in oil prices, the aggregate supply curve will shift _____ by $200 billion dollars at every price level. Show this in the figure above and label the new aggregate supply curve AS1.

b. Real GNP _____ potential GNP by $_____, causing a/an_____ gap. The price level _____ to _____.

c. Assume that the economy is currently at potential real GNP. Show the effect of a decline in input prices and label the new aggregate supply curve AS2. Real GNP _____, and the price level _____.

Concept: Classical long-run aggregate supply curve

6. The economy shown in the figure below is currently operating at its potential level of real GNP.

a. Show the effect of an increase in aggregate demand. Label the new aggregate demand curve AD1.
b. According to classical macroeconomics, in the short run real GNP will_____ and the price level will _____. In the long run wages and prices will _____, ensuring that real GNP _____ potential real GNP. Graphically, in the long run the short-run aggregate supply curve will shift _____.
c. Show on the figure above the classical long-run aggregate supply curve and label it LRAS.
d. Keynes argued that in a recessionary GNP gap, wages and prices _____ and automatic forces in the economy _____ (will, will not) quickly restore full employment. Keynes argued that full employment could be restored by _____ aggregate demand with _____ in government spending.

SELF-TEST FOR MASTERY

Select the best answer.

1. The aggregate demand curve shows:

   a. A positive relationship between prices and quantities.
   b. An inverse relationship between the price level and the aggregate quantity demanded.
   c. An independent relationship between the price level and the aggregate quantity demanded.
   d. An inverse relationship between the product price and the quantity of a good demanded.

2. Which of the following will not shift the aggregate demand curve?

   a. Changes in exports
   b. Changes in planned investment by businesses
   c. The price level
   d. Changes in government spending

3. A higher price level:

   a. Reduces real wealth and the level of consumption.
   b. Increases real interest rates and decreases planned investment.
   c. Increases imports and reduces exports.
   d. All of the above.
   e. A and b.

4. The aggregate _____ curve shows a relationship between real GNP produced and the price level. As potential real GNP is approached this curve _____.

   a. Demand, is downward sloping
   b. Supply, becomes steeper
   c. Supply, becomes flatter
   d. Demand, becomes steeper

5. The price level rises more rapidly as potential real GNP is approached along an aggregate supply curve because:

   a. Profit-taking firms are exploiting their market size and power.
   b. Of the profit incentive.
   c. The costs of additional units of aggregate output begin to rise more rapidly, causing firms to seek higher prices to cover these rising costs.
   d. None of the above.

6. Macroeconomic equilibrium occurs when:

   a. Aggregate demand equals price.
   b. Price equals the value of the marginal product.
   c. Market demand equals market supply.
   d. Aggregate quantity demanded equals aggregate quantity supplied.

7. Starting initially at potential real GNP, an increase in aggregate demand shifts the aggregate demand curve _____, causing real GNP to _____ and the price level to _____.

   a. Rightward, rise, rise
   b. Rightward, rise, fall
   c. Leftward, fall, fall
   d. Rightward, fall, fall
   e. Leftward, fall, rise

8. If actual real GNP exceeds potential real GNP:

   a. The economy is overheated.
   b. Prices rise more rapidly.
   c. An inflationary gap exists.
   d. Real GNP increases less for given increases in aggregate demand.
   e. All of the above.

9. Starting initially at potential real GNP, a decrease in aggregate demand
    shifts the aggregate demand curve _____, causing real GNP to _____
    and the price level to _____.

    a. Rightward, rise, rise
    b. Rightward, rise, fall
    c. Leftward, fall, fall
    d. Rightward, fall, fall
    e. Leftward, fall, rise

10. If actual real GNP is below potential real GNP:

    a. The economy is overheated.
    b. Prices rise more rapidly.
    c. An inflationary gap exists.
    d. A recessionary gap exists.

11. If domestic consumers reduce their demand for imports, aggregate demand
    will _____, causing real GNP to _____.

    a. Fall, rise
    b. Fall, fall
    c. Rise, fall
    d. Rise, rise

12. Demand-pull inflation:

    a. Is caused by rising prices.
    b. Is caused by rising input prices.
    c. Is due to the decline over time in aggregate demand.
    d. Is caused by continual increases in aggregate demand beyond the
        potential real GNP level.

13. An increase in input prices shifts the aggregate _____ curve _____,
    causing real GNP to _____ and the price level to _____.

    a. Demand, upward, fall, rise
    b. Demand, leftward, rise, rise
    c. Demand, rightward, rise, fall
    d. Supply, leftward, fall, rise
    e. Supply, rightward, rise, fall

14. Which of the following cause cost-push inflation?

    a. A one-time increase in aggregate demand
    b. Continual increases in aggregate demand
    c. A one-time decrease in aggregate supply
    d. Continual decreases in aggregate supply

15. Which of the following assumptions is crucial to the classical
    macroeconomic model's assertion that the economy has built-in forces that
    automatically eliminate unemployment and quickly move the economy to its
    potential level of real GNP?

    a. Profit motive
    b. Rigid wages and prices
    c. Flexible wages and prices
    d. Natural rate of unemployment

16. The classicists argued that an increase in aggregate demand would
    _____ in the short run, but in the long run real GNP would
    _____.

    a. Decrease real GNP, increase
    b. Increase real GNP, return to its potential level
    c. Increase real GNP, rise further, causing inflation
    d. Decrease aggregate supply, rise

17. The classical long-run aggregate supply curve:

    a. Is vertical at a level of output below potential real GNP.
    b. Is upward sloping.
    c. Is upward sloping at the level of potential real GNP.
    d. Is vertical at the level of potential real GNP.

18. John Maynard Keynes argued that:

    a. Downward nominal-wage rigidity prevented the classical self-
        correction mechanism from working to eliminate recessionary GNP gaps.
    b. The automatic forces of the market would restore the economy to full
        employment very quickly.
    c. The classical macroeconomists' argument that government spending
        should be used in recessions would not eliminate a recessionary GNP
        gap.
    d. Fluctuations in aggregate demand were the primary cause of
        recessions.
    e. A and d.

THINK IT THROUGH

1. Distinguish between demand-pull and cost-push inflation.

2. Discuss the macroeconomic effects of a significant increase in the price
    of oil.

3. Why did Keynes believe that government policies designed to change
    aggregate demand should be used in recessions?

CHAPTER ANSWERS

In Brief: Chapter Summary

1. The general price level 2. Inversely 3. Downward sloping 4. Shift the
aggregate demand curve 5. Increase 6. Decrease 7. Reduce 8. Reduces 9.
Positive 10. Rising 11. Rising 12. Rise 13. Even though there may be 14.
Increase 15. Rise 16. Cut 17. Changes in government purchases of final
products and input services 18. Recessionary 19. Demand-pull 20.
Inflationary 21. Rise 22. Increases 23. Leftward 24. Fall 25. Cost-push
26. Classical 27. Rise 28. Its potential level 29. Vertical 30. Keynesian
31. Classical 32. Government policies

Vocabulary Review

1. Demand-pull inflation 2. Change in aggregate demand 3. Inflationary GNP gap 4. Recessionary GNP gap 5. Change in aggregate supply 6. Macroeconomic equilibrium 7. Cost-push inflation 8. Aggregate quantity supplied 9. Classical model of macroeconomic equilibrium 10. Aggregate supply curve 11. Long-run aggregate supply curve (LRAS) 12. Aggregate demand 13. Keynesian model of macroeconomic equilibrium 14. Aggregate quantity demanded

Skills Review

1.

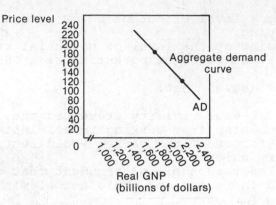

    a.   Decrease, increase, decrease b. Rise, decrease
    c.   Increases, decreases, decrease
    d. $400 billion; negative

2.   a.   Government expenditures on goods and input services; right
    b.   Planned investment spending by business; right
    c.   The willingness to consume; right
    d.   Net exports (exports less imports); right

3.   a.   1 b. 3 c. 2 d. 1 e. 3

4.   a.   Exceeds, inflationary

    b.   Falls below, recessionary

408

5. a.   Leftward

    b.   Falls below, $100 billion, recessionary; rises, 170
    c.   Increases, decreases

6. a.

    b.   Increase, rise; rise, equals; leftward
    c.   On figure above
    d.   Are rigid downward, will not; increasing, increases

Self-Test for Mastery

1. b 2. c 3. d 4. b 5. c 6. d 7. a 8. e 9. c 10. d 11. d 12. d 13.
d 14. d 15. c 16. b 17. d 18. e

Think it Through

1.   Demand-pull inflation results from continual increases in aggregate demand
when the economy is close to or beyond potential GNP. The price level rises
more rapidly when the economy is overheated along the very steep portion of the
aggregate supply curve beyond potential real GNP. In contrast to demand-pull
inflation where high inflation is associated with low unemployment, cost-push
inflation results in the simultaneous occurrence of inflation and rates of
unemployment above the natural rate of unemployment. Cost-push inflation
results from continual decreases in aggregate supply caused by increases in
input prices.

2.   An increase in oil prices shifts the aggregate supply curve leftward. The
aggregate supply curve shifts leftward (or upward) because businesses require

higher prices to cover rising oil prices in order to be induced to continue producing at their current levels of output. If prices do not rise sufficiently to fully cover the increase in oil prices, firms will cut back production. As the aggregate supply curve shifts leftward, real GNP falls, unemployment rises, and the price level increases.

3.   Keynes believed that in recessions wages and prices would not fall quickly enough to restore real GNP to its potential level without significant social costs of prolonged unemployment. Wages and prices are rigid in the downward direction in part because of institutional factors such as multi-year labor contracts. Keynes believed that recessions were due to inadequate levels of aggregate demand. Because the economy's self-adjustment mechanism would not eliminate a recessionary GNP gap in the short run, Keynes argued that government policies could be used to increase aggregate demand to a level that would restore higher levels of employment.

29

The Components of Aggregate Demand:
Consumption, Investment, Government Purchases,
and Net Exports

CHAPTER CHALLENGES

After studying your text, attending class, and completing this chapter, you should be able to:

1. List the determinants of annual consumer purchases in an economy.
2. Use a consumption function graph and the concepts of marginal propensity to consume and marginal propensity to save to show how consumption and saving in a given year vary with disposable income.
3. List the major determinants of business investment purchases and explain why such purchases are extremely unstable from year to year.
4. Discuss how government influences aggregate demand and understand why government purchases in a given year are independent of disposable income.
5. Discuss how exports and imports for a year are likely to vary with disposable income, and draw a nation's net export function graph.
6. Draw an aggregate purchases line and explain how it shows the way purchases of final products that comprise GNP will vary with disposable income in a given year.

IN BRIEF: CHAPTER SUMMARY

Fill in the blanks to summarize chapter content.

Personal consumption purchases are the major component of aggregate demand, accounting for (1)_____ (one half, two thirds) of GNP. Consumption is primarily determined by the (2)_____ (level of disposable income, real interest rate). Households on average use in excess of 90% of their disposable income for consumption purchases. Disposable income that is not consumed is saved. That percentage of consumption due to disposable income is referred to as (3)_____ (induced, autonomous) consumption. The percentage of consumption due to influences on other than disposable income is referred to as (4)_____ (induced, autonomous) consumption. Changes in autonomous consumption result from changes in aggregate household wealth, aggregate household debt, and household expectations about future income and wealth.

The consumption function is a line or curve showing an/a (5)_____ (independent, positive) relationship between consumption and disposable income. The saving function is also a line or curve showing an/a (6)_____ (independent, positive) relationship between disposable income and saving. Given that disposable income must be either consumed or saved, saving can be derived by subtracting consumption from disposable income and the saving function can be derived by subtracting the consumption function from the 45-degree line. The slope of the consumption function is called the (7)_____ (marginal propensity to consume, rate of change in consumption). For a linear curve (straight line), it is found by a change in consumption (8)_____ (divided, multiplied) by a change in disposable income. The marginal propensity to save is the slope of the saving function

411

and is defined as a change in (9)_____ (disposable income, saving) divided by a change in (10)_____ (disposable income, saving). Because disposable income must be consumed or saved, the marginal propensities to consume and save must sum to (11)_____ (zero, one).

Autonomous changes in consumption shift the consumption function, but they also shift the saving function because the saving line is derived from the consumption line. An increase in wealth (12)_____ (increases, decreases) consumption and (13)_____ (increases, decreases) saving at a given level of disposable income. The consumption function shifts (14)_____ (downward, upward) by the same amount that the saving function shifts (15)_____ (downward, upward). An increase in household debt reduces consumption (increases saving) at a given level of disposable income and vice versa. Expectations can also shift the saving and consumption functions. Expectations of a decline in future income will likely cause some households to save more and consume less out of their current income.

Investment spending is a (16)_____ (volatile, stable) component of GNP. It includes expenditures on machines, structures, equipment, and inventories. (17)_____ (Unplanned, Planned) investment purchases are those investment purchases that businesses make on the basis of profit expectations. If businesses overproduce output relative to sales, the unsold output is added to inventories. This is an increase in inventory investment even though it is unplanned. Planned investment demand is determined by the real interest rate, the real marginal return to investment, and other factors that shift the investment demand curve. A profit-maximizing business will invest up to the point at which the expected return for each additional dollar invested (the real marginal return to investment) is (18)_____ (just equal to, greater than) the opportunity cost of using a dollar to make the investment (or the real interest rate). The (19)_____ (aggregate purchases, investment demand) curve shows an inverse relationship between the real interest rate and the level of investment. A decline in the real interest rate relative to the real marginal return to investment will cause businesses to (20)_____ (decrease, increase) investment purchases.

Several factors can change the level of investment at a given real interest rate. These include: (a) expectations about aggregate demand, (b) expectations about the profitability of investments, (c) (21)_____ (disposable income, capacity utilization), (d) technological change, and (e) the tax treatment of investment and income. When plotted against disposable income, the investment function is a horizontal line at the annual level of investment. Any of the influences listed above, including the real interest rate, will shift the investment function either up or down. For example, an increase in the real rate of interest will (22)_____ (reduce, increase) investment purchases at a given level of disposable income and will shift the investment function (23)_____ (upward by the increase, downward by the reduction) in investment spending.

Government spending, like investment, is assumed to be (24)_____ (independent of, dependent on) the current year's level of disposable income. Government purchases of goods and input services constitute about (25)_____ (40%, 20%) of real GNP. The government purchases function is horizontal and shifts either up or down depending upon the change in government spending. An increase in government spending shifts the curve upward and vice versa. Government can also influence aggregate demand by changing taxes and transfer payments. An increase in taxes or a reduction in transfers (26)_____ (increases, reduces) disposable income and consumption and vice versa.

The last component of aggregate demand is net exports. Net exports are defined as the difference between exports and imports. If the difference is positive,

international trade results in an/a (27)_____ (increase, decrease) in
domestic aggregate demand. If the difference is negative, trade (28)_____
(reduces, increases) aggregate demand. Net exports are determined by the level
of disposable income and the prices of imported goods relative to domestic
prices. A/An (29)_____ (decrease, increase) in disposable income
increases imports and reduces net exports. If the international value of the
dollar (30)_____ (increases, decreases) relative to foreign currencies,
U.S. exports become less price competitive in foreign markets, reducing net
exports. The net export function shows a/an (31)_____ (positive,
inverse) relationship between net exports and disposable income.

VOCABULARY REVIEW

Write the key term from the list below next to its definition.

Key Terms

Wealth	Marginal propensity to
Aggregate household wealth	consume
Aggregate household debt	Marginal propensity to
Consumption function	save
Autonomous consumption	Planned investment
Induced consumption	purchases
Real marginal return to	Aggregate purchases
investment	

Definitions

1. _____: purchases of new or replacement residential and
nonresidential structures, producer durable equipment, and additions to
inventories that business firms intentionally make during the year.

2. _____: an estimate of the percentage of each dollar
invested that will be returned to a firm as additional revenue per year
(adjusted for the effects of changes in the price level).

3. _____: the fraction of each additional dollar of annual
disposable income that is saved.

4. _____: the market value of final goods and services that
will be purchased at any given level of income.

5. _____: the fraction of each additional dollar of annual
disposable income that is allocated to consumer purchases.

6. _____: the portion of annual consumer purchases in a
given year that responds to changes in current disposable income.

7. _____: the purchasing power of the sums of money
outstanding that households have borrowed and are currently obligated to
repay.

8. _____: the portion of annual consumer purchases that is
independent of current disposable income.

9. _____: the purchasing power of all assets owned by
households.

10. _____: a relationship between aggregate consumer purchases and disposable income in a certain year given all other determinants of consumption.

11. _____: the sum of the current values of all assets a person owns.

SKILLS REVIEW

Concept: Consumption, saving, and the consumption and saving functions

1. Below are annual data for an economy.

Disposable Income ($ billions)	Consumption ($ billions)	Saving ($ billions)
$ 0	$ 200	$ _____
250	350	_____
500	500	_____
750	650	_____
1,000	800	_____
1,250	950	_____
1,500	1,100	_____

a. Complete the table.
b. There exists a/an _____ relationship between disposable income and consumption and a/an _____ relationship between disposable income and saving.
c. Marginal propensity to consume equals _____; marginal propensity to save equals _____. The sum of the marginal propensities to consume and save equal _____.
d. Plot the consumption line in a in the figure below and plot the saving line in b. At what level of disposable income is saving zero? $_____

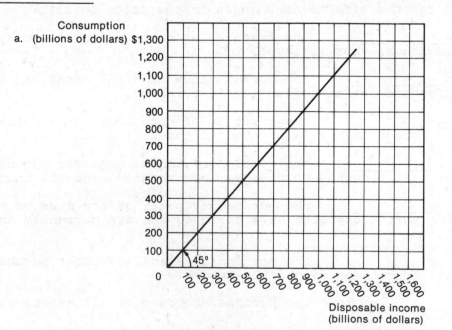

Consumption
a. (billions of dollars)

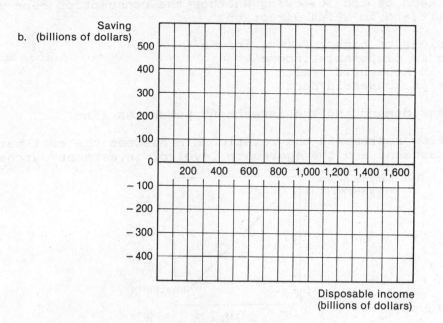

Saving
b. (billions of dollars)

Disposable income
(billions of dollars)

2. List three factors that will shift the consumption and saving lines.

a. _____
b. _____
c. _____

3. The stock market has produced impressive gains in household wealth over the last several months. Because of this, consumption increased by $200 billion at every level of disposable income. Answer the questions below based upon the data reproduced from question 1.

Disposable Income	Consumption Old	New (1)	Saving Old (2)	New (3)
$ 0	$ 200	$_____	$_____	$_____
250	350	_____	_____	_____
500	500	_____	_____	_____
750	650	_____	_____	_____
1,000	800	_____	_____	_____
1,250	950	_____	_____	_____
1,500	1,100	_____	_____	_____

a. Reproduce the saving data that you derived for question 1 in column 2 above.
b. Complete the new consumption and saving schedule assuming a $200 billion increase in consumption at every level of disposable income.
c. Plot the new consumption and saving lines in the figure above.
d. The consumption line has shifted _____ by $_____, and the saving line has shifted _____ by $_____.
e. The level of disposable income at which saving is zero is $_____ assuming the new level of consumption.

415

4. Indicate for each of the following whether the consumption line and saving line will shift and in which direction.

    a. Expectations of higher future income
    b. Increase in disposable income
    c. Decline in household wealth
    d. Increase in household debt

Concept: Investment demand and the investment purchases line

5. The figure below represents the relationship between the real marginal return on investment and the aggregate level of investment purchases for an economy.

    a. Profit-maximizing firms will engage in investment spending up to the point at which the _____ is just equal to the _____.

    b. At a real interest rate of 10%, the level of investment purchases equals $_____. If the rate of interest falls to 8%, the level of investment _____ to $_____.

    c. On the figure below, plot the economy's investment purchases line for a 10% real rate of interest.

416

d.   On the figure above, plot the investment purchases line for an 8% rate of interest.

e.   An increase in the real interest rate will shift the investment line _____, and a decrease in the real interest rate will shift the investment line _____.

6.   List five factors other than the real interest rate that will shift the investment purchases line and discuss for two of the five factors how the investment purchases line is affected.

a.   _____
b.   _____
c.   _____
d.   _____
e.   _____

Concept: Government purchases and net exports

7.   The level of government spending is assumed to be independent of the level of disposable income. Plot the government purchases line in the figure below assuming annual government purchases equal $150 billion. An increase in government purchases will shift the government purchases line _____ and vice versa. Also show in the figure the effect of a $50 billion increase in government purchases.

8. The data below show the relationship among disposable income, exports, and imports for an economy.

Disposable Income ($ billions)	Imports	Exports	Net Exports ($ billions)
$ 0	$ 0	$ 150	$ _____
400	50	150	_____
800	100	150	_____
1,200	150	150	_____
1,600	200	150	_____
2,000	250	150	_____
2,400	300	150	_____

a. Complete the table.
b. Plot the net exports line in the figure below.

Net exports
(billions of dollars)

Disposable income
(billions of dollars)

c. Net exports are _____ related to disposable income.
d. If the international value of the dollar falls relative to the foreign currencies of U.S. trading partners, assume that U.S. export goods become more price competitive abroad, resulting in an increase in exports of $50 billion at every level of disposable income. Show in the figure the effect on the net exports line. The level of disposable income at which net exports equal zero _____ to $_____.

Concept: Aggregate purchases line

9.   Derive the aggregate purchases schedule and aggregate purchases line from the table below.   (All data are in billions of dollars.)

Disposable Income	C	Ip	G	NE	Aggregate Purchases
$ 0	$200	$100	$150	$100	$_____
400	500	100	150	75	_____
800	800	100	150	50	_____
1,200	1,100	100	150	25	_____
1,600	1,400	100	150	0	_____
2,000	1,700	100	150	-25	_____
2,400	2,000	100	150	-50	_____

a.   Complete the table.
b.   Plot the aggregate purchases line in the figure below.

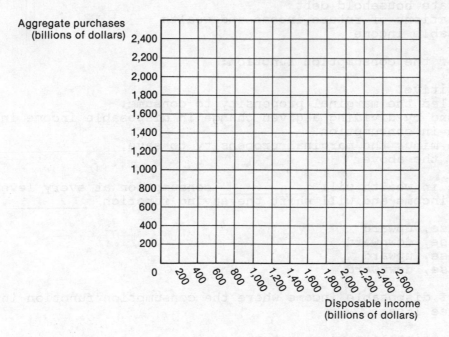

Aggregate purchases (billions of dollars)

Disposable income (billions of dollars)

SELF-TEST FOR MASTERY

Select the best answer.

1.   Consumption represents what proportion of gross national product?

   a.   One fourth
   b.   One half
   c.   Two fifths
   d.   Two thirds
   e.   Three fourths

2.   From 1960 to 1987, Americans have used what percentage on average of their disposable income for household consumption?

     a.   60%
     b.   70%
     c.   80%
     d.   Over 90%

3.   Induced consumption is caused by which of the following?

     a.   Aggregate household wealth
     b.   Aggregate household debt
     c.   Expectations of future income and wealth
     d.   Disposable income
     e.   Interest rate

4.   Autonomous consumption is influenced by all but one of the following.

     a.   Aggregate household wealth
     b.   Aggregate household debt
     c.   Expectations of future income and wealth
     d.   Disposable income

5.   The slope of the consumption function:

     a.   Is positive.
     b.   Is called the marginal propensity to consume.
     c.   Is found by dividing a given change in disposable income into a
          change in consumption.
     d.   Is one minus the marginal propensity to save.
     e.   All of the above.

6.   An increase in wealth will _____ consumption at every level of
     disposable income and will shift the saving function _____.

     a.   Decrease, upward
     b.   Decrease, downward
     c.   Increase, upward
     d.   Increase, downward

7.   The level of disposable income where the consumption function intersects
     the 45-degree line:

     a.   Is the point of maximum returns to investment.
     b.   Is the point of maximum saving.
     c.   Is the point at which saving is zero.
     d.   None of the above.

8.   Expectations of future higher income and wealth will cause the consumption
     function to shift _____ and the saving function to shift
     _____.

     a.   Upward, upward
     b.   Downward, downward
     c.   Upward, downward
     d.   Downward, upward

9. Which of the following components of aggregate demand is the most unstable?

    a. Consumption
    b. Investment
    c. Government purchases
    d. Net exports

10. Which of the following is true of planned investment expenditures?

    a. Planned investment is inversely related to the real interest rate.
    b. Planned investment is positively related to the real interest rate.
    c. Planned investment includes inventory investment resulting from unexpectedly low sales.
    d. Profit-maximizing firms plan to invest on the basis of a comparison between the nominal rate of interest and the absolute cost of the investment project.
    e. None of the above.

11. If the real rate of interest increases relative to the real marginal return to investment:

    a. Planned investment will decrease.
    b. There is an upward movement along a fixed investment demand curve.
    c. The investment line or function relating investment purchases to disposable income will shift downward.
    d. All of the above.

12. If the rate of capacity utilization falls markedly, investment spending will _____ and the investment purchases function will shift _____.

    a. Decrease, downward
    b. Increase, upward
    c. Decrease, upward
    d. Increase, downward

13. Which of the following will not shift the investment demand curve?

    a. Expectations about aggregate demand
    b. Changes in capacity utilization
    c. Changes in the real interest rate
    d. Technological change
    e. Changes in the tax treatment of investment purchases

14. In 1987, government purchases accounted for what percentage of GNP?

    a. 10%
    b. 20%
    c. 30%
    d. 40%
    e. 26%

15. The government purchases function is :

    a. Horizontal.
    b. Upward sloping.
    c. Downward sloping.
    d. Vertical.

16. Given the level of exports, as disposable income rises, imports _____ and net exports _____.

    a. Rise, rise
    b. Fall, rise
    c. Fall, fall
    d. Rise, fall

17. If the international value of the dollar increases relative to foreign currencies, U.S. exports will _____, causing both net exports and aggregate purchases to _____.

    a. Rise, rise
    b. Fall, rise
    c. Fall, fall
    d. Rise, fall

18. An increase in exports will shift the net exports curve _____ and shift the aggregate purchases line _____.

    a. Upward, downward
    b. Downward, upward
    c. Upward, upward
    d. Downward, downward

19. Which of the following defines aggregate purchases?

    a. GNP + C - S + NE
    b. C + G - NE - S + Ip
    c. C + G + Ip - S
    d. C + NE + G + Ip

20. The market value of final goods and services that will be purchased at any given level of income is known as:

    a. Aggregate purchases.
    b. Aggregate household wealth.
    c. Aggregate household debt.
    d. Aggregate household disposable income.

THINK IT THROUGH

1. Discuss the likely consequences of a crash in the stock market that results in large losses in the value of household real wealth.

2. Can you think of any reasons why it is not uncommon for businesses to invest _more_ as interest rates rise?

3. How can government influence the level of aggregate purchases other than by changing the level of government spending on goods and input services?

4. Explain how the nation's aggregate purchases function is affected when the international value of the dollar falls relative to the value of foreign currencies.

POP QUIZ   Read the news brief at the end of this and answer the questions below.

1.   Why is a high debt burden considered a threat to the economy?

2.   Mickey D. Levy of First Fidelity Bancorp is forecasting a 2.3% increase in consumption purchases for 1988, less than half the average annual increase for the first 4 years of the economic expansion that began at the end of 1982. What factors are expected to slow the rate of growth in consumer spending?

CHAPTER ANSWERS

In Brief: Chapter Summary

1. Two thirds 2. Level of disposable income 3. Induced 4. Autonomous 5. Positive 6. Positive 7. Marginal propensity to consume 8. Divided 9. Saving 10. Disposable income 11. One 12. Increases 13. Decreases 14. Upward 15. Downward 16. Volatile 17. Planned 18. Just equal to 19. Investment demand 20. Increase 21. Capacity utilization 22. Reduce 23. Downward by the reduction 24. Independent of 25. 20% 26. Reduces 27. Increase 28. Reduces 29. Increase 30. Increases 31. Inverse

Vocabulary Review

1. Planned investment purchases 2. Real marginal return to investment 3. Marginal propensity to save 4. Aggregate purchases 5. Marginal propensity to consume 6. Induced consumption 7. Aggregate household debt 8. Autonomous consumption 9. Aggregate household wealth 10. Consumption function 11. Wealth

Skills Review

1.   a.   Saving

$-200
-100
0
100
200
300
400

   b.   Positive, positive c. .6, .4; 1 d. $500 billion

423

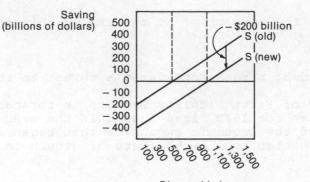

Saving (billions of dollars)

Disposable income (billions of dollars)

2. a. Changes in aggregate household wealth
   b. Changes in aggregate household debt
   c. Expectations of future income and wealth

3. a. Shown above in answer 1. a

   b.
New Consumption	New Saving
$ 400	$-400
550	-300
700	-200
850	-100
1,000	0
1,150	100
1,300	200

   c. Shown in figure above
   d. Upward, $200 billion, downward, $200 billion
   e. $1,000 billion

4. a. The consumption function will shift upward and the saving function downward.
   b. Neither the consumption nor saving functions will shift.
   c. The consumption function will shift downward and the saving function will shift upward.
   d. The consumption function will shift downward and the saving function will shift upward.

5. a. Real rate of interest, real marginal return to investment
   b. $300 billion, rises, $500 billion
   c. Shown on figure below
   d. Shown on figure below

Investment purchases (billions of dollars)

(8% real interest rate)

(10% real interest rate)

Disposable income (billions of dollars)

   e. Downward, upward

424

6. a. Expectations about changes in aggregate demand
    b. Expectations about input and product prices
    c. Capacity utilization
    d. Technological change
    e. Tax treatment of investment purchases

    Expectations of higher levels of future aggregate demand will likely cause
    businesses to revise upward their real marginal returns to investment,
    resulting in an increase in investment and an upward shift in the
    investment purchases function. Likewise, favorable tax treatment of
    investment increases the after-tax expected return from the investment
    making it more attractive. This also shifts the investment function
    upward.

7. Upward

8. a. Net Exports
        $150
         100
          50
           0
         -50
        -100
        -150

    b.

    c. Inversely
    d. Shown in figure above, increase, $1,600 billion

9. a. Aggregate Purchases
     $ 550
       825
     1,100
     1,375
     1,550
     1,925
     2,200

   b.

Self-Test for Mastery

1. d 2. d 3. d 4. d 5. e 6. d 7. c 8. c 9. b 10. a 11. d 12. a 13. c 14. b 15. a 16. d 17. c 18. c 19. d 20. a

Think It Through

1.   If households experience large losses in household wealth, they will reduce consumption expenditures and increase saving.   The consumption function will shift downward, and the saving function will shift upward.   The October 1987 crash reduced real consumer spending for a short period, but other forces that cause consumption to increase eventually offset the impact of the decline in wealth.

2.   The real rate of interest is just one of several influences affecting investment.   In an expansion, interest rates at some point usually rise, but other factors affecting investment in the opposite direction are also changing.   In an expansion, capacity utilization is rising and expectations of future growth in aggregate demand may be optimistic.   Further, there may be expectations of rising product prices and profitability of expanded capacity.   In other words, the real marginal return to investment is being revised upward faster than the increase in real interest rates.

3.   In addition to changing the level of government purchases, the government can influence the level of aggregate demand by influencing the level of disposable income and therefore consumption.   An increase in income taxes reduces disposable income and causes a reduction in household consumption and aggregate purchases and vice versa.   An increase in transfer payments to households supplements household disposable income, resulting in an increase in consumption and aggregate purchases.   A decrease in transfers reduces aggregate purchases.

4.   When the international value of the dollar falls relative to the value of foreign currencies, the prices of U.S. exports become relatively lower to foreigners as compared to their foreign-produced output.   Foreigners purchase more U.S. goods and less of their own output.   As U.S. exports rise, net

exports and aggregate purchases increase. The net export function shifts upward and, since the net export function is a component of the aggregate purchases function, the aggregate purchases function likewise shifts upward.

Pop Quiz

1. A high and rising debt burden is considered a threat to the economy because at some point consumers can no longer sustain increases in spending by borrowing. Some experts feel we have reached this point. Consumer debt to income ratios are at historic highs. This is one of the reasons that economists have been expecting a recession. Consumption makes up 65% of GNP. When consumers reduce the rate of their spending, the economy experiences a significant decline in aggregate purchases unless other components of aggregate demand are increasing.

2. Consumer spending is expected to slow in 1988 because of rising debt burdens and stagnant real disposable income. As recently as the early 1980s, consumer installment debt as a percentage of personal income was 12%. Today it is 16%--an all-time high. And this does not include mortgage debt, which has increased significantly as a percentage of income through the 1970s and into the 1980s. Average weekly pay adjusted for inflation is actually $5 lower today than it was in 1980. With rising debt ratios and stagnant real incomes, consumption spending will likely slow.

Economists Fret Over Consumer Outlays

Delicate Balance Is Required to Avoid a Slump

By Lindley H. Clark Jr.
And Alfred L. Malabre Jr.
Staff Reporters of The Wall Street Journal

Will economists ever run out of things to worry about?

Through much of the economy's long expansion and especially after the stock market crash, many forecasters feared that consumers, burdened by debt, skimpy pay gains and low savings, would slash their spending and thus spark a recession. So far, that hasn't happened.

Now, many forecasters fear that consumers may step up their spending and

Consumer Spending

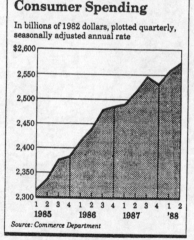

In billions of 1982 dollars, plotted quarterly, seasonally adjusted annual rate

Source: Commerce Department

thus spark—you guessed it—a recession. So far, that hasn't happened, either.

In fact, most economists don't even expect it to happen. But they also can't quite rule it out. And therefore they can't help worrying that if consumers should spend too freely now, while capital outlays and exports are surging, they could overtax the economy, accelerate inflation, force the Federal Reserve to tighten credit and, ultimately, cause a new slump.

Odd 'Bad News'

So, most economists hope that consumers keep spending—because such outlays perennially account for about two-thirds of all business activity—but that they won't spend too lavishly. Such hopes can produce odd-seeming analyses. In a recent report, Edward S. Hyman, the chief economist of C.J. Lawrence, Morgan Grenfell Inc., called a brisk increase in retail sales in June "bad news."

But despite that increase and the strong 1% gain in June consumer spending, the evidence suggests, on balance, that consumers are indeed relatively restrained.

"It's a delicate transition, getting from a consumer-led expansion to one powered by capital outlays and exports, and to do so without interruption in overall economic growth," says Donald Straszheim, the chief economist of Merrill Lynch & Co. But "the transition seems to be working. Capital spending is booming, as are exports, while consumer spending is neither racing ahead nor coming to a complete halt."

Washington's statistics mills are grinding out data, adjusted for inflation and seasonal factors, that appear to confirm that the economy is undergoing a sea change. Business fixed investment in the 1988 first half rose at a swift annual rate of 10.8%, and exports soared at a 16.8% rate. Meanwhile, consumer outlays climbed at an annual rate of only 3.4%; in last year's final quarter, which encompassed the market crash, they slipped a bit.

Trends Likely to Continue

Most economists expect these trends to continue. Mickey D. Levy, the chief economist of First Fidelity Bancorp, forecasts double-digit gains in business investment and exports this year but only a 2.3% increase in consumer outlays—less than half the average annual rise in the first four years of the current expansion.

"We're going to see very modest consumption growth," Mr. Levy predicts, calling this a "better" prospect than most forecasters had earlier anticipated. So, barring an unexpected change in government policy, consumer prices will keep rising at an annual rate below 5% at least through the next six months, he says. This, in turn, suggests continuing economic expansion through next year, he adds.

Factors that point to only slight gains in consumer spending in the months ahead are generally the same ones that earlier had prompted concern about a spending collapse.

Topping the list is consumer debt. It has surged during the economic expansion, which is nearing the six-year mark. Consumer installment debt, now above 16% of personal income, is at a record. Early in the 1980s, it was about 12%. Home-mortgage debt shows a similar progression.

Meanwhile, pay gains continue to be modest, generally failing to keep abreast of price increases. Weekly paychecks are

still edging up, on the average, but not if inflation is taken into account. Adjusted for rising prices, average weekly pay is nearly $5 less now than it was as long ago as 1980, and average hourly pay also has dwindled. A broader earnings gauge—all personal income, adjusted for inflation, taxes and population growth—has barely budged in two years.

Low Savings Rate

Moreover, the share of income saved hovers below 5%. The second-quarter savings rate, at 3.8%, topped last year's 3.2% average but remained far below the 7%-plus levels of the early 1980s.

For the second half, Charles B. Reeder, an economic consultant in Wilmington, Del., forecasts "sluggish" consumer spending, largely because of "a heavy debt burden and wage rates rising more slowly than prices." Like most forecasters, however, he doesn't expect "an actual decline in consumer spending." And F. Thomas Juster, an economist at the University of Michigan, says recent polls by its Survey Research Center find "consumers still to be confident."

Other factors less obvious than the mounting consumer debt are expected to help buoy consumers. Despite the higher debt, a Federal Reserve Board study finds that consumers' "debt-service payments have risen at a much slower rate." Among the reasons: longer loan-contract maturities and lower interest rates than those early in the decade.

Ratio of Installment Debt to Income

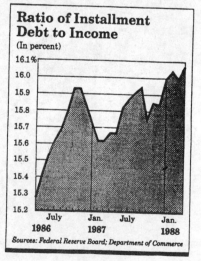

(In percent)

Sources: Federal Reserve Board; Department of Commerce

In a recent three-year period, consumer installment debt outstanding surged 64% to $551.8 billion from $337 billion, but monthly payments on that debt climbed only 38% to $10.6 billion from $7.7 billion. Significantly, delinquency rates on installment and home-mortgage loans, though relatively high, have been lower in recent months than early last year.

Demographic factors also may explain why the outlook for consumer finances may be brighter than overall debt numbers indicate. "Part of the increase in debt is related to the age profile of the population and should be considered natural and not threatening," a Dean Witter Reynolds study says.

So far in this decade, the fastest-growing population group has been the 25-to-44-year-olds—typically, the age group that, relative to income, uses the most credit. As these people age, their borrowing should ebb and their incomes should rise appreciably. Furthermore, relatively few

Index of Consumer Sentiment

First quarter 1966 = 100

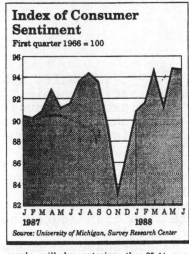

J F M A M J J A S O N D J F M A M J
1987   1988
Source: University of Michigan, Survey Research Center

people will be entering the 25-44 age bracket in the years just ahead.

Also apparently showing a brighter side is the savings picture. Although the share of income saved has long been extraordinarily low, this doesn't take into account

the surge in the value of housing and, despite the crash, of securities holdings. The Federal Reserve study finds that more than "80% of the families that have consumer installment debt also have financial

Home Mortgage Loans

Percent delinquent 30 days or more

1Q 2Q 3Q 4Q 1Q 2Q 3Q 4Q 1Q
1986   1987   1988
Source: Mortgage Bankers Association

Installment Loans

Percent delinquent 30 days or more

J A J O J A J O J
1986   1987   1988
Source: American Bankers Association

assets or home equity sufficient to permit liquidating their debts in emergencies."

Similarly, Mr. Hyman suggests that the big rise in home-mortgage debt be viewed against the big rise in the value of consumer-owned housing and land. Last year, he estimates, mortgage debt amounted to 45.6% of the value of the underlying homes and land. This was up from 37.3% at the start of the decade but slightly less than the comparable reading as long ago as the early 1960s. "Maybe the consumer isn't so leveraged," Mr. Hyman comments.

Helping sustain consumer spending is the surprising strength in employment, which partly offsets the modest size of pay

gains. Lacy Hunt, the chief economist of CM&M Group, a New York securities concern, predicts that "with such strength evident in the employment numbers—nearly four million new jobs in the past year—consumer spending certainly isn't going to collapse." He adds, "Most of the new jobs have been in the better-paid categories, including manufacturing and construction."

Nature of Job Growth

And the Labor Department estimates that "since 1982, part-time employment has accounted for only about 8% of overall job growth" and that the temporary-help industry comprises less than 1% of all payroll jobs.

Persistent strength on the job front is widely seen as a major reason for the

Population Trend Since 1980

AGE	% OF POP. IN 1980	% OF POP. IN 1987	% OF POP. IN 1995
25-34	16.8%	17.8%	15.7%
35-44	11.3	14.1	16.3
45-54	10.1	9.6	12.0
55-64	9.6	9.0	8.2

stock market crash's mild impact on consumer spending. A Federal Reserve economist says that, for all the attention accorded the market, "stock equities are among the most concentrated of all asset holdings." A Fed study shows that the top 10% of wealth-holders own over 90% of all stock. Affluent people usually aren't under heavy pressure to cut their spending.

Far more important than the stock market to consumer spending, the Fed economist says, is the housing market. He shares the consensus that consumers will keep on spending, though at a modest pace, but he cautions that "we could see an actual decline in outlays if housing turns sour and home prices drop across a broad front. Then you would see the purse strings tighten fast." No broad price drop is evident, he adds, though home prices have recently softened in some areas.

30

Aggregate Demand and Keynesian Analysis of Macroeconomic Equilibrium

CHAPTER CHALLENGES

After studying your text, attending class, and completing this chapter, you should be able to:

1. Explain the conditions required for macroeconomic equilibrium and why equilibrium sometimes occurs at a level of real GNP below the level that can provide full employment.
2. Discuss the possible causes of recessions using the Keynesian aggregate purchases aggregate production approach.
3. Discuss how the multiplier works and how it can be calculated.
4. Discuss how changes in net exports can affect aggregate demand and macroeconomic equilibrium.
5. Discuss how changes in the price level can affect aggregate demand and equilibrium real GNP.
6. Show how an inflationary GNP gap can result from an increase in aggregate demand and how an overheated economy implies that an inflationary process will decrease equilibrium real GNP.

IN BRIEF: CHAPTER SUMMARY

Fill in the blanks to summarize chapter content.

In Keynesian analysis of the macroeconomy, (1)_____ (aggregate demand, inflation) is the key cause of fluctuations in real GNP. Macroeconomic equilibrium occurs when aggregate production (2)_____ (exceeds, equals) aggregate purchases. For an economy without government purchases, taxes or net exports, another condition for equilibrium is that planned investment equal (3)_____ (consumption, saving) and unintended inventory investment (4)_____ (exceed, equal) zero. If aggregate purchases exceed aggregate production, planned investment will exceed saving and unintended inventory investment will be (5)_____ (positive, negative). This puts (6)_____ (upward, downward) pressure on real GNP. Just the opposite is true of levels of income where aggregate purchases are less than aggregate production. In equilibrium, there is no tendency for real GNP to rise or fall. Graphically, macroeconomic equilibrium occurs where the aggregate purchases line intersects the (7)_____ (45-degree, consumption) line and where the saving function intersects the planned investment line.

In Keynesian analysis, shifts in the aggregate purchases line cause expansions and recessions. For example, a/an (8)_____ (decline, increase) in planned investment will reduce aggregate purchases relative to aggregate production, resulting in an unintended (9)_____ (decline, increase) in inventory investment. Businesses will (10)_____ (increase, cut) production due to the increase in unsold output. As production and income fall, real GNP, saving, and unintended inventory investment will fall. When saving falls to equal the new and lower level of planned investment, unintended inventory investment is zero and aggregate purchases are once again equal to aggregate production but at a lower level of real GNP--a recessionary level. As real GNP falls, employment also falls. Anything that causes a downward shift in the aggregate purchases line will cause equilibrium real GNP to (11)_____ (rise, fall). Conversely, anything that causes the aggregate purchases function to shift upward will cause equilibrium real GNP to (12)_____ (increase, decrease). In the short run, the economy can attain a recessionary level of equilibrium real GNP and employment. Because of (13)_____ (downward wage and price rigidity, flexible wages and prices), Keynes believed that recessionary levels of employment would persist for long periods unless government intervened by stimulating aggregate demand. In effect, Keynes viewed the aggregate (14)_____ (demand, supply) curve as horizontal below the level of potential real GNP.

A change in (15)_____ (induced, autonomous) purchases (a shift in the aggregate purchases curve) produce larger changes in equilibrium real GNP. This is known as the multiplier effect. The (16)_____ (marginal propensity to consume, multiplier) is a number that when multiplied by either a positive or negative change in autonomous purchases gives the resulting change in equilibrium real GNP. The multiplier process occurs because income spent becomes the income of input suppliers to the industries in which the income was originally spent. Input suppliers in turn spend a portion of the new income and save a portion. When they spend, input suppliers elsewhere in the economy receive income, a portion of which they eventually spend. For the case of an economy without government or foreign sectors, this process of spending and respending continues until the change in saving (17)_____ (just equals, is greater than) the initial change in planned investment. The multiplier can be found by taking the reciprocal of (18)_____ [(1 - MPC), (1 - MPS)] or the reciprocal of the (19)_____ (MPS, MPC).

Adding the government and international sectors to the Keynesian model requires reflecting all four components of aggregate purchases in the aggregate purchases curve: C, Ip, G, and NE. The conditions for macroeconomic equilibrium also change. Aggregate production must still equal aggregate purchases, now defined as including G and NE, (20)_____ (and S = Ip continues to be, but S = Ip is no longer) valid as a condition for equilibrium. The sum of the uses of income for purposes other than purchasing domestic output (saving, taxes less transfers, and imports) must just be offset by the sum of planned investment, government purchases, and exports. That is, Ip + G + E = S + T + M or, alternatively, Ip + G + NE = S + T. The multiplier must also be modified because like saving, imports and taxes are positive functions of real income. The new multiplier can be defined as (21)_____ [the reciprocal of (1 - MRR), MRR times MPC] where the marginal respending rate (MRR) is influenced by the marginal propensity to consume (MPC), the marginal propensity to import (MPI), and the tax rate. Fluctuations in real GNP can be caused by autonomous changes in any of the components of aggregate purchases, including G and NE.

Thus far, Keynesian analysis has assumed that the price level is constant. In order to understand the inflationary implications of fluctuations in autonomous purchases, it is necessary to introduce a price variable to the Keynesian model. As an initial step, the aggregate demand curve must be derived. The aggregate demand curve shows a relationship between the (22)_____ (real disposable income, price level) and aggregate purchases. An increase in the price level will (23)_____ (increase, reduce) aggregate purchases because real wealth decreases, causing consumption to (24)_____ (rise, fall); real interest rates, rise causing planned investment to (25)_____ (rise, fall); and the prices of U.S. goods relative to foreign goods rise, causing exports to (26)_____ (rise, fall) and imports to (27)_____ (rise, fall). The aggregate demand curve is downward sloping. When the aggregate purchases curve shifts upward, causing an inflationary gap where real GNP exceeds potential GNP, the price level rises. This will eventually cause the aggregate purchases line to shift (28)_____ (to a level higher than; back down to) its original position where real GNP equals potential GNP. Thus the price variable acts as a long-run corrective mechanism, eventually returning real GNP to its potential level.

VOCABULARY REVIEW

Write the key term from the list below next to its definition.

Key Terms

Multiplier   Marginal respending rate (MRR)
Autonomous purchases   Marginal propensity to
                                  import (MPI)

Definitions

1. _____: the fraction of each extra dollar of income used to purchase imported products.

2. _____: the extra purchases that result from each extra dollar of income.

3. _____: a number that can be used to multiply a change in purchases that results in a shift of the aggregate purchases line to obtain the change in equilibrium real GNP that results from those purchases.

4. _____: purchases such as investment or autonomous consumption that cause the economy's aggregate purchases line to shift.

SKILLS REVIEW

Concept: Macroeconomic equilibrium

1. Assume that an economy does not engage in international trade and there are no taxes, transfers, or government purchases. Answer the following questions based upon the data in the table below. (All data are in billions of dollars.)

Aggregate Production	Planned Investment	Consumption	Aggregate Purchases	Unintended Inventory Investment
$ 500	$300	$ 600	$_____	$_____
1,000	300	1,000	_____	_____
1,500	300	1,400	_____	_____
2,000	300	1,800	_____	_____
2,500	300	2,200	_____	_____
3,000	300	2,600	_____	_____
3,500	300	3,000	_____	_____

a. Complete the table.
b. The conditions for macroeconomic equilibrium are that _____ equal _____ and _____ equal zero. In equilibrium, planned investment must equal _____.

432

c. Equilibrium GNP = $_____. In equilibrium, aggregate purchases = $_____, aggregate production = $_____, unintended inventory investment = $_____, saving = $_____, and planned investment = $_____.

d. Plot the aggregate purchases curve in the figure below and identify the equilibrium level of real GNP.

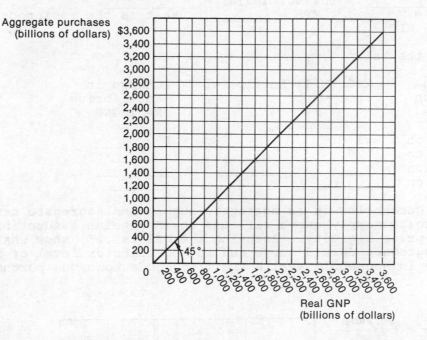

Aggregate purchases (billions of dollars)

Real GNP (billions of dollars)

e. At a level of aggregate production of $1,500 billion, aggregate purchases _____ aggregate production by $_____, resulting in an unintended inventory investment of $_____. This causes the level of real GNP to _____.

f. At a level of aggregate production of $3,500 billion, aggregate purchases _____ aggregate production by $_____, resulting in an unintended inventory investment of $_____. This causes real GNP to _____.

Concept: Changes in autonomous purchases, macroeconomic equilibrium, and the multiplier

2. For the economy shown in the table above in question 1, analyze the effect of an increase in planned investment of $100 billion. (All data are in billions of dollars.)

Aggregate Production	Planned Investment		Consumption	Aggregate Purchases		Unintended Inventory Investment	
	Old	New		Old	New	Old	New
$ 500	$300	$400	$ 600	$___	$___	$___	$___
1,000	300	400	1,000				
1,500	300	400	1,400				
2,000	300	400	1,800				
2,500	300	400	2,200				
3,000	300	400	2,600				
3,500	300	400	3,000				

a. Complete the table.

b. For the new level of planned investment, equilibrium real GNP =
    $_____.
c. On the figure above, draw the new aggregate purchases curve and
    identify the new equilibrium real GNP.
d. Equilibrium real GNP has _____ from $_____ to $_____.
    Equilibrium autonomous purchases have _____ from $_____ to
    $_____. The multiplier = _____.
e. MPC = _____, MPS = _____. What is the reciprocal of the MPS or
    (1 - MPC)?

3. Complete the table.

Change in Autonomous Purchases	MPC	MPS	Multiplier	Change in Equilibrium Real GNP
$50 billion	.8	____	_____	$ _____
-30 billion	.75	____	_____	_____
700 billion	____	.4	_____	_____
-80 billion	____	____	2	_____

4. In the figure below is an aggregate supply and aggregate demand model.
    The aggregate supply curve reflects the Keynesian assumption regarding
    wage and price rigidity. Assuming the MPS is .25, show what will happen
    to the aggregate demand curve and the equilibrium level of real GNP given
    a decline in household wealth that reduces autonomous purchases by $75
    billion.

434

5. Show on the figure below the effect of an increase in government purchases of $100 billion. Identify the new equilibrium real GNP. The multiplier = _____. If after the increase in government spending the level of equilibrium real GNP is short of potential GNP by $200 billion and government desires to increase its spending to move the economy to its potential level, how much more of an increase in government purchases is required? $_____

6. Given the initial level of aggregate purchases in the figure above, show on the figure the effect of a decline in exports of $50 billion. Equilibrium real GNP _____ from $_____ to $_____.

Concept: Aggregate demand and the price level

7. List three reasons why an increase in the price level will reduce aggregate purchases.

     a. _____
     b. _____
     c. _____

8. In the figure below, a represents three aggregate purchases curves, each associated with a different price level. Curve 1 is associated with price level P1, curve 2 with P2, and curve 3 with P3. In b, find the price level-real GNP coordinates consistent with macroeconomic equilibrium. (Plot the aggregate demand curve.)

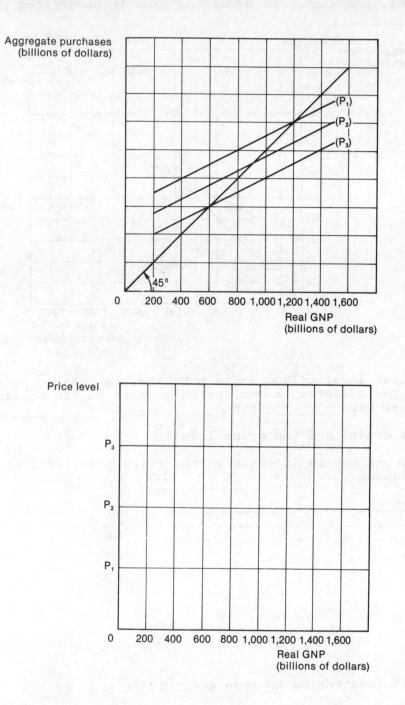

SELF-TEST FOR MASTERY

Select the best answer.

1. In Keynesian analysis, the key determinant of real GNP is:

   a. Profits.
   b. Investment.
   c. Inflation.
   d. Aggregate demand.

2. For an economy without international trade, taxes, transfers and government spending, equilibrium real GNP is achieved when

   a. Planned investment equals saving.
   b. Aggregate production equals aggregate purchases.
   c. Consumption and planned investment equal aggregate production.
   d. All of the above.
   e. None of the above.

3. Graphically, macroeconomic equilibrium occurs where:

   a. The consumption function and saving line intersect.
   b. The planned investment line and the government spending line intersect.
   c. Spending equals saving.
   d. The aggregate purchases curve intersects the 45-degree line.

4. At a level of real GNP greater than equilibrium real GNP, aggregate production _____ aggregate purchases and unintended inventory investment _____.

   a. Equals, equals zero
   b. Exceeds, is positive
   c. Is less than, is negative
   d. Equals, is negative
   e. Exceeds, equals zero

5. At a level of real GNP less than equilibrium real GNP, aggregate production _____ aggregate purchases and unintended inventory investment _____.

   a. Equals, equals zero
   b. Exceeds, is positive
   c. Is less than, is negative
   d. Equals, is negative
   e. Exceeds, equals zero

6. A decline in planned investment:

   a. Causes aggregate purchases to increase and aggregate production to decrease.
   b. Reduces aggregate purchases relative to aggregate production causing unintended inventories to rise and putting pressure on real GNP to rise.
   c. Increases aggregate purchases relative to aggregate production causing unintended inventories to rise and putting pressure on real GNP to fall.
   d. Reduces aggregate purchases relative to aggregate production causing

437

unintended inventories to rise and putting pressure on real GNP to fall.

7. If households experience a substantial increase in aggregate household wealth:

    a. Unintended inventory investment falls initially, but eventually equilibrium real GNP will rise.
    b. Unintended inventory investment rises initially, but eventually equilibrium real GNP will fall.
    c. Unintended inventory investment falls initially, but eventually equilibrium real GNP will fall.
    d. Initially equilibrium real GNP will rise, but eventually unintended inventory investment will fall.

8. If the economy is operating at a level of equilibrium real GNP below its potential real GNP:

    a. The economy is experiencing inflation.
    b. Government can move the economy toward its potential level by reducing government purchases.
    c. The economy is at full employment, but is at least not experiencing inflation.
    d. Government can move the economy toward its potential level by increasing government purchases.

9. A change in autonomous purchases produces a larger change in real GNP. This concept is represented by the:

    a. MPC.
    b. MRR.
    c. Multiplier.
    d. 1/MPI.
    e   C and d.

10. Which of the following expressions represents the multiplier?

    a. 1/MPI
    b. 1/MPC
    c. 1/MPS
    d. 1/(1 - MPC)
    e. C and d

11. If the current level of equilibrium real GNP is $2,000 billion and the MPS equals .25, an increase in planned investment of $50 billion will change real equilibrium GNP to:

    a. $1,800 billion.
    b. $2,300 billion.
    c. $3,200 billion.
    d. $2,200 billion.
    e. $2,100 billion.

12. If the MPC is .8 and a decline in consumer wealth reduces aggregate purchases by $100 billion, equilibrium real GNP will change by:

    a. -$200 billion.
    b. $200 billion.
    c. $400 billion.
    d. -$500 billion.

13. Which of the following equilibrium conditions applies to an economy with foreign trade, government spending, taxes, and transfers?

    a.   Aggregate production = aggregate purchases
    b.   C + Ip + G + NE = real GNP
    c.   Ip + G + E = S + T + M
    d.   All of the above
    e.   B and c

14. The multiplier for an economy with taxes and imports as a function of income:

    a.   Is larger than the multiplier for an economy without foreign trade, taxes, transfers, and government spending.
    b.   Is expressed as the reciprocal of the MRR.
    c.   Is expressed as the reciprocal of (1 - MRR).
    d.   Is smaller than the multiplier for an economy without foreign trade, taxes, transfers, and government purchases.
    e.   C and d

15. A/An _____ in exports can cause a/an _____ gap.

    a.   Decrease, recessionary
    b.   Decrease, inflationary
    c.   Increase, recessionary
    d.   Increase, will leave real GNP unchanged

16. Which of the following is not a reason why aggregate purchases and the price level are inversely related?

    a.   Higher prices cause higher wages, inducing firms to cut employment and production.
    b.   Higher prices reduce real wealth, decreasing consumption and aggregate purchases.
    c.   Higher prices reduce real interest rates, reducing planned investment and aggregate purchases.
    d.   Higher prices reduces exports and increase imports, reducing aggregate purchases.

17. A point on the aggregate demand curve represents a price level- real GNP coordinate at which:

    a.   Aggregate purchases equal aggregate government spending.
    b.   Aggregate demand equals aggregate purchases.
    c.   Aggregate purchases equal aggregate production.
    d.   S + C = Ip + real GNP.

18. An inflationary gap exists where equilibrium real GNP _____ potential or full-employment GNP. In the long run, an inflationary gap will cause the aggregate purchases curve to shift _____.

    a.   Equals, upward
    b.   Equals, downward
    c.   Is less than, downward
    d.   Is greater than, downward
    e.   Is greater than, upward

THINK IT THROUGH

1. Suppose that the international value of the dollar on foreign exchange markets increases, causing the prices of U.S. goods abroad to become less competitive. If exports fall, what is the likely impact on the economy?

2. If business becomes more optimistic regarding future sales such that the expected marginal rate of return to investment rises relative to the real interest rate, discuss the likely macroeconomic effects.

3. Explain intuitively the multiplier process.

CHAPTER ANSWERS

In Brief: Chapter Summary

1. Aggregate demand 2. Equals 3. Saving 4. Equal 5. Negative 6. Upward 7. 45-degree 8. Decline 9. Increase 10. Cut 11. Fall 12. Increase 13. Downward wage and price rigidity 14. Supply 15. Autonomous 16. Multiplier 17. Just equals 18. (1 - MPC) 19. MPS 20. But S = Ip is no longer 21. The reciprocal of (1 - MRR) 22. Price level 23. Reduce 24. Fall 25. Fall 26. Fall 27. Rise 28. Back down to

Vocabulary Review

1. Marginal propensity to import 2. Marginal respending rate (MRR) 3. Multiplier 4. Autonomous purchases

Skills Review

1. a.

Aggregate Purchases	Unintended Inventory Investment
$ 900	$-400
1,300	-300
1,700	-200
2,100	-100
2,500	0
2,900	100
3,300	200

   b. Aggregate purchases, aggregate production, unintended inventory investment; saving
   c. $2,500; $2,500, $2,500, $0, $300, $300

d.

Aggregate purchases
(billions of dollars)

Real GNP
(billions of dollars)

e.   Exceed, $200, -$200; rise
f.   Are less than, $200, $200; fall

2. a.   Aggregate Purchases   Unintended Inventory
Investment

Old	New	Old	New
$ 900	$1,000	$-400	$-500
1,300	1,400	-300	-400
1,700	1,800	-200	-300
2,100	2,200	-100	-200
2,500	2,600	0	-100
2,900	3,000	100	0
3,300	3,400	200	100

b. $3000
c.   On figure above
d.   Increased, $2,500, $3,000; increases, $2,500, $3,000; 5
e.   .8, .2; the multiplier

3.

Change in Autonomous Purchases	MPC	MPS	Multiplier	Change in Equilibrium Real GNP
$50 billion	.8	.2	5	$250 billion
-30 billion	.75	.25	4	-120 billion
700 billion	.6	.4	2.5	1,750 billion
-80	.5	.5	2	-160 billion

4.

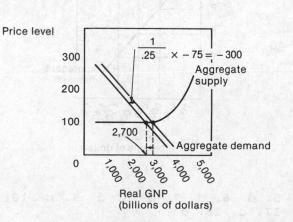

Price level

$$\frac{1}{.25} \times -75 = -300$$

Aggregate supply

Aggregate demand

Real GNP
(billions of dollars)

5.

2, $100 billion

6. Shown on figure above; decreases, $1,200, $1,100

7. a. An increase in the price level will reduce real wealth, reducing consumption and aggregate purchases.
   b. An increase in the price level will increase real interest rates, reducing planned investment and causing aggregate purchases to fall.
   c. An increase in the prices of U.S. goods relative to foreign goods increases imports and decreases exports, causing aggregate purchases to decline.

8.

Self-Test for Mastery

1. d 2. d 3. d 4. b 5. d 6. d 7. a 8. d 9. c 10. e 11. d 12. d 13. d 14. e 15. a 16. a 17. c 18. d

Think it Through

1.   If exports fall, net exports and aggregate purchases will decline. As aggregate spending declines relative to the current level of real GNP, unintended inventory investment increases. Businesses will eventually reduce the rate of production, causing real GNP to fall. As long as real GNP exceeds aggregate purchases, unintended inventory investment will be positive putting downward pressure on real GNP. Real GNP will fall to a lower equilibrium level where aggregate production and aggregate purchases are equal and unintended inventory investment is zero.

2.   If because of an optimistic outlook regarding future sales businesses revise upward their expected marginal real returns to investments, the expected marginal returns will exceed the prevailing real interest rate, causing profit-maximizing firms to increase planned investment. This will cause an autonomous increase in aggregate purchases, which in turn will produce a multiple increase in real GNP assuming that the economy initially was in equilibrium at less than full employment. If the economy was initially at full employment, the increase in planned investment will cause an inflationary gap.

3.   An increase in autonomous expenditures causes an equal increase in output and income. Businesses produce output to meet increases in spending, and households receive income for supplying inputs to the industry experiencing the autonomous spending. Input suppliers save a portion of the new disposable income and spend a portion. But when they spend, they create a demand for goods and services, which causes the producers of those items to increase production. In order to increase production, firms must hire additional inputs, providing another round of income increases to input suppliers. The multiplier process results from the spending and respending of income. At each round, output produced by the economy increases. This process continues until the initial increase in autonomous spending just equals the growth of saving. At this point, there is no additional income created and consequently no growth in spending or production.

A Complete Keynesian Model

IN BRIEF: APPENDIX SUMMARY

Fill in the blanks to summarize appendix content.

The complete Keynesian model considers aggregate purchases to be the sum of C + Ip + G + NE. Consumption, C, is a function of disposable income. In determining disposable income, DI, a net tax function is employed where net taxes collected equal the marginal tax rate times the level of (1)_____ (consumption, income). The (2)_____ (average, marginal) tax rate is the fraction of each extra dollar of income earned in a nation that is collected as taxes. Planned investment, Ip, and government purchases, G, are treated as autonomous variables. The net exports function, NE, is an/a (3)_____ (inverse, positive) function of income. Specifically, NE = exports - imports where imports are a (4)_____ (negative, positive) function of income. Thus as national income rises, imports rise relative to exports, causing net exports to (5)_____ (rise, fall).

A condition for economic equilibrium is that aggregate purchases equal aggregate production.

    Aggregate purchases = C + Ip + G + (E - M)
    Aggregate production = Y = C + S + T

Setting aggregate production equal to aggregate purchases and simplifying yields:

    (E - M) + (G - T) = S - Ip

The sum of the foreign trade balance and the government budget balance must equal the difference between saving and planned investment. This can be alternatively stated as:

    Balance of trade deficit = S - (Ip + budget deficit)

If a nation has a balance of trade deficit, domestic saving (6)_____ (falls short of, exceeds) the sum of planned investment purchases and the budget deficit.

In order to algebraically solve for the equilibrium level of real GNP and the multiplier, the individual functions for the components of aggregate purchases must be summed to obtain the aggregate purchases function. This is then set equal to the level of aggregate production, Y, and solved for Y--the equilibrium level of real GNP. The collection of coefficients preceding autonomous C, Ip, G, and E are the multipliers pertaining to each component.

    Y = C + Ip + G + NE
    Y = A + MPC[(1 - t)]Y + Ip + G + [E - MPI(Y)]
    Y = [1/(1 - MRR)]A + [1/(1 - MRR)]Ip + [1/(1 - MRR)]G + [1/(1 - MRR)]E
        where MRR = [MPC(1 - t) - MPI]

A change in planned investment, for instance, would change real GNP by [1/(1 - MRR)] times the change in (7)_____ (planned investment, real GNP).

VOCABULARY REVIEW

Write the key term from the list below next to its definition.

Key Terms

Marginal tax rate   Balance of trade deficit

Definitions

1. _____: prevails when expenditures on imported products over the year exceed receipts by domestic firms from sales of exports.

2. _____: the fraction of each extra dollar of income earned in a nation that is collected as taxes.

SKILLS REVIEW

Answer questions 1, 2, and 3 given the values below.

A = $300 billion, Ip = $400 billion, G = $500,
E = $200, MPC = .9, t = .3, MPI = .15

1. MRR = _____
    Multiplier = _____
    Equilibrium real GNP = $_____

2. If the marginal tax rate, t, is reduced to .2, what is the impact on real GNP? Real GNP _____ from $_____ to $_____.

3. If the international value of the dollar falls relative to the values of foreign currencies, exports rise. If exports rise by $50 billion, by how much will equilibrium income change? (Assume t = .2.) $_____

SELF-TEST FOR MASTERY

Select the best answer.

1. The fraction of each extra dollar of income earned in a nation that is collected as taxes is called:

    a. Net taxes.
    b. Average tax rate.
    c. Marginal tax rate.
    d. Marginal income.

2. In the complete Keynesian model, which of the following represents the consumption function?

   a. $C = A - (MPC)Y$
   b. $C = A + (MPC - t)Y$
   c. $C = MPC - A(1 - t)Y$
   d. $C = A - MPC[(1 - t)]Y$

3. In the complete Keynesian model, the multiplier is expressed as:

   a. $1/MPC$
   b. $1/(1 - MPS)$
   c. $1/(MRR - 1)$
   d. $1/(1 + MRR)$
   e. $1/\{1 - [MPC(1 - t) - MPI]\}$

4. The equilibrium condition can be expressed to yield an implication regarding a nation running a balance of trade deficit. Which of the following is a statement of that implication?

   a. Real GNP is always larger given balance of trade deficits.
   b. A balance of trade deficit implies that planned investment and the budget deficit exceed saving.
   c. A balance of trade deficit implies that domestic saving falls short of the sum of planned investment purchases and the budget deficit.
   d. None of the above.

CHAPTER APPENDIX ANSWERS

In Brief: Appendix Summary

1. Income 2. Marginal 3. Inverse 4. Positive 5. Fall 6. Falls short of 7. Planned investment

Vocabulary Review

1. Balance of trade deficit 2. Marginal tax rate

Skills Review

1. .48, 1.923, $2,692.3 billion

2. Increases, $2,692.3 billion, $3,255.8 billion

3. +$116.28 billion

Self-Test for Mastery

1. c 2. d 3. e 4. c

31

Aggregate Supply: Its Influence on Macroeconomic Equilibrium and Economic Growth

CHAPTER CHALLENGES

After studying your text, attending class, and completing this chapter, you should be able to:

1. Understand why an increase in aggregate demand can cause the price level to increase even when the economy is operating at a level below full employment.
2. Explain how a wage-price spiral and stagflation can result when an economy overheats.
3. Use aggregate demand and supply analysis to show how an unfavorable supply-side shock can cause a recession and put upward pressure on the price level, thus causing a period of stagflation.
4. Show how an increase in aggregate supply has favorable effects on macroeconomic equilibrium by putting upward pressure on real GNP while at the same time putting downward pressure on the price level.
5. Discuss long-term influences on aggregate supply and explain the economy's long-run aggregate supply curve.
6. Discuss the sources and importance of economic growth as well as its benefits and costs.

IN BRIEF: CHAPTER SUMMARY

Fill in the blanks to summarize chapter content.

If a nation's aggregate supply curve is upward sloping, increases in aggregate demand increase both real GNP and the price level. The rate of increase in the price level is likely to (1)_____ (increase, remain the same) as the economy approaches potential real GNP. If increases in aggregate demand cause an inflationary GNP gap, rising prices eventually will induce labor and other input suppliers to demand higher wages and resource prices to compensate for the loss in purchasing power due to the price level increase. This shifts the aggregate supply curve (2)_____ (rightward, leftward), thus returning the economy to (3)_____ (its potential, a recessionary) level of real GNP. But this results in still higher prices. A wage-price spiral will occur if further increases in aggregate demand take place.

(4)_____ (Expansion, Stagflation) results when the aggregate supply curve shifts to the left. Unemployment is rising while the price level is rising. If workers begin to anticipate continued increases in inflation, they ask for even higher wages, shifting the aggregate supply curve (5)_____ (rightward, leftward) by an even larger amount. Prices can be rising even when unemployment falls below the natural rate of unemployment. Stagflation can also result from (6)_____ (adverse, favorable) supply-side shocks such as sharp increases in the cost of resources that shift the aggregate supply curve leftward. But (7)_____ (adverse, favorable) supply-side shocks such as the decline in oil prices in 1986 have just the opposite effect, shifting the aggregate supply curve rightward and putting downward pressure on the price level and increasing real GNP.

In the long run, as wages and other input prices adjust to the prevailing rate of inflation and assuming that there are no other forces influencing the level of real GNP, the economy will eventually return to its potential level of real GNP at the natural rate of unemployment. The (8)_____ (long-run aggregate supply, short-run aggregate demand) curve is vertical at the potential level of real GNP. In the long run, this curve will shift to the right due to (9)_____ (decreases, increases) in the quantity of resources available for use by the economy, (10)_____ (decreases, increases) in resource productivity, improvements in technology, and improvements in the efficiency with which inputs are used.

(11)_____ (Labor productivity, The quantity of labor supplied) is the key source of real GNP growth. It is influenced by the level of work experience, education, training, (12)_____ (the amount of profit, the amount of capital per worker), the age composition of the labor force, technological improvements, and improvements in managerial techniques. The growth of capital per worker is dependent on the rate of planned investment and the (13)_____ (stock market, rate of saving). According to the text, (14)_____ (two thirds, one half) of real GNP growth from 1929 to 1982 can be attributed to increases in labor productivity, with the remainder due to increases in the quantity of labor. The increases in (15)_____ (the quantity of labor supplied, labor productivity) are primarily due to improved technology and managerial techniques, increases in the quantity of capital, and improved education and training.

Over time, even though aggregate demand is subject to cyclical variation, it exhibits a long-term upward trend. But in the long run, aggregate supply increases as well. The increase in a nation's aggregate supply satisfies its rising aggregate demand, but also (16)_____ (increases, moderates) the rate at which prices rise.

VOCABULARY REVIEW

Write the key term from the list below next to its definition.

Key Terms

Wage-price spiral   Long-run aggregate supply curve
Stagflation   Productivity
Supply-side shock

Definitions

1. _____: a measure of output per unit of input.

2. _____: a sudden and unexpected shift of the aggregate supply curve.

3. _____: exists when higher product prices result in higher wages, which in turn increase prices still further through a decrease in aggregate supply.

4. _____: term coined to describe an economy in which real GNP stagnates at a given level or actually declines from one period to the next while inflation ensues at relatively high rates.

5. _____ : shows the relationship between the aggregate
quantity supplied and the price level that would be observed if nominal
wages and other money prices were flexible enough to allow the classical
self-correction mechanism to work.

SKILLS REVIEW

Concept: Changes in aggregate demand and the price level

1. The figure below shows an aggregate demand and supply model.

Price level

Real GNP
(billions of dollars)

a. If potential real GNP equals $4000 billion, is the economy
    experiencing a recessionary or inflationary gap at ADo?
    _____ Equilibrium real GNP = $_____
b. If an increase in aggregate demand shifts the AD curve from ADo to
    AD1, the price level will _____ and the level of real GNP will
    _____.
c. If demand increases from AD1 to AD2, the price level _____ and
    the level of real GNP _____.
d. If aggregate demand increases from AD2 to AD3, the price level will
    _____ and the level of real GNP will _____.

Concept: Wage-price spiral and the long-run aggregate supply curve

2.   Suppose the economy shown in the figure below is currently in equilibrium
      at its potential level of real GNP.

Price level

AS₀

AD₀

0

Real GNP
(billions of dollars)

a.   On the figure above, show a new aggregate demand curve reflecting an
      increase in demand and label it AD1. The price level _____ while
      real GNP _____. Identify the new price level and level of real
      GNP on the figure above.
b.   Eventually, workers and other input suppliers will react to the loss
      of purchasing power resulting from the increase in the price level by
      _____. Show the impact on the aggregate supply curve
      assuming that input suppliers have completely adjusted to the new
      price level and label the curve AS1. The price level _____
      while the level of real GNP _____. Identify graphically the new
      equilibrium price and real GNP levels.
c.   Suppose that aggregate demand increases again, shifting the AD curve
      from AD1 to AD2. Show graphically and identify the new price level
      and level of real GNP. Workers will again eventually respond by
      _____, which causes the AS curve to shift _____. Show
      the new AS curve and label it AS2.
d.   The process described above produces a _____-_____ spiral.
e.   In the long run, when input suppliers have completely adjusted to the
      price level, the equilibrium level of real GNP equals _____.
      Find the long-run aggregate supply curve in the figure above and
      label it AS3. The long-run aggregate supply curve is (upward
      sloping, vertical).

Concept: Stagflation, price expectations, and supply-side shocks

3.   The figure below shows an economy at its potential level of real GNP.
      Assume that this economy has been experiencing a wage-price spiral such
      that input suppliers begin to anticipate a higher price level.

   a.   Show on the figure above, what happens to the aggregate supply curve
         when workers begin to anticipate higher prices. Label the new AS
         curve AS1. Real GNP _____, and the price level _____.
   b.   Given the aggregate demand curve and the new AS curve, AS1, assume
         that an oil price shock occurs. Show the effect on the AS curve.
         Label the new AS curve AS2. The oil price shock is known as a
         _____. Equilibrium real GNP _____ while the price level
         _____.
   c.   Rising price-level expectations and adverse supply-side shocks
         produce the dual incidence of _____ and _____, which is
         otherwise known as _____.

Concept: Economic growth and the aggregate supply and demand model

4.   List four influences that shift the aggregate supply curve rightward.

   a.   _____
   b.   _____
   c.   _____
   d.   _____

5.   In the United States, aggregate demand and aggregate supply have both
      exhibited a long-term increase. Because of downward wage-price rigidity
      or the sluggishness with which prices and wages fall, the price level over
      the long run has increased. In a in the figure below, show this process
      of economic growth. In b in the figure, show this process of economic
      growth.

a. Price level

Real GNP
(billions of dollars)

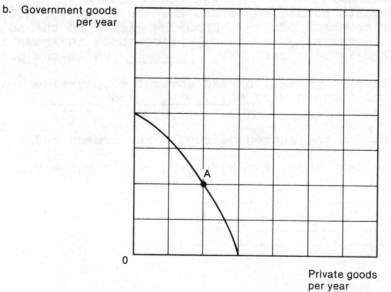

b. Government goods
    per year

Private goods
per year

SELF-TEST FOR MASTERY

Select the best answer.

1. For an economy operating on the upward sloping portion of the aggregate supply curve, an increase in aggregate demand will _____ the price level and _____ real GNP.

    a. Increase, decrease
    b. Increase, increase
    c. Decrease, increase
    d. Decrease, decrease

2. If an economy is currently operating at its potential level of real GNP, an increase in aggregate demand will:

    a. Increase the price level and produce an inflationary gap.
    b. Decrease the price level and produce a recessionary gap.
    c. Cause stagflation.
    d. Produce long-run economic growth.

3. When an economy is currently at its potential level of real GNP and experiences an increase in aggregate demand, input suppliers will eventually _____, causing the aggregate supply curve to shift _____.

    a. Withdraw from resource markets, leftward
    b. Press for higher input prices, rightward
    c. Press for higher input prices, leftward
    d. Increase the productivity of their resources, rightward

4. The process of increases in aggregate demand followed by input price pressures followed by increases in aggregate demand is called:

    a. A recession.
    b. Stagflation.
    c. The business cycle.
    d. The real output cycle.
    e. A wage-price spiral.

5. Stagflation results from which of the following?

    a. Increases in aggregate demand
    b. Increases in aggregate supply
    c. Increases in input price expectations
    d. Adverse supply-side shocks
    e. C and d

6. An oil price shock that reduces oil prices shifts the _____ curve rightward, causing real GNP to _____ and the price level to _____.

    a. Aggregate demand, fall, rise
    b. Aggregate supply, fall, rise
    c. Aggregate supply, rise, rise
    d. Aggregate supply, rise, fall
    e. Aggregate demand, rise, fall

7. An adverse supply-side shock shifts the aggregate supply curve _____ causing real GNP to _____ and the price level to _____.

    a. Leftward, fall, rise
    b. Rightward, fall, rise
    c. Leftward, rise, fall
    d. Rightward, rise, fall
    e. Leftward, fall, fall

8. Which of the following increases potential real GNP over the long run?

    a. An increase in demand
    b. Inflation
    c. Government spending
    d. Consumption
    e. None of the above

9. Which of the following shift the long-run aggregate supply curve rightward?

    a. Increases in the quantity of resources available to a nation
    b. Increases in the productivity of productive resources
    c. Improvements in technology
    d. Improvements in the efficiency with which resources are used
    e. All of the above

10. The long-run aggregate supply curve is:

    a. Upward sloping.
    b. Horizontal.
    c. Downward sloping.
    d. Vertical.

11. Which of the following is a key to the process of economic growth?

    a. Improvements in labor productivity
    b. Increases in the stock of resources
    c. Increases in the money supply
    d. Reducing the federal budget deficit

12. In order of importance, what factors are responsible for the growth in labor productivity in the United States from 1929 to 1982?

    a. Improvements in education, increases in the amount of capital per worker, increases in investment spending
    b. Increases in the capital stock, saving, cuts in income tax rates
    c. Improvements in technology and management, increases in the amount of capital per worker, improvements in education and training
    d. Saving and investment, technological improvements, increases in the quantity of labor and other resources

13. An increase in saving reduces _____ in the short run but if it is invested in physical and human capital over the long run, the level of potential real GNP will _____.

    a. Aggregate supply, decrease
    b. Aggregate supply, increase
    c. Aggregate demand, decrease
    d. Consumption, increase

14. In a growing economy, both _____ and _____ increase, but because prices do not fall as quickly or easily as they rise, the general price level over the long run _____.

    a. Aggregate demand, aggregate supply, falls
    b. Aggregate supply, unemployment, falls
    c. Inflation, unemployment, rises
    d. Aggregate demand, aggregate supply, rises

15. Supply-side shifts in the aggregate supply curve resulting from economic growth serve to:

    a. Increase inflation.
    b. Reduce the price level over time.
    c. Moderate inflation resulting from shifts in the aggregate demand curve.
    d. Increase real GNP beyond the level possible by shifts in the aggregate demand curve alone.
    e. C and d.

THINK IT THROUGH

1. Assume that an adverse-side supply shock occurs. Discuss the effects of the supply-side shock. Suppose that workers increase their expectations of inflation at the same time that the supply-side shock is occurring. Discuss the likely effects.

2. Why is the long-run aggregate supply curve independent of shifts in the aggregate demand curve?

3. Assume that the United States imports copper, which is used widely in business and industry. Discuss the effects on the U.S. economy of a major reduction in the world price of copper.

POP QUIZ   Read the news brief at the end of this chapter and answer the following questions.

1. In June of 1988 the economy appeared to be operating on what point of its aggregate supply curve?
2. Approximately what level of capacity utilization is consistent with the economy's potential level of real GNP?
3. If the economy continues to experience increases in aggregate demand, what are the likely consequences?

CHAPTER ANSWERS

In Brief: Chapter Summary

1. Increase 2. Leftward 3. Its potential 4. Stagflation 5. Leftward 6. Adverse 7. Favorable 8. Long-run aggregate supply 9. Increases 10. Increases 11. Labor productivity 12. The amount of capital per worker 13. Rate of saving 14. Two thirds 15. Labor productivity 16. Moderates

Vocabulary Review

1. Productivity 2. Supply-side shock 3. Wage-price spiral 4. Stagflation 5. Long-run aggregate supply curve

Skills Review

1. a. Recessionary gap; $1,000 billion
    b. Not change, increase
    c. Increases, increases
    d. Increase more rapidly, increase

2. a.

Price level

Real GNP
(billions of dollars)

    Increases, increases
    b. Pressing for higher wages and other input prices; increases, falls back to its potential level of real GNP
    c. Pressing for higher wages; leftward
    d. Wage, price
    e. The potential level of real GNP; vertical

3. a.

Price level

Real GNP
(billions of dollars)

    Decreases, increases
    b. Supply-side shock; falls, increases
    c. Rising unemployment and rising inflation; stagflation

4. a. Increases in the quantity of resources available to a nation
    b. Increases in resource productivity
    c. Improved technology and managerial techniques
    d. Improvements in the efficiency with which resources are used

456

5.

Price level

P_2
P_1
P_0

AS$_0$
AS$_1$
C AS$_2$

A   B

AD$_2$
AD$_1$
AD$_0$

0   Y_0 Y_1 Y_2

Real GNP
(billions of dollars)

Government goods
per year

A

(Y_0) (Y_1) (Y_2)

0

Private goods
per year

Self-Test for Mastery

1. b 2. a 3. c 4. e 5. e 6. d 7. a 8. e 9. e 10. d 11. a 12. c 13. d 14. d 15. e

Think it Through

1.   An adverse supply-side shock shifts the aggregate supply curve to the left. As aggregate supply falls relative to aggregate demand, real GNP falls and the price level rises. The dual incidence of rising inflation and rising unemployment is called stagflation. If at the same time workers have expectations of higher future price levels, the aggregate supply curve will shift even further leftward as workers press for higher wages to offset the expected higher prices. The equilibrium price level will increase even more, and the extent of unemployment will be greater. Therefore adverse supply-side shocks combined with rising price level expectations may produce a serious stagflation.

2.   Shifts in aggregate demand cause short-run changes in real GNP, but if given enough time for product and resource prices to adjust completely, the economy will return to its potential level of real GNP. For instance, if an increase in aggregate demand causes inflation, workers and other resource suppliers will in time push for higher wages and resource prices. Businesses either will require higher product prices to cover the increases in resource prices or they will reduce output at given prices. Either way, the aggregate supply curve shifts leftward and real GNP returns to its potential level in the long run. The long-run aggregate supply curve is vertical at the potential level of real GNP. Only supply-side influences such as the quantity and productivity of resources can shift the long-run aggregate supply curve rightward.

3.   A major reduction in the world price of copper is an example of a favorable supply-side shock. Businesses increase output because the

457

profitability of producing goods has increased at given price levels. The aggregate supply curve shifts rightward, putting downward pressure on the price level and increasing real GNP. In this case, a falling price level and unemployment rate occur simultaneously.

Pop Quiz

1. As of June 1988, the economy appeared to be operating at its potential level of real GNP. The economy's aggregate demand curve intersected its aggregate supply curve at the potential level of real GNP.

2. The level of economic activity beyond which inflation is likely to accelerate is a level of capacity utilization of about 82% to 83%.

3. If the economy continues to experience growth in aggregate demand, capacity utilization could reach 84% by the end of 1988. This level has indicated the beginning of considerable inflationary pressures in past expansions. Investment in capacity is occurring at a brisk pace, but the aggregate supply curve will not shift to the right fast enough to moderate inflationary pressures.

The Outlook

As Output Climbs So Do Capacity Fears

NEW YORK

The two developments, we suspect, aren't entirely unrelated. The remarkable American economy is cruising through its 70th straight month of expansion, a record for peacetime. And the cruise-control mechanism on our family's 1986 Ford Taurus station wagon remains inoperable, cruising nowhere while we await a part ordered many, many weeks ago.

There's no sure way to ascertain just how typical such experiences may be for car owners, or for that matter for owners of all sorts of other items. But evidence keeps mounting of strain on the economy's physical ability to meet demand. And the pattern sends a troubling message about the economy's possible behavior in coming months.

It suggests an environment where business activity, as it continues to gain momentum, will come under increasing difficulty, marked not only by parts shortages but dislocations ranging from costly production bottlenecks to accelerating price increases.

Early indications of such an environment can already be detected, among other places, in the fine print of this month's report of the National Association of Purchasing Management, which regularly polls more than 250 buyers at major corporations. It finds that 20 industrial products are in short supply, up from 18 in July. The scarce products include such diverse items as aluminum, paperboard, methanol and titanium dioxide.

Not surprisingly, the survey also shows that far more companies are experiencing lengthening delivery delays than prompter service, an imbalance that has prevailed now for nearly two years. The survey also lists 35 products whose prices are rising, up from 29 in July. Only one item, fuel oil, shows a drop in price.

The survey isn't so finely focused as to pinpoint the status of cruise-control parts at Ford Motor Co. However, as recently reported in this paper, Ford's car and truck assembly plants are running at capacity, with some 20% of the vehicles sold last quarter produced on overtime shifts, and the firm is weighing building new plants.

Not all manufacturers, to be sure, are keeping as busy as Ford. But there seems little question that capacity usage in general is on the rise. Indeed, it appears to be approaching levels that in the past have usually signaled the onset of strained business operations. In June, the latest month available, U.S. industry as a whole—factories, mines and utilities—used 83.1% of its capacity, after adjustment for seasonal factors. This was up from 82.9% in May and marked the highest monthly rate of operations in more than eight years.

With such a level of operations, "it seems prudent to assume that the economy has started to overheat somewhat," declares Edward S. Hyman Jr., chief economist of C. J. Lawrence, Morgan Grenfell Inc. "From here," he adds, even modest economic growth "will increase these overheating pressures."

Of course, a rapid increase in capacity would presumably serve to prevent any such pressure buildup. But as Richard B. Hoey, chief economist of Drexel Burnham Lambert Inc., remarks, increases in capacity "unfortunately are likely to be too little and too late to head off a progressive tightening of capacity utilization." He foresees, as a result, an acceleration of inflation typical of the "final stages" of a business-cycle upswing.

Parenthetically, it should be noted that economists at Goldman, Sachs & Co. estimate that plant-and-equipment outlays, adjusted for inflation, will climb a robust 8% or 9% this year, which suggests to some analysts an easing of capacity constraints. Lawrence A. Kudlow, chief economist of Bear, Stearns & Co., says that, with capital outlays "hitting new record highs, capacity worries look increasingly unrealistic."

But Mr. Hoey cautions that "a capacity boom isn't guaranteed by the investment boom." Indeed, he notes that most new spending is "for replacement purposes and has only limited benefit for capacity levels." He adds that "many of the larger plant expansions currently under way are unlikely to be fully operational until late 1989 or 1990, too late to ameliorate price pressures in the next 18 months."

A similar assessment comes from Donald H. Straszheim, chief economist of Merrill Lynch & Co., who feels that "despite a pickup in capital spending, capacity growth will continue to lag behind gains in production." By late this year, he estimates, "capacity utilization could exceed 84%," a level, he recalls, that in earlier expansions marked the onset of substantial inflationary pressure.

The record hardly encourages the hope that the current spending surge will translate rapidly and effectively into expanded production facilities. In a recent 12 months, while capital spending rose sharply, capacity edged up less than 3%. The strongest spending increases, moreover, continue to come in outlays for new equipment, which often involves replacement rather than expansion. Spending for structures, brick-and-mortar projects that are more apt to boost capacity, remains relatively weak.

Most economists, it should be added, regard capacity statistics, which the Federal Reserve Board assembles, as woefully imprecise, and Fed officials offer no ready remedy. So no one can be very certain just how much—or how little—elbowroom really does exist in the economy right now. But we do know that our cruise-control unit still needs a part.

—ALFRED L. MALABRE JR.

32
The Functions of Money

CHAPTER CHALLENGES

After studying your text, attending class, and completing this chapter, you should be able to:

1. List the four major functions of money.
2. Discuss the major components of the stock of money.
3. Explain the concept of near money and the official measures of the U.S. money stock and liquid assets held by the public.
4. Discuss the determinants of the demand for money.
5. Explain how, given the demand for money, changes in the stock of money influence interest rates and spending decisions.
6. Explain how, given the stock of money, changes in the demand for money can affect interest rates.

IN BRIEF: CHAPTER SUMMARY

Fill in the blanks to summarize chapter content.

In order to understand the operation of the macroeconomy, it is necessary to understand the role of money. But first it is necessary to define money, identify its functions, consider operational measures of money, and explain how changes in the demand for and supply of money affect interest rates and spending in the economy.

Money is defined according to its functions. Money serves as a medium of (1)_____(exchange, value), a standard of value, a standard of deferred payment, and a store of (2)_____ (exchange, value). Anything performing these functions is money. Money does not have to have intrinsic value such as (3)_____(fiat, commodity) money in order to perform these functions. Fiat money and checkable deposits are considered money not because they have intrinsic value, but because they are accepted as a medium of exchange and fulfill the other functions of money. Bonds and credit cards are (4)_____(not, also) money. Money is an asset--a store of value. Even though credit cards can be used as a medium to facilitate exchange, a liability or debt is incurred when credit cards are used.

Three of the official definitions of money are M1, M2, and M3. M1 is the sum of (5)_____(checkable, savings) deposits, currency, and traveler's checks held by the public on a given day. M2 is the sum of M1 and near monies. Near monies are assets that can easily be converted to money because they can be liquidated easily, quickly, and at little cost. M3 is the sum of M2 and (6)_____(small-, large-) denomination certificates of deposit.

Individuals and businesses hold money for two reasons: to carry out transactions in the economy and because money is an asset. Modern economies require a medium of exchange to facilitate transactions. As an economy experiences growth in nominal GNP, the number and volume of transactions increase, causing the transaction demand for money to (7)_____(increase, decrease). The degree to which receipts and payments are synchronized also affects the need for transaction money balances. In addition, expectations of future interest rates will affect the desire to hold transaction money balances because interest rates influence the (8)_____(liquidity, opportunity cost) of holding money.

Money, like other assets, has certain characteristics that make it more or less attractive to hold relative to other financial assets. Money is held as an asset not because of its income, return, or yield, but because it is (9)_____(totally riskless, liquid). Because individuals and businesses have a (10)_____ (hedging, precautionary) and speculative motive for holding money, liquidity is required to satisfy these motives. Expectations of future interest rates and bond prices affect the desire to hold money relative to other assets. Even expectations of future rates of inflation affect the desirability of holding money as an asset.

The total demand for money is the sum of the transaction and asset demands for money. The quantity of money demanded varies (11)_____(inversely, directly) with the interest rate. Higher interest rates (12)_____(decrease, increase) the opportunity cost of holding money and therefore reduce the quantity of money demanded and vice versa. The factors mentioned above that influence either the transaction or asset demand for money will affect the total demand for money. The money demand curve is (13)_____(upward sloping, downward sloping), but will shift to the right or left depending upon changes in the noninterest rate determinants of money demand, which include (a) the degree to which receipts and payments are synchronized, (b) expectations of future interest rates, stock and bond prices, and rates of inflation, and (c) the level of nominal GNP.

The interest rate is determined by the supply of and demand for loanable funds. A change in the stock of money or demand for money influences the market rate of interest. A change in the interest rate in turn influences the level of spending in the economy and GNP. For instance, given the demand for money, an increase in the supply of money will create a (14)_____(surplus, shortage) of money at the current rate of interest. Since (15)_____(more, less) money is on hand than is desired for transactions or as assets, saving and the buying of bonds are likely to (16)_____(decrease, increase). This (17)_____(decreases, increases) the supply of loanable funds resulting in an/a (18)_____ (increase, decrease) in the interest rate. Interest rates must (19)_____(fall, rise) in order to increase the quantity of money demanded to equal the higher level of the money stock. Likewise, a decline in the money stock (20)_____(increases, decreases) the interest rate.

Given the stock of money, a change in the demand for money will create either a shortage or a surplus of money at the current market rate of interest, causing the loanable funds market to be influenced such that interest rates change in the direction necessary to once again equate the supply of and demand for money. Changes in the interest rate affect interest-sensitive expenditures and thus the level of aggregate demand and GNP.

VOCABULARY REVIEW

Write the key term from the list below next to its definition.

Key Terms

Money
Commodity money
Fiat money
Checkable deposits
Commercial banks
Saving and loan associations
Mutual savings banks
Credit unions
Bonds

M1
Near monies
M2
Time deposits
M3
Transaction demand for money
Demand for money
Money demand curve
Change in money demanded

Definitions

1. _____: money that is accepted as a medium of exchange because of government decree rather than because of its intrinsic value as a commodity.

2. _____: depository institutions whose depositors are called "members" and belong to a particular organization such as a business firm or government; they make loans only to their members for the purpose of financing homes or personal goods and services.

3. _____: assets that are easily converted to money because they can be liquidated at low cost and little risk of loss.

4. _____: the sum of M2 and large-denomination certificates of deposit.

5. _____: the sum of money people wish to hold per day as a convenience in paying their bills.

6. _____: shows a relationship between the level of interest rates in the economy and the stock of money demanded at a given point in time.

7. _____: a change in the relationship between the level of interest rates and the stock of money demanded in the economy caused by a change in economic conditions.

8. _____: an item that serves the functions of money but also has value in uses other than as the medium of exchange.

9. _____: depository institutions operating in some states that are similar to savings and loan associations in that they primarily attract savings deposits and in the past have specialized in making mortgage loans; they are also owned by their depositors.

10. _____: the stock of money measured by the sum of currency, traveler's checks, and checkable deposits held by the public on a particular day of the year in the United States.

11. _____: interest-bearing accounts at commercial banks and thrift institutions for which the bank can legally request a 30-day notice before paying out the funds.

12. _____: the relationship between the sums of money people willingly hold and the level of interest rates in the economy given all other influences on the desirability of holding money instead of other assets.

13. _____: anything that is generally accepted as payment for goods or services; also serves as a standard of value, a standard of deferred payment, and a store of value.

14. _____: depository institutions that acquire funds chiefly through attracting savings deposits and have in the past specialized in making mortgage loans.

15. _____: securities issued by corporations and governments representing the promise to make periodic payments of interest and repay a debt of borrowed funds at a certain time.

16. _____: the sum of M1 and certain near monies; a measure of liquid assets held by the public.

17. _____: firms that acquire funds by accepting checkable deposits and savings deposits of households and business firms and use these funds to make loans for a wide variety of purposes.

18. _____: represents money deposited in bank accounts that can be used to write checks that are accepted to pay debts, or that can easily be converted to currency.

SKILLS REVIEW

Concept: Functions of money

1. List four functions of money.

    a. _____
    b. _____
    c. _____
    d. _____

Concept: Definitions of money; measures of money

2. Using the items given below, define M1, M2, and M3.

    Currency held by the public
    Money market mutual funds
    Money market deposit accounts
    Traveler's checks held by the public
    Checkable deposits held by the public
    Large-denomination certificates of deposit
    Savings accounts, small-denomination certificates of deposit, and
        certain other near monies

    a. M1 = _____

    b. M2 = _____
             _____

    c. M3 = _____
             _____
             _____

d. Near monies = _____

e. Silver dollars are examples of _____ money.
f. Federal Reserve Notes are examples of _____ money.
g. Why are credit cards not considered money?

Concept: **Determinants of the demand for money; money demand curve**

3. a. List and discuss three factors that influence the transaction demand for money.

   (1) _____
   (2) _____
   (3) _____

   b. List and discuss three factors that influence the asset demand for money.

   (1) _____
   (2) _____
   (3) _____

4. The data below show the relationship between the quantity of money demanded and the nominal interest rate holding all other influences unchanged.

Quantity of Money Demanded per Day ($ billions)			Interest Rate (%)
(a)	(b)	(c)	(d)
$ 740			12%
760			11
780			10
800			9
820			8
840			7

a. Plot the money demand curve on the diagram below.

Nominal interest rate (%)

Quantity of money demanded per day (billions of dollars)

b. Why is the money demand curve downward sloping?
c. List the factors that shift the money demand curve.
   (1) _____
   (2) _____
   (3) _____
d. Assume that the data above are for a level of nominal GNP of $4 trillion. Assume nominal GNP increases by $40 billion at each interest rate.
   (1) Complete column b in the table above.
   (2) Plot the new money demand curve on the figure above. The money demand curve has shifted _____.
e. Assume again that the current money demand data are reflected in column a. Assume that expectations of higher future inflation reduce the desirability of holding money as an asset, causing the demand for money to decrease by $60 billion at each interest rate.
   (1) Complete column c in the table above.
   (2) Plot the new money demand curve on the figure above. The money demand curve has shifted _____.

5. For each of the following, indicate whether the money demand curve will shift to the right or left.

   a. Technology and new banking regulations allow employers to electronically deposit paychecks in employees' checkable deposit accounts, and the accounts are automatically drafted to pay the employees' fixed monthly payments such as mortgage payments._____.
   b. Merchants allow customers to use "debit" cards whereby the merchant can electronically transfer funds for a purchase from the customer's checkable deposit account to the merchant's account._____
   c. Credit cards are used more frequently._____
   d. Employers and consumers coordinate their payments and receipts such that paychecks are received and payments are due the first of each month._____
   e. Nominal GNP increases._____

f.　The price level increases._____

g.　New highly liquid and safe financial assets become available earning a rate of interest in excess of that earned by checkable deposits._____

Concept:　Changes in the supply of and demand for money

6.　The data from question 4 above are reproduced below.

Quantity of Money Demanded ($ billions)			Interest Rate (%)
(a)	(b)	(c)	
$740			12%
760			11
780			10
800			9
820			8
840			7

a.　Assume that the stock of money is $780 billion.　Draw the money stock curve on the diagram above.　The equilibrium rate of interest is _____ %.

b.　If the demand for money changes from that shown in column a to that in column b, interest rates will _____ to _____ %.

c.　If the demand for money changes from that shown in column a to that in column c, interest rates will _____ to _____ %.

d.　On the diagrams below:
　　(1)　Show the effect of an increase in the stock of money. Interest rates _____.
　　(2)　Show the effect of a decrease in the stock of money. Interest rates _____.
　　(3)　Show the effect of an increase in both the demand for and supply of money by the same amount.　Interest rates _____.

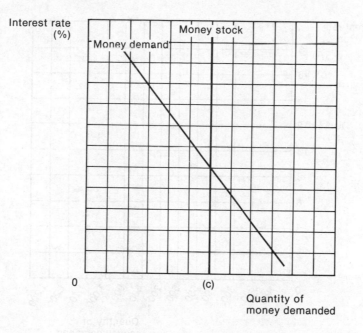

Interest rate (%)

Money demand

Money stock

0

(c)

Quantity of
money demanded

7. __Advanced Question__ Let the supply of and demand for money be given by the equations below.

MT = a - bR   where MT = transaction demand
MA = c - dR   MA = asset demand
MS = M1   MS = money stock
                          M1 = currency, checkable deposits, and
                               traveler's checks held by the public
                          R = interest rate

Constants a and c reflect the impact of noninterest rate determinants on the transaction and asset money demands, respectively. Constants b and d are the slope terms indicating the magnitude of the effect that a change in R has on MT and MA, respectively.

a. Find an equation for the total demand for money, MD.
b. Find an equation for the equilibrium interest rate. (Hint: The condition for equilibrium is that MD = MS.)
c. Using your equation for R, discuss the factors that cause R to rise or fall.
d. Given the values below, plot MA, MT, and MD on the figure below. Draw in the money stock curve. Identify on the diagram the equilibrium rate of interest.

    a = $800 billion b = $10 billion c = $400 billion
    d = $40 billion M1 = $850 billion

467

Interest rate
(%)

Quantity of
money demaned
(billions of dollars)

SELF-TEST FOR MASTERY

Select the best answer.

1. Money allows dissimilar goods and services to be valued according to a
   single common denominator--a nation's basic monetary unit, such as the
   dollar. Which of the following represent this function?

   a. Medium of exchange
   b. Store of value
   c. Standard of value
   d. Standard of deferred payment

2. Money is an asset. Which of the following represents this function?

   a. Medium of exchange
   b. Store of value
   c. Standard of value
   d. Standard of deferred payment

3. _____ money has value in exchange and intrinsic value in nonmoney
   uses.

   a. Fiat
   b. Commodity
   c. Valuable
   d. All

4. Money that, by government decree must be accepted in exchange and for the
   payment of debt is known as:

   a. Fiat money.
   b. Commodity money.

c. Demand deposits.
d. Gold.

5. One function of money that credit cards are unable to fulfill is:

   a. The medium of exchange function.
   b. The store of value function.
   c. The standard of value function.
   d. The standard of deferred payment function.

6. The sum of currency, traveler's checks, and checkable deposits held by the public is known as:

   a. M1.
   b. M2.
   c. M3.
   d. L.

7. The sum of currency, traveler's checks, checkable deposits, and certain near monies held by the public is known as:

   a. M1.
   b. M2.
   c. M3.
   d. L.

8. _____ are assets that can easily be converted to money because they can be liquidated easily, quickly, and at little cost.

   a. Large-denomination certificates of deposit
   b. Near monies
   c. Pension funds
   d. Real estate

9. Individuals and businesses hold money because:

   a. Money is necessary to carry out transactions, and it is also an asset.
   b. It is profitable to do so.
   c. It must be used to make exchanges.
   d. Nothing else can be used in a commercial transaction.

10. Which of the following financial characteristics makes money attractive as an asset?

    a. Liquidity
    b. Return or yield
    c. Risk
    d. Availability

11. A/An _____ in nominal GNP shifts the money demand curve _____.

    a. Decrease, rightward
    b. Increase, leftward
    c. Decrease, leftward
    d. Increase, rightward
    e. C and d.

12. Which of the following will shift the money demand curve leftward?

    a.   Payments and receipts become more synchronized.
    b.   The price level declines.
    c.   The level of nominal GNP decreases.
    d.   All of the above.

13. The quantity of money demanded varies _____ with the nominal interest rate. Higher interest rates _____ the opportunity cost of holding money and therefore reduce the quantity of money demanded.

    a.   Directly, reduce
    b.   Inversely, increase
    c.   Directly, increase
    d.   Inversely, reduce

14. An increase in the stock of money creates a _____ of money at the current rate of interest. This in turn_____ the supply of loanable funds, which, given the demand for loanable funds, causes the market rate of interest to _____.

    a.   Shortage, reduces, rise
    b.   Shortage, reduces, fall
    c.   Surplus, reduces, rise
    d.   Surplus, increases, fall

15. A decrease in the stock of money causes interest rates to:

    a.   Fall.
    b.   Rise.
    c.   Not change.
    d.   None of the above.

16. If the demand for money and the stock of money increased by the same amount at each interest rate, interest rates would:

    a.   Fall.
    b.   Rise.
    c.   Not change.
    d.   None of the above.

17. If the demand for money decreases, interest rates will _____ and nominal GNP will _____.

    a.   Fall, fall
    b.   Rise, fall
    c.   Fall, rise
    d.   Rise, rise

THINK IT THROUGH

1.   Can you think of any problems associated with the use of commodity money?

2.   Why can't government bureaucrats simply make up their minds and select a single definition of money? Can you think of any reasons why are there several official definitions and why these definitions change over time?

3.   Why do individuals and businesses hold money? What factors influence the desirability of holding money?

4.   Suppose you are a producer of household appliances. Further assume that most appliance purchases are made on credit. You also have observed in the past that sales increase when nominal GNP increases. What would you predict for sales if you knew that the nation's central banking authorities were deliberately reducing the stock of money?

CHAPTER ANSWERS

In Brief: Chapter Summary

1. Exchange 2. Value 3. Commodity 4. Not 5. Checkable 6. Large- 7. Increase 8. Opportunity cost 9. Liquid 10. Precautionary 11. Inversely 12. Increase 13. Downward sloping 14. Surplus 15. More 16. Increase 17. Increases 18. Decrease 19. Fall 20. Increases

Vocabulary Review

1. Fiat money 2. Credit unions 3. Near monies 4. M3 5. Transaction demand for money 6. Money demand curve 7. Change in money demanded 8. Commodity money 9. Mutual savings banks 10. M1 11. Time deposits 12. Demand for money 13. Money 14. Savings and loan associations 15. Bonds 16. M2 17. Commercial banks 18. Checkable deposits

Skills Review

1.   a.   Medium of exchange
      b.   Store of value
      c.   Standard of value
      d.   Standard of deferred payment

2.   a.   M1 = currency + traveler's checks + checkable deposits held by the public.
      b.   M2 = M1 + money market mutual funds + money market deposit accounts + savings accounts, small-denomination certificates of deposit, and certain other near monies.
      c.   M3 = M2 + large-denomination certificates of deposit.
      d.   Near monies = money market mutual funds + money market deposit accounts + savings accounts, small-denomination certificates of deposit, and certain other near monies.
      e.   Commodity
      f.   Fiat
      g.   Money is an asset, whereas a liability or debt is incurred when credit cards are used. Credit cards do not satisfy the store of value function of money.

3.   a.   (1) Nominal GNP (2) Synchronization of receipts and payments
            (3) Interest rates
      b.   (1) Interest rates (2) Expectations of inflation
            (3) Expectations of interest rates and bond prices

4. a.

Nominal interest rate (%)

Money stock = $780 billion (Question 6)

(c)

(a) (b)
(Question 4)

Quantity of money demanded per day (billions of dollars)

b. The money demand curve is downward sloping because the nominal interest rate and the quantity of money demanded are inversely related. As interest rates rise, the opportunity cost of holding money increases, which reduces the desirability of holding noninterest-bearing or low interest-yielding assets such as money.

c. (1) Synchronization of receipts and payments (2) Changes in real GNP (3) Changes in the price level (4) Expectations of inflation, interest rates, and bond prices

d. (1) (2) Rightward   e. (1) (2) Leftward

$780	$680
800	700
820	720
840	740
860	760
880	780

5. a. Left b. Left c. Left d. Left e. Right f. Right g. Left

6. a. 10% b. Increase, 12% c. Decrease, 7%
d. (1) Decrease (2) Increase (3) Remain unchanged

7. a. MD = MT + MA = (a + c) - (b + d)R
   b. Equilibrium requires that MD = MS

      M1 = (a + c) - (b + d)R

      Solving for R gives

      R = (a + c)/(b + d) - [1/(b + d)] x M1

   c. The negative sign preceding the last term in the interest rate
      equation shows that the stock of money, M1, is inversely related to
      the equilibrium interest rate. Notice that the shift terms, a and c,
      appear in the intercept of the interest rate equation. Any
      noninterest rate determinant of MT or MA that increases (a + c) will
      increase the interest rate. A change in one of these determinants
      that reduces (a + c) will reduce the interest rate. Likewise,
      changes in the slope of the transaction and asset money demand curves
      will change the interest rate.
   d. MT = 800 - 10R   MA = 400 - 40R   MD = 1200 - 50R
      R = 24 - (1/50)R

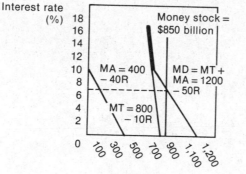

Quantity of
money demanded
(billions of dollars)

Self-Test for Mastery

1. c 2. b 3. b 4. a 5. b 6. a 7. b 8. b 9. a 10. a 11. e 12. d 13.
b 14. d 15. b 16. c 17. c

Think it Through

1.   Besides being difficult or hazardous to transport, such as was the case
with gold and silver coins, commodity money often disappears from circulation
when the market value of the commodity rises above the exchange value of money.

2.   As new financial instruments are created such as NOW accounts and money
market mutual funds, individuals in their own self-interest alter the
composition of assets that are used to meet liquidity, risk, and income needs.
Utility-maximizing choices lead us to use certain items to fulfill the
functions of money. As long as financial innovations continue to occur and as
long as the characteristics of assets change relative to one another, the money
stock will continue to evolve. As a result, the central banking authorities
must continually redefine money.

3.   Individuals hold money (a) as an asset because it is liquid and (b)
because it is an efficient way to consummate transactions. The demand for
money is inversely related to the interest rate because an increase in the
interest rate increases the opportunity cost of holding money and reduces the
quantity of money demanded. Other factors that influence the demand for money
include the synchronization of receipts and payments, the level of real GNP,

the price level, and expectations of inflation, interest rates, and bond prices.

4.   If the money stock decreases, it is likely that, other things being equal, interest rates will rise, making credit more costly to your customers. Total spending and GNP will decrease due to the higher rates of interest. Two factors therefore indicate that household appliance sales will fall: higher interest rates making credit more expensive, and a decline in nominal GNP.

33

The Banking System

CHAPTER CHALLENGES

After studying your text, attending class, and completing this chapter, you should be able to:

1. Discuss the origins of banking and explain the concept of fractional reserve banking.
2. Examine bank balance sheets and show how the balance sheets are affected when the bank makes loans.
3. Show how multiple expansion of the money stock can result from an inflow of excess reserves into banks and calculate the reserve multiplier.
4. Discuss bank portfolio management practices.

IN BRIEF: CHAPTER SUMMARY

Fill in the blanks to summarize chapter content.

In order to understand the role of money and financial institutions in the economy, it is necessary first to understand how the activities of financial institutions influence the nation's stock of money. The goldsmiths of England and the moneychangers of Italy engaged in "banking" by accepting gold for safekeeping and issuing gold receipts. In time, the receipts began to trade as a medium of exchange or money. But these early bankers discovered that (1)_____(all of the, only a fraction of the) gold had to be held in reserve at any one time to honor redemption of the gold receipts. They could therefore make loans (2)_____(equal to, in excess of) the gold they had on hand. They did this by issuing additional gold receipts--they in essence created money. The fractional reserve banking that developed meant that the stock of money (3)_____ (must equal, could be larger than) the gold reserves upon which it was based.

In depository institutions today, only a fraction of the funds acquired through deposits have to be kept back as reserves. A bank's (4)_____(total, required) reserves consist of cash and deposits held at a regional Federal Reserve Bank. But banks and other depository institutions that issue checkable deposits are required to keep reserves equal to between 3% and 12% of various deposit liabilities. A bank will balance profit, liquidity, and risk considerations in deciding the amount of (5)_____ (total, excess) reserves it desires to use to acquire income-producing assets such as loans and government securities. Excess reserves are the difference between total reserves and required reserves. While a depository institution does not have to use all of its excess reserves, it (6)_____(can, cannot) make loans or purchase securities in amounts greater than the amount it has as excess reserves. When a bank uses excess reserves to make a loan, new checkable deposits are created--money is created. Even if the borrower spends the proceeds of the loan by writing a check, the funds eventually end up in the check recipient's checkable deposit account elsewhere in the banking system.

An individual bank can increase checkable deposits or the money supply to the extent of its excess reserves by (7)_____(making loans or purchasing securities, advertising bank services), but the banking system as a whole can increase the stock of money by (8)_____(less than, a multiple of) its excess reserves. For instance, when a bank makes a loan, not only does it create new checkable deposits somewhere in the banking system, but it also passes excess reserves to other banks through the (9)_____ (financial, check clearing) system. Banks receiving deposits and reserves likewise make loans, increasing deposits and passing excess reserves to still other banks, which in turn do the same.

Each bank, however, has to keep some percentage of the new deposits back as required reserves, thus reducing the quantity of excess reserves available for loans and the quantity of reserves passed on to other banks. The percentage of deposit liabilities that must be held back is called the (10)_____ (required reserve ratio, discount rate). This process of deposit growth continues until there are no additional excess reserves in the system. At this point banks are (11)_____ (deficient, "loaned up"), meaning they have no excess reserves and can no longer make loans and create money. The stock of checkable deposits (money) can potentially expand by the reciprocal of the required reserve ratio times the quantity of excess reserves. The reciprocal of the required reserve ratio is known as the (12)_____(reserve multiplier, expansion coefficient). The process works just the opposite when banks find that their total reserves are less than required reserves. To acquire reserves or reduce required reserves in order to eliminate this deficiency, banks engage in activities that (13)_____(increase, reduce) the volume of checkable deposits.

As of January 1988, U.S. banks had reserves equal to 7.5% of total assets. Their (14)_____ (primary, secondary) reserves or government securities and other liquid securities were 18.4% of total assets. Loans accounted for (15)_____ (67%, 34%) of total assets. The largest share of funds (50%) acquired to purchase assets was obtained from saving deposits and certificates of deposits. Checkable deposits accounted for (16)_____ (40%, 20%) of total liabilities and capital. Net worth equaled 6% of total assets.

As of the beginning of the 1980s, with the enactment of the Depository Institutions Deregulation and Monetary Control Act of 1980, depository institutions such as credit unions, mutual savings banks, and savings and loan associations began to compete with banks by offering traditional banking services such as checking accounts. Whereas prior to 1980 only banks could create money, today all depository institutions with checkable deposits are involved in the process of money creation.

VOCABULARY REVIEW

Write the key term from the list below next to its definition.

Key Terms

Depository institutions	Excess reserves
Bank	Default
Financial intermediaries	Check clearing
Fractional reserve banking	Reserve multiplier
Fractional reserve ratio	Prime rate
Reserves	Collateral
Required reserve ratio	Government securities
Required reserves	Secondary reserves

Definitions

1. _____: firms that specialize in borrowing funds from savers and lending those funds to investors and others.

2. _____: a process by which a banking system creates checkable deposits by making loans in some multiple of the reserves it actually has on hand to pay withdrawals.

3. _____: balances (of a modern U.S. bank) kept on deposit with the Federal Reserve Bank in its district or a currency in its vault.

4. _____: nonrepayment of the principal and interest on a loan.

5. _____: the process of transferring Federal Reserve deposits among banks as checks are paid.

6. _____: the maximum amount of new money stock that can be created from each dollar increase in excess reserves available to the banking system.

7. _____: government securities held by banks.

8. _____: a commercial bank or thrift institution that offers checkable deposits.

9. _____: the ratio of actual reserves to total receipts for deposits.

10. _____: the difference between total reserves and required reserves of a bank held against deposits.

11. _____: interest-bearing debts of the federal government in the form of Treasury bills, Treasury notes, and Treasury bonds.

12. _____: those that make loans and offer checkable deposit and time deposit accounts for use by households and business firms.

13. _____: the dollar value of currency and deposits in Federal Reserve Banks that a bank must hold to meet current regulations.

14. _____: an asset a borrower pledges to a bank in case of default.

15. _____: the minimum percentage of deposits that a bank must hold in reserves to comply with regulatory requirements.

16. _____: the interest rate a bank charges its most credit worthy customers for short-term loans of less than 1 year.

SKILLS REVIEW

Concept: Examine a bank's balance sheet; impact of making a loan on the
          balance sheet

1.   Identify the following as either an asset (A) or a liability (L) of a
      commercial bank.

      a. ____ Certificates of deposit   g. ____ Reserve deposits at
      b. ____ Cash   Federal Reserve
      c. ____ Total reserves   h. ____ Loans
      d. ____ Bank building and   i. ____ Government secur-
              property   ities
      e. ____ Checkable deposits   j. ____ Borrowings
      f. ____ Time and saving
              deposits

2.   a.   Discuss the logic of the basic accounting identity.
      b.   Why must balance sheets balance at a given point in time?

3.   Given a balance sheet for a commercial bank, answer parts a-d assuming a
      required reserve ratio on checkable deposits of 10%.

Assets		Liabilities and Net Worth	
Cash	$ 200	Checkable deposits	$ 2,000
Reserve deposits	550	Savings and time	
Loans	6,700	deposits	5,000
Securities	1,840	Borrowings	2,400
Bank building		Net worth	600
and property	710		
Total Assets	$10,000	Total Liabilities	$10,000
		and Net Worth	

      a.   Total reserves = _____.
      b.   Required reserves = _____.
      c.   Excess reserves equal = _____.
      d.   This bank can make loans of $_____.

4.   Reserve deposits, loans, and checkable deposits are reproduced from the
      balance sheet above in the balance sheet below.

Assets		Liabilities and Net Worth	
Reserve deposits	$ 550	Checkable deposits	$2,000
Loans	6,700		

      a.   Indicate on the balance sheet above the impact of a loan of $550 to
           one of the bank's customer-depositors. Designate your entries with
           an (a). (Hint: For every entry there must be an offsetting entry.)
           Total assets have _____ to $_____, and total liabilities have
           _____ to $_____.
      b.   Assume now that the customer spends the proceeds of the loan by
           writing a check to a merchant for $550. Assume that the merchant
           deposits the check in a bank in the same Federal Reserve district and
           the check is routed to the Fed and back to the originating bank via
           the check clearing process. Indicate the impact of this on the
           balance sheet above and designate your entries with a (b). This

bank's checkable deposits have _____ to $_____, but total
reserves have _____ to $_____. Excess reserves equal
$_____. Total loans equal $_____.

c. Can this bank make loans in excess of its excess reserves? Why?
d. As a result of this loan, the stock of money has _____ by
$_____.

Concept: Multiple expansion of the money stock

5. The following assumptions pertain to the banking system:

i. Commercial Bank A has $100 in excess reserves.
ii. Required reserve ratio = 20%
iii. Other banks are presently "loaned up."
iv. All banks use all of their excess reserves to make loans.
v. Bank A makes loans to its customers that, after the check clearing
process, end up as deposits in Bank B. Similarly, Bank B makes loans
to its customers that end up as deposits in Bank C, and so on.

a. Make the final entries on each bank's balance sheet assuming
initially that Bank A makes a loan to the extent of its excess
reserves. Trace the impact from Bank A through Bank D on the balance
sheets below. (The final entries are after banks have loaned excess
reserves, customers have spent the proceeds of the loans, and the
checks have cleared.)

Bank A

Assets	Liabilities and Net Worth
Reserve deposits	Checkable deposits
Loans	

Bank B

Assets	Liabilities and Net Worth
Reserve deposits	Checkable deposits
Loans	

Bank C

Assets	Liabilities and Net Worth
Reserve deposits	Checkable deposits
Loans	

Bank D

Assets	Liabilities and Net Worth
Reserve deposits	Checkable deposits
Loans	

b. Complete the following table.

Bank	Change in Required Reserves	Change in Money Stock
A		
B		
C		
D		

c. The expansion of the money supply continues until the _____ just equals the initial excess reserves of $100. At this point, excess reserves in the banking system equal $_____. When this occurs, the money stock has increased by $_____.

6. Find the change in the money stock for the banking system by filling in the blanks below.

	Required Reserve Ratio	Change in Excess Reserves	Change in Checkable Deposits
a.	.1	+$1 billion	
b.	.2	0	
c.	.25	-$500 million	
d.	.4	+$10 billion	
e.	.5	-$5 billion	

SELF-TEST FOR MASTERY

Select the best answer.

1. Early bankers, the goldsmiths of England and the moneychangers of Italy, accepted deposits of gold for safekeeping and in return issued gold receipts. These early bankers were similar to modern bankers in that:

    a. They created a medium of exchange.
    b. They had a fractional reserve (gold) system.
    c. They accepted deposits and made loans.
    d. Gold receipts (medium of exchange) could be issued in greater volume than the gold (reserves) upon which they were based.
    e. All of the above.

2. The fractional reserve system means that:

    a. Only a fraction of bank assets at any one time may be used to create money.
    b. A bank receives only a fraction of the reserves that it needs at any given time.
    c. Only a fraction of a bank's liabilities must be held back as reserves to meet withdrawals at any one time.
    d. None of the above.

480

3. A bank's total reserves consist of:

   a. Liquid assets such as private commercial paper and Treasury bills.
   b. Cash and Treasury bills.
   c. Cash only.
   d. Cash and reserve deposits held at a regional Federal Reserve Bank.

4. A bank's required reserves are determined by:

   a. Multiplying the required reserve ratio by certain deposit liabilities.
   b. Dividing total assets by net worth.
   c. Dividing the required reserve ratio into demand deposits.
   d. The U.S. Treasury.
   e. A and d.

5. The difference between total and required reserves is known as:

   a. The required reserve ratio.
   b. Fractional reserves.
   c. Extra reserves.
   d. Excess reserves.

6. Excess reserves are important to a banker because:

   a. If they are not met, the banking regulators will shut the bank down.
   b. They represent the funds available to acquire income-producing assets such as loans and securities.
   c. They are typically deposited in special high-yielding investment accounts.
   d. They are the profits that are divided among the bank's owners.

7. An individual bank can create deposits to the extent of its:

   a. Excess reserves.
   b. Required reserves.
   c. Total reserves.
   d. Deposits.
   e. Net worth.

8. A bank is "loaned up" when:

   a. Deposits are no longer coming in.
   b. Excess reserves are negative.
   c. Excess reserves are zero.
   d. Total reserves are zero.

9. The banking system can increase the stock of money by an amount
   _____ an increase in excess reserves.

   a. Less than
   b. The same as
   c. Greater than
   d. Less than or equal to

10. The reserve multiplier is:

    a. The ratio of required reserves to total reserves.
    b. The required reserve ratio multiplied by certain deposit liabilities.
    c. The number by which the total stock of reserves changes given a change in excess reserves.
    d. The number by which the total stock of money changes given a change in excess reserves.

11. The reciprocal of the required reserve ratio is the:

    a. Depository institutions capital ratio.
    b. Reserve multiplier.
    c. Bank's required reserves.
    d. Measure of excess reserves that the banker desires to use to make loans.

12. Assume that a bank in the banking system has $1,000 in total reserves and $5,000 in checkable deposits, and the required reserve ratio on checkable deposits is 10%. This bank's excess reserves equal:

    a. Zero; it is loaned up.
    b. $250.
    c. $500.
    d. $750.

13. Assume that a bank in the banking system has $2 million in reserves and checkable deposits of $9 million, and the required reserve ratio on checkable deposits is 20%. The maximum amount of loans this bank can make is:

    a. $1 million.
    b. $500,000.
    c. $700,000.
    d. $200,000.

14. Assume that a bank in the banking system has $1 billion in reserves and checkable deposits of $6 billion, and the required reserve ratio on checkable deposits is 10%. The maximum amount by which the banking system can expand the money supply is:

    a. $4 billion.
    b. $6 billion.
    c. $8 billion.
    d. $10 billion.

15. Total reserves of the banking system of $400 billion could potentially support $_____ of checkable deposits assuming a required reserve ratio of 25%.

    a. $400 billion
    b. $700 billion
    c. $1200 billion
    d. $1600 billion

16. If a banking system is loaned up and the Federal Reserve engages in activities that withdraw reserves from the system:

    a. The money supply will expand.
    b. The money supply will decrease.

c.   The FDIC will intervene to replace the reserves.
d.   Checkable deposits will increase.

17. As of January 1988, U.S. banks on average held _____ % of their total assets as loans and _____ % of their total liabilities and capital as checkable deposits.

   a.   67, 20
   b.   40, 30
   c.   34, 58
   d.   20, 67
   e.   50, 18.4

18. As of January 1988, U.S. banks' reserves as a percentage of total bank assets equaled:

   a.   15%.
   b.   12%.
   c.   6%.
   d.   7.5%.

19. Whereas prior to 1980 only banks could create money, today because of _____ all depository institutions with checkable deposits are involved in the process of money creation.

   a.   The Federal Reserve Act
   b.   The FDIC
   c.   The Fiscal Responsibility Act of 1980
   d.   The Depository Institutions Deregulation and Monetary Control Act of 1980

20. Secondary reserves consist of:

   a.   Cash.
   b.   Cash and government securities.
   c.   Cash, reserve deposits, and government securities.
   d.   Government securities and other liquid securities.

THINK IT THROUGH

1.   Discuss the philosophy behind fractional reserve banking. What is the implication of fractional reserve banking for the multiple expansion of the money stock in terms of the role of depository institutions?

2.   Suppose you are a banker and you have difficulty predicting deposits and withdrawals. At times you unexpectedly experience large withdrawals from checkable deposits. How might this influence your decision to use excess reserves? If there are many other bankers like you in the banking system, how might the deposit expansion process be affected?

3.   Why can't a bank make loans in amounts greater than the bank's excess reserves? What would happen if more loans were extended than could be supported by excess reserves?

4.   Discuss the reserve multiplier and the multiple expansion of the money stock.

5.   What is the significance of the Depository Institutions Deregulation and Monetary Control Act of 1980 for the money expansion process?

CHAPTER ANSWERS

In Brief: Chapter Summary

1. Only a fraction of the 2. In excess of 3. Could be larger than 4. Total 5. Excess 6. Cannot 7. Making loans or purchasing securities 8. A multiple of 9. Check clearing 10. Required reserve ratio 11. "Loaned up" 12. Reserve multiplier 13. Reduce 14. Secondary 15. 67% 16. 20%

Vocabulary Review

1. Financial intermediaries   2. Fractional reserve banking 3. Reserves 4. Default 5. Check clearing 6. Reserve multiplier 7. Secondary reserves 8. Bank 9. Fractional reserve ratio 10. Excess reserves 11. Government securities 12. Depository institutions 13. Required reserves 14. Collateral 15. Required reserve ratio 16. Prime rate

Skills Review

1.   a. L b. A c. A d. A e. L f. L g. A h. A i. A j. L

2.   a.   Assets must be exactly equal to the sum of liabilities and net worth. Assets are acquired with funds that you either own or borrow. For a depository institution, assets represent the uses of funds and deposits, and borrowings and net worth represent the sources of funds.
      b.   For the accounting identity to hold, any change in assets or liabilities and net worth must have an offsetting change in the asset or liability and net worth accounts on the balance sheet. Therefore, regardless of the entries made to a balance sheet, the offsetting entries ensure that the two sides of the balance sheet always balance.

3.   a. $750 b. $200 c. $550 d. $550

4.   a.

Assets		Liabilities and Net Worth	
Reserve deposits	$ 550	Checkable deposits	$2,000
(b)	-550	(a)	550
Loans	6,700	(b)	-550
(a)	550		

Increased, $7,250; increased, $2,550
      b.   Decreased, $2000; fallen, $200, $0; $7,250
      c.   No. If this bank makes loans in excess of its excess reserves, $550, then after borrowers spend the proceeds of the loans and the checks clear, the bank will not have enough total reserves to meet its legal reserve requirement.
      d.   Increased, $550

5.   a.   Bank A

Assets		Liabilities and Net Worth
Reserve deposits	-$100	Checkable deposits
Loans	100	

484

```
                        Bank B

        Assets                   Liabilities and Net Worth

        Reserve deposits   $20   Checkable deposits $100
        Loans               80

                        Bank C

        Assets                   Liabilities and Net Worth

        Reserve deposits   $16   Checkable deposits $80
        Loans               64

                        Bank D

        Assets                   Liabilities and Net Worth

        Reserve deposits   $12.8 Checkable deposits $64
        Loans               51.2

    b.   A    ---         ---
         B    $20         $100
         C     16          80
         D     12.8        64

    c.   Increase in required reserves; $0; $500

6.  a.   $10 billion  b. $0  c. -$2 billion  d. $25 billion  e. -$10 billion
```

Self-Test for Mastery

1. e 2. c 3. d 4. a 5. d 6. b 7. a 8. c 9. c 10. d 11. b 12. c 13. d 14. a 15. d 16. b 17. a 18. d 19. d 20. d

Think It Through

1. On any given day, deposit withdrawals are only a fraction of total deposits. Therefore, to meet withdrawals banks need to keep only a fraction of total assets in the form of liquid assets such as cash and reserve deposits. The upshot of this is that banks can create deposits by making loans with excess reserves and the banking system can create a money stock that is a multiple of the reserve base upon which it rests.

2. Given the uncertainty regarding the fluctuations in checkable deposit balances, it would be wise to maintain a cushion of excess reserves as a contingency against deposit outflows that might otherwise put the bank in a deficient reserve position. Of course, in doing this you sacrifice potential income, but you also reduce the risk confronting the bank. For the banking system as a whole, this implies that some portion of excess reserves is held back, thus reducing the stock of money that can be supported by a given stock of bank reserves. The reserve multiplier will also be smaller.

3. If more loans were extended than could be funded with excess reserves, a bank would not be meeting its legal reserve requirement. This is because once the proceeds of the loans are spent and the checks clear, the bank loses total reserves equal to the loans--which are greater than excess reserves. The bank would then either have to increase total reserves by borrowing or selling other assets, or it would have to reduce checkable deposits in order to reduce required reserves.

4.   The expansion process occurs because of the fractional reserve system. A portion of a bank's excess reserves is passed on to other banks in the banking system as a result of loans and cleared checks. The only thing that prevents this expansion from occurring indefinitely is that some of the excess reserves must be held back as required reserves by those banks experiencing deposit inflows. Eventually all of the initial excess reserves will be absorbed in the banking system as required reserves, leaving none as excess reserves for further expansion of deposits. The process is an infinite geometric progression that can be solved yielding the reserve multiplier, 1/required reserve ratio, as part of the solution.

5.   The act allows credit unions, savings and loan associations, and mutual savings banks to compete with banks for checkable deposits and consumer and business loans. The significance of the act for the money expansion process is that banks are no longer the only institutions that can create money by making loans. Now all depository institutions having checkable deposits can create money by making loans. The act also brings all depository institutions offering checkable deposits under uniform reserve ratios administered by the Federal Reserve System.

34

The Federal Reserve System and Its Influence
on Money and Credit

CHAPTER CHALLENGES

After studying your text, attending class, and completing this chapter, you should be able to:

1. Discuss the organization and structure of the Federal Reserve System.
2. Examine the balance sheet of the Federal Reserve Banks and discuss the techniques used by the Fed to influence the money supply.
3. Show how the Fed's open market operations affect bank reserves, securities prices, interest rates, and the money supply.
4. Analyze the nation's money supply curve and show how desires by banks to hold excess reserves affect the quantity of money supplied.

IN BRIEF: CHAPTER SUMMARY

Fill in the blanks to summarize chapter content.

The Federal Reserve System was established in 1913. It consists of a Board of Governors, (1)_____(twelve, seven) regional Federal Reserve Banks and their branch banks, the Federal Open Market Committee, and the Federal Advisory Council. The Chairman of the Board of Governors is appointed by the President to a 4-year term, whereas the other (2)_____(three, six) board members are appointed to 14-year terms. The Federal Reserve Banks are owned by the member banks in their respective districts. The Federal (3)_____ (Advisory, Open Market) Committee is the principal policy-making body within the Federal Reserve System. It issues directives to the account manager at the trading desk of the New York Federal Reserve Bank to achieve some level of money growth during a given time period. The account manager does this by buying and selling U.S. government securities. The Fed is to some extent independent of the legislative and administrative levels of the federal government in that it does not rely upon Congressional funding, but instead earns its own operating revenues.

The major asset of the Federal Reserve System is its holdings of (4)_____ (U.S. government securities, Federal Reserve Notes). Other assets include loans to banks (discounts and advances), certificates issued by the U.S. Treasury, cash items in process of collection, coin, foreign currencies, debt obligations of federal agencies, and bank property and equipment. The largest liability of the system is (5)_____(U.S. government securities, Federal Reserve Notes). Other liabilities include deposits by banks, foreign nations, and the U.S. Treasury.

The supply of money equals the monetary base times the reserve multiplier. The (6)_____(monetary base, reserve sum) is the sum of currency in the hands of the public and total bank reserves. Total checkable deposits equal total reserves times the reserve multiplier. The Fed can influence both the monetary base (volume of reserves) and the reserve multiplier. The money expansion process is also influenced by the decisions of bankers regarding the quantity of excess reserves that are held and not used to make loans. The Fed can influence the money supply in three ways: changing the required reserve ratio, changing the (7)_____ (interest, discount) rate, and either buying or selling U.S. government securities.

An/A (8)_____(increase, decrease) in the reserve ratio does not affect total reserves, but it does reduce excess reserves and therefore contracts the money stock. An/A (9)_____ (increase, decrease) in the reserve ratio increases excess reserves and the money stock. An/A (10)_____ (increase, decrease) in the discount rate relative to the yields on short-term government securities reduces both total and excess reserves in the banking system and contracts the money supply. An/A (11)_____(increase, decrease) in the discount rate increases total and excess reserves and increases the money stock. Open market (12)_____(purchases, sales) of securities to banks reduce reserves, the monetary base, and the money supply. (13)_____(Purchases from, Sales to) the public will have the same effect if the public pays for the securities by check rather than by cash. Open market (14)_____ (purchases from, sales to) banks or the public will increase reserves, the monetary base, and the money stock. The most important of the three tools of monetary control is (15)_____ (open market operations, the discount rate, the required reserve ratio). Changes in the discount rate are important but often lag behind rather than cause changes in interest rates. The required reserve ratio, while very powerful, is not used as a money management tool.

Open market transactions affect the economy immediately in that the Fed buys and sells such a large volume of securities that securities prices and their yields (interest rates) are affected. A Fed purchase of securities (16)_____ (increases, reduces) the outstanding supply of securities held by the public and causes securities prices to (17)_____ (rise, fall) and interest rates to (18)_____ (rise, fall). A Fed sale of securities (19)_____ (increases, decreases) the supply of securities held by the public, which (20)_____ (increases, reduces) securities prices and (21)_____ (increases, decreases) interest rates. But open market transactions also affect bank excess reserves and the total stock of money. As the supply of money changes relative to the demand for money, interest rates will change. A purchase of securities (22)_____ (decreases, increases) excess reserves and (23)_____ (decreases, increases) the supply of money relative to the demand for money causing the interest rate to (24)_____ (fall, rise). A sale of securities (25)_____ (increases, reduces) excess reserves and the supply of money relative to the demand for money and causes the interest rate to (26)_____ (decrease, increase).

The supply of money is positively related to the interest rate because of the relationship between the interest rate and bankers' propensities to hold some excess reserves rather than use them for loans. Interest rates rise as the economy approaches a higher level of economic activity, but this is the time when loan demand is strong and the opportunity cost of holding noninterest-bearing assets is high. Therefore bankers (27)_____ (reduce, increase) their holdings of excess reserves. Just the opposite is generally true of recessions. The demand for loans is less, interest rates are lower, and the opportunity cost of holding reserves is lower. Bankers prefer to hold (28)_____ (less, more) excess reserves in recessions. So when interest rates are high, excess reserves held are (29)_____(smaller, larger) and the stock of money is correspondingly (30)_____(smaller, larger). Conversely, at lower rates of interest, excess reserves held are (31)_____ (smaller, larger) and the stock of money is (32)_____ (larger, smaller). This produces a/an (33)_____(vertical, upward sloping) money supply curve.

VOCABULARY REVIEW

Write the key term from the list below next to its definition.

Key Terms

Board of Governors of the
   Federal Reserve System
Regional Federal Reserve Banks
Monetary base
Federal Open Market Committee

Discount rate
Open market operations
Discount loans
Money supply

Definitions

1. _____: an arm of the Federal Reserve System; affects the amount of excess reserves available to banks by instructing the Federal Reserve Bank of New York to buy or sell government securities on the open market.

2. _____: the sum of currency in circulation and total bank reserves outstanding at any given time.

3. _____: the Federal Reserve System's purchases and sales of government securities, conducted by the Federal Open Market Committee.

4. _____: bank borrowings from the Federal Reserve System; also called advances.

5. _____: a relationship between the quantity of money supplied in the form of currency and checkable deposits and the level of interest rates prevailing at a given point in time.

6. _____: perform central banking functions for banks within each of 12 Federal Reserve districts.

7. _____: the interest rate Federal Reserve Banks charge member banks for loans.

8. _____: supervises the operation of the nation's banking system and acts as an authority to regulate the money supply.

SKILLS REVIEW

Concept: Balance sheet of the Federal Reserve; techniques to control the money stock

1. Identify each of the following as either an asset (A) or a liability (L) of the Federal Reserve.

    a. _____ U.S. government securities
    b. _____ Loans to banks (discounts and advances)
    c. _____ Deposits of the U.S. Treasury
    d. _____ Federal Reserve Notes
    e. _____ Deposits by foreign nations
    f. _____ Deposits by banks
    g. _____ Coin
    h. _____ Foreign currency

2. Determine what happens to checkable deposits in the banking system if the Fed lowers the required reserve ratio from 20% to 19%, total reserves equal $200 billion, and banks are presently loaned up. (Hint: Total checkable deposits = reserve multiplier X total reserves.)

a. Reserve multiplier (reserve ratio = 20%) = _____
b. Checkable deposits (reserve ratio = 20%) = _____
c. Reserve multiplier (reserve ratio = 19%) = _____
d. Checkable deposits (reserve ratio = 19%) = _____

3. a. Complete the table.

Reserve Ratio	Reserve Multiplier	Total Reserves	Checkable Deposits
.1	_____	$100 billion	$_____
.2	_____	100	_____
.25	_____	100	_____

b. An increase in the required reserve ratio _____ checkable deposits. A decrease in the reserve ratio_____ checkable deposits.

4. Below are balance sheets for the Federal Reserve and a commercial bank, Bank A. Assume that this and all other commercial banks are presently loaned up, no excess reserves are held, and the reserve ratio is 20%.

Federal Reserve

Assets	Liabilities and Net Worth
Loans to banks	Deposits of banks

Bank A

Assets	Liabilities and Net Worth
Reserve deposits	Borrowings

a. Assume that Bank A borrows $10 million from the Fed. Make the appropriate entries in the balance sheets above.
b. Bank A now has $_____ in excess reserves and can extend loans equal to $_____.
c. The banking system can increase checkable deposits by a maximum of $_____.
d. If the Fed increases the discount rate relative to short-term interest rates (Treasury Bill rates), the volume of discounts _____, causing bank total and excess reserves to _____, which causes a/an _____ in checkable deposits.
e. If the Fed decreases the discount rate relative to other short-term rates of interest, the volume of discounts _____, causing bank total and excess reserves to _____, which causes a/an _____ in checkable deposits.

5. Below are balance sheets for the Federal Reserve and Commercial Bank A.
    Assume that this and all other banks are loaned up, the current reserve
    ratio is 20%, and no excess reserves are held.

Federal Reserve

Assets	Liabilities and Net Worth
Securities	Deposits of banks

Bank A

Assets	Liabilities and Net Worth
Reserve deposits	
Securities	

a. The Fed purchases $25 million of securities from Bank A. Make the
    appropriate entries on the balance sheets above.
b. Bank A's total reserves _____ by $_____.
    Bank A's required reserves _____ by $_____.
    Bank A's excess reserves _____ by $_____.
c. Bank A can _____ loans by $_____ and the banking system can
    _____ checkable deposits by $_____.
d. If the Fed purchases securities from the public rather than a bank,
    would the impact on checkable deposits be any different from that
    which you showed in part c?
e. Fed purchases of U.S. government securities _____ bank excess
    reserves and the monetary base and _____ the money stock.

6. Suppose the Fed sells $20 billion in U.S. government securities to banks.
    Assume the reserve ratio is 10% and banks are loaned up.

    a. Make the appropriate entries on the balance sheets below.

Federal Reserve

Assets	Liabilities and Net Worth
Securities	Deposits of banks

All Banks

Assets	Liabilities and Net Worth
Reserve deposits	
Securities	

b. Bank total reserves _____ by $_____.
c. Checkable deposits in the banking system_____ by
    $_____.
d. If the securities are sold to the public, total checkable deposits
    _____ by $_____ if the public pays for the securities
    with checks, but _____ if payments are made with cash.
e. Assuming no cash transactions, Fed sales of securities _____
    bank reserves and the monetary base and_____ the money stock.

Concept: Money supply curve; equilibrium interest rate

7. When interest rates rise, the quantity of excess reserves held and not used _____, causing the supply of money to _____. When interest rates fall, the quantity of excess reserves held and not used _____ causing the supply of money to _____. The relationship between the interest rate and the quantity of money supplied is a _____ relationship, resulting in a _____ sloped money supply curve.

8. a.   On the diagram below, show the effect of an increase in the stock of money.

        An increase in the stock of money, given the demand for money, _____ the equilibrium interest rate.

    b.   Show on the figure above the impact of a reduction in the supply of money. A decrease in the stock of money, given the demand for money, _____ the equilibrium interest rate.

    c.   Indicate whether each of the following increases (+), decreases (-), or remains unchanged (0).

Fed Policy	Change in Monetary Base	Change in Excess Reserves	Change in Checkable Deposits
1. Increase reserve ratio	_____	_____	_____
2. Securities sales	_____	_____	_____
3. Securities purchases	_____	_____	_____
4. Decrease reserve ratio	_____	_____	_____
5. Increase discount rate	_____	_____	_____
6. Decrease discount rate	_____	_____	_____

SELF-TEST FOR MASTERY

Multiple Choice   Select the best answer.

1. The Board of Governors of the Federal Reserve System consists of how many members?

    a. 4
    b. 5
    c. 6
    d. 7
    e. 8

2. The principal policy-making body of the Federal Reserve System with regard to the regulation of the nation's money stock is:

    a. The Federal Advisory Committee.
    b. The trading desk in New York.
    c. The U.S. Treasury.
    d. The Federal Open Market Committee.

3. The major asset of the Federal Reserve System is:

    a. Bank deposits.
    b. Government securities.
    c. Treasury deposits.
    d. Federal Reserve notes.
    e. Discounts and advances.

4. The major liability of the Federal Reserve System is:

    a. Bank deposits.
    b. Government securities.
    c. Treasury deposits.
    d. Federal Reserve notes.
    e. Discounts and advances.

5. Which of the following is not a function of the Federal Reserve System?

    a. Regulation of the money supply
    b. Administering federal matching funds used in the banking industry
    c. Clearing checks
    d. Providing banks with currency and coin
    e. Making loans to banks

6. The sum of currency in circulation and total bank reserves equals:

    a. The total required reserves.
    b. The money stock.
    c. The total assets of the banking system.
    d. The monetary base.
    e. The money multiplier.

7. The Federal Reserve System controls the money supply primarily by controlling:

    a. The monetary base.
    b. Checkable deposits.
    c. The interest rate.
    d. Paper currency and coin.

8. An increase in the required reserve ratio _____ excess reserves and _____ the money stock.

    a. Increases, decreases
    b. Decreases, increases
    c. Decreases, decreases
    d. Increases, increases

9. A decrease in the discount rate _____ both total and excess reserves and _____ the money stock.

    a. Increases, decreases
    b. Decreases, increases
    c. Decreases, decreases
    d. Increases, increases

10. Sales of government securities to banks _____ total and excess reserves and _____ the money stock.

    a. Increase, decrease
    b. Decrease, increase
    c. Decrease, decrease
    d. Increase, increase

11. Federal Reserve purchases of securities _____ the money stock, and sales of securities _____ the money stock.

    a. Increase, decrease
    b. Increase, also increase
    c. Decrease, increase
    d. Decrease, also decrease

12. The most important tool for monetary control is:

    a. Changing the reserve ratio.
    b. The interest rate.
    c. The discount rate.
    d. Open market operations.

13. The least used tool of monetary control is:

    a. The reserve ratio policy.
    b. The interest rate.
    c. The discount rate.
    d. Open market operations.
    e. The statutory ability to impose price controls.

14. An open market purchase of securities by the Fed will _____ the supply of securities and cause the price of securities to _____ and interest rates to _____.

    a. Increase, increase, increase
    b. Decrease, increase, decrease
    c. Increase, increase, decrease
    d. Decrease, decrease, increase

15. Which of the following best explains the slope of the money supply curve?

    a.   Interest rates and loans are directly related.
    b.   Interest rates and total bank reserves are inversely related.
    c.   Interest rates and the monetary base are positively related.
    d.   Interest rates vary inversely with excess reserves.

16. An increase in the supply of money, given the demand for money, will:

    a.   At the prevailing interest rate cause a surplus of money, which in turn reduces the rate of interest.
    b.   At the prevailing interest rate cause no change in the stock of money or the interest rate.
    c.   At the prevailing interest rate cause a shortage of money, which in turn increases the rate of interest.
    d.   At the prevailing interest rate cause a surplus of money, which in turn decreases the rate of interest.

17. A decrease in the supply of money, given the demand for money, will _____ interest rates and _____ interest-sensitive expenditures in the economy.

    a.   Decrease, decrease
    b.   Increase, increase
    c.   Increase, decrease
    d.   Decrease, increase
    e.   Increase, will not change

THINK IT THROUGH

1. Discuss the functions of the Federal Reserve System.

2. Discuss the three tools of monetary control and how they can be used to influence equilibrium interest rates.

3. The Fed can control the rate of growth in the monetary base reasonably well over an extended period of time, but it has more difficulty achieving growth rate targets for the money supply. Can you think of any reasons why?

4. Suppose that as a manager, you are trying to decide whether to borrow short-term or long-term funds for modernization of your facilities. If you expect interest rates to rise, you will borrow by taking long-term loans at today's low interest rate. If you expect interest rates to fall, you will avoid long-term loans, preferring to borrow short-term funds until interest rates fall. What would you do if you heard that the Fed just lowered the discount rate and announced that it had been actively purchasing securities for the last several weeks?

CHAPTER ANSWERS

In Brief: Chapter Summary

1. Twelve 2. Six 3. Open Market 4. U.S. government securities 5.Federal Reserve notes 6. Monetary base 7. Discount 8. Increase 9. Decrease 10. Increase 11. Decrease 12. Sales 13. Sales to 14. Purchases from 15. Open market operations 16. Reduces 17. Rise 18. Fall 19. Increase 20. Reduces 21. Increases 22. Increases 23. Increases 24. Fall 25. Reduces 26. Increases 27. Reduce 28. More 29. Smaller 30. Larger 31. Larger 32. Smaller 33. Upward sloping

Vocabulary Review

1. Federal Open Market Committee 2. Monetary base 3. Open market operations 4. Discount loans 5. Money supply 6. Regional Federal Reserve Banks 7. Discount rate 8. Board of Governors of the Federal Reserve System

Skills Review

1. a. A b. A c. L d. L e. L f. L g. A h. A

2. a. 5 b. $1,000 billion c. 5.26 d. $1,052 billion

3. a.

Reserve Multiplier	Checkable Deposits
10	$1,000 billion
5	500 million
4	400 million

   b. Reduces, increases

4. a.

Federal Reserve

Assets	Liabilities and Net Worth
Loans to banks $10	Deposits of banks $10

Bank A

Assets	Liabilities and Net Worth
Reserve deposits $10	Borrowings $10

   b. $10 million, $10 million c. $50 million d. Decreases, fall, decrease e. Increases, rise, increase

5. a.

Federal Reserve

Assets	Liabilities and Net Worth
Securities $25	Deposits of banks $25

Bank A

Assets	Liabilities and Net Worth
Reserve deposits $ 25	
Securities -25	

   b. Increases, $25 million; no change; increase, $25 million

c.   Increase, $25 million, increase, $125 million
d.   No   e. Increase, increase

6.   a.   Federal Reserve

      Assets   Liabilities and Net Worth

      Securities $-20   Deposits of banks $-20

                   Bank A

      Assets   Liabilities and Net Worth

      Reserve deposits $-20
      Securities   20

      b.   Decrease, $20 million c. Decrease, $200 million d. Decrease, $200
            million, does not fall e. Decrease, decrease

7.   Decrease, increase; increase, decrease; positive, positively

8.   a.

      Decrease
b.   Increase
c.   Change in Monetary   Change in Excess   Change in
           Base   Reserves   Checkable
                                                Deposits

      1.   0   -   -
      2.   -   -   -
      3.   +   +   +
      4.   0   +   +
      5.   -   -   -
      6.   +   +   +

Self-Test for Mastery

1. d 2. d 3. b 4. d 5. b 6. d 7. a 8. c 9. d 10. c 11. a 12. d 13.
a 14. b 15. d 16. a 17. c

Think it Through

1.   In addition to regulating the money supply, the Fed is responsible for
maintaining the safety and solvency of the banking system, which it does
through bank regulation and oversight and acting as a lender of last resort.
The Fed also holds reserve deposits of member banks, supplies currency and coin
to banks, clears checks, makes loans to banks, aids the Treasury in the issue
of new government securities, and holds the Treasury deposits on which U.S.
government checks are written.

2.   The three tools of monetary control are the reserve ratio, the discount rate, and open market operations. If the Fed wants to expand the money supply, it can reduce the discount rate and the reserve ratio and purchase government securities. A policy designed to reduce the money stock might include increases in the reserve ratio and the discount rate and sales of government securities. In practice, the reserve ratio, while having a powerful impact on the supply of money, is not used as a device for regulation of the money supply. Open market operations together with support of the discount policy constitute the primary approach to monetary control.

3.   The Fed has more direct control over the growth of the monetary base because of the Fed's ability to buy and sell huge quantities of government securities. In contrast, the money multiplier is determined not only by the Fed via the reserve ratio, but also by the portfolio decisions of the public such as the banking system's propensity to hold excess reserves. The growth of the money supply depends on changes in both the monetary base and the money multiplier. So while the Fed can target the growth of the monetary base reasonably well over a period of several months, it is less successful in achieving its growth targets for the money stock.

4.   Both of the Fed's actions will expand the supply of money and reduce the interest rate. Because of this news, you expect interest rates to fall, which means you would be better off borrowing short-term funds and waiting until interest rates drop before you make long-term loan commitments.

35
Stabilization of the Economy Through Monetary Policy

CHAPTER CHALLENGES

After studying your text, attending class, and completing this chapter, you should be able to:

1. Discuss the mechanism through which monetary policy can affect interest rates.
2. Show how an expansionary monetary policy shifts the economy's aggregate demand curve and affects macroeconomic equilibrium.
3. Show how a contractionary monetary policy shifts the economy's aggregate demand curve and affects macroeconomic equilibrium.
4. Discuss the quantity theory of money and the possible long-term effects of monetary policy on the price level.
5. Discuss the basic ideas and implications of monetarism for monetary policy.
6. Evaluate some of the difficulties involved in choosing target goals for monetary policy.

IN BRIEF: CHAPTER SUMMARY

Fill in the blanks to summarize chapter content.

Monetary policy is used to influence the level of aggregate demand and macroeconomic equilibrium. The mechanism by which changes in the money supply influence aggregate demand is through changes in (1)_____ (prices, interest rates). Interest rates are (2)_____ (inversely, positively) related to the level of investment and other credit-sensitive expenditures. For instance, an increase in interest rates (3)_____ (reduces, increases) the level of investment which, in turn (4)_____ (reduces, increases) the level of aggregate demand and vice versa.

If the Fed wants to increase aggregate demand, it can engage in a/an (5)_____ (contractionary, expansionary) monetary policy. The Fed can expand the banking system's excess reserves. Excess reserves result in an increase in the stock of money, which reduces real interest rates and increases planned investment and aggregate demand. The effectiveness of such a policy depends on the willingness of the banking system to use the new excess reserves to make loans and on the sensitivity of investment and other expenditures to changes in the (6)_____ (interest rate, rate of inflation). If the increase in excess reserves is ultimately successful in increasing aggregate demand, real GNP and the price level increase if the economy is (7)_____ (above, below) potential real GNP. Expansionary monetary policy is useful as a tool for combating (8)_____ (recessionary, inflationary) GNP gaps and unemployment.

For the case of (9)_____ (recessionary, inflationary) GNP gaps, the Fed could withdraw reserves from the banking system. A decline in bank reserves will result in a/an (10)_____ (decrease, increase) in the real interest rate and a/an (11)_____ (decrease, increase) in planned investment and aggregate demand. As aggregate demand decreases, the price level and the level of real GNP will (12)_____ (rise, fall). A/An (13)_____ (contractionary, expansionary) monetary policy could be used to reduce inflation and bring the economy back to potential real GNP.

The long-run effect of monetary policy depends upon the demand for money, the growth of real GNP, and the growth of (14)_____ (the money stock, prices). If the income velocity of circulation of money, V, is defined as nominal GNP divided by the money stock, then the following identity emerges: (15)_____ (MQ = PV, MV = PQ). The stock of money times the income velocity of circulation equals the price level times real GNP. Velocity moves inversely with changes in the demand for money. But if velocity is constant and real GNP is assumed constant at its potential level, increases in the money stock result in (16)_____ (larger, proportionate) increases in the price level. This is the classical quantity theory of money. In the long run, the classical quantity theory of money implies a/an (17)_____ (vertical, upward sloping) aggregate supply curve at potential real GNP. An increase in the money stock increases aggregate demand (18)_____ (and results in an increase in both real GNP and the price level, but results in only an increase in the price level).

Monetarists and Keynesians believe that velocity is not constant, but the (19)_____ (monetarists, Keynesians) believe it is reasonably stable and changes in velocity are predictable. If changes in velocity are predictable, changes in the money supply can be used to influence nominal GNP. If the money stock is allowed to grow at the rate of growth of real GNP, then (20)_____ (some, no) inflation results. Inflation takes place when the money stock is allowed to grow at a rate (21)_____ (in excess of, less than) the growth rate of real GNP. Monetarists recommend constant growth of the money stock at a rate(22)_____ (equal to, less than) the economy's average growth rate of real GNP as a way to prevent inflation. Velocity has not always been stable or predictable, however. If the money supply increases at a rate faster than real GNP, inflation may not increase if velocity is (23)_____ (rising, falling).

A dilemma confronting the Fed is whether to use monetary policy to influence interest rates and aggregate demand in the short run or whether to concentrate on the long-run relationship between money growth and growth in real GNP. (24)_____ (Unfortunately, the Fed cannot, Fortunately, the Fed can) simultaneously achieve interest rate and money supply goals or targets. If real GNP or the price level increases, the demand for money will increase. In order to keep interest rates from rising, the Fed has to (25)_____ (decrease, increase) the money supply. If the goal is to keep the money supply constant in the face of an increase in money demand, then interest rates must rise. Thus controlling the interest rate means that the Fed effectively gives up control of the money stock and vice versa. This makes it (26)_____ (difficult, easy) for the Fed to achieve real GNP, employment, and inflation goals simultaneously. From the early 1940s to the mid-1970s, the Fed concentrated on controlling (27)_____ (the money stock, interest rates) as a means of stabilizing the economy. Beginning in late 1979, the Fed made an effort to concentrate on (28)_____ (the money stock, interest rates), but had to abandon the effort by mid-1982 because of the deepening recession.

VOCABULARY REVIEW

Write the key term from the list below next to its definition.

Key Terms

Stabilization policies
Monetary policy
Expansionary monetary policy
Contractionary monetary
    policy
Monetarism

Income velocity of
    circulation of money
Equation of exchange
Classical quantity theory
    of money

Definitions

1. _____: actions taken by central banks to influence money supply or interest rates in an attempt to stabilize the economy.

2. _____: action by the Federal Reserve System to decrease the monetary base or its rate of growth.

3. _____: an identity that shows the relationship between nominal GNP, the money stock, and the income velocity of circulation of money.

4. _____: a model of the long-run functioning of the economy that maintains that over the long run, changes in the money stock result in proportional changes in the price level.

5. _____: a theory of long-term macroeconomic equilibrium, based on the equation of exchange, that assumes that shifts in velocity are reasonably predictable.

6. _____: policies undertaken by governing authorities for the purpose of maintaining full employment and a reasonably stable price level.

7. _____: action by the Federal Reserve System to decrease the monetary base or its rate of growth.

8. _____: the number of times per year on average a dollar of the money stock is spent on final purchases.

SKILLS REVIEW

Concept: Monetary policy, interest rates, and aggregate demand

1.   The data below are for an economy. Using the data determine the market
      rate of interest, the level of planned investment, and the level of
      aggregate demand.

Interest Rate	Supply of Loanable Funds	Demand for Loanable Funds	Planned Investment	Aggregate Demand
(%)	($ billions)			($ billions)
14	$125	$75	$10	$2,010
13	115	80	20	2,020
12	105	85	30	2,030
11	100	90	40	2,040
10	95	95	50	2,050
9	85	100	60	2,060
8	75	105	70	2,070

a.   Equilibrium rate of interest = _____%.
b.   Planned investment = $_____; aggregate demand = $_____.
c.   The Fed engages in an expansionary monetary policy, and the supply of
      loanable funds increases by $15 billion at each interest rate. The
      new market rate of interest is _____%, planned investment
      _____ to $_____, and aggregate demand _____ to
      $_____. The aggregate demand curve shifts to the
      _____.

d.   Assume that the initial supply of loanable funds is given in the
      table above. The Fed engages in a contractionary monetary policy
      such that the supply of loanable funds decreases by $20 billion at
      each interest rate. The new interest rate is _____%, planned
      investment _____ to $_____, and aggregate demand
      _____ to $_____. The aggregate demand curve shifts
      _____.

e.   The figure below shows the aggregate demand curve for the economy
     described above. Find the point on the aggregate demand curve
     associated with part b. Now show what happens to the point for parts
     c and d. Draw new aggregate demand curves through the points
     parallel to ADo.

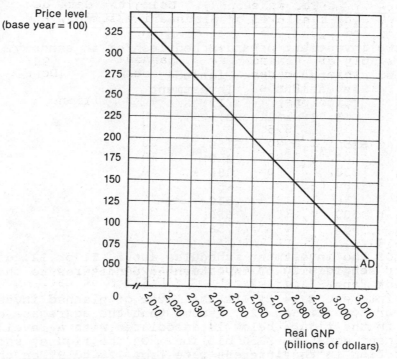

Price level
(base year = 100)

Real GNP
(billions of dollars)

Concept: Monetary policy and macroeconomic equilibrium

2.   Below is an aggregate demand and supply model of the economy.

Price level

Real GNP
(billions of dollars)

a.   Given aggregate demand ADo, the economy is experiencing an/a
     _____ (inflationary, recessionary) gap. In order to eliminate
     the gap, the Fed could _____ the money stock. This would
     _____ interest rates and _____ planned investment,
     causing the aggregate demand curve to shift _____.
b.   Given aggregate demand AD1, the economy is experiencing an/a
     _____ (inflationary, recessionary) gap. In order to eliminate
     the gap, the Fed could _____ the money stock. This would
     _____ interest rates and _____ planned investment, causing
     the aggregate demand curve to shift _____.
c.   For part a above, equilibrium real GNP will _____ and the
     equilibrium price level will _____. For part b above,

equilibrium real GNP will _____ and the equilibrium price level will _____.

3. The effectiveness of monetary policy depends upon:

a. _____

b. _____

4. Below are two investment demand schedules for an economy.

Interest Rate (%)	Planned Investment (I1) ($ billions)	Planned Investment (I2)
14	$250	$150
13	300	250
12	350	350
11	400	450
10	450	550
9	500	650
8	550	750

a. Which of the investment schedules above, I1 or I2, displays the greater sensitivity of investment expenditures to changes in the interest rate? _____

b. At an interest rate of 12% the level of planned investment is the same for both I1 and I2. Assume that the aggregate demand curve shown in the figure below is associated with a level of planned investment equal to $350 billion. On the figure, show the effect of a reduction in the interest rate from 12% to 9% on the aggregate demand curve for the case of investment schedule I1. (Assume that the aggregate demand curve shifts parallel to ADo.)

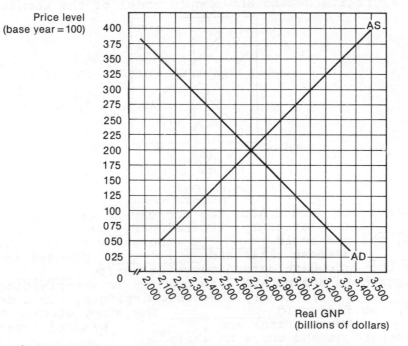

c. On the figure above, show the effect of an decrease in interest rates from 12% to 9% on the aggregate demand curve for the case of

504

investment schedule I2. (Assume that the aggregate demand curve shifts parallel to ADo.)

d. Monetary policy is _____ effective if the investment schedule is I1 and is _____ effective if the investment schedule is I2.

Concept: Classical quantity theory of money; long-term effects of money

5. a. Assume that the current level of real GNP, Q, is $2 trillion, the implicit price deflator, P, is 200, and the stock of money, M, equals $500 billion. The velocity of circulation of money equals _____.

   b. According to the classical quantity theory of money, both _____ and _____ are assumed constant. If for part a above the money stock doubles, then according to the quantity theory of money the price level, P, will _____ to _____. But if velocity falls by half its value as the stock of money doubles, the price level will _____.

   c. Which of the two aggregate supply curves in the figure below is associated with the classical quantity theory of money and is based on the assumption of flexible wages and prices? _____ If monetary policy shifts the aggregate demand curve from ADo to AD1 along the aggregate supply curve, the price level will _____ and real GNP _____.

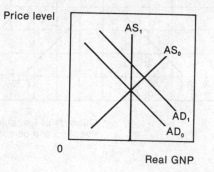

   d. The _____ believe that while velocity is not constant, it is at least predictable enough to use monetary policy to accurately influence nominal GNP.

Concept: Conflicting goals of monetary policy

6. The figure below shows an economy's loanable funds market. Assume that the Fed wants to peg interest rates at their current level as given by the demand for loanable funds, Dlf-1. Assume that because of economic expansion, the demand for loanable funds shifts outward to Dlf-2.

   a. What must the Fed do to prevent the interest rate from changing? Show this on the figure below. This monetary policy is _____ (expansionary, contractionary) and may result in _____ (more, less) inflation.

Interest rate
(%)

SLF

DLF-2

DLF-1

0

Quantity of loanable funds
supplied and demanded
per week

   b. If the Fed decided to control the stock of money, interest rates would _____. Show this on the figure above.
   c. The _____ (inability, ability) to simultaneously attain interest rate and money supply targets makes it _____ (easy, difficult) to reach macroeconomic goals such as full employment and stable prices.

SELF-TEST FOR MASTERY

Select the best answer.

1. Policies undertaken by governing authorities for the purpose of maintaining full employment and a reasonably stable price level is the definition of which of the following?

   a. Monetary policy
   b. Stabilization policies
   c. Contractionary monetary policy
   d. Expansionary monetary policy

2.   Action by the Federal Reserve System to increase the monetary base or its
      rate of growth is the definition for which of the following?

      a.   Monetary policy
      b.   Stabilization policies
      c.   Contractionary monetary policy
      d.   Expansionary monetary policy

3.   An expansionary monetary policy _____ the monetary base, causing
      the real interest rate to _____ and planned investment to _____.

      a.   Decreases, rise, fall
      b.   Increases, rise, rise
      c.   Decreases, fall, fall
      d.   Increases, rise, fall
      e.   Increases, fall, rise

4.   Which of the following is true of contractionary monetary policy?

      a.   The monetary base declines.
      b.   Real interest rates increase.
      c.   Planned investment falls.
      d.   Aggregate demand falls.
      e.   All of the above.

5.   If the economy is experiencing an inflationary GNP gap, _____
      monetary policy could be used to _____ aggregate demand and _____
      the general price level.

      a.   Contractionary, reduce, reduce
      b.   Contractionary, increase, increase
      c.   Contractionary, reduce, increase
      d.   Expansionary, reduce, reduce
      e.   Expansionary, increase, reduce

6.   Monetary policy is more effective:

      a.   The less willing bankers are to make loans.
      b.   The more responsive credit-sensitive expenditures, including
            investment, are to changes in interest rates.
      c.   The more willing bankers are to make loans with new excess reserves.
      d.   A and c.
      e.   B and c.

7.   If the economy is experiencing a recessionary GNP gap, _____
      monetary policy could be used to _____ aggregate demand and
      _____ real GNP.

      a.   Contractionary, reduce, reduce
      b.   Contractionary, increase, increase
      c.   Contractionary, reduce, increase
      d.   Expansionary, increase, reduce
      e.   Expansionary, increase, increase

8.   Which of the following is not true of the income velocity of circulation
      of money?

      a.   Velocity is defined as nominal GNP/M1.
      b.   Historically, velocity has proved to be constant.
      c.   Velocity is inversely related to the demand for money.
      d.   Changes in velocity influence nominal GNP.

9. If the price level, P, equals 1.50, real GNP is $3000 billion, and the stock of money equals $900 billion, the velocity of circulation of money equals:

    a. 4.
    b. 5.
    c. 6.
    d. 7.
    e. 8.

10. Which of the following is the equation of exchange?

    a. MP = VQ
    b. MT = Q/P
    c. MP = QT
    d. MV = PQ

11. Which of the following assumptions about the economy is central to the classical quantity theory of money?

    a. Wages and prices are rigid in the downward direction.
    b. Flexible wages and prices ensure that the economy will operate at full employment.
    c. Velocity is variable.
    d. Velocity is constant.
    e. B and d.

12. The classical quantity theory of money states that:

    a. Money is a medium of exchange necessary for the efficient functioning of the economy.
    b. Increases in the stock of money result in greater increases in the price level.
    c. Decreases in the stock of money increase the price level.
    d. Increases in the stock of money result in proportionate increases in the price level.

13. The classical quantity theory of money implies that an increase in aggregate demand:

    a. Will increase only real GNP.
    b. Will increase output, but not nominal GNP.
    c. Will increase only the price level.
    d. Will increase the price level, but will reduce nominal GNP.

14. Evidence indicates that:

    a. Velocity is unimportant.
    b. Velocity is constant.
    c. Velocity exhibits long-term trends.
    d. Velocity can increase one year, decrease the next, and increase the following year.
    e. C and d.

15. Monetarists argue that changes in the stock of money can have predictable impacts on _____ GNP assuming that _____ is reasonably stable and predictable.

    a. Real, prices
    b. Real, costs
    c. Nominal, velocity
    d. Nominal, income

16. Which of the following groups is associated with the policy recommendation that the money stock should grow only at the rate of growth in real GNP?

    a. Monetarists
    b. Keynesians
    c. Classical quantity theorists
    d. Republicans and Democrats

17. If the Fed pegs the interest rate at its current level and the demand for money increases, what must the Fed do to prevent the interest rate from changing?

    a. Increase the interest rate on nonfinancial assets.
    b. Decrease the money stock.
    c. Decrease money demand.
    d. Increase the money stock.

18. An inflationary expansion of the economy increases the demand for money. If the Fed has a policy to peg the interest rate, what is the likely consequence of its policy response?

    a. The economy will immediately fall into a depression.
    b. Inflation will fall.
    c. Inflation will rise.
    d. Unemployment will rise and inflation will fall.

19. Which of the following is true of monetary policy?

    a. From the 1940s to the present the Fed has concentrated on attaining monetary targets.
    b. From the 1940s to the 1970s the Fed emphasized interest rate stability.
    c. From late 1979 to late 1982 the Fed pegged the interest rate.
    d. The Fed has always simultaneously targeted both interest rates and the money stock.

THINK IT THROUGH

1. When the Fed increased the money supply after mid-1982, monetarists warned of impending inflation. Instead the U.S. economy has experienced stable inflation for several years. Can you think of any reasons why?

2. Discuss why monetary policy might be ineffective in a severe recession.

3. Explain how a policy to peg interest rates can cause the business cycle to exhibit more volatility.

POP QUIZ   Read the news brief at the end of this chapter and answer the
                  questions below.

      1.   What action did the Fed take and for what purpose? Discuss.
      2.   Among other goals, the Fed is trying to prevent increases in
inflation while at the same time it is also trying to maintain the
international value of the dollar within a given range. What problems are
confronted in trying to attain these goals simultaneously?

CHAPTER ANSWERS

In Brief: Chapter Summary

1. Interest rates 2. Inversely 3. Reduces 4. Reduces 5. Expansionary 6.
Interest rate 7. Below 8. Recessionary 9. Inflationary 10. Increase 11.
Decrease 12. Fall 13. Contractionary 14. The money stock 15. MV = PQ 16.
Proportionate 17. Vertical 18. But results in only an increase in the price
level 19. Monetarists 20. No 21. In excess of 22. Equal to 23. Falling
24. Unfortunately, the Fed cannot 25. Increase 26. Difficult 27. Interest
rates 28. The money stock

Vocabulary Review

1.   Monetary policy 2. Contractionary monetary policy 3. Equation of
exchange 4. Classical quantity theory of money 5. Monetarism 6.
Stabilization policies 7. Expansionary monetary policy 8. Income velocity of
circulation of money

Skills Review

1.   a. 10 b. $50 billion, $2,050 billion c. 9%, increases, $60 billion,
      increases, $2,060 billion; right d. 12%, decreases, $30 billion,
      decreases, $2,030; left

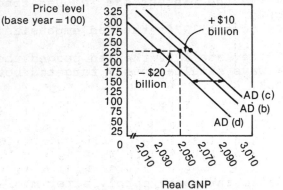

2.   a.   Recessionary; increase; decrease, increase, right
      b.   Inflationary; decrease; increase, decrease, left
      c.   Increase, increase; decrease, decrease

3.   a.   Willingness of bankers to make loans with the newly created excess
            reserves
      b.   Sensitivity of investment and other expenditures to changes in the
            interest rate

4. a. I2
   b.

Price level
(base year = 100)

Real GNP
(billions of dollars)

   c. On figure above
   d. Less, more

5. a. 8
   b. Velocity, real GNP; increase, 400; not change
   c. AS1; increase, will not change
   d. Monetarists

6. a. The Fed must increase the monetary base sufficiently to increase the stock of money equal to the increase in the demand for money. Expansionary, more

Quantity of loanable funds
supplied and demanded
per week

   b. Rise. On figure above.
   c. Inability, difficult

Self-Test for Mastery

1. b 2. d 3. e 4. e 5. a 6. e 7. e 8. b 9. b 10. d 11. e 12. d 13. c 14. e 15. c 16. a 17. d 18. c 19. b

Think it Through

1. The monetarists' warnings of inflation were based on the assumption that velocity was reasonably predictable and on the noticeable increase in the rate of growth in the money stock. According to the equation of exchange, if velocity is stable or at least predictable, increases in the money stock in excess of increases in real GNP will result in a rising price level. But velocity unexpectedly fell at times in the early to mid-1980s, offsetting the effect of increases in the money stock on nominal GNP. The deregulation of the banking industry and the introduction of financial innovations have been part of the reason for the greater volatility of velocity in the 1980s.

2.   In a severe recession, bankruptcies and the consequent loan losses might cause bankers to withhold excess reserves from the loanable funds market because of the default risks associated with loans. Investment prospects would not be expected to be very bright in a recession with firms operating with substantial excess capacity. Firms will not likely borrow to expand capacity if they are operating with excess capacity. In a severe recession or depression, an increase in the monetary base may not increase the money stock enough to reduce interest rates. And if interest rates did fall, there is no assurance that firms would borrow and spend the funds. Therefore there is a chance that aggregate demand would be little affected by an expansionary monetary policy.

3.   Suppose that the Fed has a policy to keep interest rates constant. In an economic expansion, the demand for money rises relative to the supply of money, putting upward pressure on market rates of interest. In order to keep interest rates from rising, the Fed has to increase the stock of money. This accelerates the expansion and may even result in worsening inflation. If the economy is declining and the demand for money is falling relative to the stock of money, the Fed must reduce the money supply in order to keep interest rates unchanged. But this results in further economic decline and unemployment. A policy to peg the interest rate over the business cycle will increase the instability of the economy.

Pop Quiz

1.   The Fed increased the discount rate, confirming that it is willing to slow the economy rather than risk an upsurge in inflation. The board of governors was worried that the economy's growth would be too vigorous to maintain the inflation rate at its present level. The Department of Commerce reported that hourly earnings increased at a 6% annual rate, supporting the view of those believing the economy's growth might ignite inflation. Other indications of strong growth include a high capacity utilization rate and continued increases in employment (or decreases in unemployment).

2.   In the chapter, Hyman noted that it is difficult if not impossible to achieve interest rate and money supply targets simultaneously. Likewise, if the Fed chooses to pursue domestic target goals, it may have to give up attempts to achieve international trade and finance goals. Increasing the discount rate will slow the economy and reduce the threat of inflation, but it will also increase interest rates. As domestic interest rates rise relative to foreign interest rates, foreigners purchase more U.S. financial assets. This causes the dollar to appreciate relative to foreign currencies, making U.S. goods and services less price competitive abroad. Exports would likely fall relative to imports, causing the balance of trade to worsen. As a result, attempts to reduce or prevent inflation domestically may result in an eventual deterioration of the balance of international trade.

Higher Interest

Raising Discount Rate, Fed Puts Inflation War Ahead of Dollar Policy

Action Is Likely to Push Up Greenback Even Further, Despite 7-Nation Accord

Bush Campaign Could Suffer

By ALAN MURRAY
And WALTER S. MOSSBERG
Staff Reporters of THE WALL STREET JOURNAL

WASHINGTON — Defying election-year pressures and a rising dollar, the Federal Reserve Board is raising interest rates decisively to head off a resurgence of inflation.

In a surprise step, the central bank increased its discount rate yesterday to 6.5% from 6%. Even more important, Fed officials made it clear in interviews that they plan to push up other short-term interest rates as well. The key federal-funds rate, for example, will move above the 8% level in coming days, officials said, up from about 7¾% in recent weeks. Bank prime rates, mortgage rates and other consumer-interest rates are likely to follow.

The Fed acted despite the dollar's recent strength in foreign-exchange markets. Higher interest rates, which make U.S. investments more attractive to foreign buyers, are likely to push the greenback to even loftier heights—perhaps breaking through the secret trading ranges that the major industrial nations have set to promote exchange-rate stability. In recent days, the U.S. and other governments have been battling to keep the dollar from climbing too sharply against the West German mark; they want to keep the U.S. trade deficit declining.

Domestic Considerations First

The increase in the discount rate—the rate the Fed charges on loans to financial institutions—proves once again that, when push comes to shove, U.S. officials put concern about the domestic economy above concern about a stable dollar. "The decision reflects the intent of the Federal Reserve to reduce inflationary pressures," the central bank said in announcing the increase.

"First things first," a senior Fed official explained yesterday. "You use monetary policy for domestic purposes, to fight inflation. That's the first priority."

Moreover, the push for higher interest rates, coming just a few days before the Republican convention, diminishes fears that Fed Chairman Alan Greenspan and his fellow Republican board members would shrink from fighting inflation in an election year.

"The election appears to be very far from their minds," says Scott Pardee, a former high Fed official and now vice chairman of Yamaichi International (America) Inc., a Japanese securities firm. Mr. Pardee believes that it was time for the Fed to tighten to head off potential difficulties: "The main problem they have is an economy that is strong, but not booming, and inflation that is troublesome, although not out of hand."

Markets' Reaction

Short-term interest rates and the dollar both rose after the Fed's announcement. Stock prices skidded on fears that higher rates will slow the economy. Bond prices plunged. (See story on page 3.)

Although the Fed's action yesterday isn't likely to slow the economy significantly before the November presidential election, higher rates could amplify the uncertainty that many voters already feel about the nation's economic health, thus hurting Vice President George Bush. Political-economic analysts note that in September 1980 the Fed, then led by Paul Volcker, raised the discount rate, helping wreck President Carter's re-election bid.

The timing of the Fed's move is awkward for the Reagan administration, too. The Treasury Department is going through a transition, with Secretary James Baker departing next week to take over Mr. Bush's election campaign and investment banker Nicholas Brady awaiting Senate confirmation as Mr. Baker's replacement. The move took many Treasury officials by surprise; Mr. Baker himself had said emphatically on NBC's "Meet the Press" Sunday that he didn't think the Fed had indicated any plan to raise rates.

Costly to Treasury

Moreover, the action came on the same day the Treasury was beginning its quarterly refunding operations, its offerings of new securities to replace maturing issues. As a result, it forced the government to pay higher interest rates on the securities it sells. The average yield on the three-year notes sold yesterday was 8.77%, the highest in three years.

White House spokesman Marlin Fitzwater, reading a statement approved by Secretary Baker, said that the administration is "disappointed" by the Fed's move but that "we understand there's a sound reason for it." He added that "we think the Federal Reserve has done a good job . . . the Fed's on the right course."

House Minority Leader Robert Michel of Illinois expressed some discomfort with the Fed's decision. "I don't see the signs of inflation out there," he said. But he noted that the impact of the Fed move won't be entirely negative for his party because price stability has been a Reagan "hallmark" that Republicans will stress at their convention next week.

For the Fed, the action resolved a battle that has been brewing for weeks between the presidents of the system's regional banks and the members of the Fed's board of governors. Worried by signs of strong economic growth, many of the presidents have argued that the Fed needs to raise rates. But some of the governors have resisted such suggestions, and the dispute was threatening to explode at next week's meeting of the policy-making Federal Open Market Committee, which is composed of the Reserve Board members and five Reserve Bank presidents.

The governors apparently were moved to act, however, when they discovered at their regular Monday meeting that nine of the 12 regional banks were requesting a discount-rate rise, up from only six last week. Late Monday, Chairman Greenspan called a board meeting for yesterday morning, and all six governors (one board seat is vacant) agreed to support the rate increase. They also decided to announce it in the morning, to give investors time to react before the Treasury refunding.

The rise in the discount rate brought it to its highest level since July 1986. The Fed's expected new level of just over 8% for the federal funds rate—the fee banks charge on loans to each other—would boost that rate to its high since early 1986.

U.S. officials emphasize that the Fed's move doesn't signal a defection from the general effort by the Group of Seven leading industrial nations to stabilize the dollar within a secret range of exchange rates. In addition to citing the matter of priorities, they explain that the G-7 exchange-rate system is flexible, allowing for short-term deviations and even unannounced changes in the exchange-rate ranges if economic fundamentals shift.

But the Fed's action marked the second time in less than a year that American monetary policy makers have felt compelled to meet a domestic-policy challenge at the expense of international dollar policy. Last October, in the wake of the stock-market crash, the Fed slashed interest rates to stave off a recession, even though the move drove the dollar down below levels the G-7 thought desirable. In yesterday's case, as in October, the U.S. informed its economic partners in advance of the move and, officials say, received general support for it.

A Tactical Retreat

It has been widely assumed that the upper end of the secret range is about 1.90 marks and 140 yen to the dollar, though the governments have never confirmed this. The G-7 central banks had been fighting in recent days to keep the dollar from piercing the 1.90-mark ceiling, by selling greenbacks in the currency markets. But the Fed's decision pushed the dollar firmly above 1.90 marks, and the governments beat a tactical retreat.

"With this move by the Fed, we expect the dollar to stay firm for a while," says Fred Scala, a senior currency trader at Manufacturers Hanover Trust Co. in New

York. "I expect we'll see new highs every day because the foreign-exchange market has become so interest-rate sensitive."

The officials indicate that the G-7 governments would probably avoid drastic exchange-rate actions for now and wait to see how far the dollar rises against the mark—and how long it stays high—before mounting any huge intervention campaign or changing joint exchange-rate policies.

They say other coming events—including next week's scheduled release of U.S. trade data—could moderate the dollar's rise. And they indicate that the G-7 might wait until its next scheduled meeting, around Sept. 22, before formally reconsidering whether its secret range still meshes with the fundamental positions of the world's major economies.

The lower, more stable dollar that has resulted from the G-7 effort has helped produce the desired boom in U.S. exports. Yesterday, officials said they weren't sure how much damage to the trade improvement a further surge in the greenback would cause just now. They noted that the dollar's surge, both before and after the Fed action, has been mainly against the German mark. The dollar's value against the Japanese yen has remained comfortably within the supposed ceiling of 140 yen. The officials said that if the dollar's climb remains more moderate in terms of the yen, it could have less detrimental effect on the trade balance than an overall surge.

Fed Vice Chairman Manuel Johnson and several other governors who watch financial-market indicators of inflation, rather than focus on the pace of economic growth, have tried to play down worries of inflation in recent weeks. A rising dollar, a strong bond market and stable commodity prices suggested to them that inflation fears were under control.

Employment Report Cited

But concern about inflation stepped up Friday when the Labor Department announced that employment increased strongly in July and that hourly earnings rose at a 6% annual pace. That added to the belief of many district Fed presidents that the economy couldn't continue to grow so rapidly without sparking inflation.

"The evidence suggests the economy is continuing to grow in a 3.5% to 4% range," Kansas City Fed President Roger Guffey says. "Given the strong employment numbers that have been posted recently and the high capacity utilization rates, that all adds up in my mind to the idea that inflationary pressures are quite likely to increase."

On Monday, Chairman Greenspan, who has worked to reconcile the two opposing camps, apparently was able to convince all five of his fellow governors that the time for action had come. Even Governor Martha Seger, who has dissented on many of the Fed's votes for a tighter policy, supported the move.

The Fed's Delicate Balancing Act

Rates have been pushed up...
Federal funds effective weekly average, in percent

Risking a higher dollar...
Dollar's value in W. German marks and Japanese yen, Dec. 31, 1987 = 100

...in order to cool the pace of growth in...

Prices
Change in price index for crude materials, percent

Jobs
Monthly payroll employment, in millions

Spending
Change in personal spending, percent

Sources: Labor Department; Commerce Department

In its statement, the Fed first mentioned the need to curb "inflationary pressures" and then added that "the action was also taken in light of the growing spread of market interest rates over the discount rate." The Fed hadn't changed the discount rate since last September, but it has been steadily pushing up other short-term interest rates since late March.

The increase was initially requested by the boards of all the Fed district banks except those in Chicago, Minneapolis and Dallas. Late yesterday, the Chicago and Minneapolis banks also requested a discount-rate increase.

Asked about the Fed's move yesterday, Lawrence Summers, a Harvard economist and an adviser to Democratic presidential candidate Michael Dukakis, said, "It just illustrates that the Federal Reserve is in an extraordinarily difficult position as long as we have so strong an economy coinciding with such large budget deficits."

The Fed's move puts the German government, too, in a difficult position.

For weeks, capital has been surging out of Germany. Much of it has gone into dollar-denominated holdings, helping to lift the dollar against the mark. That trend is partly due to higher U.S. interest rates, but U.S. officials and market participants also attribute it to investors' growing perception that Germany's economy is too stagnant and regulated to attract much investment. Germany's growth rate has been hovering around 2%—far below that of the

U.S. and Japan—partly because its government has been too worried about inflation to favor much stimulus.

Now, the German government and the independent central bank, the Bundesbank, face a cruel choice. They can raise interest rates to try to maintain the differential with U.S. rates and thus bolster the mark a bit. But such an increase, following a flurry of others recently, might slow German growth even further and cause the capital outflow to continue or even speed up. That might weaken the mark so much as to more than offset the bolstering effect of an interest-rate rise.

"As soon as the Bundesbank hikes rates again, it will start running the risk of choking off economic growth," says Ulrich Ramm, the chief economist of Commerzbank AG in Frankfurt. "At this point, the Bundesbank ought to wait. The higher the dollar rises, the sooner it can fall."

The Bundesbank's next scheduled opportunity to alter its key interest rates will come Aug. 25, when its policy-setting Central Bank Council returns from a four-month break. The Bundesbank yesterday left unchanged at 4.25% the rate it charges on its one-month securities-repurchase agreements, the bank's favored tool for steering German money-market rates.

Elsewhere in Europe, the effects will be much smaller. The Bank of England raised its own base rates by 0.5 percentage point Monday but insisted yesterday that its action and the Fed's weren't coordinated.

36

Stabilization of the Economy Through Fiscal Policy: Effects on Aggregate Demand and Aggregate Supply

CHAPTER CHALLENGES

After studying your text, attending class, and completing this chapter, you should be able to:

1. Discuss the federal government budget and its impact on aggregate demand in the economy.
2. Explain how expansionary fiscal policies affect the economy and show how such policies can be used to eliminate recessionary GNP gaps.
3. Explain how contractionary fiscal policies affect the economy and show how such policies can help prevent inflation.
4. Show how built-in stabilizers automatically moderate shifts in aggregate demand.
5. Discuss means of gauging the impact of fiscal policy on the economy.
6. Explain how supply-side fiscal policies can affect the economy in the long run and assess the effectiveness of recent supply-side policies.

IN BRIEF: CHAPTER SUMMARY

Fill in the blanks to summarize chapter content.

The government can influence the level of aggregate demand in both the short run and the long run through the use of fiscal policy. A budget (1)_____ (surplus, deficit) exists when government purchases exceed tax revenues. Budget (2)_____ (surpluses, deficits) occur when tax revenues exceed government purchases. Budget deficits have an/a (3)_____ (expansionary, contractionary) impact on aggregate demand, whereas budget surpluses have an/a (4)_____ (expansionary, contractionary) impact.

If the economy is experiencing a recessionary GNP gap, the government can increase real GNP by pursuing an expansionary fiscal policy. Specifically, the government can (5)_____ (decrease, increase) government purchases, increase transfer payments to individuals and organizations, or (6)_____ (decrease, increase) taxes. If the economy is in the horizontal segment of the aggregate supply curve, an expansionary fiscal policy will increase real GNP (7)_____ (without igniting, and cause) inflation. The extent of fiscal stimulus can be determined by dividing the recessionary GNP gap by the multiplier.

Tax cuts have a similar effect on aggregate demand. A reduction in taxes (8)_____ (will, will not) increase aggregate demand as much as an equivalent increase in government spending because the marginal propensities to consume and import reduce the amount of new income from the tax cut available for expenditure. If government spending is financed by an equal increase in taxes, the net effect is (9)_____ (expansionary, negative) because the government spending multiplier exceeds the net tax multiplier. The most expansionary fiscal policy is an increase in government spending

(10)_____ (financed with higher taxes, that increases the budget deficit).

If the economy has an inflationary GNP gap, the price level can be reduced by a contractionary fiscal policy. The government can (11)_____ (reduce, increase) its expenditures, (12)_____ (decrease, increase) transfers, or (13)_____ (decrease, increase) taxes. Real GNP falls toward its potential level as the price level falls. If, however, the government expands the economy when there is an inflationary GNP gap, inflation, which is already a problem, becomes worse.

Several problems are associated with the implementation of fiscal policy. For one, it is unlikely that the political process will produce the correct economic stabilization legislation. Politicians look to the next election and recognize the political problems inherent in raising taxes or cutting programs that benefit their constituencies. While it is politically much (14)_____ (more difficult, easier) to cut taxes or increase government purchases in a recession, it is much (15)_____ (more difficult, easier) to raise taxes or cut government purchases in an inflationary period.

Economic forecasting is necessary in implementing fiscal policy. Policy makers need to know where the economy is headed in order to determine the proper amount of stimulus or contraction needed. If forecasts are in error, fiscal policy (16)_____ (will, will not) likely close the recessionary or inflationary GNP gap. Lags in fiscal policy implementation also add to the difficulty of closing recessionary and inflationary gaps. The time lags include the recognition lag, the administrative lag, and the operational lag. We do not know if we have entered an expansion or a recession until weeks or even months after the occurrence. This is the (17)_____ (operational, administrative, recognition) lag. The (18)_____ (operational, administrative, recognition) lag is the length of time it takes the government to devise a policy response. And finally, the (19)_____ (operational, administrative, recognition) lag is the length of time the policy response takes to change real GNP, the price level, and the level of unemployment. Because the lengths of these lags are not known with certainty, fiscal policy may be ill timed and as a result may not close the inflationary or recessionary GNP gap.

Fortunately, the government budget still has a stabilizing impact on the economy through its automatic stabilizers--a form of (20)_____ (discretionary, nondiscretionary) fiscal policy. These include income taxes and transfer payments. The transfers that vary over the business cycle are entitlement programs such as unemployment insurance, cash assistance welfare benefits, (21)_____ (in-kind assistance, private pension benefits), and Social Security pension payments. As the economy falls into a recession, income tax revenues decline and transfers increase automatically. This (22)_____ (increases aggregate demand more than, prevents the level of aggregate demand from falling as much as) it would have otherwise. An economic expansion increases tax revenues and reduces transfer payments, which aids in restraining aggregate demand. This (23)_____ (reduces, increases) the threat of inflation. In order to determine if discretionary fiscal policy is stimulative or contractionary, it is necessary to hold constant the effect of the automatic stabilizers. This is done with the concept of the (24)_____ (balanced budget, high-employment deficit), in which government spending and revenues are compared assuming the economy is operating over the year at the natural rate of unemployment.

In addition to demand-side effects, fiscal policies can also have supply-side effects over the long run. A cut in tax rates, it is argued, will increase the after-tax returns to work, saving, and investment. If the number of labor hours increases and the levels of saving and investment increase, the

(25)_____ (aggregate supply curve will shift rightward, the aggregate demand curve will shift leftward). Evidence suggests that these effects (26)_____ (are, are not) very large, particularly in the short run. In the short run, a cut in tax rates will increase aggregate demand more than aggregate supply, implying the possibility of (27)_____ (unemployment, inflation) if the economy is on the upward-sloping portion of its aggregate supply curve. To prevent tax cuts from causing inflation and to allow sufficient time for them to have supply-side effects on the aggregate supply curve, aggregate demand will have to be restrained somewhat through reduced government spending. In addition to cuts in tax rates, legislation allowing individual retirement accounts may increase saving, and accelerated depreciation allowances and investment tax credits may (28)_____ (increase, decrease) capital formation, both of which could shift the aggregate supply curve (29)_____ (leftward, rightward).

VOCABULARY REVIEW

Write the key term from the list below next to its definition.

Key Terms

Fiscal policy	Automatic stabilizers
Government budget	High-employment deficit (or surplus)
Expansionary fiscal	Supply-side fiscal policies
policy	Accelerated depreciation allowances
Contractionary	
fiscal policy	

Definitions

1. _____: the use of government spending and taxation for the specific purpose of stabilizing the economy.

2. _____: features of the federal budget that automatically adjust net taxes to stabilize aggregate demand as the economy expands and contracts.

3. _____: generous deductions from pretax business income that are allowed when firms acquire new equipment or new purchases.

4. _____: a policy under which the government acts to restrain aggregate demand by decreasing spending or increasing taxes, or both.

5. _____: seek to influence long-run economic growth in real GNP through government subsidies and tax collections.

6. _____: a policy under which the government acts to increase aggregate demand by increasing spending or decreasing taxes, or both.

7. _____: gives the budget deficit (or surplus) that would prevail if the natural rate of unemployment were achieved.

8. _____: a plan for spending funds and raising revenues through taxation, fees, and other means, and borrowing funds if necessary.

SKILLS REVIEW

Concept: Impact of the federal budget on aggregate demand; fiscal policies to
          close recessionary and inflationary GNP gaps

1.   Assume that the economy in the figure below is currently at its potential
     level of real GNP.

a.   Identify the equilibrium price level and level of real GNP on the
     figure.
b.   Assume a decrease in autonomous spending reduces aggregate purchases
     by $125 billion. If the multiplier is 2, the aggregate demand curve
     will shift _____ by $_____. Show the new AD curve and label
     it AD1.
c.   The economy is now experiencing a/an _____ gap. Real GNP
     _____ potential GNP, and the unemployment rate _____ than
     the natural rate of unemployment.
d.   If the government wanted to reduce unemployment by closing the
     recessionary gap, it would have to _____ government spending
     by $_____.
e.   Alternatively the government could close the recessionary gap by
     _____ taxes and/or _____ transfer payments.
f.   What would be the effect if the government pursued an expansionary
     fiscal policy given the initial aggregate demand curve, ADo?

2. Assume the economy in the figure below is presently suffering from an inflationary GNP gap.

Price level

Real GNP
(billions of dollars)

a. In order to close the inflationary gap, the government could:
   (1)_____
   (2)_____
   (3)_____

b. If the economy's multiplier is 2.5 (includes price-level effects) and the decline in government spending necessary to move the economy back to its potential level of real GNP is $200 billion, potential real GNP is short of the current inflationary level of real GNP by $_____. A/An _____ in government spending of $_____ will close the inflationary gap.

c. Show on the figure above the effect of a contractionary fiscal policy. Be sure to identify the changes in the price level and real GNP.

3. List three problems associated with the implementation of fiscal policy.

   a. _____
   b. _____
   c. _____

4. Advanced Question Given the following equations, find the change in government spending necessary to close a recessionary GNP gap of $100 billion. The recessionary gap could alternatively be closed by what change in the tax rate?

```
Y  = C + Ip + G + NE      where A   = $300
C  = A + (MPC)DI                Ip  = $400
DI = Y - T                      G   = $500
T  = tY                         E   = $200
Ip = Io                         MPC = .9
G  = Go                         t   = .3
NE = E - M                      MPI = .15
M  = (MPI)Y
```

C = consumption, Y = real GNP, Ip = planned investment, G = government
purchases, NE = net exports, A = autonomous consumption, DI = disposable
income, MPC = marginal propensity to consume, T = net taxes, t = net tax
rate, E = exports, M = imports, MPI = marginal propensity to import

Concept: Built-in stabilizers and shifts in aggregate demand

5.   Assume that the economy represented in the figure below currently has a
      level of aggregate demand as shown by the AD curve, ADo.

a.   As an economy expands, taxes _____ and transfers _____. An
      increase in aggregate demand caused by a given increase in autonomous
      purchases is represented by AD1 and AD2 where one of the AD curves is
      associated with an economy having built-in stabilizers and the other
      is not. Which AD curve, AD1 or AD2, is consistent with the existence
      of built-in stabilizers? _____

b.   As an economy contracts, taxes _____ and transfers _____. A
      given reduction in autonomous purchases shifts the aggregate demand
      curve leftward from ADo. AD3 and AD4 result from the same decline in
      autonomous spending, but one of the curves is for an economy with
      automatic stabilizers and the other curve is not. Which of the two
      aggregate demand curves, AD3 or AD4, is consistent with built-in
      stabilizers? _____

c.   Built-in stabilizers _____ the fluctuations in aggregate
      demand and real GNP for given fluctuations in autonomous spending.

Concept: Supply-side fiscal policy

6. Show on the figure below the supply-side effect of a cut in tax rates. Be sure to identify the changes in real GNP and the price level.

a. A cut in tax rates will _____ the after-tax returns to work, saving, and investment and is expected to _____ the levels of hours worked, saving, and investment.
b. If the aggregate supply curve shifts _____, the price level will fall and the level of real GNP will _____.
c. Evidence indicates that the short-run effect on the aggregate supply curve of cuts in tax rates will be _____ relative to shifts in the aggregate demand curve.
d. If the economy is at its potential level of real GNP when tax rates are reduced, the price level will likely _____ unless the government _____ government purchases.

SELF-TEST FOR MASTERY

Select the best answer.

1. The use of government spending and taxation for the purpose of stabilizing the economy is called:

    a. Budget policy.
    b. Monetary policy.
    c. Fiscal policy.
    d. Trade policy.

2.   A budget deficit exits when:

a.   Tax revenue exceeds government spending.
b.   Government spending equals government revenues.
c.   Government spending exceeds government revenues.
d.   The public debt decreases.

3.   An increase in the budget deficit _____ aggregate _____.

a.   Increases, demand
b.   Increases, supply
c.   Decreases, demand
d.   Decreases, supply

4.   An increase in a budget surplus or a decrease in a budget deficit
_____ aggregate demand and _____ real GNP.

a.   Increases, reduces
b.   Increases, decreases
c.   Decreases, increases
d.   Decreases, reduces

5.   A recessionary GNP gap can be closed by which of the following?

a.   An increase in government spending
b.   A decrease in taxes
c.   An increase in transfer payments
d.   All of the above

6.   If the marginal respending rate (MRR) is .6 and the current level of
equilibrium real GNP is short of the desired level of real GNP by $250
billion, by how much will the government have to increase aggregate
demand? (Assume that the economy is in the flat portion of the AS curve.)

a. $40 billion
b. $60 billion
c. $80 billion
d. $100 billion
e. $120 billion

7.   Which of the following fiscal policies is the most stimulative in the
short run?

a.   Increases in government spending financed by borrowing (incurring a
     deficit)
b.   Increases in government spending financed by taxation
c.   Equal decreases in taxes and government spending
d.   Increases in transfers financed by taxation

8.   When the price level is responsive to changes in aggregate demand, the
multiplier will be _____ the multiplier presented in the text
chapter.

a.   Greater than
b.   Less than
c.   Equal to
d.   Twice the size of

9. Which of the following policies should be used to close an inflationary GNP gap?

   a. Increases in government spending
   b. Tax cuts
   c. Increases in transfer payments
   d. An increase in taxes

10. Which lag in the implementation of fiscal policy is due to the length of time that it takes fiscal policy to have the desired impact on the economy?

    a. Recognition lag
    b. Administrative lag
    c. Operational lag
    d. Cyclical lag

11. Automatic stabilizers:

    a. Are a form of nondiscretionary fiscal policy.
    b. Include income taxes and cash assistance to the poor.
    c. Include in-kind assistance and Social Security benefits.
    d. A and b.
    e. All of the above.

12. As the economy expands, tax revenues _____ and transfer payments _____, causing the economy to expand _____ than it would in the absence of these built-in stabilizers.

    a. Fall, rise, more
    b. Fall, fall, less
    c. Rise, fall, more
    d. Rise, fall, less
    e. Rise, rise, more

13. Built-in stabilizers result in _____ fluctuations in aggregate demand for given autonomous changes in spending than as would be the case for an economy in which built-in stabilizers did not exist.

    a. Greater
    b. More severe
    c. Smaller
    d. The same

14. Which of the following budget concepts measures the policy stance of discretionary fiscal policy--that is, whether it is expansionary or contractionary?

    a. Balanced budget
    b. Budget deficit
    c. Potential output budget
    d. High-employment deficit (or surplus)

15. A reduction in tax rates _____ the after-tax returns to work, saving, and investment, which in the long run may _____ aggregate supply.

    a. Reduces, increase
    b. Reduces, decrease
    c. Increases, decrease
    d. Increases, increase

16. Proponents of supply-side fiscal policies argue that a cut in tax rates will:

    a.   Increase the number of hours worked.
    b.   Increase the level of saving.
    c.   Increase the level of investment.
    d.   Increase potential real GNP.
    e.   All of the above.

17. Evidence indicates that a cut in tax rates in the short run will likely increase _____ more than _____, causing the price level to _____ unless government reduces _____.

    a.   Aggregate demand, aggregate supply, rise, government spending
    b.   Aggregate supply, aggregate demand, fall, transfers to the poor
    c.   Aggregate supply, aggregate demand, rise, tax rates
    d.   Aggregate demand, aggregate supply, fall, its borrowing
    e.   None of the above

THINK IT THROUGH

1.   If the current unemployment rate exceeds the natural rate of unemployment and the current government budget is in balance, the high-employment budget is in (balance/deficit/surplus). What are the effects on the economy?

2.   Conflicts such as World War II and the Vietnam War created domestic economic expansion. Explain. How does this relate to the ease or difficulty of implementing fiscal policy?

3.   Discuss the case for and against supply-side fiscal policies.

POP QUIZ   Read the news brief at the end of this chapter and answer the questions below.

1.   Some people argue that an increase in taxes will not reduce the federal budget deficit because higher taxes invite lawmakers to increase spending. Discuss Herbert Stein's response to this assertion.

2.   Historically, why have deficits increased?

3.   What assumptions are being made by the administration in projecting a decline in the deficit to $23 billion by 1993? Are any of these assumptions inconsistent with the administration's argument that tax increases will simply fuel spending rather than reduce the deficit?

CHAPTER ANSWERS

In Brief: Chapter Summary

1. Deficit 2. Surpluses 3. Expansionary 4. Contractionary 5. Increase 6. Decrease 7. Without igniting 8. Will not 9. Expansionary 10. That increases the budget deficit 11. Reduce 12. Decrease 13. Increase 14. Easier 15.

More difficult 16. Will not 17. Recognition 18. Administrative 19. Operational 20. Nondiscretionary 21. In-kind assistance 22. Prevents the level of aggregate demand from falling as much as 23. Reduces 24. High-employment deficit 25. Aggregate supply will shift rightward 26. Are not 27. Inflation 28. Increase 29. Rightward

Vocabulary Review

1. Fiscal policy 2. Automatic stabilizers 3. Accelerated depreciation allowances 4. Contractionary fiscal policy 5. Supply-side fiscal policies 6. Expansionary fiscal policies 7. High-employment deficit (or surplus) 8. Government budget

Skills Review

1. a.

    b.   Leftward, $250 billion
    c.   Recessionary GNP gap, falls below, is higher
    d.   Increase, $125 billion
    e.   Reduce, increase
    f.   Real GNP would exceed potential real GNP and the unemployment rate would fall below its natural rate, putting upward pressure on the price level.

2. a.   (1) Increase taxes (2) Reduce transfer payments (3) Reduce government spending
    b. $500 billion; decrease, $200 billion

    c.

3. a.   Political problems b. Forecasting problems c. Timing problems

4. This particular model is analyzed in the appendix that presents a complete Keynesian model. For the equations and values given, the multiplier is 1.923. Thus if the policy goal is to expand real GNP by $100 billion, divide this amount by the multiplier to determine the necessary change in government spending. ($100 billion/1.923 = $52 billion.) Government spending must be increased by $52 billion in order to increase equilibrium real GNP by $100 billion and close the recessionary GNP gap.

Alternatively, the recessionary gap can be closed by a reduction in the tax rate. The first step is to find the tax rate multiplier (change in real GNP/change in the tax rate). Dividing the tax rate multiplier into the recessionary gap of $100 billion will give the necessary change in tax rates. For those students familiar will calculus, the tax rate multiplier can be found by solving the system of equations for the equilibrium level of real GNP, Y, and taking the partial derivative of Y with respect to the tax rate, t. The tax rate multiplier is as follows:

$$\text{Tax rate multiplier} = -[MPC(Y)]/[1 - MPC + (MPC)t + MPI]$$

For the values given, the tax rate multiplier equals -4659.75. Dividing this into $100 billion gives -.021. The tax rate must be reduced from 30% to 27.9% in order to close the recessionary gap.

5. a. Increase, decrease; AD1
    b. Decrease, increase; AD3
    c. Moderate

6.

    a. Increase, increase b. Rightward, Increase c. Very small
    d. Rise, reduces

Self-Test for Mastery

1. c 2. c 3. a 4. d 5. d 6. d 7. a 8. b 9. d 10. c 11. e 12. d 13. c 14. d 15. d 16. e 17. a

Think it Through

1. If the current government budget is in balance but the economy is operating below potential real GNP, the high-employment budget would be in surplus. Thus discretionary fiscal policy would be contractionary if the economy expanded to its potential level of real GNP. Fiscal policy would act as a "drag" on the economy as it approached potential real GNP.

2. During wars, U.S. government spending has far exceeded tax revenues. The increases in the deficit during the war years created domestic economic expansion. This is powerful evidence of the ability of government budget

deficits to expand the economy in the short run. But it also points to a difficulty in the implementation of fiscal policy. National defense and security, economic stabilization, and other goals of society compete with one another. Economic stabilization may require certain budget changes, whereas the provision of national defense may require completely different budget changes. Nevertheless, any budget change that alters a deficit or surplus will have short-run macroeconomic effects that may or may not be desirable with regard to economic stabilization.

3.   During periods of stagflation, the traditional discretionary fiscal policy of aggregate demand management is unlikely to reduce inflation and unemployment simultaneously. If fiscal policy could shift the economy's aggregate supply curve rightward in the short run, real output would increase and both the unemployment rate and price level (or rate of inflation) would fall. The argument for supply-side fiscal policies is that not only would the price level and unemployment fall, but the potential level of real GNP would increase, allowing higher future living standards. All of this is based upon the belief that a cut in tax rates will have large impacts on hours worked, saving, and investment, thus shifting the aggregate supply curve rightward. Few economists would dispute the argument that tax rate cuts increase to some extent hours worked, saving, and investment. But the empirical evidence suggests that the short-run impacts of a cut in tax rates will primarily affect the aggregate demand curve rather than the aggregate supply curve. If the economy is already suffering from inflation and tax rates are cut, there will be greater rather than less pressure for prices to rise.

Pop Quiz

1.   Herbert Stein argues that increased government spending is not the direct result of higher taxes. If that were the case, why didn't government expenditures fall when taxes were cut in 1948, 1954, 1963, 1969, 1971, 1978 and 1981? Taxes were raised during World War I, World War II, the Korean War, and the Vietnam War but not by as much as government spending. The budget experience of the 1980s cannot be explained in terms of the theory that increased revenues result in increased spending. From 1980 to 1986 government spending increased by 158% of the increase in revenues. From 1986 to 1988 government spending increased by only 47% of the increase in revenues. According to Stein, "...the proportions in which the revenue (from a tax increase) would be divided between more spending and a smaller deficit are not determined by an iron law of politics."

2.   Government expenditures and revenues matched each other fairly closely until roughly the Reagan administration. Past deficits typically increased only during recessions and wars, but not during periods of prosperity and peace.

3.   In fact, the only way that the government can reach its deficit goal by 1993 is by not spending all of the increased tax revenues resulting from growth. On the one hand, the official rhetoric is that taxes should not be increased to reduce the deficit because that will increase spending; but on the other hand, the administration's budget projection assumes just the opposite.

The New Parkinson's Law

By Herbert Stein

Thirty-one years ago we all laughed at a joke called Parkinson's Law, written by a British historian. The Law was that work expands to fill the time available. I call it a joke because, like the stories about the stingy Scotsman and the mean mother-in-law, it appealed to our sense of the ridiculous but was not true. In fact, Parkinson made little attempt to prove that his Law was a law aside from telling some cute anecdotes.

Today, a version of Parkinson's Law has become an important feature of policy talk, and possibly of policy, in America. Today's Law is that government expenditures rise to meet the revenue available. This is now the primary argument used to demonstrate that a tax increase will not reduce the deficit. It has supplanted the proposition that a tax increase will not raise the revenue.

The new Law is supposed to be a corollary of the proposition that politicians are shortsighted and venal. If they have more money, they will spend it. Of course, that applies only to the other politicians, the "bad" ones—the liberals, Democrats and congressmen—not to the "good" ones like us.

But even a moment's reflection raises serious questions about the Law. If expenditures are determined by revenue, where did the $2 trillion debt come from? And if "They" spend all the revenue that the tax system yields, where did the tax cuts of 1948, 1954, 1963, 1969, 1971, 1978 and 1981 come from? Something else seems to be going on besides spending all the revenue available.

Sequence Is Important

During most of our history, until approximately the Reagan administration, expenditures and revenue were fairly close together except in wars and recessions. But that does not show that the expenditures rose to equal the revenue. It also could have been true that the revenue usually rose to equal the expenditures, which were determined by something other than the available revenue. The sequence is important.

In this century there have been three main sources of revenue increases—tax increases during wars, revenue increases from the existing tax system due to growth and inflation (creep), and tax increases to fund Social Security.

Taxes were raised during World War I, World War II, the Korean War and the Vietnam War. In no case were taxes raised enough to cover the cost of the war. In no case did expenditures rise enough after the war to absorb the revenue that would have been available if the war taxes had been retained. We did not retain enough of the war taxes even to pay off the debt accumulated during the war.

Expenditures did not rise enough to equal the rise of revenue that was produced by economic growth and inflation since World War II. The tax cuts of 1948, 1963, 1969, 1971, 1978 and 1981 gave back much of that increased revenue. Expendi-

---

Board of Contributors

If expenditures are determined by revenue, where did the $2 trillion debt come from? And if "They" spend all the revenue that the tax system yields, where did the tax cuts come from?

tures did rise during that period, absolutely and relative to gross national product, but there is no clear evidence that the rise was governed by the increased revenue. It is at least equally likely that the amount of the revenue give-back during this period was governed by the actual and prospective expenditures.

The increases in the payroll tax for Social Security were clearly motivated by the desire to pay for benefits under actual or proposed legislation. It was not because there was a lot of money in the Social Security reserves that we got the benefit increases.

For the benefit of those who may be unconvinced by my thumbnail history, I refer to a statistical analysis done by Profs. George von Furstenberg, R. Jeffery Green and Jin-Ho Jeong, "Tax and Spend, or Spend and Tax?" that was published in The Review of Economics and Statistics, May 1986. Their conclusion was summarized as follows:

"Assertions about how changes on one side of the federal budget are processed on the other cover the range of possibilities. One such assertion, tax and spend, holds that spending can be moved with prior tax action both up and down. This implies that those who raised taxes invited more spending while those who lower taxes can subdue it. . . . The evidence assembled in this paper provided no support for the first assertion [the one just cited] which was tested with quarterly data for 1954-1982."

The recent behavior of the budget is impossible to explain on the theory that expenditures closely follow revenue. Between 1980 and 1986 the increase in expenditures was 158% of the increase in receipts. That was how we got the big deficit. Between 1986 and 1988 (Office of Management and Budget estimate) the rise in expenditures was 47% of the rise in revenue. That was how we got the big reduction of the deficit.

The Administration's Scenario

If it were literally true that expenditures rise to equal revenue, there would be no way to reduce the deficit. But people who say that the deficit cannot be reduced by raising taxes do not say that the deficit cannot be reduced at all. They claim to have a different way. But their way also depends on expenditures not rising as fast as revenue. For example, the administration's scenario for reducing the deficit to $23 billion by 1993 counts on revenue rising by $349 billion between 1988 and 1993 but expenditures rising by only 65% as much. That is, it counts on "Them," the other politicians, not spending all the revenue that is expected to come from economic growth.

None of this suggests that the revenue from a tax increase would be automatically and fully reflected in a reduction of the deficit. It means that the proportions in which the revenue would be divided between more spending and a smaller deficit are not determined by an iron law of politics. The proportions will be determined by a struggle between competing claimants and its outcome is not predetermined. The president is a powerful actor in that struggle. He should not believe himself incapable of affecting the result if he makes cutting the deficit a matter of high priority.

Mr. Stein, chairman of the Council of Economic Advisers under Presidents Nixon and Ford, is a senior fellow at the American Enterprise Institute.

37

The Federal Budget Deficit and the National Debt

CHAPTER CHALLENGES

After studying your text, attending class, and completing this chapter, you should be able to:

1. Discuss the advantages and disadvantages of an annually balanced federal budget.
2. Explain how the federal budget deficit's impact on interest rates can influence private investment, economic growth, and international trade.
3. Discuss the impact of the national debt on the well-being of current and future generations.
4. Discuss some of the problems involved in measuring the federal budget deficit and explain how the deficit has been reduced in recent years to comply with the Gramm-Rudman-Hollings Act.

IN BRIEF: CHAPTER SUMMARY

Fill in the blanks to summarize chapter content.

Until the 1930s, it was believed that it was necessary to balance the budget annually. Government outlays for the year had to be financed by an equal amount of government revenue. An annually balanced budget, (1)_____ (stabilizes rather than destabilizes, destabilizes rather than stabilizes) the business cycle. In recessions, tax revenue falls and transfer payments rise, producing a federal budget deficit where federal government outlays exceed government receipts. In order to balance the budget, (2)_____ (revenues, government outlays) must be increased or (3)_____ (revenues, government outlays) reduced. But this is contractionary and will make the recession worse. In expansions, federal government surpluses may arise where taxes and other government revenues rise above government outlays. But a balanced-budget policy requires decreases in taxes or increases in government outlays, both of which are (4)_____ (expansionary, contractionary) in an economic expansion.

Deficits can be financed in two ways if taxes are not increased. The deficit can be (5)_____ (financed by selling government securities to the public, monetized), which ultimately results in an increase in the money supply. Or the deficit can be (6)_____ (financed by selling government securities to the public, monetized). In the latter case, because the Fed does not intervene and buy an equivalent quantity of securities, the money supply does not increase. Deficits are expansionary, and the method of financing deficits may add to or retard that expansionary effect. With monetization, the increase in the money stock is (7)_____ (contractionary, expansionary). The aggregate demand curve will shift farther (8)_____ (leftward, rightward) when deficits are financed by monetization. When the government sells securities to the public, the demand for loanable funds increases, causing interest rates to (9)_____(rise, fall). This causes some

(10)_____ (crowding out, crowding in) meaning that rising interest rates reduce the level of private borrowing below the level that would have prevailed if the government had not borrowed to finance budget deficits. Empirical evidence suggests that on average the crowding-out effect from government deficits is (11)_____ (large, small). On net, the expansionary effect of the deficit is still positive, (12)_____ (and larger than, but not as large as) the case of monetization. Both methods of financing are (13)_____ (more, less) expansionary, however, than increasing taxes to cover the deficit.

Deficits may also have an impact on international trade. If the financing of deficits results in higher U.S. interest rates relative to foreign rates of interest, foreigners will seek to (14)_____ (purchase, sell) the relatively higher-yielding U.S. financial assets such as U.S. government securities. But they first have to convert their foreign currencies into dollars in order to make the purchases. This increases the (15)_____ (supply of, demand for) dollars, causing the dollar's price to rise relative to those of foreign currencies. This in turn causes the relative prices of U.S. goods to (16)_____ (fall, rise) in foreign countries and the relative prices of imported goods in the United States to fall. Exports fall and imports rise, resulting in an/a (17)_____ (increase, decline) in aggregate demand. Deficits also affect international trade because deficits are expansionary and increases in the nation's disposable income cause imports to (18)_____ (fall, rise) relative to exports, causing net exports and aggregate demand to fall.

If crowding out is significant to the extent that interest rates are higher and investment spending is lower, U.S. businesses may not engage in enough development of new technology to remain competitive in world markets. A lower rate of capital growth (19)_____ (reduces, increases) the rate of growth of the economy and reduces future potential standards of living. But the government's use of resources is (20)_____ (always unproductive, not unproductive). The government subsidizes research and new technologies and encourages investment through government tax policies.

A deficit (21)_____ (reduces, adds to) the national debt, whereas a budget surplus (22)_____ (reduces, adds to) the national debt. The (23)_____ (net federal debt, national debt) is the dollar amount that the federal government owes to its creditors at a given point in time. The (24)_____ (net federal debt, national debt) is the credit extended to the federal government by those other than the Fed and government agencies. The national debt as a percentage of GNP fell from 89% in 1950 to 33% in 1980 (25)_____ (and has continued to fall to under 23%, but has risen since then to over 45%). In 1986, most of the net public debt, 84.3%, was (26)_____ (externally, internally) held by U.S. individuals, businesses, and state and local governments. The remainder of the net public debt, 15.7%, is (27)_____ (externally, internally) held by foreigners. This inflow of foreign saving acts to (28)_____ (offset to some extent, worsen) the crowding-out effect.

Two major burdens are associated with a large public debt. First, future generations will have to pay more taxes to pay interest on the debt. These additional taxes otherwise would have been used to provide additional government goods and services. Second, assuming a large crowding-out effect, a decline in investment (29)_____ (will not, will) impair the growth rate of the economy.

Several other aspects of the public debt merit consideration. Part of the national debt was incurred to acquire public capital assets. These assets have value and to some extent offset the national debt. It is prudent policy for governments to finance capital assets by borrowing, as is done in the private sector. Inflation affects the real value of the national debt. For instance, during periods of inflation and high interest rates, the real value of the national debt (30)_____ (rises, falls). The actual deficit overstates the real value of the deficit. This constitutes a transfer of purchasing power from the government's creditors to the government. During periods of low and stable inflation and low interest rates, the real value of the national debt is higher, in effect transferring purchasing power from the government to the holders of government securities. Here the actual deficit (31)_____ (understates, overstates) the real value of the deficit.

Deficits can be reduced by increasing taxes, government fees and charges and other receipts, by reducing government outlays, or by the sale of public assets. The sale of public assets to private business interests is known as (32)_____ (competitive bidding, privatization). The Reagan administration has been reluctant to reduce expenditures for Social Security benefits or national defense, which together make up 70% of federal government outlays. Another 15% is pledged to interest payments on the national debt. This leaves all other government programs representing only 15% of federal government outlays. It is politically very difficult to eliminate the deficit by cuts in that 15% of the budget alone. Because the Reagan administration resisted tax increases, the deficit continues to remain very large.

VOCABULARY REVIEW

Write the key term from the list below next to its definition.

Key Terms

Crowding-out effect   Internal debt
National debt   External debt
Net federal debt   Privatization

Definitions

1. _____: the portion of the national debt owed to citizens of other nations.

2. _____: the dollar amount that the federal government owes to its creditors at a given point in time.

3. _____: the process of selling government assets to private business interests.

4. _____: the portion of the national debt owed to those other than the Fed and government agencies.

5. _____: the portion of the national debt owed to the nation's own citizens.

6. _____: the reduction in private investment purchases caused by higher interest rates that result from borrowing by the government to cover its budget deficit.

SKILLS REVIEW

Concept: Annually balanced budget

1. Assume that the economy shown in the figure below is at its potential level of real GNP and the federal budget policy is to balance the budget.

a. Suppose the level of aggregate demand falls from ADo to AD1. As real GNP _____, tax revenues _____ and transfer payments _____, causing the budget to be in _____.

b. Because of the balanced-budget policy, the government must _____ or _____, both of which shift the AD curve _____. Show this graphically on the figure above and identify the change in equilibrium real GNP.

c. Assume that the economy is once again at its potential level of real GNP and aggregate demand increases to AD2. As real GNP _____, tax revenues _____ and transfers _____, causing the budget to be in _____.

d. In order to balance the budget, the government must _____ or _____, both of which shift the AD curve _____. Show this graphically on the figure above and identify the change in equilibrium real GNP.

e. Given initial changes in aggregate demand, a balanced-budget policy results in _____ (larger, smaller) fluctuations in real GNP.

Concept: Deficits, interest rates, crowding out, and international trade

2.   The figure below shows a loanable funds market for an economy.

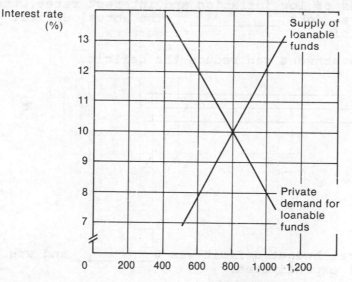

a.   Suppose the government enters the loanable funds market to borrow
     $200 billion at the prevailing rate of interest to finance the
     deficit. Government borrowing _____ the demand for loanable funds
     by $200 billion at every interest rate. Show this on the figure
     above and identify the change in the interest rate. Interest rates
     _____ to _____ %, causing investment spending and other
     credit-sensitive expenditures to _____ by $_____.
b.   As investment spending _____, the economy's future rate of
     growth will be _____.
c.   If the economy is in a deep recession, it is likely that investment
     spending is _____ to changes in interest rates. In a deep
     recession, crowding out is _____.

3.   If deficits increase U.S. interest rates relative to foreign rates of
      interest:

a.   Foreign demand for U.S. dollars _____ (increases, decreases).
b.   The price of the U.S. dollar _____ (rises, falls) relative to the
     prices of foreign currencies.
c.   U.S. goods and services become _____ (more, less) price
     competitive abroad.
d.   Exports _____ (rise, fall) and imports _____ (rise, fall).
e.   Net exports and aggregate demand _____ (increase, decrease).
f.   Equilibrium real GNP _____ (increases, decreases).

Concept: Burden of the national debt, measuring and reducing the deficit

4.   List and describe the two major burdens of the national debt.

a.   _____
b.   _____

5. a. During periods of high inflation and interest rates, the real value of the net federal debt _____. The actual deficit _____ the real deficit.

   b. During periods of low inflation and interest rates, the real value of the net federal debt _____. The actual deficit _____ the real deficit.

6. List three ways government can reduce the deficit.

   a. _____
   b. _____
   c. _____

SELF-TEST FOR MASTERY

Select the best answer.

1. In 1986, the federal budget deficit was $_____ and was equal to _____% of federal expenditures.

   a. $100 billion, 16%
   b. $100 million, 23%
   c. $200 million, 22%
   d. $220 billion, 22%

2. Which of the following prevails when federal government receipts for a year exceed government outlays?

   a. High-employment budget
   b. Balanced budget
   c. Federal budget deficit
   d. Federal government surplus

3. What was true of budget policy prior to the 1930s?

   a. The budget should be balanced annually.
   b. Recessions produced deficits, requiring a contractionary budget response.
   c. Expansions produced surpluses, requiring an expansionary budget response.
   d. The budget actually destabilized the economy.
   e. All of the above.

4. Of the ways listed below for financing or eliminating a deficit, which policy is the least expansionary?

   a. Tax financing
   b. Sale of government securities to the public
   c. Monetization
   d. None of the above

5. Of the ways listed below for financing or eliminating a deficit, which policy is the most expansionary?

    a. Tax financing
    b. Sale of government securities to the public
    c. Monetization
    d. Privatization

6. A deficit financed by monetization results in an aggregate demand curve:

    a. That lies to the left of the AD curve when deficits are financed by taxes.
    b. That lies to the left of the AD curve when deficits are financed by selling government securities to the public.
    c. That does not shift.
    d. That lies to the right of the AD curve when deficits are financed by selling government securities to the public.

7. If a deficit results in _____ interest rates and _____ private investment, there is said to be _____ .

    a. Higher, less, crowding out
    b. Higher, less, monetization
    c. Lower, more, crowding in
    d. Lower, less, crowding out
    e. B and c

8. Empirical studies suggest that the impact of federal budget deficits on interest rates:

    a. Is very large.
    b. Is large and has caused our international trade problems.
    c. Is small.
    d. Rises and falls with fluctuations in real GNP.

9. If the budget deficit causes _____ U.S. interest rates relative to foreign interest rates, imports will _____ and exports will _____ .

    a. Lower, rise, rise
    b. Higher, rise, fall
    c. Higher, rise, rise
    d. Higher, fall, fall
    e. Lower, fall, fall

10. An increase in the budget deficit will eventually _____ the nation's disposable income, which _____ imports and _____ aggregate demand below what it would be in the absence of international trade.

    a. Decrease, decreases, increases
    b. Increase, decreases, decreases
    c. Decrease, increases, decreases
    d. Increase, increases, decreases
    e. Decrease, decreases, decreases

11. Which of the following terms represents the credit extended to the federal government by those other than the Fed and government agencies?

    a. All private securities holders
    b. Government debt
    c. National debt
    d. Net federal debt

12. Which of the following terms is defined as the dollar amount that the
    federal government owes to its creditors at a given point in time?

    a.   All private securities holders
    b.   Government deficit
    c.   National debt
    d.   Net federal debt

13. Today the national debt as a percentage of GNP is over:

    a.   22%.
    b.   19%.
    c.   63%.
    d.   45%.

14. Most of the national debt is _____ held, which means that when the
    debt is repaid there is _____ in aggregate demand.

    a.   Internally, a significant reduction
    b.   Internally, no change
    c.   Externally, no change
    d.   Externally, a significant reduction
    e.   Internally, an increase

15. The externally held debt was what percentage of the total net public debt
    in 1986?

    a.   12%
    b.   50%
    c.   84.3%
    d.   15.7%

16. During periods of high inflation and high interest rates, the actual
    deficit _____ the real deficit, resulting in a gain to _____
    at the expense of _____.

    a.   Overstates, the government's creditors, the government
    b.   Overstates, the government, the government's creditors
    c.   Understates, the government, the government's creditors
    d.   Understates, the government's creditors, the government

17. Which of the following acts establishes deficit reduction targets?

    a.   Deficit Reduction Act of 1981
    b.   Tax Reform Act of 1986
    c.   Monetary Decontrol Act of 1980
    d.   PL 1492
    e.   Gramm-Rudman-Hollings Act

18. Which of the following are reasons why the federal budget deficit has not
    been reduced significantly in the 1980s?

    a.   The Reagan administration was unwilling to increase taxes to
         eliminate the deficit.
    b.   The administration was reluctant to cut Social Security benefits
         and national defense spending, both of which together constitute 70%
         of federal government spending.
    c.   An increasing portion, now 15%, of the federal government's outlays
         is pledged as interest payments to holders of the public debt.
    d.   It has proved politically very difficult to eliminate the deficit

entirely by cutting the government programs that make up the
remaining 15% of government outlays.
e.   All of the above.

THINK IT THROUGH

1.   If the economy is at its potential level of real GNP and the government
budget deficit increases, which method of deficit financing would you favor and
why? Would it be better to raise taxes or borrow?

2.   "A balanced-budget amendment is necessary to keep lawmakers fiscally
responsible and to stabilize the economy." Do you agree? Explain.

3.   Discuss the implications for the relationship between the budget deficit
and international trade given studies that suggest that government deficits do
not have large crowding-out effects.

CHAPTER ANSWERS

In Brief: Chapter Summary

1. Destabilizes rather than stabilizes 2. Revenues 3. Government outlays 4.
Expansionary 5. Monetized 6. Financed by selling government securities to the
public 7. Expansionary 8. Rightward 9. Rise 10. Crowding out 11. Small
12. But not as large as 13. More 14. Purchase 15. Demand 16. Rise 17.
Decline 18. Rise 19. Reduces 20. Not unproductive 21. Adds to 22. Reduces
23. National debt 24. Net federal debt 25. But has risen since then to over
45% 26. Internally 27. Externally 28. Offset to some extent 29. Will 30.
Falls 31. Understates 32. Privatization

Vocabulary Review

1. External debt 2. National debt 3. Privatization 4. Net federal debt 5.
Internal debt 6. Crowding-out effect

Skills Review

1.   a.   Falls, fall, rise, deficit
       b.   Increase taxes, reduce government outlays, leftward

537

c. Increases, rise, fall, surplus
d. Reduce taxes, increase government outlays, rightward
e. Larger

2. a. Increases, rise, 11%, fall, $100 billion

b. Falls, reduced
c. Unresponsive, very small or nonexistent

3. a. Increases b. Rises c. Less d. Fall, rise e. Decrease f. Decreases

4. a. Future generations will have to pay more interest on the debt instead of receiving government goods and services in return for those taxes. If the percentage of the net federal debt externally held increases, the payment of interest results in an outflow of purchasing power from the United States, resulting in a lower level of aggregate demand than otherwise would be the case.

   b. If the crowding-out effect is substantial, a growing federal debt will decrease private investment and reduce the growth rate of the private capital stock. This slows the growth of worker productivity and real GNP and results in lower living standards than would have been the case if investment spending had not been crowded out. The inflow of foreign saving resulting from the externally held debt, however, serves to moderate the crowding-out effect.

5. a. Falls; overstates b. increases; understates

6. a. Increase taxes, charges and fees b. Reduce government outlays
   c. Sale of public assets

Self-Test for Mastery

1. d 2. d 3. e 4. a 5. c 6. d 7. a 8. c 9. b 10. d 11. d 12. c 13. d 14. b 15. d 16. b 17. e 18. e

Think it Through

1. If a deficit must be incurred at the level of potential real GNP, then the least expansionary form of financing should be used to prevent excessive overheating of the economy. A deficit will produce an inflationary GNP gap, but it can be minimized by selling U.S. government securities to the public rather than monetizing the deficit. At least the sale of securities to the public will not add fuel to the fire by expanding the money stock. With

monetization, in contrast, the money stock increases, resulting in a larger inflationary gap. At potential real GNP, it would be preferable to finance government outlays with tax increases. On net, there would still be an expansionary effect producing an inflationary gap, but the gap would be smaller than if the expenditures were financed by borrowing.

2. Regarding fiscal responsibility, a balanced budget does not necessarily mean a cap on spending or taxes. Higher taxes allow higher spending, but if lawmakers want to spend sums in excess of current revenues they can simply increase taxes. With regard to stabilization of the economy, a balanced-budget policy would destabilize rather than stabilize the economy. A decline in real GNP produces a recessionary gap and results in a deficit, which must be eliminated by increasing taxes or cutting government outlays, both of which make the recession worse. An increase in real GNP beyond potential real GNP produces an inflationary gap, which results in a budget surplus. The surplus can be eliminated by increasing government outlays or cutting taxes, both of which make inflation worse. A balanced-budget rule would not allow the policy flexibility needed for dealing with recessions and inflationary periods.

3. Large budget deficits have been blamed for worsening the U.S. balance of trade. The argument is that rising budget deficits caused U.S. interest rates to rise relative to those prevailing abroad. Foreigners increased their demand for U.S. dollars so that they could purchase U.S. financial assets such as government securities. The increase in the price of the dollar relative to the prices of foreign currencies reduced the price competitiveness of U.S. goods abroad and resulted in a reduction in net exports. This prevented aggregate demand and equilibrium real GNP from attaining a higher level. If empirical evidence shows that the impact of deficits on interest rates is small, then the high interest rates that were in part causing the deterioration of net exports must be due to factors other than federal budget deficits. The point is that theoretical cause-and-effect relationships may or may not have important quantitative impacts on the economy even though it is commonly believed by the public that those relationships are significant.

38

Tradeoffs Between Inflation and Unemployment and the Theory of Rational Expectations

CHAPTER CHALLENGES

After studying your text, attending class, and completing this chapter, you should be able to:

1. Discuss the historical tradeoff between annual inflation and unemployment in modern economies through the use of the Phillips curve.
2. Show how shifts in aggregate supply can affect the tradeoff between the goals of reducing inflation and reducing unemployment.
3. Understand how rational expectations of changes in the price level can affect the behavior of workers and investors and influence macroeconomic equilibrium.
4. Understand some of the difficulties of implementing stabilization policies and explain how rational expectations about the effect of stabilization policies might frustrate achievement of their goals.

IN BRIEF: CHAPTER SUMMARY

Fill in the blanks to summarize chapter content.

In the 1950s, A.W. Phillips investigated the relationship between the unemployment rate and the rate of change in wages for Great Britain. He discovered what appeared to be a very stable (1)_____ (direct, inverse) relationship between the unemployment rate and wage inflation. As the unemployment rate fell, the rate of wage inflation increased and vice versa. The Phillips curve was consistent with models of the economy that emphasized changes in aggregate (2)_____ (demand, supply) as the source of fluctuations in real GNP and the price level. Using data for the (3)_____ (1970s, 1960s), a stable Phillips curve (expressed as a relationship between the unemployment rate and the rate of change in prices) seemed to explain the unemployment-inflation experience of the United States. Policy makers believed that it was possible to choose the desired unemployment rate-inflation rate along the Phillips curve by using demand-management policies. The Phillips curve analysis assumes that the aggregate supply curve shifts rightward in an/a (4)_____ (erratic, predictable) manner. Further, it does not consider the role of inflation expectations.

In the 1970s and 1980s the Phillips curve for the United States has (5)_____ (not remained stable but has shifted due to, remained stable in part because of) supply-side shocks and changes in inflation expectations. For instance, the oil-price shocks of the early 1970s caused the aggregate supply curve to shift (6)_____ (leftward, rightward) more than the aggregate demand curve shifted (7)_____ (leftward, rightward) resulting in a rising price level at a time when the economy was experiencing increases in the rate of unemployment. Between 1978 and 1980, as unemployment rose from 6% to 7%, the rate of inflation rose from 8% to over 13% per year. These events directly (8)_____ (support, counter) the belief that the

Phillips curve is stable over the long run. Over short periods, such as 1986 and 1987, the Phillips curve tradeoff between inflation and the unemployment rate was present, but over the long run the Phillips curve shifts. Supply-side shocks that increase input prices increase the rate of inflation for given unemployment rates and shift the Phillips curve (9)_____ (downward, upward). Supply-side shocks that reduce input prices, such as the decline in oil prices in 1986, shift the Phillips curve (10)_____ (downward, upward).

There are two major competing theories of how we form expectations. One theory holds that we form expectations adaptively. Our expectations are dependent solely on past observations of the variable to be forecast. The other major theory, the theory of (11)_____ (aggregate expected demand, rational expectations), holds that individuals use all information, past and present, including relevant economic models, in their forecasts of economic variables. This theory assumes that the expected value of the forecast variable equals the actual future value of that variable. This doesn't mean that individuals forecast correctly all the time; rather it means that forecasting errors will not be systematically high or low in the long run.

If an increase in aggregate demand is anticipated, it is argued that rational individuals will use this information in forming inflation expectations. If labor, for instance, expects higher inflation as a result of an anticipated increase in aggregate demand, they will press for higher wages as a way of maintaining the real value or purchasing power of their wage income. If wages and other input prices rise at exactly the same rate as prices, real wages and real input prices will not change, (12)_____ (causing, and there is no reason for) employers to alter their current rates of employment and production. Thus the rational expectations theory holds that anticipated changes in aggregate demand, which include changes caused by fiscal and monetary policy, will be (13)_____ (completely, partially) offset by input suppliers as they react to anticipated changes in inflation. The aggregate supply curve shifts leftward by (14)_____ (the same amount as, less than) the aggregate demand curve shifts rightward. The price level increases, but real GNP and employment remain unchanged.

Increases in inflation expectations cause the Phillips curve to shift (15)_____ (downward, upward). If inflation expectations rise, labor and other input suppliers will renegotiate contracts, thus increasing unit production costs and causing firms to raise prices. Inflation rises at given levels of unemployment. The (16)_____ (Keynesian model, accelerationist hypothesis) argues that attempts by policy makers to reduce the rate of unemployment below the natural rate with expansionary fiscal or monetary policy will work only in the (17)_____ (long run, short run). In the (18)_____ (long run, short run), input suppliers will increase their inflation expectations and press for higher input prices when they discover that inflation is higher than expected. This causes the unemployment rate to return to its natural level.

Counter cyclical policy requires that policy makers first determine if macroeconomic problems are the result of demand-side or supply-side shocks. If they are due to demand-side shocks, the first problem of stabilization efforts is (19)_____ (to implement policy, forecasting shifts in aggregate demand). Second, the government must respond quickly to offset the undesired change in aggregate demand. Third, the extent to which monetary and fiscal policy should be used depends upon the predicted impacts of changes in the money supply or the government deficit. The ability of policy to offset an undesired change in aggregate demand depends to some extent on whether the policy change is anticipated or unanticipated. Policy will likely be (20)_____ (more, less) effective if it is unanticipated.

Some economists argue that policy makers often make errors that result in economic instability. They argue that policy exacerbates business cycle fluctuations and should not be used. They suggest that policy makers (21)_____ (use a policy rule such as a constant rate of money growth, always balance the budget) rather than use discretionary fiscal and monetary policy. Another view holds that stabilization policy has nevertheless (22)_____ (reduced, increased) the severity of economic fluctuations since the end of World War II. (23)_____ (Fiscal, Incomes) policies such as jawboning, wage-price guidelines, and wage-price controls have been used in addition to monetary and fiscal policy to control inflation. Wage-price controls are (24)_____ (frequently, rarely) used in peacetime because they distort the price system and contribute to the variability of inflation.

VOCABULARY REVIEW

Write the key term from the list below next to its definition.

Key Terms

Phillips curve   Policy rule
Disinflation   Incomes policies
Rational expectations   Wage-price guidelines
Accelerationist hypothesis   Wage-price controls

Definitions

1. _____: argues that attempts by policy makers to reduce the unemployment rate below the natural rate can succeed only in the short run.

2. _____: a preannounced government rule that will inform the public of future economic stabilization policies.

3. _____: refers to use by individuals of all available information, including any relevant economic models, in their forecasts of economic variables.

4. _____: policies that seek to curb inflation by directly influencing both prices and wages without reducing aggregate demand through the use of monetary or fiscal policy.

5. _____: a sharp reduction in the annual rate of inflation.

6. _____: rules established by government authorities that result in control of prices, wages, and their rate of increase.

7. _____: a curve showing the hypothesized inverse relationship between annual unemployment and annual inflation in a nation.

8. _____: standards established by government authorities that seek to keep wage and price increases within certain bounds over a period.

Concept: **Shifts in the aggregate supply curve and the inflation-unemployment tradeoff**

1. The figure below shows an economy at its potential real GNP of $3,000 billion with a natural unemployment rate of 6%. The price level is 100, and the rate of inflation is zero.

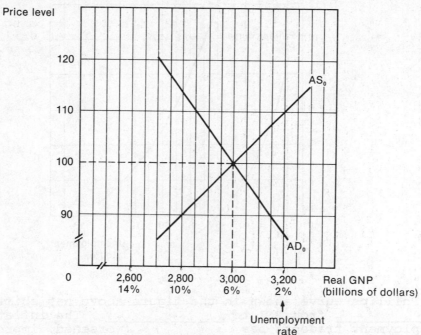

a. Assume that autonomous increases in aggregate demand shift the AD curve by $100 billion at every price level. The aggregate demand curve shifts _____. Show this on the figure above and label the new AD curve AD1.

b. Now assume that in addition to the increase in aggregate demand, a supply-side shock increases input prices, shifting the AS curve by $200 billion at every price level. The aggregate supply curve shifts _____. Show this on the figure above and label the new AS curve AS1.

c. The price level has _____ from 100 to _____, resulting in a _____ % change in the price level. Real GNP _____ from $3,000 billion to $_____, and the unemployment rate _____ from 6% to _____ %.

d. On the figure below, find the point representing the initial rate of
    inflation, 0%, and initial rate of unemployment, 6% and label that
    point A. Now find the coordinate that represents the new rate of
    change in the price level and the new rate of unemployment from part
    c and label that point B.

e. The Phillips curve shown in the figure above has shifted
    _____ from PC1 to _____. The inflation-
    unemployment tradeoff has _____ (worsened, improved).
    Adverse supply-side shocks that increase input prices shift the
    Phillips curve _____.

2. Given the level of aggregate demand, a favorable supply-side shock that
    decreases input prices will shift the aggregate _____ curve
    _____ and will shift the Phillips curve _____. The unemployment-
    inflation tradeoff _____ (worsens, improves).

Concept: **Rational expectations, the AD-AS model, and implications for stabilization policy**

3. Suppose the economy shown in the figure below, like that in the first figure, is at potential real GNP where the natural rate of unemployment is attained with a zero rate of inflation.

a. Assume that an increase in the money supply that shifts the aggregate demand curve rightward by $150 billion at every price level is fully anticipated by the public. Show the new AD curve and label the curve AD1. According to rational expectations theory, if the increase in aggregate demand is fully anticipated, input suppliers push for _____ input prices, causing the AS curve to shift _____ by $_____ billion. Show the new AS curve in the figure above and label it AS1. After the shifts in the AD and AS curves, the price level _____ from 100 to _____, resulting in a _____% change in the price level. Real GNP and the rate of unemployment _____.

b. In the figure below, plot the initial rate of change in the price level and unemployment rate. Now plot the new rate of change in the price level and unemployment rate found in part a. Draw a line connecting the two points.

Inflation rate (%)

Unemployment rate (%)

c. The proponents of the rational expectations theory view the Phillips curve as _____(downward sloping, vertical). Anticipated increases in aggregate demand _____ real GNP and the unemployment rate, although the rate of inflation _____.

d. According to the rational expectations theory, if changes in the federal budget deficit or the money supply are completely anticipated, fiscal and monetary policy are _____ (effective, ineffective) in altering real GNP and the rate of unemployment.

4. List two criticisms of the rational expectations theory.

a. _____

b. _____

Concept: Accelerationist hypothesis and stabilization policy

5.   The economy shown in the figure below is currently operating at its
     potential level of real GNP with an inflation rate equal to zero.

   a.   Suppose policy makers want to reduce the unemployment rate below
        the natural rate of unemployment to 3% by using expansionary fiscal
        policy. Equilibrium real GNP must rise to $3150 billion in order to
        reduce the unemployment rate to 3%. Show the new aggregate demand
        curve in the figure above and label the AD curve AD1.
   b.   The price level rises from 100 to _____, producing a _____ %
        change in the price level. Workers and other input suppliers will
        eventually revise their expected rates of inflation from 0% to
        _____. As this happens, wages and other input prices _____,
        causing the aggregate _____ curve to shift _____ until real GNP
        equals $_____. Show the new aggregate supply curve and label
        the AS curve AS1.
   c.   If government once again expands the economy in an effort to reduce
        the unemployment rate below the natural rate, real GNP will _____,
        the rate of unemployment will _____, and the price level will
        _____. The effects on real GNP and the unemployment rate _____
        in the long run as input suppliers react to the realization that
        actual inflation exceeds expected inflation. The price level
        is_____ in the long run.
   d.   According to the accelerationist hypothesis, fiscal and monetary
        policy are able to affect real GNP and the unemployment rate in the
        _____, but not in the _____.

SELF-TEST FOR MASTERY

Select the best answer.

1. In the 1950s, A.W. Phillips investigated the relationship between:

    a. Wage and price inflation.
    b. Output and price changes.
    c. The unemployment rate and the rate of change in wages.
    d. The unemployment rate and the rate of change in prices.

2. The U.S. Phillips curve in the 1960s:

    a. Shifted erratically.
    b. Appeared to be stable.
    c. Shifted consistently upward.
    d. Shifted downward during the first half of the decade.

3. The Phillips curve tradeoff implies:

    a. That if the curve is stable, society must accept increases in inflation in exchange for decreases in unemployment.
    b. That if the curve is unstable, society must accept increases in inflation in exchange for decreases in unemployment.
    c. That if the curve is stable, society must accept increases in inflation in exchange for increases in unemployment.
    d. That if the curve is unstable, society must accept falling unemployment when inflation falls.

4. Which of the following can cause the Phillips curve to shift?

    a. An increase in inflation expectations
    b. A decrease in inflation expectations
    c. An adverse supply-side shock increasing input prices
    d. A favorable supply-side shock decreasing input prices
    e. All of the above

5. The oil-price shock of 1973 had the effect of shifting the aggregate supply curve _____ by _____ than the aggregate demand curve shifted _____. The outcome was stagflation.

    a. Rightward, less, leftward
    b. Rightward, less, rightward
    c. Leftward, less, leftward
    d. Leftward, less, rightward
    e. Leftward, more, rightward

6. The U.S. Phillips curve in the 1970s:

    a. Was stable.
    b. Shifted upward due to supply-side shocks and rising inflation expectations.
    c. Shifted downward due to supply-side shocks.
    d. Shifted downward in the first half of the decade and upward in the second half.

7. In the 1980s, the Phillips curve has shifted _____ in part because of _____ and _____.

   a. Downward, declines in oil prices, falling inflation expectations
   b. Upward, increases in oil prices, rising inflation expectations
   c. Downward, rising wages, falling prices
   d. Upward, falling wages, rising prices
   e. None of the above

8. Which of the following terms represents a sharp reduction in the rate of inflation?

   a. Crawling inflation
   b. Deflation
   c. Hyperinflation
   d. Disinflation
   e. B and d

9. Which of the following theories of expectations holds that individuals form expectations by looking only to past values of the variable to be forecast?

   a. Rational expectations theory
   b. Certainty equivalent theory
   c. Expected value analysis
   d. Adaptive expectations theory

10. Which of the following theories of expectations holds that individuals use all information available in forming expectations?

   a. Rational expectations theory
   b. Certainty equivalent theory
   c. Expected value analysis
   d. Adaptive expectations theory

11. Rational expectations theory implies that anticipated changes in aggregate demand:

   a. Affect real GNP and the price level only in the long run.
   b. Will be completely offset by the actions of input suppliers as they react to their inflation expectations.
   c. Will always affect real but not nominal GNP.
   d. Will result in economic expansion over the long run.
   e. A and d.

12. Which of the following theories holds that efforts by policy makers to reduce the unemployment rate below the natural rate of unemployment will be successful only in the short run?

   a. Adaptive expectations theory
   b. Rational expectations theory
   c. New classical-RE model
   d. Accelerationist hypothesis

13. An increase in inflation expectations causes input suppliers to push for _____ input prices, which _____ unit production costs and prices. This results in a/an _____ shift in the Phillips curve.

   a. Higher, increase, downward
   b. Lower, decrease, downward
   c. Lower, increase, upward

d.   Higher, increase, upward
e.   Lower, decrease, upward

14. The first problem of stabilization policy is to:

a.   Predict the impact of changes in the money stock or the
     government deficit on the economy.
b.   Quickly implement countercyclical policies.
c.   Predict shifts in aggregate demand.
d.   Follow a policy rule.

15. The second problem of stabilization policy is to:

a.   Predict the impact of changes in the money stock or the
     government deficit on the economy.
b.   Quickly implement countercyclical policies.
c.   Predict shifts in aggregate demand.
d.   Follow a policy rule.

16. The third problem of stabilization policy is to:

a.   Predict the impact of changes in the money stock or the
     government deficits on the economy.
b.   Quickly implement countercyclical policies.
c.   Predict shifts in aggregate demand.
d.   Follow a policy rule.

17. Incomes policies have proved _____ in reducing wage and price
     inflation over the long run and as a result are used _____ during
     peacetime.

a.   Successful, frequently
b.   Unsuccessful, often
c.   Successful, infrequently
d.   Unsuccessful, only rarely

18. Which of the following are examples of incomes policies?

a.   Jawboning
b.   Wage-price guidelines
c.   Wage-price controls
d.   Tax cuts
e.   A, b, and c

THINK IT THROUGH

1.   "At times during the 1970s and 1980s in the United States, the rate of
inflation and the rate of unemployment moved in the same direction. This is
evidence that the Phillips curve does not exist and policy makers need not pay
any attention to the tradeoff it implies." Analyze this statement.

2.   Identify the implication of rational expectations theory regarding the
ability of monetary and fiscal policy to affect real GNP and the rate of
unemployment. This policy implication depends upon several important
assumptions: (a) individuals form expectations rationally, (b) wages and prices
are flexible, and (c) all markets are competitive markets that constantly

clear--are in equilibrium. How might this policy implication change if wages and prices are in fact slow to adjust?

3.   Use the accelerationist hypothesis to describe an inflationary process that begins with demand-pull inflation and is followed by cost-push inflation to be followed again by demand-pull inflation and so on. In other words, how can the accelerationist hypothesis be used to explain a wage-price spiral?

CHAPTER ANSWERS

In Brief: Chapter Summary

1. Inverse 2. Demand 3. 1960s 4. Predictable 5. Not remained stable, but has shifted due to 6. Leftward 7. Rightward 8. Counter 9. Upward 10. Downward 11. Rational expectations 12. And there is no reason for 13. Completely 14. The same amount as 15. Upward 16. Accelerationist hypothesis 17. Short run 18. Long run 19. Forecasting shifts in aggregate demand 20. More 21. Use a policy rule such as a constant rate of money growth 22. Reduced 23. Incomes 24. Rarely

Vocabulary Review

1. Accelerationist hypothesis 2. Policy rule 3. Rational expectations 4. Incomes policies 5. Disinflation 6. Wage-price controls 7. Phillips curve 8. Wage-price guidelines

Skills Review

1.   a.   Rightward

b.   Leftward
c.   Increased, 110, 10%; falls, $2,950 billion, rises, 7%

d.

e.   Upward, PC1; worsened; upward

2.   Supply, rightward, downward; improves

3.   a.

Higher, leftward, $150 billion; rises, 110, 10%; remain unchanged

b.

c.   Vertical; do not change the level of; increases
d.   Ineffective

4.   a.   Individuals do not have access to all information, nor do they make
          use of all available information.
     b.   Wages and other input prices are slow to adjust due to the existence
          of annual and multi-year contracts.

5.   a.

Price level

(Long-run) effect of actions taken by input suppliers and workers

(Short-run) expansionary fiscal policy

Real GNP (billions of dollars)

b.   110, 10%; 10%; rise, supply, leftward, $3,000 billion
c.   Increase, decrease, rise; vanish, higher
d.   Short run, long run

Self-Test for Mastery

1. c 2. b 3. a 4. e 5. e 6. b 7. a 8. d 9. d 10. a 11. b 12. d 13. d 14. c 15. b 16. a 17. d 18. e

Think It Through

1.   The Phillips curve and the tradeoff it implies between the rate of inflation and the unemployment rate does indeed exist in the short run when the economy is not buffeted by supply-side shocks and changes in inflation expectations. Supply-side shocks and changes in inflation expectations shift the Phillips curve. But at a given point in time the economy operates on a Phillips curve that is not necessarily stable. Increases in aggregate demand that reduce the unemployment rate below the natural rate will cause inflation unless the Phillips curve is shifting, in which case inflation may increase or decrease as the unemployment rate falls. For instance, if an increase in aggregate demand is accompanied by a favorable supply-side shock that shifts the aggregate supply curve rightward more than the aggregate demand curve shifts rightward, the unemployment rate falls while the price level falls. The Phillips curve is shifting downward at the same time that the unemployment rate is falling. Policy makers need to be aware that the inflation-unemployment tradeoff will likely present itself in the short run, although it is likely to shift over the long run and therefore is not a reliable guide to the long-run tradeoff.

2.   Rational expectations theory holds that monetary and fiscal policy changes will be anticipated by the public. For example, an anticipated increase in the money stock will produce expectations of rising inflation, which will cause workers and other input suppliers to push for higher input prices. This increases unit production cost,s causing firms to increase prices at given levels of output. The aggregate supply curve shifts leftward as the aggregate demand curve shifts rightward. There is no change in real variables such as real GNP and the unemployment rate, only increases in the price level. Thus it is argued that anticipated monetary or fiscal policy will not be effective in altering real GNP or unemployment rates and should not be used. If, however, wages and other input prices are slow to adjust as they certainly are due to the existence of multi-period contracts, leftward shifts in the aggregate supply curve will lag behind the rightward shift in the aggregate demand curve, resulting in higher real GNP and a lower rate of unemployment in the short run. It is argued that the length of time it takes for complete adjustment may well be quite long, resulting in a "long" short run.

3.   Suppose policy makers want to reduce the unemployment rate below the
natural rate of unemployment. If the economy is at its potential level of real
GNP and expansionary monetary or fiscal policy is used, demand-pull inflation
results as real GNP rises and the unemployment rate falls. In time, input
suppliers will realize that actual inflation exceeds expected inflation and
will push for higher input prices, causing the aggregate supply curve to shift
leftward. Now the unemployment rate is rising and the rate of inflation is
worsening--cost-push inflation is occurring. But suppose policy makers persist
in their efforts to reduce the unemployment rate and once again use
expansionary policy. This causes inflation to worsen still further but reduces
the unemployment rate below the natural rate. As was the case previously,
workers and other input suppliers will eventually realize that actual inflation
is outpacing expected inflation, which will cause them to press for higher
input prices. Again the aggregate supply curve shifts leftward, returning the
unemployment rate to its natural level, but at still higher rates of inflation.
Activist demand-management policy that tries to keep the rate of unemployment
below the natural rate of unemployment will only succeed in creating a wage-
price spiral in the long run.

39

International Trade, Productivity, and the Economics of Less Developed Countries

CHAPTER CHALLENGES

After studying your text, attending class, and completing this chapter, you should be able to:

1. Understand the underlying basis for international trade and the gains in well-being possible from free trade with foreign nations.
2. Discuss the principle of comparative advantage and show how productivity changes in specific industries can affect their comparative advantage in international trade.
3. Discuss controversies regarding free trade vs. protection of U.S. industries from foreign competition in light of the basic theory of international trade.
4. Analyze the impact on the economy of tariffs, import quotas, and other trade restrictions.
5. Discuss some of the unique economic problems of less developed countries and the causes of low per capita income and slow economic growth in those nations.

IN BRIEF: CHAPTER SUMMARY

Fill in the blanks to summarize chapter content.

Nations engage in international trade because it is mutually beneficial for all trading nations to do so; otherwise they would not trade. Some nations may have a/an (1)_____ (comparative, absolute) advantage in producing goods, meaning that with a given complement of resources, one nation can produce more of an item than another nation with the same quantity of resources. But the presence of an absolute advantage in the production of an item does not indicate whether a nation should specialize in and export that good or whether the good should be imported. A country should specialize in and export those goods for which it has an/a (2)_____ (absolute, comparative) advantage and import those goods for which other countries have a comparative advantage. A nation has a comparative advantage in the production of a good relative to another nation if it produces the good at (3)_____ (lower, higher) opportunity cost than its trading partner.

Nations that trade on the basis of comparative advantage (4)_____ (gain at the expense of their rivals, mutually gain from trade). On an international scale, resources are used more efficiently as nations produce output based upon comparative advantages. World output, income, and living standards are (5)_____ (higher, lower) as a result of specialization and trade than would be the case in the absence of trade. All trading partners gain, although not equally. The distribution of the gains from trade is determined by the (6)_____ (foreign exchange rate, terms of trade)--the rate at which goods can be traded or exchanged for one another on international markets. A nation will be induced to trade goods for which it has a comparative advantage for import goods if it can obtain the imported goods at prices below the domestic opportunity cost of production. The real terms of trade are determined by (7)_____ (government, world demand and supply). For trade incentives to exist, the terms of trade must be (8)_____ (below, above) the opportunity cost of producing each additional unit of the good a nation desires to import. When countries specialize in and export those goods for which they have a comparative advantage and import goods for which other nations have a comparative advantage, the consumption possibilities curve of each nation lies (9)_____ (outside, inside) the production possibilities curve.

Changes in productivity can affect a nation's competitiveness in international markets. If a nation experiences slower technological growth or lower levels of investment in human and physical capital relative to those of its trading partners, in time it may lose its (10)_____ (absolute, comparative) advantage in those industries where international competitiveness requires improvements in productivity. The nation that invests more heavily in things that enhance productivity will eventually (11)_____ (gain, lose) a comparative advantage relative to the lagging nation and will capture a share of the international market that it previously did not have. Productivity growth (growth in output per labor hour) in the United States from 1981-1985 was among the (12)_____ (highest, lowest) for industrialized nations at about (13)_____ (10%, 1%) per year. This has been cited as a reason for the decline in the competitiveness of some U.S. export industries. The primary cause of the low productivity growth is believed to be the low rate of annual (14)_____ (government, investment) spending as a percentage of domestic production relative to other nations, particularly Japan. Increased government regulation and (15)_____ (a liberal Congress, higher energy prices) have also been cited as factors contributing to the productivity decline of the 1970s.

As comparative advantage changes, nations losing the comparative advantage in a good no longer export that good. Industry sales and output fall, causing some workers with specialized skills to become unemployed and other suppliers of specialized inputs to experience a decline in income. Both the owners of the declining industry and its input suppliers are harmed. But this has to be balanced against the widespread gains to society when a nation produces on the basis of comparative advantage. Changes in comparative advantage are painful in the short run, but nations are better off in the long run by specializing in and exporting those goods for which they have a comparative advantage and trading for those goods for which they do not.

Several arguments, however, have been advanced for protecting domestic industries. It is argued that some industries may need to be protected from international competition to maintain production capacity (16)_____ (vital to national security, necessary to be self-sufficient). Protecting (17)_____ (large and established industries, new and emerging "infant" industries) from the rigors of international competition is considered a way of allowing an industry to grow in a sheltered environment until it attains sufficient economies of scale to compete internationally. Industries experiencing changes in comparative advantage can be spared some of the short run costs to specialized input suppliers and owners by receiving some protection from foreign rivals. Some industries are protected from what is viewed as unfair competition by foreign governments that subsidize their export industries. Arguments against free trade derive from changes in the (18)_____ (distribution of income that occur, efficiency with which goods are produced) as some industries fail and lose their comparative advantage.

Two methods of import protection are import tariffs and import quotas. A (19)_____ (quota, tariff) is a tax on an imported good. The intention is

to reduce imports and increase the sales of domestic products. A tariff
(20)_____ (raises, lowers) the price of the imported good to the consumer,
(21)_____ (increases, reduces) the net price to the foreign producer, and
generates tax revenue for the government. A/An (22)_____ (tariff, import
quota) is a limit on the quantity of foreign goods that can be sold in a
nation's domestic market. Like the tariff, an import quota (23)_____
(increases, reduces) the quantity of imported goods sold and (24)_____
(raises, lowers) the price to the consumer, but unlike a tariff, the import
quota also (25)_____ (lowers, raises) the price received by the foreign
producer. If the demand for the imported good is inelastic, the foreign
producer (26)_____(is always worse off, may be better off) operating with
a quota. Further, quotas raise no revenue for government. But protectionism
invites retaliation from trading partners. If a nation's trading partners also
impose import tariffs and quotas, all of the trading nations (27)_____
(lose, gain) because the level of international trade is lower and consumers in
each country are paying higher prices than necessary.

(28)_____ [Newly industrialized countries, Less developed
countries (LDCs)] have very low real per capita GNPs. This is because of (a)
(29)_____ (high, low) rates of saving and capital accumulation, (b) poorly
skilled and educated workers, (c) lagging technological know-how, (d)
(30)_____ (high, low) population growth and unemployment, and (e) political
instability and government policies that discourage production. These nations
are dependent on foreign trade to acquire capital and technology necessary for
increases in their standard of living. But unless they export enough to
acquire the foreign exchange to purchase the imported goods, these nations will
not be able to advance significantly without the help of gifts or loans from
foreign nations.

VOCABULARY REVIEW

Write the key term from the list below next to its definition.

Key Terms

Specialization	Consumption possibilities
Mutual gains from	curve
international trade	Tariff
Absolute advantage	Import quota
Comparative advantage	Real per capita output
Real terms of trade	Less developed country
	(LDC)

Definitions

1. _____: shows combinations of two goods a nation can
consume given its resources, technology, and international trade.

2. _____: the actual market exchange rate of one good for
another in international trade.

3. _____: a tax on imported goods.

4. _____: a nation has a comparative advantage over a
trading partner in the production of an item if it produces that item at
lower opportunity cost per unit than its partner does.

5. _____: a limit on the quantity of foreign goods that can be sold in a nation's domestic markets.

6. _____: a nation has an absolute advantage over other nations in the production of an item if it can produce more of the item over a certain period with a given amount of resources than the other nations can.

7. _____: a measure of output per person in a nation; calculated by dividing real GNP by population.

8. _____: on average, citizens in all trading nations gain from exchanging goods in international markets.

9. _____: a country whose real GNP per capita is generally much less than $1000 per year.

10. _____: use of labor and other resources in a nation to produce the goods and services for which those resources are best adapted.

SKILLS REVIEW

Concept: Absolute vs. comparative advantage, terms of trade, gains from trade

1. The domestic production possibilities of two nations, nation A and nation B, for two goods, cases of wine and boxes of cheese, are shown below.

Production Possibilities

	Nation A	Nation B
Wine (cases)	1 million	600,000
Cheese (boxes)	500,000	400,000

a. Plot the production possibilities curve for each nation in a and b in the figure below.

b. Assuming each nation has the same quantity of resources, 1000 workers, and both nations produce only wine, the number of cases of wine per worker in nation A of _____ cases _____ the number of cases of wine per worker of _____ cases in nation B. Similarly, if both nations produce only cheese, the number of boxes of cheese per worker in nation A of _____ boxes _____ the number of boxes of cheese per worker in nation B of _____ boxes. Nation A has a/an _____ advantage in the production of both wine and cheese. Nation A's production possibilities curve _____ nation B's production possibilities curve.

c. In nation A, the opportunity cost of producing a case of wine is _____ boxes of cheese and the opportunity cost of producing a box of cheese is _____ cases of wine. The slope of nation A's production possibilities curve is _____, which means that the opportunity cost of producing an additional box of cheese is _____ cases of wine.

d. In nation B, the opportunity cost of producing a case of wine is _____ boxes of cheese and the opportunity cost of producing a box of cheese is _____ cases of wine. The slope of nation B's production possibilities curve is _____, which means that the opportunity cost of producing an additional box of cheese is _____ cases of wine.

2. Regarding the problem above, nation A has a comparative advantage in the production of _____, whereas nation B has a comparative advantage in the production of _____. Nation A should specialize in and export _____ and should import _____. Nation B should specialize in and export _____ and should import _____. For nation A to be induced to trade for _____, it must give up less _____ than that implied by its domestic opportunity cost of _____. For nation B to be induced to trade for _____, it must give up less _____ than that implied by its domestic opportunity cost of _____. Trade will be mutually beneficial to both nations if 1 box of cheese trades for between

_____ and _____ cases of wine. Alternatively, trade will result if 1 case of wine trades for between _____ and _____ boxes of cheese.

3. a. Assume that the terms of trade for cheese are set exactly between the two quantities of wine you cited in question 2 above. Alternatively, assume that the terms of trade for wine are set exactly between the two quantities of cheese you cited above. What are the terms of trade?

    1 box of cheese = _____ cases of wine
    1 box of wine   = _____ boxes of cheese

    b. Given the terms of trade, in a and b in the figure above plot the consumption possibilities curve for each nation.
    c. If nation A specializes in wine and keeps 800,000 cases for its domestic consumption and trades 200,000 cases to nation B, how many boxes of cheese can it get in return? _____ boxes Given nation A's domestic opportunity cost of cheese of _____ cases of wine, it can domestically produce only _____ boxes of cheese by sacrificing 200,000 cases of wine. Trade results in a gain of _____ boxes of cheese over what was possible in the absence of trade.
    d. If nation B trades cheese for 200,000 cases of nation A's wine, how much cheese will it have to trade? _____ boxes of cheese. Given B's domestic opportunity cost of wine of _____ boxes of cheese, it can domestically produce 200,000 cases of wine only by sacrificing _____ boxes of cheese, but it only has to give up _____ boxes of cheese through international trade to acquire the same quantity of wine. Trade results in a gain of _____ boxes of cheese over what was possible in the absence of trade.

Concept: Protectionism, tariffs, and quotas

4. List four arguments in favor of protectionism.

    a. _____
    b. _____
    c. _____
    d. _____

5. In a and b in the figure below are shown the domestic and import markets for shoes.

a.   Suppose that domestic shoe manufacturers and their input suppliers are able to win an import tariff of $10 per pair of imported shoes. Show the new import supply curve in b above. The $10 tariff causes the price to the consumer to _____ to $_____ and the net price to foreign shoe manufacturers to _____ to $_____. Sales of imported shoes _____ to _____ million pairs. The tariff has raised tax revenue of $_____. Show these effects in b.

b.   In a, assume that the decline in import sales causes an increase in domestic shoe demand by an equal amount at each price level. The domestic demand for shoes shifts _____ by _____ million pairs of shoes. Domestic shoe prices _____ to $_____ and sales _____ to _____ million pairs.

c.   In effect, the tariff redistributes income from _____ and _____ to the owners and input suppliers of the protected domestic shoe industry.

d.   If an import quota had been used instead to achieve the lower level of import sales that you found in part a above, the price of imported shoes paid by the consumer and received by the foreign producer _____ to $_____. The domestic market price of shoes _____ to $_____, and sales _____ to _____ million pairs of shoes. In this case, the government receives _____ tax revenue and the foreign producer may experience a/an _____ in total revenue if the demand for imported shoes is sufficiently inelastic. Show the case of an import quota in b in the figure above.

SELF-TEST FOR MASTERY

Select the best answer.

1. If a nation has a/an _____ in the production of an item, it can produce more of the item with a given quantity of resources than can other nations.

    a. Special advantage
    b. Comparative advantage
    c. Absolute advantage
    d. Mutual gain

2. A nation's comparative advantage is determined by:

    a. The total cost of production.
    b. The quantity of resources required to produce a unit of output.
    c. The opportunity cost of producing an item relative to a trading partner's opportunity cost of producing the same item.
    d. Specialization in the production of all goods.

3. If nations trade on the basis of comparative advantage, a nation should specialize in and _____ those goods for which it has a comparative advantage and should _____ those goods for which other nations have a comparative advantage.

    a. Export, import
    b. Import, export
    c. Export, export
    d. Import, import

4. If nations trade on the basis of comparative advantage:

    a. A nation can gain only at the expense of trading partners.
    b. Exporting nations gain and importing nations lose.
    c. Importing nations gain and exporting nations lose.
    d. All trading partners mutually gain.

5. A nation will be induced to trade for imported goods if the nation can give up _____ goods through international trade for the imported item than implied by its domestic _____ cost of production.

    a. More, total
    b. More, opportunity
    c. Fewer, variable
    d. Fewer, opportunity

6. Which of the following refers to the rate at which goods are exchanged for one another in international markets?

    a. Exchange rate
    b. Terms of trade
    c. Specialization
    d. Opportunity cost
    e. None of the above

7. If nations trade on the basis of _____ advantage, the consumption possibilities curve lies _____ the production possibilities curve.

    a. Absolute, inside
    b. A unique, parallel to
    c. Comparative, parallel to
    d. Comparative, outside

8. When a nation's productivity growth lags behind that of its trading partners, in time it may:

    a. Lose its comparative advantage in some industries.
    b. Gain a comparative advantage as a result of the lag in productivity growth.
    c. Diversify with "infant" industries.
    d. Experience a reduction in the opportunity cost of producing the good.

9. Lagging productivity growth of a nation relative to its trading partners:

    a. Results in a loss of comparative advantage in some industries.
    b. Results in an increase in the opportunity cost of producing some goods relative to that of foreign rivals.
    c. Results in a loss of income to the owners and specialized input suppliers in the industries experiencing lagging productivity growth.
    d. All of the above.

10. The United States from 1981 to 1985 experienced an average rate of growth of ____% in its output per worker, which was among the _____ for industrialized nations.

    a. 1, lowest
    b. 3.5, lowest
    c. 10, highest
    d. 8, highest

11. Which of the following have been cited as reasons for the slow productivity growth in the United States in the 1970s?

    a. Average annual net investment of 6% of domestic production
    b. Increased government regulation to improve working conditions and the environment
    c. Rising energy prices
    d. All of the above
    e. None of the above

12. Which of the following is not an argument in favor of protectionism?

    a. National security
    b. Reducing structural unemployment
    c. Protecting infant industries
    d. Protecting U.S. industries against subsidized foreign producers
    e. Goal of self-sufficiency

13. Which of the following is a tax on an imported good?

    a. Income tax
    b. Import quota
    c. Rationing tax
    d. Tariff

14. A tariff does which of the following?

    a. Increases the price of the imported good to the consumer
    b. Decreases the net price received by the foreign producer
    c. Increases the price of the domestic good
    d. Redistributes income from domestic consumers and foreign producers to the protected industry
    e. All of the above

15. Which of the following places a limit on the quantity of a foreign good that can be imported into a domestic market?

    a. Import capacity limit
    b. Import quota
    c. Export quota
    d. Tariff

16. An import quota does which of the following?

    a. Increases the price of the imported good to the consumer
    b. Increases the price received by the foreign producer
    c. Increases the price of the domestic good
    d. Redistributes income from domestic consumers to the protected domestic exporter
    e. All of the above

17. Which of the following is a country whose real GNP per capita is generally less than $1000 per year?

    a. A newly industrialized country
    b. A less developed country
    c. An industrialized country
    d. A socialist state

18. Which of the following is not a reason for low per capita output in a country?

    a. Low rates of saving and investment
    b. Poorly skilled and educated workers
    c. High population growth and unemployment
    d. Lagging technology
    e. Socialism

THINK IT THROUGH

1. "In international trade, one nation's trade surplus (exports in excess of imports) must be another nation's trade deficit (imports in excess of exports). Therefore the mercantilists must be correct in saying that a nation should encourage exports and discourage imports." Evaluate this statement.

2. The United States has lost its international competitiveness in some basic industries, particularly those that produce standardized goods with large economies of scale. Can you think of any reasons why?

3. If a nation employs protectionist measures such as tariffs or quotas and trading partners retaliate in kind, discuss some likely consequences.

POP QUIZ   Read the news brief at the end of this chapter and answer the
                questions below.

1.   In the first half of 1988, the U.S. trade deficit was $70 billion, but it
narrowed from $84.45 billion in the first half of 1987. In June of 1988, the
trade deficit widened to $12.54 billion from $9.76 billion the previous month.
Discuss the changes in imports and exports for the month of June that produced
this widening gap.

2.   How did the U.S. trade deficit change with major trading partners? In
light of this chapter, discuss how the United States benefits from trade even
though its deficit with several major trading partners widened in June of 1988.

CHAPTER ANSWERS

In Brief: Chapter Summary

1. Absolute 2. Comparative 3. Lower 4. Mutually gain from trade 5. Higher
6. Terms of trade 7. World demand and supply 8. Below 9. Outside 10.
Comparative 11. Gain 12. Lowest 13. 1% 14. Investment 15. Higher energy
prices 16. Vital to national security 17. New and emerging "infant"
industries 18. Distribution of income that occur 19. Tariff 20. Raises 21.
Reduces 22. Import quota 23. Reduces 24. Raises 25. Raises 26. May be
better off 27. Lose 28. Less developed countries (LDCs) 29. Low 30. High

Vocabulary Review

1. Consumption possibilities curve 2. Real terms of trade 3. Tariff 4.
Comparative advantage 5. Import quota 6. Absolute advantage 7. Real per
capita output 8. Mutual gains from international trade 9. Less developed
countries (LDCs) 10. Specialization

Skills Review

1.   a.

   b.   1,000, exceeds, 600; 500, exceeds, 400; absolute; lies farther from
         the origin than
   c.   1/2, 2; -2, 2
   d.   2/3, 1.5; -1.5, 1.5

2.   Wine, cheese; wine, cheese; cheese, wine; cheese, wine, cheese; wine,
      cheese, wine; 1.5, 2; 1/2, 2/3

3.　a.　1.75 cases of wine, 7/12 box of cheese
　　b.　Shown on figure above
　　c.　116,667; 2, 100,000; 16,667
　　d.　116,667; 2/3, 133,333; 116,667; 16,667

4.　a.　National security
　　b.　Protect infant industries
　　c.　Reduce structural unemployment
　　d.　Protect U.S. industries against subsidized foreign producers

5.　a.

Price per pair

Millions of
pairs of shoes
supplied and demanded
per year

Price per pair

Millions of
pairs of shoes
supplied and demanded
per year

　　　　Rise, $45, fall, $35; fall, 40; $400 million
　　b.　Rightward, 10; increase, $45, rise, 205
　　c.　Consumers, foreign producers
　　d.　Increase, $45; increases, $45, rise, 205; no, increase

Self-Test for Mastery

1. c 2. c 3. a 4. d 5. d 6. b 7. d 8. a 9. d 10. a 11. d 12. e 13.
d 14. e 15. b 16. e 17. b 18. e

Think It Through

1.　A nation's wealth is not defined in terms of the foreign currency (or gold
during the mercantilist era) earned from trade surpluses, but by the total
goods consumed by the nation in part as a result of international trade.　A
nation may run a trade deficit yet still consume more goods than if the nation
engaged in no international trade.　It is true that a trade deficit means a
lower level of domestic aggregate demand and level of real GNP, but that level
of real GNP may be higher than it would have been if the nation did not produce
and trade on the basis of comparative advantage.

2.　The United States has experienced lagging productivity growth in several
of its heavy industries--those that produce standardized goods and whose firms
realize substantial economies of scale.　Other nations have had more rapid
productivity growth in some of these industries, taking away the comparative
advantage once enjoyed by the U.S. industries.　New techniques of production
were being introduced abroad at a time during which many U.S. plants were aging
and becoming obsolete.　U.S. firms were not investing enough in new plant and
equipment and technology to maintain their relatively lower opportunity cost of
production.　Several foreign nations that have captured the comparative
advantage from the United States have done so by investing a greater percentage
of their domestic production in physical capital and technology.　They also
have an advantage in having a relatively less costly labor force.

3.　If all trading nations are engaging in protectionist measures, all lose in
that the volume of international trade will be lower, the level of world output

and living standards will be lower, and household real incomes will be lower because the prices of imported and domestic goods will be higher than in the absence of trade restrictions.

Pop Quiz

1.   The U.S. trade deficit increased in June because imports for the month exceeded exports. Imports increased by 5.7% and included the following changes: imports of capital goods increased by 10%, imports of consumer goods increased 8%, auto imports increased 12.5%; however, food, feeds, and beverage imports fell 4%, oil imports fell 9.3%, and imported industrial supplies fell 2.8%. Exports fell by 2.4% and included the following changes: exports of capital goods fell by 6%, auto and auto parts exports fell by 7.3%, food, feeds, and beverage exports fell 7.2%, but exports of industrial supplies increased 3.2% and exports of consumer goods increased 2.4%.

2.   Although the U.S. trade deficits with Canada and Taiwan increased, the U.S. trade deficits with Japan, Western Europe, and various oil-producing nations declined. The U.S. trade deficit implies a lower level of aggregate demand and equilibrium real GNP than would be the case if the United States did not have a trade deficit. However, by specializing in and exporting those goods for which it has a comparative advantage and importing those goods for which other nations have a comparative advantage, the United States may enjoy higher domestic standards of living even with a trade deficit than if the nation engaged in no international trade.

U.S. Trade Gap Widened in June To $12.54 Billion

Result, After 42-Month Low In May, Came as Imports Rose 5.7% to a Record

By David Wessel

Staff Reporter of The Wall Street Journal

WASHINGTON—The nation's merchandise trade deficit worsened in June, as a strong U.S. economy boosted imports to a record.

The Commerce Department put the deficit at $12.54 billion, substantially widened

from the revised $9.76 billion reported for May. The May gap was a 42-month low.

Imports rose 5.7% to $39.35 billion in June as Americans bought more foreign-made capital goods, consumer products and autos. Exports fell by a modest 2.4% to $26.81 billion, but they remain well above year-earlier levels. The deficit worsened with all major trading partners.

Slow and Difficult

Although the U.S. trade picture still appears brighter than last year, the report underscores how slow and difficult the process of closing the trade gap will be. "The June deficit confirms . . . the willingness of the U.S. to consume more than we can actually afford," said James Howell, a Bank of Boston economist.

"Our economy is drawing a larger-than-expected quantity of goods into the coun-

try, and we're probably running into bottlenecks in getting goods out of the country," said James Cochrane, an economist with Texas Commerce Bancshares Inc. in Houston.

Surging imports suggest that the Federal Reserve Board, which already has pushed interest rates higher, is likely to force them still higher, economists said. "We're going to have to keep import demand slow and that means more of a lift for short-term interest rates," warned Robert Barbera, a Shearson Lehman Hutton Inc. economist.

Monthly trade figures can be misleading because they are volatile. Commerce Secretary C. William Verity insisted that the underlying trend in the U.S. trade position "remains favorable," noting that the trade deficit in the second quarter was narrower than those in each of the preceeding three quarters.

First Half

In the first half of this year, the U.S. trade deficit was $70 billion, narrowed from $84.45 billion in the first half of 1987. The trade figures are adjusted for usual seasonal fluctuations, but not for higher prices. If the effects of higher prices are removed, the improvement in the trade deficit is far more impressive, Mr. Verity said.

The Commerce Department said U.S. imports of capital goods rose 10% in June to $9.22 billion, a reflection of the continued U.S. boom in capital spending. Imports of consumer goods were up 8.5% to $8.68 billion. And auto imports rose 12.5% to $7.51 billion, mainly because of more imported Canadian cars.

Imports of food, feeds and beverages fell 4% in June to $2.08 billion, and imports of industrial supplies dropped 2.8% to $10.74 billion. Oil imports, which aren't adjusted for seasonal fluctuations, fell 9.3% to $3.57 billion, as both the volume of imports and the price declined.

On the export side, the Commerce Department said exports of capital goods dropped 6% in June to $8.69 billion. Ex-

ports of autos and parts fell 7.3% to $2.25 billion. And exports of foods, feeds and beverages declined 7.2% to $2.72 billion. But exports of industrial supplies were up 3.2% to $7.37 billion and consumer-goods exports rose 2.4% to $1.97 billion.

Major Partners

The trade deficit with major U.S. trading partners widened in June, but the deficits with Japan, Western Europe, the Organization of Petroleum Exporting Countries and the newly industrializing countries of Asia all were lower than in June 1987.

The trade deficit with Canada, America's largest trading partner, rose to $1.4 billion in June from $1.04 billion in May and was more than double its $530.5 million level in June 1987. An increase in imports of Canadian autos and parts accounted for much of the change. The auto industry's trade deficit with Canada widened to $826.1 million in June from $621 million in May and $226.9 million in June 1987.

But Commerce Department officials warned that for the past several months Canadian customs data—upon which the U.S. relies—have understated U.S. exports, forcing subsequent revisions in the department's reports. The figure for U.S. exports to Canada in May was revised up by $300 million.

The trade deficit with Taiwan widened a substantial 30% in June to $1.23 billion, and is now larger than the U.S. deficit with any single country except Japan and Canada. This occurred even though Taiwan bought $200 million of non-monetary gold in June, and $300 million in May, in what U.S. officials have described as a "gimmick" to shrink its reported trade surplus with the U.S. Taiwanese central-bank officials said in July they were suspending the gold purchases.

The seasonally adjusted trade deficit for May originally was estimated at $10.93 billion. Before seasonal adjustments, the Commerce Department said the trade deficit in June was $12.62 billion, up from $9.51 billion in May.

U.S. Merchandise Trade Deficits

(In billions of U.S. dollars, not seasonally adjusted)

	JUNE '88	MAY '88	JUNE '87
Japan	$4.40	$4.12	$5.35
Canada	1.40	1.04	0.53
Western Europe	1.91	1.20	2.93
NICs*	2.72	2.35	3.70

*Newly industrialized economies, including Singapore, Hong Kong, Taiwan, South Korea

Source: Commerce Department

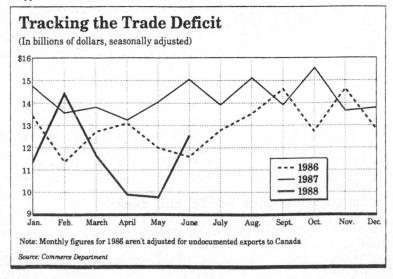

Tracking the Trade Deficit

(In billions of dollars, seasonally adjusted)

- - - 1986
— 1987
— 1988

Note: Monthly figures for 1986 aren't adjusted for undocumented exports to Canada

Source: Commerce Department

40

The Economics of Foreign Exchange and the Balance of International Trade

CHAPTER CHALLENGES

After studying your text, attending class, and completing this chapter, you should be able to:

1. Understand how international transactions between the United States and the rest of the world involve the exchange of dollars for units of foreign currency.
2. Use supply and demand analysis to show how exchange rates of one currency into another are established in foreign exchange markets.
3. Use aggregate supply and demand analysis to show the impact of changes in the real exchange rate of the dollar on macroeconomic equilibrium.
4. Explain the causes of currency appreciation and depreciation in foreign exchange markets and discuss the evolution of the current international monetary system.
5. Understand how a balance of trade deficit in the United States in a given year implies an increase in net foreign acquisition of U.S. financial and other assets in that year.

IN BRIEF: CHAPTER SUMMARY

Fill in the blanks to summarize chapter content.

International trade requires the exchange of currencies. The (1)_____ (foreign exchange rate is, terms of trade are) the price of one nation's monetary unit in terms of the monetary unit of another nation. The (2)_____ (stock market, foreign exchange market) is a market in which currencies are exchanged. Here the forces of supply and demand determine the rate at which any two currencies are exchanged. For example, a U.S. importer wants to purchase foreign goods with dollars but foreign exporters want to be paid in their own currencies. An exchange of currency must take place. For a fee, the importer can use dollars to purchase a bank draft denominated in foreign currency from a U.S. bank. This constitutes (3)_____ (a demand for, an increase in the supply of) the foreign currency.

Equilibrium in the foreign exchange market occurs where the supply of and demand for a currency are equal--where the supply and demand curves for a currency intersect. If the price of a currency (expressed in terms of units of another currency) is higher than the equilibrium exchange rate, a (4)_____ (shortage, surplus) of the currency will cause a decline in the exchange rate. If the exchange rate is below the equilibrium exchange rate, a (5)_____ (shortage, surplus) of the currency results in an increase in the exchange rate. Influences that shift the demand or supply curves will alter the exchange rate between two currencies. Several factors can affect the equilibrium exchange rate of the U.S. dollar: (a) foreign demand for U.S. exports, (b) U.S. demand for imports, (c) real interest rates in the United States relative to those in foreign nations, (d) profitability of direct investment in U.S. businesses and real estate relative to profitability of similar investments in foreign nations, (e) expectations of an increase in the price of the dollar in terms of foreign currency, and (f) the price level (6)_____ (established by the Bretton Woods agreement; in the United States) relative to the price levels in foreign nations.

If real interest rates in the United States rise relative to interest rates in Great Britain, for instance, the British will increase their (7)_____ (supply of, demand for) U.S. dollars in the foreign exchange markets in order to purchase higher-yielding U.S. financial assets. As the demand for dollars rises relative to the supply of dollars, the exchange rate of the dollar (8)_____ (falls, rises). The dollar will be exchanged for more British pounds than previously. Conversely, the British pound will be exchanged for (9)_____ (more, fewer) U.S. dollars. The dollar (10)_____ (depreciates, appreciates) and the pound (11)_____ (depreciates, appreciates). British goods valued in dollars fall in price, and U.S. goods valued in British pounds increase in price. As a result, U.S. goods exported to Great Britain become (12)_____ (more, less) price competitive with British domestic output. Likewise, in the United States, British imported goods become (13)_____ (more, less) expensive relative to U.S. domestic output.

A higher rate of interest in the United States increases the real exchange rate between the pound and dollar, causing U.S. exports to Britain to (14)_____ (rise, fall) and U.S. imports from Britain to rise. U.S. net exports (15)_____ (fall, rise), causing the aggregate demand curve to shift (16)_____ (rightward, leftward). But an appreciation of the dollar also reduces the dollar prices of imported raw materials and other inputs, which shifts the aggregate supply curve (17)_____ (rightward, leftward). It is expected that the change in aggregate demand is larger than the change in aggregate supply, causing equilibrium real GNP and the price level to (18)_____ (rise, fall).

Conversely, a depreciation of the dollar makes U.S. goods (19)_____ (more, less) price competitive abroad while increasing the relative prices of imports to the United States. U.S. exports (20)_____ (fall, rise) and imports (21)_____ (fall, rise), causing net exports to rise. An increase in net exports shifts the aggregate demand curve (22)_____ (rightward, leftward). The aggregate supply curve shifts leftward because the prices of imported inputs (23)_____ (decrease, increase). On net, the increase in aggregate demand will outweigh the decrease in aggregate supply, causing equilibrium real GNP and the price level to (24)_____ (fall, rise). These changes may take some time to develop. Empirical evidence indicates that it may take up to 2 years before changes in exchange rates significantly affect import prices. This, of course, depends upon the profit goals of foreign producers. If foreign producers wish to maintain prices in foreign markets, they may absorb most of the change in exchange rates as lower profits. If import prices remain unchanged relative to other prices, there is no reason for net exports to change.

The foreign exchange market described above is a free market often referred to as a (25)_____ (fixed, floating or flexible) exchange rate market. Prior to the 1930s, however, exchange rates were fixed within narrow limits. This was accomplished by the gold standard, under which currencies were convertible into (26)_____ (gold, the U.S. dollar) at fixed rates. This meant that each currency had (27)_____ (several exchange rates, a unique exchange rate) relative to every other currency. Exchange rates remained fixed as long as the gold price of each currency remained (28)_____ (flexible, unchanged). Nations concerned with domestic macroeconomic problems would often devalue their currency rather than allow an outflow of gold that would reduce the nation's money stock. Devaluation alters exchange rates, however. This system was replaced in 1944 by the (29)_____ (managed float, Bretton Woods system) in which the values of foreign currencies were tied to the U.S.

dollar rather than to gold. The United States abandoned its role as the guarantor of exchange rate stability when it chose to suspend convertibility of the dollar into gold in (30)_____ (1971, 1961). In 1973, the United States and other nations abandoned the fixed exchange rate system in favor of the (31)_____ (modified gold standard, flexible exchange rate system). Today the foreign exchange market is characterized as a managed float rather than a freely floating or flexible exchange rate system. The Federal Reserve System and foreign central banks intervene in the market to effect desirable changes in exchange rates.

The balance of payments for a nation shows the net exchange of the nation's currency for foreign currencies from all transactions between that nation and foreign nations in a given year. In the United States the balance of payments consists of the current account and the capital account. The (32)_____ (capital, current) account shows the effect of the volume of goods and services traded on international markets, including changes in investment income and other miscellaneous transactions. The balance (33)_____ (on the current account, of trade) represents the difference between the value of merchandise exports and imports. The balance (34)_____ (on the current account, of trade) is more comprehensive in that it measures U.S. net exports for the year, including transactions involving services, investment income, and transfers. As recently as 1981, the United States had a surplus in its current account balance but had a large merchandise trade deficit.

In 1985, the current account registered a (35)_____ (deficit, surplus) of over $117 billion. This means U.S. citizens supplied $117 billion more to foreigners than foreigners supplied in foreign currencies to Americans. A net outflow must be offset (financed). When the current account is in deficit, the United States must sell assets or borrow to finance the deficit. These transactions are shown in the (36)_____ (capital, current) account. As foreigners purchase U.S. financial and real assets at a rate greater than U.S. citizens purchase those assets abroad, the net inflow of dollars just offsets the current account deficit.

VOCABULARY REVIEW

Write the key term from the list below next to its definition.

Key Terms

Foreign exchange rate
Foreign exchange market
Foreign exchange
Currency appreciation
Currency depreciation
Purchasing power parity
Gold standard
Balance on current account
  of the balance of
  payments

Bretton Woods system
International Monetary
  Fund (IMF)
Special drawing right (SDR)
International balance of
  payments
Balance of trade
Managed float
Real exchange rate
Nominal exchange rate

Definition

1. _____: the price of a unit of one nation's currency in terms of a unit of a foreign currency.

2. _____: the price of one nation's monetary unit in terms of the monetary unit of another nation.

3. _____: the sacrifice of goods and services that foreign buyers must make when they use their own currency to purchase goods of the first nation worth one unit of that nation's currency.

4. _____: a market in which buyers and sellers of bank deposits denominated in the monetary units of many nations exchange their funds.

5. _____: an international monetary system that required that currencies be converted into gold at a fixed price.

6. _____: the money of one nation held by citizens of another nation either as currency or as deposits in banks.

7. _____: describes the current international monetary system, under which central banks affect supply of and demand for currencies in ways that influence equilibrium in foreign exchange markets.

8. _____: occurs when there is an increase in the number of units of one nation's currency that must be given up to purchase each unit of another nation's currency.

9. _____: established under the Bretton Woods agreement; set rules for the international monetary system to make loans to nations that lack international reserves of dollars.

10. _____: occurs when there is a decrease in the number of units of one nation's currency that must be given up to purchase each unit of another nation's currency.

11. _____: an international monetary system developed in 1944 and based on fixed exchange rates, with the value of foreign currencies tied to the U.S. dollar.

12. _____: a principle that states that the exchange rate between any two currencies tends to adjust to reflect changes in the price levels in the two nations.

13. _____: a paper substitute for gold that is created by the International Monetary Fund and is distributed to member nations to use as international reserves.

14. _____: a statement showing the net exchange rate of a nation's currency for foreign currencies from all transactions between that nation and foreign nations in a given year.

15. _____: the difference between the value of merchandise exported by a nation's firms and the nation's imports of foreign-produced goods.

16. _____: measures U.S. net exports for the year, including transactions involving services, investment income, and transfers.

SKILLS REVIEW

Concept: Foreign exchange rates and foreign exchange markets

1. The figure below represents a foreign exchange market for the U.S. dollar and the Canadian dollar.

Price (number of Canadian dollars)

Millions of U.S. dollars per day

a. Given demand curve Do and supply curve So, the equilibrium exchange rate between the Canadian and U.S. dollar is 1 U.S. dollar = _____ Canadian dollars or alternatively, 1 Canadian dollar = _____ U.S. dollars.

b. A U.S. good valued at $1000 in U.S. dollars would cost _____ Canadian dollars. A Canadian good valued at 100 Canadian dollars would cost _____ U.S. dollars.

2. List six factors that influence the exchange rate of the dollar.

a. _____
b. _____
c. _____
d. _____
e. _____
f. _____

3. Referring to the figure above, suppose real interest rates in the United States rise relative to interest rates abroad, causing the demand for dollars to increase to D1.

a. What are the new exchange rates?

(1) 1 U.S. dollar = _____ Canadian dollars
(2) 1 Canadian dollar = _____ U.S. dollars

b. The U.S. dollar has _____, and the Canadian dollar has _____.

c. A U.S. good valued at 1000 U.S. dollars now costs _____ Canadian dollars. A Canadian good valued at 100 Canadian dollars now costs _____ U.S. dollars.

d. U.S. goods become _____ price competitive in Canada, and Canadian goods become _____ price competitive in the United States.

4. Referring to the figure above, given the initial demand curve, Do, assume that U.S. firms increase their imports from Canada, causing the supply of U.S. dollars to shift to S1.

    a. What are the new exchange rates?

        (1) 1 U.S. dollar = _____ Canadian dollars
        (2) 1 Canadian dollar = _____ U.S. dollar
    b. The U.S. dollar has _____, and the Canadian dollar has
        _____.
    c. A U.S. good valued at 1000 U.S. dollars now costs _____ Canadian
        dollars. A Canadian good valued at 100 Canadian dollars now costs
        _____ U.S. dollars.
    d. U.S. goods become _____ price competitive in Canada, and Canadian
        goods become _____ price competitive in the United States.

Concept: **Changes in real exchange rates and equilibrium real GNP and the price level**

5. The figure below represents an economy.

    a. A depreciation of the U.S. dollar relative to the Canadian dollar
        makes U.S. goods _____ price competitive in Canada and Canadian
        goods _____ price competitive in the United States. U.S.
        exports _____, imports _____, and net exports _____.
    b. Given the initial aggregate demand and supply curves, ADo and ASo,
        the change in net exports indicated above shifts the AD curve to
        _____ (AD1, AD2).
    c. The price of imported inputs in U.S. dollars _____, causing the AS
        curve to shift to _____ (AS1, AS2).
    d. Equilibrium real GNP _____ from Yo to _____.

6. Refer to the figure above in answering this question.

    a. An appreciation of the U.S. dollar relative to the Canadian dollar
        makes U.S. goods _____ price competitive in Canada and Canadian
        goods _____ price competitive in the United States. U.S. exports
        _____, imports _____, and net exports _____.
    b. Given the initial aggregate demand and supply curves, ADo and ASo,
        the change in net exports indicated in part a above shifts the AD
        curve to _____ (AD1, AD2).
    c. The prices of imported inputs in U.S. dollars _____, causing the AS
        curve to shift to _____ (AS1, AS2).
    d. Equilibrium real GNP _____ from Yo to _____.

Concept: International balance of payments

7. Identify which of the following represent a <u>capital account</u> and which represent a <u>current account</u> transaction in the balance of payments and state whether the transaction results in an <u>inflow</u> or <u>outflow</u> of U.S. dollars.

    a.   U.S. exports of services increase.
    b.   Foreigners purchase U.S. Treasury bills.
    c.   Automobile imports into the United States decrease.
    d.   Transfers to foreigners increase.
    e.   U.S. firms purchase factories abroad.
    f.   Rich oil sheiks purchase Texas ranch land.
    g.   Hitachi receives income from its U.S. plants.
    h.   Foreigners increase imports of U.S. merchandise goods.
    i.   U.S. citizens purchase stock in foreign enterprises.

Capital or Current Account?	Inflow or Outflow?
a. _____	_____
b. _____	_____
c. _____	_____
d. _____	_____
e. _____	_____
f. _____	_____
g. _____	_____
h. _____	_____
i. _____	_____

SELF-TEST FOR MASTERY

Select the best answer.

1. A market in which buyers and sellers of bank deposits denominated in the monetary units of many nations exchange their funds is known as:

    a.   The loanable funds market.
    b.   The money market.
    c.   The capital market.
    d.   The foreign exchange market.

2. If the price of a dollar in terms of units of a foreign currency is above the equilibrium exchange rate, a _____ exists, which will put _____ pressure on the equilibrium exchange rate of the dollar.

    a.   Shortage, downward
    b.   Shortage, upward
    c.   Surplus, downward
    d.   Surplus, upward

3. If a $10,000 U.S.-made automobile is sold in France and the exchange rate between the dollar and the franc is $1 = 8 francs, the U.S. automobile sold in France will cost _____ francs.

   a. 20,000
   b. 40,000
   c. 60,000
   d. 80,000
   e. 100,000

4. The exchange rate between the dollar and the franc is $1 = 8 francs, and the price of a bottle of imported French wine is $5. If the exchange rate changes to $1 = 4 francs, the dollar price of the French wine _____ to $_____.

   a. Falls, $2.50
   b. Rises, $10
   c. Rises, $20
   d. Does not change

5. An increase in foreign demand for U.S. exports will _____ demand for the dollar, causing the dollar to _____.

   a. Decrease, appreciate
   b. Increase, depreciate
   c. Increase, appreciate
   d. Decrease, depreciate

6. An increase in U.S. demand for imports will _____ the _____ U.S. dollars, causing the dollar to _____.

   a. Increase, demand for, appreciate
   b. Increase, supply of, appreciate
   c. Decrease, supply of, depreciate
   d. Decrease, demand for, appreciate
   e. Increase, supply of, depreciate

7. If real interest rates in the United States rise relative to interest rates abroad, the _____ dollars will _____, causing the dollar to _____.

   a. Demand for, increase, appreciate
   b. Demand for, increase, depreciate
   c. Supply of, decrease, depreciate
   d. Supply of, increase, appreciate

8. If the rate of inflation in the United States rises relative to the rate of inflation in foreign nations, U.S. exports _____ and imports _____, causing the demand for dollars to _____ and the supply of dollars to _____.

   a. Increase, decrease, rise, fall
   b. Decrease, increase, fall, rise
   c. Increase, increase, fall, fall
   d. Decrease, decrease, rise, rise

9. The price of a unit of one nation's currency in terms of a unit of a foreign currency is called:

   a. The nominal exchange rate.
   b. The real exchange rate.

c. Foreign exchange.
d. Purchasing power parity.
e. None of the above.

10. Empirical evidence suggests that:

   a. Import prices respond very quickly to changes in exchange rates.
   b. Net exports respond within a year to changes in the exchange rate of the dollar.
   c. Import prices are slow to respond to changes in exchange rates, taking up to 2 years to be affected.
   d. There is an immediate link between exchange rates and import prices.

11. An increase in the real exchange rate of the dollar causes aggregate demand to _____ and aggregate supply to _____, resulting in a/an _____ in real GNP.

   a. Decrease, decrease, decrease
   b. Increase, increase, increase
   c. Increase, decrease, decrease
   d. Increase, increase, decrease
   e. Decrease, increase, decrease

12. A depreciation of the dollar causes aggregate demand to _____ and aggregate supply to _____, resulting in a/an _____ in real GNP.

   a. Decrease, decrease, decrease
   b. Increase, increase, increase
   c. Increase, decrease, increase
   d. Increase, increase, decrease
   e. Decrease, increase, decrease

13. The Bretton Woods agreement:

   a. Represented a new international monetary system.
   b. Tied the value of foreign currencies not to gold but to the dollar.
   c. Was established in 1944.
   d. Also established the International Monetary Fund.
   e. All of the above.

14. The present international monetary system is best described as a:

   a. Fixed exchange rate system.
   b. Purchasing power parity system.
   c. Flexible exchange rate system.
   d. Managed float.

15. Which of the following summarizes the transactions involving the international exchange of goods and services, investment income, and other miscellaneous transactions?

   a. Balance of trade
   b. Statistical discrepancy
   c. Current account
   d. Capital account

16. Which of the following is the difference between the value of merchandise exported and merchandise imported?

    a.   Balance of trade
    b.   Balance on the current account
    c.   Budget balance
    d.   Balance of payments

17. Which of the following measures net exports for the year, including transactions involving services, investment income, and transfers?

    a.   Balance of trade
    b.   Balance on the current account
    c.   Budget balance
    d.   Balance of payments

18. When the current account is in deficit, the capital account must

    a.   Be balanced.
    b.   Be zero.
    c.   Not add to the deficit.
    d.   Have an equal and offsetting surplus.

THINK IT THROUGH

1.   How can the Fed, through domestic monetary policy, cause the U.S. dollar to depreciate?

2.   How can the Fed, through direct intervention in foreign exchange markets, cause the U.S. dollar to depreciate?

3.   If the U.S. dollar depreciates, what are the likely economic consequences?

POP QUIZ   Read the news brief at the end of this chapter and answer the questions below.

1.   Lindley Clark cites two reasons for the recent climb in the exchange rate of the U.S. dollar. What are they?

2.   According to the article, why would Japan, Britain, and West Germany be hesitant to intervene to slow the appreciation of the dollar?

CHAPTER ANSWERS

In Brief: Chapter Summary

1. Foreign exchange rate is 2. Foreign exchange market 3. A demand for 4. Surplus 5. Shortage 6. In the United States 7. Demand for 8. Rises 9. Fewer 10. Appreciates 11. Depreciates 12. Less 13. Less 14. Fall 15. Fall 16. Leftward 17. Rightward 18. Fall 19. More 20. Rise 21. Fall 22. Rightward 23. Increase 24. Rise 25. Floating or flexible 26. Gold 27. A unique exchange rate 28. Unchanged 29. Bretton Woods system 30. 1971 31.

Flexible exchange rate system 32. Current 33. Of trade 34. On the current account 35. Deficit 36. Capital

Vocabulary Review

1. Nominal exchange rate 2. Foreign exchange rate 3. Real exchange rate 4. Foreign exchange market 5. Gold standard 6. Foreign exchange 7. Managed float 8. Currency appreciation 9. International Monetary Fund (IMF) 10. Currency depreciation 11. Bretton Woods system 12. Purchasing power parity 13. Special drawing right (SDR) 14. International balance of payments 15. Balance of trade 16. Balance on the current account of the balance of payments

Skills Review

1. a. 1.5, 2/3
    b. 1,500, $66.67

2. a. Foreign demand for U.S. exports
    b. U.S. demand for imports
    c. Real interest rates in the United States relative to those in foreign nations
    d. Profitability of direct investment in U.S. businesses and real estate relative to profitability of similar investments in foreign nations
    e. Expectations of an increase in the price of the dollar in terms of foreign currency
    f. The price level in the United States relative to the price levels in foreign nations

3. a. 2, 1/2
    b. Appreciated, depreciated
    c. 2,000; 50
    d. Less, more

4. a. 1, 1
    b. Depreciated, appreciated
    c. 1,000; 100
    d. More, less

5. a. More, less; rise, fall, increase
    b. AD1
    c. Rises, AS2
    d. Increases, Y1

6. a. Less, more; fall, rise, decrease
    b. AD2
    c. Falls, AS1
    d. Decreases, Y4

7. a. Current, inflow
    b. Capital, inflow
    c. Current, outflow
    d. Current, outflow
    e. Capital, outflow
    f. Capital, inflow
    g. Current, outflow
    h. Current, inflow
    i. Capital, outflow

579

Self-Test for Mastery

1. d 2. c 3. d 4. b 5. c 6. e 7. a 8. b 9. a 10. c 11. e 12. c 13. e 14. d 15. c 16. a 17. b 18. d

Think It Through

1.   If the Fed pursues an expansionary monetary policy that reduces the real rate of interest in the United States relative to interest rates abroad, Americans will increase their demand for foreign currencies by supplying more dollars to the international foreign exchange markets in order to purchase higher-yielding foreign financial assets. The increase in the supply of dollars relative to demand will cause the dollar to depreciate. The expansionary monetary policy will also increase the nation's income, causing imports to increase. In order to increase imports, Americans must supply dollars to acquire foreign exchange to purchase the foreign goods. This too will cause the dollar to depreciate. If the expansionary monetary policy is also inflationary such that the rate of inflation in the United States rises relative to foreign rates of inflation, U.S. exports will fall and imports will rise. This will cause foreign demand for the dollar to fall and the supply of dollars to increase, also resulting in depreciation of the dollar.

2.   If the Fed wished to depreciate the dollar, it could purchase foreign currencies with its dollar holdings, causing the demand for foreign currencies to rise and the supply of dollars to increase. This in turn would cause the dollar to depreciate relative to the foreign currencies purchased by the Fed.

3.   If the dollar depreciates, U.S. goods become less costly in foreign currencies, increasing their price competitiveness in foreign markets. Likewise, foreign goods become more costly in dollars, decreasing their price competitiveness in the United States. U.S. imports of foreign goods decrease, and U.S. exports to foreign nations increase. The increase in net exports causes the aggregate demand curve to shift rightward. But foreign inputs now cost more in dollars. As production costs rise, the aggregate supply curve shifts leftward. On net, however, real GNP increases.

Pop Quiz

1.   According to the article, the dollar has appreciated because the U.S. downing of an Iranian airliner in the Persian Gulf raised fears of a possible international crisis. Money tends to flow to "safe-haven" currencies such as the dollar when there are mounting fears of international instability. It is noted that increases in U.S. exports and foreign investors' optimism regarding the inflation outlook in the United States were also responsible for the rise in the exchange rate of the dollar. Exports create a demand for the dollar, causing its exchange rate to rise. If foreign investors expect U.S. inflation to remain stable, they will be more likely to invest in U.S. dollar-denominated securities. This too creates a demand for the dollar, causing it to appreciate.

2.   All of these nations are enjoying strong economies. If they intervened in foreign exchange markets to prevent the appreciation of the dollar, they would have to purchase their own currencies with their dollar holdings. The increase in the supply of dollars keeps the dollar from appreciating, and the increased demand for foreign currencies prevents the foreign currencies from depreciating relative to the dollar. These actions, however, keep foreign currencies from depreciating and foreign export industries from becoming more price competitive in the United States. "Defending" the dollar against appreciation means that foreign nations sacrifice an increase in net exports and income.

The Outlook

Should the Dollar Find Its Own Market Level?

NEW YORK

Anyone who wonders why Japan hesitates to let the yen become an international currency should consider the continuing convolutions of the U.S. dollar. Not only the U.S. but most major countries want to manage the dollar to suit their own convenience. Japan may be an industrial giant, but it has no desire to subject the yen to that sort of nonsense.

The dollar has been climbing lately, at least temporarily reversing the drop that began in February 1985. Early last week, the dollar spurted on foreign markets for reasons entirely separate from U.S. economic management. The accidental U.S. downing of an Iranian passenger plane in the Persian Gulf, killing all 290 persons aboard, raised fears of a new international crisis. In an international crisis, investors seek a safe-haven currency, and the dollar still is perceived to be the best around.

The rise in the dollar stems in large part from the increase in U.S. exports, which has shrunk the merchandise trade deficit. The dollar's rise, moreover, lessens inflation fears, since it tends to make imports less expensive. An analysis by Lawrence H. Meyer & Associates of St. Louis notes that the rise leads foreign investors to become more optimistic about the dollar's future and thus more willing to buy dollar securities, helping to push the dollar higher. "A stronger dollar," the firm says, "hints that the dollar may have bottomed."

Jerry L. Jordan, chief economist of First Interstate Bank of Los Angeles, is convinced that the dollar "has seen its lows for this cycle." He says Federal Reserve Chairman Alan Greenspan "is building up credibility as an inflation-fighter. He hasn't quite moved into the spot Paul Volcker held as the second most powerful man in the U.S., but he's making progress."

Some analysts argue that the stronger dollar will end the upsurge of U.S. exports, just as the weaker dollar started it. A few contend that the dollar not only will have to fall but will have to drop sharply to continue the improvement in the U.S. trade balance. The fact is that no one can be absolutely certain what level of the dollar is needed to sustain exports—or just what the future level of the dollar will be. The dollar's current strength is based heavily on a foreign perception that the U.S. is beginning to get its house in order. Evidence to the contrary could send the dollar down.

All of this is happening, it should be noted, when neither the Federal Reserve nor any other major central bank has much appetite to push the dollar significantly lower or higher. The Fed prefers peace and quiet in presidential election years, so its preference presumably would be a dollar that stabilized at about the current level—at least, between now and November. So far, Fed Chairman Greenspan has commented only that he sees no reason for the dollar to go lower. The U.S. hope obviously is that the dollar now is low enough to permit continued strength in U.S. exports.

Some central banks have sold dollars in an effort to slow the gains of the U.S. currency, but others are hesitant. If the Bank of Japan sells dollars it soaks up yen, tending to weaken the Japanese economy, now in the midst of a consumer-fueled boom. Japan knows it may eventually have to tighten credit to cool off the boom, but presumably it would prefer to base the timing on its domestic needs, not on the buoyant dollar.

The British and West Germans also have strong economies, which could be weakened by new dollar sales. Some foreigners find the current situation strange. A German banker quoted in this newspaper last week said he found it hard to believe that Germany would have to defend its mark when it has a low inflation rate, high current account surpluses and a booming export economy.

For the present, market factors seem to be working in favor of the dollar. "The question is how foreign net demand for our assets will compare with our net demand for foreign goods," Mr. Jordan says. "Our net demand for foreign goods is going down,

while net foreign demand for our assets has picked up sharply." The U.S. is still bringing assets home from abroad, while foreigners continue to buy assets here.

One reason the outlook for sales of assets to foreigners is strong is that the inflation rates seem to be moving in our favor. The foreign perception is that U.S. inflation has stabilized, at a time when other major industrial countries are worrying about rising inflation.

Time will tell. The U.S. has found that a nation with an international currency can largely ignore inflation, trade deficits and budget deficits for a long time without disaster. But no one can ignore such fundamental factors forever.

For the near term, the Federal Reserve needs to continue to provide investors, foreign and domestic, assurance of its determination to prevent a surge of inflation, a task that is complicated by higher food prices stemming from the Midwest drought. It's unlikely that much reduction of the budget deficit will be forthcoming until after the election, if then, but it would be helpful if the presidential candidates gave more evidence that they appreciated the seriousness of the problem.

In the long run, the fundamental factors must prevail. But it's no wonder that Japan prefers to keep the yen out of the uncertainties that persist until the fundamentals assert themselves. What is surprising is that government officials don't remember that the exchange rate is a market price and thus decide to let the dollar find its own level.

—Lindley H. Clark Jr.

41

Economics and Ideology: Socialism vs. Capitalism

CHAPTER CHALLENGES

After studying your text, attending class, and completing this chapter, you should be able to:

1. Discuss the ideas of Karl Marx and the ideological underpinnings of socialism.
2. Discuss modern socialist economies, particularly that of the Soviet Union.
3. Explain central planning as a means of allocating resources in a command economy.
4. Discuss issues involved in evaluating economic performance in modern economies.

IN BRIEF: CHAPTER SUMMARY

Fill in the blanks to complete the chapter summary.

(1)_____ (Capitalism, Socialism) is associated with private ownership of resources, freedom of enterprise, and an economy in which markets allocate resources. (2)_____ (Capitalism, Socialism), in contrast, is associated with government ownership of productive resources and central planning. Prices and resource allocation are determined by central planners rather than by markets.

According to Karl Marx, only (3)_____ (labor, capital) produces value. Even capital is the past product of labor. Marx argued that capitalists hire labor at subsistence wages, generating a (4)_____ (marginal revenue product, surplus value)--the wages paid to labor are less than the value of the worker's production. Capitalists therefore exploit workers and will continue to do so until the working class revolts and establishes a socialist state. Most workers, however, earn incomes well above a subsistence level in market economies. Marx did not foresee the enormous gains made in (5)_____ (profits, labor productivity) as a result of technology and capital formation. Over time, the (6)_____ (supply of, demand for) labor has outpaced the (7)_____ (supply of, demand for) labor, resulting in increases in real wages. The working class has not revolted in a manner envisioned by Marx because of gains in real living standards and social policy designed to alleviate some of the failures of market systems.

The Soviet Union is a (8)_____ (market, command) economy in which resources are allocated by central planners who set production goals. The (9)_____ (Gosplan, Politburo) is the central planning board for the Soviet Union and drafts 5-year plans listing production goals for the economy. The government sets prices to ensure the satisfaction of the output goals. Prices of many goods have been kept artificially low as a way of subsidizing consumption. But when prices are set below the level that equates supply and demand, (10)_____ (surpluses, shortages) become a problem. Shortages

can be eliminated with a (11)_____ (lump sum, turnover) tax if it is
equal to the difference between the price that would equate supply and demand
and the lower subsidized price. Shortages are reduced, but only from a
reduction in quantity demanded. Quantity supplied remains fixed at the
planners' production target.

As of January 1, 1988, the Soviet economy began to institute reforms such as
putting (12)_____ (10%, 60%) of Soviet enterprises on a self-financing
basis. These firms are required to earn a profit or they will be shut down.
Managers (13)_____ (will be, will not be) able to decide what is to be
produced and how to produce it. In fact, many prices will be determined by
markets rather than by central planning. Even prior to these reforms, farmers
were allowed to sell produce in markets from private plots. These plots are
considerably more productive than collective farms in producing food,
accounting for as much as (14)_____ (25%, 75%) of Soviet agricultural
output. Economic incentives are also used to motivate Soviet labor and existed
prior to the reforms instituted at the beginning of 1988. In 1987, private
enterprise was legalized in 29 areas, primarily in crafts and services. These
changes will be beneficial to the Soviet economy. Managers will no longer have
incentives to just meet output targets or exceed those targets, but will now
have incentives to minimize costs in order to generate profits. This will
result in a (15)_____ (less, more) efficient use of resources.

Other socialist systems vary in the degree to which central planning and
markets are relied upon to allocate resources. In (16)_____ (North
Korea, Yugoslavia), for example, most businesses are state owned but worker
managed. Profits from these firms are used for investment in the enterprise or
are divided among the firm's workers. In other nations, such as Great Britain,
some large industrial enterprises are publicly owned, but the remainder of the
economy is organized as a market economy.

In evaluating capitalism and socialism, important considerations include:
(a) the extent to which the pursuit of self-interest and market exchange of
goods and services produce results that coincide with a general consensus
regarding national goals, (b) the way an economic system distributes well-being
among members of a society, (c) the achievement of technological efficiency,
(d) freedom of choice and responsiveness to consumer demands, and (e) economic
growth and fluctuations.

VOCABULARY REVIEW

Write the key term from the list below next to its definition.

Key Terms

Economic system	Gosplan
Socialism	Materials balance
Labor theory of value	Consumer sovereignty
Surplus value	Turnover tax
Command economy	Indicative planning
Centrally planned economy	

Definitions

1. _____: an economy in which politically appointed committees plan production and manage the economy to achieve political goals.

2. _____: the central planning board for the Soviet Union.

3. _____: an economy in which resource allocation decisions are determined largely by the central planning authorities who set production goals.

4. _____: exists when the supply of each intermediate product equals its demand as an input in some other productive process.

5. _____: defined by Karl Marx as the difference between a worker's subsistence wage and the value of the worker's production over a period.

6. _____: the responsiveness of the market economy to changes in consumer demand.

7. _____: maintains that only labor can produce something worth paying for.

8. _____: a sales tax used to raise revenue for the government; often used in planned economies to eliminate shortages in consumer markets.

9. _____: an economic system that is usually associated with government ownership of resources and central planning to determine prices and resource use.

10. _____: a system in which government encourages voluntary compliance by industrial and labor interests to coordinate economic decisions so as to achieve politically determined objectives.

11. _____: an accepted way of organizing production, establishing rights to ownership and use of productive resources, and governing economic transactions in a society.

SKILLS REVIEW

Concept: Production targets, shortages, the turnover tax, and black markets

A competitive market for a good is shown in the figure below.

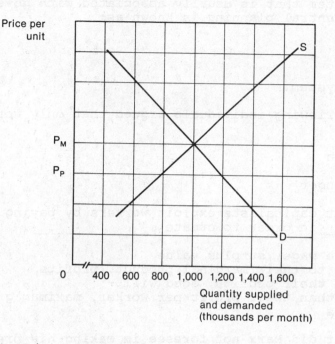

a. Assume that this market economy now becomes a command economy in which central planners set production targets. Show the effect of a production target of 800,000 units where planners establish a price of Pp per unit. At the controlled price of Pp, there exists a _____ of _____ units.

b. If the official government price is raised to the previous market level of Pm, there exists a _____ of _____ units.

c. In order to eliminate the _____ and still maintain the production target of 800,000 units, a turnover tax equal to the difference between _____ and the _____ could be used. However, if a turnover tax is used in this manner, consumers in the command economy pay _____ prices and consume _____ output than they did previously in the market economy.

d. Black markets will likely develop because some consumers will be willing to pay _____ prices than a government price like Pp in order to have additional units of the good. Even if a turnover tax eliminates shortages, black markets will likely still exist because the marginal cost of supplying an additional unit of a good will likely be _____ than the government price that eliminates shortages.

Select the best answer.

1. An economic system that is usually associated with government ownership of resources and central planning is known as:

    a. Capitalism.
    b. Fascism.
    c. Socialism.
    d. A market system.

2. Which of the following individuals argued that only workers create value?

    a. Adam Smith
    b. George Bush
    c. Karl Marx
    d. Karl Menninger

3. Marx argued that capitalists exploit workers by paying them a _____ in order to create _____.

    a. Subsistence wage, surplus value
    b. Wage equal to their marginal product, profits
    c. Portion of their profits, good will
    d. Wage less than their profit per worker, maximum growth for their enterprises

4. What main factor did Marx not foresee in making his prediction that workers would not rise above a subsistence standard of living?

    a. Population growth
    b. Growth in household consumption
    c. Growth in labor productivity
    d. Advances in technology
    e. C and d

5. The Soviet Union is an example of a:

    a. Market economy.
    b. Mixed-market system.
    c. Democratic socialist state.
    d. Command economy.

6. Which of the following is the Soviet Union's central planning board?

    a. Ministry of Industry
    b. Soviet Monetary Alliance
    c. Perestroika
    d. Gosplan

7. As of January 1, 1988, economic reforms were initiated in the Soviet Union. Which of the following is an economic reform?

    a. Requiring some soviet enterprises to earn a profit
    b. Allowing managers of some enterprises to decide what to produce and how to produce it
    c. Allowing many prices to be determined by markets
    d. All of the above

8. A turnover tax is:

    a. Used to reduce surpluses.
    b. Used to finance the Soviet economic reforms.
    c. Used to reduce shortages.
    d. The difference between the cost of a good and the price that equates supply and demand.

9. One advantage of a planned economy is that:

    a. It is more efficient.
    b. It responds more rapidly to changes in consumers' desires.
    c. It has achieved the highest living standards in the world.
    d. It can avoid fluctuations in aggregate demand and thus avoid the costs associated with business cycles.

10. Which of the following is true regarding private enterprise in the Soviet Union?

    a. The Soviet economic reforms have privatized collective farms.
    b. Private farm plots account for as much as 25% of the Soviet Union's total agricultural output.
    c. In 1987, private business was legalized in 29 areas.
    d. Most individuals engaged in private enterprise are in crafts or services.
    e. B, c, and d

11. In which of the following nations is a majority of enterprises state owned but worker managed?

    a. People's Republic of China
    b. France
    c. Yugoslavia
    d. Argentina

12. In which of the following nations is government ownership of or financial interest in large industrial enterprises common?

    a. United Kingdom
    b. France
    c. Italy
    d. All of the above
    e. A and c

13. Which of the following nations uses indicative planning--where private industry cooperates with the government to achieve political goals?

    a. Great Britain
    b. Yugoslavia
    c. Soviet Union
    d. United States
    e. France

14. In assessing the merits of capitalism vs. socialism, which of the following considerations are important?

    a.   The extent to which the pursuit of self-interest and market exchange of goods and services produce results that coincide with a general political consensus regarding national goals

    b.   The way an economic system distributes well-being among members of a society

    c.   The achievement of technological efficiency

    d.   Freedom of choice and responsiveness to consumer demands

    e.   All of the above

THINK IT THROUGH

1. Identify and briefly discuss some of the main differences between capitalism and socialism.

2. Several nations have returned state-owned enterprises to the private sector, whereas other socialist nations have instituted major market-based reforms. Can you think of any reasons why?

POP QUIZ   Read the news brief at the end of this chapter and answer the questions below.

1. Outline Angola's new economic plan. What is Angola's motivation for employing market-based reforms?

2. How do Angolans cope with the lack of product quantity and variety at state stores and a virtually worthless currency?

CHAPTER ANSWERS

In Brief: Chapter Summary

1. Capitalism 2. Socialism 3. Labor 4. Surplus value 5. Labor productivity
6. Demand for 7. Supply of 8. Command 9. Gosplan 10. Shortages 11. Turnover 12. 60% 13. Will be 14. 25% 15. More 16. Yugoslavia

Vocabulary Review

1. Centrally planned economy 2. Gosplan 3. Command economy 4. Materials balance 5. Surplus value 6. Consumer sovereignty 7. Labor theory of value 8. Turnover tax 9. Socialism 10. Indicative planning 11. Economic system

Skills Review

Price per unit

S₁ (Target production)
Turnover S
Tax, T

$P_P + T$
P_M
P_P

Target output = demand

At price = P_M, shortage = 200

D

At price = P_P, shortage = 400

400 600 800 1,000 1,200 1,400 1,600

Quantity supplied and demanded (thousands per month)

    a.   Shortage, 400,000
    b.   Shortage, 200,000
    c.   Shortage, the subsidized price, price that would equate supply and
        demand; higher, less
    d.   Higher, less

Self-Test for Mastery

1. c 2. c 3. a 4. e 5. d 6. d 7. d 8. c 9. d 10. e 11. c 12. d 13. e 14. e

Think It Through

1.   Capitalism relies on self-interest, private ownership, and markets to allocate resources. Socialism is distrustful of self-interest (the profit motive) and in the extreme case of a command economy, resources are allocated with extensive central planning. Capitalism rewards input suppliers on the basis of the quantity and productivity of inputs supplied. This is not necessarily so if markets are imperfectly competitive. A socialist state earns a profit from state-owned resources and redistributes it to workers in the form of wages and services. Modern mixed economies try to achieve equity in the distribution of income through transfer payments. In a competitive market economy, firms have an incentive to keep costs as low as possible, resulting in technological efficiency. Managers in socialist states often confront a much different set of costs and incentives, which reward managers not for minimizing costs, but for meeting production targets. In capitalist economies with competitive markets, consumers are sovereign. There is free choice in consumption, the employment of inputs, and the production of output. In a socialist state, individual freedoms are much less important than the achievement of political goals. A capitalist system is subject to recurrent ups and downs in real GNP and the rate of unemployment. The incidence of business cycles can be lessened considerably in command economies because aggregate demand is strictly controlled. If there are ups and downs in production, they are likely the result of supply-side shocks rather than fluctuations in aggregate demand.

2.   Competitive economies that rely on markets to allocate resources realize a higher level of technological efficiency than economies that rely on central planning. In a market system, self-interest coordinates decisions such that resources are allocated to their most productive employments. Workers are free to offer their labor services to the highest bidder. Entrepreneurs bring resources together to produce goods desired by consumers in hopes of earning a profit. Economic survival in a competitive economy requires technological

efficiency. Firms that are unable to produce at minimum possible unit costs will exit the market in the long run. Even in the case of modern mixed economies having many imperfectly competitive markets, the level of efficiency is much higher than in command economies. Most socialist nations are recognizing the power of incentives. As noted in the text, the Soviet Union is embarking on major market-based reforms that require the pursuit of self-interest in order to succeed.

Pop Quiz

1.   The economic plan Angola intends to implement is similar to those being implemented in other socialist countries. The plan calls for autonomy for managers and decentralization in decision making. It also involves returning land to farmers and businesses to entrepreneurs in order to encourage private sector production. Prices will be determined by the market, and wages will be tied to labor productivity. Angola has turned to market incentives not because of a radical ideological shift from Marxism, but because the war against Unita, the rebel army supported by the United States and South Africa, is expensive and requires an economy that can produce enough output to support the war effort. Angola is using capitalism to defend Marxism!

2.   A thriving black market exists in Luanda, Angola. Here almost any good, including imported goods, can be found and at prices well below the official prices in state stores. The state stores have limited variety and encounter shortages. The "official" prices are ridiculously high and bear no relationship to market forces. In fact, either dollars or kwanzas are used to purchase beer at state stores for $12 or 30,000 kwanzas. The beer is then taken to the black market and sold for $15 in kwanzas, which can be traded for other goods on the market. "Money is meaningless...Beer has meaning." Angolans cope with scarcity in state stores and a worthless currency by having an efficient black market that produces true market prices.

In Marxist Angola, Capitalism Thrives, Using Beer Standard

* * *

Black Market at City Dump Outdraws State's Stores, Where Cigarettes Cost $60

By Roger Thurow
Staff Reporter of The Wall Street Journal

LUANDA, Angola—Capitalism literally has ended up on the scrap heap in this fervently Marxist country.

On the top of a hill overlooking this decaying port city, smack in the middle of a dump, a thriving black market coexists profitably with the garbage and flies. Vendors' prices are guided by the hand of Adam Smith rather than by state planners devoted to Karl Marx. The nearly worthless local currency is pegged to the price of beer. Anyone with the time to browse through this vast outdoor bazaar will find everything the socialist stores on the streets below are supposed to have, but don't.

The vendors first set up their stalls at the dump because it was a convenient open space. Now, garbage is taken only to the fringes of the market. Everyone, it seems, shops here: peasant farmers, factory workers, bureaucrats, soldiers, bankers, diplomats. Even state economists come looking for inspiration and ideas, as well as turnips and onions.

Destroyed by War

"We're studying this market, which is a very efficient market," says Victor Nunes, a Finance Ministry official responsible for overseeing Angola's ambitious economic adjustment program. "We have much to learn from it."

As Angola tries desperately to resuscitate its gasping socialist economy, it is taking a crash course in capitalism. A new economic plan, not coincidentally, is being launched at the same time Luanda is pushing for membership in the International Monetary Fund. The plan is similar to those being tinkered with in other run-down socialist countries: decentralizing economic decision-making, giving more autonomy to managers of businesses, encouraging the private sector, returning land to farmers and shops to entrepreneurs, harnessing prices to market forces and salaries to productivity, promoting foreign investment.

The catalyst for Angola's economic restructuring is the 13-year war against the rebel army known as Unita, which is supported by South Africa and the U.S. The war has devastated the economy, potentially one of the richest in Africa. More

mines than maize is planted in the countryside, much of which is controlled by the guerrillas. The industries of the big cities have ground to a halt from lack of material and spare parts. Skilled managers, always scarce here, are drafted as soldiers.

"We have come up with a slogan," says Dumilde das Chagas Simoes Rangel, Angola's trade minister. "Develop the economy to fight the war; fight the war to defend the economy."

Thus, if capitalism is what it takes to defend Marxism in Angola, so be it. "It is possible," says Mr. Nunes, "to construct socialism with rational economic means."

Like the free market. In the past, the state tried mightily to crush the illegal black markets, which account for the bulk of the country's economic activity. Today, however, the police on duty at the black markets are responsible for crowd control, not crowd dispersement. The state has decided to fight capitalism with capitalism, rather than with bulldozers and truncheons.

"We have to combat the parallel market with economic mechanisms," says Mr. Nunes, favoring the word "parallel" over "black."

At the moment, the black market is winning easily. Because of the deregulated prices and the more realistic exchange rate, many imported goods go directly from the port of Luanda to the unofficial markets, bypassing the state stores that stand forlorn and empty.

Empty Shelves

In downtown Luanda, a drugstore crumbling under a burned-out neon sign offers only a couple of packages of sinus pills and some dental floss. Its glass cabinets are empty, except for one that displays color posters of stomach ulcers. In contrast, the black market has a long row of vendors offering everything from antacids and aspirin to cough medicine and laxatives.

Also available on the black market: fruit, vegetables and fish; bubble gum, underwear and gin. Soap comes from Brazil, skin lightener from England, antihistamines from Switzerland, spaghetti from Bulgaria and soda pop from West Germany (though there is little from the U.S., which doesn't have diplomatic relations with Angola).

These are the things people want, not the bulky paraffin cookers or the industrial-type waffle irons ordered by the central planners and made here or in Russia. Even the name of the market reflects consumer choice: Roque Santeiro, the title of a popular Brazilian soap opera that is broadcast regularly in this former Portuguese colony.

'Money Is Meaningless'

Throughout Luanda, dollars and beer are the currencies of choice, favored over the local currency, the kwanza.

If anybody paid attention to the official rate of 30 kwanza to the dollar (nobody does), he would have to pay more than $60 for a packet of Marlboros or a can of orange pop. A heavy metal ashtray in the shape of a bug—its wings open up to collect the ashes—would cost more than $150 at a state store.

At the black market rate of 2,000 kwanza per dollar, the cigarettes and pop cost less than $1 each, and the ashtray is a steal at less than $3.

"Money is meaningless," says a budding economist who is wiling away Luanda's midnight-to-5 a.m. curfew by attending an all-night party. "Beer has meaning."

Imported Beer

He explains the two ways to get on the beer standard. If you have dollars, you simply head to one of the government-run hard-currency shops and buy a case of imported beer—Heineken, Beck's, Stella Artois—for $12. (Dollars aren't hard to get in Angola, at least for those in the middle class, who often travel abroad.)

But those who have only kwanza can get in on the deal, too. Typically, workers draw, as part of their salaries, coupons that can be redeemed at grocery stores run by their employers. These stores also have plenty of imported beer.

Having acquired a case of beer, you head to the neighborhood black market and cash in the 24 cans for 30,000 kwanza. (Recently, Stella Artois has been devalued to 15,000 kwanza because of unsubstantiated rumors here that it causes impotence.) This is worth $15 at the black-market rate and $1,000 at the official rate. Suddenly, you are rich, and you can load up on vegetables, fish, soap and clothes or even a plane ticket to Lisbon. The latter costs roughly two cases of beer.

Rich Food and Chic Clothes

The black marketeer, in turn, sells the

individual cans of beer for a nice profit: at 2,000 kwanza a can, he will collect 48,000 kwanza for a case. Everybody's happy.

"It works quite nicely," says the student economist at the all-night party. Because he hopes to work one day for the Bank of Angola, he agrees to speak on the condition he won't be identified. "You can get anything you want in Angola."

The party, attended by Luanda's young jet set, is proof of that. A feast unimaginable to all but a few Angolans is spread over several tables: lobster, prawns, beef, pork, chicken, cakes, pies and pastries. The bar is stocked with liquor from around the world, and the women are dressed in outfits from Lisbon, Paris and Rome.

The student giggles, somewhat embarrassed by these riches. "On the surface, Luanda looks miserable," he says. "But things aren't always as they seem."